SOCIAL INEQUALITY AND SOCIAL STRATIFICATION IN US SOCIETY

Christopher B. Doob
Southern Connecticut State University

Boston Columbus Indianapolis New York San Francisco Upper Saddle River
Amsterdam Cape Town Dubai London Madrid Milan Munich Paris Montreal Toronto
Delhi Mexico City Sao Paulo Sydney Hong Kong Seoul Singapore Taipei Tokyo

Editorial Director: Craig Campanella
Editor in Chief: Dickson Musslewhite
Publisher: Karen Hanson
Editorial Assistant: Joseph Jantas
Director of Marketing: Brandy Dawson
Executive Marketing Manager: Kelly May
Marketing Assistant: Janeli Bitor
Director of Production: Lisa Iarkowski
Senior Managing Editor: Maureen Richardson
Production Editor: Shelly Kupperman
Production Project Manager: Maggie Brobeck

Art Director, Cover: Jayne Conte
Cover Image: Blend Images/Alamy
Media Director: Brian Hyland
Lead Media Project Manager: Tom Scalzo
Supplements Editor: Mayda Bosco
Full-Service Project Management and Composition:
Chitra Ganesan/PreMediaGlobal
Printer/Binder: RR Donnelly/Harrisonburg
Cover Printer: RR Donnelly/Harrisonburg
Text Font: 10/12 ITC Garamond

Credits and acknowledgments borrowed from other sources and reproduced, with permission, in this textbook appear on the appropriate page within text or on page 367.

Library of Congress Cataloging-in-Publication Data
Doob, Christopher Bates.
    Social inequality and social stratification in US society /
Christopher B. Doob. — 1st ed.
        p. cm.
    Includes bibliographical references and index.
    ISBN-13: 978-0-205-79241-2
    ISBN-10: 0-205-79241-3
1. Equality—United States. 2. Social stratification—United States.
I. Title.
    HM821.D66 2011
    305—dc23

                                        2011040457

10 9 8 7 6 5 4 3 2 1

ISBN 10:   0-205-79241-3
ISBN 13: 978-0-205-79241-2

CONTENTS

Part 1   The Foundation of Social Stratification and Social Inequality

Chapter 1   THE ROAD TO SOCIAL INEQUALITY: A CONCEPTUAL INTRODUCTION   1

The Rise of the Global Economy   3

The Conceptual Skeleton: Social Reproduction and the Impact of Capital Types   10

Forms of Capital   12

Social Reproduction and Schooling   14

Conclusion   17

Chapter 2   IN MARX'S WAKE: THEORIES OF SOCIAL STRATIFICATION AND SOCIAL INEQUALITY   23

The Davis-Moore Theory of Social Stratification   24

Marxist Theory of Capitalism and Social Stratification   25

The Economic Structure of Marxist Theory   25

Marx's Capitalist Class System   27

Marx on Revolution and Its Aftermath   28

Commentary   28

The Marxist Impact Illustrated: Three Social-Stratification Theories   31

Weber's Theory of Class, Status, and Party   31

Wright's Perspective on Class   35

Perrucci and Wysong's Theory of Class   36

The Power-Elite Theories   38

Mills's Power-Elite Perspective   38

Domhoff's Theory of the Upper-Class-Centered Corporate Community   39

Dye's Theory of the Institutional Elite   42

Conclusion   44

Chapter 3   REPEAT PERFORMANCE: GLOBALIZATION THROUGH TIME AND SPACE   48

The Rise and Fall of World Systems   48

Conditions in the Development of World Systems   51

Social Stratification and Social Inequality in the Global Setting   55

The Global Spectrum: From the Very Rich to the Very Poor 59

Three Semiperipheral Locations 62

Unions against Sweatshops 65

Squatter Communities: A Global Surge 68

Conclusion 71

Chapter 4 FOUNDATION FOR SOCIAL INEQUALITY: CONCEPTS AND STRUCTURES 77

On Your Own: Class, Ideology, and Social Mobility 78

Class in the United States 78

The American Ideology 82

Fixation on Social Mobility: Where Is the American Dream? 87

The Invisible Empire and Its Calculus of Control 91

The Elite Policy-Making Process 91

The Burgeoning Business of Lobbying 94

Campaign Giving 98

The Power of the Press 100

Public Policy 105

Conclusion 113

Part 2   Class, Race, and Gender

Chapter 5 HEADING THE HIERARCHY: UPPER CLASS OR SUPERCLASS? 121

Getting Rich: From the High Seas to Hi Tech 122

The Early Years 122

From the Robber Baron Era to 1970 124

The Globalization Phase 125

The Old Rich versus the New Rich 127

Born to the Upper Class 129

Wealthy Families 129

Schooling for the Rich 131

Elite Social Clubs 135

Managing Upper-Class Wealth and Income 137

The American Corporate Leadership 137

The Superclass and the Power Elite 140

Conclusion 142

Chapter 6 THE BADLY BESIEGED MIDDLE CLASS 148

The Emergence of the Middle Class 148

Industry's Impact on the Middle Class 149

The Two Middle Classes 152

Income and Jobs 152

Families and Education 156

The Ecology of Class 158

Establishment of the Middle-Class Life 160

Childhood 160

Schooling 162

Networking: It's Who You Know 165

The Lean, Mean Middle-Class Work Machine 167

Middle-Class Workforce Changes Involving Downsizing, Outsourcing, and Temp Work 169

The Middle-Class Struggle with Reemployment 172

The Middle Class's Slippery Slope for Making Ends Meet 174

Conclusion 177

Chapter 7 WORKING CLASS: ESTRANGED FROM ENTITLEMENT 186

Working-Class History 186

The Union Response 189

An Overview of the Working Class 194

Working-Class Development 196

Childrearing 196

Schooling 198

Community Ties 199

Working-Class Employment: Can the Dream Survive? 201

Working-Class Jobs Today 203

Blue-Collar Workers' Challenges 207

Conclusion 210

Chapter 8 AMERICAN POVERTY: THE DREAM TURNED NIGHTMARE 216

The American Poor through the Centuries 217

Governmental Efforts to Reduce Poverty 218

Who Is Poor? 220

The Pain of Family Poverty 225

Poor Children's Childcare and Schooling   227
   Childcare in Poverty Areas   227
   Poor Children's Education   228
Low-Income Communities and Their Social Capital   237
Poor People's Work   240
   The Prospects of Low-Income Employment   242
   Battling on Up?   244
The Welfare Reform Era   245
   Running the TANF Gauntlet   246
   Evaluation of Welfare Reform   248
Conclusion   253

Chapter 9   RACISM: A PERSISTENT AMERICAN PRESENCE   261
Passage to Racism   264
   Who's White and Who's Not   269
   Modern Racial Isolation and Oppression   271
The Varied Impact of Race on Families   272
The Influence of Race on Peer and Friendship Patterns   275
   Minorities' Frequent Preference for Racially Homogenous Peers   277
Race, Schooling, and Academic Success   278
   Direct Effects   279
   Impact of Stereotype Threat   281
Collision of Mass Media and Race   283
   Racial Minorities' Participation   283
Work and Racial Inequality: Contributing Factors   286
   Disadvantaged Context: Minority-Group Members' Unrelenting Battle against Poverty   286
   Stereotype Fallout and the Employment Process   291
Conclusion   295

Chapter 10   WOMEN'S OPPRESSION: SEXISM AND INTERSECTIONALITY   305
A History of Second-Class Citizenry   306
The Persistence of Sexism   308
   The Family Impact   310
   The Influence of Peers   311
   Schools and the Gendered Hidden Curriculum   313
   The Representation of Females in the Mass Media   315
   Women in the Modern Work World   318

Sexism and Intersectionality: Prospects for a Double Negative 324

Intersectionality: Black and Hispanic Women 325

Intersectionality: Lesbians' Challenge for Equality 330

Intersectionality: Poor Immigrant Women 332

Intersectionality: Black Students in Special-Education Programs 335

Conclusion 338

Part 3   Addressing Inequalities

Chapter 11 ASTRIDE WITH THE BEST AND THE WISEST 348

Contemplating Strategies for Change 348

Critical Arenas 352

The Schooling Revolution 352

The Revitalization of the Economy 356

Another Way 360

Conclusion 362

Photo Credits 367

Glossary 368

Index 374

PREFACE

The title for this book and the subject matter are conventional, but I have sometimes used less common types of sources to help reveal the workings of social inequality and social stratification. They are:

- **Historical information:** Whether the topic is the upper class, the poor, women, or racial minorities, it seems informative to provide historical material. Significant subjects such as the way wealthy individuals deal with the government or the middle class's treatment of the poor or the working class are not patterns that materialized full blown in the twenty-first century. The history of such patterns reveals important clues about why their significance persists. It is comparable to witnessing an actual conversation about a topic instead of just its terse ending. In Chapters 3 and 5 to 10, an opening section examines major historical events that have influenced current trends. For students the material can be both interesting and instructive.
- **Qualitative data:** To augment the steady flow of quantitative information that forms the foundation of analyses throughout the text, qualitative sources help reveal individuals' and small groups' thoughts and activities that accompany people's struggles with the socioeconomic order. Such research is particularly helpful in displaying the complexity of intersectionality, which addresses the impact of two or more statuses on women's lives.
- **A consistent conceptual skeleton:** Individuals' success in stratified settings often relies heavily on their access to valued resources—types of capital which involve finances, schooling, social networking, and cultural influences. Analyzing the impact of capital types throughout the text helps map out the prospects for individuals, families, and also classes to maintain or alter their economic, political, and social prospects. A steady flow of additional theories or concepts often plays a contributory role.

The text divides into three parts. The opening section contains four foundational chapters, namely an introduction, one about theory emphasizing the centrality of a conflict perspective, another that examines the development and impact of globalization, and a fourth that discusses the conceptual and structural elements underlying social inequality and social stratification. The following six chapters provide portraits of the major Americans classes as well as analyses of how race and gender link to inequalities in the United States. The last chapter considers attempts to reduce social inequality.

At the end of each chapter, I have included a list of important concepts that are highlighted in the previous pages along with discussion topics, research papers, and relevant websites. Clearly there are more activities here than most courses will use. My intention is to give instructors a variety of choices.

ACKNOWLEDGEMENTS

Karen Hanson has been a very effective editor with various contributions to this project. A special thanks to Maggie Brobeck at Pearson, Chitra Ganesan at PreMediaGlobal, and Shirley Jackson at Southern. I am also grateful to Linda Atkinson and Nick Doob for their continuous support. In addition, in doing what she always does—commenting on the entire manuscript and serving as a frequent sounding board—Teresa Carballal has probably been more valuable than ever before. Many thanks to the talented reviewers for this project—Diane Kayongo-Male (South Dakota State University), Steve Marson (University of North Carolina at Pembroke), and Tanetta Andersson (Case Western Reserve University).

Anyone with a comment or question should contact me at doobc1@southernct.edu.

SUPPLEMENTARY MATERIALS

Instructor's Manual and Test Bank (ISBN 0205001149): The Instructor's Manual and Test Bank has been prepared to assist teachers in their efforts to prepare lectures and evaluate student learning. For each chapter of the text, the Instructor's Manual offers different types of resources, including detailed chapter summaries and outlines, learning objectives, discussion questions, classroom activities, and much more.

Also included in this manual is a test bank offering multiple-choice, true/false, fill-in-the-blank, and/or essay questions for each chapter. The Instructor's Manual and Test Bank is available to adopters at http://www.pearsonhighered.com.

MyTest (ISBN 0205020631): The Test Bank is also available online through Pearson's computerized testing system, MyTest. MyTest allows instructors to create their own personalized exams, to edit any of the existing test questions, and to add new questions. Other special features of this program include random generation of test questions, creation of alternative versions of the same test, scrambling question sequence, and test preview before printing. Search and sort features allow you to locate questions quickly and to arrange them in whatever order you prefer. The test bank can be accessed from anywhere with a free MyTest user account. There is no need to download a program or file to your computer.

PowerPoint Presentations (ISBN 020502243X): Lecture PowerPoints are available for this text. The Lecture PowerPoint slides outline each chapter to help you convey sociological principles in a visual and exciting way. They are available to adopters at http://www.pearsonhighered.com.

MySearchLab: MySearchLab contains writing, grammar, and research tools and access to a variety of academic journals, census data, Associated Press news feeds, and discipline-specific readings to help you hone your writing and research skills. In addition, a complete eText is included. MySearchLab can be purchased with the text (ISBN 0205231675) or separately (ISBN 0205239927).

CHAPTER 1

The Road to Social Inequality: A Conceptual Introduction

In *Raggedy Dick* by Horatio Alger, Jr., the hero, a young bootblack, jumped from a ferry boat into turbulent waters after a small boy, who had fallen overboard. Dick nearly drowned but managed to save the boy and received praise for his courageous act. Shortly afterward the boy's father, who conveniently owned a counting house (accounting firm), gave Dick a job at $10 a week—three times what he earned as a bootblack (Alger 1985, 127). The lad was on his way.

Such fortunate developments typically happened to Alger's heroes. They were hardworking, ambitious, intelligent, generous, honest, street-wise, opportunistic boys determined to advance themselves from modest origins to elevated positions in society. Inner drive and talent were the primary reasons for their positive outcomes. In *Struggling Upward*, Alger indicated that his hero had elevated himself from poverty to wealth—that luck played a role, "but above all he . . . [was] indebted for most of his good fortune to his own good qualities" (Alger 1985, 280).

In the late nineteenth-century era of wide-ranging economic inequality, Alger's host of well over a hundred novels about dedicated, high-minded poor young white boys relentlessly seeking fortune and fame was very popular. Many Americans firmly believed that they lived in a land of open opportunity, where the virtue of hard work inevitably produced the rewards of wealth, power, and prestige—"rags to riches" as the phrase goes.

But while such transformations have occurred, the position throughout this book is that select groups—higher-class members, whites, and males—have had better opportunities and, therefore, more extensive rewards—than lower-class people, racial and ethnic minorities, and women.

This text's mission is to examine the processes that have produced and sustained those inequalities. Besides the conventional quantitative studies and statistics, the upcoming chapters contain both historical and qualitative sources, broadening and deepening the reader's grasp of the topics at hand. In addition, the relentless use of certain concepts—social reproduction and four types of capital, which are introduced in this chapter—help to structure a coherent overall organization and to reveal "the fine print" of American social inequality and social stratification. At this juncture it is necessary to introduce the course's most fundamental concepts.

Sociologists recognize the prevalence of **social inequality**, a situation in which individuals, families, or members of larger structures like neighborhoods or cities vary in access to such valued resources as wealth, income, education, healthcare, and jobs. Sometimes people's inequalities can change—for instance, a large number of working-class individuals might obtain a substantial pay boost, raising their wages as well as their ranking among the nation's earners. Like the members of all classes, however, their location in the class structure, which is a prominent type of social stratification, generally remains fairly stable when compared to the previous generation's.

Any society displays **social stratification**, a deeply embedded hierarchy providing different groups varied rewards, resources, and privileges and establishing structures and relationships that both determine and legitimate those outcomes.

Most people within a given society consider that its social-stratification systems represent the natural order of things. Respondents in various studies have indicated that people possessing greater wealth and power tend to have a range of more desirable traits than those who are less affluent or powerful (Beeghley 2008; Chan and Goldthorpe 2007; Della Fave 1980). This text examines class, racial, and gender stratification. Within the American class system, middle-class individuals' chances for advanced education and high-paying jobs have been better than working-class people's opportunities. A persistent suspicion expressed throughout the text is that growing economic inequality between affluent members of the upper and upper-middle class, and people in other classes is a precursor of a stratification system featuring a smaller middle class and concomitantly a larger working class. All in all, systems of class, racial, and gender stratification provide the conceptual foundations for analyzing trends in social inequalities.

A third central concept is **ideology**, which is the complex of values and beliefs that support a society's social-stratification systems and their distribution of wealth, income, and power. The American ideology, which emphasizes the centrality of individual achievement, equal opportunity, and the importance of hard work, receives politicians', business leaders', and media spokespeople's frequent endorsement, but the actual workings producing social inequalities and social stratification tend to remain unexamined—the fine print hidden behind the ideology's bold public claims. As the world's wealthiest nation, one might expect that the United States would spend more on its impoverished members, resulting in less social inequality than in other developed nations. Such a conclusion, however, overlooks the powerful influence of the country's ideology, which both lionizes individuals fixated on the pursuit of wealth and criticizes, even demonizes, the less successful, particularly the poor. The potency of American ideology will be apparent throughout the text, which provides various measures to show that among developed nations the United States has some of the highest levels of social inequality.

This chapter describes the development of the global economy and its impact on the American workforce. Then discussion focuses on certain central concepts, social reproduction and forms of capital, which analyze the process providing some people better opportunities and rewards than others. Finally sociological research comparing working-class and middle-class schooling illustrates these concepts.

Much of this chapter, in fact most of this text, focuses on the United States. As a foundation for understanding social inequality in American society, however, it is essential to lead off with a broader view of major developments since World War II. Then the discussion returns to a decidedly more sociological analysis.

THE RISE OF THE GLOBAL ECONOMY

Globalization is the increasing integration of nations in an age featuring highly reduced costs for communication and transportation along with the lowering of such "artificial barriers" as treaties or tariffs restricting the movement of goods, services, financial capital, and technology across borders (Stiglitz 2002, 9–10). Multinational corporations, many of which are American based, have been driving forces in globalization, demonstrating that the largely unregulated movement internationally of capital, goods, and technology leads to accelerated profit making.

Is globalization new? The term is fairly new, with the verb "globalize" first appearing in the *Merriam Webster Dictionary* in 1944. However, early efforts toward globalization reach back thousands of years. For instance, in 325 BCE, merchants established overland trade routes between the Mediterranean, Persia, India, and central Asia (Ludden 2008). Since the 1970s, however, a greatly expanded globalization process has developed. While globalization involves a variety of issues, including education, agriculture, or infrastructure, the current emphasis is on the economic dimension, which powerfully impacts social inequality.

Globalization has produced certain distinct economic changes. First, many nations once considered underdeveloped have begun producing quality goods. Computer-based manufacturing plants located in southeast Asia and Latin America have started to compete favorably with factories in developed countries in western Europe and North America, pressuring American corporate executives to downsize or close their plants. Second, at present advanced technology helps coordinate international economic activities. Because of the use of both modern computers and telecommunications, multinational corporations can decentralize their activities, locating subsidiaries around the world and effectively monitoring their activities from corporate headquarters. Finally the global economy has created an international workforce, with both white- and blue-collar jobs susceptible to being shipped overseas. The option to use alternative workers gives corporate executives greater clout when negotiating American employees' wages and benefits.

The global economy has rapidly expanded trade over time, with the wealthier nations leading the way. The estimate is that about two thirds of international financial transactions involve the United States, western Europe, and Japan (Brecher, Costello, and Smith 2000, 2–3; Perrucci and Wysong 2008, 109).

At the end of World War II, the international economic picture was distinctly different. Most prominent nations possessed severely damaged economies and infrastructures that made them incapable of effectively providing food, shelter, and other basic necessities to their citizenry. The major exception to this outcome was the United States, which emerged from the war with its economy intact, ready to undertake a massive international business expansion. For nearly 30 years, the United States controlled three quarters of the world's invested capital and two thirds of its industry. The government helped subsidize this dominance, developing a $22 billion foreign aid package to western Europe known as the Marshall Plan. The funding was earmarked for purchasing American agricultural and industrial products and bringing European nations into a global federation headed by the United States—both moves that helped solidify the preeminence of American business.

Global economics, however, has seldom been a stable entity. By the middle 1970s, the once war-ravaged nations of western Europe and Japan had recovered and were becoming rising industrial powers. As a result these countries were less inclined to import American industrial and agricultural goods. Meanwhile the profits of US corporations declined in the domestic market, falling from a return on investment of 15.5 percent in the late 1960s to below 10 percent after 1975.

Who or what is responsible for the decline? Corporate leaders, politicians, and media spokespeople have criticized various groups for contributing to the American business slowdown—organized labor for pushing too hard for salaries and benefits, thereby making American products too expensive for the competitive market; American workers, whether unionized or not, for being overpaid, complacent, and prone to shoddy production; and increased environmental and health-and-safety legislation for raising business costs.

What such corporate leaders and media spokespeople have conveniently ignored is the fact that American business ventures usually focus on short-term profits, largely abandoning such demanding but effective tactics as purchasing updated, more efficient technology, building new plants, engaging in research and development, and seeking new markets. In addition, Congress has established many tariffs, protecting domestic American business from outside competition. Shielded from that competition, however, American corporations often operate inefficiently, turning out inferior products, especially in the automotive industry.

As the global economy developed, American corporate leaders modified their stance on governmental protection. If they were going to expand their businesses and be welcomed abroad, they needed to permit foreign investment at home. These leaders lobbied Congress to lower tariffs on foreign imports, and between the 1970s and 2000 a steady decrease occurred (Dye 2002, 18–19; Perrucci and Wysong 2008, 111–13).

Sociologist Richard Sennett designated the global economic system the "new capitalism," which features certain novel traits. First, with the collapse of the Bretton Woods system of monetary management, national boundaries no longer restrict investors. Now they can seek wealth anywhere on earth. Banks have been major players, with American, Japanese, and German financial organizations in the forefront. David Rockefeller, former CEO of the prominent Chase Manhattan Bank, indicated that if Chase wanted to remain a prominent player in US banking, it had no option but to engage in the frantic international competition for foreign business (Rockefeller 2002, 197–98). In the twenty-first century, the same competitive pressure has persisted. Charles O. Prince III, Citigroup's chief executive, once admitted that he was aware that his aggressive deal-making would get the financial conglomerate in serious trouble, but he felt powerless to pull back, declaring, "As long as the music is playing, you've got to get up and dance" (Goodman 2010, 4).

Second, in this expanding market offering accelerated wealth, the new shareholders have often been impatient, fixated on making quick profits. As later examples in the text indicate, a frantic rush for profits—a feeding frenzy—can develop when wealthy business people see a choice prospect of making a lot of money. In this frenetic atmosphere, corporate leaders generally believe that the companies best equipped for profit making are those that are flexible and dynamic; the traditional ideal of a solid, stable firm no longer prevails. To promote a quick-profits corporate agenda, executives become increasingly enamored of downsizing and outsourcing (Sennett 2006, 37–44). For decades, largely unheeded by most Americans, some expert observers have indicated that American corporate leaders have acted more like bankers than big-business executives, appearing more interested in buying and selling companies than in the painstaking, critically important tasks of producing and selling goods and services. Robert Lekachman, an economist, concluded that corporate leaders "see more opportunities in tax dodges and mergers than in the painfully slow process of developing new products." In this revised business setting, only a select few are winners. Lekachman observed that "[w]hat we're getting now is investment which rewards stockholders and senior executives and devastates the communities in which corporations operate" (*The Business of America . . .* 1984).

Globalization has changed people's economic prospects. The payoff for corporate leaders and investors has been impressive. American multinationals are positioned to pursue any competitive advantage, locating plants to benefit from "low wages, cheaper raw materials, advantageous monetary exchange rates, more sympathetic governments, or proximity to markets" (Perrucci and Wysong 2008, 115). Corporations are not penalized for eliminating US jobs and are allowed to dismiss any employees as long as discrimination does not occur. In addition, big-business leaders bringing money earned abroad back to the United States pay a very low tax rate because it is simply assumed that those profits are used to maintain or create American jobs (Hira and Hira 2005, 76–81).

American corporate investment in the global economy has expanded rapidly over time. In 1970 US firms invested $75 billion abroad, with the figure rising to $167 billion in 1978. Between 1982 and 2007, that dollar value grew steadily, averaging an increase of over 12 percent per year in the decade between 1999 and 2008 (Ibarra and Koncz 2008; Jackson 2009). Figure 1.1 provides data that display the expanding American corporate investment abroad over a 26-year time span.

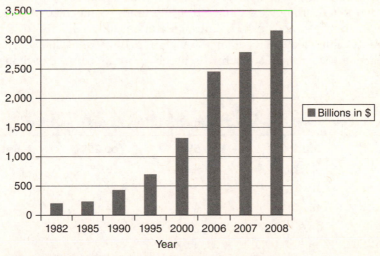

FIGURE 1.1   American Corporations' Investment Abroad over Time

Between 1982 and 2008, corporate investment abroad increased steadily, including a robust 13.3 percent rise between 2007 and 2008. The 2008 figure of $3,162 billion is over 15 times as large as the $207.8 billion total for 1982.

Sources: Marilyn Ibarra and Jennifer Koncz. 2008. "Direct Investment Positions for 2007: Country and Industry Detail." U.S. Bureau of Economic Analysis. http://www.bea.doc.gov/scb/pdf/2008/07%20 July0708_dip.pdf. James K. Jackson. 2009. "U.S. Direct Investment Aboard: Trends and Current Issues." Congressional Research Service. (November 5). http://relooney.fatcow.com/0_New_6184.pdf.

While globalization provides large corporations huge profits, it has punished many Americans economically. Sociologists Maxine Baca Zinn and D. Stanley Eitzen indicated that starting in the middle 1970s, many Americans experienced workforce changes involving declines in earnings, factory employment, and union support (Zinn and Eitzen 2005, 17). It is hardly surprising that data from the General Social Survey gathered between 1977 and 2002 indicated that over time, perceived job insecurity has increased, with workers who are black, less educated, less well paid, or part-time expressing greater concern (Fullerton and Wallace 2007).

As the book progresses, all of these issues are examined, revealing the specific conditions causing many in the labor force to lose out. Of the 3.6 million, long-tenured (three or more years on the job) workers displaced between January 2005 and December 2007, 45 percent lost or left their jobs due to a company or plant leaving, 31 percent had their positions eliminated, and 24 percent faced insufficient work (U.S. Bureau of Labor Statistics 2008b). An additional 4.6 million individuals who were short-tenured (with less than three years on the job) were displaced during that same time period, producing a total of 8.2 million individuals removed from their positions (U.S. Bureau of Labor Statistics 2008a).

The global economy has had a polarizing impact on American income. As Table 1.1 indicates, between 1980 and 2007, the richest 1 percent of the population increased its share of income by 14.3 percent, and the top 25 percent boosted theirs by 12 percent. In contrast, especially to the top 1 percent, the bottom 50 percent has seen its share decline by 5.5 percent (Prante 2009).

Business leaders' relative income increases have been particularly impressive. The ratio of the average chief executive officer's (CEO's) annual income compared to an average worker's earnings expanded from 24 times as much in 1965 to 107 times more in 1990, then zoomed to 525 times greater in 2000, and fell to 339 as much in 2008 year (Collins 2009; Executive PayWatch 2010; Mishel 2006). That last ratio indicates that the CEO earns as much in scarcely more as half a day than the worker in a year.

TABLE 1.1 Income Shares of Selected Segments of Tax Payers over Time

Year	Top 1%	Top 5%	Top 25%	Bottom 50%
1980	8.5%	21%	56.7%	17.7%
1985	10	22	58	17.3
1990	14	27.6	62.1	15
1995	14.6	28.8	63.4	14.5
2000	20.8	35.3	67.2	13
2005	21.2	35.8	67.5	12.8
2007	22.8	37.4	68.7	12.2

The more affluent the segment of tax payers, the more their share of the national income has increased over time. Inevitably the reverse pattern applies to the bottom 50 per cent, who over 27 years have received a dwindling portion.

Source: Gerald Prante. 2009. "Summary of Latest Federal Individual Income Tax Data." *The Tax Foundation.* http://www.taxfoundation.org/news/show/250.html.

Economist Paul Krugman observed that back in the hardship years, when CEOs scraped by with incomes averaging scarcely 40 times workers' salaries, they felt grossly underpaid. Professors at business schools came to the rescue, arguing that CEOs were being greatly undervalued, treated like bureaucrats who were compensated the same whether they made money or lost it. To motivate these critical leaders, the professors argued, companies needed to offer them special incentives. Stock options, opportunities to buy one's company's shares, which increase in value if the stock rises, are widely considered the most effective enticements to motivate business executives to produce profits and boost stock prices. With such an arrangement, which is seldom available to business leaders in other countries, these executives have benefited immensely, especially those working for companies which illegally backdate the purchase date to when the stock price was low, permitting executives to buy much more stock in a given transaction than the current price allows. As a result since the early 1990s, the average CEO has become increasingly wealthy even though research indicates that companies' profits bear little or no statistical relationship to CEOs' expanded incentives (Krugman 2006).

While affluent Americans have done well, the overall economic picture indicates that this wealthiest nation has had greater economic inequality than other developed nations. The **Gini index**, which is a measurement of a nation's statistical distribution of income or wealth inequality, verifies this conclusion: The higher a country's score, the greater the inequality. In 2010 the Gini index measuring family income was 45 for the United States and was higher than the scores for 92 other countries, including all the developed nations—those in western Europe and also Australia, Japan, and New Zealand (CIA—The World Factbook 2010). A difficulty with the Gini index is that like the system for rating (football) quarterbacks, its results, while often cited, are complicated to compute and, in fact, the formula is usually unknown to those who use the data.

Another, more easily understood measure of countries' economic inequality involves a comparison between the percentage of the national income a wealthy segment and a poor segment obtain. One study found that between 1970 and 2000 when compared to individuals in six western European countries, the top 20 percent of Americans in income had a greater percentage of income and the bottom 20 percent a smaller percentage than their counterparts in the other nations (Hoff 2002).

A similar result emerges when researchers calculate the income ratio of countries' 10 percent most affluent to the 10 percent least affluent. Among the 24 developed nations possessing the highest quality-of-life indices, Japan displayed the least disparity between the richest and poorest tenths, with a ratio of 4.5 for the richest to poorest tenth followed by the Czech Republic at 5.3 and Finland at 5.6. The United States scored a ratio of 15.9, obtaining the greatest disparity between the richest and poorest tenth of the 24 major developed nations on the list (United Nations Development Programme 2009). Table 1.2 provides the comparative ratios for these countries.

The United States not only produces greater economic inequality than other developed nations but also higher rates of physical and mental illness, lower life expectancy, and higher crime. Historian Tony Judt concluded that the affluence of a country has less impact on its citizens than its social inequality. He indicated that inequality is "corrosive," rotting from the inside and taking some time to reveal itself. He added that: "in due course competition for status and goods increases" along with "a growing sense of superiority (or inferiority) based on their possessions" and the hardening of "prejudice

TABLE 1.2 Ratio of a Developed Nation's Richest 10 Percent in Income to Its Poorest 10 Percent

Country	Ratio	Country	Ratio
1. Japan	4.5	13. France	9.1
2. Czech Republic	5.3	14. The Netherlands	9.2
3. Finland	5.6	15. Canada	9.4
4. Norway	6.1	15. Ireland	9.4
5. Sweden	6.2	17. Greece	10.2
6. Austria	6.9	18. Spain	10.3
6. Germany	6.9	19. Italy	11.6
8. Korea (Republic of)	7.8	20. Australia	12.5
9. Denmark	8.1	20. New Zealand	12.5
10. Belgium	8.2	22. Israel	13.4
11. Poland	9.0	23. United Kingdom	13.8
11. Switzerland	9.0	24. United States	15.9

Among the major developed nations classified by the United Nations' Economist Intelligence Unit as having the leading quality-of-life indices, the United States displayed the highest ratio of the income for the most affluent 10 percent to the income for the least affluent 10 percent. In short, this measurement suggests that the United States has greater economic inequality than any other developed nations.

Source: United Nations Development Programme. 2009. "Ratio of the Richest 10% to Poorest 10%." *Human Development Reports.* http://hdrstats.undp.org/indicators/145.html.

toward those on the lower rungs of the social ladder." In addition, "crime spikes and the pathologies of social disadvantage becomes even more marked" (Judt 2010, 19). Judt's is a broad, bold claim, and yet nothing in this text disputes it.

Presently a small group of scholars has been attempting to determine if economic inequality might contribute to widespread financial risk and failure. David Moss, a well known economic historian, learned that striking statistical correlations appeared between economic inequality and both bank collapses and financial deregulation, which is a topic in Chapter 4. Specifically, as the Great Depression approached in 1928, the top 10 percent of earners obtained an inordinately high 49.3 percent of all income and the top 1 percent 23.9 percent; in 2007 on the eve of the modern financial crisis, the respective numbers were impressively close—49.7 and 23.5 percent. The scholars examining this topic have suspected that such income inequalities might encourage wealthy individuals to engage in actions that put the entire financial system at risk. For instance, with growing affluence Wall Street leaders become more powerful, prompting them to push for increased deregulation and a rising danger of increased financial instability (Story 2010).

For many modern Americans, the impact of social inequality is greatest on the job. Barbara Garson wrote about "the electronic sweatshop," representing "a combination of twentieth-century technology and nineteenth-century scientific management in turning the . . . [business] of the future into the factory of the past" (Garson 1989, 10).

As a highly successful multinational, Walmart not only produces goods in many countries but also has retail outlets around the world, including 189 stores in 101 Chinese cities.

Walmart has been a prominent proponent of this approach, applying industrial principles to the retail market by combining the use of informational technology with a harsh, punitive work regime. Walmart's core technology, known as "enterprise systems" or ES, uses sophisticated computer hardware and software to standardize and monitor the full set of tasks a company's employees perform. With ES, Walmart has electronic tags, sensors, and "smart" chips to locate products at various steps in the production and distribution processes. Informed by ES, supervisors and managers "drill down"—an important phrase in the ES parlance—and immediately locate any potential culprit—a clerk in Omaha who sent a package to the wrong destination, an inefficient warehouse team in San Diego, or an underachieving salesperson in Baltimore.

For the corporation's bottom line, ES has been a huge success. Walmart employees' productivity has been about 41 percent higher than that of its competitors while wages have been considerably lower. However, even without ES, most American businesses have generally followed the same pattern. Between 1995 and 2006, the national increase in workers' productivity exceeded the growth in real wages by 340 percent (Head 2007, 42).

Systems like ES produce distinct consequences. To begin, recognizing that their employers are fixated on the bottom line and consider them dispensable, job holders often display little loyalty. It is a far cry from the so-called "giving/getting compact" that prevailed for about three decades after World War II and involved a company's commitment to fairly certain lifetime employment along with good pay and benefits in exchange for workers' unflagging loyalty and hard work (Yankelovich 1981). One business analyst suggested that whereas workers and management previously had a shared fate in a stable marriage, now employees face a lifetime of marriages and divorces, sometimes emerging better and sometimes worse but with the companies possessing the upper hand in deciding when termination occurs (Hacker 2006, 67).

In particular, trust no longer prevails. Trust involves both formal situations such as the recognition that the other party in a contract will meet the prescribed standards and informal trust, which develops gradually over time in fairly stable organizations as individuals work with each other in a variety of situations including stressful ones. Richard Sennett illustrated the change in informal trust by describing employees' response to accidents that occurred 30 years apart in two industrial corporations. The earlier situation involved a factory fire, where a circuit of fire hose nozzles broke. The workers knew each other well enough to function as a smooth team, efficiently putting out the fire while ignoring the manager's distracting orders. The later accident resulted from a malfunctioning air-conditioning system, which spewed noxious gases. Many individuals panicked while others wanted to organize but were at a loss how to do it. People did not know and trust each other well enough to have established a foundation for working together in this stressful situation (Sennett 2006, 63–72). After the second accident, one manager was critical of working arrangements, concluding that the plant was only "superficially organized on paper" (Sennett 2006, 67).

Workers are hardly the only critics of modern big business. Respondents give a mixed assessment of multinationals, the chief global players. In an international survey by the McKinsey Quarterly, 68 percent of corporate executives indicated that large corporations make a generally or somewhat positive contribution to the public good. In contrast, only 48 percent of consumers concurred (Brown 2007, C5).

Now the focus shifts from the global economy, which provides the setting for modern social inequality, to an examination of concepts for analyzing that topic.

THE CONCEPTUAL SKELETON: SOCIAL REPRODUCTION AND THE IMPACT OF CAPITAL TYPES

Do Americans inhabit a social world where large numbers of people are socially mobile, living out a version of the rags-to-riches story, or do they tend to die in the classes into which they are born? The focus here is **social reproduction**, which is an emphasis on the structures and activities that transmit social inequality from one generation to the next. The definition suggests the relevance of historical analysis, which is the opening topic in Chapters 4 through 9. Furthermore, research and theory on the topic has tended to reach a distinct conclusion—which, according to sociologist Jay MacLeod, "attempts to show how and why the United States can be depicted more accurately as the place where 'the rich get richer and the poor stay poor' than as 'the land of opportunity'" (MacLeod 2009, 7–8). In short, these analyses tend to conclude that the social-stratification system holds most Americans in place, making it fairly likely that they will end up in class positions that are similar to their parents'.

Researchers have examined social reproduction in various institutional contexts, particularly educational ones. Basil Bernstein's (1990; 2000) British working-class respondents grew up in homes where shared knowledge and values developed speech patterns that put them at distinct disadvantage in schools' more complex middle-class language settings. Samuel Bowles and Herbert Gintis's (1976; 2003) research concluded that with students' eventual location in the workforce in mind, administrators structured various schools differently, emphasizing rules and behavioral control for working-class students but encouraging a more participatory classroom, less supervision, and a larger set of course electives for their middle-class counterparts. Jay MacLeod's (2009) informants were black and white boys growing up in public housing and struggling, usually unsuccessfully, against impinging circumstances to be successful in school and in the work world.

Social inequality impacts people both objectively and subjectively (Wacquant 1989, 15). An affluent, upper-class individual might have the optimal financial backing to subsidize his or her drive for educational and occupational success, but this person might lack the self-confidence and optimistic outlook that a less affluent, working-class person possesses. The first person has the objective advantage and the second one the greater subjective edge. In referring to "habitas," sociologist Pierre Bourdieu recognized that subjective outlooks toward social inequality can involve groups or categories. A **habitas** is the set of attitudes, behavior, and experiences maintained by the people sharing a distinct social world. The social world can be narrow such as the one inhabited by neighborhood residents or broad such as that which all working-class women share. The concept serves as a connector between the inner consciousness and the limitations or potentials the social world provides, influencing people to act in distinctive ways. The habitas members of a given class maintain contributes to social reproduction, sustaining the existing structures and cultural standards, including class-based inequalities (Bourdieu 1977b, 82–83; Bourdieu 1998, 8; Giroux 2001, 89; Kusserow 2004, xi; MacLeod 2009, 15).

Other social theorists emphasized that the process is not deterministic, with "discontinuities, contradictions, and resistance in the reproduction process" (Walford 1986, 183). Social reproduction is a potent reality, but individuals can sometimes elude it. College students can be successful in this regard. Starting in the early 1970s, many colleges and universities admitted what became a substantial number of black and Hispanic students, often providing them financial aid. These sites of higher education have generally subscribed to the position that they are providing "compensatory sponsorship" for disadvantages these students of color have faced. Most of these schools have not extended such opportunities to low-income white applicants (Grodsky 2007). However, a substantial number of colleges and universities do take family income into account, regardless of students' race. For instance, since 2003 at the University of Virginia, a financial aid program has assured that low-income students do not need to take out loans to attend the school (Kinzie 2009).

In addition, college administrators increasingly recognize the difficulties modern students face, supplying a variety of timely services that can empower individuals and help challenge social reproduction. My university, for example, provides an Office of Study Skill Enrichment, a Writing Center, a Tutorial Center, and Student Supportive Services. When such facilities and their personnel are effective, students have an improved chance to develop a positive strategy for success, planning their college lives so that they make maximum use of opportunities that can advance them. Admittedly times are tough, but many college personnel are trying to address pressing student problems, reaching out quickly and firmly to individuals whom they might help.

What are the key factors that contribute to determining people's location in social-stratification systems and whether or not social reproduction occurs? I introduce four of them in the following section.

Forms of Capital

Capital refers to resources that people possess or acquire, finding them valuable in various settings (Spillane, Hallett, and Diamond 2003, 3). These capital forms are critical tools for obtaining economic, political, and social success. In fact, the quantity and quality of capital available to different classes replicate their location in the class hierarchy, representing a potent thrust toward social reproduction. Four types of capital—financial, cultural, human, and social—have been extensively studied and are interrelated to each other.

FINANCIAL CAPITAL concerns monetary items such as wages and salaries or purchasable items such as computers or books that can contribute directly or indirectly to obtaining various valued resources representing other types of capital (Bourdieu 1990, 132–33; Spillane, Hallett, and Diamond 2003, 4; Young 2004, 59). A direct contribution might be the expensive purchase of four years of tuition, room, and board at an elite private college, which is a type of human capital. On the other hand, an indirect contribution might involve payment for membership in a social club which offers useful contacts (social capital) that can lead to a job offer or promotion. Financial capital can also subsidize a lifestyle that influences the content of cultural capital.

CULTURAL CAPITAL comprises broadly shared outlooks, knowledge, skills, and behavior passed from one generation to the next (Bourdieu 1977a; Bourdieu 1990, 124–25; Kingston 2001, 89–90; Lamont and Lareau 1988; Lareau and Weininger 2003, 587–88; MacLeod 2009, 13). All adults possess cultural capital, though certain varieties, notably those maintained by higher classes, are more helpful than others for educational and occupational success and advancement. Some earlier definitions of the concept indicated that it should focus on such refined interests as art, music, and etiquette, but sociologists Annette Lareau and Elliot B. Weininger observed that Pierre Bourdieu, who created the concept, suggested that cultural capital also incorporates broader capacities such as technical or interpersonal skills (Lareau and Weininger 2003, 580). Lareau and Weininger's use of the term is consistent with Bourdieu's sense of it. They indicated that in school systems some parents effectively mobilize their cultural capital—in this instance their experience and knowledge of how to promote desired educational outcomes—to meet with teachers and other school personnel to facilitate their children's successful movement through the system. Middle-class parents have more appropriate cultural capital for this purpose than their working-class and poor counterparts (Laureau and Weininger 2003, 596–97). Families' cultural capital can affect the human capital their members obtain.

HUMAN CAPITAL involves the attainment of skills, knowledge, and expertise people acquire to be successful in various valued ways (Brooks 2007; Coleman 1988, S100; Spillane, Hallett, and Diamond 2003, 3; Svendsen and Svendsen 2003, 609; Young 2004, 59). Individuals usually receive human capital from schooling and job training. In addition, someone might obtain it from a formal or an informal apprenticeship such as working for a carpenter, plumber, labor leader, corporate official, judge, or another experienced job

At dinner family members not only share food but also can offer each other information, ideas, advise, and support—in short, cultural capital.

holder. A developed nation like the United States strongly emphasizes the importance of schooling, and less educated employees are often disadvantaged in the job world. Sites for the development of human capital such as the colleges students attend can provide social capital, with selected individuals and groups becoming valuable contacts.

SOCIAL CAPITAL, often called "social networking," refers to those individuals, networks, groups, and organizations that can assist participants in pursuing valued objectives (Coleman 1988, S98; Furstenberg and Hughes 1995, 581; Kao 2004, 172; Lin 2000, 786; Portes 1998, 3; Portes 2000, 2–3; Putnam 1995, 664–65; Sennett 2006, 63). Recent uses of the concept have extended it from a resource individuals or small groups possess to one located within communities or even nations (Portes 2000, 3–5). People's social capital— for instance their relationships with high-status business associates—can help to increase their financial capital, sometimes dramatically. Finally some social scientists have made an additional distinction, referring to "political capital" when individuals use social capital in the political realm (Magno 2008; Robertson 2008). The reference to social capital takes the interrelations of the four capital types full circle.

Each of the four forms can interact with any other, but one principle about these interrelations stands out: That in line with the prevailing prospect of social reproduction, a given individual, family, or community often has a relatively consistent quality of capital in the four different areas.

Throughout the text these four types of capital are prominent, displaying influence in class formation and social reproduction—both at the macro and the micro levels. Consider how human capital might develop on both dimensions. At the macro level, the state-controlled system of funding public education, which relies heavily on local property tax, produces wide variation in the quality of public schools. At a micro level, classroom activity involving affluent and poor schools is likely to contrast sharply, with the latter facilities much more likely to display large classes, more inexperienced and less well-paid teachers, and lower quality learning materials.

The following study on schooling provides an initial chance to see an illustration of social reproduction, featuring contributions that capital types make to the process.

SOCIAL REPRODUCTION AND SCHOOLING

Historically and even currently, many analysts of American society have described the education system as the great equalizer—the place where all children, regardless of how humble their background, can receive the quality schooling that will make occupational success possible. But is this an accurate observation about American education?

This outlook ignores ignores the role of class. A **class** is a large category of similarly ranked people located in a hierarchy and distinguished from other large categories in the hierarchy by such traits as occupation, education, income, and wealth (Gilbert 2011, 263). Chapter 2 indicates that some sociologists have defined class differently, most notably subdividing a nation's citizens strictly according to their relationship to the economy. While such classifications have had a major impact on sociological thinking, the present definition is the foundation for modern sociological usage. In this section and in subsequent chapters, it will become apparent that the members of different classes have varied access to capital sources, affecting their placement in the social-stratification system.

To begin, it is hardly surprising that financial capital affects people's educational opportunities. Middle-class families have more money to spend on schooling, using it for such costs as private schooling, tutoring, or college payments. As Chapter 7 indicates, insufficient funding is a prominent reason some working-class students leave college. Financial capital also impacts children's education in another way. Because the American system of public-school funding depends heavily on property tax, children in more affluent residential districts have better schools—smaller classes, better paid teachers, and higher quality supplies (Frank 2007; Slavin 1999; Warren 2007). Middle-class parents also possess other advantages that can promote their children's educational progress.

The family of origin provides cultural capital that can affect children's schooling success in different ways. First, parents have a chance to help their offspring learn both to reason and to develop verbal skills. In a study of 88 black and white primarily working- and middle-class children, sociologist Annette Lareau found that middle-class parents were more inclined than their working-class counterparts to reason with their children—not simply to give them orders—and to encourage them to engage in thoughtful conversation. As a result the middle-class students obtained more effective early development of skills that helped them relate to teachers and peers in school (Lareau 2007, 542–43).

Second, cultural capital also concerns parents' outlook on their children's college attendance. In a study focused on 80 white middle-class and working-class respondents living in a medium-sized northeastern city, sociologist Thomas Gorman observed that the respondents' class membership distinctly predicted the likelihood of obtaining this kind of capital. A working-class woman explained, "We were more or less raised that education was not important for the female" (Gorman 2000, 700). In contrast, an accountant from a middle-class background indicated that while his parents never mentioned it, they always assumed that he would go to college (Gorman 2000, 703)

In addition, working-class parents tend to develop less educationally related social capital than their middle-class counterparts. In Lareau's study Ms. Driver, a working-class white woman whose daughter had a serious reading disability, was pleased that school officials were seeking to determine why the girl had difficulty, but she had not requested it. Furthermore she had only a vague grasp of the problem. For instance, Ms. Driver noted that her daughter Wendy "goes to Special Ed. I think it's two classes a day . . . I'm not one hundred percent sure—for her reading. It's very difficult for her to read what's on paper. But then—she can remember things. But not everything. It's like she has a puzzle up there" (Lareau 2007, 546). Without clearly understanding the issue, Ms. Driver could hardly assist the teachers in addressing it.

In contrast, Ms. Marshall maintained a distinctly different habitas, staying fully informed about her daughter's school issues and feeling entitled to be an active participant in resolving any difficulties. She was an African American, middle-class mother who used her professional skills and experience to supply detailed information that would help teachers effectively address her daughter Stacey's individualized needs. Discussing a gymnastics instructor, Ms. Marshall told Lareau, "And sometimes teachers have to learn how to, you know, meet the needs of the kid. Her style, her immediate style was not accommodating to Stacey" (Lareau 2007, 545).

Like their parents the children in the two classes had different experiences developing social capital. Most of the working-class respondents in Gorman's study grew up with the idea that, as one truck driver phrased it, they were "not college material" (Gorman 2000, 702). Such an outlook made it unlikely that they had close contacts and friendships with their college-bound classmates. Middle-class students, however, found themselves with educationally beneficial social capital—immersed in a social network composed of "academically oriented friends" and "caring teachers and administrators" (Gorman 2000, 705). One middle-class respondent, who became a chemist, indicated that she received good grades and belonged to several important student organizations. She added, "I can't think of one person I associated with in high school that didn't go to college" (Gorman 2000, 705).

While social capital influences schooling, this most common type of human capital, in turn, influences people's access to jobs and thus their financial capital. About half of Gorman's working-class subjects regretted either dropping out of high school or not going to college, recognizing that limited schooling greatly restricted their employment possibilities. The remaining working-class respondents, most of whom were skilled laborers, were quite happy with their positions. One electrician indicated that he was pleased with both his pay and job content. He explained, "I don't want to wear a shirt and tie . . . , not have stress on me" (Gorman 2000, 710). Once again, however, the middle-class respondents often fared better. As college graduates who frequently had advanced degrees, the majority were content with their high-paying, often satisfying positions. A lawyer declared, "Well, I've reached my occupational goal. I'm a partner in a fairly good law firm. I guess I'll continue to practice law and improve my standing in the law firm and improve my abilities as an attorney" (Gorman 2000, 710).

TABLE 1.3 Working- and Middle-Class Uses of Capital in the Pursuit of Schooling

	Examples Involving Working-Class Respondents	Examples Involving Middle-Class Respondents
Cultural Capital	Parents often providing little guidance through the educational process and downplaying the importance of school and children's ability to do well at it	Parents supporting and often guiding their children's educational progress and emphasizing the importance of schooling, especially college
Social Capital	Few academically oriented peers or positive teacher contacts that might have promoted academic success	Immersion in school networks enhancing the pursuit of education
Human Capital	Frequent negative memory of school performance and of school itself	Widespread sense of having received the benefits of education
Financial Capital	About half Gorman's respondents dissatisfied with the nature of and payment from their jobs; about half content with their work	A clear majority of Gorman's subjects satisfied with the content of their work and their accomplishments on the job

Source: Thomas J. Gorman. 2000. "Reconsidering Worlds of Pain: Life in the Working Class(es)." *Sociological Forum.* V. 15, pp. 693–717; Annette Lareau. 2007. "Unequal Childhoods: Race, Class, and Family Life," in David B. Grusky and Szonja Szelényi (eds.), *The Inequality Reader: Contemporary and Foundational Readings in Race, Class, and Gender,* pp. 537–48.

The above description has emphasized that a complex of interacting types of capital provides one set of class members better educational and occupational opportunities than the other. Perusing studies on higher education, social scientists Robert Haverman and Timothy Speeding addressed the impact of such forces on people's schooling. They suggested that compared to their lower-income, less educated (working-class) counterparts, affluent, well-educated (middle-class) parents are better equipped to "invest time, money and influence to ensure their children's academic success from preschool through graduate school" (Haveman and Smeeding 2006, 128).

Clearly the middle-class parental investment pays off. In 1975 a college graduate's income was 47 percent higher than a high school graduate's income. By 2007 that margin had spiked to 83 percent (U.S. Census Bureau 2008). The economic payoff for higher education seems likely to continue. Table 1.3 summarizes the impact that class-based capital types produce on schooling.

In sum, the preceding material has supported Jay MacLeod's claim that social reproduction usually prevails, with Americans more often locked into class settings than unrestricted and free in a land of open opportunity. Beyond this general conclusion, the context of class-based living is diversified. The upcoming chapters provide details—information about the various structures, processes, and groups affecting Americans' class-based outlooks, behavior, and opportunities.

The final section summarizes all the text's chapters.

Conclusion

The first chapter contains key terms and ideas that provide a foundation for the investigation of social inequality and social stratification—first, definitions and discussion of the fundamental terms social inequality, social stratification, and ideology; then basic information about the development of the modern global economy and an overview of its impact; the introduction of the concepts social reproduction along with four types of capital, all of which prove useful in analyzing social inequality and social stratification, and finally the use of these terms in examining working-class and middle-class people's differing educational and occupational opportunities.

The second chapter, which involves theories of social stratification, highlights the contributions of such theorists as Karl Marx, Max Weber, and Eric Wright, and in addition, there is a section that provides a summary of several power-elite theories, which anticipate later discussions, indicating how wealthy, powerful interests affect major economic and political policies. The third chapter examines social stratification and social inequality in a global context, considering the development of world systems and globalization's impact on people in developing countries. The fourth chapter discusses prominent ideological and structural factors that have promoted social inequality and social stratification; the power elite's major activities and the three principal areas of

public policy are included. The following four chapters examine the major class categories—the upper class, the middle class, the working class, and the poor. Extensive social research provides information about respondents in different classes. Limited information about these investigations, however, has appeared in texts on social inequality and social stratification—in particular, the fine body of qualitative studies is noticeably absent. The next two chapters discuss two critical types of discrimination—racism and sexism. The text finishes with a conclusion, which analyzes various initiatives addressing some of the nation's most pressing educational and occupational problems of inequality.

At this juncture I would like to stress an avoid-the-baby-with-the-bathwater issue. This chapter began with reference to the type of open, free society that Horatio Alger praised. I applaud the spirit of that idea: Historically our citizens have prided themselves on their hard-working, dedicated, resilient approach to life. What seems unfortunate has not been the exciting possibilities the ideology suggests but the power elite's persistent refusal to address the crushing reality of social reproduction, meaning that a vast array of Americans face systemic restraints inhibiting or eliminating their chances to be successful. Why these unequal outcomes occur and the consequences in diverse people's lives seem to be revealing, ever-interesting issues well worth addressing in the pages ahead.

Key Terms in the Glossary

Capital *12*
Class *14*
Cultural capital *12*
Financial capital *12*
Gini index *7*
Globalization *3*
Habitas *11*

Human capital *12*
Ideology *2*
Social capital *13*
Social inequality *2*
Social reproduction *10*
Social stratification *2*

Discussion Topics

1. What is globalization? What are two reasons it represents a "new capitalism"?
2. Discuss "winners" and "losers" in the modern American economy, providing information from the chapter and other sources.
3. Define the four types of capital examined in the chapter, supplying clear illustrations of each.

4. Is social reproduction likely to persist in our society? Is this a difficult issue to discuss? Do you find social reproduction a troublesome reality? Describe a set of conditions that would help eliminate it.

Research Papers

1. Pick an American corporation. Based on your research, provide as much detail as possible indicating how over time globalization has affected the company's profits, production, and workers.
2. From Table 1.2's list of countries, choose one with the greatest and one with the least disparity between the richest and the poorest. Then gather information about each country, learning what conditions in the two nations promote their respective outcomes.
3. Focus on a family or a neighborhood you know well, indicating in detail the extent to which

social reproduction applies. Provide detailed information about the influential people—parents, other relatives, peers, teachers, counselors, work associates, and others. Incorporate types of capital if they prove useful.

4. Choose two of the types of capital discussed in this chapter and write an essay describing how they differ for wealthy, middle-income, and poor people. At some point during the paper, indicate how the two types of capital might interrelate, influencing each other.

Informative Websites[1]

Two Nobel Prize-winning American economists Paul Krugman (http://www.michigandaily .com/content/daily.com/content/lecture-frugman-talks-globalization-downturn) and Joseph Stiglitz (http://www .opendemocracy.net/globalization-vision_reflections/stiglitz_3931.jsp.) make informal comments about contemporary globalization, which both experts consider a complicated but inordinately important topic.

This Website (https://www.cia.gov/library/ publications/the-world-factbook/ rankorder/2172rank.html) provides Gini indices for 102 nations. It is apparent that

some countries, most likely the wealthier ones with a larger workforce for such purposes, supply more updated measures. International data on the ratio of a country's richest 10 percent to its poorest 10 percent (http://hdrstats.undp.org/en/ indicators/160.html) provide some notable, perhaps unexpected outcomes. For instance, one might expect that the more developed nations would display less economic inequality. That, however, is not necessarily the case. Such nations as Bangladesh, Burundi, Ethiopia, and especially Azerbaijan with a ratio of 2.9, have low ratios, and that is because they have greater

---

[1]The Websites appear in the order that the linked topics are discussed in the text. In addition, throughout the text, I am including a few exemplary TV series, which are available as DVDs.

economic uniformity than developed nations—namely shared poverty.

The United States has always been a country possessing hundreds of largely volunteer organizations that attempt to provide information about and seek solutions to the various social problems and social inequalities that exist in our world. United for a Fair Economy (http://www.faireconomy.org/)

and MoveOn (http://www.moveon.org/) are two well-known examples.

It might be interesting and even revealing to go to your school's Website and investigate the services provided to students. In addition, fellow students might have helpful suggestions. Sometimes looking into such issues can be very rewarding.

Bibliography

Alger, Horatio, Jr. 1985. *Ragged Dick and Struggling Upward*. New York: Viking Press. Originally published in 1868 and 1890 respectively.

Beeghley, Leonard. 2008. *The Structure of Social Stratification in the United States*, 5th ed. Boston: Pearson Allyn & Bacon.

Bernstein, Basil. 1990. *The Structuring of Pedagogic Discourse: Volume IV: Class, Codes and Control*. London: Routledge.

Bernstein, Basil. 2000. *Pedagogy, Symbolic Control and Identity: Theory, Research, Critique*, revised ed. Lanham, MD: Rowman & Littlefield.

Bourdieu, Pierre. 1977a. "Cultural Reproduction and Social Reproduction," pp. 487–510 in Jerome Karabel and A. H. Hawley (eds.), *Power and Ideology in Education*. New York: Oxford University Press.

Bourdieu, Pierre. 1977b. *Outline of a Theory of Practice*. Cambridge: Cambridge University Press.

Bourdieu, Pierre. 1990. *The Logic of Practice*. Stanford: Stanford University Press.

Bourdieu, Pierre. 1998. *Practical Reason: On the Theory of Action*. Stanford: Stanford University Press.

Bowles, Samuel, and Herbert Gintis. 1976. *Schooling in Capitalist America*. New York: Basic Books.

Bowles, Samuel, and Herbert Gintis. 2003. "*Schooling in Capitalist America* 25 Years Later." *Sociological Forum* 18 (June): 343–48.

Brecher, Jeremy, Tim Costello, and Brendan Smith. 2000. *Globalization from Below: The Power of Solidarity*. Cambridge, MA: South End Press.

The Business of America . . . 1984. California Newsreel.

Brooks, David. 2007. "A Human Capital Agenda." *New York Times* (May 15): A19.

Brown, Paul B. 2007. "In Corporations They Don't Trust." *New York Times* (June 9): C5.

Chan, Tak Wing, and John H. Goldthorpe. 2007. "The Social Stratification of Theatre, Dance, and Cinema Attendance," pp. 525–36 in David B. Grusky and Szonja Szelényi (eds.), *The Inequality Reader: Contemporary and Foundational Readings in Race, Class, and Gender*. Boulder: Westview Press.

CIA—The World Factbook. 2010. "Country Comparison: Distribution of Family Income—Gini Index." https://www.cia.gov/library/publications/the-world-factbook/rankorder/2172rank.html.

Coleman, James. 1988. "Social Capital in the Creation of Human Capital." *American Journal of Sociology* 94: S95–S120.

Collins, Chuck. 2009. "The Audacity of CEO Greed." Institute for Policy Studies. http://www.ips-dc.org/articles/1043.

Della Fave, Richard. 1980. "The Meek Shall Not Inherit the Earth: Self-Evaluation and the Legitimacy of Stratification." *American Sociological Review* 45 (December): 955–71.

Dye, Thomas R. 2002. *Who's Running America? The Bush Restoration*, 7th ed. Upper Saddle River, NJ: Prentice-Hall.

Executive PayWatch. 2010. "Trends in CEO Pay." http://www.aflcio.org/corporatewatch/paywatch/pay/.

Frank, Robert H. 2007. *Falling Back: How Rising Inequality Harms the Middle Class*. Berkeley: University of California Press.

Fullerton, Andrew S., and Michael Wallace. 2007. "Traversing the Flexible Turn: U.S. Workers' Perception of Job Security, 1977–2002." *Social Science Research* 36 (March): 201–21.

Furstenberg, Frank F., Jr., and Mary Elizabeth Hughes. 1995. "Social Capital and Successful Development among At-Risk Youth." *Journal of Marriage and the Family* 57 (August): 580–92.

Garson, Barbara. 1989. *The Electronic Sweatshop: How Computers Are Transforming the Office of the* Future *into the Factory of the Past*. New York: Penguin Books.

Gilbert, Dennis. 2011. *The American Class Structure in an Age of Growing Inequality*, 8th ed. Los Angeles: Pine Forge Press.

Giroux, Henry A. 2001. *Theory and Resistance in Education: Toward a Pedagogy for the Opposition*. Westport, CT: Bergin & Garvey.

Goodman, Peter S. 2010. "Sluggers and Bankers in the Strikeout Era." *New York Times* (January 17). "Week in Review," p. 4.

Gorman, Thomas J. 2000. "Reconsidering Worlds of Pain: Life in the Working Class(es)." *Sociological Forum* 15: 693–717.

Gray, Sandra Leaton. 2004. "Defining the Future: An Interrogation of Education and Time." *British Journal of Sociology of Education* 25 (July): 323–40.

Grodsky, Eric. 2007. "Compensatory Sponsorship in Higher Education." *American Journal of Sociology* 112 (May): 1662–1712.

Hacker, Jacob S. 2006. *The Great Risk Shift: The Assault on American Jobs, Families, Health Care, and Retirement and How You Can Fight Back*. New York: Oxford University Press.

Haveman, Robert, and Timothy Smeeding. 2006. "The Role of Higher Education in Social Mobility." *The Future of Children* 16 (Autumn): 125–50.

Head, Simon. 2007. "They're Micromanaging Your Every Move." *New York Review of Books* 54 (August 16): 42–44.

Hira, Ron, and Anil Hira. 2005. *Outsourcing America: What's Behind Our National Crisis and How We Can Reclaim American Jobs*. New York: Amacom.

Hoff, Derek. 2002. "Statistical Appendix: Income Inequality in Seven Nations—France, Germany, Italy, Japan, Sweden, the United Kingdom, and the United States," pp. 401–09 in Oliver Zunz, Leonard Schappa, and Nobuhiro Hiwatari (eds.), *Social Contracts under Stress: The Middle Classes of America, Europe, and Japan at the Turn of the Century*. New York: Russell Sage Foundation.

Human Development Report 2007/2008. "Inequality Measures: Ratio of Richest 10% to Poorest 10%." http://hdrstats.undp.org/indicators/145.html.

Ibarra, Marilyn, and Jennifer Koncz. 2008. "Direct Investment Positions for 2006." U.S. Bureau of Economic Analysis. http://www.bea.doc.gov/scb/pdf/2008/07%20July0708_dip.pdf.

Jackson, James K. 2009. "U.S. Direct Investment Aboard: Trends and Current Issues." Congressional Research Service. (November 5). http://relooney.fatcow.com/0_New_6184.pdf.

Judt, Tony. 2010. "Ill Fares the Land." *New York Review of Books* 57 (April 29): 17–19.

Kao, Grace. 2004. "Social Capital and Its Relevance to Minority and Immigrant Populations." *Sociology of Education* 77 (April): 172–75.

Kingston, Paul W. 2001. "The Unfulfilled Promise of Cultural Capital Theory." *Sociology of Education* (Extra Issue) 74: 88–99.

Kinzie, Susan. 2009. "U-VA. President Says He Will Step Down." *Washington Post* (June 13). http://www.washingtonpost.com/wp-dyn/content/article/2009/06/12/AR2009061203817.html.

Krugman, Paul. 2006. "Incentives for the Dead." *New York Times* (October 20): A23.

Kusserow, Adrie S. 2004. *American Individualism: Child Rearing and Social Class in Three Neighborhoods*. New York: Palgrave Macmillian.

Lamont, Michele, and Annette Lareau. 1988. "Cultural Capital: Allusions, Gaps and Glissandos in Recent Theoretical Developments." *Sociological Theory* 6 (Fall): 153–68.

Lareau, Annette. 2007. "Unequal Childhoods: Class, Race, and Family Life," pp. 537–48 in David B. Grusky and Szonja Szelényi (eds.), *The Inequality Reader: Contemporary and Foundational Readings in Race, Class, and Gender*. Boulder: Westview Press.

Lareau, Annette, and Elliot B. Weininger. 2003. "Cultural Capital in Educational Research: A Critical Assessment." *Theory and Society* 32: 567–606.

Lin, Nan. 2000. "Inequality in Social Capital." *Contemporary Society* 29 (November): 785–95.

Ludden, David. 2008. "A Quick Guide to the World History of Globalization." http://www.sas.upenn.edu/~dludden/global1.htm.

MacLeod, Jay. 2009. *Ain't No Makin' It: Aspirations and Attainment in a Low-Income Neighborhood*, 3rd ed. Boulder: Westview Press.

Magno, Cathryn. 2008. "Refuge from Crisis: Refugee Women Build Political Capital." *Globalisation, Societies and Education* 6 (June): 119–30.

Mishel, Lawrence. 2006. "CEO-to-Worker Pay Imbalance Grows." Economic Policy Institute. www.epi.org/content.cfm/webfeatures_snapshots_20060621.

Oliver, Melvin L., and Thomas M. Shapiro. 2006. *Black Wealth/White Wealth: A New Perspective on Racial Inequality*, 2nd ed. New York: Routledge.

Perrucci, Robert, and Earl Wysong. 2008. *The New Class Society: Goodbye American Dream?*, 3rd ed. Lanham, MD: Rowman & Littlefield.

Portes, Alejandro. 1998. "Social Capital: Its Origins and Applications in Modern Society." *Annual Review of Sociology* 24: 1–24.

Portes, Alejandro. 2000. "The Two Meanings of Social Capital." *Sociological Forum* 15 (March): 1–12.

Prante, Gerald. 2009. "Summary of Latest Federal Individual Income Tax Data." The Tax Foundation. http://www.taxfoundation,org/news/show/250.html.

Putnam, Robert D. 1995. "Tuning In, Tuning Out: The Strange Disappearance of Capital in America." *PS: Political Science and Politics* 28 (December): 664–83.

Robertson, Susan L. 2008. "Reflections on Education, Democracy and Social Change." *Globalisation, Societies and Education* 6 (June): 101–03.

Rockefeller, David. 2002. *Memoirs*. New York: Random House.

Sennett, Richard. 2006. *The Culture of the New Capitalism*. New Haven: Yale University Press.

Slavin, Robert E. 1999. "How Can Funding Equity Ensure Enhanced Åchievement?" *Journal of Education Finances* 24:519–28.

Social Register Association. 2008. "Welcome to the Official Web Site of the Social Register Association." http://www.socialregisteronline.com/.

Spillane, James P., Tim Hallett, and John B. Diamond. 2003. "Forms of Capital and the Construction of Leadership: Instructional Leadership in Urban Elementary Schools." *Sociology of Education* 76 (January): 1–17.

Stiglitz, Joseph E. 2002. *Globalization and Its Discontents*. New York: W.W. Norton & Company.

Story, Louise. 2010. "Slicing the Pie: New Research Raises a Question: Do Widening Gaps between Rich and Poor Necessarily Lead to Financial Crisis?" *New York Times* (August 22). "Week in Review," p. 5.

Svendsen, Gunnar Lend, and Gert Tinggaard Svendsen. 2003. "On the Wealth of Nations: Bourdieuconomics and Social Capital." *Theory and Society* 32: 607–31.

United Nations Development Programme. *2009.* "Ratio of the Richest 10% to Poorest 10%." *Human Development Reports*. http://hdrstats.undp.org/indicators/145.html.

U.S. Bureau of Labor Statistics. 2008a. "Displaced Workers Summary." (August 20). http://www.bis.gov/news.release/disp.nr0.htm.

U.S. Bureau of Labor Statistics. 2008b. "Reasons for Job Losses among Displaced Workers." (August 22). http://www.bls.gov/opub/ted/2008/aug/wk3/art05.htm.

U.S. Census Bureau. 2008. Table A–3. "Mean Earnings of Workers 18 and Over, by Educational Attainment, Race, Hispanic Origin, and Sex: 1975 to 2007." *Current Population Survey*. http://www.census.gov/population/socdemo/education/cps2008/tabA-3.csv.

Wacquant, Loic J. D. 1989. "The Rise of Advanced Marginality: Notes on Its Nature and Implications." *Benjamin E. Mays Monograph Series* 2 (Fall): 7–20.

Walford, Geoffrey. 1986. "Ruling-Class Classification and Framing." *British Educational Research Journal* 12: 183–95.

Warren, Elizabeth. 2007. "The New Economics of the Middle Class: Why Making Ends Meet Has Gotten Harder." Testimony Before Senate Finance Committee, May 10, 2007. http://finance.senate.gov/hearings/testimony/2007test/051007testew.pdf.

World Bank 2006. 2006. "Inequality Measures: Gini Index." http://hdr.undp.org/hdr2006/statistics/indicators/147.html.

Wright, Erik Olin. 2005. "Foundations of a Neo-Marxist Class Analysis, pp. 4–30 in Erik Olin Wright (ed.), *Approaches to Class Analysis*. Cambridge: Cambridge University Press.

Yankelovich, Daniel. 1981. "New Rules in American Life: Searching for Fulfillment in a World Turned Upside Down." *Psychology Today* 14 (April): 35–91.

Young, Alfred A., Jr. 2004. *The Minds of Marginalized Black Men: Making Sense of Mobility, Opportunity and Future Life*. Princeton: Princeton University Press.

Zinn, Maxine Baca, and D. Stanley Eitzen. 2005. "Economic Restructuring and Systems of Inequality," pp. 16–19 in Thomas M. Shapiro (ed.), *Great Divides: Readings in Social Inequality in the United States*, 3rd ed. New York: McGraw-Hill.

CHAPTER 2

In Marx's Wake: Theories of Social Stratification and Social Inequality

After World War II, the United States was prospering, with little concern about economic woes, global terrorism, or environmental destruction. Yes, enemies existed—the Soviet Union and China, in particular—but for most people these distant threats had little impact on daily existence.

The title of a popular sitcom captured a sense of the era—"Happy Days." In the program set in the 1950s, a number of teens went about their pleasant, light-hearted activities, often meeting at a diner called Arnold's, where while wolfing down milkshakes, sodas, ice cream, and sandwiches, they kidded each other about the myriad trivia of high-school life. In that "happy days" era, little attention went to such potentially divisive social-stratification topics as class, race/ethnicity, and gender. Little reference to social inequality occurred, even in sociology courses and books.

At the time the dominant voice in the field belonged to Talcott Parsons, who wrote in *The Social System* that his subject matter featured "an integrated structure of action elements . . . brought together in a certain kind of ordered system" (Parsons 1951, 36). With the use of such words as "integrated" and "ordered," Parsons emphasized that the system he described was stable, in equilibrium. Change, conflict, social stratification, and social inequality were not prominent concerns.

By the late 1960s, however, the content of sociology, including its theory, had begun to change. Civil-rights activity in the South, protest against the Vietnam War, and then a few years later the emergence of the women's liberation movement helped develop considerable interest in and concern about a number of inequality-related issues.

This chapter has four main sections. The structural-functional theory presented in the opening part contrasts sharply with the conflict perspectives in the following two sections, where Marxist theory plays a dominant role. Then the fourth section, featuring three theories, examines the issue of the power elite, which concerns the influential set of individuals who establish and implement the primary policies for running the country.

While the material in this chapter presents the work of sociologists who are experts in formulating theories about social activity, they are hardly the only individuals developing theories. Many people of varied backgrounds produce or subscribe to theories about a host of issues—about childrearing, global warming, world peace, and many more. A **sociological theory**, which is the focus here, is a combination of observations and insights providing a systematic explanation of social life. The upcoming theory offers a sharp contrast to the other theories examined in this chapter.

THE DAVIS-MOORE THEORY OF SOCIAL STRATIFICATION

Spearheaded by Parsons's work, **structural-functional theory** is a perspective suggesting that groups in interaction tend to adjust to one another in a fairly stable, conflict-free way. Kingsley Davis and Wilbert E. Moore (1945) produced a well-known version of structural-functional theory, arguing that social stratification is inevitable and necessary. They contended that because some positions require special ability or training, individuals qualified to do these jobs are in short supply. For medical doctors the arduous, taxing years of training, which are costly and restrict them in earning money, are a sacrifice they would not endure without the likelihood that they would eventually be well paid. Indeed, Davis and Moore claimed, because of the importance of what they do and the scarcity of individuals with their qualifications, medical doctors and others in functionally critical occupations must be well compensated, demonstrating the inevitable necessity for social stratification in modern societies. For an individual in an elevated profession like medicine, the benefits of high placement in the social-stratification system include a lot of money, but there needs to be more. Davis and Moore's characterization of such jobs was that "the position must be high in the social scale—must command great prestige, high salary, ample leisure, and the like" (Davis and Moore 1945, 244).

In the structural-functional tradition, Davis and Moore described a smoothly running social-stratification system in which people in elevated positions receive sufficient rewards "to draw talent and motivate training" (Davis and Moore 1945, 247).

As a member of the same sociology department at Princeton, Melvin Tumin rejected the Davis and Moore theory, dismissing the idea that individuals in well-paid positions are compensated for talent and training. In rebuttal Tumin raised several points:

- Well-paid people are not necessarily more valuable than less affluent individuals. For instance, for the survival of a factory, the unskilled workers are as essential as the engineers. Without both categories of employees doing their jobs effectively, the factory will collapse.
- Instead of job payment linked to an elusive functional contribution, the key requirement for receiving high income is bargaining power (Tumin 1953, 388). As a modern example not provided by Tumin, prominent professional athletes and entertainers do not necessarily make a major contribution to the well-being of society, but their popularity buttressed by agents and managers who negotiate for them leads to lucrative contracts. Or, to return to Davis and Moore's example of medical doctors, evidence supporting Tumin's focus on bargaining power indicates that the American Medical Association (the AMA) has used its considerable influence to pare down the number of doctors. Starting in 1904 the Council on Medical Education of the AMA pressured state medical boards to shut down many medical schools and to curtail the number of students at those remaining. Between 1900 and 2002,

the US population increased nearly 300 percent but the number of medical schools, most of which lost students, declined by 26 percent (Steinreich 2004). The key here was an organization's influential role in restricting the numbers of individuals trained as doctors. In short, the AMA used its bargaining power to establish and maintain a scarcity of doctors, thereby keeping their fees high.

• Finally Tumin believed that Davis and Moore overstated the sacrifice doctors and others preparing for high-status jobs experience. He pointed out that the parents, not the students themselves, generally pay for the schooling. Tumin indicated that "this cost tends to be paid out of income which the parents were able to earn generally by virtue of *their* [his italics] privileged positions in the hierarchy of stratification" (Tumin 1953, 390). To Tumin's thinking most medical students are not sacrificing economically but are the apparent beneficiaries of at least two generations of social reproduction. Far from sacrificing, Tumin continued, well-educated students receive psychic benefits from their schooling or training. These include a life of greater freedom and flexibility than most full-time workers. In addition, there is "the much higher prestige enjoyed by the college student and the professional-school student as compared with persons in shops and offices" (Tumin 1953, 390).

Tumin described a social-stratification system not based on individuals' talent and training but on the influence occupational groups or their lobbyists can exert favoring high salaries. Such a conclusion fits into an intellectual tradition opposing the structural-functional approach. **Conflict theory** is a perspective contending that the struggle for wealth, power, and prestige in society should be the central concern of sociology. This approach is useful for analyzing topics involving social inequality and social stratification, where focus is on the process by which the members of different classes and other stratified groups receive greatly varied access to income, wealth, power, and prestige. The towering figure in conflict theory has been Karl Marx.

MARXIST THEORY OF CAPITALISM AND SOCIAL STRATIFICATION

Karl Marx was a philosopher, political, economic, and sociological theorist, and revolutionary, who lived and worked in a tumultuous era during which unrest and rebellion were common. Marx frequently addressed the stormy contemporary realities—for instance, describing the major economic events in late 1840s France that produced an "eruption of the general discontent" (Marx 1959, 286). Facing many competitive socialist thinkers, Marx sometimes attacked and ridiculed their doctrines (Tucker 1978, xxxiii). He was an unrelenting critic of capitalism but also its victim. From the late 1840s to the middle 1850s, Marx and his family lived in poverty, with only three of his seven children surviving to adulthood (Singer 2000, 5).

Marxist theory contributes significantly to the study of social stratification and social inequality, a contribution grounded in economic analysis.

The Economic Structure of Marxist Theory

Marx believed that the mode of production has a dominant influence on the development of a society's structures and activities. The **mode of production** is a nation's organized system for developing goods and services such as feudalism, capitalism, or socialism. In a well-known passage, Marx indicated that the mode of production "conditions the social,

In 2011 thousands of unionized public workers met at the Wisconsin capitol to protest the governor's bill eliminating most of their collective-bargaining rights. The reality conflict theory addresses is apparent—that the political and economic elite and average citizens often have sharply opposing interests.

political and intellectual life process in general. It is not the consciousness of men that determines their being, but, on the contrary, their . . . [mode of production] that determines their consciousness" (Marx and Engels 1968, 182).

Marxist theory focuses on **capitalism**, a system in which economic production features private ownership in pursuit of profit. Widely considered the foremost critic of capitalism, Marx nonetheless acknowledged its contribution in promoting international economic advancement. Marx and his long-time collaborator Frederick Engels indicated that industrial capitalism "during its rule of scarce one hundred years, has created more massive and more colossal productive forces than have all preceding generations together" (Marx and Engels 2005, 46). While lauding the material accomplishments of capitalism, Marx opposed its system of private ownership and the exploitation of workers that accompanied it.

In analyzing capitalism and other modes of production, Marxist theory distinguished a core pair of concepts. The **substructure** involves the material conditions of production such as gathering and hunting, agriculture, or industrial development. The type of substructure determines the **superstructure**, which concerns the noneconomic parts or institutions of society—for instance, the political system, medicine and healthcare, the family, or education. An industrial society, where most healthy adults are fully employed 40 hours a week or more in diverse occupations, possesses a complicated superstructure. To govern such a society, a well-developed political system is necessary; in addition, to prepare people to perform adequately in this complex work world, extensive schooling and training are essential; furthermore families must function adequately to nurture children through their formative years, providing them the cultural capital to interact effectively in the complex, business-driven world (Marx 1920).

An element of the superstructure that greatly interested Marx was the capitalist class system. As with all parts of the superstructure, Marx contended that the capitalist mode of production determines its structure and activities.

Marx's Capitalist Class System

Marx focused on two classes, which differ in their relationship to the **means of production**—the factories, farms, and businesses, where goods and services are developed and dispersed. The **bourgeoisie** is the class with ownership of the various means of production. Wide-ranging power and control over business activity and all sectors of the superstructure follow from that ownership. The **proletariat** involves the workers, who do not own the means of production. They must labor for wages because they have no other source of income (Marx and Engels 1959, 4).

Engels indicated that in the late nineteenth century most Americans denied that a class struggle between the bourgeoisie and proletariat could develop in the United States. However, workers were experiencing exploitative conditions that were similar to those their European counterparts encountered, and so they unionized and engaged in widespread strikes, encouraging a shared consciousness "of the fact that they formed a new and distinct class of American society: a class of—practically speaking—more or less hereditary wage workers, proletarians" (Engels 1959, 490).

Capitalism, Marx contended, is a brutal system, driven by the bourgeoisie's unrelenting push for ever-expanding profits. The value of a product is largely based on the monetary worth of a worker's labor. However, according to Marx, workers only receive a small, subsistence portion of the value of their labor. The **surplus value**, which is the difference between a product's economic worth and the worker's payment, provides the bourgeoisie with ever-expanding profit and the proletariat with a steadily declining standard of living. Marx strongly condemned the capitalist system when he wrote:

> The bourgeoisie . . . has pitilessly torn asunder the motley feudalities that bound man to his "natural superiors," and has left remaining no other nexus between man and man than naked self-interest, than callous "cash payment."
>
> (MARX AND ENGELS 2005, 43)

To keep control of capitalism, the bourgeoisie has used several powerful tools. One is **ideology**, which involves the complex of values and beliefs that support a society's social-stratification systems and their distribution of wealth, income, and power. Because of the bourgeoisie's ideological control, **false consciousness** prevails—the proletariat's inability to perceive that the established economic and political forces inevitably maintain their domination and exploitation (Gagné and McGauchey 2002; Rosen 1996). Marx did not use the term, but he wrote about the context in which the process unfolds.

Many politicians are masters at promoting false consciousness. A fairly modern example would be the "trickle-down" economics of the Reagan administration, which claimed, with considerable major media support, that various tax breaks involving reduced taxes on capital gains, corporate profits, and wealthy people's income would eventually benefit the overall population by encouraging companies to invest more heavily in the economy and creating more jobs for members of various classes, higher wages, and a general upturn in the economy (Etebari 2003). Such a projected outcome is consistent with the American ideology, which has always contended that the more restricted government's input in business—in this instance cutting taxes—the more capitalism thrives. While trickle-down economics has not come to pass, some modern politicians have continued to assert its validity.

All in all, Marx concluded, the bourgeoisie's use of ideology to influence the proletariat's thinking has proved effective. He observed, "The class which has the means of material production at its disposal has control at the same time over the means of mental production" (Marx 1978a, 172). Chapter 4 illustrates this claim, analyzing major corporations' powerful impact on mass-media content.

A second source of domination the bourgeoisie can tap is the government, which, Marx believed, simply exists to serve ruling class interests. Since its officials represent the bourgeoisie, the proletariat with its opposing interests loses out. According to Marx, the government "is nothing but a machine for oppression of one class by another" (Marx 1978b, 628).

In addition to the bourgeoisie and proletariat, Marx described two other classes, providing useful information for Erik Wright and other theorists seeking to update and refine Marx's analysis. They are the **petite bourgeoisie**, a small-business class, whose members never accumulate enough profit to expand their holdings and to challenge the bourgeoisie's economic supremacy; and the **lumpenproletariat**, the portion of the working class comprised of society's dregs—swindlers, brothel-keepers, beggars, and such—who are disengaged from the revolutionary struggle. Members of these two classes are minor characters in Marx's story, which focuses on the two principals—the bourgeoisie and the proletariat. Philosopher Lewis S. Feuer suggested that like other prophets Marx was a dualist, seeing history as a "conflict between good and evil, the children of light and the children of darkness" (Feuer 1959, xviii).

Marx on Revolution and Its Aftermath

Capitalism, Marx declared, is a system where the interests of the two major classes directly oppose each other. Because of their relentless domination by the bourgeoisie, the proletariat eventually understands and rejects false consciousness, realizing the only hope for improving their situation is to organize resistance among their fellow workers. Joined by some marginal members of the bourgeoisie, the organized proletariat becomes large and powerful enough to overthrow its tormenters, fervently believing that revolution has become the sole option. Marx and Engels wrote, "The proletarians have nothing to lose but their chains. They have a world to win" (Marx and Engels 1959, 41)

After the revolution, socialism replaces capitalism. According to Marx, **socialism** is an economic system in which the proletariat controls the means of production and the distribution of profits. A radical change has occurred, featuring the elimination of the exploitative bourgeoisie and its ownership of the means of production.

What have critics emphasized about Marxist theory?

Commentary

Marx's theoretical work demonstrates both weaknesses and strengths.

WEAKNESSES

- Max Weber, whose theory is examined next, was an early critic of Marxism. According to Weber's biographers, he felt Marx's work featured "an untenable monocausal theory" (Weber 1946, 46–47). Like many others Weber emphasized that Marx focused on one factor—the economic mode of production—as the determinant of developments in the social world and failed to acknowledge that other factors like political power, values, or the mass media can function as independent variables.

- Marxist theory does not acknowledge the widespread separation of business ownership and control. Marx believed that control followed from ownership. In fact, during his lifetime the bourgeoisie usually both owned and ran their companies, but as corporations have grown larger and more complex, specialized managers have become increasingly necessary to oversee business activity (Wright 1978, 67–68).

- Marx and Engels significantly underestimated the role played by the middle class (petite bourgeoisie), feeling that it would disappear in the struggle between the bourgeoisie and the proletariat. In truth, the middle class has often played an important part in modern capitalism, sometimes serving as a buffer or intermediary between the potentially clashing capitalists and workers (Muravchik 2002, 36).

- Marx proved incorrect about who led the revolutions that reorganized nations. It was not the proletariat but well-educated middle-class individuals who created government bureaucracies that often served their personal interests and failed to promote socialist goals (Harrington 1972, 74).

- With his fixation on the overthrow of capitalist nations, Marx was wrong about where the major revolutions occurred—not in the capitalist economies but in feudal systems like Russia, China, and Cuba (Muravchik 2002, 37). These countries had highly repressive regimes which kept most of the proletariat desperately poor, deprived of basic human rights, and receptive to revolution once capable leadership arose.

Countering its weaknesses, Marxist theory is recognized for its important contributions.

STRENGTHS

- Proponents of Marx's theory contend that its analysis of capitalism captures a sense of the system's basic qualities. Referring to *The Communist Manifesto*, perhaps Marx and Engels's most celebrated work, a scholar noted that the system they depicted seems fully modern, emphasizing "a relentless drive to expand and . . ." [to develop] "society's productive capacities to levels undreamed of in early centuries" (Gasper 2005, 96). Besides conveying the general spirit of capitalism, Marx also described complicated, subtle qualities of this economic system that continue to reveal themselves in the contemporary world. For instance, he was concerned with the subject of new technology replacing labor power and driving down the value of commodities, and also was troubled about the formation of a **reserve army of labor**, namely the bourgeoisie's purposeful maintenance of a distinct level of unemployment as a bargaining chip for keeping wages low (Milward 2000, 186–87). In modern times the nation has always had such an entity, which has fluctuated in size, registering 3.8 percent of the workforce of ages 16 and over in 1948, then rising to 9.6 percent in 1983, dropping to 4 percent in 2000, and climbing to 9.5 percent in 2010

(Bureau of Labor Statistics 2010). In addition, Marx emphasized the fundamental link between capitalism and class. Sociologist Anthony Giddens observed that the theory stressed that the exploitative relationship between the bourgeoisie and the proletariat produces a class struggle, "which constitutes the essential core of capitalism as a social and economic system" (Giddens 1973, 85).

• Marxist theory has made an important contribution to the development of class analysis itself. Marx examined such significant issues as the emergence of class-based economic interests and the developing consciousness of class groups (Berberoglu 2005, 10; Ollman 1968, 580). Sociologist Charles H. Anderson indicated that Marx's division of the citizenry within capitalism remains broadly accurate—with very few qualifying as capitalists and the rest classified as working-class, or at least non-capitalist. Anderson wrote, "In terms of objective interest, that interest can only be defined as profit for the capitalist class and as material and social well-being for the working class. The two objective interests are today totally and unqualifiedly incompatible" (Anderson 1974, 124).

• Finally, with his analysis of ideology and false consciousness, Marx encouraged later scholars to examine how leaders' public statements are prone to bias and distortion in situations where the stakes involve wealth, power, and control. Michael Harrington concluded that Marxist analysis has an unusually clear-eyed, concrete perception of these topics, relentlessly using a fact-based approach to ferret out class bias and privilege and reveal the associated ideology justifying the elite's advantages (Harrington 1976, 192). Table 2.1 provides highlights of the Marxist theory.

The significant effect of Marxist thinking is apparent in theory and research on social inequality and social stratification, including Max Weber's contributions.

TABLE 2.1 Central Concepts and Ideas in the Marxist Theory of Capitalism and Social Stratification

1. Core concept: Mode of production, with the substructure determining the superstructure

2. Mode of production determining the class structure: In capitalism, two classes, the bourgeoisie and proletariat differing in their relationship to the means of production; bourgeoisie receiving ever-expanding profit; proletariat obtaining wages which decline in value over time

   2a. Social forces supporting bourgeoisie's control: a powerful ideology bolstered by false consciousness; an oppressive government

3. Proletariat's exploitation promoting the spread of conflict with the bourgeoisie, leading to eventual revolution. Emergence of socialism, with the proletariat in control

4. Commentary: A number of criticisms overshadowed by several broad points emphasizing Marxist theory's lasting contributions

---

Sources: Karl Marx. 1920. *The Poverty of Philosophy*; Karl Marx. 1959. "Excerpts from *The Class Struggles in France, 1848 to 1850*," pp. 281–317 in Lewis S. Feuer (ed), *Marx & Engels: Basic Writings on Politics & Philosophy*; Karl Marx. 1978. "The Civil War in France," pp. 618–52 in Robert C. Tucker (ed.), *The Marx-Engels Reader*; Karl Marx. 1978. "The German Ideology: Part I," pp. 146–200 in Robert C. Tucker (ed.), *The Marx-Engels Reader*, 2nd ed. New York; Karl Marx and Friedrich Engels. 1959. "Manifesto of the Communist Party," pp. 1–41 in Lewis S. Feuer (ed.), *Marx & Engels: Basic Writings on Politics & Philosophy;* Karl Marx and Friedrich Engels. 1968. *Selected Works in One Volume*; Karl Marx and Friedrich Engels. 2005. "The Annotated Communist Manifesto," pp. 37–90 in Phil Gasper (ed.), *The Communist Manifesto: A Road Map to History's Most Important Document.*

THE MARXIST IMPACT ILLUSTRATED: THREE SOCIAL-STRATIFICATION THEORIES

Weber's theory differs from the other two, which are more aligned with the Marxist perspective, building on its strengths and updating it.

Weber's Theory of Class, Status, and Party

Weber's living situation differed sharply from Marx's. During his working years, decades of peace and widespread prosperity made it possible for distinguished professors like him to lead an affluent existence. In other ways, however, he struggled. Throughout his life Weber suffered bouts of severe depression interspersed with periods of intense intellectual work. During the active times, he painstakingly examined complicated contemporary issues, strongly and proudly supporting the drive to create a nation state and yet also fighting for individual freedom; expressing pride in having been a German officer but describing the Kaiser, the army's commander-in-chief, as a shameful individual; and growing up as a self-consciously masculine member of the upper-middle-class with dedication to duels and drinking but encouraging the first female labor official in Germany and addressing members of the women's emancipation movement early in the twentieth century. Weber sympathized deeply with poor working people, but a Marxist revolution struck him as a "bloody carnival," which could not possibly produce effective structural change (Gerth and Mills 1946, 11, 24–26, 41). Marx's ideas were always a source of Weber's attention.

Since Weber criticized Marxist thought for its alleged monocausality, it is hardly surprising that his study of social stratification was decidedly not monocausal, assessing three central dimensions in conflict theory—class, status, and power. In analyzing class, Weber, like Marx, examined economic issues, but he described a system that is more diversified in its stratification systems and much less concerned about capitalist exploitation. Table 2.2 compares Marx's and Weber's theories.

CLASS According to Weber, a class is a set of individuals with similar chances for gaining income and wealth in the business world (Weber 1946, 181). Weber indicated that the force creating class is "unambiguously economic interest, and indeed, only those interests involved in the interests of the market" (Weber 1999, 85).

Weber designated more classes than Marx. While owners of companies and workers are included, Weber's classification considered many occupational settings that vary widely in income, wealth, and life chances (Weber 1946, 182–83). For instance, the owner of a small warehouse or office building might barely make a profit while the proprietor of a discount merchandising chain might be a multimillionaire or a billionaire. Similar diversity exists among workers. A member of a company's custodial staff and one of its managers are both unpropertied, but the latter might earn 50 times as much as the former.

Weber indicated that individuals' class position, namely their income and wealth, influences the second factor in his social-stratification analysis.

STATUS Weber described status as an estimation of a person's honor or prestige (Weber 1946, 146–47). Unlike classes, status groups, loosely speaking, are communities in which members share a broadly similar lifestyle. Income and wealth are not the only

TABLE 2.2 Comparative Features of Marx's and Weber's Theories

	Marx	Weber
The theorist's context	A tumultuous era in which unrest and rebellion were frequent	A settled, physically comfortable time period but a tormented inner life
Source(s) of social stratification	Focus on the mode of production determining social stratification and all other elements in the superstructure	Examination of class, status, and power
Analysis of capitalism	Emphasis on the bourgeoisie's economic and political supremacy and their exploitation of the proletariat	A description of various classes in contemporary capitalism with little attention to the system's exploitation
Prospect of revolution	An inevitability resulting from the proletariat's growing discontent mobilizing a movement to overthrow the bourgeoisie	No prospect of its success but charismatic missions possessing revolutionary overtones

Sources: Karl Marx. 1959. "Excerpts from *The Class Struggles in France, 1848 to 1850*," pp. 281–317 in Lewis S. Feuer (ed.), *Marx & Engels: Basic Writings on Politics & Philosophy*; Karl Marx. 1978. "The Civil War in France," pp. 618–52 in Robert C. Tucker (ed.), *The Marx-Engels Reader*; Karl Marx. 1978. "The German Ideology: Part I," pp. 146–200 in Robert C. Tucker (ed.), *The Marx-Engels Reader*, 2nd ed.; Karl Marx and Friedrich Engels. 1959. "Manifesto of the Communist Party," pp. 1–41 in Lewis S. Feuer (ed.), *Marx & Engels: Basic Writings on Politics & Philosophy*; Karl Marx and Friedrich Engels. 1968. *Selected Works in One Volume*; Karl Marx and Friedrich Engels. 2005. "The Annotated Communist Manifesto," pp. 37–90 in Phil Gasper (ed.), *The Communist Manifesto: A Road Map to History's Most Important Document*; Max Weber. 1946. *From Max Weber: Essays in Sociology*. Hans Gerth and C. Wright Mills (eds.); Max Weber. 1999. *Max Weber: Essays in Economic Theory*. Richard Swedberg (ed.).

factors determining status, but they play a significant role. Somewhat quaintly, Weber concluded that in modern democracies "it may be that only the families coming under approximately the same tax class dance with one another" (Weber 1946, 187).

The principal distinction between class and status, Weber suggested, is that class ranking is based on people's production and acquisition of goods while membership in status groups derives from the consumption of goods, which promotes distinctive lifestyles (Weber 1946, 193).

To be accepted in a certain status group, an individual often must follow strict behavioral standards or meet certain precise qualifications. For instance, to be recognized as a gentleman, a person needs to dress and behave appropriately; or to be accepted into what Weber called the circle of "esteemed" families, one's heritage must include several generations of wealth and a widely supported conviction among this elite status group that the family in question maintains a suitable background, values, and behavior. Those accepted into the select set of esteemed families have distinct advantages (Weber 1946, 188)—in modern times marriage to other members of the esteemed set, valuable social contacts that can advance financial or political interests, and access to high-level positions in various corporations.

Some goods or services a status group obtains might have little impact on their everyday living. **Conspicuous consumption** is lavish expenditure on high-priced goods and services in order to flaunt one's wealth. Thorstein Veblen, the economist who coined the term, indicated that costly gifts and elaborate dinner parties serve as examples (Lerner 1948, 117). Conspicuous consumption tends to be wasteful, spending money on goods or services that might have been used for some practical end. From the Middle Ages onward, ample lawns served as a means for the landed gentry to display the fact that in many cases they could afford to sacrifice large plots of potential grazing land (Seth's Blog 2010).

Some connection exists between class and status groups. Members of higher classes with greater wealth and income are likely to have lifestyles differing from those with less financial capital. Weber suggested that occupational groups produce status groups (Weber 1946, 193). Dentists and construction workers are likely to have on-the-job clothing, food preferences, recreational choices, and housing types and location that are distinctly different.

Both status groups and classes link to Weber's third dimension of social stratification.

PARTY Individuals "live in a house of power," Weber indicated (Weber 1946, 194). Indeed, he suggested, parties are about power, with their members seeking specific outcomes in a deliberate, planned manner by imposing their will on others. Parties can represent the interests of either class or status groups, but often they support a combination of both. In modern societies parties refer not only to political parties but also unions, consumer groups, business organizations, foundations, civic groups, and many more.

Weber visualized parties exercising three types of **authority**—power derived from a person's location within an organization or structure. The first, bureaucratic authority, is widely dispersed in modern societies:

1. **Bureaucratic system of authority:** It is a structure that systematically administers the tasks controlling an organization's operation. The bureaucratic system of authority developed in such ancient societies as China, Japan, and India, and today it exists in all modern public and private organizations. Some of the basic characteristics of this system are that:
   • Laws or administrative rules control the bureaucratic structure.
   • A hierarchy exists, with those in higher positions supervising those at the lower rungs.
   • The bureaucracy requires written records, which are carefully recorded and preserved (Weber 1946, 196–98; Weber 1999, 100–01).
   Weber was impressed with bureaucratic systems, indicating that in the capitalist market economy they permitted activities to be "discharged precisely, unambiguously, continuously, and with as much speed as possible" (Weber 1946, 215). Modern sociologists, however, have often emphasized a negative side, indicating that the bureaucrats themselves can become inflexible supporters of the rules, with both their clients and the organization itself adversely affected (Merton 1968, 177–78). Many comedians have developed routines that mock bureaucrats' rigidity or callousness— for instance the emergency-room official who requires the profusely bleeding patient to fill out lengthy medical forms in triplicate.
2. **Traditional system of authority:** This system is usually patriarchal, with the dominant individual, whether a husband, father, master, chieftain, lord, or king, maintaining legitimacy based on established belief. It is a situation in which the rules are

sacred, with violation leading to anger and perhaps violent reaction (Weber 1946, 296–97). The traditional patriarchal standard practice was that the eldest son would succeed his father as king, chief, or simply owner of the family plot of land. With obvious exaggeration but also more than a sliver of truth, many have observed that America was settled by second and third (etc.) sons and their families.

3. **Charismatic system of authority:** At the core of this system, there is an individual who pursues a mission driven by a powerful sense of divine purpose and draws followers who are committed to that mission. It might be a quest for political independence, a push for the end of racial oppression, or an effort to establish a new religion. Neither leaders nor followers engage in a charismatic mission for economic gain. They are outsiders who want significant change in society. Unlike the other two systems, the charismatic variety contains little or no structure or established rules. Charismatic authority is volatile, only lasting as long as followers maintain personal allegiance to the leader and his or her mission (Weber 1946, 248–50).

This reality appears to make successful charismatic leaders like Malcolm X and Martin King vulnerable to assassination. Kill the leader and the mission dies too. Charisma has become a common term, seemingly referring to charm or perhaps sex appeal. What has disappeared from this modern usage is Weber's sense that the charismatic individual appeals to people not because of a nice smile or winning personality but because he or she is leading what followers consider a crucially important mission to which they are committed.

While all three of these men have been considered charismatic, only Martin Luther King, Jr., meets Weber's standard. He emerged as a prominent civil-rights leader from outside the established political system while the Kennedys, in contrast, were elected officials.

Overall, however, modern usage of Weber's concepts has remained true to the original meanings. Sociologists have found his emphasis on three dimensions of social stratification—class, status, and party (power)—helpful, encouraging a broader look at the topic than Marx's economically focused analysis.

Some sociologists, especially those attuned to social inequality and social stratification, have suggested that Weber's analysis was too uncritical of capitalism. His examination of class focused on the varied life chances that classes possess in a market economy and avoided the often conflicting relations between classes. In particular, Weber gave little attention to one of Marx's central ideas—capitalists' exploitation of the working class (Wright 2002, 850–51). In contrast, the upcoming theories clearly display an affinity to Marxist thinking.

Wright's Perspective on Class

As a graduate student in the 1970s, Erik Wright felt that it was essential for proponents of Marx's theory "to engage in serious and systematic quantitative research." He stressed two reasons—that because quantitative analysis is the "central terrain of academic sociology," such investigations would establish the theory's legitimacy; and that "some of the important questions" supporters of the theory ask "can be illuminated" through this research (Wright 1989, 3).

Wright agreed with Marx that ownership of the means of production should be a factor in determining class placement, but he contended that others traits—control over the production process, control over employees, and job holders' skills—are also important in determining class location (Wright 1978, 64–74; Wright 1997, 20–26; Wright 2005):

Control over ownership: Owners make basic decisions about investment and expansion such as where to invest corporate profits or whether to take over another company.

Control over the production process: Managers or other authorities must develop a strategy about production—for instance, whether to increase, decrease, or maintain the production level of ice cream or cell phones.

Control over the employees: The focus here involves the range of supervision—whether it is over an entire organization, a portion of it, or over nobody. Foremen, for instance, are workers in charge of distinct plant operations (Wright 1978, 64–74).

Skill level: Some people acquire distinct abilities through training or special talent, providing a valuable contribution to an organization. Within a company, employees can range in skill level from highly credentialed managers or consultants to manual workers with few or no formal qualifications and training (Wright 1997, 20–26).

The following examples illustrate how Wright used these four factors in determining classes (Wright 1978, 96–108):

• According to Wright, Marxist-style owners such as a Henry Ford or John D. Rockefeller are "employers." These people own the companies, exerting control over their financial future. They are the dominant players in production decisions, and, in addition, these individuals are positioned at the top of the company hierarchy, exercising control over the entire workforce. Such employers are not likely to possess extensive business expertise, and Wright indicated that in the highly competitive modern corporate setting what he labeled "expert managers" have assumed an expanded role in the production process.

- Low-level managers, whom Wright labeled "managers," have no control over either ownership or production but do oversee their portion of the hierarchy. These employees require well-developed social skills for getting along with superiors, equals, and subordinates. Some formal credentials are normally required such as a college degree.
- "Experts" are highly successful, well-credentialed scientists, with a Ph.D., special training, and talent for developing advances in a highly technical research specialty. They have no ownership of the means of production but do supervise their staff. By making cutting-edge scientific breakthroughs, these individuals bring honor and research funding to a university and increased profit to a business.
- Wright's "workers" are employees with no ownership of the means of production, no control over production, no supervisory role, and no special talent or training. They might be service employees in a fast-food restaurant or members of a custodial staff or construction crew.

Like Wright, Robert Perrucci and Earl Wysong have shared Marx's perception that the capitalist system has shaped the formation of the modern class structure.

Perrucci and Wysong's Theory of Class

In a Marxist tradition, Perrucci and Wysong described an elite, which they labeled "the privileged class" or "superclass." These people, who represent 1 to 2 percent of the nation's residents, obtain six- to seven-figure incomes annually from business ownership and/or investment.

The elite's close allies are Perrucci and Wysong's "credentialed class"—composed of managers, specifically mid- and high-level managers, and top officers of corporations and public organizations with salaries in the six- and seven-figure range and often advanced degrees in such fields as business, the law, and accounting and represent about 13 to 15 percent of the population; and "professionals" such as physicians, lawyers, and academic individuals at prestigious universities with terminal degrees in their respective fields and salaries ranging from $100,000 a year to high six figures and comprising about 4 to 5 percent of the American people.

Economically speaking, the three elevated classes represent "the privileged classes"—"the haves"—and the remaining approximately 80 percent are "the new working class"—"the have nots," wage earners with supervised work and often possessing limited skills and job security. At the top of the second segment are what Perrucci and Wysong called "the comfort class" composed of such occupational groups as nurses, police personnel, small-business owners, machinists, carpenters, and plumbers, who possess less education and skills than privileged-class members. Many of these job holders receive highly controlled management supervision and frequently risk abrupt termination because of the impact of both new technology and downsizing. Thousands of individuals in this class are tempted to avoid unpleasant supervision by starting their own businesses, but while some succeed, many are too poorly funded, suggesting that self-employment in the new working class is a risky business. Incomes in this class range between $35,000 and $50,000, with membership representing about 10 percent of the country's residents.

Perrucci and Wysong designated the largest section of the "have nots" as "the contingent class," meaning that the people in question are particularly vulnerable to losing their jobs. About half of the population are "wage earners," obtaining about $30,000 a year in such positions as machine operators, sales and clerical staff members, low-level supervisors, and skilled craft workers. Their job insecurity is likely to be greater than that faced by members of the new working class. A small portion of the contingent class, comprising about 3 to 4 percent of all people, are "self-employed personnel" running low-volume businesses, with few or no staff members. Examples include owners of small retail stores and restaurants that seldom generate much income and are highly vulnerable to failure.

Finally Perrucci and Wysong described an additional 10 to 15 percent of the population forming "the excluded class"—those at the bottom of the occupational structure, possessing little formal education and training and moving in and out of the labor force in largely unskilled, temporary jobs (Perrucci and Wysong 2008, 22–31).

This scheme emphasizes social inequality, especially economic inequality involving a privileged, affluent 20 percent and a nonprivileged, nonaffluent 80 percent. No middle class exists. Table 2.3 indicates how Marxist analysis influenced each of the three theories just discussed.

TABLE 2.3 Marxist Theory as a Point of Departure for Other Theories of Social Stratification

Theorist	Central Idea of the Theory
Max Weber	To develop a theory of social stratification that unlike Marx's is not unidimensional. Thus his analysis of three dimensions: class, status, and party (power)
Erik Wright	To quantify Marxist theory, moving beyond Marx's position that ownership/nonownership of the means of production represents the exclusive determinant of class and instead to propose four variables impacting class formation: control over ownership; control over means of production; control over employees; and skill level
Robert Perrucci and Earl Wysong	Displaying a Marxist-like economic distinction between "the haves" and "the have nots." Extension of Marx's class system, featuring seven occupationally based classes

Source: Robert Perrucci and Earl Wysong. 2008. *The New Class Society: Goodbye American Dream?*, 3rd ed.; Lanham, MD: Rowman & Middlefield; Max Weber. 1946. *From Max Weber: Essays in Sociology.* Hans Gerth and C. Wright (eds.). New York: Oxford University Press; Max Weber. 1999. *Max Weber: Essays in Economic Theory.* Richard Swedberg (ed.); Erik Olin Wright. 1978. *Class, Crisis and the State*; Erik Olin Wright. 1989. "The Comparative Project on Class Structure and Class Consciousness: An Overview." *Acta Sociologica.* V. 32, pp. 3–22; Erik Olin Wright. 1997. *Class Counts: Comparative Studies in Class Analysis.* Erik Olin Wright. "The Shadow of Exploitation in Weber's Class Analysis." *American Sociological Review.* V. 67, pp. 832–53; Erik Olin Wright. 2005. "Foundations of a Neo-Marxist Class Analysis, pp. 4–30 in Erik Olin Wright (ed.), *Approaches to Class Analysis.*

Besides the theories just discussed, another set of theories Marx's ideas influenced focuses on the role that a select group of leaders play in running society.

THE POWER-ELITE THEORIES

A **power elite** is a number of high-status people, particularly in prominent corporate and political positions, who largely control the process of determining a society's major economic and political policies. Before American social scientists were analyzing power elites, a structural-functional theory, which failed to examine the power-elite issue, was the dominant theory addressing policy development. **Pluralism** is a theory concluding that a dispersion of authority and control exists within government. As a result of this alleged condition, advocates of pluralism claimed that:

- Authority generally will be used for decent purposes because its various sites of power will counterbalance each other, keeping coercive use at a minimum.
- Minorities will possess the authority to veto policies opposing their interests, and as recognized partners in the power game, they will cooperate with other groups over time.
- Political resolution will require constant negotiation among the various centers of power. This process will give the different participants a chance to learn how to produce successful outcomes benefiting all contending parties (Dahl 1967; 1982).

In contrast, the power-elite theorists perceive a huge imbalance of power. C. Wright Mills, for instance, concluded that for corporate leaders "no powers effectively and consistently countervail against them" (Mills 1956, 125).

Mills's Power-Elite Perspective

Like the social-stratification theorists just discussed, Mills both incorporated and revised Marxist ideas. While he shared Marx's recognition of a dominant wealthy and powerful class, Mills believed that the source for that power lay not only in the economic realm but also in the political and military arenas (Domhoff 2006, 547).

Writing in the 1950s, Mills asserted that little knowledge of the power elite existed—that many citizens, including some of the elite, believed that there was no such group; and that others believed, though often vaguely, that "a compact and powerful elite" existed. Some prominent individuals knew that Congress had permitted a handful of political leaders to make critical decisions about peace and war; and that two atomic bombs had been dropped in Japan in the name of the United States, but neither they nor anyone they knew had been consulted (Mills 1956, 4–5). Mills's *The Power Elite* sought to inform people about this unpublicized topic.

According to Mills, the power elite belongs to a privileged class whose members recognize their mutual exalted position in society. As a rule "[t]hey accept one another, understand one another, marry one another, tend to work and to think, if not together at least alike" (Mills 1956, 11). It is a well-regulated existence where education plays a critical role. Youthful upper-class members attend prominent preparatory schools, which not only open doors to such elite universities as Harvard, Yale, and Princeton but also to the universities' highly exclusive clubs. These memberships in turn pave the way to the prominent social clubs located in all major cities and serving as sites for important business contacts (Mills 1956, 63–67).

The upper-class men who receive these special privileges have the background and contacts to enter the three branches of the power elite. These are:

The political leadership: Mills contended that since the end of World War II corporate leaders had become more prominent in the political process, with a decline in central decision-making for professional politicians.

The military circle: In Mills's time a heightened concern about warfare existed, making top military leaders and such issues as defense funding and personnel recruitment very important. Most prominent corporate leaders and politicians were strong proponents of military spending.

The corporate elite: According to Mills, in the 1950s when the military emphasis was pronounced, it was corporate leaders working with prominent military officers who dominated the development of policies. These two groups tended to be mutually supportive (Mills 1956, 274–76).

Mills contended that the power elite has an "inner core" composed of individuals able to move from one institutional area of power to another—a general who becomes a political consultant or a politician who becomes a corporate executive. These people have more knowledge and a greater breadth of interests than their colleagues. Prominent bankers and financiers, who Mills considered "almost professional go-betweens of economic, political, and military affairs," are also members of the elite's inner core (Mills 1956, 288–89).

The Power Elite has distinct limitations. Mills provided little detail about the contemporary elite's activities. For instance, he never mentioned either the Council on Foreign Relations or the Committee on Economic Development, two elite-dominated, policy-making organizations that were already prominent players in his time. In addition, through no fault of his own, Mills described an era when it was still possible to analyze the power elite by focusing only on the United States. The subsequent expansion of globalization has made his theory appear anachronistic (Rothkopf 2009, 117).

On the other hand, Mills was a pioneer, propelling his power-elite theory into a pluralism-dominated academic world, where his novel ideas, according to G. William Domhoff, "caused a firestorm in academic and political circles, leading to innumerable reviews in scholarly journals and the popular press, most of them negative." Over time, however, *The Power Elite* has become a classic, recognized as "the first full-scale study of the structure and distribution of power in the United States," using the complete set of theoretical and research tools then available (Domhoff 2006, 547). Both Domhoff's and Thomas Dye's theories have built upon Mills's conclusions, providing more detail about such issues as the make-up of the ruling group and the process by which policies are established and implemented. Their more contemporary works supply recent information about this powerful group's role in society.

Domhoff's Theory of the Upper-Class-Centered Corporate Community

Sociologist G. William Domhoff borrowed two important ideas from Mills—that the power elite has members primarily born into the upper class and that the cohesion created by their shared background and lifestyle helps promote that leadership group's successful activity. Domhoff described the power elite as largely upper-class people who have leadership roles in business and government and a major commitment to retaining the prevailing rules and laws that sustain the current income and wealth distribution (Domhoff 2010, 115). The power elite, in short, is the dominant instigator of social reproduction.

Domhoff concluded that upper-class status and power-elite membership are not synonymous. Some upper-class individuals are "playboys and socialites," with little involvement in politics. On the other hand, some members of the power elite have middle-class and occasionally working-class origins and gradually worked their way to the top (Domhoff 2005a).

Like Mills, Domhoff indicated that the corporate class has a privileged secondary school and college and university background; New Englanders who graduated from private schools were more likely than upper-class students from other areas to have attended Ivy League universities while their private-school counterparts from outside New England have been more likely to have graduated from prominent state universities (Domhoff 2010, 58–59).

At the structural core of the power elite lies a corporate community composed of profit-seeking organizations embedded in a common network featuring what Domhoff referred to as interlocking directorates. An **interlocking directorate** is a formal connection between two major corporations which develops when an officer from one company serves on the board of directors of another. For 2004 the average number of interlocking directorates among 1,996 leading corporations was just 6.1. The largest, wealthiest corporations, however, had 20 or more, including General Electric with 24 and Citigroup with 25 (Domhoff 2010, 34).

Interlocking directorates can prove useful in specific ways. For instance, corporate leaders find that an effective, safe tactic for promoting various company interests is to join the board of a major media corporation. Thus in 2004 the Washington Post Company elected Melinda Gates, a former Microsoft executive and the wife of founder Bill Gates, to its board of directors. Donald Graham, the co-chairman of the Post said, "She's a well-qualified director, somebody with a good strong technology background and helps to run a very large organization" (Ahrens 2004, E02). What Graham omitted was that the Post leadership's long-time influence with Washington politicians could prove particularly helpful in Microsoft's continuing battle against the enforcement of antitrust legislation.

Besides interlocking directorates helping the companies involved, the executives themselves are distinctly advantaged, particularly "the inner circle" of company leaders who are simultaneously located on boards of two or more large companies. Michael Useem noted that some attributes members of interlocking directorships possess include:

- Access to diverse information, providing a broader grasp of the business community as well as an aura of stature and legitimacy not available to less connected colleagues.
- Membership in a cohesive, powerful group, where inner-circle leaders know each other well and relate to each other extensively.
- A distinct tendency for these individuals to share an upper-class background, which has provided social, cultural, human, and financial capital paving the way to the inner circle.

- Involvement in major policy-making groups such as the Committee for Economic Development and the Business Roundtable, which upcoming chapters indicate play a major role in policy development (Useem 1984, 61–71).

All in all, Domhoff noted that several studies done over time have concluded that the 15–20 percent of corporate directors who sit on two or more boards and form the inner circle unite the big-business world in a largely like-minded corporate community (Domhoff 2010, 36–37). He conceded, however, that the function of interlocking directorates can be overstated. While these connections can be useful for establishing their members' prominence and serve as a means of passing useful information from one corporation to another, the spread of influence is limited. Domhoff suggested that people's own social networks function similarly. "Obviously, you know your friends, and often know some of their other friends, but you certainly don't know the friends of these 'friends of friends'" (Domhoff 2005b).

Domhoff stressed the importance of building social capital for those seeking to join the power elite. The process starts in exclusive prep schools, then moves on to elite colleges and universities, and finally involves upper-class clubs. At each juncture the prospective power-elite members have privileged opportunities to develop friendships and useful contacts with a host of other similarly placed individuals.

The most prominent of these elite organizations is the Bohemian Club, where two weeks a year well-connected economic and political leaders gather for a host of relaxing activities as well as informal opportunities to discuss important policy issues (Domhoff 1974; Domhoff 2005b, 56–60). At one time 45 percent of the nonresident members of the Bohemian Club belonged to the Social Register or to other upper-class directories (Domhoff 1974, 30).

Domhoff obtained statistical information, suggesting a distinct connection between membership in elite social clubs like the Bohemian Club and participation in important policy-making organizations. He found that 673 of the 797 largest corporations had at least one high-level executive simultaneously represented in one of 15 exclusive social clubs and in policy-making organizations—clubs like the Bohemian Club and Links and policy-making organizations like the Business Roundtable and Committee for Economic Development (Domhoff 1975, 179). Because of their executives' multiple organizational connections, top corporations have simultaneous access to privileged information and influence.

In assessing Domhoff's theory, political scientist Thomas Dye felt that it overstated the role that upper-class individuals play in the power elite. Dye pointed out that Domhoff used three factors to calculate class of origin—listing in the Social Register (of the upper class); attendance at a prestigious preparatory school; and membership in a prominent social club. Dye indicated that both the first and the third criteria could be attained after moving up from a middle-class background and thus hardly served to prove that the people in question were born into the upper class. To qualify as upper class in origin in Dye's estimation, an individual needed to have attended a prestigious preparatory school and to have had a parent in a top position in a major corporation, bank, newspaper, the military, or some other prominent organization. Using these criteria, Dye found that the portion of the power elite originating from the middle class is about 70 percent and the segment from the upper class only 30 percent—very different from Domhoff's claim that upper-class individuals numerically dominate the power elite (Dye 2002, 151). While these two theorists differ in their figures for power-elite members' class of origin, they also have another important difference. For Dye, power-elite participation is less about class membership than about one's organizational affiliation.

Dye's Theory of the Institutional Elite

Dye's position is that the basis for power-elite membership is institutional power, namely an influential position within a prominent private or public organization. He specified 7,314 top institutional positions, involving 5,778 individuals, some of whom had two or more interlocking directorates. According to Dye, the power elite controls over half of the nation's industrial and financial assets; over half the assets of private foundations; the television networks, major newspapers, and media conglomerates; major civic and cultural organizations; and the primary activities of the three major branches of the federal government (Dye 2002, 139–40).

Dye suggested that this leadership group "is recruited from the well-educated, prestigiously employed, older, affluent, urban, white, Anglo-Saxon, upper-class and upper-middle-class male populations of the nation" (Dye 2002, 147). Some of Dye's key findings:

> *Age:* Corporate leaders average about 60 years old; heads of foundations, law, education, and civic organizations about 62; government-sector members about 56.
>
> *Gender:* Women are barely represented among corporate leadership in the institutional elite and contribute only 20 percent in the political realm; they appear among top position holders only in cultural affairs, education, and foundations.
>
> *Ethnicity:* White Anglo-Saxons dominate in the power elite, with Protestants representing about 80 percent of the top business leaders and about 73 percent of members of Congress.
>
> *Education:* Nearly all the leaders are college-educated with almost half having advanced degrees. About 54 percent of the big-business leaders and 42 percent of the government elite are graduates of just 12 heavily endowed, prestigious universities.
>
> *Social clubs:* Most holders of top positions in the power elite possess memberships in one or more social clubs, including about a third belonging to a small number of especially prestigious clubs in major cities like New York and Washington. Dye's conclusion: that these memberships are a result of individuals' elite status and not an independent source of power for the institutionalized elite (Dye 2002, 147–49).

The core of the elite—what Domhoff and Useem called the inner circle—are Dye's "multiple interlockers." Because of their presence on at least two boards of directors for major companies, this small percentage of the institutional elite has a greater range of communication and a wider scope of influence than their peers on just one board—individuals Dye designated "specialists." Dye concluded that multiple interlockers' exposure to extensive information prompts them to represent broad interests, encouraging them to act on behalf of a wide range of elite structures. In particular, multiple interlockers are well placed to link the corporate world with politicians, foundations, think tanks, policy-making groups, universities, and cultural and civic organizations (Dye 2002, 140, 142). They are an exclusive group, predominantly affluent white males.

TABLE 2.4 Comparisons of the Power-Elite Theories

	Mills	Domhoff	Dye
Members' origin	Upper class	Largely upper class	Upper and middle class
Educational background	Privileged early schooling and attendance at prominent private colleges and universities	Exclusive preparatory schools and attendance at well-known private and public universities and colleges	Well educated with preference for 12 well-endowed private universities
Social clubs	Status elevators for climbing to high-status positions	Important locations for building contacts, obtaining information, and using influence	Memberships acquired from one's high status and not significant in furthering elite's goals
Major players	Three higher circles of power—the economic, political, and military	A corporate community developed into a common network	Nearly 6,000 individuals in important, diverse organizations filling over 7,000 top institutional positions
The elite of the elite	Unspecified number of individuals comprising an inner core and located simultaneously within two areas of power	Inner circle formed by 15–20 percent of the elite, whose well-informed influential members are involved in interlocking directorates	Multiple interlockers representing a small percentage of the institutional elite and very active in linking corporations to various influential structures
Major activities	Interaction and intercommunication among elite groups, with little detail about the process of policy formation	Control over foundations, think tanks, and policy-making groups providing a major impact on public policy	Control over foundations, think tanks, and policy-making groups, providing a major impact on public policy

Sources: G. William Domhoff. 2005. "Who Rules America?: Power at the National Level." http://sociology.ucsc.edu/who-rulesamerica/power/national.html; G. William Domhoff. 2005. "Who Rules America?: Interlocking Directorates in the Corporate Community." http://sociology.ucsc.edu/whorulesamerica/power/corporate_commun...; G. William Domhoff. 2006. "*The Power Elite* 50 Years Later." *Contemporary Sociology.* V. 35, pp. 547–50; G. William Domhoff. 2010. Who Rules America?: Politics & Social Change, 6th ed.; Thomas R. Dye. 2002. *Who's Running America? The Bush Restoration,* 7th ed.; C. Wright Mills. 1956. *The Power Elite.*

Fortune 500 CEOs are a prominent source for multiple interlockers, and in 2010 only 16 (3.2 percent) of them were minorities and 15 (3 percent) female (Cox 2010; CNNMoney .com 2010).

Like Domhoff, Dye analyzed the intricate multi-organizational process where power-elite members control the development of major economic and political policies. Table 2.4 compares the three power-elite theories. In Chapter 4 this group's activities are examined at length, but meanwhile the focus shifts to some fundamental points about the theories already examined.

Conclusion

What are the most useful ideas in this chapter?

- Karl Marx and Erik Wright contended that selected economic factors serve as the determinants of class position. However, the reality is that the overwhelming number of researchers studying class have measured it in a largely Weberian manner, featuring occupational categories and usually including income/wealth and education. So in order to incorporate these valuable studies, I have needed to use a definition of class similar to theirs in this text.
- Upcoming chapters discuss the influence and control the power elite exerts. While previous material suggests some disagreement between Domhoff and Dye, they agree on a set of basic points: that there exists a highly educated, super-class-backed, corporate-centered group, possessed of an inner circle of especially well connected members and mobilized to promote economic and political policies that serve their interests. This is a fundamentally important proposition applying throughout the book.
- Both sets of theories in this chapter link to the concept of social reproduction introduced in Chapter 1. For instance, the Marxist theory suggests that because of its ownership of the means of production, the bourgeoisie controls the economy, keeping most wealth and power in its members' hands. The power-elite theories provide a consistent perspective, indicating how that dominant group uses various means—such as interlocking directorates, social clubs, and memberships in various elite organizations—to insulate themselves as they pursue policies that perpetuate their great wealth and power. In contrast, the structural-functional theories briefly examined in this chapter—the Davis-Moore and pluralism perspectives—are nearly oblivious to power and conflict and never analyze the issue of social reproduction.
- Finally certain contemporary realities addressed in Chapter 1—soaring corporate profits and top executives' salaries contrasted with stagnant or declining income prospects for the majority of citizens—suggest that Marx's emphasis on persistently opposed interests between the capitalist leadership and other classes remains a robust reality today. The following chapters amplify this conclusion.

Key Terms in the Glossary

Authority *33*
Bourgeoisie *27*
Bureaucratic system of authority *33*
Capitalism *26*
Charismatic system of authority *34*
Conflict theory *25*
Conspicuous consumption *32*
False consciousness *27*

Ideology *27*
Interlocking directorate *40*
Lumpenproletariat *28*
Means of production *27*
Mode of production *25*
Petite bourgeoisie *28*
Pluralism *38*
Power elite *38*
Proletariat *27*
Reserve army of labor *29*

Socialism *28*
Sociological theory *24*
Structural-functional theory *24*
Substructure *26*
Superstructure *26*
Surplus value *27*
Traditional system of authority *33*

Discussion Topics

1. Indicate why the Davis-Moore theory belongs in the structural-functional category. Then evaluate its conclusions.
2. What are three major points the Marxist theory makes? Summarize two important weaknesses and two strengths.
3. Discuss Weber's social-stratification perspective, emphasizing its differences from Marxist theory.
4. What are Wright's variables for determining class? Describe two of the classes that he designated.
5. Compare Mills's, Domhoff's, and Dye's theories on three important traits. Does Domhoff's or Dye's theory appear to provide a more convincing assessment of the power elite?

Research Papers

1. Find research information that further evaluates Marx's theory, providing detailed information that develops the weaknesses and strengths discussed in the chapter. If one particular issue stands out and offers considerable detail, then consider making it the paper's focus.
2. Using a database for academic journals like JSTOR or SocIndex, locate an article where the respondents' class is a central issue in the study. I suggest choosing a qualitative investigation since it will be likely to provide detailed data about respondents that will prove useful. Read the article, summarize its major points and conclusions, and then—this is a critical part of the assignment, not simply a minor part of it—indicate what the study suggests about the utility of either Weber's or Marx's theory.
3. Develop the following thesis, which some Americans support: "No American power elite exists, except in the feverish minds of some deluded academics." " What is the evidence on the topic? Information supporting both the pluralism and power-elite perspectives applies here.

Informative Websites

The MX-Files (http://www.appstate.edu-stanovskydj/marxfiles.html) provides the full text of Marx's major writings along with biographies, critiques, and other source material.

Erik Wright's home page (http://www.ssc.wisc.edu/-wright/) contains a summary of this eminent specialist's Sociology 621—"Class, State, and Ideology: An Introduction to Marxist Social Science," which examines the concepts and theories that have developed in the Marxist tradition.

G. Williams Domhoff (http://sociology.ucsu.edu/whorulesamerica/) has an ongoing Website, which supplies basic information about the power elite and also updated research and data.

Bibliography

Ahrens, Frank. 2004. "Melinda Gates Joins Washington Post Company as Director: Ex-Microsoft Executive Elected to Board." *Washington Post* (September 10): E02.

Anderson, Charles H. 1974. *The Political Economy of Social Class*. Englewood Cliffs, NJ: Prentice-Hall.

Berberoglu, Berch. 2005. *An Introduction to Classical and Contemporary Social Theory: A*

Critical Perspective. Lanham, MD: Rowman & Littlefield Publishers.

Bureau of Labor Statistics. 2010. "Where Can I Find the Unemployment Rate for Previous Years?" *Current Population Survey*. http://www.bls.gov/cps/prev_yrs.htm.

CNNMoney.com. 2010. "Women CEOs." *Fortune 500*. http://money.cnn.com/magazines/fortune/fortune500/2010/womenceos/

Cox, Gena. 2010. "Racial Minorities May Not Get Corporate Leadership Opportunities Because They Do Not Fit the 'Leadership Prototype.'" The Way to Lead.com. http://thewaytolead.com/2010/04/08/racial-minorities-may-not-get-corporate-leadership-opportunities-because-they-do-not-fit-the-%E2%80%9Cleadership-prototype%E2%80%9D/.

Dahl, Robert A. 1967. *Pluralist Democracy in the United States: Conflict and Consent*. Chicago: Rand McNally.

Dahl, Robert A. 1982. *Dilemmas of Pluralist Democracy*. New Haven: Yale University Press.

Davis, Kingsley, and Wilbert E. Moore. 1945. "Some Principles of Stratification." *American Sociological Review* 10 (April): 242–49.

Domhoff, G. William. 1974. *The Bohemian Grove and Other Retreats*. New York: Harper & Row.

Domhoff, G. William. 1975. "Social Clubs, Policy-Planning Groups, and Corporations: A Network Study of Ruling-Class Cohesiveness." *The Insurgent Sociologist* 5: 173–84.

Domhoff, G. William. 2005a. "Who Rules America?: Power at the National Level." http://sociology.ucsc.edu/whorulesamerica/power/national.html.

Domhoff, G. William. 2005b. "Who Rules America?: Interlocking Directorates in the Corporate Community." http://sociology.ucsc.edu/whorulesamerica/power/corporate_community.html.

Domhoff, G. William. 2006. "*The Power Elite* 50 Years Later." *Contemporary Sociology* 35 (November): 547–50.

Domhoff, G. William. 2010. *Who Rules America? Power, Politics & Social Change*, 6th ed. New York: McGraw-Hill.

Dye, Thomas R. 2002. *Who's Running America? The Bush Restoration*, 7th ed. Upper Saddle River, NJ: Prentice-Hall.

Engels, Friedrich. 1959. "The Labor Movement in the United States," pp. 489–97 in Lewis S. Feuer (ed.), *Marx & Engels: Basic Writings*

on Politics & Philosophy. Garden City, NY: Anchor Books.

Etebari, Mehrun. 2003. "Trickle-down Economics: Four Reasons Why It Just Doesn't Work." United for Fair Economy. http://www.faireconomy.org/research/TrickleDown.html.

Feuer, Lewis S. 1959. "Introduction," pp. ix–xxi in Lewis S. Feuer (ed.), *Marx & Engels: Basic Writings on Politics & Philosophy*. Garden City, NY: Anchor Books.

Gagné, Patricia, and Deanna McGauchey. 2002. "Designing Women: Cultural Hegemony and the Exercise of Power among Women Who Have Undergone Elective Mammoplasty." *Gender & Society* 16 (December): 814–38.

Gasper, Phil (ed.). 2005. *The Communist Manifesto: A Road Map to History's Most Important Document*. Chicago: Haymarket Books.

Gerth, Hans, and C. Wright Mills (eds.). 1946. *From Max Weber: Essays in Sociology*. New York: Oxford University Press.

Giddens, Anthony. 1973. *The Class Structure of the Advanced Societies*. London: Hutchinson & Company.

Hans Gerth and C. Wright Mills (eds.). 1946. *From Max Weber: Essays in Sociology*. New York: Oxford University Press.

Harrington, Michael. 1972. *Socialism*. New York: Saturday Review Press.

Harrington, Michael. 1976. *The Twilight of Capitalism*. New York: Touchstone Books.

Lerner, Max (ed.). 1948. *The Portable Veblen*. New York: Viking Press.

Marx, Karl. 1920. *The Poverty of Philosophy*. Chicago: Charles H. Kerr Publishing.

Marx, Karl. 1959. "Excerpts from *The Class Struggles in France, 1848 to 1850*," pp. 281–317 in Lewis S. Feuer (ed.), *Marx & Engels: Basic Writings on Politics & Philosophy*. Garden City, NY: Anchor Books.

Marx, Karl. 1978a. "The Civil War in France," pp. 618–52 in Robert C. Tucker (ed.), *The Marx-Engels Reader*, 2nd ed. New York: W.W. Norton & Company.

Marx, Karl. 1978b. "The German Ideology: Part I," pp. 146–200 in Robert C. Tucker (ed.), *The Marx-Engels Reader*, 2nd ed. New York: W.W. Norton & Company.

Mark, Karl, and Friedrich Engels. 1959. "Manifesto of the Communist Party," pp. 1–41 in Lewis S. Feuer (ed.), *Marx & Engels: Basic Writings on Politics & Philosophy*. Garden City, NY: Anchor Books.

Marx, Karl, and Friedrich Engels. 1968. *Selected Works in One Volume*. New York: International.

Marx, Karl, and Friedrich Engels. 2005. "The Annotated Communist Manifesto," pp. 37–90 in Phil Gasper (ed.), *The Communist Manifesto: A Road Map to History's Most Important Document*. Chicago: Haymarket Books.

Merton, Robert K. 1968. *Social Theory and Social Structure*, 3rd ed. New York: Free Press.

Mills, C. Wright. 1956. *The Power Elite*. New York: Oxford University Press.

Milward, Bob. 2000. *Marxian Political Economy: Theory, History and Contemporary Relevance*. London: Macmillan Press Ltd.

Muravchik, Joshua. 2002. "Marxism." *Foreign Policy* No. 133 (November–December): 36–38.

Ollman, Bertell. 1968. "Marx's Use of 'Class.'" *American Journal of Sociology* 73 (March): 573–80.

Parsons, Talcott. 1951. *The Social System*. Glencoe, IL: Free Press.

Perrucci, Robert, and Earl Wysong. 2008. *The New Class Society: Goodbye American Dream?* 3rd ed. Lanham, MD: Rowman & Middlefield.

Rosen, Michael. 1996. *On Voluntary Servitude: False Consciousness and the Theory of Ideology*. Cambridge: Harvard University Press.

Rothkopf, David. 2009. *Superclass: The Global Power Elite and the World They Are Making*. New York: Farrar, Straus and Giroux.

Seth's Blog. 2010. "Revisiting Conspicuous Consumption." http://sethgodin.typepad .com/seths_blog/2010/04/revisiting-conspicuous-consumption.html.

Singer, Peter. 2000. *Marx: A Very Short Introduction*. New York: Oxford University Press.

Steinreich, Dale. 2004. "100 Years of Medical Robbery." Ludwig von Mises Institute. June 10. http://www.mises.org/ story/1547.

Tucker, Robert C. 1978. Introduction," pp. xix–xxviii in Robert C. Tucker (ed.), *The Marx-Engels Reader*, 2nd ed. New York: W.W. Norton & Company.

Tumin, Melvin. 1953. "Some Principles of Stratification: A Critical Analysis." *American Sociological Review* 18 (August): 387–94.

Useem, Michael. 1984. *The Inner Circle: Large Corporations and the Rise of Business Political Activity in the U.S. and the U.K.* New York: Oxford University Press.

Weber, Max. 1999. *Max Weber: Essays in Economic Theory*. Richard Swedberg (ed.). Princeton: Princeton University Press.

Wright, Erik Olin. 1978. *Class, Crisis and the State*. London: NLB.

Wright, Erik Olin. 1989. "The Comparative Project on Class Structure and Class Consciousness: An Overview." *Acta Sociologica* 32: 3–22.

Wright, Erik Olin. 1997. *Class Counts: Comparative Studies in Class Analysis*. Cambridge: Cambridge University Press.

Wright, Erik Olin. 2002. "The Shadow of Exploitation in Weber's Class Analysis." *American Sociological Review* 67 (December): 832–53.

Wright, Erik Olin. 2005. "Foundations of a Neo-Marxist Class Analysis, pp. 4–30 in Erik Olin Wright (ed.), *Approaches to Class Analysis*. Cambridge: Cambridge University Press.

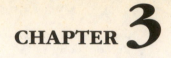

Repeat Performance: Globalization through Time and Space

In the midst of the lively conversation, the elegant, 90-year-old woman said, "Please excuse me. There's something I want to share with you." A moment later she came back with a letter, which she had received at the turn of the twentieth century. The writer was a young Englishman she had met during a transatlantic voyage. He was explaining to his 15-year-old correspondent how exciting it was to be growing up in the nation whose empire stretched around the globe. "What's particularly impressive," he wrote, "is that in spite of our modest size, the magnificent phrase still rings true: 'Rule, Britannia! Rule the waves.' And that's going to be the reality for centuries to come." How strange it felt listening to the young man's words while realizing that the world's once dominant nation was now sharply reduced in the course of less than one slender lifetime.

Yes, he was wrong. In fact, as we see with modern world systems, once a nation attains dominance, it is on the brink of decline, and soon a repeat performance makes another nation dominant. In this chapter we examine the development and demise of world systems, which significantly affect citizens' economic and political opportunities around the planet. Then the focus shifts to global social stratification, with distinctive differences apparent between core nations and the less developed peripheral and semi-peripheral countries. Throughout the chapter it is clear that not only classes but nations themselves vary in access to capital resources. In particular, certain types of capital such as technology and education affect social inequality within countries. The final section indicates how the context of the global age impacts class groups, ranging from the wealthy to the poor.

First, however, it is necessary to place the global age in context.

THE RISE AND FALL OF WORLD SYSTEMS

The past 400 years of human history have featured three time periods in which a single country—Holland (the United Provinces) 1620–72, Great Britain 1815–73, and the United States 1945–67—established **hegemony**, a situation in which one nation has sufficient power and influence to impose its rules and goals globally in the economic, political, military, diplomatic, and even cultural realms (Wallerstein 1984, 38). The leaders of hegemonic powers prefer to use consensus instead of coercion. While the height of US hegemonic power has passed, its military bases in over 130 countries, the continuing prominence of large numbers of American-headquartered multinationals, and its well-funded if financially challenged government mean that the country continues to be the major player in the global setting.

In the 1970s and 1980s, Immanuel Wallerstein, Christopher Chase-Dunn, and a number of other scholars concluded that because countries are not isolated but are economically and politically interrelated with many others, then the world system is the most accurate and revealing perspective for analyzing the structures and functions of modern nations. The **modern world system** is a capitalist global economy which contains multiple states and a single dominant international division of labor. When a particular system is fully established, one nation maintains hegemonic control, extending its influence throughout the global entity (Chase-Dunn 1989, 2; Wallerstein 1974, 7). During the history of world systems, nations have varied in their wealth, power, and the roles played.

World-system analysts examining the international division of labor divide countries into three types—the core, the semiperipheral, and the peripheral, roughly the rich, the middle-income, and the poor. A **core nation** is a country which possesses a successful industrial history, exerts both political and economic influence in the world system, and enjoys a high standard of living. The core nations are western European countries, the United States, Japan, Australia, and New Zealand. A majority of the world's 10 percent most affluent citizens, who own 85 percent of global wealth, reside in the core nations. Western Europe has 29 percent of that total, the United States 25 percent, and Japan 20 percent. A **semiperipheral nation** is an independent state which has achieved a moderate level of industrialization and development. In Asia they include South Korea (the Republic of Korea), Singapore, Hong Kong, and Malaysia and in Latin America Argentina, Brazil, and Mexico. A **peripheral nation** is a member of the poorest, least powerful, and least industrially developed set of countries, which are primarily located in Africa, Asia, and Latin America (Bradshaw and Wallace 1996, 44–45; Davies, Sandstrom, Shorrocks, and Wolff 2006; Wallerstein 1974). Some descriptions in this chapter cite all three types of nations; in other instances the semiperipheral and peripheral categories are combined as "developing" nations. Table 3.1 indicates that the three types of countries not only vary enormously in income but also in life expectancy.

Across time, income inequality between the core and peripheral countries has widened. In 1820 estimates indicated that the most affluent 20 percent of the population earned three times as much as the poorest 20 percent. In 1870 that ratio rose to 7 to 1, then 30 to 1 in 1960, 60 to 1 in 1990, 74 to 1 in 1997, and 82 to 1 in 2003 (Pieterse 2002, 1025; Prabhakar 2003, 323). It is abundantly clear that in contemporary times most workers in the peripheral nations have been increasingly losing out compared to their core-nation counterparts.

Furthermore the relationship between core nations and the other two categories of countries has been exploitative, with the wealthy states seeking two major benefits—raw materials and cheap labor. The raw materials include a variety of minerals and metals essential for manufacturing such products as automobiles, weapons, computers, and a lengthy list of other items. It is safe to say that without these raw materials the core countries' wealth would be greatly diminished. To obtain raw materials, the European powers established colonies on every continent except Europe.

TABLE 3.1 Global Inequality: Per Capita Income and Life Expectancy in Selected Core, Semiperipheral, and Peripheral Countries

Core nations	Per capita income	Life expectancy
Switzerland	$55,510	82
United States	47,930	78
United Kingdom	46,040	80
Canada	43,640	81
Germany	42,710	80
Australia	40,240	81
Japan	38,130	83
Italy	35,460	82
Semiperipheral nations	**Per capita income**	**Life expectancy**
Israel	$24,720	81
South Korea (Republic of Korea)	21,530	80
Mexico	9,990	75
Brazil	7,300	72
Malaysia	7,250	74
Argentina	7,190	75
Peripheral nations	**Per capita income**	**Life expectancy**
Indonesia	$1,880	71
Bolivia	1,460	66
India	1,040	64
Bangladesh	520	66
Rwanda	440	46
Ethiopia	280	55
Liberia	170	58

Global inequality in income ranges widely. Not surprisingly the data here suggest that people living in more affluent countries have a greater chance of living longer.

Source: World Bank. 2010. "GNI per Capita. PPP (current international $)." http://data.worldbank.org/indicator/NY.GNP.PCAP.CD. "Life Expectancy at Birth." http://data.worldbank..org/indicator/SP.DYN.LEOO.IN.

Outsiders from core nations also sought cheap labor, sometimes engaging in slavery. Before the end of the slave trade, 12 million Africans had been captured and transported to an alien, oppressive life in distant, hostile lands. While slaves were used to perform a variety of tasks, the majority of those in the Caribbean, Brazil, and the southern United States labored on sugar, tobacco, and cotton plantations (Bradshaw and Wallace 1996, 45–48; Chirot 1977, 22).

Slavery, of course, has been abolished, and since World War II colonies have proved too costly to maintain, leading to their sovereignty. So is it safe to say that those poor countries are no longer exploited for their raw materials and labor? The answer is decidedly negative, and the key players shaping this modern reality are multinationals, which have developed in the context of modern world systems. A **multinational** is a large corporation which both produces and sells goods or services in various countries. Profit and a desire for free, unrestricted business activity determine the global choices, including decisions about contracts with feeder (supplier) factories, which manufacture goods for the multinationals. In the modern phase of the world-systems process, multi-nationals have attained massive wealth and power. In 2011 Walmart, the giant retail-store chain, was at the top of the revenues heap with a $421 billion yearly intake, followed by three huge oil companies—Royal Dutch Shell, Exxon Mobil, and BP (CNN Money 2011).

The process producing these three hegemonic systems has involved a common set of factors (Wallerstein 1980; Wallerstein 1984, 39–40).

Conditions in the Development of World Systems

As each system developed, a fairly uniform set of factors unfolded—first, expansion in three critical economic domains, namely agriculture/industry, commerce, and finance; then the formation of an ideology emphasizing free trade; third, the growth of military might to insure a stable setting for doing business; and finally the demise of the hege-monic power and a restructuring of the system (Wallerstein 1984, 40–42):

THE FUNDAMENTAL ECONOMIC ISSUES OF AGRICULTURE/INDUSTRY, COMMERCE, AND FINANCE Comparing the Dutch and American experiences, one finds broad similarities and specific differences. The Dutch fishing industry was very successful, and a major contributor was the fifteenth-century invention of the *haringbuis* or buss, a fishing boat which not only had extensive cargo space but possessed a unique combination of speed, maneuverability, and seaworthiness. The buss provided sufficient deck space to gut and salt fish, preserving the fish and permitting the boats to stay out from six to eight weeks. Using their busses, the Dutch dominated the North Sea herring fishery, the Iceland cod industry, and the Spitzbergen whale hunt. The Dutch also were ingenious at growing crops. Possessing little land, they became experts in draining large areas and perfecting intensified agriculture. Such industrial crops as flax, hemp, hops, and dyes grew well in Dutch soil. The United Provinces not only produced industrial crops but also became the top manufacturer of industrial goods. Textile production centered in the northern Netherlands, and it grew steadily for a century until the 1660s when formidable British competition began to replace it.

The Dutch were also heavily involved in shipbuilding, a highly organized and mechanized activity, with such labor-saving devices as wind-powered sawmills, block and tackles, and great cranes to move heavy items. As a precursor to the twentieth-century automobile business, Dutch shipbuilding required a number of ancillary indus-tries, producing spare parts, rope, nautical instruments, and sea charts. In its hegemonic heyday, the United Provinces engaged in a number of other world-leading industries, including the production of paper, books, armaments, crockery, tanned hides, cut tobacco, and soap (Wallerstein 1980, 39–44).

Equipped with an array of high-quality goods that were delivered by a huge fleet of ships, Dutch merchants were in a strong position. The nation's international trade flour-ished, expanding tenfold between 1500 and 1700. In 1670 the United Provinces shipped three times more tonnage than Great Britain, its closest rival, and more than the tonnage of Britain, France, Spain, Portugal, and Germany combined (Wallerstein 1980, 46).

The Dutch fishing fleet's finely built ships made them tempting prey for pirates.

British merchants found the Dutch operation dazzling, watching in amazement and envy as their commercial fleet recaptured Baltic and Mediterranean markets lost earlier to the British (Ormrod 2003, 34). The nation's reputation as the world's dominant commercial force survived well beyond the actual fact. As late as 1728, the author Daniel DeFoe referred to the Dutch as "the Carryers of the World, the middle Persons in Trade, the Factors and Brokers of Europe" (Wilson 1941, 4). However, not all observers were admiring. British patriots deeply resented the fact that merchants from the United Provinces were so profit-hungry that if the price were right they would willingly trade with Spain, both countries' mortal enemy (Kennedy 1987, 68).

In seventeenth-century Holland, many people were making substantial amounts of money, and they needed a safe and secure location for their capital. *De Wisselbank van Amsterdam* became that location, with its deposits rising sixteenfold through the century. The bank's growing wealth allowed it to develop a substantial credit function, greatly adding to its wealth. In addition, the stability of Dutch currency made it the preferred money of the day, permitting low interest rates and attracting further investment (Wallerstein 1980, 58–59).

As the Dutch world system was declining, the roots of what would eventually be the American system were developing. In the seventeenth and eighteenth centuries, core industries developed in New England, featuring shipbuilding, cod fishing, the distillation of rum, and light manufacture; in addition, colonial merchants made profit carrying products between the colonies and Great Britain. Eventually New England merchants, farmers of the middle colonies, and the southern plantations owners realized that it would serve their common interest to divest themselves of British colonial control.

In the nineteenth century, agricultural exports, including slave-grown cotton, were money-making ventures. At that time the northern industrial sector was developing a variety of products, and in the opening decades of the twentieth century, the export of cotton textiles, a variety of machines, electrical appliances, and automobiles was success-ful and expanding (Chase-Dunn 1989, 182–83). American industrial development caught and surpassed its major rivals. For instance, in 1855 the British originated the Bessemer process to produce high-grade steel at a low cost. Then the Germans developed a more efficient, low-cost process, but shortly afterwards the United States exceeded both coun-tries, producing 70 percent of the world's steel within 30 years of the introduction of the Bessemer process (Bunker and Ciccantell 2005, 187). Such an energetically innovative approach is generally missing from modern American big business.

As it rose to hegemonic supremacy following World War II, the United States initi-ated the Marshall Plan, which helped war-ravaged European countries reestablish them-selves economically. The government provided $12.4 billion over four years to both allies and former enemies, and those nations primarily used the money to buy large amounts of food, feed, fertilizer, machines, vehicles, equipment, and fuel from American companies. In the late 1940s, the Marshall Plan served as a major financial tool, solidifying the world-wide dominance of American business (Chirot 1977, 149–50; Kaplinsky 2005, 223).

THE DEVELOPMENT OF AN IDEOLOGY, WHICH IS THE COMPLEX OF VALUES AND BELIEFS THAT SUPPORT A SOCIETY'S SOCIAL-STRATIFICATION SYSTEMS AND THEIR DISTRIBUTION OF WEALTH, INCOME, AND POWER The hegemonic power normally seeks an unrestrict-ed international flow of capital and labor along with various political freedoms. A major reason for supporting free trade is that then the dominant nation does not need to pay for the administrative control that establishing tariffs would entail. Often free trade serves hegemonic powers well. However, if it does not, then they have promoted tariffs. In the nineteenth century, Great Britain, the hegemonic power, was much more supportive of free trade for French, German, Dutch, and Spanish colonies than for its own, which of-ficials felt required protective tariffs for its products. After World War II, the United States carried the hegemonic baton, promoting the general idea of free world trade but often favoring tariffs to protect its own products. Furthermore during this era, a host of former colonies became independent countries, and most of their leaders supported the United States's hegemony and **ideology** (Chase-Dunn 1989, 160, 275; Chase-Dunn, Kawano, and Brewer 2000, 80–81; Martin 2008, 172–73; Wallerstein 1984, 41).

All in all, it is laughable to suggest that major powers consistently support restriction-free international trade. From 1974 to 2004, the World Trade Organization, the core-nation-controlled body on international trade, permitted tariffs and other restrictions that affected apparel firms' investment and outsourcing decisions. The absence of trade re-strictions often comes at a price—for instance, American firms' permission to import clothing from Mexican factories without those factories facing duties or quotas as long as the products use fabrics created in the United States (Collins 2003, 49–50).

THE ROLE OF THE MILITARY While dominant powers in the world system often present themselves as peace-loving, their leaders have recognized the necessity of a strong mili-tary presence. In fact, each of the three major world powers established its hegemony by winning wars covering an approximate 30-year span—the Dutch in the Thirty Years' War from 1618 to 1648, the British in the Napoleonic Wars from 1792 to 1815, and the Americans in the two world wars occurring between 1914 and 1945 (Wallerstein 1984, 41–42). A close relationship exists between hegemonic wealth and military power. The Netherlands' commercial success permitted the country to develop the world's largest navy as well as the only army comparable to Spain's. Admiral Alfred Thayer Mahan, the leading nineteenth-century authority on sea power, declared the "United Provinces owed their consideration and power to their wealth and their fleets" (Mahan 1889, 97).

While the relationship between wealth and military power is significant, another factor comes into play. Unlike such countries as France, Germany, Spain, and Russia which have had potential adversaries sharing the same land mass, Great Britain and the United States have had physical separation from potential enemies. Thus these two eventual hegemonic powers had less need than other nations to form a large, costly standing army, spending the money instead on economic development and, particularly in the British case, naval expansion (Chase-Dunn 1989, 161).

Since the 1950s the expenditure for the American military has been enormous, with major corporations supporting an active world-wide military presence and receiving large contracts for a wide variety of goods and services. The eye-popping reality is that the US military expenditure is close to half—about 45 percent—of the global total (Frank and Paul 2010; Shah 2010). In his farewell address, President Dwight D. Eisenhower, once a celebrated army general, warned about the growing threat of a "military-industrial complex," and several topics raised in the upcoming two chapters address that issue (Chirot 1986, 241–42).

THE RESTRUCTURED WORLD SYSTEM   Each of the three systems developed after a lengthy war, and afterward the new hegemonic power sought to establish economic and political stability on its own terms (Wallerstein 1984, 42–43). Before World War II was over, in fact, British and American representatives met in Bretton Woods, New Hampshire, to plan a stable economic structure that would promote world financial growth (Kaplinsky 2005, 12–13). The Bretton Woods conference was a distinctly hegemonic performance, favoring the United States. At one point the renowned economist John Maynard Keynes, the chief British representative, declared that the Americans "plainly intend to force their conceptions through, regardless of the rest of us" (*New York Times* 2009). While Keynes and his compatriots grumbled, they acknowledged that the money the Marshall Plan provided would overcome not only British but other European countries' opposition to American directives at Bretton Woods.

One important outcome of the conference was the formation of several global organizations, notably the International Monetary Fund (IMF), the World Bank (WB), and the General Agreement on Tariffs and Trade, which eventually became the World Trade Organization (WTO). Since the 1980s these organizations have eliminated most restrictions on trade, greatly benefiting multinationals and handicapping the formerly protected peripheral and semiperipheral countries (Kaplinsky 2005, 13–14; Kentor and Boswell 2003, 302; Robinson 2000, 90).

Writing from the vantage point of having been the chairman of President Clinton's Committee on Economic Advisors, the distinguished economist Joseph E. Stiglitz concluded that while the IMF officially seeks to ensure global economic health, its real agenda is very different. Stiglitz added that IMF support for free trade "may not have contributed to global economic stability, but it did open up vast markets for Wall Street" (Stiglitz 2002, 207).

In fact, such open systems tend to promote their own demise. First, that very openness encourages the spread of the hegemonic power's technologies. Foreign competitors will have ample opportunity to develop newer, more efficient technologies along with more recent, better organized plants. Bombed into ruin during World War II, the Japanese auto industry rebuilt with cutting-edge technology to become formidable competition for its American rival. Second, in order to establish themselves as world leader in the production and sale of goods, the companies residing in the hegemonic power must steadily raise employees' pay.

It is a precarious situation. Competing firms in other countries, which almost inevitably have a lower standard of living, can pay their employees less, permitting these companies to undersell their competitors in the hegemonic power (Wallerstein 1984, 45).

A decisive moment has arrived. Wallerstein wrote, "Once the clear productivity edge is lost, the structure cracks" (Wallerstein 1984, 45). The US hegemonic decline started in the 1970s (Wallerstein 2003, 13). However, while the United States no longer has hegemonic control, a host of American multinationals with great wealth and influence has meant a persistent economic prominence. Daniel Chirot claimed that American leadership "in the capitalist world is far from over. For better or for worse, there is no country in the system that will have the power to determine its course as much as the United States . . . well into the twenty-first [century]" (Chirot 1986, 230).

Table 3.2 lists the principal factors in the preceding discussion of world systems. The upcoming international analysis displays persistent evidence of US multinationals' influence.

SOCIAL STRATIFICATION AND SOCIAL INEQUALITY IN THE GLOBAL SETTING

Modern world systems have always been in flux, with the production and distribution of such goods as clothes and sport shoes gradually globalizing over time. In the 1960s I spent a few weeks alone in a small town in northern Italy, eventually feeling somewhat homesick and looking forward to any conversation in English. Then one day I saw a young red-haired man sitting in a park. Approaching him, I examined his clothes. He had American jeans, often referred to as Levi's, and high-top, black-and-white US Keds. At that time the United States was either the principal or only market for those products, which were made exclusively in the United States. He had to be an American. Sure enough!

TABLE 3.2 Major Elements of World-Systems Analysis

A. Three nations which established hegemonic control: Holland 1620–72; Great Britain 1815–73; United States 1945–67

B. Three types of countries in world systems: core; semiperipheral; and peripheral

C. Four conditions in hegemonic development

  1. Economic growth: agriculture-industry, commerce, and finance

  2. Ideology emphasizing free capital and labor; core nations promoting ample protective tariffs for their companies' products

  3. Strong military necessary to establish hegemonic control

  4. A restructuring of the previous world system, with the new hegemonic power trying to produce the economic and political stability that best serves its interests

---

Sources: Christopher Chase-Dunn. 1989. *Global Formation: Structures of the World Economy*; Christopher Chase-Dunn, Yukio Kawano, and Benjamin D. Brewer. 2000. "Trade Globalization since 1796: Waves of Integration in the World System." *American Sociological Review.* V. 65, pp. 77–95; Immanuel Wallterstein. 1974. *The Modern World-System: Capitalist Agriculture and the Origins of the European World-Economy in the Sixteenth Century*; Immanuel Wallterstein. 1980. *The Modern World-System II: Mercantilism and the Consolidation of the European World Economy, 1600–1750*; Immanuel Wallterstein. 1984. *The Politics of the World-Economy: The States, the Movement, and the Civilizations.*

Now the situation is different. Multinationals sell jeans, sport shoes, and many other consumer items once available only in the United Sates in stores throughout the world. As upcoming analysis indicates, the multinationals responsible for such products establish policies that impact on semiperipheral and peripheral nations' economies and class structures. One word of caution: A given country's economic development emerges gradually over time. While modern multinationals exploit many very poor countries and contribute to their persistent poverty, those countries, which were once colonies, have usually experienced a lengthy, destructive relationship with core nations, that significantly antedates the multinational era. The peripheral nations have been victims, with the majority of citizens deprived of effective schooling and decently paying jobs; these individuals are often very poor, but overall they are neither unmotivated nor intellectually challenged. Most Americans are somewhat aware of a similar process occurring on their soil. Much like colonial powers, the US government systematically deprived Native Americans of both their land and traditional way of life, exploiting them mercilessly and transforming them into the poorest, least educated, unhealthiest racial group in the country.

The core states, which have historically been the exploiters, have a fairly different class structure from the one that exists in the widely exploited peripheral and semiperipheral countries. Within the core nations, a fairly uniform level of affluence and work tasks means that the class structure tends to be fairly consistent from country to country (Bereberoglu 2009; Ishida 1989, 69). A composite of several sociological schemes suggests the following set of classes:

- The capitalist class whose members control the nations' multinationals and possess a disproportionate share of wealth. Within countries variations among capitalist class members exist; for instance, in 2005 by one measure (not the one described in Chapter 1), American CEOs made 39 times more than the average factory workers while in other countries the figure was less—23 times more in France and just 17 times more in Spain.
- The professional/management (upper-middle) class, whose participants are well educated, often with advanced degrees, and generally well paid.
- The lower-middle class composed of small-business owners, clerks, and salespeople, possessing sufficient schooling to qualify for these jobs and enough income to accumulate modest savings.
- The working class, which includes both skilled and unskilled job holders. Members possess limited formal education and considerable variation in job complexity and income. For instance, carpenters, plumbers, electricians, and welders are much more skilled and better paid than assembly-line workers or custodians.
- The poor, whose members obtain the least schooling and fairly few job skills. Poor people's job situation varies considerably, with some permanently unemployed and others working full-time and receiving a low wage (Berberoglu 2009, 36; Clement 1990; Giesecke 2008; Hashimoto 2000; Müller, Lüttinger, König, and Karle 1989; Sicakyuz 2008).

While class has a major impact on people's job prospects, gender can play a significant role. A confidential report ordered by Walmart revealed that in 1995 in many categories of employment, the conglomerate was paying its US female workers 19 percent less than their male counterparts and that men were five-and-a-half times more likely to receive a promotion to a managerial position. In spite of receiving this information, Walmart executives made few adjustments in their hiring and promotion policies, and in 2010 in a class-action suit, as many as 1.5 million present and former employees were eligible for financial compensation. However, in 2011, in a 5 to 4 decision, the Supreme Court ruled that the class-action suit against Walmart was invalid, not establishing the existence of a general policy of discrimination against all female employees (Bario 2010; Biskupic 2011; Fisher 2010).

In contrast to the core countries, the semiperipheral and peripheral nations have their own fairly uniform set of classes, which generally provide less financial and human capital and more social reproduction than the core countries supply.

- The upper class is either corporate and engaged in industrial and commercial enterprises or is landowning and involved in crop and livestock production; in addition, top political leaders primarily live and work in the national capital.
- The upper-middle-class contains a small number of well-educated professionals and high-level government officials.
- The self-employed lower-middle-class involves artisans, shopkeepers, clerks, and small business people.
- The peasant class provides assorted agricultural products and either owns or leases their land.
- The working class includes industrial, clerical, and service job holders as well as temporarily unemployed individuals.
- The informal sector of people engages in a wide range of small illegal businesses, which can be fairly stable money makers; some of the poor are permanently unemployed and/or homeless (Berberoglu 2009, 53; Hoffman and Centeno 2003; Robinson 2000).

Multinationals' investment in semiperipheral and peripheral nations has consistently been exploitative, undermining those nations' economies in several ways:

STRUCTURAL DISTORTION IN THE ECONOMY   Historically core states have used less developed nations as sources for extraction of minerals, crops, or natural resources like timber, coal, or oil. The extraction work is largely unskilled and low-paid, offering jobs that are a far cry from the more diversified opportunities that exist in core nations, where a wide range of production and sales jobs develop (Chirot 1986, 99; Kerbo 2006). Even when manufacturing moves to poor countries, benefits for the local workforce are modest. Multinationals' heavy investment permits them to gain control over various political and economic processes in the host nation, structuring job activities to maximize their profits. As a pair of sociologists suggested, the giant companies become "the only game in town" (Kentor and Boswell 2003, 310).

AGRICULTURAL DISRUPTION   When multinationals invest in agriculture in less developed countries, the rules of the game once again emphasize maximized profit. Mechanized farming and extended use of land become the order of the day. Food prices rise, and poor peasants find it increasingly difficult to locate land to grow their crops. Agricultural disruption is hardly a new process. It is well known that a blight was the immediate cause of the so-called "potato famine" which between 1845 and 1852 drove over a million Irish citizens to migrate to the United States. What is less well known is that starting long before the blight, much of the country's best land was used for exported products, particularly livestock which continued to be shipped to England, often under heavy guard, throughout the seven-year famine (Kerbo 2006; Kinealy 2002).

TOP-LEVEL COLLUSION   As a rule, the relationship between a developing nation's political leadership and multinationals' representatives becomes intimate, mutually self-serving, and corrupted, paving the way for multinationals to maximize profits, often at most local citizens' expense. Illustrations later in this chapter involve India, China, Brazil, and Mexico.

OPEN MARKETS   Since the United Provinces obtained hegemonic power, core nations have generally supported unrestricted trade. Their multinationals usually possess the vast resources to dominate commercial arrangements, often in developing nations undermining fledgling industries. Frequently the core nations' call for open markets is distinctly hypocritical. As the dominant multinationals located in such countries as Germany, Japan, and the United States were establishing themselves, they depended on import tariffs or other protections from foreign competition. In fact, some of those measures persist. The United States and the European Union continue to pay their agribusinesses substantial subsidies, allowing them to underprice foreign farmers, many of which are small, struggling, and located in developing nations (Kerbo 2006).

In the fierce global economy, it is hardly surprising that a UN Human Development Report in 2005 indicated that compared to 15 years earlier, 18 of the world's poorest nations had declining income and life expectancy (Ismail 2007, 33).

Since the 1980s an additional factor has intensified the global pursuit of profit. Large institutional investors, which are major big businesses, have accumulated enough collective savings to exert significant impact on financial markets, pushing for accelerated cash flow to shareholders. Corporate officials pass on this sense of urgency to the leaders of the feeder factories which manufacture their products. The leading multinationals have become adept at the practice. Walmart has developed into the world's largest retailer by pressuring its suppliers to compete with each other to manufacture the least expensive products. To obtain a similar result, a British multinational used a variety of techniques, including so-called "cross-cutting," where the retailer obtains a price quote from one supplier, then contacts a second with the intention of undercutting it, and finally returns to the original supplier (Kaplinsky 2005, 176). It is hardly a hospitable employment setting for workers in feeder factories. In 2006 about 66 million people, the majority of whom were women, assembled goods for a global market. Many faced long hours, low wages, environmental threats, sexual harassment, and union repression (Palpacuer 2008).

The previous set of points has emphasized that the multinational-driven global system has tended to undermine peripheral and semiperipheral states. Do the core nations, which created colonies and later multinationals, bear the full responsibility for poor countries' degraded conditions? Modern-world-systems theory emphasizes the significant negative contribution of those nations. It is important, however, to acknowledge two additional conditions: that many poor countries have suffered incompetent or corrupt leadership that helped drain the nations resources, and that sometimes a state's relationship with multinationals has led to national economic improvements (Bradshaw and Wallace 1996, 51–52). In fact, Doug Schuler, a marketing specialist, examined available data on international business and concluded that in developing countries, multinationals generally provide better wages and working conditions than local companies (*Magazine of Rice University* 2005). It should be added, however, that as information supplied throughout this chapter indicates, the impact multinationals have on developing nations is broader in scope than just wages and working conditions.

Furthermore other factors besides globalization can come into play affecting people's life chances. In examining 143 countries, researchers at the International

Monetary Fund learned that additional conditions influencing a given nation's social inequality included technology, education, and sectional shifts. Another source suggests the impact of the government's involvement:

TECHNOLOGY   Across all world regions, there has been a steady growth in nations' distribution of information and communications technology. Individuals schooled to use such advanced skills will widen the income gap from those without such skills. This factor is the most prominent one that has driven a recent acceleration of economic inequality across nations.

EDUCATION   Increased education is likely to provide better access to higher-skilled, better-paying positions.

SECTIONAL SHARE OF EMPLOYMENT   Shifts in type of work can significantly impact many people's incomes. If industrial development sharply expands in a country, the new job holders might experience a distinct income growth compared to farmers.

GOVERNMENTAL CONCERN FOR PUBLIC WELFARE   A study of social inequality in 60 nations found that whether or not a nation has a large public sector that provides the citizenry effective schooling, healthcare, and other benefits significantly impacts income inequalities, particularly for the poorest states. The presence of multinationals has a major effect. A federal government's ability to provide such benefits depends heavily on its economic welfare, and the extent of multinationals' involvement in countries can decisively influence that condition. However, it is not just a question of money; a critical necessity concerns political officials' commitment to its citizens' needs (Hoffman and Centano 2003; International Monetary Fund 2007; Lee, Nielsen, and Alderson 2007).

Assessments of social inequality demonstrate that poor individuals and families are losing out compared to their more affluent compatriots. However, one should remember that income information about social inequality reveals a significant part but not the entire story of people's economic condition. Mexico serves as a case in point. Between 1985 and 1994, the income differences between high- and low-skilled workers increased. At the same time, changing tariff policies increased the disposable income for all households, with wealthier households obtaining a 6 percent increase and their poorer counterparts a 2 percent increase, leading to a 3 percent reduction in the national level of poverty (International Monetary Fund 2007, 42).

The prevailing conditions in modern world systems provide the context for the development of various contemporary class trends.

THE GLOBAL SPECTRUM: FROM THE VERY RICH TO THE VERY POOR

Semiperipheral and peripheral nations display sharp economic inequalities, with those at the top very rich. Russia is a striking case in point. A single event initiated the ferocious race for wealth. The so-called "loans for shares" was a rigged government sale of a host of publicly owned resources that included factories, mines, minerals, transportation systems, oil, gas, and coal. President Clinton and a team of Harvard advisors strongly supported this sale, concluding that it would assure that the transformation of socialism to capitalism would be permanent.

Those who secured the lion's share of state resources used hardcore criminal techniques—assassinations, massive theft, and illegal stock manipulations and buyouts—to build their empires. In addition, many critics, including former President Putin, pointed out that these wealthy individuals failed to take the time and trouble to expand their businesses, choosing instead to focus on such quick-profit approaches as stock speculation, investment in banking, and buyout of mineral-processing plants (Kramer 2006, 3.1; Petras 2008, 319–21).

Interestingly at least one clear exception exists to the Russian pattern for becoming very rich. Oleg V. Deripaska, who may be the wealthiest Russian, got his start working on the shop floor of a Siberian smelter. He became a physicist and then an industrialist, developing a massive aluminum business. While his commercial ventures do no appear squeaky clean, it seems apparent that unlike most Russian billionaires Deripaska has been building his company. The key, he explained, has been cheap electricity from Siberian hydropower. "It's like a physics equation," he asserted. "If a country imports energy or energy-related products, it means the country will not be able to produce aluminum" (Kramer 2006, 3.1).

While Russia has about 50 billionaires, China has about 20. Like their Russian counterparts, few if any Chinese billionaires grew up rich. Instead of extensive financial capital, their families provided valuable social capital, links to political officials from whom they could purchase land, import and export licenses, and various public enterprises such as housing projects and factories. In the 1980s as this collusion thrived, the Chinese Communist Party became a huge bribe-taking apparatus, displacing both urban workers' housing and rural villages to provide wealthy real-estate speculators and construction-company owners opportunities to enrich themselves. Leading capitalists have found that a government patron cannot only help secure their access to valuable resources but can also assist them in avoiding labor regulations that would have required them to pay for such costs as pensions, health insurance, and environmental protection (Petras 2008, 322–24; So 2003, 368).

Unlike their Chinese or Russian counterparts, most of India's 35 billionaires were born rich, part of the privileged upper class, and became richer. A number of government policies have created a billionaire's paradise, particularly in new economic zones, where wealthy business men can avoid taxes and restrictive labor legislation and reap huge profits on rapidly rising real-estate values. Meanwhile the issues that benefit the wealthy contribute to an economic nightmare for low-income workers, who experience eviction, rising prices, and poor job prospects (Desai 2007, 3–4; Petras 2008, 325–26.

Like India several Latin American countries have national economic policies that promote wealthy individuals' drive for further enrichment. Both the IMF and the WB played important roles in developing the modern Mexican and Brazilian economies. Their policies permitted wealthy people to buy telecommunications, banking, and other formerly public facilities and also to receive tax exemptions and subsidies. Furthermore the policies promoted declining social services, increasing state repression of labor unions, growing regressive taxation, and bankrupting of small farmers, peasants, and rural workers. Brazil and Mexico contain 30 of Latin America's 38 billionaires. (Hoffman and Centeno 2003; Petras 2008, 321–22).

Billionaires' rise in semiperipheral nations effectively fits a Marxist model, highlighting the bourgeoisie's profit fixation. In all of the countries just considered, the largely IMF-backed policies that benefit the wealthy are harmful, sometimes drastically harmful for most of the populace. The upcoming section illustrates how current global economic and political realities impact various sets of job holders. Table 3.3 provides international

TABLE 3.3 World and Regional Estimates of the Working Poor in Developing Nations over a Decade

	1997: US $2 per day or less (in millions or workers)	1997: US $2 a day or less as percentage share in total employment
World	1,426.6	57.1%
Central and southeastern Europe[1]	30.6	20.6
East Asia	558.1	78.2
Southeast Asia & the Pacific	156.4	69.6
South Asia	415.4	86.6
Latin America & the Caribbean	53.0	27.6
Middle East	10.4	24.6
North Africa	19.4	42.3
Sub-Saharan Africa	183.3	85.5

	2007: US $2 per day or less (in millions of workers)	2007: US $2 a day or less as percentage share in total employment
World	1,210.4	40.8%
Central and southeastern Europe	21.2	13.1
East Asia	258.6	32.3
Southeast Asia & the Pacific	145.9	53.6
South Asia	478.8	80.1
Latin America & the Caribbean	40.1	16.1
Middle East	13.4	21.7
North Africa	19.0	30.5
Sub-Saharan Africa	233.4	82.0

[1]The nations included in this category are Europe's least developed and are not European Union members.

This table, which focuses on the working poor, indicates that over a decade each of the eight geographical areas represented here displayed a declining percentage of job holders making less than US $2 a day. The data also suggested substantial regional differences in poverty, with in 2007 82 percent of employees in Sub-Saharan Africa and 80 percent in South Asia making $2 a day or less while only 13 percent of their counterparts in central and southeastern Europe earned so little.

Source: International Labour Organization. 2009. Box 201. "World and Regional Estimates of Working Poor." *Key Indicators of the Labour Market Programme: Poverty, Working Poor and Income Distribution.* http://www.ilo.org/public/english/employment/strat/kilm/download/kilm20.pdf.

data about both poverty and inequality, demonstrating that while various regions' percentages of working poor making $2 or less a day has declined over time, regional inequality prevails, with South Asia and Sub-Saharan Africa having over 80 percent of their working poor earning such a small sum.

The harsh challenges employees in developing nations often face are apparent in the upcoming discussions of work in China, Latin America, and India; unionization in global sweatshop settings; and squatters' struggle to survive.

Three Semiperipheral Locations

CHINA   China's expanded participation in world trade has been notable. Although other low-wage markets have grown, none can match its increase in exports since 1990. Competing nations have been startled. In Mexico, one of China's chief rivals, it was as if there was a "great sucking sound" of jobs migrating to China (Kaplinsky 2005, 132).

In China, where business and political leaders work closely together, the government usually provides the dormitories where factory workers live. The housing provision is for individuals not families, and since the tenants are migrants, not citizens of the locale, the state can impose distinct residency controls. If they lose their jobs, they also lose their housing. Because workers are completely dependent on the factory and the state for both their employment and residence, they usually accept long hours at low pay (Pun and Yu 2008).

Dong, for instance, was a 23-year-old migrant worker from a fairly poor village in Hunan. As the eldest daughter, her father asked her to quit school at 16. She moved to Shenzhen, where she lived in a state-owned dormitory and worked for a feeder factory. Dong explained that she realized that working in unpleasant conditions in a strange city would be a major challenge. "But I thought it was still worth it to try, and it was a chance for me to look at the outside world" (Pun 2004, 31).

Almost every year Dong returned to her poor village, bringing about 2,000 yuan ($240) to her family, which was more than its total income. The family was happy with her contribution, and she was pleased to help them. However, the work took its toll. Dong said, "The working hours are too long. It's too hard." She returned home one New Year's exhausted, thinking she would not go back to the city. "I stayed home for two months and I slept, slept all the day" (Pun 2004, 31). Feeling restored and with a boyfriend in a nearby village, Dong returned to factory work, concluding that even though her job was difficult and exploitative, it represented a last chance to enjoy her personal freedom outside the village before settling down to married life.

The long working hours that Dong and other industrial workers in feeder factories often experience have become one issue in the anti-sweatshop movement in the United States and western Europe directed against Walmart, Reebok, Nike, and other multinationals. Those companies, in turn, have at least gone through the motions of pressuring their suppliers to upgrade their working conditions and payment. A study of two Chinese supplier factories for Walmart found that in anticipating the investigators' questions, managers supplied their employees uniform answers, particularly involving working hours, rest days, and wages. Interviewed later in their dormitories, the workers admitted that they did not approve of the false answers management required them to give. However, they feared that not only would they get in trouble if they told the truth, but management had convinced them if they failed to support the denial of sweatshop conditions the regular flow of orders to the company might cease (Pun 2005, 107).

These factories' activities represent **hegemonic despotism**, a condition where modern firms can control operations by threatening workers with downsizing or even plant closure. Indeed companies' ample opportunities to relocate mean they can pit worker groups in different areas against each other, undercutting their efforts to unionize or improve wages and working conditions (Collins 2003, 10).

Walmart has become highly successful at implementing hegemonic despotism. The giant chain has dramatically increased its number of stores and its share of the American toy market. As previously noted, the key to Walmart's growth has been its system of getting the lowest prices possible by forcing suppliers to compete against each other. The majority of Walmart's supplier factories are Chinese, and the company's pricing strategy has worked well in the Chinese dormitory system, where workers have little recourse to accepting an exploitative, punitive job setting (Pun and Yu 2008).

In the twenty-first century, Chinese factories have received extensive attention regarding dangerous working conditions. For instance, in Suzou, 137 workers obtained serious nerve damage from exposure to a toxic agent used to clean the glass screens of Apple's iPhone. One 27-year-old man had become so hypersensitive to cold that even when indoors he needed to wear down-insulated clothes. In a loud, angry voice, he explained that he was much too young for such an inconvenience. He added, "Only 50- or 60-year-old men wear something like this" (Barboza 2011, B1). Apple officials said they would alter dangerous conditions at the plant and monitor injured workers' progress, but a dozen employees who had suffered contamination said that Apple never contacted them. Meanwhile, these individuals indicated, administrators at the feeder factory had pressured many injured workers to resign, offering cash supplements that would eliminate the company's liability (Barboza 2011).

LATIN AMERICA   The involvement of Latin American countries in the global system also has distinctive features. First, many of these countries have a long history of core nations' economic dominance during which there was a formation of a national upper class, which became wealthier and more powerful than their counterparts in most other developing states. Second, over time this class deeply entrenched itself economically and politically, often emphasizing sharp racial differences to help establish class distinctions. Finally many of the Latin American nations have failed to address less affluent citizens' needs. Modern political officials have tended to perpetuate colonial governments' role— namely, to facilitate big business's goals (Hoffman and Centeno 2003, 381–83; Lee, Nielsen, and Alderson 2007, 85).

Not surprisingly employment in the Latin American global economy is a difficult experience. Many Mexicans work in factories where they produce low-cost clothing for exportation. In the village of San Sebastián, one plant had 14,000 workers, most of whom were Indians from nearby settlements. The law required that if employees were on the job for more than 30 days, they had to register to obtain medical and other services. Scarcely half the workers at the factory felt they could afford the benefits; after 29 days they quit and were rehired. Most individuals were on the assembly line, producing jeans and shirts. A significant drawback was that since the factories did not provide necessary training, the majority of workers were unqualified for their jobs.

Wages were based on the number of pieces assembled and tended to slightly exceed the official minimum wage of $3 a day (Berruecos 2008, 1704–05). A researcher told José, a manager in a clothing-manufacturing plant, that the wages seemed very low. José agreed but noted that other local firms had similar standards. Certainly, he conceded, pay was lower than in the United States and many other nations. However, José added, "compared to here, it [the pay] is not. And we offer them a future, we offer them a chance for advancement and many other things. So I think we're helping" (Berndt 2003, 272–73). Perhaps the point to reemphasize is that such factories are often either the only or the best game in town.

In some factories, however, job qualities are better. The Mexican subsidiary of Dannon, a French firm best known in the United States for yogurt, established several highly unusual practices. First, in a country where workers describe bosses as "gods" or "tyrants," the Dannon leadership downplayed rank differences, emphasizing that employees could call their superiors by their first names and see them without appointments. A machine operator evaluated his supervisor. "If I have any doubts, I approach him [my boss] and he can help me resolve my problem." A project manager agreed, indicating that employees "did not work as boss and workers but as friends" (d'Iribarne 2002, 250).

Throughout the factory the dominant, often mentioned expression was that "We are all Dannon," a statement conveying a sense that everywhere Dannon products were sold the company's image was the reflection of all its employees. Besides its positive personnel policies, the corporation displayed unusual financial support for workers, paying them better than competitors and offering more flexible hours and greater job security (d'Iribarne 2002, 248).

INDIA   Like Mexican job holders, Indian employees face diverse working circumstances. Overall it is a poor, primarily rural nation, where about half the country's workers are either farm owners or farm laborers. Examining consumers' expenditures in the 1980s and 1990s, one finds that the greatest increase has been in the lower-middle income—households spending between US $129 and $301 per month—and less growth has occurred among those in the upper-middle contingent spending over $344 a month (Desai 2007, 6–7).

Nonetheless in the twenty-first century, the Indian professional and management class has done well. Government employees receive salaries that are often adjusted for inflation and that include fairly regular increases. Professionals in the private sector, however, have been India's major middle-class winners. Since the government's willingness to accept multinationals' presence in the early 1990s, information technology (IT) has steadily expanded, with the software industry growing by 50 percent annually between 1990 and 1998. Estimates indicated that over 200 Fortune 500 corporations outsource some of their software needs to Indian companies. Besides software development and programming, the Indian IT industry provides overseas customers call centers, accounting, and data entry. In spite of offering steady raises, Indian companies find it increasingly difficult to hold onto their software programmers, who are in frequent contact with overseas customers and find it fairly easy to migrate to Europe and the United States. (Desai 2007, 9–11).

For Indian IT specialists, however, money is not the only consideration in locating jobs. A study of 60 women in the IT industry indicated that many respondents strongly valued autonomy and self-reliance and like Shirin, a 25-year-olf graphics specialist, viewed their careers as a means of maintaining a vibrant sense of self. She said, "If you have to achieve something, you cannot stay in one job. It's very stagnant water" (Radhakrishnan 2006, 9). Shirin explained that to qualify for new jobs she needed updated knowledge and skills and that only in such an expanding professional context would she feel a sense of accomplishment.

Unlike Shirin most Indian workers must make wages their priority. At Phoenix International, a supplier factory for Reebok, the experienced, largely literate employees received subminimum wages, and it was only after the formation of a union that a change occurred. In addition, any mistakes workers made on the job led to such punishments as beatings or painful confinement in the burning hot sun. In fact, the formation of the union flowed from an incident where a pregnant woman suffered the latter punishment. The union made workers feel empowered and less fearful of discussing the many serious problems they encountered. An employee explained, "It is difficult to believe that the Reebok persons didn't know of the unpaid extra working hours, the lack of rest intervals, the arbitrary fines [in violation of] labor laws" (D'Mello 2003, 38–39). While the union did win workers various rights, the victory was short-lived. In 2000 the plant was illegally closed, putting 2,000 individuals out of work.

What roles do unions play in improving global workers' lives?

Unions against Sweatshops

At a World Trade Organization meeting in Seattle in November 1999, thousands of protesters opposing multinationals' global policies were a vocal presence. Jay Mazur, the activist president of the Union of Needletrades, Industrial and Textile Employees, asserted that globalization had reached a turning point where elites no longer could make basic decisions behind closed doors. The future, Mazur said, would involve "a contested terrain" in which deregulation, big business domination and corruption, and the dismissal of ordinary citizens' compelling interests would be relentlessly under attack. Yet the current reality is bleak. Mazur concluded, "Globalization is leaving perilous instability and rising inequality in its wake" (Mazur 2000, 79).

While the "contested terrain" Mazur cited is unquestionable, its appearance is more likely to occur in some countries than in others. An examination of 84 developing nations indicated that after foreign investment occurred, the presence of one potent factor was most likely to promote conflict and unrest—a country's possession of a large working class whose wages and working conditions foreign investment would be likely to impact (Rothgeb 2002). In selected nations such a class has been active and militant.

In the early 2000s, in Chinese medium-sized towns and villages, where multinationals' feeder factories have been prominent, working-class people protested against the forced relocations, political corruption, tax abuses, and other actions that have benefited wealthy people and corporations at their expense. In 2005, China experienced more than 70,000 public protests in urban factories and villages. In May 2007, in a small city, over 10,000 citizens rioted against local tax escalations, setting their rich adversaries' buildings and cars on fire (Bensman 2006, 7; Petras 2008, 324).

Global workers producing goods for multinationals usually labor in sweatshops, where the following negative conditions are prevalent:

Unstable employment and low compensation. Such conditions fail to provide "a living wage," which means sufficient income to survive decently in that particular locale.

Exposure to difficult, dangerous working conditions. Major issues involve fire safety, the presence of toxic material and chemicals, and the absence of clean water. Serious if slightly less pressing, workers often suffer crowding and excessive heat or noise.

Sexism and racism. Testimonies indicated that selected women and racial groups have been objects of discrimination, obtaining lower pay, less advantageous job arrangements, and, in the case of women, exposure to sexual harassment and assault. In Panoptimex, a feeder factory in Juárez, Mexico, which made televisions for the multinational CEW, women were young, generally under 20, and usually composed about three quarters of the assembly-line workers. A researcher observed that the supervisors, who were all men, engaged in "monitoring efficiency and legs simultaneously, their gazes focused sometimes on fingers at work, sometimes on the nail polish that adorns them" (Salzinger 2007, 174). The supervisors also propositioned the workers, who often submitted to their advances, thinking, usually mistakenly, that it would lead to promotion. Throughout the global economy, where work is tedious and stressful, the majority of managers believe that women are more docile, compliant employees. In the highly controlled modern garment industry, where inspectors have begun to evaluate employees' output in greater detail, factory owners and managers tend to feel that women can more readily deal with the stress and criticism, making them increasingly valued job holders. Throughout the western hemisphere, Mexican women have a reputation for possessing two highly desirable traits—the ability to both patiently and competently perform the tedious, repetitive tasks that occur in manufacturing and information processing and the willingness to submit to patriarchal leadership.

Captive and child labor. In various countries in Asia and Africa, workers remain in forced servitude until a debt is paid. Sometimes those workers are children; in addition, child labor is common in the textile and apparel industries, particularly in Bangladesh, India, and Pakistan.

Ineffectual monitoring. The emphasis on cheap prices make it unlikely that the inspections multinationals sometimes initiate will yield significant reforms. These giant companies besieged by international criticisms of making huge profits from sweatshop labor have felt pressured to respond, officially ordering feeder factories or subsidiaries to eliminate or curtail sweatshop conditions. However, because of management's intimidation, employees often mislead the examiners, or local companies simply ignore the violations. Both the multinationals and their feeder factories are firmly committed to keeping product prices as low as possible, and most violations are cost-effective (Collins 2003, 156–57; Esbenshade 2004; Heintz 2004, 226; Rivoli 2003, 224–26; Roman 2004, 104–05; Wright 2007, 194–95).

Have unions proved useful in curtailing sweatshop conditions? It depends. In some factories such as Taiwan-owned facilities located in Vietnam a strict tradition of corporate control exists, with management suppressing all independent union activity. A manager explained, "I can breed my own cells to monitor the deviant behavior. If I find someone who likes to criticize the company, well, we have a 'graveyard' [very unpleasant work setting], and (s)he will be sent there and buried." A Vietnamese worker's observation was consistent. He avoided the union because it "is useless and provides me [with] nothing" (Wang 2005, 49).

The Kukdong plant in Mexico, a Nike feeder factory, also had a company union that management required employees to join. In this case workers became militant, seeking to develop a union that would address their grievances and goals. Graham Knight and Don Wells, the social scientists who studied the plant, found the struggle between workers and management involved three stages.

First, an opening protest occurred, starting in December 2000. In a setting featuring low wages, compulsory unpaid services provided to management, and inadequate transportation subsidies, employees decided to boycott the cafeteria, which had substandard food that made some workers sick and caused them to miss time on the job. The absence of a union that would express people's grievances was glaringly apparent. One respondent explained that the company union proved worthless, remaining uninvolved when employees seeking a better wage were fired. The workers had a plan, initiating their protest with the food boycott, which developed into a successful collective effort that was less jarring than a strike but involved 90 percent of the workforce (Knight and Wells 2007, 89). The fact of the matter was that even though the workers' actions were not jarring, their adversaries remained unwilling to accept even the mildest version of uncooperative behavior. Various repercussions occurred.

Second, management personnel acted, and the protest accelerated. It started in early January when corporate union officials fired five protest leaders. Workers, in turn, occupied the factory compound, demanding the individuals' reinstatement. Police attacked the protesters, causing sufficient injury that 15 of them had to be hospitalized. The police's harsh response encouraged further militance as union advocates fanned out throughout nearby neighborhoods to gain residents' support. An important detail was that most of the factory workers had strong roots in the area and could use their social capital to bolster their cause. In upcoming months the workers' mobilization broadened. Several protest leaders toured the United States, speaking to media personnel and student groups. Activists' targets dispersed, including not only Nike officials but also representatives of various American universities which used Nike apparel and belonged to a pair of high-profile associations that monitored and reported on conditions in the international garment industry. During the protest phase, a significant change had occurred. Now the Kukdong laborers were no longer focused on grievances directed against them but were committed to obtaining their rights. A leader spoke out forcefully in favor of eliminating the company's union, which had always treated workers harshly (Knight and Wells 2007, 91). The Kukdong workers were convinced that they needed their own union—one that worked for them.

Third, following the publicity the protests created, four investigations of the Kukdong plant occurred, indicating various violations of the Nike code the company's supplier plants were supposed to follow. By March the workers had established their own union—the Sindicato Independiente Trabajadores de la Empresa de Kukdong Internacional de México (SITEMEX). While the company's union persisted, trying to use intimidation and bribery to further its agenda, SITEMEX decisively prevailed, becoming the workers' effective representative at the plant. By April SITEMEX received certification as the legal union at Kukdong (Knight and Wells 2007, 92–93).

Knight and Wells observed that the three phases of the protest were closely interrelated, building upon each other. For instance, the Kukdong workers were quickly able to advance from their initial protest, the cafeteria boycott, to a second stage, providing American students and reporters extensive publicity about their cause. Effective preparatory work with universities and media companies made this progression possible (Knight and Wells 2007, 93).

The authors noted that proponents of the anti-sweatshop movement saw the Kukdong victory as a triumph of international labor solidarity confronting corporate power. Conceding that universities, mass-media organizations, and other outside structures had a role, the authors noted that the Kukdong protest also featured a local dimension. Knight and Wells concluded that the international and local dimensions of the protest were highly interdependent, with each making a critical contribution to the creation of SITEMEX (Knight and Wells 2007, 98).

   The labor struggle at the Han Young welding factory in Tijuana, Mexico, appears to support Knight and Wells's conclusion. In this earlier instance, even though the workers' effort to unionize received widespread support, including backing from both the Mexican and American presidents, the situation ended in almost total defeat, with all participants fired and the plant relocated. Curiously external pressures actually worsened the situation. It turned out that the workers' most formidable adversaries were not the company but other powerful interests. The Han Young Company and Hyundai, its major client, were actually willing to reach a resolution with the union. However, as the effort to unionize at Han Young received growing publicity, the state commerce secretary and the Mexican Businessmen's Association became increasingly determined to prevent it. The secretary and members of the Association met with the owner of Han Young and explained that they were determined to make an example of his workers and that if he did not break the union, officials would shut down his plant (Williams 2003). It appears, in short, that outside support can prove useful if, as in the case of the Kukdong factory, local union activists are in a strong bargaining position; if, however, as in the Han Young case, powerful opposition confronts unionization, then even robust outside support is not likely to help establish the union.

   Factory workers struggle to make a living. Their lives are difficult but usually less desperate than squatters' experience.

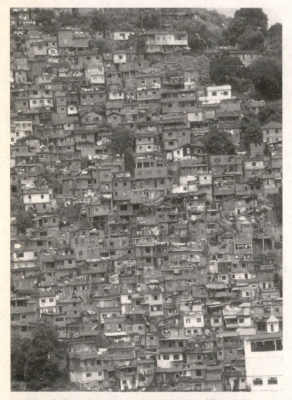

In Brazil the squatter communities like this one in Rio de Janeiro are called favelas.

Squatter Communities: A Global Surge

Squatters are simply individuals or families who settle on land that does not belong to them. In 2005 there were about a billion squatters on the planet, and with about 70 million individuals a year leaving rural areas for cities, the expectation is that by 2030 the squatter total will reach two billion, or about one in four people (Neuwirth 2006, 9–11). While squatters tend to be poor, often very poor, that is not always the case. They vary in income, work, aspirations, and class (Neuwirth 2006, 14).

   Political scientist Janice Perlman (de la Rocha, González, Perlman, Safa, Jelia, Roberts, and Ward 2004) described a set of four conditions promoting squatter communities. Her research involved Brazil, where in Rio de Janeiro alone there are at least 600 squatter communities (Neuwirth 2006, 39). The conditions are:

Growing inequality. During its global phase, Brazil has eliminated a substantial number of unskilled jobs and increased positions for university-trained professionals, making it one of the economically most unequal countries in the world.

Surplus population. In the early 2000s, Brazil's unemployment rate was one of the highest in its history, with many people losing jobs and unlikely to work again. Furthermore the majority of workers were poorly paid and/or were exploited in temporary jobs, often making it difficult or impossible to live outside squatter communities.

Retrenchment of the welfare state. Programs related to the poor are focused on surveillance and control. Compared to Europe or even the United States, Brazil has provided much less support for poor people.

Stigmatization. Are people maligned for living in squatter communities? Perlman asked her respondents about eight sources of discrimination they might encounter, and this issue received the most reference—by 66 percent of the research subjects. Stigmatization promotes isolation and a diminished opportunity to make the contacts necessary to break out of a squatter residency.

When one examines a squatter community like Kiberia in Nairobi, Kenya, these factors impinge.

Kiberia, Africa's largest squatter community, lies in a valley and is primarily composed of mud blockhouses. Each structure contains as many as 20 rooms, which are about 10 feet by 10 feet. Ventilation is poor, coming through the door and sometimes a small window. The one room must meet all family needs, serving as a living room, dining area, kitchen, washroom, study, bedroom and even, if going outside at night is dangerous, a temporary toilet (Neuwirth 2006, 70–73).

The local government does not recognize Kiberia, providing no sewers, no electricity, and no water supply. To obtain water, residents must pay 10 times as much as more affluent people living in a neighborhood with municipally supplied water. Furthermore during those fairly frequent times when water is scarce, the price of city-controlled water remains stable, but the street supply triples or quadruples in cost, making it 30 or 40 times more expensive than municipal water (Neuwirth 2006, 80–81).

In Kiberia, water is an illegal source of money-making and so is housing. The Provincial Administration, a generally inactive collection of tribal chiefs and elders, controls the government land where Kiberia is located. For a substantial, under-the-table fee, this group permits wealthy investors to build squatter housing. Investigator Robert Neuwirth indicated that since the cost of developing such properties is low and requires minimal upkeep, owners make substantial profits (Neuwirth 2006, 94). Tenants who are late with the rent are quickly thrown out. A resident emphasized that renters are always subservient to landlords (Neuwirth 2006, 4).

While life in Kiberia is difficult, even oppressive, many residents are proud, hard-working individuals who have struggled to make a decent living. Neuwirth indicated that upon meeting him, many people quickly brought out their high-school diplomas or photos to build the case that they were not the unworthy inhabitants of a squatter town but were well educated, responsible individuals holding good jobs (Neuwirth 2006, 70).

Kiberia residents have varied backgrounds and lifestyles. Michael Obera's job as a clerk in the City Council paid over 9,000 shillings a month (around $120) and represented a middle-class income, but he struggled economically because the city was always two months behind in issuing paychecks. Obera lived in Kiberia because renting elsewhere was too costly; outside the squatter community, two rooms for himself, his wife, and four children would have consumed his entire salary (Neuwirth 2006, 71–72).

Unlike Obera's job, employment inside Kiberia is part of the **informal sector**, which involves jobs and businesses that government neither monitors nor taxes. Neuwirth observed a teenaged hauler with an enormous burlap bag full of cabbages belonging to a woman too frail to carry them. Such workers have semiofficial locations where they remain, and if they poach on someone else's territory, a fight is likely. Depending on how heavy the load and the distance covered, the hauler could make up to 50 shillings a load, perhaps 250 shillings ($3) a day. It is hard work but good earnings for Kiberia (Neuwirth 2006, 75–76).

Within the squatter community, running a well-located hotel can be both a demanding and lucrative livelihood. Sabina Ndunge, who was the sole support of her six children and owned Bombers Pisa Motel, opened her hotel at 5 A.M. and closed at 9:30 P.M. She bought all her food at a local market 10 minutes walk from her location. Economics prompted her not to have meat in her stews, keeping the expense down. In fact, the cost with meat would have been three or four times greater. Ndunge, who had run her hotel since 1988, would have liked to see such improvements as paved road, permanent buildings, and access to healthcare but only if her expenses did not rise. Her business required keeping her prices low—only possible if the products and services she needed to run the hotel stayed cheap (Neuwirth 2006, 76).

Winnie Kioko was another business woman in Kiberia. She worked as a seller of potatoes. Every week she rented space in a truck, rode to the Rift Valley, and bought potatoes, which she sold to stores and restaurants. Her earnings were about 4,000 shillings ($48) a month. Kioko was a member of a 15-person merry-go-round to which each woman contributed 1,000 shillings every two weeks. Twice a month someone received the kitty. At one point Kioko had additional expense and lacked the money to buy potatoes. For six months she stopped making her weekly trips for potatoes until the 15,000-shilling payment from the merry-go-round allowed her to get started again. Merry-go-rounds emphasize spending, not saving; joining one is a practical way of recognizing that at times individuals like Kioko need extra money for business expenses, old debts, or perhaps a medical bill. Interestingly only women participate in merry-go-rounds; neither women nor men could explain why this was the case (Neuwirth 2006, 90–91).

Kiberia's residents, people like Michael Obesa, Sabina Ndunge, and Winnie Kioko, lived in a squatter community where the informal sector dominated. That reality suggests that such individuals' lives are similar in certain respects to the American underclass—the poorest of the poor—discussed in Chapter 8. Clearly the inhabitants of Kiberia have limited access to valued types of capital.

Consider Michael Obera, whose middle-class salary represented a reasonable amount of financial capital, which would suggest some economic security. However, he encountered the stress and inconvenience that government employees in many peripheral nations face—that their countries' underfunded treasuries periodically run out of cash. Harsh economic conditions also played a central role in Sabina Ndunge's life, forcing her to choose her dishes' ingredients carefully so that customers could afford them and prompting her to support improvements in the community only if they would not increase her expenses. Finally Winnie Kioko, while possessing the least financial capital of the three, displayed robust social capital, using her merry-go-round to raise the money required to restart her business.

These three individuals and many other members of the Kiberia squatter community were hard-working, resourceful, and fairly successful. Their lives, however, were precarious, always impacted by the volatile local and national economy and the conditions cited earlier which promote squatter communities. In most families social reproduction appears highly probable. It seems unlikely that children growing up in a squatter community will have access to the human and financial capital that would make it possible for them to advance to a more prosperous way of life. In sum, they count among the largest losers in the modern global system.

Does this community have a future? Elsewhere in Nairobi the government demolished squatter communities to replace it with better housing. Michael Obera, however, suggested that improvements would increase rents, forcing many families to create new squatter towns (Neuwirth 2006, 98). Once again, it is apparent that squatter residents have very fragile lives, vulnerable to various impinging forces.

However, Neuwirth's representation of life in Kiberia might be overly pessimistic. In a review of his book, David Satterthwaite indicated that Neuwirth failed to mention the Kenyan Homeless People's Federation, a squatters' organization which had developed savings schemes and was negotiating with a government agency to prevent mass evictions (Satterthwaite 2008, 234).

Globally the best solution would probably involve home ownership. A nationwide program focused in Peruvian squatter neighborhoods revealed that when people became property owners, their economic investment in housing improvement increased more than two thirds—not only because of pride of ownership but also because of greatly diminished fear of being evicted (Field 2005). The utility of such a program seems clear. The problem is that subsidizing the requisite world-wide home ownership is expensive— nearly $300 billion to buy housing for the huge number of squatters, which will increase by about 670 million people between 2005 and 2020. The sum is enormous, but it becomes conceptually less daunting on appreciating that it is about $3 a year per person on the planet (Neuwirth 2006, xiii).

Prospects are not good for many global residents. Let us consider the chapter's principal main points, which tend to support that contention.

Conclusion

Historically three nations—Holland, Great Britain, and the United States—have established hegemony, dominating the world system for a period of time. In the modern world system, countries divide into three types based on economic level—in declining affluence they are the core, the semiperipheral, and the peripheral. During the first two hegemonic phases, the core nations exploited their colonies, benefiting from their raw materials and cheap labor. In the modern era, multinationals have attained massive wealth and power investing in developing nations.

The formation of a modern world system results from a set of four conditions—expansion in three fundamental economic domains, namely agriculture/industry, commerce, and finance; the formation of an ideology emphasizing free trade; the growth of military might; and the decline of the hegemonic power and a restructuring of the system.

Because of their countries' contrasting economic and political structures, the class systems in core and developing nations are distinctly different, with poverty and low income, limited modern technology, and restricted schooling more prevalent in semiperipheral and peripheral states. Multinationals' investment in developing nations has undermined their economies in various ways.

While multinationals significantly impact the poorer countries, other factors affecting social inequality within them include technology, education, sectional share of employment, and governmental concern for public welfare.

In the context of the modern world system, citizens in developing nations have had highly varied experiences and levels of success. Billionaires in Russia, China, India, and Latin America have diverse backgrounds but share the common experience of profitably colluding with their own governments. In contrast, ordinary global workers in China, Mexico, and India experience highly controlled, poorly paid jobs. In such factories as Dannon's Mexican subsidiary, workers have been well paid and treated humanely. In India, IT professionals receive good salaries and often have various job options.

Many workers in developing countries, however, face sweatshop conditions, which include low wages, exposure to difficult, dangerous working conditions, sexism and racism, captive and child labor, and ineffectual monitoring. Can unionization mobilize to combat these conditions? Sometimes. A critical condition appears to be an effective opportunity for the union to develop and expand its influence without lethal opposition from impinging powers—in a case study presented, the opposition came from a government official and a businessman's association.

Squatter communities, which are rapidly expanding, contain many of the planet's poorest people. Certain conditions, namely growing social inequality, surplus population, retrenchment of the welfare state, and stigmatization, have promoted these settlements. Kiberia, a squatter community in Nairobi, Kenya, displays a variety of lifestyles and occupations among its largely hard-working residents struggling to survive a relentlessly demanding existence.

Little information in this chapter suggests that social reproduction is under siege. Table 3.4 briefly illustrates that conclusion by providing observations about access to capital for the global affluent and the global poor.

A final thought about the inequities of the global economy. Throughout human history individuals and groups have often been effective at confronting formidable immediate threats—the marauding bear or tiger, the opposing army, or the devastating epidemic. In contrast, the modern global economy poses

TABLE 3.4 Contrasting Capital Access among the Global Affluent and Poor		
	Affluent[1]	**Poor**
Financial capital	The opportunity to use these resources for a variety of purposes related to living well and increasing one's wealth, including investment in various global businesses	Necessity to seek low-paying jobs, with 80 percent of workers in South Asia and Sub-Saharan Africa making less than $2 a day
Human capital	Possession of sufficient funds to prepare youth educationally to benefit from the nation's involvement in modern business such as India's growing participation in IT	Very limited opportunities for schooling and training, sometimes failing to prepare their workers to perform their assembly-line jobs properly
Social capital	Effective connection to groups willing to promote their interests. Most notably, the mutually beneficial if corrupt association between developing nations' wealthy business people and their governments	General lack of access to valuable connections. Exceptions include squatter communities' use of merry-go-rounds or unusual employment settings providing extensive worker supports—for instance, at Dannon's Mexican subsidiary or SITEMEX at the Kudkong plant

[1]A broad category of people extending from the wealthy to middle-class managers and professionals

serious, slowly growing problems like expanding world poverty and homelessness that are least threatening for the nations possessing the most resources to confront them. Is there a reasonable prospect of mobilizing a major movement to alter global inequities? What would be an effective strategy for spearheading it?

Key Terms in the Glossary

Core nation *49*
Hegemonic despotism *62*
Hegemony *48*
Ideology *53*

Informal sector *70*
Modern world system *49*
Multinational *51*
Peripheral nation *49*

Semiperipheral nation *49*
Squatters *68*

Discussion Topics

1. List and describe the four factors in the development of world systems.
2. What are three prominent means by which multinationals have undermined developing nations' economies?
3. Evaluate the following statement: The patterns permitting individuals in developing nations to become billionaires loosely fit a Marxist model.
4. Define hegemonic despotism and indicate how Chinese governmental policies support that condition. Make certain to include Walmart in the discussion.
5. If factory workers in a developing nation plan to start a union, what basic guidelines should they keep in mind?
6. Comment on this claim: The residents of squatter communities are simply society's failures, namely individuals and families without the fortitude and perseverance to be successful in the work world.

Research Papers

1. Is a fourth hegemonic power likely to arise? To address this question, analyze all four conditionss that have produced hegemonic powers and attempt to determine what contemporary evidence related to these factors suggests as an outcome.
2. The text indicates that in 2005 China experienced over 70,000 public protests in factories and villages. Gather material about these protests, indicating instances of union input, preferably one involving the organization and/or strengthening of a union effort. Evaluate the action's success, suggesting whether it made effective use of local conditions that could promote the union's goals. What impact have these protests had in both the factory and the locale?
3. Pick a squatter community—perhaps Kiberia in Kenya, Geeta Nagar in India, Rocinha in Brazil, or some other one for which extensive information is available. Describe life in this community, providing detail about how inclusion in a modern world system affected the development and maintenance of this squatter community and also ideas about the most promising means of improving residents' prospects for obtaining human and financial capital.

Informative Websites

Immanuel Wallerstein's speech "America and the World: The Twin Towers as Metaphor" (http://www.wallerstein.com/America-and-the-world-the-twin-towers-as-metaphor/) provides an incisive view of the United States after its loss of hegemony and in the years following September 11.

Now for another viewpoint on a topic discussed several times in this chapter: The Walmart Foundation (http://walmartstores.com/communitygiving/203.aspx) describes this massive multinational's contribution to addressing such issues as schooling, hunger relief, and disaster response.

UNITEHERE! provides a website (http://www.unitehere.org/international/) which summarizes the connections to international unions maintained by this coalition of American and Canadian workers, many of whom are women and/or minority-group members in such low-wage job sectors as food service, textiles, manufacturing, and airport labor.

A lively overview of squatting (http://money.howstuffworks.com/squatting1.htm), introduces such topics as squatters' relationships with the law and the landlord's point of view, and discusses a variety of international squatting communities.

Bibliography

Barboza, David. 2011. "Workers Poisoned at Chinese Factory Wait for Apple to Fulfill a Pledge." *New York Times* (February 23): B1+.

Bario, D. 2010. "Report on Walmart Sex Discrimination Foreshadowed Massive Class Action." *The Am Law Daily*. http://amlawdaily.typepad.com/amlawdaily/2010/06/walmart-report.html.

Bensman, David. 2006. "China on the Capitalist Road." *Dissent* 53 (Summer): 7–8.

Berberoglu, Berch. 2009. *Class and Class Conflict in the Age of Globalization*. Lanham, MD: Rowman & Littlefield.

Berndt, Christian. 2003. "El Paso del Norte . . . Modernization Utopias, Othering and Management Practices in Mexico's *Maquiladora* Industry." *Antipode* 35 (March): 264–85.

Berruecos, Luis. 2008. "The Quality of Social Existence in an Indian Community in Mexico due to Globalization." *American Behavioral Scientist* 51 (August): 1694–1712.

Biskupic, Joan. "Supreme Court Limits Walmart Sex Discrimination Case." *USA TODAY* (June 21). http://www.usatoday.com/money/industries/retail/2011-06-20-walmart-sex-bias-case_n.htm.

Bradshaw, York W., and Michael Wallace. 1996. *Global Inequalities*. Thousand Oaks, CA: Pine Forge Press.

Bunker, Stephen G., and Paul S. Ciccantell. 2005. "Space, Matter, and Technology in Globalization of the Past and Future," in Christopher Chase-Dunn and E.N. Anderson (eds.), *The Historical Evolution of World-Systems*. New York: Palgrave-Macmillan.

Chase-Dunn, Christopher. 1989. *Global Formation: Structures of the World-Economy*. Cambridge, MA: Basil Blackwell.

Chase-Dunn, Christopher, Yukio Kawano, and Benjamin D. Brewer. 2000. "Trade Globalization since 1795: Waves of Integration in the World-System." *American Sociological Review* 65 (February): 77–95.

Chirot, Daniel. 1977. *Social Change in the Twentieth Century*. New York: Harcourt Brace Jovanovich.

Chirot, Daniel. 1986. *Social Change in the Modern Era*. New York: Harcourt Brace Jovanovich.

Clement, Wallace. 1990. "Comparative Class Analysis: Locating Canada in a North American and Nordic Context." *Canadian Review of Sociology & Anthropology* 27 (November): 462–86.

CNNMoney.com. 2011. "Global 500: Our Annual Ranking of the World's Largest Corporations." http://money.cnn.com/magazines/fortune/global500/2011/eshtml http://money.cnn.com/magazines/fortune/global500/2011/full_list/

Collins, Jane L. 2003. *Gender, Labor, and Power in the Global Apparel Industry*. Chicago: University of Chicago Press.

Davies, James, Susanna Sandstrom, Anthony Shorrocks, and Edward N. Wolff. 2006. "The Global Distribution of Household Wealth." *Free Online Library*. http://www.thefreelibrary.com/The+global+distribution+of+household+wealth-a0159646788.

de la Rocha, Mercedes González, Janice Perlman, Helen Safa, Elizabeth Jelin, Bryan R. Roberts, and Peter M. Ward. 2004. "From the Marginality of the 1960s to the 'New Poverty' of Today: A LARR Research Forum." *Latin American Research Review* 39 (February): 183–203.

Desai, Sonalde. 2007. "Globalization and the Changing Power of the Indian Middle Classes." American Sociological Association annual meeting. pp. 1–20.

d'Iribarne, Philippe. 2002. "Motivating Workers in Emerging Countries: Universal Tools and

Local Adaptations." *Journal of Organizational Behavior* 23 (May): 243–56.

D'Mello, Bernard. 2003. "Reebok and the Global Footwear Sweatshop." *Monthly Review* 54 (February): 26–40.

Esbenshade, Jill. 2004. *Monitoring Sweatshops: Workers, Consumers, and the Global Apparel Industry*. Philadelphia: Temple University Press.

Field, Erica. 2005. "Property Rights and Investment in Urban Slums." *Journal of the European Economic Association* 3 (April–May): 279–90.

Fisher, Daniel. 2010. "Ninth Circuit Gives Wal-Mart a Big Headache." *Forbes* (April 26). http://blogs.forbes.com/docket/2010/04]26/ninth-circuit-gives-wal-mart-a-big-headache/.

Frank, Barney, and Ron Paul. 2010. "Why We Must Reduce Military Spending." *The Huffington Post* (July 6). http://huffingtonpost.com/rep-barney-frank/why-we-must-reduce-milita_b_636051.html.

Giesecke, Johannes. 2008. "The Impact of Class on Social Inequality, Winners and Losers of the Income Dynamics in Germany between 1998 and 2005." American Sociological Association annual meeting. pp. 1–16.

Hashimoto, Kenji. 2000. "Class Structure in Contemporary Japan." *International Journal of Sociology* 30 (Spring): 37–64.

Heintz, James. 2004. "Beyond Sweatshops: Employment, Labor Market Seniority and Global Insecurity." *Antipode* 36 (March): 222–26.

Hoffman, Kelly, and Miguel Angel Centeno. 2003. "The Lopsided Continent: Inequality in Latin America." *Annual Review of Sociology* 29 (June): 363–90.

International Monetary Fund. 2007. "World Economic Outlook: Globalization and Inequality." http://www.imf.org/external/pubs/ft/weo/2007/02/index.htm.

Ishida, Hiroshi. 1989. "Class Structure and Status Hierarchies in Contemporary Japan." *European Sociological Review* 5 (May): 65–80.

Ismail, Mohd Nazari. 2007. *The Globalisation Debate: A Case of Barking Up the Wrong Tree*. Kuala Lumpur, Malaysia: University of Malaya Press.

Kaplinsky, Raphael. 2005. *Globalization, Poverty and Inequality: Between a Rock and a Hard Place*. Cambridge, UK: Polity Press.

Kennedy, Paul. 1987. *The Rise and Fall of the Great Powers: Economic Change and Military Conflict from 1500 to 2000*. New York: Random House.

Kentor, Jeffrey. 1981. "Structural Determinants of Peripheral Urbanization: The Effects of International Dependence." *American Sociological Review* 46 (April): 201–11.

Kentor, Jeffrey, and Terry Boswell. 2003. "Foreign Capital Dependence and Development: A New Direction." *American Sociological Review* 68 (April): 301–13.

Kerbo, Harold. 2006. *World Poverty in the 21st Century: The Modern World System and the Roots of Global Inequality*. New York: McGraw-Hill.

Kinealy, Christine. 2002. *Irish Famine: The Great Calamity 1845–52*. New York: Palgrave-Macmillan.

Knight, Graham, and Don Wells. 2007. "Bringing the Local Back In: Trajectory of Contention and the Union Struggle at Kukdong/Mexmode." *Social Movement Studies* 6 (May): 83–103.

Kramer, Andrew E. 2006. "Out of Siberia: A Russian Way to Wealth." *New York Times* (August 20): 3.1.

Lee, Cheol-Sung, François Nielsen, and Arthur S. Alderson. 2007. "Income Inequality, Global Economy and the State." *Social Forces* 86 (September): 77–111.

Magazine of Rice University. 2005. "Examining the Pros and Cons of Global Capitalism." (Fall). http://www.rice.edu/sallyport/2005/fall/sallyport/capitalism.html.

Mahan, A. T. 1889. *Influence of Sea Power upon History: 1600 through 1783*. London: Sampson Low, Marston, Searle & Rivington.

Martin, William G. 2008. "Conclusion: World Movement Waves and World Transformations," pp. 168–80 in William G. Martin (ed.), *Making Waves: Worldside Social Movements, 1750–2005*. Boulder: Paradigm Publishers.

Mazur, Jay. 2000. "Labor's New Internationalism." *Foreign Affairs* 79 (January/February): 79–93.

Müller, Walter, Paul Lüttinger, Wolfgang König, and Wolfgang Karle. 1989. "Class and Education in Industrial Nations." *International Journal of Sociology* 19 (Fall): 3–40.

Neuwirth, Robert. 2006. *Shadow Cities: A Billion Squatters, a New Urban World*. New York: Routledge.

New York Times. 2009. "Bretton Woods System." (August 28). http://topics.nytimes.com/topics/reference/timestopics/subjects/b/bretton_woods_index.html.

Ormrod, David. 2003. *The Rise of Commercial Empires: England and the Netherlands in the*

Age of Mercantilism, 1650–1770. Cambridge, UK: Cambridge University Press.

Palpacuer, Florence. 2008. "Bringing the Social Context Back In: Governance and Wealth Distribution in Global Commodity Chains." *Economy and Society* 37 (August): 393–419.

Petras, James. 2008. "Global Ruling Class: Billionaires and How They 'Make It.'" *Journal of Contemporary Asia* 33 (May): 319–29.

Pieterse, Jan Nederveen. 2002. "Global Inequality: Bringing Politics Back In." *Third World Quarterly* 23 (December): 1023–46.

Prabhakar, A.C. 2003. "A Critical Reflection on Globalization and Inequality: A New Approach to the Development of the South." *African and Asian Studies* 2: 307–45.

Pun, Ngai. 2004. "Women Workers and Precarious Employment in Shenzhen Special Economic Zone, China." *Gender and Development* 12 (July): 29–36.

Pun, Ngai. 2005. "Global Production, Company Codes of Conduct, and Labor Conditions in China: A Case Study of Two Factories." *China Journal* 54 (July): 101–13.

Pun, Ngai, and Xiaomin Yu. 2008. "When Wal-Mart and the Chinese Dormitory Labour Regime Meet: A Study of Three Toy Factories in China." *China Journal of Social Work* 1 (July): 110–29.

Radhakrishnan, Smitha. 2006. "Rethinking the Nation as Global: Gender, Class, and the Making of IT India." American Sociological Association annual meeting. pp. 1–19.

Rivoli, Pietra. 2003. "Labor Standards in the Global Economy: Issues for Investors." *Journal of Business Ethics* 43 (March): 223–32.

Robinson, William I. 2000. "Neoliberalism, the Global Elite, and the Guatemalan Transition: A Critical Macrosocial Analysis." *Journal of International Studies and World Affairs* 42 (Winter): vi–107.

Roman, Joseph. 2004. "The Trade Union Solution or the NGO Problem? The Fight for Global Labour Rights." *Development in Practice* 14 (February): 100–09.

Rothgeb, John M., Jr. 2002. "Foreign Investments, Privatization, and Political Conflict in Developing Countries." *Journal of Political and Military Sociology* 30 (Summer): 36–50.

Salzinger, Leslie. 2007. "Manufacturing Sexual Subjects: 'Harassment,' Desire, and Discipline on a Maquiladora Shopfloor," pp. 161–83 in Denise A. Segura and Patricia Zavella (eds.), *Women and Migration in the U.S.-Mexico Borderlands.* Durham: Duke University Press.

Satterthwaite, David. 2008. "Review." *International Journal of Urban and Regional Research* 32 (March): 233–35.

Shah, Anup. 2010. "World Military Spending." Global Issues. http://www.globalization.org/article/75/world-military-spending.

Sicakyuz, Achrene. 2008. "Europe Takes Aim at CEO Bonuses; Leaders across the Political Spectrum Are Expressing Hostility to the Surging Incomes of Corporate Bosses." *New York Times* (October 4): C2.

So, Alvin Y. 2003. "The Changing Pattern of Classes and Class Conflict in China." *Journal of Contemporary Asia* 33: 363–77.

Stiglitz, Joseph E. 2002. *Globalization and Its Discontents.* New York: W. W. Norton & Company.

Wallerstein, Immanuel. 1974. *The Modern World-System: Capitalist Agriculture and the Origins of the European World-Economy in the Sixteenth Century.* New York: Academic Press.

Wallerstein, Immanuel. 1980. *The Modern World-System II: Mercantilism and the Consolidation of the European World Economy, 1600–1750.* New York: Academic Press.

Wallerstein, Immanuel. 1984. *The Politics of the World-Economy: The States, the Movement, and the Civilizations.* Cambridge, UK: Cambridge University Press.

Wallerstein, Immanuel. 2003. *The Decline of American Power.* New York: New Press.

Wang, Hong-zen. 2005. "Asian Transnational Corporations and Labor Rights: Vietnamese Trade Unions in Taiwan-Invested Companies." *Journal of Business Ethics* 56 (January): 43–53.

Williams, Heather L. 2003. "Of Labor Tragedy and Legal Farce: The Han Young Factory Struggle in Tijuana, Mexico." *Social Science History* 27 (Winter): 525–50.

Wilson, Charles Henry. 1941. *Anglo-Dutch Commerce in the Eighteenth Century.* Cambridge, UK: Cambridge University Press.

Wright, Melissa W. 2007. "The Dialectics of Still Life: Murder, Women, and Maquiladoras," pp. 184–202 in Denise A. Segura and Patricia Zavella (eds.), *Women and Migration in the U.S.-Mexico Borderlands.* Durham: Duke University Press.

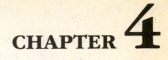

Foundation for Social Inequality: Concepts and Structures

Consider the following set of contemporary points about American social inequality:

- The United States now possesses more social inequality than any other major industrialized nation.
- Since 2001 the country has produced a steady increase in both the number of poor and those who are uninsured.
- Income inequality has been growing, with the biggest gains to the top 5 and 1 percent of households.
- At the financial pinnacle, a steady increase has occurred in the number of billionaires. In 2009, it took $950 million to attain the Forbes 400 of richest Americans.
- The social inequality is nonpartisan, with the Gini index increasing just as much under William Clinton as under George W. Bush. Widening disparities resulted from three decades of policies tilted toward major corporations and large asset owners and away from all nonaffluent groups. Public policies involving taxes, wages, and spending have had a major impact on these inequalities (Collins and Yeskel 2005; Miller and Greenberg 2009).

How, one might wonder, did these inequalities develop? Two sets of background information contribute to an understanding—conceptual elements and structural or interactional data. The first section examines the concepts and ideas that underpin the American sense of how society works and should work. The second involves the structures and activities—the institutions, organizations, agencies, and practices—that shape the central economic and political policies. George Ritzer, a sociological theorist, has developed a framework for social action that coincides with this chapter's content.

According to Ritzer, the major levels of social analysis involve two dimensions—the macro versus micro dimension and the subjective, revealing people's feelings and desires, versus the objective dimension, relating to material objects. Combinations involving these four categories produce four types of subjects for sociological study:

The macro-subjective: Large-scale nonmaterial phenomena such as culture, norms, ideology, and class

The micro-subjective: Small-scale nonmaterial mental processes such as a community's or even a family's beliefs or perceptions

The macro-objective: Large-scale material structures such as institutions, major corporations, or even society itself

The micro-objective: Small-scale material entities such as classrooms, families, or social clubs (Ritzer 1980; Ritzer 1989; Ritzer 2008, 376–77).

While the second section features the objective issues, the upcoming discussion focuses on subjective topics, in both instances primarily, but not entirely at the macro level. Later chapters contain extensive material about both micro types.

ON YOUR OWN: CLASS, IDEOLOGY, AND SOCIAL MOBILITY

If a theme runs through the three subjects in this section, it is the idea that individuals and families are free agents—on their own. The traditional outlook on this position is that individuals and families possess the freedom to make their own decisions and chart their own destiny. Generally little attention has gone to the fact that left on their own, many groups are vulnerable to powerful pressures and crises. As the upcoming chapters demonstrate, the less affluent people are, the greater their vulnerabilities. In this section it becomes clear that with the emphasis involving being on their own, many Americans downplay class membership, focusing instead on the preeminence of the individual and the family. It is abundantly clear that both of the other topics discussed here—the American ideology and the pursuit of social mobility—contain ideas consistent with the emphasis about being on one's own. An analysis of class is the foundation for the rest of this section.

Class in the United States

As the definition in Chapter 1 noted, a **class** is a large category of similarly ranked people distinguished from other categories in the hierarchy by such traits as occupation, education, income, and wealth (Gilbert 2011, 263). In doing research, social scientists generally use measures of occupation, income/wealth, and education to distinguish classes (Dye 2002, 150). However, the extensive research on class has displayed a wide variety of measurements, differing on such issues as whether to focus on one or more variables; whether the research site should be a single town or city, or the entire nation; or whether the class placement should be subjectively or objectively determined (Perry-Jenkins 2005, 454). Even the analysts who subscribe to the following classification are likely to differ in their estimated percentages of people comprising the various classes.

This text presents an extensively used six-class scheme based on several variables but featuring occupation, thus locating it in the Weberian tradition. In this classification occupation, education, and income are distinctive for each class:

1. The first of two privileged categories is the upper class or superclass, with income from investments and inheritance, and some members holding top corporate positions; education from prestigious college and universities, sometimes including post-graduate work; a typical household income of about $2 million yearly; and a total of about 1 percent of the population.
2. The second privileged group is the upper-middle class, involved in high-level management, professional work, and ownership of medium-sized businesses; education

featuring college graduation and often post-graduate study; a yearly income of about $150,000; and a 14 percent segment of the people. This class includes "the working rich," a small but growing set of wealthy professionals—some doctors, lawyers, dentists, and ranking but not top corporate officials who earn hundreds of thousands of dollars a year or more—often enough to qualify them as upper-class members. However, they are not part of that class because their income derives from fees and salaries, not investments.

3. The first of two majority classes (in numbers) is the middle class, sometimes designated the lower-middle class, employed in crafts, lower management, semi-professional, and nonretail sales work; at least high-school completion and often some college credits; income about $70,000 a year; and a total of about 30 percent of the population.

4. The second category within the majority set is the working class, composed of low-paid craftspeople, clerical workers, and retail-sales employees; a frequent possession of a high-school certificate; earnings of about $40,000 a year; and representation of about 30 percent of US inhabitants.

5. The higher of the two lower classes is the working poor, with jobs in service work, labor, and clerical activities; education involving at least some high-school attendance; income about $25,000 a year; a 13 percent segment of the people.

6. Finally the underclass involves individuals who are unemployed or working part-time, often outside the mainstream work structure, and can be dependent on public assistance or other government subsidy; income about $15,000 a year; and nearly a 12 percent portion of the populace (Gilbert 2011, 244–49; Marger 2011, 56–61).

About 90 percent of respondents place themselves in the middle class (meaning either the upper middle or middle categories in the above scheme) when asked to choose between that designation and either upper or lower class (Dye 2002, 150). A national survey giving more options also revealed a leaning toward the middle-class preference. Among the respondents, 2 percent placed themselves in the upper class, 17 percent in the upper-middle class, 45 percent in the middle class, 27 percent in the working class, and 8 percent in the lower class (Samuelson 2006). A more recent ABC News Poll revealed a fairly similar outcome. Forty-five percent of respondents considered themselves middle-class, 39 percent working-class or below, and an additional 14 percent upper-middle-class or better (ABC World News Poll 2010). In short, two national surveys revealed that about three of five individuals interviewed considered themselves in the middle-class range. Describing themselves as middle-class, I would argue, is a way of suggesting they are typical Americans, thus downgrading or even dismissing the significance of class and implying that people should be judged solely as individuals.

Economist Michael Zweig suggested that several factors appear to promote Americans' tendency to describe themselves as middle-class rather than working-class. One issue is social mobility. Because of the national push to advance one's economic and social position, working-class origin is widely considered a stigma, simply a condition to escape. Second, consumerism comes into play, with middle-class buying patterns featured in various media outlets. Finally mass-media policies play an important role; newspapers, radio, television, and magazines pay little or no attention to the working class, and unions, which have historically served people in many working-class jobs, receive limited or negative coverage (Zweig 2000, 39-56).

Perhaps what is most notable about class is that outside sociology and other academic spheres it is seldom a topic of discussion. Why is that? Sociologist Gregory Mantsios asserted that "[i]n politics, primary and secondary education, and to the mass media, formulating issues in terms of class is unacceptable, perhaps even un-American" (Mantsios 2007, 183).

Sociologist Diana Kendall has offered a related argument, featuring a useful concept. **Media framing** is the process of packaging information and entertainment in order to produce a distinct impact on an audience. The process involves a series of decisions about what is informative and entertaining—such decisions as how much coverage to give a story or whether to give it a positive or negative spin. Media framing is particularly apparent with news, but it also occurs with entertainment (Kendall 2005, 7). All in all, leaders in the major media determine that to placate corporate sponsors and to promote entertainment, their best course of action is to offer a superficial look at class and social inequality, trivializing them. Kendall indicated that "the media either play class differences for laughs or sweep the issue under the rug so that important distinctions are rendered invisible" (Kendall 2005, 229).

The general avoidance or de-emphasis of class-related issues in the media and also in schools means that most Americans do not perceive shared class interests, making common cause unlikely. Most notably this trend undermines union organizing.

Nonetheless, situations arise in which class differences, though often not discussed as such, create a distinct conflict. In the late 1990s, in Burlington, Vermont, the city lost its supermarkets. A referendum took place to determine what would be the replacement—a standard supermarket, that featured bargain items that poor and working-class families often valued, or a more health-conscious, somewhat more expensive store, which middle-class people favored. Feelings were strong, with angry testimonies at one meeting indicating that lower-income individuals refused to have a group of residents stopping them from buying the white bread and red meat that they preferred. The issue, however, ran deeper than food choices.

One local observer suggested that there was a class-based background to this conflict—that for the first time since high school the lower-income residents were in face-to-face relationship with the upper-middle-class individuals, who were top students and teachers' favorites. "So there are years of resentment that have bottled up . . . these people" (Alvarez and Kolker 2001). The commenter had no research data at hand, and yet what he said about differing class experiences in school will generally be supported in later chapters.

While most Americans seldom refer to class or discuss class-related issues, they are well aware that one of the factors associated with class—income and wealth—varies widely. Income and wealth, which are often discussed interchangeably, have distinctly different meanings. **Income** involves individuals' earnings obtained through wages, salaries, business profits, stock dividends, rents, and other means. **Wealth** is people's economic assets—their cars, homes, stocks, bonds, and real estate, which can be converted into cash. More affluent families have greater income and wealth than less affluent families, but, in particular, they possess a greater portion of all wealth.

Table 4.1 demonstrates that between 1980 and 2007 only those individuals in the highest designated income bracket ($100,000 and over) substantially increased their percentage of the total national income (U.S. Census Bureau 2008; U.S. Bureau of the Census 2010).

TABLE 4.1 Percent Distribution of Total Income for Families over Time[1]

	Under $15,000	$15,000–$24,999	$25,000–$34,999	$35,000–$49,000
1980	10.3%	12.1%	12.6%	18.9%
1990	10.2	11.6	11.3	16.8
2000	8.1	9.7	10.7	15.0
2004	9.2	10.3	10.6	14.5
2007	7.9	9.0	9.6	13.7
	$50,000–$74,999	$75,000–$99,000	$100,000 and over	
1980	24.5%	12%	9.6%	
1990	22.6	13.4	15.2	
2000	20.7	14.3	21.5	
2004	20.4	13.6	21.4	
2007	19.6	14.3	25.8	

[1]All data except the figures for 2007 are in constant 2005 dollars.

Families with income of $100,000 a year or more, who approximately represent Dennis Gilbert's two privileged classes, more than doubled their proportion of the total income over 27 years. Except for the next most affluent category of families, which modestly increased its percentage over time, every other category decreased its proportion of income in that time period.

Sources: U.S. Bureau of the Census. 2008. Table 673. "Money Income of Families—Percent Distribution by Income Level in Constant (2005) dollars: 1980 to 2005." *Current Population Reports*, Series pp. 60–231. http://www.census.gov/compendia/statab/2008/tables/08s0673.pdf; US Bureau of the Census. 2010. Table 682. "Money Income of Families Distribution by Family Characteristics and Income Level." *Statistical Abstract of the United States: 2010*. http://www.census.gov/…income_expenditures_poverty_wealth.html.

As far as wealth distribution is concerned, it has remained very stable, with Gilbert's capitalist class, the top 1 percent, holding a consistently disproportionate share over time—33.8 percent of all wealth in 1983 and 34.3 percent in 2004. Most wealth, nearly 85 percent of it, is in the possession of the most affluent 20 percent of the population. It is among the superrich that the greatest expansion in wealth has occurred. Between 1983 and 2004, the number of households with a net worth (in 1995 dollars) of $10 million increased from 66,500 to 344,888—more than a fivefold increase (Wolff 2007). However, the economic decline did affect the wealthiest Americans. In 2009 the number of billionaires, which was 473 the previous year, dipped below 400, with a mere 371 individuals qualifying for this exclusive membership (Kroll 2008; Miller and Greenberg 2009).

Wealth, or the lack of it, is one determinant of lifestyle. In Chapter 2 the examination of Max Weber's social-stratification theory indicated that status-group members have distinctive lifestyles. A **lifestyle** is a particular set of behavioral patterns involving social relations, childrearing practices, language usage, and other activities deriving from members' consumption patterns (Gilbert 2008, 245). American classes are large and diverse, containing within them groups with varied lifestyles. Money can have a significant impact. Abundant amounts of cash allow the rich to purchase mansions, vacations, airplanes, and other amenities not available to other classes, and these items contribute to a uniquely privileged lifestyle.

One final issue about this topic might be called "the ecology of class"—that the members of any class tend to live and work in physical areas that provide either important advantages or disadvantages compared to individuals in other classes. In any city a substantial difference in quality exists between the schooling, hospital care, library facilities, and municipal services that affluent and poor districts receive.

While Americans are broadly aware of the existence of classes, they seldom appear to analyze their fellow citizens as members of them. Instead they see individuals as largely autonomous entities, subject to the broad ideological forces now discussed.

The American Ideology

As we saw in Chapter 2, **ideology** involves a complex of values and beliefs that support a society's distribution of wealth, income, and power. The images and vision an ideology provides often distract people from recognizing their society's inequalities. The United States possesses a "rags-to-riches" ideology, which was perhaps most famously represented in the Horatio Alger novels.

It is an ideology that presidents and other public personages have widely praised, describing a country where unparalleled individual success is uniquely available. Announcing his run for the presidency, Ronald Reagan declared that ours is truly a land of opportunity, "never mean and always impatient to provide a better life for its people in a framework of basic fairness and freedom" (Reagan 1979).

In 2005 the *New York Times* conducted a nationwide survey, asking respondents whether it is possible to start out poor and become rich. Eighty percent of those questioned said yes, leading the analyst to conclude that there remains strong faith in a Reagan-like American Dream (Connelly 2005). These data would appear to be distinct evidence of **legitimation**—individuals' willing acceptance of the dominant ideology and institutions and the social inequalities they promote.

Extensive evidence exists in support of this legitimation. Even during the Great Depression of the 1930s when widespread unemployment and growing poverty might have produced enthusiasm for a redistribution of income, only one third of respondents in a nationwide survey backed the idea of a ceiling on income, with the remainder turned over to the government as taxes. Then in 1981 another survey item raised the possibility of a top limit on earning set at $100,000. Eighty percent rejected this idea, including substantial numbers of the very poor (Ladd 1994, 38–39)

Marx's concept of false consciousness seems applicable here. Whether it is a proposed limit on income or the upcoming issue of individual achievement, most Americans appear convinced that the rags-to-riches ideology superclass members like Ronald Reagan have favored also supports their own interests. Ideology tends to capture people's minds, precluding a hard look at the facts before them. It seems safe to conclude that it creates false consciousness, helping to promote economic and political elites' interests at ordinary citizens' expense.

Many scholars have written about the American ideology, and some of the specific features have included the upcoming topics—individual achievement, hard work, equality of opportunity, and support for the capitalist order (Bellah et al 1996; Hochshild 1981; Huber and Form 1973; Ladd 1994; Marger 2011, 218–29; Williams 1970, 452–500).

INDIVIDUAL ACHIEVEMENT   The idea of individual achievement is that each person is dependent on his or her own abilities, talents, and efforts for obtaining valued rewards, especially income and wealth. The focus of achievement has traditionally been the work world, notably business, which is the main avenue for becoming rich. But while much of the attention involving individual achievement has focused on obtaining wealth, the most admired Americans have featured an array of more general laudable traits that are firmly in the Horatio Alger tradition. Sociologist Robert Merton indicated that a fitting model for American individual achievement has been Abraham Lincoln, who not only displayed an array of stellar personal qualities but was "eminently successful in climbing the ladder of opportunity from the lowermost rung of laborer to the respectable heights of merchant and lawyer" (Merton 1968, 480–81).

It appears that one reason professional sports are so popular in the United States is that they represent high-level individual achievement—top athletes pitted against the most formidable opponents. Sometimes journalists or the athletes themselves use warfare analogies, referring to being "in the trenches" or "taking no prisoners." In 2010 shortly after three basketball superstars—LeBron James, Dwayne Wade, and Chris Bosh—had arranged to play together on the Miami Heat, Michael Jordan, one of the top all-time players, was asked whether he would have made such a move two decades earlier. Speaking as a "warrior" from another era, Jordan replied that he never would have contacted Larry Byrd and Magic Johnson (along with Jordan the best players of that era),

In recent years Kobe Bryant (right) and Pau Gasol of the Los Angeles Lakers have won two National Basketball Association championships, making it nearly certain that American sports fans would consider them high-level individual achievers.

"and said, 'Hey, let's get together and play on one team . . .' In all honesty, I was trying to beat those guys" (ESPN.com News Service 201).

In focusing on individual achievement, Americans tend to downplay the significance of family-of-origin differences in financial, human, cultural, and social capital. The focus is on the single person's success . . . or failure. In studying middle-class adolescents in crisis, sociologist Elliott Curie was struck by how many of their parents seemed to believe that in this highly competitive, achievement-oriented society "even the most vulnerable must learn to handle life's difficulties by themselves—and that if they cannot it is no one's fault but their own" (Currie 2004, 122).

A national celebration of individual achievement, however, does not mean that Americans are inevitably successful. In a test given to 15-year-olds in 30 developed nations, American students scored below 16 other countries in science and below 23 others in math (Planty et al 2008; *Washington Post* 2007). Is the work ethic stronger in those countries?

IMPORTANCE OF HARD WORK   In *The Protestant Ethic and the Spirit of Capitalism*, Max Weber argued that the Puritans, who subscribed to Calvinist theology, had a strong influence on the development of capitalism. The Puritan god was considered an aloof, inscrutable being deciding "the fate of every individual and [regulating] the tiniest details of the cosmos from eternity" (Weber 1958, 104). Supposedly human beings existed simply for the glorification of God and were expected never to question His decisions, accepting them on faith. One critical article of faith involved the doctrine of predestination, which asserted that before birth people were destined either for salvation or damnation. While nothing could be done to earn salvation, the Calvinist religion suggested that what individuals should do was simply assume they were among the elect and dedicate themselves to an effective performance of their worldly tasks, and they would "attain certainty of their own election and justification in the daily struggle of life" (Weber 1958, 111). Thus, Weber contended, Puritans were given "a positive incentive to asceticism." They were driven to work hard, to be austere and highly organized, and to be successful—not to become wealthy but because they were dedicated to the glory of God and, of course, their own salvation.

For the Puritans the source of the incentive to work lay in the relationship individuals had with God. Weber wrote, "In practice this means that God helps those who help themselves. Thus the Calvinist, as it is sometimes put, himself creates his own salvation, or, as would be more correct, the conviction of it" (Weber 1958, 115). As historian Daniel T. Rodgers phrased it, these early settlers were "laborers for their Lord, . . . engaged in a task filled with hardship, deprivation, and toil" (Rodgers 1978, 4). By the nineteenth century, that "preoccupation with toil" was a fundamental characteristic of American business activity (Rodgers 1978, 5).

Rodgers and Weber were analyzing the **work ethic**—the conviction that unrelenting commitment to one's job is necessary both for occupational success and for building character. It is a prominent part of the American ideology, and in a sociological study of 130 millionaires, Paul G. Schervish and his associates encountered frequent allusions to the importance of hard work. For instance, a man whose family had been rich for several generations endorsed the common belief that people became wealthy because they were "motivated to work a little bit harder than the next guy. . . . or had the greater incentive . . . [accumulat[ing] a little bit more than the next guy" (Schervish, Coutsoukis, and Lewis 1994, 223).

One international survey found that when asked whether "hard work offers little guarantee of success," 63 percent (nearly two thirds) of respondents in the United States disagreed compared to a distinctly smaller 51 percent in Italy, 46 percent in France and the United Kingdom, and 38 percent in Germany (Ladd 1994, 80)—hardly a surprising difference considering the prominence of the American emphasis on the work ethic.

With Americans, however, evidence suggests that they not only work hard but that they are invested in their jobs. Writer Studs Terkel spent three years interviewing individuals in over a hundred different jobs, and he learned that "those we call ordinary are aware of a sense of personal worth—or more often a lack of it—in the work they do" (Terkel 1974, xxiv).

Furthermore in a national survey, 87 percent of respondents indicated that they were either positive or very positive about their jobs. Most of those interviewed said that their work gave them a sense of identity as opposed to a small number who contended that their jobs were merely something necessary for making a living (*Wall Street Journal* 2003b).

Are Americans generally concerned about people's chances to be successful?

EQUALITY OF OPPORTUNITY   Traditionally American culture has emphasized **equality of opportunity**, a situation where people possess broadly similar chances for success in business, politics, and other prized endeavors. From its inception the United States was committed to break from the British tradition emphasizing royalty, nobility, and hierarchical privilege locking people into a rigid class structure.

During the nineteenth century, the country achieved distinct progress in restricting class privilege by eliminating such practices as imprisonment for debt and slavery and initiating provisions for common citizens to obtain land and public education. While acknowledging these accomplishments, sociologist Robin M. Williams, Jr., conceded that "[m]odern America, of course, shows inequalities of wealth, power, and prestige; and there is far from being equality of opportunity to acquire these things" (Williams 1970, 474).

Since its inception in the nineteenth century, the American public-school system has been touted as a vehicle of equal opportunity. Many biographies or autobiographies of wealthy, successful men and women, who have risen from poverty or economically modest backgrounds, have praised teachers and schools that have been critical in their development. Education has had a large impact on people's lives. Analyzing the relationship between schooling and occupational success, sociologist Dennis Gilbert observed that "the good jobs go primarily to those who have completed college—about a quarter of young men and women" (Gilbert 2008, 141). As we see in upcoming chapters, various classes have distinctly varied quality and quantity of schooling available to them.

Supporters of the three ideological points just described are likely to endorse the American economic system.

PREEMINENCE OF LIBERAL CAPITALISM   **Liberal capitalism** is a combination of a democratic political system and a capitalist economy, supporting free trade and unrestricted economic competition. From Chapter 2 we should recall that **capitalism** is a system in which economic production features private ownership in pursuit of profit.

Over the past 200 years, it has been apparent that liberal capitalism has been an effective system for producing prosperity and economic growth, with central planning and government intervention proving less effective. In the United States, liberal capitalism has received widespread endorsement, not only because it has produced more goods and services but because the system is sufficiently open to let many individuals pursue their personal plans to obtain wealth and success (Anderson 2007).

The historian Henry Steele Commager lauded the spirit of American enterprise. He wrote, "The American knew that nothing was impossible in his brave new world. . . . Progress was not, to him, a mere philosophical ideal but a commonplace of experience" (Commager 1947, xi and xiv). The touchstone of progress, sociologist Robin Williams, Jr., suggested, has been an ever-expanding per capita gross national product (Williams 1970, 469).

Overwhelmingly Americans have supported liberal capitalism. Both of the two major political parties are committed to the system, with most candidates for elected office receiving a significant amount of their financial support from corporate givers. Unlike most other countries, which have some type of proportional representation permitting minority parties to receive seating in their legislatures, the American system is winner-take-all, making it rare that a representative of a third party, perhaps someone critical of liberal capitalism, is elected (Alesina, Glaeser, and Sacerdote 2001).

A corollary of the American support for liberal capitalism is Thomas Jefferson's idea "that the government which governs least, governs best" (Reed 2006). Keep government off people's backs, with business activity minimally legislated and regulated. In these regards other modern nations restrict capitalism more extensively. Later in this chapter, some consequences of limited regulation are discussed.

Americans have tended to have faith that liberal capitalism will deliver. A Gallup Poll found that while only 2 percent of respondents considered themselves rich, nearly a third, 31 percent, expected to be rich some day. Not surprisingly those who were between 18 and 29 were most optimistic, with 51 percent anticipating future wealth. In addition, expectations also rose as income went up, with 51 percent of those making over $75,000 believing they would become rich (*Wall Street Journal* 2003a). This survey was done in 2003. Perhaps the results would have been less upbeat several years later.

After examining the preeminence of liberal capitalism and other elements of the American ideology, a reader might wonder how legitimacy developed in this instance. Sociologist L. Richard Della Fave (1980) indicated that laboratory studies and surveys of social-stratification systems showed that the closer the correspondence between individuals' elevated self-esteem and their possession of valued resources, the greater the system's legitimacy. A system is considered highly legitimate when those at the top of the social hierarchy feel good about themselves while those in the lower classes do not. Furthermore people tend to apply a similar evaluation of others, displaying greater esteem toward affluent individuals. Those at the top are usually positioned to solidify their success. For instance, they are often able to stage or control encounters with subordinates, impressing on them the extent of their domination. In contrast to the poor, affluent individuals have the resources to maintain their privacy, keeping any indiscretions largely hidden. My guess is that many members of the power elite grasp all or most of the preceding insights.

The American ideology has supported people's belief in social mobility.

Fixation on Social Mobility: Where Is the American Dream?

Social mobility is the movement of an individual or group up or down in a social hierarchy such as a class system. Does the American ideology with its emphasis on individual achievement and hard work provide realistic guidelines for achieving upward mobility? Researchers Roberta Rehner Iversen and Annie Laurie Armstrong's answer would be negative, highlighting the following myths about social mobility:

Myth 1: **"Initiative gets you in the door."** The authors indicated that in the United States education is considered the key to success, with schooling and training the basis for increased pay and better jobs and the belief that schooling can overcome any existing inequalities. However, in the twenty-first century, a growing number of workers are facing a situation involving "deskilling," where the introduction of new machines means that semiskilled operatives replace skilled craftsmen in a variety of working-class class jobs. Deskilled job holders include individuals who load ships, do short-order cooking, typeset, and bake. Semiskilled employees face work settings where initiative as represented by the contributions of education and skill training can do little to promote social mobility.

Myth 2: **"Hard work pays off."** The traditional corporation provided job stability and career ladders, which permitted workers to move up in both responsibility and income. Recent studies included in Chapters 6 question the persistence of this pattern, indicating that globalization, downsizing, and outsourcing have eliminated many secure career paths. It is a situation that is good—flexible—for employers, but employees in a wide range of jobs can experience insecurity and loss of morale, with the realization that hard work is often no longer likely to pay off.

Myth 3: **"Pull yourself up by your bootstraps."** This position is highly consistent with the idea of individual achievement—that wholly or almost wholly on one's own the self-reliant person can be upwardly mobile. The fact is that through American history young people's upward mobility has received support from vocational learning in schools, apprenticeships, and networks of family members, friends, and acquaintances. Today, however, the majority of entry-level workers lack all or most of these resources. Many are school dropouts, often undereducated or underskilled, deprived of supportive networks, and thus unprepared to be successful in a work world where, especially at lower levels, it has become increasingly difficult to move upward (Iversen and Armstrong 2006, 14–19).

As the third myth suggests, families are often essential supports for young people's upward mobility, providing financial capital for schooling, which has become increasingly critical for occupational success, and also supplying cultural and social capital (Bowles and Gintis 2002; Rytina 2000). As the focus shifts to the measurement of social mobility, it is helpful to keep in mind the impact of structural conditions on individuals' prospects for upward mobility.

A pair of concepts highlight important realities about social mobility. **Intergenerational mobility** is a measure of social mobility comparing a child's and a parent's class location. Major studies of social mobility use international mobility as their focal concept. **Structural mobility** is a type of social mobility where either technological or institutional change creates an increase or decrease in jobs within a certain class. Since the 1970s the introduction of computers and automation has produced structural mobility, reducing millions of blue-collar and later white-collar jobs (Theriault 2003, 126–27). In addition, large numbers of workers have been the victims of changing institutional policies, where many corporations have accelerated both downsizing and outsourcing. The growing presence of these two sources of structural mobility has meant job losses and income reduction, producing a "downward intergenerational drift among young adults from middle-income (or upper-middle-income) families who cannot find jobs that will allow them to replicate their parents' income levels or living standards" (Perrucci and Wysong 2008, 64). In the mid-twentieth century, however, upward social mobility was more prevalent.

The early studies of intergenerational mobility focused on fathers and their sons. In 1962 Peter M. Blau and Otis Dudley Duncan did research on 20,700 employed men interviewed by the Current Population Survey, and 11 years later David L. Featherman and Robert M. Hauser replicated the earlier research, examining 33,600 employed men. The results were quite similar. In 1962 60 percent of the sons were upwardly mobile and 23 percent downwardly mobile. In 1973 the respective percentages were 60 and 26 (Blau and Duncan 1967; Featherman and Hauser 1978, 93). In both studies, in short, upward mobility was more than double downward mobility.

Traditionally Americans have believed in upward mobility. In fact, a nationwide *New York Times* survey conducted in 2005 found that when respondents were asked to indicate what were the chances of moving up in class compared to 30 years earlier, 40 percent indicated greater, 35 percent the same, 23 percent less, and 2 percent gave no answer (Connelly 2005). It is hardly a pessimistic result, with three in four asserting that the opportunity for upward mobility was better or the same as 30 years before.

As globalization has advanced, however, upward mobility has declined. An analysis of national data from the General Social Survey for 1972–1979 and 1995–2004 compared men with their fathers for eight major occupational categories. The result was that in the 1970s, 48 percent were upwardly mobile, 34 percent stable, and 19 percent downwardly mobile. In 2000 the respective percentages were 41, 33, and 27 (Gilbert 2008, 130). This comparison shows that in the more recent year upward mobility was less and downward mobility greater than in the earlier time.

Information from the nationally conducted Panel Study of Income Dynamics compared children's income between 1994 and 2000 with their parents' earnings from 1967 to 1971; the researchers divided income into five quintiles adjusted for changing dollar value. Forty-two percent of children born into the lowest category remained in that quintile, meaning that 58 percent rose into higher income groups. However, a substantial segment of that 58 percent—24 percent—only rose to the second category—$32,701 to $51,900—and therefore 66 percent of the children, about two thirds—born into the lowest income group, remained in the two lowest income categories. In the third income group—$51,901 to $70,800—39 percent were downwardly mobile, 24 percent stayed the same, and 38 percent were upwardly mobile. Then, in the most affluent quintile, $98,001 and above, 57 percent were downwardly mobile compared to parents, and 42 percent stayed the same (Hertz 2006). Table 4.2 summarizes the findings in this research.

Given the meaning of social mobility, the lowest income group cannot be downwardly mobile nor the wealthiest upwardly mobile. With those considerations taken into account, it is nonetheless notable that the three more affluent groups displayed consistently less upward mobility and the two poorer quintiles distinctly more.

TABLE 4.2 Economic Mobility Prospects for Different Income Groups in the Panel Study of Income Dynamics[1]

		$0 to $32,700	$32,701 to $51,900	$51,901 to $70,800
Economic mobility from family of origin, 1967–71	Down	----	24%	39%
	Same	42%	26	24
	Upward	58	56	38
Comment		About two thirds in the two lower income quintiles (64%)	An approximate split between the upwardly mobile and the other two categories	About equal percentages of downward and upward mobility

		$70,801 to $98,000	$98,001 and above
Economic mobility from family of origin, 1967–71	Down	51%	58%
	Same	25	42
	Upward	24	----
Comment		Essentially a balance between downward mobility and the other two categories	Upward mobility not conceptually possible. High rate of downward mobility.

[1]While rounding off figures can cause the quintile totals to be either slightly less or more than 100 percent, the second lowest quintile totals 106 percent, suggesting a reporting error in the study.

Source: Tom Hertz. 2006. "Understanding Mobility in America." http://www.americanprogress.org/issues/2006/04/Hertz_MobilityAnalysis.pdf.

Structural mobility seems relevant, with technological change as well as downsizing and outsourcing promoting the loss and diminishment of both while-collar and high-paying blue-collar jobs but also the growth of service positions, which has improved the employment possibilities for some individuals born into low-income families.

While a segment of poor families in the study experienced upward mobility, those who remained at the bottom were poorer in 1998 relative to those at the top than counterparts 30 years earlier, and many were inclined, for reasons to be examined in the chapter on poverty, to stay trapped where they were (Bradbury and Katz 2007). Data from the Panel Study of Income Dynamics indicated that individuals who started in low-income jobs were more likely to experience upward mobility if they worked full time, stayed in good health, and obtained more schooling, particularly beyond high school (Theodos and Bednarzik 2006).

While some low-income families were upwardly mobile, children born to parents in the top quintile had the greatest likelihood of making it to the top, and the chances of making it to the highest income quintile decreased as one's parents' income declined.

All in all, this study revealed notable conclusions about social mobility in absolute terms—that is, the value of children's compared to parents' earnings (adjusted for inflation)—and relative terms—the two generations' respective locations on the economic ladder. The chief findings were:

- About one third of the children were upwardly mobile in both income senses. As Table 4.2 indicates, upward mobility was most pronounced in the two lowest quintiles—over half in the lowest.
- Slightly more than a quarter of children were holding their own, earning more income than their parents but maintaining the same position as the previous generation in the income distribution.
- A small group of children, about 5 percent, were earning more money than their parents but falling behind them on the dimension of relative mobility.
- About a third of the respondents fell behind their parents in both family income and comparative class ranking. Downward mobility prevailed in over half the two most affluent quintiles (Isaacs 2007a).

Americans' prospects for upwardly mobility have become less prevalent than in many other countries. A comparison of the United States and 11 other developed nations indicated that the impact of American parents' income on their children's income was greater than the effect in nine of the eleven other countries. In the United States, Italy, and Great Britain, about 50 percent of parents' earnings advantage or disadvantage passed on to children while in Denmark, Australia, Norway, Finland, and Canada, the younger generation inherited less than 20 percent of the parental income impact. This result asserts what many Americans would consider a heresy—that the Horatio Alger rags-to-riches story is much more likely to unfold in these five nations than in the United States.

The income impact American parents have also appears unusually strong in affecting children's scholastic achievement. Secondary-school students in 30 nations took a science test, and based on two measurements, the American children's results displayed either the first or the fourth highest association between parents' income and children's test scores. Once again, the United States demonstrated a more pronounced tendency toward social reproduction than almost all other nations included in the study (Corak 2006; Isaacs 2007b; Organization for Economic Co-operation and Development 2010; Rampell 2010).

Let me conclude with two significant points about this important, ever-unfolding topic. First, as with any concept, it is important when writing or speaking about social mobility to keep its meaning firmly in mind—focus on the idea of upward or downward movement in a social hierarchy. Sometimes analysts, even sociologists, lose that focus. For instance, a prominent text has a discussion on the topic, indicating that families are a prime resource for upward mobility and that wealthy, particularly upper-class families are helpful. The fact of the matter, however, is that while upper-class families often promote their children's occupational success, they do not help them become upwardly mobile. It is not conceptually possible, because the children are already at the top of the class hierarchy. Remember: Stay focused on the core meaning of the concept.

Second, like many sociologists I would welcome another large-scale social-mobility study along the lines of the pair of massive investigations conducted in the 1960s and 1970s. Unquestionably the twenty-first-century version needs to recognize the diversity of modern society, displaying the various intersectional combinations of gender and race and including the often ignored Native Americans.

Throughout this section we have seen evidence of Americans' support for the Horatio Alger myth—rags to riches. The focus shifts to important activities which a select few seek to dominate, insuring a society where their elite interests reign supreme.

THE INVISIBLE EMPIRE AND ITS CALCULUS OF CONTROL

As the lengthy, sometimes bitter contest for the 2008 Democratic nomination between Hillary Clinton and Barack Obama stayed locked in the media spotlight, a common misconception once again seemed creditable: that the prime movers and shakers in the power elite are prominent, highly scrutinized individuals. Such people can provide entertaining media theatre, but the actual economic and political policies are often formulated elsewhere, by less known or largely unknown individuals. Not only are the individuals who make prominent policies frequently obscure, but, in addition, the organizations involved receive little public attention. Their activities are well organized, systematically executed, unspectacular, and singularly important. Robert Perrucci and Earl Wysong referred to the existence of an "invisible empire." It is invisible in that the various groups and organizations that are responsible for the activities are out of the public view, and politicians and the media seldom provide more than the barest information about these structures. Furthermore it is an empire in that "the privileged-class leadership has crafted a far-flung and widely dispersed collection of resources, organizations, and processes into a coherent political force that ensures the perpetuation of its interests" (Perrucci and Wysong 2008, 142).

The factors contributing to this political force are the policy-making process, lobbying, campaign spending, the power of the press, and public policy, namely taxation, the budget, and regulation. In military parlance it seems apparent that the power elite has well-equipped arsenals with refined, efficient weaponry for defeating adversaries on each of these competitive battlefields.

The Elite Policy-Making Process

The superclass provides most of the funding for the various groups discussed here. The four-part process begins with foundations, involves think tanks and universities, and features policy-making groups. Both superclass and upper-middle-class individuals function within these different structures, and the most powerful and influential among them participate extensively in interlocking directorates.

FOUNDATIONS Among the over 66,000 foundations in the United States, only a few are well enough funded to produce a significant impact on policies. A **foundation** is a tax-free organization which spends money on research, education, the arts, and many other endeavors. Upper-class corporate leaders control large foundations, which possess well-credentialed boards and staff. Foundation money comes from dividends they receive on substantial blocks of corporate stock, with a small group of wealthy organizations making the lion's share of major foundations' contributions. In the mid-2000s, the top 100 foundations awarded $11.2 billion in grants annually, fully 37 percent of all foundation giving. The wealthiest foundations generally have interlocking directorates with each other and with a wide range of large corporations, providing input for a fairly unified power-elite policy.

Often foundations provide "seed money" for looking into issues members of the superclass consider important. In addition, their funding goes to think tanks. Between 1990 and 2000, over a third of the $1 billion spent by 24 conservative think tanks came from foundations (Alterman 2004; Domhoff 2010, 91–92; Dye 2002, 174; Perrucci and

Wysong 2008, 164–65). Without foundation money, think tanks and policy-making groups would be seriously handicapped.

THINK TANKS A **think tank** is an organization that does the most detailed research and analysis in the policy-formation process. While research and analysis are primary functions, public relations can also be important, with many think tanks producing newsletters, reports, and media interviews promoting favored policies. In the most prominent, well funded think tanks, the researchers are individuals with advanced training and degrees from prominent universities. There exist about twice as many conservative as liberal think tanks, and the conservative ones are generally better funded, receiving $295 million between 2003 and 2005 while their liberal counterparts obtained $75 million.

The three most prominent conservative think tanks are the Brookings Institution, the American Enterprise Institute, and the Heritage Foundation, with the first two organizations having some influential politicians and economists associated with them. In addition, both the Brookings Institution and the American Enterprise Institute have about 60 percent of their directors sitting on the boards of major corporations. These interlocks help to provide corporate leaders information about the think tank activities and to build support for favored policies (Domhoff 2010, 97–98; SourceWatch 2005). Like all the organizations in the policy-making process, the think tanks require university support.

UNIVERSITIES The nation contains about 4,000 colleges and universities, but in 2007 there were only 62 qualified as "billion dollar universities"—those with endowments of $1 billion or more. Besides great wealth these schools have disproportionate interplay with the power elite. They receive about two thirds of all college and university endowment, and the wealthiest and most prominent such as Harvard, Yale, Stanford, University of Texas, and Princeton provide education for large numbers of eventual corporate and political leaders as well as future members of foundations, think tanks, and policy-making groups. Many trustees at the wealthiest, most prominent private universities come from major corporations. In addition, the presidents of well known universities sometimes serve as board members at major corporations or become important political appointees. Finally universities are the location for some of the research that think tanks and policy-making groups use (Christie 2007; Domhoff 2010, 99–100; Dye 2002, 129).

POLICY-MAKING GROUPS These are the organizations that formulate important economic and political policies. Their membership features heads of major corporations, banks, and law firms, important government officials, and prominent people from universities, foundations, and the mass media. These individuals need to review the policy-related research done by foundations, think tanks, and universities. At the groups' meetings, members have a chance to question experts from think tanks and universities, familiarizing themselves with the issues at hand. Discussion occurs on the policy direction(s) to take, and leaders make deliberate efforts to establish a consensus among the members. Once consensus is established, these organizations use various media forms including journal articles, books, and press releases as well as interviews, speeches, and lobbying to influence both politicians and the general public. Three of the most prominent policy-making groups are the Council on Foreign Relations (CFR), the Committee for Economic Development (CED), and the Business Roundtable (BR).

The Council on Foreign Relations is the major policy-making group dealing with foreign affairs. Founded in 1921, CFR commissions studies on foreign-policy issues and then initiates discussions and seminars among its members and leading government officials in order to reach consensus. While most of the 3,900 members of the CFR do nothing more than receive reports and attend large banquets, the board of directors, whose members are usually powerful, influential people from business and politics, tend to be active participants.

The Committee for Economic Development was founded in the 1940s with the idea of both preparing for the possibility of another major depression and of having in place a plan that would override any proposals that a liberal-labor coalition might develop. CED contains about 200 corporate members along with a small number of college presidents. Like the CFR the CED uses study groups examining reports produced by academic experts. The difference is that at the CED the results of committee deliberations are released, with footnotes indicating where members had differences of opinion. The CED, which was once a moderate-conservative organization, changed its general stance and became more decisively conservative in the middle 1970s at a time of rising oil prices, rapid inflation, and growing unemployment (Domhoff 2010, 104–11; Dye 2002, 124–27).

Finally the Business Roundtable (BR) which was founded in 1972, is an organization in which members are the chief executive officers of about 160 of the nation's largest corporations, which collectively have a huge economic impact. These corporations generate $4.5 trillion in sales a year, employ over 10 million workers, and pay 40 percent of all American corporate income taxes. BR receives over $3 million in dues a year, which funds lobbying for specific bills members want passed by Congress and signed into law by the President. BR also tries to shine a positive light on big business. For instance, in 2006 BR leaders tried to convince government officials that it should not be compulsory for companies to reveal corporate executives' golden parachute benefits or deferred compensation (Domhoff 2010, 111–13; Dye 2002, 127; Norris 2006; Schwartz and Lohr 2008, 7). Another public-relations effort involved BR's attempt to counter survey evidence showing widespread public disapproval of big business's emphasis on short-term profits and frequent disregard for anyone else's interests. John J. Castellani, the Roundtable's president, said "A lot of pain and suffering has come from business's wrongdoing, and we must again foster trust" (Deutsch 2005). To help regain that trust, BR developed a corporate ethics program and then later started what it calls Sea Change, an initiative to encourage business to maintain environmentally sound growth.

The Business Roundtable was a prominent player in promoting a major set of policies involving all four components of the invisible empire.

THE NEOCONSERVATIVE POLICY MOVEMENT   In the late 1970s and early 1980s, what observers describe as a "neoconservative" policy movement emerged and has continued to remain influential. Support for these emerging positions originated from two sources—the failure of established fiscal practice to prevent the stagnant economy of the 1970s; and the mobilization of the corporate community and its allies. Many observers believed that the election of Ronald Reagan and the more conservative Congress that arrived with him were responsible for these policies; however, some of the new conservative practices actually preceded Reagan's election by several years.

The major players in this neoconservative economic surge included several of the organizations just discussed—think tanks like Heritage Foundation and the American Enterprise Institute along with policy-making groups, particularly the Business Roundtable. Some of the outcomes of this effort have included the passage of the Economic Recovery Tax Act of 1981, the largest tax cut in US history and one that has distinctly favored wealthy people; loosening of clean water and air standards that business had found too costly; and preliminary investigation promoting welfare reform, namely cutting welfare rolls and releasing into the workforce millions of individuals ill equipped or prepared to support themselves and their families (Jenkins and Eckert 2000). Table 4.3 provides some more detail about elite groups' efforts to produce these policies.

Presently the neoconservative movement continues, with leaders' activities remaining obscure to the public. For instance, Bruce Kovner, the manager of Caxton Associates, the world's largest hedge fund, has been an important player, controlling wide-ranging activities helping to develop economic and political policies. While Kovner is shy, humble, even self-deprecating, his actions reverberate. He has used his wealth and connections to corporate and political leaders to become very influential. In particular, for several years Kovner was the chairman of the American Enterprise Institute, which under his direction promoted the most potent neoconservative ventures in a generation—notably support for a militarily backed democratization of the world, beginning with the Middle East and the Iraq War; and advocacy of an unrestricted free market, where all or most government regulations on commercial activity were either removed or severely reduced.

At the American Enterprise Institute, Kovner had an arsenal of intellectuals, between 50 and 100 people, who could produce a steady flow of well-written reports and op-eds that barraged the public with the Institute's neoconservative point of view. The positions expressed favored wealthy and powerful interests, shortchanging most segments of the population. For instance, one of Kovner's associates suggested that the idea of a living wage, something like $12 an hour, is a sinister plot that seeks to bring socialism to American cities. Like the poor the working class was also under fire. At AEI Kovner and his colleagues were highly critical of unions, with one report supported by several confusing charts indicating that between 1947 and 2000 unions cost the US economy over $50 trillion in lost income and output (Thompson 2008, 20; Weiss 2005). In later chapters I examine both unions and the living wage, suggesting that most evidence supports very different conclusions.

AEI and a vast range of other organizations frequently engage in lobbying.

The Burgeoning Business of Lobbying

Lobbying is the process by which individuals or groups attempt to influence government officials to support legislation or policies sought by their clients, who can be corporations, professional and trade associations, or consumer and environmental groups. Lobbyists include former government officials, former politicians, lawyers, public-relations specialists, and corporate executives specialized in relations with government. The lobbyist tries to convince the politician that it is either in his or her interest to support the client's wish or, at least, that providing support will not be damaging to the politician. To win over the politician, the lobbyist offers financial support, which politicians need to meet the steep cost of campaigning (Domhoff 2010, 176–77; Dye 2002, 121–22).

TABLE 4.3 The Policy-Making Process and Neoconservative Goals: An Illustration of Interconnected Activities among the Four Types of Elite Organizations

1. **Universities:** In particular, involvement features the "billion-dollar" universities, which have large endowments primarily from wealthy individuals and corporations and have educated many of the individuals participating in the three other types of groups. Some ties between prominent universities and other elite groups are particularly intimate. For instance, the Hoover Institution, a major think tank which participated in this policy-making process, is located on campus at Stanford University, establishing extensive, mutually beneficial contacts between the two structures.

2. **Foundations:** Organizations which provide the initial direction to and funding for think tanks. Two foundations—Castle Rock and John M. Olin—donated to all three think tanks involved in these policy-making activities; two—Lynde and Harry Bradley and Sarah Mellon Scaife—funded two of the represented think tanks. Top foundation board officials are leading members of prominent corporations or law firms; the majority have one or more degrees from prominent universities, often from the Ivy League.

3. **Think tanks:** Three were involved here—the American Enterprise Institute, the Heritage Foundation, and the Hoover Institution. Prominent board officials have occupational and educational credentials similar to their foundation counterparts. Academic researchers working for these organizations presented studies to think tank leaders, who discussed and debated them at length.

   Some specific initiatives taken at think tanks to help develop the neoconservative policies:

   a. In the 1970s at the American Enterprise Institute, economists Norman Ture and Robert Mundell wrote several reports arguing that progressive taxes requiring the wealthiest to pay the highest rate, and welfare spending discouraged business investment and thus were major causes of a stagnant economy.

   b. In 1978 at the Hoover Institution, economist Martin Anderson presented a proposal on welfare reform, which provided the foundation for neoconservatives' drive to change the system.

   c. In the 1970s, as part of the American Enterprise Institute's Governmental Regulation Program, Murray Weidenberg produced a report arguing that environmental and workplace regulations, which were troublesome costs for many corporations, were a major source of inflation.

4. **Policy-making groups:** In this instance three—the Business Roundtable, the US Chamber of Commerce, and the National Association of Manufacturers—were involved in the consensus-building and lobbying of the public and Congress necessary to achieve their common goals. Outgrowths of these new efforts included:

   a. The Tax Reform Act of 1986, primarily benefiting corporations and wealthy individuals

   b. The Personal Responsibility and Work Opportunity Act of 1996, which reorganized and cut funding for the welfare system

   c. Mobilized Congressional opposition against further costly environmental and workplace regulations and reduction of the impacts of the Clean Air and Clean Water Acts

Source: Some of the details come from J. Craig Jenkins and Craig Eckert. 2000. "The Right Turn in Economic Policy: Business Elites and the New Conservative Economics." *Sociological Form.* V. 15, pp. 307–38.

Two types of lobbying exist. First, federal lobbying entails various specific individuals or groups, often corporate ones, seeking a "fixer" who can "open doors," which is a prominent activity in Washington. These clients want to influence policy making in Congress and federal agencies. When thinking about lobbying, most people have this type in mind. Second, class-wide lobbying is more focused. It involves coalitions of powerful corporate groups subsidizing lobbyists' intervention in the political process to initiate legislation or other specific actions promoting upper-class interests (Dye 2002, 121–22; Perruccci and Wysong 2008, 143–44). These two types of lobbying are quite different.

FEDERAL LOBBYING   To serve their wealthy clients, Washington lobbying firms employ thousands of lobbyists. Attorneys are widely represented, because they often have the knowledge, skills, and contacts to influence congressional members and agency personnel. About 240 former congressional members and agency heads as well as 2,200 former government employees are registered lobbyists. Former House members who become lobbyists are most likely to have served on the money committees—Commerce and Ways and Means. Ex-congressional lobbyists can earn up to $2 million a year (Perrucci and Wysong 2008, 146-47; Santos 2006, 52).

Figure 4.1 shows the steadily increased expenditure for congressional lobbying over 11 years. In 2008 the $3.3 billion total meant $17.4 million for every day Congress was in session or $32,523 per legislator per day (Center for Responsive Politics 2009c). In the 12-year span between 1998 and 2010, the five industries spending the most for congressional lobbying were pharmaceuticals/health products $1.9 billion; insurance $1.4 billion; electric utilities $1.3 billion; computers/Internet $1.1 billon; and business associations $1 billion (Center for Responsive Politics 2010).

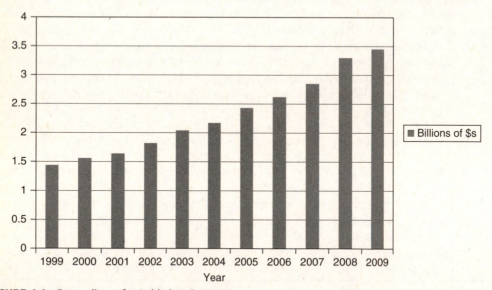

FIGURE 4.1   Expenditure for Lobbying Congress

The data show that in 11 years there was a relentless escalation in the amount of money spent by corporations, labor unions, and other organizations and individuals on lobbying Congress. This expenditure rose from $1.45 billion in 1999 to $1.82 billion in 2002 and in spite of the economic downturn continued to spiral upward, reaching $3.49 billion in 2009.

Source: Center for Responsible Politics. 2010. "Lobbying Database." http://www.opensecrets.org/lobby/index/.

With their potent social capital, former politicians can produce highly lucrative lobbying results, both for themselves and their clients. A controversial case in point has been The Carlyle Group, a Washington-based investment firm extensively involved in buying low-valued defense-contract companies, obtaining lucrative contracts for those companies, and then selling them at a substantial profit. To pursue these activities, Carlyle has employed a former British prime minister, a former Philippines president, a Saudi prince, a former secretary of state, and most impressively former president George H.W. Bush, who served the company for 10 years. Bush was an extremely useful pick-up because he had maintained a nearly 30-year relationship with the very wealthy Saudi Arabian leadership, which did much of its purchasing of military products through Carlyle connections. Bush became a lobbyist for Saudi military leaders, opening doors with Pentagon officials and business leaders to help his clients obtain weaponry and aircraft (Dye 2002, 122; Freeman 2004).

To various observers Bush, the first former president to craft a commercial relationship with the Pentagon, was embroiled in a blatant conflict of interest in which, according to Charles Lewis, Director of the Center for Public Integrity, a nonprofit news organization, the senior Bush "earned money from private interests that worked for the government of which his son was president" (Leser 2004). The payments Bush and his Carlyle associates obtained from the Saudis were considerable, about $1.4 billion (Freeman 2004).

While a number of federal lobbying situations such as the one involving The Carlyle Group and former President Bush receive some publicity, class-based lobbying epitomizes the invisible government, with all or most of the work done behind the scenes, hidden from public view.

CLASS-BASED LOBBYING This activity concerns well organized corporate initiatives where wealthy business interests are pitted against organized labor and/or citizen and consumer groups on what tend to be minimally publicized issues both sides consider economically and politically significant. Such wealthy policy-making groups as the Business Roundtable, the Conference Board, and the Committee for Economic Development are at the core of this type of lobbying.

An illustration of class-based lobbying was the passage of the Class Action Fairness Act (CAFA) of 2005. The Business Roundtable and the US Chamber of Commerce coordinated this event, which involved 100 major corporations, 475 lobbyists, and millions of dollars in campaign contributions, lobbying, and advertising costs. In return for their expenditure, the corporate clients became the beneficiaries of a law which shifted consumers' or workers' class-action suits seeking damages of $5 million or more from state to federal courts, where rulings tend to oppose the plaintiffs (those bringing the cases against the companies) (Perrucci and Wysong 2008, 170).

A firm supplying legal services to various large corporations was enthusiastic about CAFA. A document issued by the firm indicated that the new law was valuable for businesses with a national customer base. It stated, "For the most part, such companies no longer have to fear being hauled into a state court in a notoriously plaintiff-friendly county" (Wilson, Sonsini, Goodrich, and Rosati 2005).

For plaintiffs CAFA has distinct disadvantages. One of the reasons class-action suits brought to federal courts are often quickly dismissed is that unlike state judges, whose only required standard is their own states' statutes, federal judges faced with large class-action suits must address all plaintiffs' respective state laws, which often provide diverse, even contradictory directives for the case at hand.

The new law serves the corporate community well. It was passed at a time when President Bush had appointed 204 federal judges out of the total of 836. Invariably these judges and later Bush appointees were conservative, likely to support big business and not its opponents. During a hearing on the bill, Senator Richard Durbin of Illinois, a staunch opponent of CAFA, declared, "This isn't the Class Action Fairness Act—this is the Class Action Moratorium Act" (Little 2005).

Like lobbying, campaign giving involves large sums of money.

Campaign Giving

Congressional candidates require substantial sums of money for two interrelated reasons. First, the American political system is highly individualistic, with success dependent on name recognition and personal image. As a result wealthy donors and fund raisers are essential for candidates seeking to defeat opponents, who are engaged in an equally costly venture. Wealthy backers are particularly important at the primary stage when expensive TV advertising promoting name recognition and clarification of one's positions are critical in helping to start a campaign. Second, the electoral apparatus plays a significant role. Italy, Germany, Japan, Russia, Sweden, Spain, and most of the world's leading democracies have some version of **proportional representation**, where the electoral formula attempts to match the national or regional votes a party receives with its legislative seats. In such a system, a party's vote total determines candidates' prospects, with office seekers often receiving financial support from their parties and sometimes being seated even if they did not win their own district. Small parties representing nonaffluent interests can often have an impact. The American system, in contrast, is winner-take-all, and finishing second is worthless for the candidate. Office seekers are largely left on their own to develop financial support, which becomes a critical concern since the amount of money raised distinctly increases the likelihood of winning (Alexander 1976, 44; Domhoff 2010, 159–62; *Fairvote* 2009). Sociologist G. William Domhoff concluded that American politics "is like a high-stakes poker game: Anyone is welcome as long as they can raise millions of dollars to wager" (Domhoff 2010, 160).

The amount of money spent on American political campaigns dwarfs the costs elsewhere. For instance, the total 2008 expenditure for all elections was $5.2 billion and $2.4 billion just for the presidential race. In European elections a ceiling on spending exists. In France, for instance, the two finalists in the second round of presidential elections can spend no more than $31.4 million. In the British 2005 general elections, roughly the equivalent of the US congressional and presidential elections, all the parties that won seats spent only $61.4 million—about one eighty-fifth the American total (French Embassy 2006; OpenSecrets.org 2010; ukpolitical.info 2005).

Certainly money has been the key. In 1979 the Federal Election Commission (FEC) decided that donors could give unrestricted amounts of money to state parties but not to a particular candidate. In practice, it became possible to specify that the money would be earmarked to defeat a particular opponent, though the favored candidate could not be named. This type of financial support for a party on behalf of an unspecified yet specified candidate became known as "soft" money. Soft money contributions for both parties rose from $46 million in 1992 to $150 million in 1996 and then to over $250 million in 2000. Still "hard" money donations designated for specific candidates were much greater—over

$400 million in 2000. In 2002 the Bipartisan Campaign Reform Act eliminated the soft-money option, but the cap on individual donations was raised, allowing a person to give a maximum of $95,000 over two years to a party and its candidates.

Changes in the financing of political contests has continued. The 2004 election produced a major innovation that benefited both political parties. Advocacy organizations, called 527s after the section of the tax code that legalizes them, can receive unrestricted sums from contributors as long as they stay independent of the political party and its candidates, not even communicating with them. The organizations 527s support focus on issues—feminists interests, governmental deregulation, tax reform, environmental cleanup, or whatever—and while they are not allowed to endorse parties or candidates, their positions are likely to bolster both a party and its candidates. In the 2004 election, all donations from 527s totaled $599 million, dropped to $385 million in the 2006 midterm election, and then rose to $506 million in 2008. The absence of contributors' limits make enormous donations possible. In 2008 five individuals gave about $5 million each (Center for Responsive Politics 2009a; Coddington, DeBarros, Novak, Piggott, and Roig 2008).

Campaign contributions come from both individual giving such as the money from participants in 527s and from PACs. A **PAC**, or political action committee, is a private fund-raising group often affiliated with a corporation, labor union, or citizen group, permitting participants an additional $5,000 contribution on top of their individual giving. PACs exist to elect or defeat candidates or to support or oppose legislation. Both parties receive large amounts of money from these committees. In the years 2009 and 2010, 17 of the top 20 PAC contributors gave more money to Democrats than Republicans (Center for Responsive Politics 2009b).

While the individual contributions to PACs are small, merely $5,000 per candidate per election, the impact of certain PACs, especially corporate PACs, is formidable because they exist within the corporate community, where interlocking directorates and widely shared information and common interest can develop a massive, coordinated support for selected candidates.

In 2003 and 2004, corporate PACs contributed to Congressional candidates in the following manner. These PACs:

- Gave to candidates from both parties but slightly more to Republicans.
- Provided about 11 times more contributions to incumbents than to challengers (Perrucci and Wysong 2008, 155–59).

The last point suggests that corporate PAC voting tends to be very practical—going with the likely winner over a possible ideological preference. A study of 1980 elections supported this trend. A comparison of the PACs for 394 major corporations and individual giving from 592 executives within those corporations concluded that the PACs were much less ideological, generally giving to incumbents, particularly influential incumbents, regardless of their party. These practices were most pronounced when corporations depended on government business, which presumably incumbents were best positioned to help them obtain. For instance, Rockwell International, a major defense contractor, gave 59 percent of its PAC money to incumbent Democratic candidates while its chairman and its president directed 100 percent of their contributions to Republicans. Many other corporations displayed a similar split pattern between PACs' and individuals' giving (Burris 2001).

PACs find it much more beneficial to contribute to Congressional contests than to presidential races. In the 2008 elections, PACs' contributions represented the following percentages of individual donations:

- In House contests: 61 percent
- In Senate elections: 30 percent
- In the presidential race: less than .4 percent

Obviously PAC involvement ranges varies greatly depending on the office (Center for Responsive Politics 2009c; Federal Elections Commission 2009).

A fundamental reality of campaign giving is that traditionally the lion's share of the donations have come from high-income individuals. In the 2000 presidential election, the most affluent 13 percent of households, which had yearly income of $100,000 or more, provided 86 percent of the contributions of $200 or more (Overton 2004, 76). One half the $2.7 billion in gifts in the 2006 Congressional elections came from individuals in the upper 1 percent of earnings (Domenitz 2008). In the 2008 presidential election, 60 percent of all donations were over $200, and presumably individuals needed to be fairly affluent to afford such a sum. However, Barack Obama received massive support from a large, economically diverse group that gave much less in past presidential contests; about 44 percent of Obama's contributors were female, and they gave 42 percent of his total funds (Federal Elections Commission 2009; Weintraub and Levine 2009). Does the last finding herald a renewed attack on social reproduction in politics, with wealthy donors' dominant influence more effectively challenged than in the past, or is it merely an exception to the pattern?

A recent development makes it appear that the big donors will continue to dominate the lobbying process. In 2010 a divided Supreme Court ruled in the *Citizens United v. Federal Election Commission* case that the federal government has no authority to limit corporate contributions to political candidates—that such limitations would represent a restriction in free speech. Dissenters on the Court declared that it was a grave error to consider corporate speech expressed through contributions as similar to common speech. The result of this decision, opponents asserted, was to permit wealthy, powerful interests an even greater political impact (Liptak 2010). The United States, which was already the undisputed leader in campaign spending, now seems to be widening its lead.

Campaign giving involves the mass media since a sizable segment of the money obtained from it goes to candidates' television and radio advertisements.

The Power of the Press

Toward the end of his career, Theodore White, the celebrated chronicler of presidential elections, concluded that the American mass media is inordinately influential, "determin[ing] what people talk about and think about—an authority that in other nations is reserved for tyrants, priests, parties, and mandarins" (White 1973, 327).

Decades after White's statement the power of the press has changed in one important respect: It has become more centralized. Media analyst Ben H. Bagdikian indicated that in 1983 the men and women who headed the 50 or so dominant mass-media corporations "could have fit comfortably in a modest hotel ballroom." Twenty years later that number was reduced to five, who "could fit in a generous phone booth" (Bagdikian 2004, 27). What happened?

By the 1990s what have become the big five media conglomerates had expanded impressively. During those years these organizations and their allies engaged in successful lobbying, and as a result Congress passed a major piece of legislation. Robert W. McChesney, a professor of communications, indicated that "[t]he 1996 Telecom Act was . . . the product of the largest corporate lobbies all salivating at the prospect of rewriting the law to provide them a larger slice of the action" (McChesney 2003). In addition, a brief reference in the act gave digital spectrum, the publicly owned space used for high-definition channels and worth about $70 billion, to the media conglomerates free of charge. Had those giants been charged a fair price, the payment would have permitted a significant tax cut for the entire middle class or perhaps served as a major source of funding for a national healthcare program (Moyers 1999). Except for the business and trade press, which praised the passage of the act as valuable to owners and investors, the new law received almost no news coverage.

The Telecommunications Act of 1996 altered existing restrictions on ownership limits. Previously a media owner could possess no more than 12 television channels, 12 radio stations, and 12 newspapers. After the passage of the Telecom Act, individuals could own an unlimited number of television channels as long as they represented less than 35 percent of the market, and there was no longer a ceiling on radio-station ownership. The new legislation set loose a feeding frenzy, a frantic scramble for the available prizes. It was a situation encouraging aggressive activity, with those companies not pushing for increased acquisitions vulnerable to takeover (McChesney 1999, 21). Clearly, with what had once been 50 companies becoming five and then six in 2010, only the wealthiest and most powerful mass-media corporations survived as independents.

This small number of conglomerates and their subsidiaries have a huge impact. A national survey indicated that television was the major source of news and information for 56 percent of the respondents, and newspapers were a distant second at 23 percent. The major media companies controlled about 75 percent of prime-time viewing (Khan 2003). Table 4.4 lists the major holdings of these six conglomerates.

The media conglomerates are not only large and wealthy, but they also have interlocking directorates. In 2004 the five giant media groups and the five largest newspaper corporations had 118 directors who sat on the boards of 288 national and international corporations. These interlocking directorates provide the opportunity for media leaders to exchange information with and to influence prominent leaders from the general corporate community. In addition, these prominent media groups extend their sources of information and potential influence by appointing prominent ex-politicians to their boards (Thornton, Walters, and Rouse 2006, 245–47).

A final comment involving prominent media leadership is that a small number of newspapers, particularly the *New York Times*, *USA Today*, the *Wall Street Journal*, and the *Washington Post*, are "must" reading for high-level government officials, who require a steady stream of major news stories and opinion pieces to engage in informed discussion with their peers. In addition, these four dailies and a few others, which constitute the national press, disseminate their articles, producing many of the news stories and most of the opinion pieces on national issues published in the nation's 1,800 newspapers (Dye 2002, 100).

TABLE 4.4 The Big Five Mass-Media Conglomerates

	General Electric/ Comcast[1]	Walt Disney	News Corp
Total revenues, 2009	$157 billion	$36.1 billion	$30.4 billion
Major TV holdings	NBC and Telemundo	ABC TV Network	Fox Broadcasting Co.
Major subsidiaries owned	26 TV stations	277 radio stations, music and book publishing companies	Such publications as *Wall Street Journal*, *TV Guide*, and *New York Post*; book publishers including National Geographic and FX
Other notable cable outlets owned or partially owned	Bravo, History Channel, ScyFy Channel, MSNBC, Oxygen	ESPN, Disney Channel, A&E, Lifetime	HarperCollins, National Geographic and FX

	Time Warner	Viacom	CBS
Total revenues, 2009	$25.8 billion	$13.6 billion	$13 billion
Major TV holdings	CNN, TBS, TNT, HBO	MTV, VH1, Nickelodeon/ Nick-at-Nite	CBS TV
Major Subsidiaries Owned	150 magazines including *Time*, *Sports Illustrated*, *Fortune*, and *People*	MTV Radio, BET Radio, Nickelodeon Magazine	30 TV stations and CBS Radio with 130 stations; the publisher Simon & Schuster
Other notable cable outlets owned or partially owned	Cinemax, Cartoon Network	Comedy Central	Showtime

[1]In 2010 General Electric sold a controlling interest in its conglomerate to Comcast.

Sources: Free Press. "Ownership Chart: The Big Six." http://freepress.net/ownership/chart/main; Mafruza Khan. 2003. "Media Diversity at Risk." http://www.corpwatch.org/article.php?id=6850; Robert Perrucci and Earl Wysong. 2008. *The New Class Society: Goodbye American Dream?*, pp. 205–07; Wikinvest. 2009. "Wiki Analysis." http://www.wikinvest.com/stock/CBS_(CBS).

In spite of the wealth and power the major media groups possess, one should not conclude that media reports always serve the corporate elite's interests. For instance, at times the media leadership is unwilling or unable to squash stories, involving such topics as corporate corruption, environmental accidents, illegal lobbying, or military personnel's murder of civilians or torturing of prisoners (Domhoff 2006, 128). Most of the time, however, media personnel pursue their standard agenda.

MEDIA DOING BUSINESS   The major media seek to develop money-making policies that promote a large number of viewers and readers and also champion the corporate community's interests, often subordinating the public's welfare. Two major means to accomplishing these goals are media hype and an opinion-shaping strategy.

Hype about the News   The underlying issue about hype and the news involves media companies' need for large audiences. Without them the companies cannot sell expensive time segments to advertisers, who pay $100,0000 to $500,000 for a 15- to 30-second time slot on any of the prime-time programs. The more people who watch, the more the media company can charge the advertisers. A fairly precise sense of the viewing audience's size comes from the electronic boxes that the A.C. Nielsen Company and other independent services place in a national sample of American homes.

For TV companies, therefore, drawing lots of viewers is critical. Most media executives believe that the way to do that is by hyping bad news. Whether the topic is government, business, the schools, the military, or politics, hype features violence, abuse, corruption, drugs, sexual debauchery, and various other negatives. The resulting public response has been cynicism, distrust, a sense of powerlessness, and disaffection toward political activism—in short, "television malaise" (Dye 2002, 107–08; Robinson 1976).

Hype about the news is fairly obvious to many people, but some of the tactics used in opinion shaping are hard to detect.

The Opinion-Shaping Strategy   While it is often low-keyed, the major media companies show vigilant support for large corporations' perspectives and policies. Three tactics that shape opinions include deck stacking, selective reporting, and spin control.

Deck stacking is the process of loading most of the positions in the media companies—the editors, managers, and reporters—with unshakably loyal personnel. The elite professionals, some of whom make multiple millions of dollars a year, strongly support corporate ownership's interests and generally avoid issues that would be directly or indirectly critical of them (Perrucci and Wysong 2008, 222–32).

The deck stackers' efforts on behalf of corporate policy can be fairly subtle. For instance, the Sunday-morning talk shows are widely thought to be programs where politicians and policymakers, left and right politically, discuss and debate the pressing issues of the day. However, the deck stackers who have chosen the guests have been highly selective, often picking individuals sympathetic to corporate interests. The group Media Matters for America classified each of the nearly 7,000 individuals who appeared between 1997 and 2005 on ABC's *This Week*, CBS's *Face the Nation*, and NBC's *Meet the Press*, the leading Sunday-morning talk programs. Among politicians Republican/conservatives edged out Democrats/progressives by 52 to 48 percent during Clinton's second term. In Bush's first five years in office, Republicans/conservatives dominated, 58 to 42 percent. Throughout the Bush tenure, conservative journalists, whose questions and comments were likely to support corporate interests, represented about two thirds of the interviewers. The most frequent guest during the entire time period was conservative/Republican Senator John McCain, who appeared 124 times (Media Matters for America 2006).

Besides the guests appearing on these shows, the topics covered also favored the corporate elite's interests. During the late 1990s, Essential Action, a nonprofit organization that provides information on topics neglected or avoided by the mass media and policymakers, did a quantitative study of four Sunday morning programs—NBC's *Meet the Press*, NBC's *The McLaughlin Group*, CBS's *Face the Nation*, and ABC's *This Week*. The task was to learn to what extent these high-profile programs addressed issues about the workings of corporate power. A major finding was that topics linked to corporate power—environmental pollution, corporate crime, labor unions, corporate welfare (government-provided economic boosts to big business), national healthcare, renewable energy, business deregulation, and the increase of corporate profits—constituted less than 4 percent of the shows' discussion subjects. In addition, the research found that the vast majority of guests were politicians and government officials, people who tended to examine issues in a cautious, uncontroversial way, studiously avoiding reference to corporate power as well as any criticism of corporations. (Essential Action 2000).

A second tactic in the opinion-shaping strategy is **selective reporting**, which is a biased coverage of news issues that promotes corporate interests and downplays, denigrates, or ignores issues and groups challenging these interests. Selective reporting involves both corporations and their frequent adversaries—labor unions. A survey conducted with CEOs of the 1,000 largest industrial corporations in the United States indicated that two thirds concluded that mass-media coverage of their businesses was good or excellent, and only 6 percent felt it was badly done (Bagdikian 1997, 57). Obviously these executives did not feel that selective reporting victimized them. In contrast, labor supporters tended to respond quite differently.

Labor scholar William J. Puette examined television news programs from the 1970s and 1980s. He found that the media's presentation of unions was largely unsympathetic, even harsh, conveying the idea that these organizations were narrow-minded special interests whose presence hurt the country. The prominent media, notably television, often stereotyped union members as lazy, insubordinate, and unproductive. Above all, media critics of organized labor claimed, the unions' demands for ever-rising pay and benefits undermined the country's ability to compete in the global economy. Puette concluded that "television portrayals tend to emphasize the pettiness or foolishness of union bargaining goals" (Puette, 1992, 153).

Other supposedly negative union traits also obtain media attention. When members of the United Food and Commercial Workers union (composed of clerks, cashiers, and other workers) went on strike in southern California in 2004, their chief grievance, which was supermarket workers' reduction in health benefits, received little coverage. Instead news reports featured stories about strikers' disruptive behavior such as 100 union supporters shutting down a Safeway store for an hour by forming a conga line that moved through the store. As the strike advanced into its fourth month, the coverage became increasingly critical, highlighting the conclusion that workers' selfishness created nagging inconvenience for shoppers (Kendall 2005, 147–48). For instance, an article quoted a customer who said, "I feel bad (for the strikers) . . . but this has been going on long enough." The account cited the strike's adverse impact on 800 stores and also on large numbers of customers and employees (Keefe 2004, C1).

Like selective reporting, spin control is subtle and obscure to the general public. **Spin control** involves various media practices meant to mobilize an audience's support for a corporate or superclass outlook. It includes the use of persuasive terms, references, and images as well as forms of advertising or public-relations activities. Spin control often confuses or muddles public thinking (Perrucci and Wysong 2008, 230). In Marxist terminology it is an attempt to create false consciousness.

In April 2008 the *New York Times* broke a story about the Guantanamo Bay detention center that represented a fairly elaborate effort at spin control, where media personnel were in partnership with politicians, government officials, and retired military officers. Several years earlier, criticism had been widespread about the detention center for terrorism suspects at Guantanamo Bay (Cuba), with Amnesty International referring to it as "the gulag of our time." The Bush administration's response was to send a planeload of prominent ex-military officers to the detention center for a carefully orchestrated tour. The men on the flight along with several dozen others represented more than 150 military contractors as either lobbyists or consultants, and, in addition, many were affiliated with prominent television networks or radio stations or wrote frequent op-ed pieces. The ties to contractors were seldom revealed to the public and sometimes not even to the networks. A reporter concluded that available evidence demonstrated that Bush officials had pressured the press "to transform the analysts into a kind of media Trojan horse—an instrument intended to shape terrorism coverage from inside the major TV and radio networks" (Barstow 2008, 1).

All the major networks employed individuals from this group of ex-military officers, with Fox News having the largest contingent. In interviews participants spoke about the powerfully seductive atmosphere in which their contact with the Bush administration took place. They met with Secretary of Defense Donald Rumsfeld in his private conference room, where the media analysts obtained embossed name tags, were served with the best government china, and received requests for advice and counsel along with warmly grateful thank you notes from Rumsfeld himself. Paul E. Vallely, a former Fox News analyst and retired Army general, was responsible for this episode of spin control. He called his plan "MindWar"—using network TV and radio "to strengthen our national will to victory" (Barstow 2008, 25). The operation featured spin control where the government, major TV networks, and retired military leaders were all basic components in the administration's concerted public-relations effort to mobilize TV audience's support for its military policy. In the months leading up to the Iraq invasion, this group of widely respected ex-officers emphasized in the national media what became a familiar set of conclusions: [that] "Iraq possessed chemical and biological weapons, and might one day slip some to Al Qaeda; an invasion would be a relatively quick and inexpensive 'war of liberation'" (Barstow 2008, 25).

Many of the ex-military officials found the financial and prestige rewards that came with their media positions good reasons to be public proponents of the administration's stance on the war on terror. Others, however, became disillusioned. Kenneth Allard, a former NBC analyst, said he began to see a huge discrepancy between what optimistic insiders told him privately about the war's potential contribution and what his own inquiries and various publications revealed. "Night and day," Mr. Allard said, "I felt we'd been hosed" (Barstow 2008, 24).

As we have noted, the mainstream media give little or no effective coverage of many issues that impact on social inequality. Topics dealing with public policy are often cases in point. One might argue that just as we as individuals need medical experts' information about our physical condition to stay healthy, the citizenry requires thorough communication about the upcoming topics to develop an informed understanding about the health of the nation. As it stands, most people have neither knowledge nor interest in public-policy issues, and so superclass domination persists with limited opposition.

Public Policy

Three issues linked to the federal government affect who gains or loses income or wealth. The topics are taxation, the budget, and regulation, with business oversight included within the last topic.

TAXATION   Extensive lobbying occurs in this area, and the results usually serve superclass interests. Historical evidence shows that the proportion of income tax paid by individuals and corporations has altered dramatically between 1934 and 2010, with the percentages paid by individuals more than tripling and the corporate segment remaining fairly steady (Budget for Fiscal Year 2010a). Figure 4.2 displays changes in these percentages over time.

While the individual proportion of income tax has risen, those in the highest brackets have received substantial tax breaks. To begin, an often overlooked point is that about half of all personal income goes untaxed, with the lion's share of these advantages benefiting wealthy people who receive various loopholes, exemptions, and deductions (Dye 1998, 241; Zepezauer 2004). A prominent case in point involves the tax exemption corporate executives receive when they reinvest money with their companies. Pulitzer prize-winning reporter David Kay described a hypothetical CEO who received $105 million the previous year. That executive might keep $5 million, paying $2 million in taxes, living on $3 million for the year, and reinvesting the remaining $100 million with the company, which will need to pay taxes on the sum because it is reported as profit. Each year companies pay more and more for their executives' profits, further enriching them and passing the costs on to workers. Kay indicated why workers suffer. He declared, "[I]t's not the competition from the guys down the street, [but] competition from the guys in your own executive suite, who are taking all the money in the pay pool." (Levine 2004, E1).

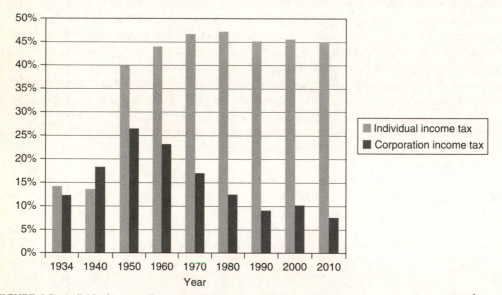

FIGURE 4.2   Individual Income Tax versus Corporate Income Tax as Percentage of the Federal Tax Total[1]

[1]Excise and payroll taxes are other federal types.

Between 1934 and 2010, the percentage of federal income tax individuals paid increased fairly steadily while the corporate proportion generally dropped. The two proportions of tax were quite similar in 1934, but in 2010 the individual percentage was about six times greater.

Source: Budget for Fiscal Year 2010. 2010. Table 2.1. "Receipts by Source: 1934–2014." http://www .gpoaccess.gov/usbudget/fy10/pdf/hist.pdf.

Such outcomes oppose the widely supported idea of a progressive income tax—that those most capable of affording the cost will make larger payments and, as a result, the distribution of after-tax income will be more equal than the distribution of pre-tax income. In the twenty-first century, however, such an outcome has emphatically not occurred. Two tax cuts signed into law by President George W. Bush—the Economic Growth and Tax Relief Reconciliation Act of 2001 and the Jobs and Growth Tax Relief and Reconciliation Act of 2003—offered much more reconciliation to the affluent than anyone else. When fully in effect, these two tax cuts reduce taxes for the poorest 20 percent of households by 0.4 percent; by 2.3 percent for the middle 20 percent; by 6.8 percent for the top 1 percent; and 7.6 percent for households with incomes over $1 million (Aron-Dine 2008). Over time the wealthy have been the primary beneficiaries of a declining tax burden, with federal tax for the wealthiest 1 percent of families going from 44.4 percent in 1980 to 30.4 percent in 2004 (*Wall Street Journal* 2007).

Thomas Dye, an expert on public policy, commented on federal taxation, indicating that the version that is most beneficial for the majority of American citizens "is universal, simple, and fair . . . But the federal tax system is very nearly the opposite: it is complex, unfair, and nonuniversal" (Dye 1998, 241).

Arguably the most significant word in the preceding statement is "complex." The quality about the federal tax system that promotes both false consciousness and spin control is its complexity—that it contains extensive technical detail that only accounting experts can understand. Dye suggested that the system could be simpler, but that would be unlikely to appeal to influential, wealthy groups.

In fact, changes in the federal taxation system favoring average citizens are hard to enact. A major consideration is that the United States has a cumbersome federal system of taxation: Three governmental authorities exist—the presidential administration, the Senate, and the House of Representatives—and on any proposed change in the system, certainly on any bill supporting the controversial possibility of a more progressive income tax, these three authorities would probably produce sufficiently different versions that a compromise measure would prove difficult to attain (Messere, Kam, and Heady 2003, 208).

Like taxation, budgeting is high on the superclass agenda.

BUDGETING   Many individuals and groups develop budgets, but public varieties including the federal budget differ from others in several respects. First, a public budget, unlike those produced by families or small businesses, involves a number of individuals and groups with varying positions and amounts of influence about the budgetary choices. The presidential administration, which provides the initial budget, the Congress, which can alter its particulars, and various lobbying groups all influence the content of the federal budget. Second, unlike a private budget, a public budget such as the federal version produced each year makes the distinction between those who produce the budget—the politicians—and those who must pay for it—the citizenry. The politicians can force the people to pay for expenditures they do not approve, but the citizenry can vote those politicians out of office. Finally a public budget such as the national budget is a vehicle for public accountability (Rubin 1995, 190), with the Office of Management and Budget Website now issuing yearly reports providing data extending from the past, usually 1940 on most issues, to the present.

Two major conditions currently influence budgetary activities. First, party differences are often apparent. Republicans are less likely than Democrats to support increased health and welfare programming, funding for family planning, reduction in defense spending, and federal aid to cities (Keefe and Hetherington 2003, 149). Second, in recent decades, the executive budgetary office has become more active. Previously that office had acted quite defensively, scrutinizing requests from departments and bureaus, finding waste and eliminating it, and generally acting as "the protector of the public purse." With Ronald Reagan's arrival, however, that office began taking wide-ranging initiative with Congress, cutting many programs and becoming less responsive to monetary requests from various government agencies, particularly those dealing with poverty (Rubin 1995, 191–92).

In fact, American federal budgets generally allot a smaller portion for oppressed citizens' needs than other affluent countries do. In the opening years of the twenty-first century, the United States had a higher proportion of low-paying jobs than six northern European countries and Canada. Nonetheless those countries spent much more on social transfers to the poor or near poor than the United States. For instance, starting in 1999, Great Britain allotted .9 percent of its Gross Domestic Product for low-income families with children, reducing in four years child poverty by 23 percent. In all seven of these countries, the child-poverty rate was below 10 percent while in the United States it was 22 percent (Smeeding 2006, 202).

In contrast, the federal government spends huge sums on defense—about 713 billion in 2010 (*Budget for Fiscal Year* 2010, 2010b). Beyond the real issue of national security, sociologists Robert Perrucci and Earl Wysong contended that a primary effect of military spending is "to juice the profits of military contractor firms and to feed . . . [the] highly paid scientists, engineers, and civilian employees who work in government, industry, and universit[ies]" (Perrucci and Wysong 2008, 184–85).

Meanwhile federal funding for Temporary Assistance to Needy Families, the primary federal aid for poor people, was about $23 billion (*Budget for Fiscal Year* 2010, 2010b)—about 3.2 percent the funding for defense. Other widely valued social programs such as Medicare, which provides supplemental medical subsidy to seniors; affordable housing, which can keep poor families from going homeless; and Head Start, a popular, effective initiative for very young poor children, were all cut during George W. Bush's two terms in office (Kuttner 2007). Table 4.5 lists defense and family-support budgetary allotments over time, indicating that the public-assistance percentage of the budget has declined steadily through the years and promoting the conclusion that this shrinking expenditure is a significant contributor to the United States having one of the highest rate of poverty among the most affluent nations.

While the budget and taxation are subjects of public policy receiving some media and public attention, the third topic, regulation, has often been a largely invisible reality. That obscurity, however, does not mean that it is an insignificant issue.

REGULATION AND BUSINESS OVERSIGHT   The government creates organizations that are supposed to engage in regulation. A **regulatory agency** is an independent governmental investigatory commission established by Congress to develop standards for some specific commercial activity and then to enforce those standards. The first regulatory agency was the Interstate Commerce Commission, which was formed in 1887 because of widespread complaints that the railroads were abusing their economic power, setting

TABLE 4.5 Payment for Public Assistance and Defense over Time (In millions of dollars)		
Year	**Public assistance to families (In millions of dollars and as percentage of budget outlays)**	**Defense spending (In millions of dollars and as percentage of budget outlays)**
1940	$279 (2.9%)	$1,660 (17.5%)
1950	1,123 (2.6%)	13,724 (32.3%)
1960	2,059 (2.2%)	48,130 (52.2%)
1970	4,142 (2.1%)	81,692 (41.8%)
1980	6,924 (1.2%)	133,995 (22.7%)
1990	12,246 (1.0%)	299,331 (23.9%)
2000	18,730 (1.0%)	294,495 (16.5%)
2010	22,638 (0.7%)	712,853 (23.4%)

While the portion of the federal budget devoted to defense spending has varied through the years, the budgetary percentage for public assistance, though always modest, has relentlessly declined. The sharply contrasting payments make it abundantly clear that superclass interests target one area and deemphasize the other.

Source: Budget for Fiscal Year 2010. Historical Tables. 2010. Table 3.1 "Outlays for Superfunction and Function, 1940-2014" and Table 11.3 "Outlays for Payments for Individuals by Category and Major Program, 1940-2014." http://www.gpoaccess.gov/usbudget/fy10/pdf/hist.pdf.

exorbitant rates in some areas and flagrantly bribing state and city governments. The sitting president appoints replacements for departing commissioners serving in 50 regulatory agencies, and the Senate must give its approval. Invariably these individuals share the president's values and aims and are often business people from the areas they are supposed to regulate.

Two broad perspectives on the regulatory agencies exist. One view suggests that these organizations possess considerable discretionary power, allowing them to play a major, even dominant role in the regulatory process. Supporters of this viewpoint would argue that agency professionals' elevated values and their expertise are qualities that promote their effectiveness. A second position claims that the political environment dominates agency personnel. Interest groups, congressional committees, and changing economic and technological conditions often control regulatory outcomes, backers of this viewpoint say (Meier 1995, 265–66).

In the twenty-first century, activities within many regulatory agencies often support the second outlook. Some prominent examples:

The Federal Communications Commission (FCC): Duties involve the licensing and regulation of all radio and television broadcasting including cable and satellite telecommunications. In 2003 the FCC relaxed several longtime media ownership rules, making it easier for the media conglomerates created by the Telecommunications Act of 1996 to extend their enormous wealth and power (McChesney 2003). In addition, the FCC protected the media giants' control by eliminating previous standards requiring independent programming. As a result the major television networks have taken over the production of many programs, driving small entrepreneurs, often headed by women and minorities, out of business (Khan 2003). The FCC represents wealthy, powerful interests, and in a moment of rare candor, one FCC chairman declared, "The job of the FCC is to regulate fights between the super wealthy and the super super wealthy. The public has nothing to do with it" (McChesney 2003).

The Food and Drug Administration (FDA): Responsibilities concern the establishment of safety standards for most kinds of food, drugs, vaccines, construction, and veterinary products. In 2006 a survey conducted with 5,918 FDA scientists found that hundreds of these individuals felt that the agency's mission to protect public health and safety was compromised when high-level bureaucrats pressured investigators to approve drugs in spite of the latter group's reservations about their safety. Disillusioned by these working conditions, many first-rate scientists left the agency (Union of Concerned Scientists 2007). The FDA commissioners were generally supporting this problematic situation.

The Environmental Protection Agency (EPA): The primary task involves safeguarding the natural environment, namely air, water, and land. Under Christine Todd Whitman, the former governor of New Jersey, the EPA was politicized, covering up the dangers of asbestos and electronic waste in the dust following the 9/11 attacks in New York City. In addition, energy industry leaders, who had been big donors to George W. Bush's campaign, pushed the administration to relax clean-air standards, and they usually succeeded, with Bush engaging in several initiatives to help the energy industries, most notably breaking his campaign promise to regulate carbon-dioxide emissions. Isolated and disillusioned, some EPA officials resigned (Drew and Oppel 2004; SourceWatch 2007).

The Nuclear Regulatory Commission (NRC): This agency focuses on the oversight of all activities involving nuclear reactors, materials, and waste. According to the Union of Concerned Scientists, which has studied nuclear-power safety issues since the early 1970s, the NRC has done a good job establishing safety regulations but a poor job enforcing them. For instance, the Inspector General's office issued a report highlighting NRC's repeated failures to enforce fire regulations. Since 1994 the NRC had known that 17 US reactors had inadequate fire protection, but they have failed to resolve the problem. In the future this safety issue is likely to be magnified as a number of companies encouraged by subsidies and incentives in the 2005 Energy Bill apply for licenses to build new plants. Many critics suggest that the NRC staff needs to reassess their responsibilities, currently paying too much attention to matters that minimally influence safety and not enough to such critical dangers as fires or leaks (Lochbaum 2008; Pietrangelo 2008).

Minerals Management Service (MMS): This obscure group's focus involves the regulation of oil and gas exploration and development. The agency became renowned for its wild parties and widespread absenteeism. Steady, conscientious work was hardly the order of the day. Leaders' prevailing position was that costs were too high and benefits too low to justify what independent experts considered critical equipment improvements—in one particular case, $500,000 for a mandatory shutoff switch, which would have prevented the Gulf oil spill (Elliott 2010; Skrzyeki 2010).

While issues linked to regulatory activity generally receive little public attention, one distinct exception exists—the subprime mortgage crisis. "Subprime mortgage" is a euphemistic financial term for high-interest loans to individuals who normally are unable to qualify for loans—middle-class families with too much debt or working-class or poor families with unstable work histories or little collateral. Lenders compensate for the greater risk they take either by charging higher interest rates or offering adjustable loans that increase over time. In the 1990s subprime lending was rare but began to surge— from 8.6 percent of all loans in 2001 to 20.1 percent in 2006.

Then crisis hit. The combined impact of rising interest rates on mortgages and a deteriorating economy featuring layoffs, stagnant wages, and rising cost of living made it impossible for many home buyers to meet their mortgage payments. Before the subprime upheaval has finished, it is likely that two million families will have lost their homes (Atlas and Dreier 2007).

A typically troubling case involves Milagros Munoz, a dental assistant who bought a brick duplex a short distance from the clinic where she worked. "When I did the closing," she said, "instead of being happy . . . like some people, they're ecstatic, they wanna pop the champagne and say 'Look, I got a house!' . . . all I did was cry. I said, 'Mom, I don't feel right . . . something's wrong'" (Jahr 2008). Unfortunately she was right. Her broker must have realized that she was a poor financial risk, and so to bolster her loan eligibility, he listed her yearly income, which was under $30,000 a year, as $65,000. Like many others Munoz was the victim of an Adjustable Rate Mortgage or "Exploding ARM,"

Some of the families that lost their homes because of the housing crisis have ended up in tent cities like this one in Sacramento.

which starts with a low interest rate that "resets" after two years and then zooms upward dramatically in the remaining 28 years of the loan. Munoz's broker never explained about the Exploding ARM, and suddenly she faced a monthly mortgage increase of $700. "[T]here's no way in the world I can catch up," she said (Jahr 2008). A critical but common omission was that no regulatory official carefully reviewed this case, seeking to protect the buyer.

Unregulated business activity resides at the foundation of the housing crisis. From 1945 until the late 1970s, the banking system was well organized, with at least five agencies playing a prominent role in the process of helping people to make safe and satisfying home purchases. However, the wealthy and powerful banking community lobbied for change. They got it—the Depository Institutions Deregulatory and Monetary Control Act of 1980, which, among other things, minimized and simplified regulation and made subprime lending more feasible (Atlas and Dreier 2007; Francis 2007). Inexperienced clients now lost most regulatory protection, and unscrupulous lenders could often forget about oversight.

Congressmen Barney Frank, a long-time crusader for low-cost housing, observed that in the portion of the banking industry that is regulated, no significant difficulties for mortgage holders have occurred. It is a very different matter, however, in the unregulated portion, where subprime lending has concentrated. Frank wrote, "To the extent that the system did work, it is because of prudential regulation and oversight. Where it was absent the result was tragedy for hundreds of thousands of families who have lost, or soon will lose, their homes" (Frank 2007).

Besides the area of governmental regulatory protection, another realm where the oversight of business has been mishandled has involved the credit-rating process, where such private agencies as Moody's and Standard & Poor's provide the ratings. These organizations, which oddly enough are paid by the businesses they evaluate, produce ratings that convey to investors a supposedly accurate sense of the financial soundness of the corporation in question. A high rating means that when individuals buy a company's bonds or stocks, they can feel secure that the business will survive and prosper and that their investment will be a sound one. Moody's and Standard & Poor's most publicized mistake was their failure to make an accurate, honest evaluation of bonds backed by home mortgages, contributing significantly to the economic woes within the housing industry.

However, credit-rating agencies' larger failure has involved their flawed assessment of top financial corporations. They have provided many prominent companies high-grade ratings even though they consistently took on increasing debt and risk. Why were the credit-rating firms such pushovers? The answer is painfully simple. Had they thoroughly evaluated the top financial organizations and in many instances downgraded them, it would have required a costly, time-consuming reevaluation of thousands of other firms whose own ratings derived from their relations with the highly rated top organizations.

The result would have been a slowdown in short-term profit-making, which as we have observed several times has become a fixation of American business. In the past outside regulation was effective, but as preceding examples suggest, this pattern no longer prevails. A pair of financial writers concluded, "The tyranny of the short term has extended itself with frightening ease into the entities that were meant to, one way or another, discipline Wall Street, and force it to consider its enlightened self-interest" (Lewis and Einhorn 2009, 9).

Americans, however, have a mixed reaction to overseeing business. In a nationwide survey conducted shortly after the $700 billion federal bailout of major corporations in 2008, 41 percent of Americans said businesses faced too much or the right amount of regulation compared to 45 percent who said they confronted too little. However, when asked whether regulation was partly responsible for the nation's financial and housing crises, 73 percent agreed, 19 percent disagreed, and 8 percent were unsure (*Los Angeles Times*/Bloomberg Poll 2008). David Ruder, an expert on financial regulation, agreed that loose regulation had made a major contribution to those crises and that both in the United States and in other core nations stricter financial regulation seems necessary. However, Ruder indicated, it is not going to be easy to achieve this goal. The finance, insurance, and real-estate industries, which make major contributions through lobbying, are fierce opponents of increased regulation. Battling over this issue lies ahead. Ruder concluded, "We very well may come out of this horrible situation with a better version of American capitalism—it'll be a little tamer; it'll be a little more regulated" (Berenson 2008: 4).

Moving through the murky territory of American policy making, we have seen few areas where the superclass interests have not dominated, often to the detriment of the general American public. That theme is apparent in the upcoming overview of the chapter.

Conclusion

This chapter analyzes the concepts and structures underlying social inequality. The three principal concepts are class, ideology, and social mobility. The text uses a popular six-class scheme. Overall Americans have tended to ignore or downplay class, more strongly emphasizing individuals' autonomous impact. Discussions of ideology focus on specific segments of it like individual achievement and the preeminence of liberal capitalism, which not only receive widespread support but appear to sustain current types of social inequality. The situation involving social mobility is less optimistic than in the past. Recent studies indicate both less upward mobility than in the 1960s and 1970s and less upward mobility than in various other developed nations.

In examining the invisible government, this chapter seeks to reveal important information about its central structures and activities. The elite's policy-making process involves four types of wealthy and powerful groups—foundations, think tanks, universities, and policy-making groups. Lobbying and campaign giving

are activities in which the power elite is heavily involved, using its influence and money to promote preferred policies. In addition, corporate and political leaders support the major mass media and, in turn, those organizations establish policies and practices that serve the elite.

The public-policy issues of taxation, budgeting, and regulation and business oversight provide the fruits of the power elite's effort to shape public policy. As far as their own financial interests are concerned, they have largely been successful. On the other hand, the results for the nation and the globe have been destructive.

Throughout the chapter social reproduction plays a robust role. The superclass with its corporate and top political underpinnings possesses the lion's share of precious resources, namely types of capital, which its members use not only to enrich and empower themselves but to enact laws and practices promoting policies that entrench social inequality. Consider:

- *Financial capital:* Great wealth is central. Without huge sums of money available to them, the media giants could not expand their holdings. Paying large sums for lobbying and campaign spending, major corporations are able to purchase support for legislation and help elect candidates promoting their goals in various areas of public policy. Superclass wealth also subsidizes the power elite's influence over public policy.

- ***Social capital:*** Two types:
  a. **Internal:** Within the corporate community, superclass members have interlocking directorates which facilitate information sharing and cooperative decision making. Four types of elite organizations—universities, foundations, think tanks, and policy-making groups—are the settings for developing superclass social capital, which promotes well informed, cohesive decision making.
  b. **External:** Superclass members use lobbying and campaign spending to purchase political support, especially from incumbents.
- ***Cultural capital:*** Beginning in their preschool years, superclass individuals start obtaining the manners, perceptions, values, and skills necessary to function well in their elite world. Chapter 5 examines these issues.
- ***Human capital:*** As both Chapters 2 and 5 indicate, the superclass can afford high-quality schooling, which provides its members the credentials for top corporate and political positions and access to other elite individuals and groups.

The superclass has many capital resources available to promote its favored policies. However, as upcoming chapters explain, other classes have capital assets that can contribute to positive economic and political outcomes. In 2007 the United Auto Workers (UAW) signed an innovative contract with General Motors (GM). Recognizing that GM had been losing money, the union made concessions, backing off on desired pay raises and settling for bonuses, and not holding GM responsible for retirees' healthcare but insisting GM pay billions of dollars into a trust fund for those health costs. It was a compromise contract both sides could accept—a positive outcome.

The extent to which such an outcome can be generalized, however, is problematic. Ninety-two percent of the workforce is not unionized and thus lacks the collective clout UAW showed, and a survey by Sibson Consulting found that even though the economy was improving between 2003 and 2006, workers were increasingly less satisfied with their work and their lives (Trumbull 2007).

In the chapters ahead, it is apparent that Americans' varied access to capital types means diverse opportunities and outcomes.

Key Terms in the Glossary

Capitalism *85*

Class *78*

Deck stacking *103*

Equality of opportunity *85*

Foundation *91*

Ideology *82*

Income *80*

Intergenerational mobility *87*

Legitimation *82*

Liberal capitalism *85*

Lifestyle *81*

Lobbying *94*

Media framing *80*

PAC *99*

Proportional representation *98*

Regulatory agency *108*

Selective reporting *104*

Social mobility *87*

Spin control *104*

Structural mobility *87*

Think tank *92*

Wealth *80*

Work ethic *84*

Discussion Topics

1. Consider the definition of class in this chapter and recall other designations from Chapter 2. What seems to be the most effective definition and why?
2. Does the American ideology affect social inequality? Explain, making references to some of its specific features.
3. In the next two decades are Americans likely to alter their expectations about social mobility? Discuss.
4. What kinds of sources would a student researcher use to obtain detailed information about the policy-making process? Starting with Internet references provided in this chapter, begin to compile a preliminary list.
5. Discuss the two types of lobbying. Is the American lobbying system beneficial for most Americans? Should there be legislation changing it?
6. How do deck stacking and spin control promote social inequality?
7. Comment on the strengths and weaknesses of the American tax system.
8. What changes in the federal budget would most effectively reduce social inequality?
9. Is government regulation necessary? Discuss this topic, bringing in the subprime mortgage crisis and other modern regulatory-related issues.

Research Papers

1. Produce a paper analyzing the relationship between one or more key elements of the American ideology and American capitalism.
2. What has happened to the Horatio Alger rags-to-riches story? Use studies of social mobility to address this question. Speculate about the future.
3. A promising way to learn about the "invisible government" involves a focus on a specific organization which participates in it—a think tank, a corporation, or a policy-making group. Choose such an organization and describe its activities contributing to power-elite policies, detailing and evaluating the organization's relationship with other groups involved in the process. This chapter's bibliography can provide a start for locating prospective sources.
4. Pick one of the three principal areas of public policy. Research the topic thoroughly. The opening section of the paper should summarize current conditions. Its core should be a hard-headed, well-documented analysis that describes the most effective ways to alleviate contemporary inequalities. Keep in mind that power-elite resistance is inevitable, and thus any proposals need to have the potential of receiving strong public support.

Informative Websites

Gilmore Girls is a comedy-drama TV series that that ran from 2000 to 2007. The setting is a cohesive Connecticut community, and the story revolves around a single mother and her daughter and often features relationships, sometimes conflicts between members of different classes.

The American Enterprise Institute (http://www.aei.org) is probably the most influential conservative think tank. This website indicates the myriad activities in which this very active organization engages.

The array of topics at the sites for the Council on Foreign Relations (http://www.cfr.org/) and the Committee for Economic Development (http://www.ced/org/) make it clear that these two, very powerful policy-making groups are strongly committed to public relations. The positions various writers take are distinctly conservative, with highly trained experts addressing a topic.

The Center for Responsive Politics, a liberal think tank, (http://www.opensecrets.org/lobby/) supplies updated federal data about lobbying, addressing such specific issues as the top spenders by industry, the top lobbying firms, and the top issues where lobbying occurs.

The widely respected Union of Concerned Scientists (http://www.ucsusa.org/scientific_integrity/abuses_of_science/?) provided a report entitled "Freedom to Speak? A Report Card on Federal Agency Media Policies," which examined regulatory agencies' scientific integrity, including a report card grading the degree of freedom 15 important agencies allow their researchers to speak publicly about the work.

Bibliography

ABC World News Poll. 2010. "Within the Middle Class, Four in 10 Are Struggling." http://abcnews.go.com/images/PollingUnit/1106a1MiddleClass.pdf.

Alesina, Alberto, Edward Glaeser, and Bruce Sacerdote. 2001. "Why Doesn't the United States Have a European-Style Welfare State?" *Brookings Papers on Economic Activity* 2001: 187–254.

Alexander, Herbert E. 1976. *Financing Politics*. Washington, DC: Congressional Quarterly Press.

Alterman, Eric. 2004. "Think Again: 'Ideas Have Consequences: So Does Money.'" *Center for American Progress*. http://www.american-progress.org/issues/2004/10/b222111.html.

Alvarez, Louis, and Andrew Kolker. 2001. *People like Us: Social Class in America. Center for New American Media*. http://www.pbs.org/peoplelikeus/about/doccredits.html

Anderson, Kim. 2007. "Liberal Capitalism: The Will to Happiness." *Policy* (Summer). http://www.cis.org.au/Policy/summer%2007-08/anderson_summer 07…

Aron-Dine, Aviva. 2008. "Have the 2001 and 2003 Tax Cuts Made the Tax Code More Progressive?" *Center on Budget and Policy Priorities*. http://www.cbpp.org/3-11-08tax.htm.

Atlas, John, and Peter Dreier. 2007. "The Conservative Origins of the Sub-Prime Mortgage Crisis." *The American Prospect* (December 18). http://prospect.org/article/conservative-origins-sub-prime-mortgage-crisis-0.

Bagdikian, Ben H. 1997. *The Media Monopoly*. Boston: Beacon Press.

Bagdikian, Ben H. 2004. *The New Media Monopoly*. Boston: Beacon Press.

Barstow, David. 2008. "Behind TV Analysts, Pentagon's Hidden Hand: Courting Ex-Officers Tied to Military Contractors." *New York Times* (April 20): 1+.

Bellah, Robert N., Richard Madsen, William E. Sullivan, Ann Swidler, and Steven M. Tipton. 1996. *Habits of the Heart: Individualism and Commitment in American Life*, 2nd ed. Berkeley: University of California Press.

Berenson, Alex. 2008. "How Free Should a Free Market Be?" *New York Times* (October 5): "Week in Review," p. 1+.

Bernstein, Basil. 1990. *The Structuring of Pedagogic Discourse: Volume IV: Class, Codes, and Control*. London: Routledge.

Blau, Peter M., and Otis Dudley Duncan. 1967. *The New Occupational Structure*. New York: Free Press.

Bowles, Samuel, and Herbert Gintis. 2002. "Schooling In Capitalist America Revisited." *Sociology of Education* 75 (January): 1–18.

Bradbury, Katharine, and Jane Katz. 2007. "Are Lifetime Incomes Growing More Unequal? Looking at New Evidence on Family Income Mobility," pp. 423–27 in David B. Grusky and Szonja Szelenyi (eds.), *The Inequality Reader: Contemporary and Foundational Readings in Race, Class, and Gender*. Boulder: Westview Press.

Budget for Fiscal Year 2010a. Historical Tables. 2010. Table 2.1. "Receipts by Source: 1934–2014." http://www.gpoaccess.gov/usbudget/fy10/pdf/hist.pdf.

Budget for Fiscal Year 2010b. Historical Tables. 2010. Table 3.1 "Outlays for Superfunction and Function, 1940–2014." http://www.gpoaccess.gov/usbudget/fy10/pdf/hist.pdf.

Budget for Fiscal Year 2010c. Historical Tables. 2010. Table 11.3 "Outlays for Payments for Individuals by Category and Major Program, 1940–2014." http://www.gpoaccess.gov/usbudget/fy10/pdf/hist.pdf.

Burris, Val. 2001. "The Two Faces of Capital: Corporations and Individual Capitalists as

Political Actors." *American Sociological Review* 66 (June): 361–81.

Center for Responsive Politics. 2009a. "527s: Advocacy Group Spending in the 2008 Elections." http://www.opensecrets.org/527s/index.php.

Center for Responsive Politics. 2009b. "Top PACs." http://www.opensecrets.org/pacs/toppacs.php.

Center for Responsive Politics. 2009c. "Washington Lobbying Grew to $3.3 Billion Last Year, Despite Economy." http://www.opensecrets.org/news/2009/01/Washington-lobbying-grew-to-32.html.

Center for Responsive Politics. 2010. "Top Industries." https://www.fecwatch.org/lobby/top.php?index.Type=i.

Christie, Les. 2007. "Harvard Leads Billion-Dollar Endowment Club." *CNNMoney.com*. http://money.cnn.com/2007/01/22/pf/college/richest_endowment_fun…

Coddinton, Ron, Anthony DeBarros, Kristen Novak, Rhyne Piggott, and Carlos Roig. "Track the Flow of Campaign Contributions."*USA Today* (September 19). http://www.usatoday.com/news/politics/election2008/campaign-finance-tracker.htm#q2.

Collins, Chuck, and Felicia Yeskel. 2005. "Billionaires R Us." *AlterNet*. http://www.alternet.org/workplace/27168.

Commager, Henry Steele. 1947. *America in Perspective*. New York: Random House.

Connelly, Marjorie. 2005. "How Class Works." *New York Times* (May 15). http://www.nytimes.com/packages/html/national/20050515_CLASS_GRAPHIC/index_04.html.

Corak, Miles. 2006. "Do Poor Children Become Poor Adults? Lessons from a Cross Country Comparison of Generational Earnings Mobility." *Institute for the Study of Labor (Bonn)*. http://ftp.iza.org/dp1993.pft.

Currie, Elliott. 2004. *The Road to Whatever: Middle Class Culture and the Crisis of Adolescence*. New York: Metropolitan Books.

Della Fave, L. Richard. 1980. "The Meek Shall Not Inherit the Earth: Self-Evaluation and the Legitimacy of Stratification." *American Sociological Review* 45 (December): 955–71.

Deutsch, Claudia H. 2005. "How Surveys Show That Big Business Has a P.R. Problem." *New York Times* (December 9): C1.

Domenitz, Janet. 2008. "The Real Power of Campaign Donations." *Boston Globe* (June 23): http://www.boston.com/bostonglobe/editorial_opinion/oped/articles/2008/06/23/the_real_power_of_campaign-donations/.

Domhoff, G. William. 2010. *Who Rules America? Power, Politics, & Social Change*, 6th ed. New York: McGraw-Hill.

Drew, Christopher, and Richard A. Oppel, Jr. 2004. "Air War: Remaking Energy Policy: How Power Lobby Won Battle of Pollution Control at E.P.A." *New York Times* (March 6). http://query.nytimes.com/gst/fullpage.html?res=9507E3DA1EFF9…

Dye, Thomas R. 1998. *Understanding Public Policy*, 9th ed. Upper Saddle River, NJ: Prentice-Hall.

Dye, Thomas R. 2002. *Who's Running America? The Bush Restoration*, 7th ed. Upper Saddle River, NJ: Prentice-Hall.

Elliott, Justin. 2010. "The Sex and Oil Scandals of the Minerals Management Service." *TPMMuckraker* (May 6). http://tpmmuckraker.talkingpointsmemo.com/2010/05/mms_flashback_sex_drugs_oil.php.

ESPN.com News Services. 2010. "Jordan Wouldn't Have Called Magic, Bird." http://sports.espn.go.com/nba/news/story?id=5391478.

Essential Action. 2000. "Sunday Morning Political Talk Shows Ignore Corporate Power Issues." http://www.essentialaction.org/spotlight/report/talkingheads.html#rep.

FairVote. 2009. "The Winner-Take-All Problem." http://www.fairvote.org/?page=107.

Featherman, David L., and Robert M. Hauser. 1978. *Opportunity and Change*. New York: Academic Press.

Federal Election Commission. 2009. "Contributions to All Candidates by State." http://www.fec.gov/DisclosuresSearch/mapApp.do.

Francis, David R. 2007. "Government Regulation Stages a Comeback." *Christian Science Monitor* (September 10): 14.

Frank, Barney. 2007. "Lessons of the Subprime Crisis." *Boston Globe* (September 14). http://www.boston.com/news/globe/editorial_opinion/oped/articles/2007/09/14/lessons_of_the_subprime_crisis/.

Freeman, John. 2004. "All in the Family; 'House' Tells How Saudis Enriched Bushes, Got Special Favors." *Hartford Courant* (March 14): G3.

French Embassy. 2006. "Political Party Funding in France." (April 4). http://www.ambafrance-uk.org/Politics-party-funding.html.

Gilbert, Dennis. 2008. *The American Class Structure in an Age of Growing Inequality*, 7th ed. Thousand Oaks, CA: Pine Forge Press.

Gilbert, Dennis. 2011. *The American Class Structure in an Age of Growing Inequality*, 8th ed. Thousand Oaks, CA: Pine Forge Press.

Hertz, Tom. 2006. "Understanding Mobility in America." *Center for American Progress*. http://www.americanprogress.org/issues/2006/04/Hertz_MobilityAnalysis.pdf.

Hochschild, Jennifer I. 1981. *What's Fair? American Beliefs about Distributive Justice*. Cambridge, MA: Harvard University Press.

Huber, Joan, and William H. Form. 1973. *Income and Ideology*. New York: Free Press.

Isaacs, Julia B. 2007a. "Economic Mobility of Families across Generations." *Pew Charitable Trusts: Economic Mobility Project*. http://www.economicmobility.org/assets/pdfs/EMP_FamiliesAcrossGenerations_ChapterI.pdf.

Isaacs, Julia B. 2007b. "International Comparisons of Economic Mobility." *Pew Charitable Trusts: Economic Mobility Project*. http://www.economicmobility.org/assets/pdfs/EMP_InternationalComparisons_ChapterIII.pdf.

Iversen, Roberta Rehner, and Annie Laurie Armstrong. 2006. *Jobs Aren't Enough: Toward a New Economic Mobility for Low-Income Families*. Philadelphia: Temple University Press.

Jahr, Nichoas. 2008. "Subprime Crimes from Wall Street to Brooklyn and Beyond." *Brooklyn Rail: Critical Perspective on Arts, Politics and Culture (March)*. http://www.brooklynrail.org/2008/03/express/subprime-crimes.

Jenkins, J. Craig, and Craig M. Eckert. 2000. "The Right Turn in Economic Policy: Business Elites and the New Conservative Economics." *Sociological Forum* 15 (June): 307–38.

Keefe, Bob. 2004. "Growing Strike Wearing on Customers, Workers." *Austin American-Statesman* (February 6): C1.

Keefe, William J., and Marc J. Hetherington. 2003. *Parties, Politics, and Public Policies in America*. Washington, DC: CQ Press.

Kendall, Diana. 2005. *Framing Class: Media Representation of Wealth and Poverty in America*. Lanham, MD: Rowman & Littlefield.

Khan, Mafruza. 2003. "Media Diversity at Risk." *Corpwatch*. http://www.corpwatch.org/article.php?id=6850.

Kroll, Luisa. 2008. "The World's Richest People: World's Billionaires." *Forbes* (March 5). http://www.forbes.com/2008/03/05/richest-billionaires-people-billion…

Kuttner, Robert. 2007. "Get Serious, Democrats." *Boston Globe* (January 6): A11.

Ladd, Everett Carll. 1994. *The American Ideology: An Explanation of the Origins, Meaning, and Role of American Political Ideas*. Storrs, CT: Roper Center for Public Opinion Research.

Leser, Eric. 2004. "Carlyle Empire." *Culture Change* (April 29). http://www.culturechange.org/CarlyleEmpire.html.

Levine, Bettijane. 2004. "STYLE & CULTURE; Beware the Ides Of April; If You're Not Super Rich, You Might Have a Problem with the Tax System." *Los Angeles Times* (April 7): E1.

Lewis, Michael, and David Einhorn. 2009. "The End of the Financial World as We Know It." *New York Times* (January 4): "Week in Review," pp. 9–10.

Liptak, Adam. 2010. "Justices, 5–4, Reject Corporate Spending Limit." *New York Times* (January 21): A1+.

Little, Amanda Griscom. 2005. "Erin Brockovich, Drop Dead." *Salon.com*. http://dir.salon.com/story/opinion/feature/2005/02/12/class_action.

Lochbaum, David. 2008. "Fixing the Nuclear Regulatory Commission." *Bulletin of the Atomic Scientists* (February). http://www.thebulletin.org/web-edition/features/fixing-the-nuclear-re…LosAngelesTimes/Bloomberg Poll. 2008. (October 10–13).

Mantsios, Gregory. 2007. "Class in America—2006," pp. 182–98 in Paula S. Rothenberg (ed.), *Race, Class, and Gender in the United States*, 7th ed. New York: Worth.

Marger, Martin N. 2011. *Social Inequality: Patterns and Processes*, 5th ed. New York: McGraw-Hill.

McChesney, Robert W. 1999. *Rich Media, Poor Democracy*. Urbana: University of Illinois Press.

McChesney, Robert W. 2003. "The FCC's Big Grab: Making Media Monopoly Part of the Constitution." *Counterpunch* (May 16). http://www.counterpunch.org/mcchesney05162003.html.

Media Matters for America. 2006. "If It's Sunday, It's Conservative: An Analysis of the Sunday

Talk Show Guests on ABC, CBS, and NBC, 1997–2005." http://mediamatters.org/items/200602140002.

Meier, Kenneth J. 1995. "Regulation: Politics, Bureaucracy, and Economics," pp. 265–77 in Stella Z. Theodoulou and Matthew A. Cahn (eds.), *Public Policy: The Essential Readings*. Upper Saddle River, NJ: Prentice-Hall.

Merton, Robert K. 1968. *Social Theory and Social Structure*, 3rd ed. New York: Free Press.

Messere, Ken, Flip de Kam, and Christopher Heady. 2003. *Tax Policy: Theory and Practice in OECD Countries*. Oxford, England: Oxford University Press.

Miller, Matthew, and Duncan Greenberg. 2009. "The Forbes 400." *Forbes.com*. http://www.forbes.com/2009/forbes-400-buffett-gates-ellison-rich-list-09-intro.html.

Moyers, Bill. 1999. "Free Speech for Sale." *Films for the Humanities and Sciences*.

Norris, Floyd. 2006. "Which Bosses Really Care If Shares Rise?" *New York Times* (June 2): C1.

OpenSecrets.org. 2010. "Cash Counter Widgets from OpenSecrets." http://www.opensecrets.org/action/countdownwidgets.php.

Organization for Economic Cooperation and Development. 2010. "A Family Affair: Intergenerational Social Mobility across OECD Countries." *Economic Policy Reforms Going for Growth*. http://www.oecd.org/dataoecd/17/42/44566315.pdf.

Overton, Spencer. 2004. "The Donor Class: Campaign Finance, Democracy, and Participation." *University of Pennsylvania Law Review* 153 (November): 73–118.

Perrucci, Robert, and Earl Wysong. 2008. *The New Class Society: Goodbye American Dream?* 3rd ed. Lanham, MD: Rowman & Littlefield.

Perry-Jenkins, Maureen. 2005. "Work in the Working Class: Challenges Facing Families," pp. 453–72 in Suzanne M. Bianchi, Lynne M. Casper, and Rosalind Berkowitz King (eds.), *Work, Family, Health and Well-Being*. Mahwah, NJ: Lawrence Erlbaum Associates.

Pietrangelo, Anthony R. 2008. "The NRC Must Ensure Current Levels of Safety and Performance as Nuclear Fleet Expands." *Bulletin of the Atomic Scientists* (July 11). http://www.thebullletin.org/web-edition/roundtables/the-future-of-the-nuclear-regulatory-commission.

Planty, Michael, William Hussar, Thomas Snyder, Stephen Provasnick, Grace Kena, Angelina KewalRamani, and Jane Kemp. 2008. "The Condition of Education 2008." *National Center for Education Statistics*. http://nces.ed.gov/pubs2008/2008031.pdf.

Puette, William J. 1992. *Through Jaundiced Eyes: How the Media View Organized Labor*. Ithaca, NY: ILR Press.

Rampell, Catherine. 2010. "Are You Better Off than Your Parents Were?" *Economix: Explaining the Science of Everyday Life*. (February 10). http://economix.blogs.nytimes.com/2010/02/10/are-you-better-off-than-your-parents-were/.

Reagan, Ronald. 1979. "Intent to Run for President." Ronald Reagan Presidential Foundation & Library. http://www.reaganfoundation.org/reagan/speeches/speech.asp?spid=4.

Reed, Bruce. 2006. "Governing Well Is the Best Revenge." *Cato Unbound*. http://www.cato-unbound.org/2006/10/04/bruce-reed/governing-well-i…

Ritzer, George. 1980. *A Multiple Paradigm Science*, rev. ed. Boston: Allyn & Bacon.

Ritzer, George. 1989. "On Levels and 'Intellectual Amnesia.'" *Sociological Theory* 7 (Fall): 226–29.

Ritzer, George. 2008. *Modern Sociological Theory*, 7th ed. New York: McGraw-Hill.

Robinson, Michael. 1976. "Public Affairs Television and the Growth of Political Malaise." *American Political Science Review* 70 (June): 409–32.

Rodgers, Daniel T. 1978. *The Work Ethic in Industrial America: 1850–1920*. Chicago: University of Chicago Press.

Rubin, Irene S. 1995. "The Politics of Public Budgets," pp. 185–200 in Stella Z. Theodoulou and Matthew A. Cahn (eds), *Public Policy: The Essential Readings*. Upper Saddle River, NJ: Prentice-Hall.

Rytina, Steven. 2000. "Is Occupational Mobility Declining in the U.S.?" *Social Forces* 78 (June): 1227–76.

Samuelson, Robert J. 2006. "Myths and the Middle Class." *Washington Post* (December 27): A19.

Santos, Adolfo. 2006. *Do Members of Congress Reward Their Future Employers? Evaluating the Revolving Door Syndrome*. Lanham, MD: University Press of America.

Schervish, Paul G., Platon E. Coutsoukis, and Ethan Lewis. 1994. *Gospels of Wealth: How the Rich Portray Their Lives*. Westport, CT: Praeger.

Schwartz, Nelson D., and Steve Lohr. 2008. "Looking for Swing Votes in the Boardroom." *New York Times* (August 17): Sunday Business, p. 1+.

Skrzycki, Cynthia. 2010. "BP Oil Spill: Is BP the Walrus?" *GlobalPost* (June 23). //http://www.globalpost.com/dispatch/global-green/100623/bp-oil-spill-cleanup.

Smeeding, Timothy M. 2006. "Government Programs and Social Outcomes: Comparison of the United States with Other Rich Nations," pp. 149–218 in Alan J. Auerbach, David Card, and John M. Quigley (eds.), *Public Policy and the Income Distribution*. New York: Russell Sage Foundation.

SourceWatch. 2005. "Think Tanks." http://www.sourcewatch.org/index.php?title=Think_tanks.

Terkel, Studs. 1974. *Working*. New York: Pantheon Books.

Theodos, Brett, and Robert Bednarzik. 2006. "Earnings Mobility and Low-Wage Workers in the United States." *Monthly Labor Review* (July): 34–47. http://www.bls.gov/opub/mir/2006/07/art4full.pdf.

Theriault, Reg. 2003. *The Unmaking of the American Working Class*. New York: New Press.

Thompson, Gabriel. 2008. "Meet the Wealth Gap." *Nation* 286 (June 30): 18+.

Thornton, Bridget, Britt Walters, and Lori Rouse. 2006. "Corporate Media Is Corporate America," pp. 245–62 in Peter Phillips (ed.), *Censored 2006: The Top 25 Censored Stories*. New York: Seven Stories Press.

Trumbull, Mark. 2007. "For U.S. Workers, Anxious Times." *Christian Science Monitor* (October 2): 1.

ukpolitical.info. 2005. "Election Campaign Spending by Political Parties." http://www.ukpolitical.info/Expenditure.htm.

Union of Concerned Scientists. 2007. "Summary of the FDA Scientist Survey." http://www.ucsusa.org/scientific_integrity/interference/fda-scientists-…

U.S. Census Bureau. 2008. Table 673 "Money Income of Families—Percent Distribution by Income Level in Constant (2005) Dollars: 1980 to 2005." *Current Population Reports*, pp. 60–231, http://www.census.gov/compendia/statab/2008/tables/08s0673.pdf.

U.S. Bureau of the Census. 2010. Table 682. "Money Income of Families Distribution by Family Characteristics and Income Level." *Statistical Abstract of the United States*: 2010. http://www.census.gov/…income_expenditures_poverty_wealth.html.

Wall Street Journal. 2003a. "Is This a Great Country?" (April 1): A14.

Wall Street Journal. 2003b. "America Works." (August 29): A8.

Wall Street Journal. 2007. "How the Income Share of Top 1% of Families Has Increased Dramatically." (January 11): B6.

Washington Post. 2007. "Today's News." (December 5): C13.

Weber, Max. 1958. Originally published in 1905. *The Protestant Ethic and the Spirit of Capitalism*. New York: Charles Scribner's Sons.

Weintraub, Ellen L., and Jason K. Levine. 2009. "Campaign Finance and the 2008 Elections: How Small Change(s) Can Really Add Up." *St. John's Journal of Legal Commentary* 24: 461–77.

Weiss, Philip. 2005. "George Soros's Right-Wing Twin. *New York Magazine* (July 24). http://mymag.com/nymetro/news/people/features/12353/.

White, Theodore. 1973. *The Making of the President, 1972*. New York: Bantam.

Williams, Robin M., Jr. 1970. *American Society*, 3rd ed. New York: Alfred A. Knopf.

Wilson, Sonsini, Goodrich & Rosati. 2005. "Class Action Fairness Act Signed into Law." http://www.wilsononsini.com/WSGR/Display.aspx?SectionName=publications/PDFSearch/clienttalert_classification_fairnessact.htm.

Wolff, Edward N. 2007. "Recent Trends in Household Wealth in the United States: Rising Debt and the Middle-Class Squeeze." *Levy Economics Institute*. http://www.levy.org.

Zepezauer, Mark. 2004. *Take the Rich Off Welfare*. Cambridge: South End Press.

Zweig, Michael. 2000. *The Working Class Majority: America's Best Kept Secret*. Ithaca, NY: ILR Press.

CHAPTER 5

Heading the Hierarchy: Upper Class or Superclass?

Lobbyists for the managers of hedge funds, who make unregulated investments for the very rich, have convinced Congress that the 20 percent profit share they receive on deals is not regular income—taxed up to 35 percent—but a capital gains—taxed at 15 percent—even though the managers are not risking their own money as a capital-gains deduction requires. This tax break has helped these managers make huge chunks of money—in 2007 $22.5 billion for the top 25 managers, on average about $900,000 million each, with the number one individual clearing $3.7 billion. In the first year of the modern financial crisis, these 25 managers still earned $11.6 billion (Anderson 2008; Story 2009).

Even some very wealthy people have criticized how the taxation system works. Warren Buffett, one of the richest men in the world, admonished his fellow billionaires, saying they were paying a lower tax rate than the workers who clean their offices. And he offered any of them $1 million if they could prove otherwise.

A billionaire who managed one of the leading hedge funds admitted that the situation in which he and his colleagues have been "making egregious amounts of money paying low or no taxes is really becoming laughable. . . . The . . . guys I know admit they do not have an argument that can hold water" (Ignatius 2007, A19).

How is such an outcome possible? As Chapter 4 indicates, wealthy, powerful individuals and groups have various means to promote their goals. In this instance they have the pervasive impact of lobbying and campaign giving. In the summer of 2007, congressional Democrats wanted to raise taxes on hedge funds, but Charles Schumer, a Democratic senator from New York, protested, saying jobs and companies affected would leave New York City. Even Schumer's allies disputed this claim, indicating that these robust firms were hardly so fragile that the prospect of increased taxes would force them to leave. Schumer, in fact, was taking a position inconsistent with his long-held support for middle-class constituents' economic struggles. So why did Schumer champion low taxes for hedge-fund managers? Schumer was chairman of the Democratic Senatorial Campaign Committee, and hedge-fund companies, had donated large sums of money—$2 million between January and June 2007—to that committee. In turn, Schumer became a well placed supporter of hedge funds. Besides being the third-ranking Democrat in the Senate, he was the only Democrat serving on both of the committees, Banking and Finance, that have jurisdiction over decisions about hedge-fund taxation (Hernandez and Labaton 2007).

Throughout this chapter we see that the American superclass is able to use its financial and social capital to influence politicians to produce favorable outcomes. A look at the historical development of the upper class reveals that such a pattern has developed over time. In shifting to the present day, our attention focuses on the impact of family, education, and social clubs on upper-class members' development. The significance of wealth—attaining it and keeping it—leads to an examination of the processes of managing upper-class wealth and income. The last major section involves the corporate world, focusing on the superclass's participation at the top corporate levels and in the policy-making structures introduced in Chapter 4.

This chapter analyzes the most privileged segment of the population—the upper class or superclass. While many upper-class people have little involvement in public policy, others, namely superclass members, are active in this process. Whether referred to as upper-class or superclass, these families' income and wealth derive from business ventures, inheritance, and top corporate positions. Many are well educated, having graduated from prestigious colleges and universities, sometimes receiving graduate degrees. The yearly household income is typically about $2 million, and the upper class represents about 1 percent of the population (Gilbert 2011, 244–45). Social reproduction has often been an explicit goal, particularly for the power-elite members among the rich, who have sought to make certain that the economic and political policies they help develop assure that the succeeding generation retains a lion's share of wealth and power.

The account of the upper class begins with a look back in time to an era in which wealth first materialized, at least for a few, early in American history.

GETTING RICH: FROM THE HIGH SEAS TO HI TECH

One might divide the development of American wealth into three eras—the seventeenth through the nineteenth centuries, ranging from early privateering to the dawn of robber baroning in the 1860s; the century extending from then until the 1970s; and the current postindustrial/global phase. Two categories of wealthy—the old and the new rich—have emerged over time.

The Early Years

Before banking and manufacturing became prominent in the nineteenth century, most affluent people had little actual money. However, these individuals had plenty of wealth in the form of land, mansions, livestock, jewels, carriages, and slaves. Some of them were decidedly rich. Robert Carter of Westmoreland, Virginia, owned over 300,000 acres of fine grazing land, more than 1,000 slaves, an ironworks, a flour mill, and a renowned mansion (Beebe 2009, 3–4).

During that era violence proved an effective way to build wealth. Some prerevolutionary merchants plundered gold, silk, and ivory in the waters off India and Arabia. This piracy produced great wealth, with Frederick Philipse's huge New York estate providing the most conspicuous display. The surveyor-general of customs complained to his London headquarters that "pyrates" were welcomed in most ports, and governors fully supported their plundering. By the 1760s it was apparent that many of the colonies' richest families owed their prosperity to war, piracy, and privateering (governmentally authorized attacks on enemy shipping).

During the revolution privateering was an especially lucrative activity; between 1775 and 1782, some 2,000 colonial vessels captured about 3,000 British ships worth what was then the enormous sum of $18 million. Historian Kevin Phillips wrote, "Booty underpinned postwar preeminence everywhere in New England" (Phillips 2002, 13). A troublesome question comes to mind: Did these violent, wealth-producing activities significantly influence the formation of American business practices?

After the Revolutionary War, shipping, often augmented by privateering, was the greatest source of wealth. By the 1790s Salem, which was the port launching the many ships that captured 458 vessels during the revolution, had a number of seafaring millionaire families at a time when such wealth was rare.

Both during and after the war, wealthy individuals made money from government contracts. Robert Morse, the superintendent of finance, became a spectacularly rich man. Unconcerned about any impinging conflict of interest, he gave one quarter of the wartime contracts reaching his office to his own firm.

The wealthy managed to get the inside track on the moneymaking side of any government venture. In 1781 the Bank of the United States was founded to aid the new federal government in its wartime currency and debt management. Within a few years, a host of complaints asserted that an upper-class clique controlled the Bank, which primarily gave loans to wealthy Philadelphians. When these rumors were at their height, Stephen Girard, a wealthy ship owner, was able to block the Bank's charter renewal, buy the building, and open his own Girard Bank. With the support of the Madison administration, many millions of federal money were transferred to the new bank, making the owner so wealthy that when the government was strapped for funds during the War of 1812, Girard bailed it out (Phillips 2002, 12–20).

By the 1840s the country had 150 to 200 millionaires, primarily living in New York, Philadelphia, and Boston (Phillips 2002, 26–27). Between 1850 and 1870, wealth was concentrated in the hands of a few people. The richest 2 percent held between 35 and 45 percent of the wealth while the most affluent 5 percent possessed 50 to 60 percent of it (Soltow 1989, 180).

The fact that individuals were rich was hardly a guarantee of being cultured, sophisticated, or even well mannered. Once arriving at a party, John Jacob Astor, the wealthiest man in New York City, greeted the hostess by wiping his hands on her dress. Cornelius Vanderbilt, who replaced Astor as the city's most affluent individual, was seldom a guest at elegant parties because he constantly swore, spat, and manhandled the female servants (Phillips 2002, 29).

While Astor, Vanderbilt, and many other early rich men pursued wealth in largely solo ventures, some of their prominent contemporaries would create a **corporate community** comprised of a number of large businesses and banks which form a network for such mutual benefits as sharing information and developing economic and political policies. The first corporate community involved wealthy textile owners in New England, and by 1845 a group of 80 men known as "the Boston Associates" controlled 31 textile companies representing 20 percent of the nation's textile business.

Chapter 2 introduced a concept—**interlocking directorate**, the definition of which is a formal connection between two major corporations that develops when an officer from one company serves on the board of directors of another. Interlocking directorates facilitate information sharing and policy development and have been a prominent contributor to the effectiveness of corporate communities. Seventeen members of the Boston corporate community became directors of local banks, managing 40 percent of all banking capital in the city. Twenty served on the boards of six insurance companies, and 11 functioned as directors for five railroads. Other large cities, particularly New York City, were also creating corporate communities (Dalzell 2003; Domhoff 2010, 26–27).

As the number of wealthy individuals grew, certain patterns about their development became apparent. While some rich men had worked their way up from poverty, most had not. An examination of records involving the richest 1 percent in four locales—New York City, Brooklyn, Philadelphia, and Boston between the late 1820s and the middle 1840s—showed that a high percentage came from wealthy and/or prominent families—from 95 percent in New York City to 81 percent in Brooklyn (Pessen 1990, 85–86). Viewing such evidence, historian William Miller concluded that "poor boys who became business leaders have always been more conspicuous in American history books than in American history" (Pessen 1990, 79). Historical support for the Horatio Alger rags-to-riches claim, Miller suggested, is minimal. Instead social reproduction has been a dominant upper-class trend.

Still, the rags-to-riches notion stayed alive, in part perhaps because a few major figures of the robber baron era like John D. Rockefeller and Andrew Carnegie rose from humble beginnings to become fabulously rich.

From the Robber Baron Era to 1970

The Civil War provided a chance to make fortunes. A number of corporate and banking giants of the latter 1800s—J.D. Rockefeller, Andrew Carnegie, J.P. Morgan, and Jay Gould—avoided soldiering, usually by hiring substitutes, and began making their fortunes. These capitalists were pioneers in such basic industries as railroads, iron, coal, and oil along with banking and other financial services necessary to support business development (Phillips 2002, 35–37). They became known as "robber barons" because their harsh, unregulated business practices often destroyed the competition.

During this period some top leaders monopolized business activities. In the 1880s J.P. Morgan in railroads and John D. Rockefeller in oil consolidated their respective industries, accumulating wealth that dwarfed any previous personal riches (Gilfoyle 2002, 281). David Rockefeller observed that within one mammoth oil company his grandfather successfully integrated all the elements of the industry—"from production at the wellhead to the final delivery to the customer. Standard [his corporation] was the first modern, fully integrated enterprise" (Rockefeller 2002, 7). Such advances were very lucrative. Between 1873 and 1890, the great fortunes doubled or tripled, with Rockefeller and Carnegie each possessing between $200 and $300 million. It was a wide-open period without government regulation. The economy flourished, and the gross domestic product (measuring the nation's economic production) rose from $72 billion in 1860 to nearly $170 billion in 1880 (Rothkopf 2009, 98).

Millionaire Frederich Townsend Martin proudly explained that he and his big-business colleagues openly used their wealth and the politicians it could buy to protect their economic and political interests. These corrupted individuals would mobilize "against any legislation, any political platform, any presidential campaign that threatens the integrity of our estates" (Josephson 1962, 352). While it is still possible to use money to exert powerful influence on politicians, no modern capitalist has the temerity to speak publicly with such brutal honesty.

The late nineteenth century was an era in which the rich felt completely in control—the so-called Gilded Age when their wealth was fully on display. Economist and sociologist Thorstein Veblen (1899) coined the term **conspicuous consumption**—lavish expenditure on high-priced goods and services in order to flaunt one's wealth. A contributing factor in these demonstrations was the role of the mass media, namely newspapers and magazines, in doing what the media have been doing ever since—depicting wealthy people's personal appearance and their physical locations as "handsome" or "beautiful." In particular, the society page, which became very popular at this time, revealed some of the prominent details of wealthy people's lives such as their trips on luxury ocean liners or their lavish parties at either fancy New York hotels or their Newport mansions (Kendall 2005, 21–23). An 1897 costume ball at the famous Waldorf featured many guests dressed as renowned historical figures. The aforementioned John Jacob Astor, wearing a sword covered in jewels, portrayed Henry IV of France, and 50 women appeared as Marie Antoinette (Henwood 2008, 14). Epitomizing media leaders' perceptions during that era, a well-known journalist told a class of college students, "Only the rich man is interesting" (Wecter 1937, 349).

For the upper class, the good times continued in the twentieth century. At that juncture J.D. Rockefeller became the country's first billionaire, and Andrew Carnegie was next in line with a half-billion-dollar fortune. The absence of an income tax served wealthy people well. The number of millionaires increased steadily, rising from 5,000 in 1900 to 7,000 in 1914 (Phillips 2002, 49).

With World War I, as with the Revolutionary and Civil Wars, companies supplying the military made huge amounts of money. For instance, the DuPont Company profits went from $6 million in 1914 to $82 million in 1916. The stock value of such major wartime companies as Bethlehem Steel and General Motors soared, with Bethlehem Steel going from $33 a share in 1914 to $600 a share in 1918. In the 1920s and 1930s, technology helped build fortunes. Telephones and electricity became significant money-making inventions, but the automobile assumed a dominant role as Henry Ford became the nation's second billionaire. The growth of the auto industry produced a ripple effect in such major businesses as steel, oil, plate glass, tires, and highway construction (Phillips 2002, 55–58).

Once again, in World War II, those industries working for the government profited greatly. After the War, as Chapter 1 indicated, the United States dominated world industry, and the American upper class flourished. The number of millionaires went from 27,000 in 1953 to 80,000 in 1962, and then to 90,000 in 1965. Many of the country's richest individuals have been inheritors, with members of the Mellon, Rockefeller, and DuPont families representing 12 of the 25 wealthiest individuals in 1957 (Phillips 2002, 79–82).

In recent years the upper-class wealthy have continued to thrive, receiving considerable support from various government initiatives.

The Globalization Phase

In the early 1970s, globalization and technological change began to impact American business, producing a host of new rich people. While Chapter 1 examined the transformation process, little attention went to the role that the federal government has played in establishing fortunes.

Each year the government awards about $815 billion in "wealthfare" to corporations and rich individuals—about 47 percent (nearly half) of what it takes yearly to run the federal government (Zepezauer 2004, 1). The largest issues include:

Military waste, fraud, and incompetence: $224 billion a year. The American military budget is enormous, equal in size to the total cost for the next 22 national military budgets combined. The massive expenditure provides a range of military contractors extensive opportunities to enrich themselves, often wastefully or fraudulently. Between 1985 and 1995, $28 billion was lost, either in transactions with weapons contractors or in financial mismanagement. Contractors' charges for specific items have often been nonsensical. For instance, McDonnell Douglas sold the navy large numbers of a small metal nut for $2,043 each; Grumman Aerospace charged the air force $898 for a single plain metal bolt; and then Boeing originally planned to bill the air force $2,548 for a pair of pliers but dropped the price to a mere $748 when the client balked.

Big-business influence on the federal government has altered the way in which combat is conducted. During the Iraq War, so-called security contractors, historically known as mercenaries, were able to obtain lucrative deals for their services, comprising a much larger, more expensive presence than in previous wars. The functions the security contractors provide are similar to those the military or police offer, but often the scale is smaller. Not only were mercenary forces in Iraq very costly, but they were often undisciplined and violent, initiating a number of deadly shootouts with Iraqi civilians. In August 2007 more security contractors had died in the Iraq War than all the coalition forces combined.

Multinationals' tax avoidance: $137 billion a year. Because multinationals have extensive dealings with their foreign branches, they can freely transfer profits out of and expenses into the United States, thereby minimizing domestic profitability on paper and depriving the country of about $50 billion a year in tax revenues. Multinationals have various other means of avoiding taxes. For instance, US companies can officially establish their corporate headquarters in a tax haven such as the Cayman Islands, Antigua, or Bermuda. Once they have paid their incorporation fee, they are official residents of that country. While companies can conveniently remain in the United States, their tax obligation is to the new host, which charges much less. In 2004 American multinationals paid an overall federal tax rate of about 2.3 percent on $700 billion in foreign profits.

Low taxes on capital gains: $90 billion a year. Besides hedge funds, which were discussed earlier, stocks, bonds, and real estate are prominent sources of wealth that benefit from the capital-gains designation.

Accelerated depreciation: $85 billion a year. Historically businesses have been able to receive annual tax breaks for the declining values of buildings and equipment. In 1971 the Nixon administration issued an executive order allowing companies to anticipate depreciation, writing off the costs of wear-and-tear before they occurred and receiving a lump sum that amounted to an interest-free loan from taxpayers. It was a bonanza for corporations, producing a sharp drop in taxes (Krugman 2007, A29; Siegel 2009; Zepezauer 2004).

Substantial subsidies of major industries: Another legislative aid the federal government provides has been the subsidy of certain major industries. By 1965 the federal government underwrote almost two thirds of biomedical research, which has been crucial for the development of the drugs that have sustained a thriving pharmaceutical industry. That subsidy, though down to about 40 percent, continues presently. Then in the TV business, the passage of the Telecommunications Act of 1996 gave each television network an additional six megahertz of spectrum, representing a bonus worth about $70 million overall in exchange for a vague assurance to provide public-service programming (Phillips 2002, 248; SourceWatch 2007). This is only the latest example of a well-developed pattern of gift-giving to the major media companies. "The free distribution of the public-owned electromagnetic spectrum to U.S. radio and television companies," a critic asserted, "has been one of the greatest gifts of public property in history" (McChesny 1999, 142).

However, in spite of these governmental supports, many leading American corporations have recently struggled. In 2009 the following American multinationals—General Motors, Citigroup, Fannie Mae, Ford Motor, TimeWarner, and ConocoPhillips—were six of the eight global corporations suffering the year's greatest losses. All but Ford Motor and TimeWarner received massive federal bailouts (Global 500 2009; Van der Galien 2009). Furthermore, decreasing dividends from stocks and other major investments indicated that the economic worth of the most affluent 1 percent may have declined between 2007 and 2009 (Leonhardt and Fabrikant 2009, A16).

As we have seen, each new era has brought with it opportunities for obtaining wealth. Whether or not people are born wealthy seems to make a significant difference in their outlooks and behavior.

The Old Rich versus the New Rich

Sociologist E. Digby Baltzell, a member of the upper class himself, described the old rich as groups of families descended from successful families of the previous or earlier generations. The old rich, in short, have a track record of established wealth, prominence, and respectability. Baltzell noted that "they are brought up together, are friends, [with] a distinctive style of life and a kind of primary group solidarity which sets them apart" (Baltzell 1989, 7).

Political scientist Thomas R. Dye, who designated the largely eastern, established old rich "yankees," observed that this contingent of wealthy people has included the descendants of the major entrepreneurial families of the Industrial Revolution—the Rockefellers, Fords, Mellons, DuPonts, Vanderbilts, Astors, and others. This faction also contains leaders of established corporations, major law firms, and prominent banks and investment companies (Dye 2002, 159).

While there has been considerable variation in how individuals respond to being born into wealth and prominence, many feel comfortably settled at the top of the hierarchy. As one old-rich individual half-seriously queried, "Why would anybody want to strive for anything if all the really important prizes had been handed out in the maternity ward at New York Hospital?" (Lapham 1988, 16).

The old rich families have an organization that celebrates their upper-class status—the Social Register. Founded in 1886 it has a membership of about 25,000, including individuals who are descendants of the association's founding group. In order to join the association, families must obtain letters of recommendation from several active members, and then an advisory board evaluates the candidates. On its website the Social Register Association stated that "[s]ince its inception, the Social Register has been the only reliable, and the most trusted, arbiter of Society in America" (Social Register Association 2008). Its members are at the top of the American social hierarchy. The *Social Register* represents an emphatic upper-class effort to reinforce the boundary of what Max Weber would consider its status group, marking its distinct separation from all others, especially from the new rich.

As befits their status, many of the old rich maintain a restrained, dignified lifestyle. Dr. Nina Chandler Murray, a member of the Poor family of Standard & Poor's, the credit-rating firm, declared that people with her upbringing "had a honed discipline of what was expected." She added, "Showing off money was a sin. It was not that status was not important," but now the rule "is '[i]f you've got it, flaunt it'" (Fabrikant 2005, 26).

The last reference was to the new rich, who have been building large numbers of massive mansions in Nantucket, where Dr. Murray's summer home was located. Often coming from the West or Southwest, the new rich, whom Thomas R. Dye called "cowboys," have obtained all or most of their assets themselves. Their sources of wealth have included computer technology, business machines, oil drilling, real-estate development, particularly in the Southwest, discount drugs and merchandising, fast foods, and insurance (Dye 2002, 159; Keister 2005, 61–68). One observer noted that like the robber barons of the Gilded Age, the new rich have embraced conspicuous consumption, "construct[ing] huge mansions, outdo[ing] one another in buying high-end status symbols like megayachts" (Fabrikant 2005, 1). In spite of such exorbitant consumption, the new rich tend to be more toned down than their Gilded Age counterparts. For instance, many major Wall Street operatives have forsaken the traditional business suit for what has become known as "hedge-fund casual"—open-necked shirts and khakis (Henwood 2008, 14).

Megayachts such as these shown in Malta's Grand Harbor are likely to belong to members of the new rich.

Dye surmised that because the new rich have often struggled and succeeded on their own, they have been less supportive of such liberal concerns as welfare and immigration reform than the old rich, who grew up in a liberal tradition where they became more concerned than the new rich about helping those less fortunate than themselves (Dye 2002, 159).

While Dye's conclusion has often been cited, a study revealed that it was inaccurate. Sociologist Val Burris examined the politics of the Forbes 400 richest Americans along with several samples of wealthy people from earlier decades and found that the "yankees" were more conservative than the "cowboys." Burris learned that the old rich tended to grow up as members of the Republican party, which has strongly supported wealthy people's property rights and opposed labor unions and wealth distribution. In contrast, the new rich coming from less affluent backgrounds were more likely to have been born into Democratic households, where liberal concerns were more prevalent, and in many cases this early influence persisted (Burris 2000).

Whether referring to the old or new rich, it is difficult to visualize the vastness of great wealth. One attempt to convey that vastness features the obscure Larry Ellison, the eleventh richest person in the world. In 2007 Ellison would have needed to spend $30 million a week or $183,000 per hour to avoid increasing his wealth (Brooks 2007, A13). As Figures 5.1 and 5.2 demonstrate, upper-class members possess a substantial share of the nation's wealth and income. While over time the upper-class portion of net worth (wealth and income) has stayed fairly stable at about one third of the nation's total, this group's income percentage has relentlessly increased. Clearly the abundance of financial capital can benefit upper-class children.

BORN TO THE UPPER CLASS

Upper-class individuals possess various types of capital to promote their families' needs and interests. Each of the chapters dealing with class, race, and gender has a developmental section that demonstrates members' relationship to social reproduction.

Wealthy Families

In her study of upper-class women, sociologist Diana Kendall's respondents emphasized the importance of nurturing their children's academic, social, and professional skills as foundations for success in adulthood (Kendall 2002, 81). Susan Ostrander's sociological study of upper-class women reached a similar conclusion, indicating it is a popular myth that the rich leave raising children to servants. As one respondent said, "The proper development of the next generation of privilege is far too important to be left to hired hands" (Ostrander 1984, 71). This person seemed to be suggesting that the cultural capital—the language, the habits, and intimate knowledge required for upper-class membership—is not something an outsider can effectively impart.

Sometimes upper-class parents have special resources to provide their children unusually enriching experiences. In the mid-twentieth century, David Rockefeller, the long-time CEO of Chase Manhattan Bank, and his wife took their children on many international trips and often filled their various homes with guests from around the world "so that from an early age the children [were] exposed to a variety of interesting and accomplished people—such as Pablo Casals, the great cellist; Pedro Beltran, the prime

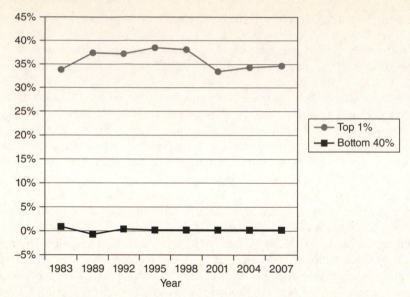

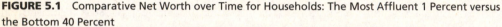

FIGURE 5.1 Comparative Net Worth over Time for Households: The Most Affluent 1 Percent versus the Bottom 40 Percent

In 1983 the top 1 percent of households possessed 33.8 percent of the national wealth and income. In the next 24 years, that figure stayed very stable, registering 34.6 percent in 2007. For the least affluent 40 percent, stability also prevailed, with this massive number of Americans locked in at less than half a percent of all net worth. Numerically these trends appear to be a powerful display of social reproduction, with the total net worth for the lowest 40 percent of households declining over the 24 years from one 38th to one 178th the wealthiest 1 percent's portion.

Source: Edward N. Wolff. 2010. "Some Trends in Household Wealth in the United States: Rising Debt and the Middle-Class Squeeze—An Update to 2007." Levy Economic Institute of Bard College. http://www.levyinstitute.org/pub/wp-589.pdf.

minister of Peru; [and] Nate Pusey, the president of Harvard" (Rockefeller 2002, 323). This is a rarefied cultural capital few children encounter.

Whether it is the Rockefellers or a parent from a century earlier, old-money parents have been very concerned about family continuity. This issue is apparent in a letter from Theodore Roosevelt, Sr., to his son Theodore Roosevelt, Jr., later the twenty-sixth American president. The father indicated that for a father it is rewarding to watch his son's steadily increasing maturity, and the son, in turn, "enjoys relieving his father of part of . . . [his] responsibilities . . . , and these cares prepare the boy to take the father's place in the great battle of life" (Aldrich 1988, 196). The statement emphasizes the parents' investment in preparing their children well to perform their adult roles. Otherwise, the thinking goes, the secure future of both the child and the family appears to be at serious risk.

Among the old rich, the operative family has usually extended well beyond the nuclear unit to include grandparents, aunts and uncles, and various levels of cousins. Nelson W. Aldrich, Jr., a member of the old rich himself, concluded that "the best way to describe Old Money families is to call them families of cousins" (Aldrich 1988, 55).

Some of the extended upper-class families meet regularly, once or twice a year or every other year. Two functions are served: to get reacquainted and to discuss business-related issues. The Weyerhaeuser family, which owns one of the largest pulp-and-paper

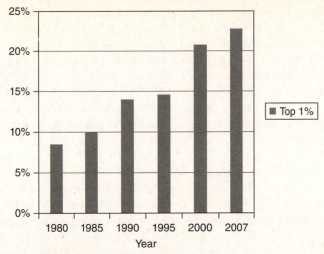

FIGURE 5.2   The Upper-Class Portion of Income over Time

Over a 27-year span, the wealthiest 1 percent of individuals has nearly tripled their share of the total income, rising from 8.4 percent in 1980 to 22.8 percent in 2007.

Source: Gerald Prante. 2009. "Summary of Latest Federal Individual Income Tax Data." *The Tax Foundation: Summary of Latest Individual Income Tax Data.* http://www.taxfoundation.org/publications/show/250/html.

empires in the world, has arranged its gathering to coincide with the annual meeting of the Weyerhaeuser Company (Allen 1987, 105–06). For youthful members these gatherings can be important chances to develop productive cultural and social capital.

Children's education is a major concern for upper-class parents.

Schooling for the Rich

In one study a wealthy respondent explained, "After the obstetrician told me I was pregnant, the first phone call I made was to my husband to tell him. The second call I made was to [an elite private school] to put my [unborn] child on the school's waiting list for four years down the road" (Kendall 2002, 81).

Wealthy children's informal education is likely to start at an early age—for instance, at prestigious preschools where they begin to learn appropriate class-linked manners and etiquette and also to develop relationships with members of the other sex. At age eight or nine, many children are enrolled in junior cotillions, where they continue to pursue the "social graces," which require them to sit up straight in their chairs and, above all, to behave as young ladies and gentlemen (Domhoff 2010, 57; Kendall 2002, 90). According to one instructor, for girls acting like young ladies includes "sitting cross-ankled but never with legs crossed." To qualify as young gentlemen, boys are supposed to sit with feet flat on the floor or if their feet do not reach the floor, they should not wriggle them. One upper-class woman told Diana Kendall that such instruction provided "a very long-term investment in a child's life . . . representing something they will have with them forever. It enforces the polite training they receive at home" (Kendall 2002, 90–91). She concluded, in short, that the combined impact of upper-class preschools' and families' instruction represent a potent package of cultural capital.

As upper-class children reach their teens, many of them attend one of the prominent boarding schools. Founded in the last half of the nineteenth and early twentieth centuries, these schools, often called preparatory (prep) schools, have become a fundamental building block in an upper-class subculture. Sociologist G. William Domhoff described these schools as the "lynchpins in the upper-class educational system" (Domhoff 2010, 57).

Upper-class and upper-middle-class boarding schools, which have expanded from dozens to several hundred, have developed a distinctive lifestyle. Prominent features have included patterns of hazing new students and requiring school blazers and ties, attendance at chapel services, and participation in such elite sports as squash and crew. Some terminology comes from the British system in which the principal is designated rector or headmaster and students are in forms, not grades. In particular, the teachers and administrators at these schools are concerned with developing character, recognizing that their student body will produce many future leaders of the country. Headmasters' speeches, which often contain references to successful alumni, stress this point (Domhoff 2010, 57–58).

Writer Nelson W. Aldrich, Jr., indicated that historically the teachers at the most elite prep schools were demanding and tough, seeking to indoctrinate their students "in all the values and virtues of competitive self-reliance, almost as if they too, could be self-made men and women" (Aldrich 1988, 146). Their position was that life is an unrelenting struggle with many major hurdles, including students' rapidly approaching competition to get into elite universities like Yale, Princeton, and Harvard. Nobody has taken the American ideology more seriously than these educators of the country's upper-class members. At Phillips Exeter, one of the most renowned prep schools, an alumnus confessed that "[e]ach day after lunch during my first year, I went back to my room and cried . . . "[Daily activity involved] "bitter engagements with life, but without them I would never have matured" (Aldrich, 1988, 147). As part of the cultural capital they imparted, these teachers and administrators relentlessly emphasized the need to be tough and resilient—to develop character—an appropriate challenge for these boys who would one day run what all considered the most important country in the world.

A similar emphasis persists. The headmaster of a well-known northeastern prep school recently proclaimed that while academics is very important "[c]haracter education is our most important commitment. We insist that our students follow the school's ideals and principles" (Howard 2008, 119). The message often produces the desired impact. Keegan, an A student at Bradvik, a private school in a wealthy midwestern community, indicated that most of his contemporaries had learned to be successful at school so that they could be successful later in life. Keegan offered an analogy about cultural capital that seems to come from the same tradition as the Exeter alumnus previously quoted. The effort, he explained, was like competition at a track meet. Runners would train so that the first three laps pose little problem. However, Keegan noted that as the race drew toward its close, "you have to put everything you have into it to succeed. You can decide whether to just get by or run extra hard in the final lap" (Howard 2008, 54).

While these elite schools' cultural tradition remains consistent over time, changes have occurred—for instance in the student body's gender, racial, and ethnic makeup. What were once all-male facilities now are co-ed. A study of 18 very prestigious boarding schools indicated a steady increase in the number of African American students, with a nearly 10 percent growth between 1999 and 2003 (*Journal of Blacks in Higher Education* 2003, 58–59).

In 2006 five of the most acclaimed New England boarding schools pledged to provide more financial aid and no longer to reject students because of family income. "We don't want to be a school that caters to wealthy families in the Northeast," David Beim, an Exeter trustee, explained. "We want to reach out to families across the country who come from different backgrounds" (Vaznis 2006, B1).

Since upper-class parents carefully plan their children's schooling, it seems likely that diversifying prep schools' student bodies has hardly been a haphazard move. Lengthy deliberation probably occurred, perhaps involving think tank or other superclass-sponsored input. Positions promoting the outcome might have included the belief that racial, ethnic, and income diversity provide a favorable public image for the schools and also the realization that bright students from minority and/or low-income backgrounds are a potentially valuable resource, who can be educated to become reliable, productive upper- or upper-middle-class contributors to superclass interests.

Regardless of students' class of origin, boarding schools provide a unique experience. Baltzell indicated that isolated from their families and outside friends, these young people often develop a close relationship with their fellow students and teachers. These individuals have served as "surrogate families," and classmates often become an individual's most valued friends and contacts (Baltzell 1989, 303). Similarly a graduate of the elite Hill School explained that "the simple fact of sharing the same life for a period of years" meant he perceived the school as "his second family" (Wolff 1989, 224). These surrogate family contacts can be valuable. In one study a respondent explained, "Where I went to boarding school, there were girls from all over the country, so I know people from all over. It is helpful when you move to a new city and want to get invited into the local social club" (Ostrander 1984, 85). These family-like prep-school contacts, in short, can become potent sources of social capital.

Like the prep-school experience, study at an elite college or university is an important step in an upper-class individual's development. In the late 1980s, Baltzell asserted that it was "more advantageous, socially and economically to have had a mediocre academic record at Harvard, Yale, or Princeton than to have been Phi Beta Kappa at a less prominent college" (Baltzell 1989, 319). In *Money and Class in America: Notes and Observations on Our Civil Religion*, Lewis H. Lapham claimed that "[a] Yale education was a means of acquiring a cash value . . . [W]hat was important was the diploma, the ticket of admission to Wall Street, the professions, the safe havens of big money" (Lapham 1988, 19).

It was also important, upper-class leadership believed, to control who received this ticket of admission. By the 1920s various leaders at the most prominent Ivy League universities concluded that the percentage of "undesirable" Jews, students whose families recently immigrated from Poland and Russia, had risen too high. The decision was to set quotas on Jews, promoting an admissions policy that emphasized "good character" and "manliness" more than academic achievement. Now students had to write a personal letter, provide a list of extracurricular achievements, and supply letters of recommendation from trusted individuals like teachers, alumni, and headmasters, preferably from elite schools. To evaluate the greatly enlarged body of information that candidates submitted, universities created admissions offices. Upper-class leaders felt that the curtailment of Jews' admission was critical. Not only were they worried about stiff competition in business and education, but many felt that most Jews were deficient—inferior physical beings who were too bookish to display the "manliness" necessary to defend the nation (Karabel 2005, 98, 130–32).

In modern times preferential treatment for upper-class students continues. The most prestigious 100 or so universities and colleges favor admittance for students whose parents have a history of giving them large donations. In addition, some schools show preferences for celebrities' children, whose presence can enhance the institution's reputation. Each year the fund-raising office supplies the admissions bureau with a list of these advantaged applicants, "who are often accepted even if they rank near the bottom of their high school classes or have SAT scores 300–400 points below some rejected applicants" (Golden 2007, 5). One might wonder how preferred students end up performing academically. At Duke University, which developed a well organized system for recruiting wealthy students, a former admissions officer indicated that these individuals were the weakest portion of the applicant pool (Golden 2007, 78). At Brown University, which has an unusually high number of celebrity children, 20 percent of the overall student body graduates with high honors, but none of the celebrity children have qualified; 12 percent of the celebrity group compared to about 30 percent overall have received honors in their major (Golden 2007, 94).

While the highly celebrated universities and colleges give many upper-class students preferential treatment, those schools have grown and diversified, and in the process the upper-class proportion of the student body has dropped (Domhoff 2010, 58). Meanwhile upper-class students have been attending a greater number of colleges, entering about 200 of the total of 2,300 four-year institutions. These prestigious, well-known schools include the Ivy League (e.g., Brown, Cornell, Harvard, and Princeton), the top 20 private universities (e.g., Chicago, Duke, and Stanford), the top 20 state universities (e.g., California-Berkeley, North Carolina, Texas, and UCLA), and small elite colleges (e.g., Amherst, Bowdoin, Oberlin, Reed, and Swarthmore). As graduates these upper-class individuals often obtain advanced degrees, eventually entering business, various professions, politics, and other enterprises (Perrucci and Wysong 2008, 270).

Whether they are old or new rich, affluent Americans tend to be well educated. An examination of the Forbes 400, a list of the wealthiest individuals in the United States, over half of whom belong to the new rich, indicated typical members had a bachelor's degree and often a postgraduate degree, too (Keister 2005, 72).

Besides the human capital—the knowledge and skills they impart—the most prominent colleges and universities are also sources of important social capital. In 1908 admissions officials from Columbia University asked the headmaster of the elite Horace Mann School in New York City why more graduates did not attend their distinguished university. The headmaster was direct, saying Columbia did not attract enough students with social advantages, and thus there was "little opportunity of making friendships of permanent value." It is naïve, the headmaster continued, to think upper-class students only want academic learning from a college—that no less important are "associations and friendships that might be formed within the student body" (Powell 1996, 44–45). The sole way this episode is outdated is the era in which it occurred: The headmaster's point is decidedly contemporary.

The friends and associates made at elite universities' "eating clubs" have often been valued contacts throughout graduates' lives. At Harvard the most exclusive eating clubs have been Porcellian, A.D., and Fly; at Yale, Scroll and Key, Skull and Bones, and the Fence Club (Allen 1987, 25; Baltzell 1989, 330–31). At Harvard, Franklin D. Roosevelt applied to the Porcellian and was rejected, later explaining it was "the greatest disappointment of my life" (Viser 2007, M11). Roosevelt's wife believed that the incident produced

The nondescript building in which Skull and Bones, a social club at Yale University, is housed does not suggest the valuable social capital its members have often obtained from their participation in the club.

an "inferiority complex," which helped the future president identify with marginalized people (Karabel 2005, 17).

Since Roosevelt's time the popularity of eating clubs has remained. At Princeton, where critics, including a recent university president, contend that these groups bolster the elite status of rich students, a substantial number still eagerly seek entry into such prestigious organizations as the Ivy Club and the University Cottage Club (Hu 2007, 4).

While eating clubs can provide valuable contacts during the college years, the pursuit of social capital often accelerates after graduation.

Elite Social Clubs

In the first half of the twentieth century, most wealthy American men lived in cities, and many belonged to metropolitan clubs, where they often went for lunch or dinner or sometimes even weekend parties. Soon after World War II, many rich families started moving to large suburban estates, and country clubs became frequent sites for family members, offering a variety of social and recreational events. The metropolitan clubs primarily became places where members had lunch, an occasional relaxing afternoon, or perhaps a meeting (Domhoff 2010, 61–63). They remain important sites for recreation and building social capital.

The most exclusive social clubs are in the oldest cities—Boston, New York City, and Philadelphia. Others, which are well respected, have developed in such major cities as Pittsburgh, Chicago, and San Francisco. The most exclusive social clubs are two in New York City—the Links and the Knickerbocker (Allen 1987, 25).

It is difficult to join such clubs. To begin, it is expensive. The initiation fees, annual dues, and other expenses range from several thousands yearly in downtown clubs to tens of thousands annually in some country clubs. Those capable of payment then confront the screening process. A club member must nominate an aspirant, who needs to obtain letters of recommendation from three to six members, and then faces a 10- to 12-person admissions committee. Negative votes from two or three of these individuals can prevent entrance into the social club (Domhoff 2010, 61).

Personal wealth has never been the sole basis for attaining membership in exclusive clubs. The individual and family must meet the admissions committee's standards for values and behavior. Old money prevails over new money as the Rockefeller family experience suggests. John D. Rockefeller, the family founder and the nation's first billionaire, joined the Union League Club, a fairly respectable but not top-level metropolitan club; John D. Rockefeller, Jr., belonged to the University Club, a step up from his father; and finally his son John D. Rockefeller, III, reached the pinnacle with his acceptance into the Knickerbocker Club (Baltzell 1989, 340).

Upper-class men and women often join clubs in several cities, creating a nation-wide pattern of overlapping memberships. Several dozen men, most of whom are very wealthy, belong to three or more clubs and also sit on several corporate boards. In fact, the interconnections between social clubs and corporations appear extensive. One study assessed the club memberships of the chairpersons and outside directors of the 20 largest industrial corporations. It revealed that while these corporate individuals frequently joined upper-class social clubs, they were particularly likely to be members of very exclusive clubs. For instance, at least one director from 12 of the 20 top corporations belonged to the Links Club, which is a favored meeting location for the national corporate leadership (Domhoff 2010, 62).

The Bohemian Club is another highly exclusive social club whose all-male membership features the country's neoconservative elite. Each July it conducts a two-week retreat at its 2,700-acre location in Bohemian Grove 75 miles north of San Francisco. The principal club members are leading corporate CEOs and directors, major politicians, celebrities, and other prominent upper-class individuals. On the weekends the total count of members and guests ranges between 1,500 and 2,500. An opening ceremony called the Cremation of Care announces that the busy Bohemians can put aside their normal responsibilities and enjoy plays, concerts, lectures, and such outdoor recreations as canoeing, swimming, and trapshooting.

Amidst the good times, however, serious networking takes place, including occasional campaigning for the presidency. In 1967 Richard Nixon made what he considered his most important, satisfying speech on the way to the presidency. In 1995 George H.W. Bush gave a talk in which he described his son George W. as possessing the virtues that would qualify him to be a fine future president. Then four years later as the election year approached, father brought son to the Bohemian Club to meet many of his rich and powerful fellow club members, who could provide substantial promotional and financial support for the run to the presidency (Domhoff 2010, 66).

The Bohemian Club's yearly retreat is an event that has been repeated for over a century, and its potential impact is vast. Half jokingly, journalist Alexander Cockburn indicated that every July many of the nation's top economic and political leaders will meet "in a gloomy grove of redwoods in northern California preparing to banish care . . . as members of the Bohemian Club. Along the way, they will hash out the future of the world" (Cockburn 2001, B15).

Superclass members show the same deliberate use of capital resources in dealing with their finances that they demonstrate in other important areas of living.

Managing Upper-Class Wealth and Income

If an individual or family has extensive financial assets, what is the best course of action for increasing it? There is a pair of options rich people are likely to choose:

- A **family office** is an organization formed when family members pool some of their resources and hire experts to evaluate investments, charitable activities, and perhaps even political donations. The existence of family offices is significant, because they can be the means by which a fortune from an earlier generation remains under the control of a single authority and is not dispersed into many descendants' hands, losing the economic clout needed for maximum wealth accumulation. In 2008 an estimated 4,000 family offices handled fortunes of $100 million or more (Domhoff 2010, 76–77). For very wealthy families, these organizations can be quite large. At one time the Rockefellers' family office, which is called Rockefeller Family and Associates, had over 200 clerks, accountants, lawyers, and financial advisers (Allen 1987, 108). Obviously such an organization is expensive to maintain, but it has managed to keep what was once the nation's largest fortune under centralized control. Only wealthy clients can qualify for the full range of benefits a family office provides. For Merrill Lynch to provide these services, a family needs to have $100 million to invest (Frank 2004).
- In addition, there are holding companies, which can provide the functions of a family office if the family is small and cohesive. These organizations are used to make collective investment for family members and to create new companies in which they own substantial shares. Warren Buffett, one of the wealthiest Americans, has operated through a holding company, Berkshire Hathaway. Along with his fellow investors, who include his son Howard, he sits on the boards of several companies in which they are invested (Domhoff 2010, 77).

As Table 5.1 indicates, the upper class mobilizes different types of capital to promote social reproduction for itself—namely, perpetuation at the top. A basic reason for this upper-class advantage is the possession of corporate wealth.

THE AMERICAN CORPORATE LEADERSHIP

As we noted in Chapter 2, American corporate leaders come from both upper-class and upper-middle-class backgrounds. The current focus in on top corporate leaders, who, regardless of their personal class of origin, are sufficiently wealthy to be located in the upper class.

TABLE 5.1 Advantages from a Configuration of Upper-Class Capital Sources

1. Financial capital
   a. Life enhancers: First-rate food, housing, medical care
   b. Temporal and spatial empowerment to simplify living and improve its quality (discussed in the last section)
   c. Superior education, enhancing life chances
   d. Wealth that family offices, holding companies, and other investment groups can expand
   e. Donation of large sums through lobbying, campaign giving, and foundation and think tank support to promote economic and political interests and goals

2. Cultural capital
   a. Families that are dedicated to providing the values, information, manners, outlooks, and other qualities necessary to produce successful entrants into the upper class
   b. Preschool and school instruction developing a sense of being a member of the elite

3. Human capital
   a. Quality schooling for preparing individuals to enter high-level corporate and professional positions
   b. From infancy the opportunity to obtain valuable cultural and social capital at school

4. Social capital
   a. One's own family, which is often well connected through its extended kinship network
   b. Lasting friendships and acquaintances developed among one's schoolmates in elite boarding schools
   c. Connections developed in elite college and graduate schools, particularly in highly exclusive eating clubs
   d. Benefits of memberships in upper-class metropolitan and country clubs
   e. Contacts and information provided by service on various high-level corporate boards of directors or boards for universities, foundations, think tanks, and policy-making groups

Within the American corporate structure, top managers have more authority than their counterparts in foreign big business. One reason is that putting managers instead of family owners in charge prevents claims of monopolistic control sometimes leveled against powerful foreign family groups that manage large blocks of multi-company stock. A second factor promoting professional management has been the increasing demands created by modern technology and complex planning, which often necessitate well-trained experts in top positions. In addition, founding families sometimes suffer the illusion that they can hire managers and remain in charge, with stockholders following their lead. Finally American corporate managers often gain control because over time many wealthy owners turn to philanthropy and require competent individuals to run their businesses (Becht and DeLong 2002; Becht and DeLong 2005).

It is a different pattern from the late nineteenth and early twentieth centuries, when the country's rich and powerful men controlled the corporations they created—Andrew Carnegie at United States Steel, Andrew Mellon at the Alcoa and Mellon Bank, Henry Ford at the Ford Motor Company, J.P. Morgan at J.P. Morgan & Company, and John D.

Rockefeller at Standard Oil Company. In 1900 when Carnegie, Rockefeller, and the other early tycoons were still active, 24 percent of the 200 largest nonfinancial firms were under professional management's control. That figure rose to 41 percent in 1929 and to over 80 percent in 1974 (Dye 2002, 24; Herman 1981, 66).

A small number of individuals currently represent top management. The typical major corporate boardroom consists of about 15 people. However, only a few, about six, are "inside" directors, who make most important decisions, and these include the chairman of the board, the chief executive officer (CEO), the president, and several top vice presidents. "Outside" directors, who do not belong to the company's management, usually accept the inside directors' judgment (Dye 2002, 21).

The corporate structure features a "management-by-objective" system in which the lowest segment of managers collects targets and objectives from their subordinates and makes a commitment to their immediate superiors to achieve various goals. Starting with their subordinates' projections, that group of managers then transmits their own set of goals to the next level of managers up the line. Ultimately the commitments reach from the lowest-level product managers or account executives to the CEO (Jackall 2010, 19-20).

Within this interlocking system, CEOs are all-powerful, with managers up and down the line engaging in endless discussions about the CEOs' plans, ideological leanings, style, and preferences. Managers have various ways of characterizing the CEOs' power. One researcher indicated that these descriptions "range from the trite 'When he sneezes, we all catch cold' to the more colorful 'When he says "Go to the bathroom," we all get the sh—ts'" (Jackall 2010, 23).

Some CEOs have more control within their companies than others. The very powerful are more likely to appoint board members who are demographically more similar to themselves—in age, educational level, and other traits—than the less powerful CEOs, whose new board members are more likely to match up with the existing board (Westphal and Zajac 1995). It is likely that CEOs feel most empowered building a top-level structure with individuals sharing their backgrounds.

Who are these individuals at the top of the corporate hierarchies? One expert suggested that their success was less likely to come from a fortunate birth than from success in big business. If not upper class in origin, high-level managers usually come from the upper-middle class and attend prominent universities and colleges, frequently from the Ivy League. Those with hopes of moving into top corporate positions must have the appropriate educational credentials. In the past the most common degree was a masters of business administration (MBA) from a leading business school—Harvard, Stanford, Wharton, or Columbia (Jackall 2010, 44). Nowadays over half of the corporate presidents of the 500 largest corporations possess a variety of degrees, not only MBAs but also law degrees and PhDs. Increasingly top corporate leaders have backgrounds in finance and law unlike their predecessors, who were more likely to have come from advertising, engineering, research, and sales. This shift demonstrates that modern corporations' most pressing, perplexing problems involve finance, taxation, and government regulation (Dye 2002, 26).

Rising through the ranks, corporate managers, particularly the most successful ones, must possess a set of traits, which are outlined in Chapter 6. No two analysts provide an identical description of those traits, but the following statement by Howard Morgans, the former president of Procter & Gamble, indicates that a candidate trudging toward the corporate summit must project a sense of being "loyal to a fault, tolerably bright, fairly creative, politically agile, always tough, sometimes flexible, unfailingly sociable and . . . seem superior to a dozen men who are almost as good" (Dye 2002, 25). This quotation strongly supports the idea that social traits and style play a significant role in corporate managers' advancement. Among the wealthiest, best connected executives, a select few move into the power elite, where they join the potent but largely invisible network that plays a major role in establishing national policy.

Economist Paul Krugman suggested that the power elite's policy-making activities are ideologically based—that the conservative leadership has "long idealized the Gilded Age, regarding everything that followed . . . as a diversion from the true path of capitalism" (Krugman 2008, A29). In particular, their optimal arrangement features a world unencumbered by income tax or by government regulation. The largely conservative superclass has been willing to devote substantial amounts of money and time to promote such outcomes.

The Superclass and the Power Elite

In Chapter 2 we examined G. William Domhoff's and Thomas Dye's contemporary theories of the power elite. While there are disagreements, they share certain common outlooks: that upper-class membership is a prominent trait; that these individuals have been well educated at the nation's top colleges and universities; that many of them share membership in well-known exclusive clubs; that major players are leaders from the corporate sphere and other major organizations; that an inner circle exists within the power elite; and that the power elite's command of foundations, think tanks, and policy-making groups produces a major impact on national policy (Domhoff 2010; Dye 2002).

While direct access to the power elite is impossible to obtain, researchers have drawn certain inferences about their members from available data, including political donations (Burris 2005; Lorien 2006). In examining 781 corporate elite members from 1,060 of the largest US corporations, sociologist Val Burris found that these top officials demonstrated patterns of political donations more similar to those individuals with whom they shared membership on corporate boards than with colleagues in their same industry or region.

Working on corporate boards together seems to foster cohesiveness. In the course of their shared activity, Burris suggested, these major corporate executives use each other as sources of information and guidance on both economic and political matters. Trust develops (Burris 2005, 273). Michael Useem's interviews conducted in the early 1980s confirmed this pattern.

In his study of top corporate executives, Useem spoke with a prominent industrialist who was sitting on four corporate boards and had a long, distinguished record of government service. When asked to name individuals who would effectively represent big-business interests to government officials, he listed six men he considered exemplary, possessing corporate and governmental experience much like his own. He noted that these executives, though busy with their own corporate duties, "are down in Washington undertaking responsibilities, beyond the requirements of their own operation. They are heading [such policy-making groups as] the Business Roundtable and the Business Council" (Useem 1984, 97).

While the members of all classes network, wealthy and powerful individuals and organizations have access to particularly potent social capital, working with their own kind for common policies and goals. To some extent that reality is physically observable. For instance, many major think tanks are located on a stretch of Massachusetts Avenue in Washington, DC. There is the Carnegie Endowment for International Peace and next door is the much larger Brookings Institution. The influential Institute for International Economics is across the street, and other think tanks are located nearby. Upon establishing these organizations, their founders gained extensive political contacts. When in 1910 Andrew Carnegie started the Carnegie Endowment, he obtained instant access to top leaders around the world (Rothkopf 2009, 122–23).

In a similar fashion, superclass members' involvement in the public-policy process inevitably proves beneficial for them. At this juncture, consider three of the types of elite policy-making groups discussed in Chapter 4; at the moment the focus is on superclass participation.

To begin, foundations, which are tax-free organizations spending money on such activities as research, education, and the arts, have boards of directors or trustees whose members are often upper-class. Research on the 12 largest foundations revealed that half the trustees were superclass members. Such individuals are productively connected with other members of their class. A study of large foundations concluded that over a third of their top leaders were members of upper-class social clubs, and the board members of the 50 largest foundations generally attended Ivy League or other prominent, wealthy universities. A number of neoconservative organizations such as the Bradley, Olin, and Scaife foundations remain under the donating families' leadership, which directly controls how its money promotes the neoconservative agenda (Domhoff 2010, 91–92; Perrucci and Wysong 2008, 165).

Foundations are major supporters of think tanks, which are organizations devoted to research, analysis, and public relations. Conservative think tanks outnumber their liberal counterparts two to one, and the conservative groups outspend the liberals three to one. Between 2001 and 2006, 24 neoconservative think tanks spent over $1 billion. A study found that just 12 wealthy foundations provided half the funding for the American Enterprise Institute, a leading neoconservative think tank, and 85 percent or more of the financing for other prominent neoconservative think tanks. Superclass members are well represented on the boards of these organizations, strongly influencing their policies, but they participate minimally in their daily activities (Domhoff 2010, 98; *Harvard Law Review* 2002, 1504; Perrucci and Wysong 2008, 166). With the superclass's financial support, the wealthy think tanks can mobilize quickly to promote important interests. For instance, in February 2007, Richard C.J. Somerville and hundreds of other prominent scientists issued a report stressing the costly necessity of rapidly cutting carbon emissions to avoid a devastating impact from global warming. Shortly afterwards the American Enterprise Institute, which receives significant funding from Exxon Mobil, offered a number of environmental experts $10,000 each to write essays criticizing the scientific accuracy of the report (Schorr 2007).

Think tanks often do studies on selected topics for policy-making groups. Top corporate executives who have acquired inside positions in their firms and belong to interlocking directorates are prime candidates to serve on such prominent policy-developing organizations as the Business Roundtable, the Council on Foreign Relations, and the Committee for Economic Development (Useem 1984, 103–05).

The Business Roundtable, which focuses on lobbying for business interests and promoting positive public relations, is an organization with a superclass membership composed of 161 CEOs from major corporations, including the 15 largest. Based on a company's size, dues range from $10,000 to $35,000 a year, producing a budget of at least $3 million a year (Domhoff 2010, 111–13; Dye 2002, 127).

The Council on Foreign Relations, which studies and deliberates about foreign policy issues, is the largest policy-making organization. Its membership of about 3,900 members draws heavily from the superclass, with major executives from large corporations being well represented. While 37 percent of the top 500 industrial companies have at least one officer or director in this organization, 70 percent of the top 100 and 92 percent of the top 25 belong. In addition, 21 of the top 25 banks and 16 of the biggest 25 insurance companies have Council membership.

The Committee for Economic Development, which studies reports about economic issues and then formulates policy, also has a strong superclass representation. Its core membership is about 200 higher-level executives from major corporations, a small number of university presidents, and a few prominent economists and public-administration experts (Domhoff 2010, 104–11; Dye 2002, 124–27).

We have seen how the power elite has profoundly impacted the American economy. For instance, in the 1970s, a carefully organized set of policies promoted reduced taxes, especially for the wealthy, and the steady erosion of the welfare safety net (Jenkins and Eckert 2000). Starting with legislation in the 1980s, the wealthy banking community successfully lobbied for reduced regulation (Atlas and Dreier 2007; Francis 2007). The rich range of financial and social capital available to the power elite gives their members enormous influence, allowing them to move toward and often attain desired outcomes. A hypothetical though currently unheeded alternative would be that these elite individuals would consider themselves the guardians of the national economy, appreciating that it is not only a moral but a practical necessity to focus beyond their group interests and to alleviate various destructive conditions affecting large numbers of less affluent citizens.

An interesting study discussed in the conclusion makes it clear that some wealthy Americans do have a broader agenda than simply enriching themselves. Before addressing that research, however, I summarize the chapter's major conclusions.

Conclusion

The upper class is at the pinnacle of American economic and political ascendancy, best positioned within the class structure to obtain high-quality financial capital and also social capital—in the latter area through social clubs, interlocking directorates, policy-making activities, and class-based lobbying—and then to use these resources to communicate about and to consolidate class interests. In the last two chapters, we have seen that even with superior resources available to them, upper-class members of the corporate world face highly competitive, even fierce challenges to success—in reaching and staying on top of the corporate ladder, in satisfying demanding stockholders, or in surviving in businesses like the major media where takeovers are often imminent.

Upper-class families are in an advantageous position to raise their children to reproduce their success. Socialization in both home and school is often exacting, imparting valuable cultural capital so that these young people can competently fill prominent roles in society. It is notable that upper-class mothers are often so invested in their children's socialization that in the earlier years many of them personally engage in most of the child-rearing activities. Among other things these mothers want their children to be empowered—an issue featured in a sociological study of millionaires, which provided a detailed look at wealthy Americans' world.

This research, which featured 130 millionaires, with only five possessing less than $5 million, found that the respondents benefited from both the skills and the advantages that came with being rich. To begin, the investigators learned that their research subjects possessed three types of empowerment—temporal, spatial, and psychological—contributing to a strong sense of personal freedom. Table 5.1 mentions two of these types of empowerment as advantages the upper class obtains from financial capital.

Temporal empowerment is the advantage received when wealthy people hire various workers—housekeepers, gardeners, accountants, personal secretaries, investment experts, and others—who spare them various mundane demands most others must face. In addition, millionaires possess spatial empowerment, which means they benefit from such luxuries as chauffeured limousines with tinted glass as well as helicopters and airplanes, permitting them to move about the country and the world with unusual speed and ease (Schervish, Coutsoukis, and Lewis 1994, 3–5). In the twenty-first century, multi-millionaires and billionaires have been buying large, long-haul airliners designed for 300 to 400 passengers but reconfigured for carrying no more than a couple of dozen people and sometimes also Rolls Royces and racehorses. One observer noted that these consumers often take a dynamic approach, "starting out, for example, with a Boeing 737 and eventually moving up—the next best thing is the Boeing 787 Dreamliner, which lists for about $150 million and up" (Sharkey 2006, C1).

Unlike the other two types, psychological empowerment is not unique to the wealthy. Two phases of psychological empowerment exist:

- Individuals in question are confident, believing they are both capable of becoming wealthy and are entitled to do so. These people downplay a sense of risk as they move from a safe situation, say salaried work, to independent, self-directed entrepreneurial activity.
- Future millionaires look inward, evaluating their behavior, and focus on developing an efficacious approach that will ensure the accomplishment of their goals (Schervish, Coutsoukis, and Lewis 1994, 5–6).

One multi-millionaire, who made his fortune as an appliance distributor, appeared to have both of the phases in mind when he said, "I've eliminated three words from my vocabulary: 'If' and 'I wish.' Most people who use those words are losers" (Schervish, Coutsoukis, and Lewis 1994, 5–6). Respondents in this research often emphasized individual achievement, but they readily sought help when it proved useful.

Such individuals were likely to display what this research team called **hypergamy**—the ability to transcend normal rules and restrictions. For instance, a real-estate magnate indicated that wealth allowed him to cut through red tape and other barriers. This man explained, "I can pick up the phone and call a congressman who's heard my name and I can have the impact of one million votes with a phone call" (Schervish, Coutsoukis, and Lewis 1994, 8).

Hypergamy involves the use of social capital, specifically the exploitation of political or business connections. One real-estate and pension-management mogul asserted, "If I want to call a federal senator right now, I just pick up the phone and he'll f---ing take my call 'cause I give them money 'cause they're whores [laughter], they're whores" (Schervish, Coutsoukis, and Lewis 1994, 264).

While some superclass members might be contemptuous of the politicians they subsidize, they continue to contribute to them. The potential for corruption is ever-present. Focusing on corporate leaders' contributions to elected officials, a political economist observed, "Politicians may seek popular support by responding to public outrage, but they do not bite the hand that feeds them. Since pro-business policies are necessary, much is off-limits for legislative debate" (Tabb 2007, 39). Therein lies a major problem for the curtailment of social inequality. If the superclass uses its financial and social capital manage to solidify and advance its agenda with elected politicians, how can the other classes with less money and access effectively promote their interests with politicians on such inequality-related topics as welfare subsidy, military spending, tax reform, or big-business regulation?

Finally since the superclass is a particularly powerful leadership group, one might evaluate the kind of role model it provides. In the past two chapters, a pair of major self-interested themes have emerged: that through public-policy lobbying, superclass individuals have relentlessly pushed for increasing their already mammoth piece of the wealth/income pie; and that the corporate component of the class has focused on short-term profits and downplayed or ignored businesses' long-term healthy growth. What impact do such priorities have on the American people?

Key Terms in the Glossary

Conspicuous consumption *125*
Corporate community *123*
Family office *137*

Hypergamy *143*
Interlocking directorate *123*

Discussion Topics

1. Evaluate this statement: It seems reasonable to conclude that the earliest rich Americans lived by a strict moral code.
2. Examine three ways that the federal government provides wealthfare to top corporations.
3. What are major differences between the old rich and the new rich?
4. Besides financial support how do wealthy families help their children to be successful?

5. Why did G. William Domhoff describe prominent boarding schools as "the lynchpins in the upper-class educational system"?
6. Analyze the role that social clubs play in rich people's lives, distinguishing between the upper class and the superclass.
7. What are important traits that top corporate executives need to possess?
8. Develop this idea: Power-elite members tend to associate and work with individuals sharing similar traits and outlooks.

Research Subjects

1. Write about the old rich versus the new rich, discussing their contrasting outlooks and priorities and locating outside case-study material that differentiates between the two types of wealthy people.

2. Analyze this thesis: Upper-class education clearly illustrates the concept of social reproduction. Obtain information from various sources extending from preschool programs through college and even postgraduate education.

3. Develop a short paper indicating whether or not interlocking directorates truly contribute to coherent power-elite policies. Use G. William Domhoff's *Who Rules America?: Power, Politics, and Social Change* and various other sources, including those mentioned in the chapter.

4. Choose a major CEO and research him/her, providing detailed information about his/her rise to the top and style of management. In addition, indicate whether this individual appears to belong to the power elite, supplying detail to support the conclusion.

5. Focus on power-elite policy formation, choosing any significant issue, especially those cited in the last two chapters, and indicate how the superclass input of money and power affects the activities of groups involved in the process.

Informative Websites

Learn about the Social Register (http://www .socialregisteronline.com/contact/). The site includes a brief history of the organization and (in "Frequently Asked Questions") the necessary steps to apply for membership. Good luck!

This site supplies information about the 25 corporations which have been the largest recipients of federal funding for their participation in the Iraq War. (http://businesspundit.com/ the-25-most-vicious-iraq-war-pr…)

This website provides a substantive introduction to Phillips Academy Exeter, one of the most renowned prep schools. (http://www.exeter .edu/about_us/about_us.aspx).

Historically Yale (http://www.yale.edu/) and Harvard (http://www.harvard.edu/) have been the top choices for upper-class college education.

While this chapter has referred to the power elite as "the invisible empire," many of the prominent organizations within it are highly visible and willing, even eager, to discuss their public activities. A case in point is the Business Roundtable (http://www.business roundtable.org/about), which played a central role in the neoconservative movement in the 1970s and continues to be a major participant in policy development.

Bibliography

Aldrich, Nelson W., Jr. 1988. *The Mythology of America's Upper Class*. New York: Alfred A. Knopf.

Allen, Michael Patrick. 1987. *The Founding Fortunes: A New Anatomy of the Super-Rich Families in America*. New York: E.P. Dutton.

Anderson, Jenny. 2008. "Wall Street Winners Get Billion-Dollar Paydays." *New York Times* (April 18): A1+.

Baltzell, E. Digby. 1989. *Philadelphia Gentlemen: The Making of a National Upper Class*, 2nd ed. New Brunswick, NJ: Transaction Publishers.

Becht, Marco, and J. Bradford DeLong. 2002. "One Boardroom Fits All?" *Foreign Policy* 131 (July/August): 88–89.

Becht, Marco, and J. Bradford DeLong. 2005. "Why Has There Been So Little Block Holding in America?" pp. 613–66 in Randall Morck (ed.), *A History of Corporate Governance around the World: Family Business Groups to Professional Managers*. Chicago: University of Chicago Press.

Beebe, Lucius. 2009. *The Big Spenders: The Epic Story of the Rich Rich, the Grandees of America and the Magnificoes, and How They Spend Their Fortunes*. Mount Jackson, VA: Axios Press.

Brooks, Arthur C. 2007. "What's Wrong with Billionaires?" *Wall Street Journal* (March 19): A13.

Burris, Val. 2000. "The Myth of Old Money Liberalism: The Politics of the *Forbes* 400

Richest Americans." *Social Problems* 47: 360–78.

Burris, Val. 2005. "Interlocking Directorates and Political Cohesion among Corporate Elites." *American Journal of Sociology* 111 (July): 249–83.

Cockburn, Alexander. 2001. "Commentary; Redwoods; Tutus and Power; They Meet, They Frolic and They Plot How to Run the Planet." *Los Angeles Times* (June 21): B15.

Dalzell, Robert F., Jr. 2003. "Book Review." *Journal of American History* 90 (June): 220–21.

Domhoff, G. William. 2010. *Who Rules America? Power, Politics, & Social Change*, 6th ed. New York: McGraw-Hill.

Dye, Thomas R. 2002. *Who's Running America? The Bush Restoration*, 7th ed. Upper Saddle River, NJ: Prentice-Hall.

Fabrikant, Geraldine. 2005. "Richest Are Leaving Even the Rich Behind." *New York Times* (June 5): 1+.

Francis, David R. 2007. "Government Regulation Stages a Comeback." *Christian Scientist Monitor* (September 10): 14.

Frank, Robert. 2004. "Rich, Richer, Richest: Private Banks' Class System; Firms Create Tiers of Service to Court the Super-Wealthy; What You Get for $100,000." *Wall Street Journal* (September 8): D1.

Gilbert, Dennis. 2011. *The American Class Structure in the Age of Growing Inequality*, 8th ed. Thousand Oaks, CA: Pine Forge Press.

Gilfoyle, Timothy J. 2002. "Making an American Upper Class." *American History* 30 (June): 279–87.

Global 500. 2009. "Global 500: Our Ranking of the World's Largest Corporations." *CNNMoney. com.* http://money.cnn.com/magazines/fortune/global500/2009/full_list/.

Golden, Daniel. 2007. *The Price of Admission: How America's Ruling Class Buys Its Way into Elite Colleges: And Who Gets Left Outside the Gates*. New York: Three Rivers Press.

Harvard Law Review. 2002. "The Political Activity of Think Tanks: The Case for Mandatory Contributor Disclosure." 115 (March): 1502–24.

Henwood, Doug. 2008. "Our Gilded Age." *Nation* 286 (June 30): 14+.

Herman, Edward S. 1981. *Corporate Control, Corporate Power*. New York: Cambridge University Press.

Hernandez, Raymond, and Stephen Labaton. 2007. "In Opposing Tax Plan, Schumer Supports Wall Street over Party." *New York Times* (July 30): A1+.

Howard, Adam. 2008. *Learning Privilege: Lessons of Power and Identity in Affluent Schooling*. New York: Routledge.

Hu, Winnie. 2007. "More Than a Meal Plan." *New York Times* (July 29): Section 4A, p. 22.

Ignatius, David. 2007. "A Backlash against Billionaires." *Washington Post* (July 19): A19.

Jackall, Robert. 2010. *Moral Mazes: The World of Corporate Managers,* 2nd ed. New York: Oxford University Press.

Jenkins, J. Craig, and Craig Eckert. 2000. "The Right Turn in Economic Policy: Business Elites and the New Conservative Economics." *Sociological Form* 15 (June): 307–38.

Josephson, Matthew. 1962. *The Great American Capitalists, 1861–1901*. New York: Harcourt, Brace, and World.

Journal of Blacks in Higher Education. 2003. "Young Blacks at the Nation's Highest-Ranked Private Boarding Schools." (Autumn): 56–59.

Karabel, Jerome. 2005. *The Chosen: The Hidden History of Admission and Exclusion at Harvard, Yale, and Princeton*. Boston: Houghton Mifflin Company.

Keister, Lisa A. 2005. *Getting Rich: America's New Rich and How They Got That Way*. New York: Cambridge University Press.

Kendall, Diana. 2002. *The Power of Good Deeds: Privileged Women and the Social Reproduction of the Upper Class*. Lanham, MD: Rowman & Littlefield..

Kendall, Diana. 2005. *Framing Class: Media Representations of Wealth and Poverty in America*. Lanham, MD: Rowman & Littlefield.

Krugman, Paul. 2007. "Hired Gun Fetish." *New York Times* (September 28): A29.

Krugman, Paul. 2008. "Bad Cow Disease." *New York Times* (June 13): A29.

Lapham, Lewis H. 1988. *Money and Class in America: Notes and Observations on Our Civil Religion*. New York: Weidenfeld & Nicolson.

Leonhardt, David, and Geraldine Fabrikant. 2009. "After 30-Year Run, Rise of the Super-Rich Hits a Sobering Wall." *New York Times* (August 21): A1+.

Lorien, Jasny. 2006. "Networks of Political Donations: A Study of Interlocking Directorates."

American Sociological Association annual meeting. pp. 1–29.

McChesny, Robert. 1999. *Rich Media, Poor Democracy*. Urbana: University of Illinois Press.

Ostrander, Susan A. 1984. *Women of the Upper Class*. Philadelphia: Temple University Press.

Perrucci, Robert, and Earl Wysong. 2008. *The New Class Society: Goodbye American Dream?* 3rd ed. Lanham, MD: Rowman & Littlefield.

Pessen, Edward. 1990. *Riches, Class, and Power: America before the Civil War*, 2nd ed. New Brunswick, NJ: Transaction Publishers.

Phillips, Kevin. 2002. *Wealth and Democracy: A Political History of the American Rich*. New York: Broadway Books.

Powell, Arthur G. 1996. *Lessons from Privilege: The American Prep School Tradition*. Cambridge, MA: Harvard University Press.

Rockefeller, David. 2002. *Memoirs*. New York: Random House.

Rothkopf, David. 2009. *Superclass: The Global Power Elite and the World They Are Making*. New York: Farrar, Straus and Giroux.

Schervish, Paul G., Platon E. Coutsoukis, and Ethan Lewis. 1994. *Gospels of Wealth: How the Rich Portray Their Lives*. Westport, CT: Praeger.

Schorr, Daniel. 2007. "What the World Needs Now Is to Reduce Carbon Emissions; In the US, States May Lead the Way in Proposing Tougher Standards." *Christian Science Monitor* (February 9): 9.

Sharkey, Joe. 2006. "For the Super-Rich, It's Time to Upgrade the Old Jumbo Jet." *New York Times* (October 17): C1.

Siegel, Paul. 2009. "Multinational Tax Loopholes." http://www.learningfountain.com/blog/archives/00001153.htm.

Social Register Association. 2008. "Welcome to the Official Website of the Social Register Association." http://www.socialregisteronline.com/.

Soltow, Lee. 1989. *Men and Wealth in the United States, 1850–1870*. New Haven: Yale University Press.

SourceWatch. 2007. "Telecommunications Act of 1996." http://www.sourcewatch.org/index.php?title=Telecommunications_Act_of_1996.

Story, Louise. 2009. "Smiling through a Down Year: Top 25 Hedge Fund Managers Made $11.6 Billion in 2008." *New York Times* (March 25): B1+.

Tabb, William K. 2007. "The Power of the Rich," pp. 35–45 in Michael D. Yates (ed.), *More Unequal: Aspects of Class in the United States*. New York: Monthly Review Press.

Useem, Michael. 1984. *The Inner Circle: Large Corporations and the Rise of Business Political Activity in the U.S. and U.K*. New York: Oxford University Press.

Van der Galien, Michael. 2009. "67% Oppose Bailout Plan for General Motors." *Poli Gazette* (May 31). http://www.poligazette.com/2009/05/31/67-oppose-bailout-plan…

Vaznis, James. 2006. "Costly Boarding Schools Offer More Aid." *Boston Globe* (April 18): B1.

Veblen, Thorstein. 1899. *The Theory of the Leisure Class*. New York: MacMillan.

Viser, Matt. 2007. "No Ordinary Museum." *Boston Globe* (March 18): M11.

Wecter, Dixon. 1937. *The Saga of American Society: A Record of Social Aspiration, 1607–1937*. New York: Charles Scribner's Sons.

Westphal, James D., and Edward J. Zajac. 1995. "Who Shall Govern? CEO/Board Power, Demographic Similarity, and New Director Selection." *Administrative Science Quarterly* 40 (March): 60–83.

Wolff, Tobias. 1989 *This Boy's Life: A Memoir*. New York: Harper & Row.

Zepezauer, Mark. 2004. *Take the Rich Off Welfare*. Cambridge: South End Press.

CHAPTER 6

The Badly Besieged Middle Class

Testifying before the Senate Finance Committee, Harvard law professor Elizabeth Warren characterized the recent financial plight of many middle-class Americans. Warren stated that traditionally the poor was the only economically challenged class. Nowadays, however, "[t]he division is between those who are prospering and those who are struggling, and much of the middle class is now on the struggling side" (Warren 2007). In fact, many of those middle-class people who are struggling are professionals, college graduates, and sometimes, individuals with advanced degrees (Mooney 2008, 5).

Throughout its history the American middle class has been intensely involved in seeking economic success. Within the upcoming sections—about the history of the middle class; the two middle classes; the impact provided by families, schools, and social networks; and the analysis of the middle-class economic world—it is apparent that middle-class people have persistently pursued social mobility, seeking to defy the forces of social reproduction. To begin, the history of the middle class emphatically demonstrates that trend.

THE EMERGENCE OF THE MIDDLE CLASS

Early visitors to the United States commented on Americans' love of movement. In 1815 while traveling widely, Morris Birkbeck, an Englishman, observed a steady stream of stage coaches, wagons, and horseback riders, concluding "you have before you a scene of bustle and business, extending over a space of three hundred miles, which is truly wonderful" (Birkbeck 1818, 35–36). Some of the activity involved families' migration westward to buy farmland. In a country which was 80 percent rural, family farming was the dominant occupation. At the turn of the nineteenth century, that trend persisted. The annual sale of western lands vaulted from a hundred thousand acres in the 1790s to five times that figure after Thomas Jefferson in 1804 completed the Louisiana Purchase, which added a huge landmass to the continental United States (Appleby 2001, 38).

In the 1830s about 80 percent of people owned the property on which they worked. Upward mobility was prevalent, with half the men becoming elite businessmen in the first 50 years of the nineteenth century coming from a poor or working-class background. It was an open era, at least for men of northern European origin. Abraham Lincoln, a devotee of the work ethic, was optimistic about people's prospects. He declared, "Property is the fruit of labor... that some should be rich shows that others may become rich, and hence is just encouragement to industry and enterprise" (Mills 1956, 8).

During this era, however, many middle-class individuals were neither rich nor likely to become so. Besides owning farms, they also ran modest businesses—"handicrafters and tradesmen of small but independent means" (Mills 1956, 5). Independence, C. Wright Mills emphasized, was a key feature in men's work lives, but for many a change occurred even before the onset of industrialization—when the growth and spread of railroads established national markets controlled by merchant capitalists and forced formerly independent farmers or tradesmen to work for those capitalists (Mills 1956, 21).

The first half of the nineteenth century was a time of explosive commercial growth, and it showed in middle-class businessmen's behavior. During this era Europeans complained of "the drawn faces and frantic busyness of . . . Americans . . . and the universal preoccupation with what Charles Dickens damned as the 'almighty dollar'" (Rodgers 1978, 5). Invariably Europeans commented on Americans' disinterest in leisure and preoccupation with work. Francis Grund, a Viennese immigrant, who had spent 10 years living in Boston, indicated that "it is as if all America were but one gigantic workshop, over the entrance of which there is the blazing inscription, 'No admission here except on business'" (Rodgers 1978, 6).

During this era middle-class men found themselves released from an earlier personal standard featuring rootedness in the community. Now the focus was on "self," and ministers, businessmen, lawyers, and other prominent spokesmen emphasized that to be successful in this open, expanding economy they should relentlessly seek self-improvement, recognizing that hard work was more important than talent in attaining wealth and prominence (Rotundo 1983, 25).

Employed outside the home and preoccupied with their own development, middle-class men were less involved with the family than their eighteenth-century counterparts, who were usually home-centered patriarchal figures in control of most domestic activities, even childrearing (Illick 2002, 57–58). As the Industrial Age arrived, middle-class women became the dominant figures in domestic life (Brady 1991, 85–86; Rotundo 1983, 30).

Industry's Impact on the Middle Class

The development of American industry profoundly affected middle-class work and family life. C. Wright Mills estimated that in the early 1800s just as mercantile capitalism was underway, 80 percent of workers were self-employed businessmen. By 1870 when industrial capitalism was well established, the figure had dropped to 33 percent (Mills 1956, 63). At the dawn of the twentieth century, the growth of American business promoted the expansion of various middle-class jobs—for clerks, salespeople, managers, and even professionals (Moskowitz 2001, 173).

Growing up in a self-employment tradition, however, men were reluctant to join companies and work for others. The managerial challenge was to convince recent college graduates entering the business world that employment in a commercial bureaucracy was not selling out a cultural ideal that emphasized economic independence. Whether in Atlanta, Chicago, or Los Angeles, company recruiters told their best prospects that modern business represented a successful trade-off among desires for security, autonomy, and financial success (Davis 2001, 203–04). Recruiters asserted that working for a successful corporation ambitious young men had a chance to be gainfully employed for life, obtaining promotion after promotion and riding ever upward with the company's advancement.

The company ladder was an important factor in workers' recruitment. All employees, according to the prevailing claim, had a chance to move up the rungs from lowly to high positions. Most business leaders believed that effective promotion systems were good for their companies, and they discussed them extensively in executive circles. Managers made most promotions from within the company, agreeing, as a 1919 study indicated, that businesses "which do not adopt the policy of making promotions from the inside cannot hope to maintain a force of ambitious capable workers" (Davis 2001, 207). As a 1950s sociological analysis indicated, such a system encouraged middle-class job holders' unwavering loyalty to their employers, committing themselves to become "organization men." The prevailing belief was that an employee should stick with one company—that individuals looking for improved opportunities elsewhere were not serving their current businesses well (Whyte 1956).

Compared to office employees, small business owners faced more challenges. To stay independent and to protect their enterprises, they recognized that the best strategy was to form associations and agreements that regulated prices, wages, and production and that their common interests encouraged them to enforce those rules with fines, boycotts, and sometimes even violence. Many occupational groups formed associations. At the turn of the twentieth century in Chicago, for instance, some of the small-business people with active associations were plumbers, carpenters, cooks, drapers, jewelers, liquor dealers, masons, tailors, retail druggists, and undertakers (Cohen 2001, 195–96). While some of these businesses were successful, many were not. Owners often found themselves either going bankrupt or forced to do wage work to keep their enterprises afloat (Applegate 2001, 110; Beckery 2001, 288).

During the nineteenth century, the middle-class economic world changed considerably, and the family also altered, becoming increasingly focused on preparing its members for their part in the expanding industrial setting. Experts in both England and the United States stressed the importance of the stay-at-home middle-class mother, who was widely judged more virtuous than her mate. Publishers issued a host of advice books, helping formerly rural families make the transition to city life. In line with the growing trend, the advice books emphasized that the mother, not the father, had the more prominent family role (Brady 1991, 88–89; Illick 2002, 58–59).

The mother was the person best positioned to assume the formidable responsibility of developing her children, who "were now being described as born into the world with minds as blank slates" (Illick 2002, 58). The mother, in short, was supposed to provide the foundational writing on that slate, determining whether or not her children would be successful in life.

Parents, particularly mothers, supplied guidance. Gently but forcefully, middle-class women would teach their children to follow their commands, learning self-control in the process. Children were required to develop a conscience so that their own guilt would monitor them. Since boys spent more time outside the home, the prevailing belief was that they particularly needed the support of a conscience. In fact, middle-class mothers were consistently concerned about preparing boys for the challenges of the industrial work world. It was normally expected that from the age of six, boys would become active, tough, and emotionally restrained, engaging in strenuous physical activity, especially the sports of football and baseball. The expectations for most daughters were that like their mothers they would marry, have a family, and run the household. So girls had the chance to learn from their mothers about their future life—everything from domestic skills to the emotional connections between women. Often daughters expressed regret about parting from their mothers at marriage and requested their presence when they gave birth (Brady 1991, 101; Illick 2002, 62–65).

A key requirement for the middle-class family was the home—intended to be a well protected, comfortable place to live. In the Middle West, municipal leaders, usually local merchants, formed vigilante committees to clean up their municipalities, establishing law-abiding towns and cities where a prosperous middle class led an active, secure social life (Wills 2000, 599–600). A different strategy developed in large eastern cities. To escape the filth, sickness, noise, and crime of urban life, many middle-class families moved to the suburbs. This relocation was expensive, with home buyers required to make a down payment of at least half the purchasing price. Few young people could afford such an amount, and as a result the suburbs of the time displayed a distinctly middle-aged character (Blumin 1989, 275–80).

Through the first three quarters of the twentieth century, the middle class was generally prosperous, except during the Great Depression of the 1930s. In the decades following that economic crisis, the government introduced a number of social programs, including Social Security, unemployment insurance, the GI Bill (providing college payments to returning war veterans), and federal housing loans that offered significant support to middle-class families (Mooney 2008, 1).

However, these government supports were much more available for certain individuals, particularly whites as opposed to blacks. In 1935, with backing from the federal government, the Home Owners Loan Corporation examined real estate in 239 cities, developing "residential security maps," which indicated the level of confidence investors could have in the quality of their investments. The evaluators were particularly concerned about African Americans, invariably giving black neighborhoods the lowest ratings. This initiative helped establish the use of **redlining**, which is the discriminatory practice of refusing to provide mortgage loans or property insurance or only providing them at accelerated rates for reasons not clearly associated with any conventional assessment of risk. The term originated because lenders and insurers actually circled in red the areas they declared off-limits for their services (Doob 2005, 95; Massey and Denton 1993, 51–52). Without housing loans blacks were often greatly disadvantaged in their efforts to move into middle-class neighborhoods. Sociologists Melvin L. Oliver and Thomas M. Shapiro considered this issue part of a much larger government effort, which "[f]rom the first codified decision to enslave African Americans . . . has erected major barriers to black economic self-sufficiency" (Oliver and Shapiro 2006, 260). Chapter 9 provides further information about the impact of discriminatory treatment of blacks in the realm of housing.

Meanwhile in the course of the prosperous twentieth century, many middle-class jobs increased, especially for whites. Between 1910 and 2000, the number of accountants and auditors expanded 13 times; college presidents, professors, and instructors multiplied 12 times; and engineers grew nine times. The number of computer specialists, who only appeared in substantial numbers in the late 1950s, mushroomed 95 times between 1960 and 2000 (Wyatt and Hecker 2006, 42). Figure 6.1 indicates that the upper-middle-class portion of the workforce in the professions and management has increased steadily over time, particularly since 1990.

Until now we have examined the middle class as a single entity, but it can be subdivided.

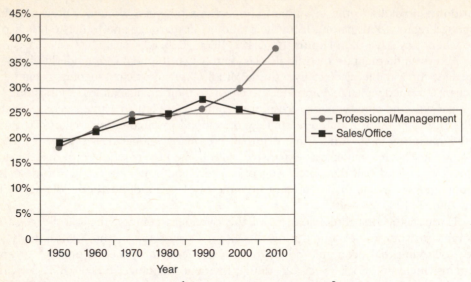

FIGURE 6.1   Middle-Class Occupations'[1] Proportion of the Workforce[2]

[1]In 1950 through 1970, technical workers were a small component of the professional category.
[2]Workers' minimum age was 14 year old in 1950 through 1970 and then rose to 16 years in 1980.

While the proportions of the workforce for both types of middle-class occupations have increased over time, professional/managerial positions have recently risen sharply—from 26 percent in 1990 to 38 percent in 2010.

Sources: Bureau of Labor Statistics. 2001. Table 10. "Employed Persons by Major Occupation, Annual Averages, 1987–2000." *Report of the American Workforce, 2001*. Website: http://www.bls.gov/opub/ rtaw/pdf/table 10.pdf; Bureau of Labor Statistics. 2010. *A-19*. "Employed Persons by Occupation, Sex, and Age." *Current Population Survey*. http://www.blsgov/web/cpseea19.pdf; U.S. Bureau of the Census. 1971. No. 347. "Employed Persons by Major Occupation Group and Sex: 1950 to 1971." *Statistical Abstract of United States: 1971*, 92nd ed. http://www.census.gov/prod/www/abs/statab/1971/-1994 .htm; U.S. Bureau of the Census. 1981. No 675. "Employed Persons by Sex, Race, and Occupation: 1972 and 1980." *Statistical Abstract of the United States: 1981*. http://www.census.gov/prod/www/abs/ statab/1981-1994.htm.

THE TWO MIDDLE CLASSES

Both middle classes appear to share a common set of aspirations, which include home ownership, a car for each adult, a college education for children, health protection, retirement security, and family vacations (U.S. Department of Commerce 2010). Nonetheless the upper-middle class and the middle class (sometimes referred to as the lower-middle class) are fairly different in their characteristics, with the economic dimension serving as a reasonable starting point.

Income and Jobs

While income is a major factor determining whether jobs qualify as middle class, the nature of the work is also relevant. The Bureau of Labor Statistics and other authoritative sources generally consider all white-collar positions middle class, involving professional or semi-professional, administrative, or sales functions.

White-collar job holders are well educated or fairly well educated individuals who perform nonmanual tasks in offices. On the other hand, blue-collars positions reside in the working class. **Blue-collar** job holders have obtained a high-school diploma or less schooling and do manual work, normally receiving an hourly wage. Some white-collar employees such as many secretaries or clerks receive salaries under the middle-class minimum while individuals in the skilled trades such as the majority of plumbers and welders enjoy a solid middle-class income.

Upper-middle-class people, comprising about 14 percent of the population, have a yearly income that averages about $150,000, with a small percentage making considerably more. These affluent individuals, who include lawyers, doctors, or high-level executives, belong to a subcategory which sociologist Dennis Gilbert has called "the working rich," and they can earn hundreds of thousands of dollars a year. They might be specialty physicians such as radiologists or oncologists, partners in elite law firms, or even professors at prominent universities, who can make large sums writing or consulting. They fall into the upper-middle and not the upper class because their incomes derive from professional fees or executive salaries and not from money-producing assets. (Gilbert 2011, 244, 246; Perrucci and Wysong 2008, 26–27). Table 6.1 displays the proportion of the national net worth (wealth plus income) over time for upper-middle-class households.

Occupationally the members of this class work as professionals, high-level managers, and medium-sized business owners (Gilbert 2011, 244, 246). Benefits of their jobs often include autonomy, prestige, and pursuit of a variety of tasks, many or all of which are interesting and even intellectually stimulating.

For physicians, professional development begins in medical school, where the volume of information that must be quickly learned often seems overwhelming. "It's like trying to drink from a fire hose," one student said. "It's impossible to learn everything put before you" (Coombs 1998, 11–12). While in the beginning many students feel overwhelmed, the survivors eventually realize that they must make compromises about how much they learn in order to avoid breaking down from stress or exhaustion (Coombs 1998, 13). To be accepted as doctors, aspirants must demonstrate a working knowledge of the

TABLE 6.1 Upper-Middle-Class Households' Percentage of Total Net Worth over Time

Year	Net worth holders in the 2–20 percentiles
1983	47.5%
1989	46.2%
1992	46.6%
1995	45.4%
1998	45.3%
2001	51%
2004	50.3%
2007	50.5%

Data on the 19 percent of households directly following the top 1 percent, a slightly larger segment than the upper-middle class, indicated a stable, even slightly increasing proportion of the total net worth over time.

Source: Edward N. Wolff. 2010. "Recent Trends in Household Wealth in the United States: Rising Debt and the Middle-Class Squeeze—an Update to 2007." The Levy Economic Institute. http://www.levy.org/pubs/wp_589.pdf.

massive field of medicine. Throughout their training, especially during the (third) clinical year, students try to avoid public mistakes and blunders—clinicians' criticism can be quick and embarrassing—and appear to be dignified, competent doctors (Conrad 1988).

Survey data indicate that physicians are fairly happy with their work. In fact, one study revealed that over 80 percent of doctors with direct patient-care responsibilities were content with their careers (Landon 2004). Research with 6,590 physicians engaged in 42 specialty areas indicated sharp differences in satisfaction levels. In particular, individuals in pediatric specialties claimed the greatest satisfaction while those involved in various types of surgery expressed the least (Finney 2009; Leigh, Tancredi, and Kravitz 2009).

Lawyers, like physicians, have distinct standards for what qualifies as professional expertise. Research on lawyers indicates that two principal factors determine how prestigious they consider a colleague's work:

- First, the nature of the activities, whether they are simple and accessible such as the preparation of standard-form wills or highly specialized and intellectually stimulating such as a complicated patent application or a high-profile criminal trial
- Second, the type of clients, whether they represent large, prominent organizations or wealthy clients, or nonaffluent individuals or families (Sandefur 2001).

The American Bar Association's survey of 800 lawyers found that 55 percent were satisfied with their careers. However, many highlighted significant problems, including long hours, sharply rising costs for expert witnesses, and a decline in civility among lawyers (Kane 2008; Ward 2007).

In spite of the economic downturn, high-level managers also appear satisfied with their work. A 2009 survey of 3,187 business leaders averaging $206,000 per year found that 70 percent were satisfied or very satisfied with their jobs, up from 61 percent in 2008 and 47 percent in 2006. Individuals' specialities made a significant difference, with marketing showing the highest rating and sales the lowest. The most prominent factors adversely affecting these executives' job evaluations were limited advancement opportunities, insufficient compensation, and deficient challenge and opportunity for growth (Mayclim 2009).

Big business has recognized the necessity for expertise among high-level managers. In recent years as finance, taxation, and governmental regulation have become increasingly important challenges facing large corporations, management prospects have increasingly sought advanced degrees in economics, accounting, or the law (Dye 2002, 26). Whether in management or in the professions, specialty training literally pays off. The highest paying occupations include business executives, physician specialists, and dental specialists, who normally have obtained extensive postgraduate education (Bureau of Labor Statistics 2008a).

While upper-middle-class work has always been demanding and exacting, the job setting has steadily deteriorated for many people in recent decades. Respondents in a study of 250 managers in eight large industrial plants spoke emotionally about the transformation that had taken place in their companies, where in the era of downsizing a "community of purpose" has replaced the previous "community of loyalty." One manager explained, "Loyalty comes with trust and believing, and this has been cast out across the whole company as being not the way to run things" (Heckscher 1995, 8).

The declining economy has posed various problems for young upper-middle-class individuals. Coming out of college, they often confront the work world with a substantial, five-figure student loan debt. On the job, employees are likely to experience layoffs, salary freezes, long hours, and limited employer loyalty. Financial constraint means that now, unlike several decades ago, these people find it impossible to support the combined costs of children, a house, medical coverage, and retirement savings that young upper-middle-class individuals previously could maintain without severe difficulty. In fact, many young professionals cannot visualize retiring, believing they cannot possibly save enough to cover both living and medical expenses for old age (Mooney 2008, 16–17).

Middle-class individuals, who are in lower-paying positions than their upper-middle-class counterparts, face similar prospects. They represent about 30 percent of the population and average about $70,000 a year; their jobs include low-level managers, semiprofessionals such as the police, nurses, teachers, small-business owners, foremen, clerks and secretaries, and nonretail salespeople like insurance or real-estate agents (Gilbert 2011, 244, 246–47).

These jobs are less prestigious than upper-middle-class positions, and as a result the incumbents are less authoritative, sometimes encountering difficult relations with superiors or members of the public or facing troublesome conditions at work. It is hardly surprising that these middle-class employees tend to have extensive complaints about their jobs.

Police officers are a case in point. A well researched overview of American police work found more than 30 stress factors on the job, including incompetent or overly demanding supervision, an absence or shortage of career development opportunities, distorted and unfavorable press accounts, extensive criticism from both minority and majority citizens, and the biological and psychological stresses of frequent shift changes (Miller and Braswell 2002, 125–29; Rodgers 2006, 242–45). Surveys involving police officers' job satisfaction in various regions show contrasting results. While about 80 percent of police officers in Washington, DC, and Lafayette, Louisiana, were generally satisfied with their employment, only 45 percent in Detroit and 58 percent throughout Oklahoma were positive about it (Carlan 2007).

Nurses also show varied contentment with their positions. A national survey of hospital nurses indicated that the type of location influenced job satisfaction. Individuals in maternal/newborn and pediatric units, for instance, tended to be more positive about work than their colleagues in medical/surgical and emergency settings. Overall, nurses were content with their peer interactions and professional-development opportunities and were displeased with their decision-making roles and pay. In addition, they were moderately satisfied with their level of autonomy and relations with physicians (*Nursing* 2005; *RN* 2005). A continuous irritant concerned the control imposed by doctors, who, according to a pair of specialists, have maintained "a medical monopoly" (Group and Roberts 2001, 475).

Teachers also display varied job satisfaction, which is affected by such school-site factors as the amount of support from their principals and colleagues, the size of workloads, and the availability of both interesting, informative courses to teach and effective classroom resources. Those without positive conditions are likely to leave teaching. In the first three years, 22 percent of new teachers quit their jobs (Gulwadi 2006; Johnson and Birkeland 2003). Ranya, for instance, a middle-aged Asian American woman, found herself in a suburban high school where she looked forward to teaching science. However, she discovered that nobody had ordered books or supplies, and so she was forced to go five weeks without them. Furthermore her courses were very hard to teach well, containing students of diverse backgrounds and abilities who were largely taking the course as a requirement. Before accepting the job, Ranya had told administrators that because she was new to teaching, she would need experienced colleagues' help. She received none, even after asking several colleagues for assistance. The researchers concluded that considering that since "she had no prior experience, little preparation, a challenging teaching assignment, minimal collegial support, and no books or supplies for the first six weeks of school, it is hardly surprising that Ranya decided to leave teaching" (Johnson and Birkeland 2003, 596).

While the jobs in the two middle classes vary substantively, the income trends have been quite similar. The U.S. Census Bureau found that both upper-middle-class positions in management and the professions and middle-class jobs in sales and administrative support rose in yearly income from the early 1980s to 2000. At that juncture they started to decline (U.S. Census Bureau; 2007a; U.S. Census Bureau 2007b), becoming another source of stress for middle-class workers.

Although class is a major factor impacting people's lives, others are simultaneously influential. Feminist researchers have been particularly attuned to this reality, and an important concept, which receives extensive attention in Chapter 10, should be mentioned. **Intersectionality** is the recognition that a woman's oppressions, limitations, and opportunities result from the combined impact of two or more influential statuses—in particular, her gender, race, class, age, and sexual preference (Barvosa 2008, 76–77; Dill, McLaughlin, and Nieves 2007, 629; Lengermann and Niebrugge 2008, 353; Mullings and Schulz 2006, 4–5). For instance, a variety of studies indicated that while physicians are well-paid overall, men are generally better paid that women—that the major factor producing the difference is women's childcare duties, which cut both their hours and their earnings. With each additional child, male doctors' income increased, apparently unaffected by childcare, while a new child meant a loss for their female counterparts. One investigation concluded that women physicians received an 11 percent loss in income for being married, a 14 percent decline for having one child, and a 22 percent loss for two or more children (Bashaw and Heywood 2001; Kehrer 1976; Sasser 2005). This is only one of innumerable illustrations involving middle-class occupational groups, showing that gender and other factors can significantly impact people's degree of success.

Table 6.2 provides data about middle-class income. Besides income and jobs, families and schooling in the two classes appear to be distinctly different.

Families and Education

When researchers mention middle-class studies on families, they usually are referring to upper-middle-class respondents. For instance, one review of investigations involving young children in the 1990s indicated that the majority of the many studies on the attachment between parents, particularly mothers and their children, has involved upper-middle-class families (Demo and Cox 2000, 879). Why other middle-class subjects receive little attention was not explained. It might be that, whether conscious or not, researchers tend to merge the lower-middle class with the working class. For instance, in one study the researcher described his working-class respondents as filling a number of "blue-collar/lower-white-collar occupations" (Gorman 2000, 699). That appears to be a clear blending of the two classes, with the middle-class component essentially absorbed. In another study the researchers indicated that their middle-class families contained at least

TABLE 6.2 Income Shares for Portions of the Middle Class over Time

Year	Top 2 to 10 percent	Top 2 to 25 percent
1980	23.7%	48.2%
1985	23.7	48
1990	28.8	52.1
1995	25.6	48.8
2000	25.2	46.3
2007	25.2	45.9

These data demonstrate that since about 1990 the top 2 to 10 percent of earners, who represent the majority of upper-middle-class workers, and the top 2 to 25 percent of job holders, who comprise over half the overall middle class, have generally obtained a declining share of the total income.

Source: Gerald Prante. 2009. "Summary of Latest Federal Individual Income Tax Data." *The Tax Foundation: Summary of Latest Individual Income Tax Data.* http://www.taxfoundation.org/publications/show/250/html.

one member who was a manager or possessed some highly credentialed skill (Horvat, Weininger, and Lareau 2003, 326). Once again, the lower segment of the middle class appeared to be shut out. While data involving families and schooling in the two middle classes seems skewed toward the upper-middle-class, the research is informative.

In particular, children growing up in upper-middle-class families have advantages in access to capital over other, less elevated middle-class peers: better financial resources to spend on education, housing, and a various other items; higher-quality human capital as the upcoming discussion on education indicates; more effective social capital involving family and community connections; and better cultural capital because parents' education and middle-class experience lead to more effective guidance.

Schooling is a prime advantage. Upper-middle-class individuals are usually college-educated and often have advanced degrees. In fact, as we noted earlier, some fields put a premium on specialty training—for instance, in medicine where radiologists and oncologists earn twice as much as less specialized family physicians (Perrucci and Wysong 2008, 26) and in business where future managers recognize that advanced degrees in finance, taxation, and government regulation will help promote their advancement through the ranks (Dye 2002, 26).

College graduation is a prerequisite of the upper-middle class. A study of American children born between 1966 and 1970 found that when the respondents were divided into four income segments, those in the most affluent quarter, a broad approximation of upper-middle-class families, represented about 50 percent of all college graduates (Haveman and Smeeding 2006). These individuals have a distinct earning advantage. For instance, in 1979 income for college graduates was 31 percent higher than the income of people who had not completed college. By 1993 that difference had become 53 percent (Weir 2002, 192). Using 2009 data, Figure 6.2 indicates the widely ranging income differences for Americans with varying amounts of schooling. Clearly college graduation and postgraduate education contribute significantly to earnings.

However, simply graduating from college does not assure that individuals will obtain good-paying jobs. A national survey of college graduates indicated that the key to gaining such positions has been **functional literacy**—the capacity to use basic skills in reading, math, and the interpretation of documents in work situations. College graduates

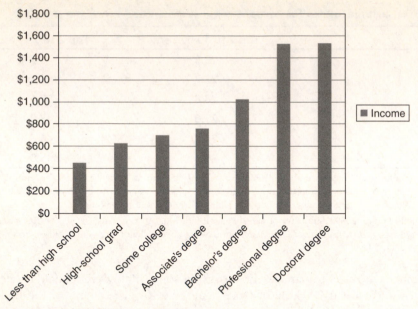

FIGURE 6.2   Amount of Education and Weekly Income

Clearly education pays, most emphatically for upper-middle-class individuals with advanced degrees.

Source: Bureau of Labor Statistics. 2010. "Education Pays." http://www.bls.gov/emp/ep_chart_001.htm.

who scored higher on a functional literacy test tended to have good-paying jobs where a college degree was the standard; those scoring lower on the test ended up with positions requiring only a high-school diploma (Pryor and Schaffer 1997).

Middle-class people, who are less well educated than upper-middle-class individuals, are usually high-school graduates, sometimes attend college, and in some instances graduate from college (Gilbert 2011, 246–47). Getting the degree can be difficult to accomplish. A national survey found that about 75 percent of students enrolled in community colleges expected to transfer to a four-year institution. Within five years only 17 percent who had entered community college in the mid-1990s actually made the switch. With college being expensive and representing a financial sacrifice, many hard-pressed adults find it difficult or impossible to commit to higher education. In 1995 Andy Blevins dropped out of college after his freshman year and worked in a supermarket, eventually becoming a produce buyer. It was interesting work, paid well, and provided health benefits and a 401(k) retirement plan. Such positions usually go to someone with a four-year college degree. In spite of possessing the job, however, Blevins regretted dropping out of college. He felt like he was "on thin ice." Everything could slip away if he lost his position. What kind of job could he expect to get—a guy without a college degree? (Leonhardt 2005, A14).

The Ecology of Class

Besides the advantages already described, upper-middle-class individuals are favored in another area—the **ecology of class**, the largely unrecognized or acknowledged impact that residential or occupational location has on quality of life. Because of higher income as well as political influence, upper-middle-class individuals live and work in areas that often have high-quality schools, lower crime, and effective municipal services (such as garbage pick-up, road repair, library services, or healthcare). The ecology of class is readily apparent in the American public-education system, where district property tax plays a major role in school funding, creating financial inequalities between poor and affluent school districts not found in most other postindustrial nations, which distribute school funding at the federal level. In the 1960s James Bryant Conant, the former president of Harvard, described the American system as one fostering "inequality of opportunity" and advocated that in the name of equal opportunity, the states and to a lesser extent the federal government should assume the responsibility for public-school funding (Conant 1967). Like many in his wake, Conant recognized that the American method of public-school funding has been a highly efficient mechanism for promoting social reproduction. Middle-class, especially upper-middle-class families, literally pay the price for expensive housing so that their children's schooling is high-quality.

In other situations the impact of the ecology of class can be instantly life-altering. The quality of a hospital's services generally reflects the area in which it is located. Thus when upper-middle-class architect Jean Miele had a heart attack after lunch while working in midtown Manhattan, the emergency medical technician in the ambulance gave him the choice of two nearby hospitals, both of which were licensed to perform the latest emergency cardiac care. He chose Tisch Hospital, and within two hours an experienced

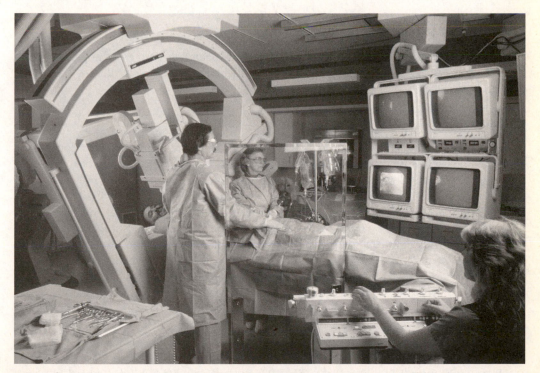

It is probable that the patient receiving this angioplasty treatment is middle-class.

cardiologist had performed angioplasty, reopening a closed artery and implanting a stent to keep it that way. Two days later Miele returned home; thanks to quick, competent treatment damage to his heart was minimal.

For Will Wilson, a transportation coordinator for an electricity company living in a lower-middle-class area, treatment was less effective. Wilson's heart attack occurred four days before Miele's while he was in his apartment. Wilson also had a choice of two nearby hospitals, but in his less affluent, middle-class area, neither was licensed to perform angioplasty. He picked Brooklyn Hospital, where a doctor gave him a drug to break up the clot blocking the artery. It was unsuccessful. The next morning Wilson was sent to a hospital in Manhattan where angioplasty was performed. The doctor admitted that Wilson would have been better off if the procedure had been done sooner. After five days Wilson returned home.

A year later Jean Miele had recovered. He was exercising regularly, had lost weight, and had effectively low critical measurements for recovering heart-attack patients—blood pressure and cholesterol. In contrast, Will Wilson's heart attack was a setback. His heart function remained impaired, and his blood pressure and cholesterol were a little high. While not as serious as Miele about exercising, Wilson was primarily disadvantaged in recovery because of less effective medical treatment—in particular, the delay in receiving angioplasty (Scott 2005). Clearly the ecology of class impacted these two men very differently.

Although differences between the two middle classes can be important, most social-scientific literature does not distinguish between the two. Therefore throughout the rest of the chapter, the distinction between the two classes is dropped, and reference is simply to the middle class.

ESTABLISHMENT OF THE MIDDLE-CLASS LIFE

Middle-class members' conscientious use of available capital sources is apparent when analyzing three topics affecting preparation for the adult world—childhood, schooling, and networking.

Childhood

A century ago middle-class individuals had distinctly different opinions about family life. Should middle-class women be permitted to go to college, to work, and to vote, or should they continue to fulfill the traditional, stay-at-home role? Debates on this and many other family-related issues appeared in public speeches and writings (Brady 1991, 103).

Modern Americans continue to have different conceptions about the family. For instance, they engage in varied styles of childrearing. Sociological studies conducted through the 1980s and 1990s concluded that authoritative parenting characterized by a combination of parental warmth, support, and control (some rules establishing limits) is generally more beneficial for children, creating a greater sense of trust, security, and self-confidence, than either a permissive style, setting few if any rules and restrictions, or an authoritarian approach, requiring unquestioning obedience to parental directives (Demo and Cox 2000, 880).

"Helicopter parents," who hover over their children during the college years, are recent illustrations of authoritative parenting. They keep in close touch by e-mail and cell phones, helping their children make decisions and sometimes chiding them about such issues as studying or grades. A team of writers noted, "To faculty and staff, such parents are often viewed as a buzzing annoyance. Yet a surprising number of first-year college students are now reporting that they're quite OK with their parents' academic doting" (Gordon and Kim 2008, B1). In fact, a nationwide UCLA survey indicated that 84 percent of freshmen concluded that mom and dad showed the right amount of involvement in making the decision about where to go to college. As far as parents' participation in choosing college courses and activities, almost 75 percent of the freshmen felt that they handled those issues well (Gordon and Kim 2008, B1).

Research on middle-class children's socialization shows that their parents provide a number of valuable sources of capital that age peers from working-class and poor backgrounds generally do not obtain. In a study of children belonging to these three classes, sociologist Annette Lareau (2002; 2003; 2007) described the transmission of capital resources:

- Cultural capital: Middle-class parents spent a lot of time helping their children learn to express themselves effectively. Many also painstakingly explained the reasoning for the decisions and orders they issued, encouraging their children to appreciate that living well requires a careful study of the complicated, sometimes threatening modern world.
- Human capital: With a sense of developing their children's skills and discipline, middle-class parents frequently signed up boys and girls for various adult-run activities, sometimes as many as three or four per week or even more. These activities included athletic teams, music lessons, dance classes, and art training. When needed, parents also helped with homework.
- Social capital: Middle-class parents either directly intervened on their children's behalf, or they could locate friends, colleagues, other parents, or hired professionals to help solve physical, psychological, or legal problems their children faced.

As a result of the investments in capital their parents provide, middle-class children are likely to feel a sense of entitlement—an outlook the parents are likely to encourage. For instance, when nine-year-old Alex and his mother were on the way to the doctor, she suggested that he should be thinking of possible questions. During the examination the doctor told Alex's mother that on height he was in the ninety-fifth percentile. Alex interrupted, asking, "I'm in the what?" The doctor explained, mentioning that he was compared to other ten-year-olds.

ALEX: I'm not ten.

DOCTOR: Well, they graphed you at ten . . . they usually take the closest year
           to get that graph.

ALEX: All right.

(LAUREAU 2002, 767)

It is apparent that Alex readily engaged in a conversation with his doctor, even challenging him and offering an opinion; children who felt less entitled might have been reluctant to do so.

Other research complements Laureau's findings, indicating specific emphases that occur in middle-class socialization. A 1990s study of parental values based on a representative sample of Americans 18 and over indicated that the more education parents had, the more likely they were to value autonomy, the capacity to make informed, uncontrolled decisions, and to want such conditions for their children. In particular, women in positions that were privileged and exhibited autonomy—for instance, managers, professionals, and supervisors—were especially likely to value autonomy and transmit this value to their children (Xiao 2000).

Other research also revealed that middle-class mothers' job content can affect the socialization they provide their children. A study of 500, primarily upper-middle-class families with middle-school and high-school students indicated that women employed in the sciences and mathematics offered daughters and sons equitable supports and challenges while others, equally well educated in such fields as business and the law, tended to favor their sons. Since mothers are often more involved with their children than fathers, the varied approach shown by these women in different occupations seemed likely to encourage divergent outcomes (Maier 2005).

In contrast to the child-friendly childrearing patterns just described, Elliott Currie's research on substance-abuse victims revealed a drastically different brand of socialization. His informants, primarily middle-class individuals who were former university students, had generally grown up in families in which it was easy to fail and difficult to find sustained attention or consistent approval. The respondents' parents tended to advocate a "sink-or-swim" approach, bringing up their children to navigate life largely on their own and often complaining that they made demands for tolerance and nurturance that parents should not need to provide (Currie 2004, 47–49). For instance, Tracy belonged to a family where children were always expected to compete well. Her father, an excellent athlete and a successful research physician, was a relentless source of pressure. Tracy explained that "[w]hat I felt was good was never good enough . . . And then when I was all in the drug world, it's like everything I did was good" (Currie 2004, 78). The drug world, in short, offered support Tracy never received at home.

Currie acknowledged that some of the parents had difficult lives—were out of work or hard pressed to maintain a middle-class standard—but what stood out to him in this study was the parents' conviction that they should seldom help their children and that no matter how great the youths' vulnerability, the preeminent importance of individuals' competitive struggle for success required them to handle life's demands and difficulties by themselves. These children received little or none of the nurturing support and guidance many middle-class peers obtained. Feeling overwhelmed, most of them dropped out of college and turned to substance abuse (Currie 2004, 121–22).

One of the important impacts of middle-class childrearing is its preparation of children to be successful in school. A researcher indicated that a major difference between middle- and working-class individuals looking back on their youth was that the middle-class members recalled knowing they were going to go to college while the working-class respondents, even if they hoped to go to college, seldom made such an assumption (Gorman 2000, 714).

Schooling

Robert E. Slavin, an expert on public-school funding, declared, "To my knowledge, the United States is the only nation to fund elementary and secondary education based on local wealth" (Slavin 1994, 98). By "local wealth" Slavin meant that the primary source of American public-school funding has been local property tax. Throughout a state, homes and businesses are assessed at a standard rate, and inevitably significant disparity in district tax payments results because the value of the assessed property in different locales varies considerably. The result is that the wealthier districts, which make larger tax payments, have more money to spend on schooling. Educator Jonathan Kozol asserted that the American system of public-school funding creates "savage inequalities" (Kozol 1991). Within other developed nations, the system tends to equalize funding among districts, sometimes providing greater support to schools with more extensive needs. In the Netherlands, for instance, schools generally receive money based on the number of students, but when children are disadvantaged, poor and/or minority, they receive larger allotments because their needs are greater (Slavin 1994, 98–99; Slavin 1999, 520).

American middle-class parents seek to live in areas where school quality is good. Many find themselves facing a dilemma: Should they buy a house that is larger and more expensive than they need in order to obtain access to good schools or buy a house within their budget and have their children attend subpar schools? (Frank 2007, 44–45). Many choose the first option and as a result face large mortgages, which is a prominent factor contributing to the recent acceleration of middle-class debt (Warren 2007).

Another challenge involves social-capital management to advance their children's educational interests. Middle-class parents are likely to use two tactics:

- Some of them seek out other parents or teachers for information and advice—for instance, guidance on which teacher would be most effective with one's child. A study found that middle-class parents frequently pursued such issues while working-class and poor parents seldom did (Horvat, Weininger, and Lareau 2003, 337–38). Some parents seek to develop a regular communication with their children's teachers. One middle-class father walked his daughter to her classroom every day. He would keep an eye out for the teacher whom he would see "once, twice, three times a week. And I ask is everything all right? And I mean it sincerely because if there's something I can do as a parent, then I want to know about it and I'll try to do it" (Fields-Smith 2007, 197).
- In addition, middle-class mothers and fathers often enlist the help of professionals when they feel their children need such services. For instance, when one mother learned that her son's teacher felt he had a learning disability, the mother, with a master's in clinical psychology, brought in her own psychologist, who contested the teacher's evaluation, concluding the boy had above-average intelligence and abilities. School officials were forced to reevaluate the child's situation (Horvat, Weininger, and Lareau 2003, 335).

Middle-class parents' involvement in their children's schooling underlines their recognition of its importance. Some middle-class parents are able and willing to invest in private schools, concluding that the knowledge, skills, and heightened self-image their children receive make the expense worthwhile. For instance, Donna attended an all-girls private school, which emphasized the development of self-reliant, independent young women seeking success in the competitive modern world. Donna explained "that you are learning . . . to be a strong person and . . . not afraid of anybody or anything or let anybody tell you what you can't be. . . . it sounds like a brochure, but it really is true" (Proweller 1998, 53).

Public schools, too, can have well organized objectives regarding students' optimal development. A study of two California school districts—one was suburban upper-middle-class and the other urban working-class and poor—indicated sharp differences in educational philosophy and approach, with important implications for teachers' socialization and ultimately children's education. The suburban district's officials recruited widely, visiting various universities, particularly a research university with a master's in teaching program. The intention was to find the best candidates sharing the program's philosophy, which emphasized professional autonomy for teachers and capacity building for students. A principal in the district explained, "Teachers that we hire are very creative and capable. We need to give teachers opportunities to use their creativity to really think about their teaching and kids" (Achinstein, Ogawa, and Speiglman 2004, 579). This district's leadership, in short, had a clear plan to produce a high-quality schooling experience for students and also the resources to implement it. One might wonder whether students whose teachers used such an open-ended approach would test well. They did, with 80 percent of the schools in the suburban district averaging at least a passing score on state-adopted achievement tests while only 8 percent of the schools in the urban district, where a much more structured approach to teaching prevailed, met that standard (Achinstein, Ogawa, and Speiglman 2004, 583). Besides the better test scores in the upper-middle-class area, it is likely that this district benefited from the fact that the prevailing teaching style was quite compatible with its students' socialization.

Even in successful school districts, the quality of schooling differs. Research on 452 sixth graders from two suburban middle-class middle schools found distinct differences among teachers on such dimensions as maintenance of high performance standards, effectiveness of rule setting, and the display of nurturance, fairness, and motivation (Wentzel 2002). Using initiative and contacts, middle-class parents can sometimes learn about teachers' strengths and weaknesses and manage to have their students placed with more promising teachers.

As their children progress through the grades, middle-class parents become increasingly concerned about their children getting into the college of their choice. They recognize the importance of a college degree as either preparation for the job world or as the educational foundation for postgraduate training. We have already encountered information showing the economic impact of a college degree. Another reality in middle-class parents' lives is its expense. Between 1987 and 2007, the cost of a college degree doubled (Warren 2007). An informed estimate indicated that by 2025 the price of an education at a four-year private college will be $500,000 and that the cost for out-of-state residents at state universities will be $250,000 or more (Ornstein 2007, 228).

Besides the issue of expense, applicants to top colleges and universities face fierce competition to gain entrance. In some regards those chosen for admission are distinctly different from their counterparts of several generations earlier. Sociologist Jerome Karabel indicated that if in the year 2000, exactly a century after he entered Harvard, Franklin Roosevelt had returned as a freshman he would have been shocked to see that nearly half the members of the class were women and that racial minorities, over half of whom were Asian, made up over a third of it (Karabel 2005, 536).

However, at Harvard and many other elite schools, another, less visible trend lurks behind the display of gender and racial diversity. As competition to enter the most prominent, prestigious colleges and universities has increased, privileged upper-class and upper-middle-class parents have followed a conscientious preparation—in particular, enrolling their children in the most successful elementary and secondary schools, developing athletic, musical, or artistic skills that will impress admissions committees, and using expensive tutoring services to prepare them for the Standard

Aptitude Tests. Overall these preparations produce the desired outcomes. As a result the most prestigious colleges or universities tend to exclude nonaffluent students. A study of the nation's 40 leading universities indicated that Yale, Princeton, and Harvard ranked twenty-fifth, thirty-eighth, and thirty-ninth respectively in economic diversity. Clearly family-linked advantages make a huge contribution (Karabel 2005, 537–46). Jerome Karabel wrote, "Though in principle open to everyone, the elite colleges are in truth a realistic possibility only for those young men and women whose families endow them with the . . . [financial] capital implicitly required for admission" (Karabel 2005, 549). In short, social reproduction dominates.

Like human capital, social capital also plays an important role in middle-class individuals' successful development.

Networking: It's Who You Know

Middle-class people often have access to potentially helpful family members, friends, and community individuals and groups as well as various professionals or experts that members of the less affluent and less prominent classes either cannot connect to or cannot afford. Middle-class people are joiners—open to information and influence from various members of their class.

Sometimes middle-class individuals band together for mutual benefit. For instance, they can mobilize social capital to fight crime in their neighborhoods, keeping them safe, stable places to raise children. The upcoming study focused on a middle-class neighborhood in Chicago called Groveland, which adjoins poor, high-crime areas. In this situation the use of social capital featured two approaches.

Adults within the community used extended family and friendship ties to exercise informal social control. Alberta Gordon participated in this process, indicating that she did not hesitate telling children when they were doing something wrong, "[a]nd no problem going to their parents because I know their parents" (Pattillo 1998, 762). Informal social control in action was apparent when Ms. Spears, another community member, saw a teenage girl wearing an electronic pager often used by drug dealers. She asked her to whom it belonged. Her father, the girl indicated. Ms. Spears followed with a mix of questions and orders: "What are you doing with a beeper? You don't need a beeper. Give it back. . . I don't care if it's yo' brother's, mother's, father's . . . It's not becoming" (Pattillo 1998, 762). Which she did.

The informal approach produced small successes. However, gangs and drug dealing are formidable opponents, and so the middle-class residents of Groveland often pursued more formal sources of social capital, involving educational, religious, police, and business organizations, whose staff members often lived in Groveland. For instance, when a group of local clubs organized an anti-drug march, a number of neighborhood businesses donated material and food. The United Church of Christ hosted several community meetings where local residents made specific demands of the alderman, the police, and a local public-school principal. One complaint involved the presence of three drug houses in the area, two of which were eventually closed down. A second issue involved the presence of gang recruiters in the elementary school playground. Following the meeting the police began surveillance of the playground (Pattillo 1998, 764).

Like Groveland a small neighborhood in Cleveland known as Prince Heights or Upper Prince stood out from its urban surroundings as the one locale "for miles where the yards are manicured, the houses well kept, and the neighbors know each other" (Maag 2008, A18). The driving force for local improvement was Daniel Lewis, a supervisor for the Cleveland Transit Authority. Every time a house went up for sale, Lewis encouraged a family member to buy it. Lewis's daughter explained that her father taught his children that "middle-class isn't about economics . . . It's a mindset. You work hard. You take care of your house and your neighborhood and the people around you" (Maag 2008, A18). Middle-class status, Lewis seemed to suggest, was less about financial capital than about other capital types.

Prince Heights has been a healthy, vibrant, middle-class neighborhood in a locale where drug trafficking and violent crime had always been a nearby presence. In June 2008 Daniel Lewis was killed in his yard, the innocent victim of a drive-by shooting. After Lewis's death some neighbors wanted to place teddy bears at the crime scene, but his wife opposed the action, suggesting instead that it would be more faithful to her husband's memory to mobilize the social network he had promoted and develop a powerful community group to protect their neighborhood.

Switching from urban communities like Groveland and Prince Heights with their family, friendship, and neighborhood social capital to the primarily middle-class professional hi-tech world of social networking represents a sharp shift. In fact, can one even claim that the hi-tech business world has social capital? Certainly employees use various forms of telecommunications to exchange details about everyday job activities (Bishop and Levine 1999; Hyde 2003, 158–59). Debate exists about whether the social networks established in such instances feature the use of social capital or not. Some analysts conclude that social capital is not involved because of participants' fixation on work-related issues and no involvement of family, friends, and community (Cohen and Fields 2000; Hyde 2005). However, one should keep in mind that the standard for qualification on this issue is not a sharp one—that some groups representing social capital previously cited in this chapter have been work associates or hired professionals, decidedly not intimates for the people in question.

Since the 1990s e-mail and the Internet have promoted social networks that are not restricted by physical space; that allow many people, hundreds and even thousands or millions, to be contacted at once; and that with attachments and websites permit the transmission of text, documents, photos, and videos. In addition, within these computer-generated systems, bidirectional communication exists, allowing individuals receiving information to provide feedback (Dellarocas 2003; Wellman 2001, 2031). Adult Internet users tend to be college educated, affluent, white, and under the age of 55 (DiMaggio, Hargittai, Neuman, and Robinson 2001, 311). However, the user group has broadened.

While computer-generated networks are growing, research produces mixed results on the topic of whether these systems build social capital. A study of 169 Pittsburgh-area families who used computers with Internet connections over two years found that high levels of Internet use corresponded with declines in communication with both family members and friends (Kraut, Patterson, Lundmark, Kiesler, Mukophadhyay, and Scherlis 1998). Another, much larger investigation featuring a representative sample of over 4,000 families indicated that a quarter of respondents using the Internet five hours a week or more felt that it reduced the time spent with friends and family (Nie and Erbring 2000). In contrast to these two sets of findings, various researchers have felt that computer networks have contributed to people's social capital, enhancing their sense of community. One expert noted, "It is becoming clear that the Internet is not destroying community but is resonating with and extending the types of networked community that have already become prevalent in the developed Western world" (Wellman 2001, 2002).

A case in point involves **social-networking sites**, which are Internet organizations that are seeking to build online communities of people sharing interests and activities. A host of these sites have developed, with MySpace and Facebook the most widely used. On its website, Facebook's publicity statement indicated that anyone can join the site, using a school or work e-mail address to register and then present a detailed profile of whatever one wants to convey about his or her past, present, and future. Facebook connects to a wide variety of networks, whose members belong to schools, companies, small businesses, or physical regions like towns. This social-networking site started in early 2004, and within about four-and-a-half years had 100 million users around the world (Facebook 2008).

The use of such sites is expanding. One observer admonished, "If you have avoided social-networking sites like Linkedin and Facebook with the excuse that they are the domain of desperate job hunters or attention-seeking teenagers, it's time to reconsider" (Tribble 2008, C6). A case in point would be technology consultant Josh So, who found out that his corporate division was about to be eliminated. Within hours of updating his online job résumé on LinkedIn, So learned about openings that led to four interviews. A week later he had two offers, and then in under a month his employer counteroffered with a position in another division, bumping up his salary $25,000. Based on his experience, Mr. So advised, "Build your own inner circle of people you know are good—people you know will get you places" (Tribble 2008. C6).

As the upcoming section indicates, once losing their jobs, employees in the modern work world are generally less successful than Josh So was.

THE LEAN, MEAN MIDDLE-CLASS WORK MACHINE

The business world is the heart of the American middle-class economy. What qualities do middle-class individuals entering this setting need in order to be successful? Robert Jackall's well-known sociological study of management in two companies—one with 11,000 staff members manufacturing a variety of chemicals and the other with 20,000 employees producing textiles—provided a set of prominent qualities (Jackall 2010, 18–19). These factors include:

Education: In Jackall's study the more prestigious firm recruited managers from such celebrated business schools as Harvard, Stanford, and Wharton. The less respected company sought to hire young managers from less prominent business schools in its locale—in the South or Southwest (Jackall 2010, 44). The importance of postgraduate schooling for those entering the business world has grown. A survey done in 2008 by the Graduate Management Admissions Council indicated that the number of applications to programs providing master of business administration degrees surged 77 percent from 2007, up from a 64 percent increase the previous year (Damast 2008). Some business abilities, however, are not learned in school. Experts point out that in such areas as fund management and investment banking, the requisite skills are more likely to be learned on the job than in classes (Ip 2008).

Hard work: Jackall indicated that individuals who want to succeed in management not only need to work hard but have to be perceived as hard workers, constantly on the move and improving their output. An executive vice president at the textile firm spoke about the unrelenting effort necessary. Certain individuals, he asserted, stood out. "You can spot it the first six months. They have suggestions at meetings. They come into a business and the business picks up. They don't go on coffee breaks . . ." (Jackall 2010, 48).

Self-control: While working hard in what is often a pressure-packed atmosphere is essential, the individual seeking to climb the corporate ladder must demonstrate self-control. When interviewed managers stressed the importance of hiding feelings and intentions behind a relaxed, smiling, affable exterior. Corporate life, they seemed to imply, was a game that demanded a perfect poker face (Jackall 2010, 51).

Hitting the numbers: To be successful in business, a person must contribute to the profit commitments that upper-level management has established for his or her work unit. However, making money in itself is insufficient to ensure an individual's advancement in management (Jackall 2010, 66).

Acting as a team player: Ambitious corporate managers soon realize that they must master this role where they learn to get along with others, fit in, recognize trouble and if possible stay away from it, and always appear unthreatening and pleasant, hiding ambition. The object is to make both one's superiors and peers feel comfortable (Jackall 2010, 53–54).

Obtaining a patron: Prominent corporate officials provide protégés a chance to advance—giving them opportunities to showcase their talents or introducing them to other high-level executives who might also help their progress. The patron-protégé relationship is a reciprocal one, with junior members making certain that their superiors receive all critical information to produce effective decisions and providing unswerving loyalty to them in exchange for the benefits previously mentioned. Over time as patrons invest heavily in junior managers, they become committed to making certain that those individuals do not fail because failure would diminish senior executives' reputation for picking winners (Jackall 2010, 65–66). As several of these observations suggest, choosing protégés is not a selfless decision. Not surprisingly a study featuring data from 282 patrons indicated that they were more likely to choose protégés based on their perception of perceived ability than of junior executives' perceived need for support (Allen, Poteet, and Russell 2000). Female executives have recognized that women's most promising prospects for patrons are likely to be members of their own sex. "A lot of women recognize that they got a break from women on the way up," said Patricia O'Brien, dean of the Simmons Graduate School of Management. "They want to return the favor" (Aoki 2001, F1). Regardless of protégés' gender, CEOs are potentially the most helpful patrons. Upper-management personnel who use flattery, opinion conformity, and favor-rendering with their CEOs are more likely to receive board appointments at either firms where their bosses already serve or to obtain such positions at boards to which their CEOs are connected through interlocking directorates (Westphal and Stern 2006).

The above set of principles has applied for decades, especially in firms with more stable job ladders. However, with technological advances and the increase in downsizing/outsourcing, corporate jobs have often become less secure. A study of five industries, three of which feature middle-class employees—financial services, semiconductors, and software—found distinct differences in firms' job prospects. For instance, good, long-term job ladders are most likely to exist in large growing firms, but some small expanding companies also have first-rate job ladders. While good jobs exist, holding on to them can be challenging. In the semiconductor, financial services, and software industries, research revealed that shrinking firms often forced established workers to compete for their jobs against new employees (Brown, Haltiwanger, and Lane, 2006, 70–78).

In the three high-skilled industries included in this study, worker turnover was very high. Only one of four workers in the semiconductor industry, one of five in financial services, and just one of seven in the software business remained on the job more than five years (Brown, Haltiwanger, and Lane 2006, 68).

Many middle-class workers now feel that their tenure with a given firm will be brief—only as long as they feel enthusiastic about their tasks and the company finds their contribution useful. A middle-manager commented that after "three years, four years, you've shot all your bullets, you've done all you can do in my kind of job, and it's time to move on to something else" (Heckscher 1995, 142). Many middle-class workers maintained intense loyalty to their companies in the past, but as working conditions changed toward the end of the twentieth century, it sharply declined.

Middle-Class Workforce Changes Involving Downsizing, Outsourcing, and Temp Work

In the late 1980s and early 1990s, according to investigative reporter Barbara Ehrenreich, corporate executives' attitude toward middle-class employees changed. "Blue-collar workers were always thought to be disposable," she asserted, "but now they started looking at white-collar workers as just expenses to eliminate" (Doster 2006). These executives were engaging in **downsizing**—the deliberate reduction of permanent employees in an effort to provide an organization more efficient operation and/or cut costs. The introduction of new technology, extensive corporate restructuring, and outsourcing of jobs to foreign locations all promote downsizing. Both large and small corporations pursue the practice, with massive firms like IBM, AT&T, and GM reducing their heavily middle-class workforce by 10 to 20 percent (Perrucci and Wysong 2008, 3). Several nationally conducted studies indicated that compared to workers in the 1980s, employees in the 1990s, both middle- and working-class, experienced a shorter duration for their jobs (Newmark, Polsky, and Hansen 2000) and a greater likelihood of losing their positions (Bernhardt, Morris, Handcock, and Scott 2000; Valletta 2000). Starting in the 1990s, income instability became more prevalent among well educated workers (Hacker 2006, 28).

In the twenty-first century, data on downsizing indicate significant job losses. Between January 2005 and December 2007, 3.6 million workers with three or more years on the job lost their positions because of company closings or moves, insufficient work, or the elimination of their positions. Data supplied on middle-class jobs indicated 1.1 million positions lost in management, professional, and related occupations and nearly a million in sales, clerical, and related positions (Bureau of Labor Statistics 2008b).

In interviews with 77 recently unemployed mid- and top-level managers, a team of researchers found that at the time of their termination 60 percent of the research subjects felt a "deep sense of betrayal, a lack of loyalty on the company's part and a sense of cold dismissal" even when they received fairly generous severance packages.

The pain this young woman feels has been experienced by millions of middle-class workers who like her have been downsized in recent years.

Some respondents described a "freezing out" process, feeling slowly shut out of the loop, and finding [later] "that there were meetings held, [and] you weren't invited." The laid-off workers often felt treated disrespectfully, with no forewarning of dismissal. Employees received an e-mail, a voice-mail, or "a 30-second conversation . . . your job has been eliminated . . . come in on the weekend to clean out your office" (Mendenhall, Kalik, Spindel, and Hart 2008, 197).

Downsizing has received extensive attention and media coverage as individuals lost their jobs and often struggled both to find another job and to maintain their previous lifestyle. Initially concern about outsourcing was muted. **Outsourcing** is companies' subcontracting of services to other companies instead of continuing to provide those services themselves. Outsourcing can occur with firms in the immediate area or elsewhere in the United States, but a substantial amount of it involves companies in foreign countries. Outsourcing featuring middle-class jobs started slowly. In the early 1990s, Indian animators began to produce Saturday morning cartoons. Soon afterwards Indians' "hidden hands" were starting to do Amazon.com book orders (Sheshabalaya 2005, 3).

From the 1990s on, outsourcing steadily increased, but data on the subject are limited. It is notable that the federal government, which spends $130 billion yearly on research, provides no statistics on the topic, and companies have failed to supply their own (Hira and Hira 2005, 43–44). Apparently the power elite mobilized in this area. Soon after George W. Bush was elected president, the Business Roundtable, an influential corporate policy-making group discussed in earlier chapters, sought to persuade the president to ignore public complaints about downsizing and outsourcing (Sheshabalaya 2005, 33). The government supplies some information about downsizing, but the decision not to publicize outsourcing statistics seems consistent with the Business Roundtable's preference.

Official silence, however, has not stopped specialists' estimates. John C. McCarthy, a financial expert, made a much-discussed prediction that 3.3 million white-collar American jobs would be outsourced overseas by 2015 (Forrester Research 2008). Besides computer software, other hard-hit areas have included architecture, accounting, engineering, information technology, and call-center operation. Nearly every major technology company, including Microsoft, Hewlett-Packard, Compaq, Yahoo, Google, IBM, and Electronic Data Systems, have been obtaining various services from abroad (Hira and Hira 2005, 44–49).

India has become a nation that can mobilize a large, competent middle-class workforce for outsourced jobs. The country has a population of over a billion people, a well-developed educational and high-tech infrastructure, and middle-class citizens willing to work cheaply, perhaps for 15 percent an American's salary (Sheshabalaya 2005, 3–7).

Not all observers agree that outsourcing is a problem for the American workforce. The Association for Computing Machinery, whose members are various types of computer professionals, conducted a year-long study to assess the impact of outsourcing to countries like India and China and concluded that the impact in the computer industry was exaggerated—that more hi-tech jobs would be created than lost and that in spite of offshore outsourcing, employment in the information-technology industry was the highest it had been in the last few years. Ronil Hira, a professor of public policy, whose research was previously cited, was a consultant in the study. Hira's diplomatic evaluation was that the Association report took "a feel-good" stance on the outlook for jobs (Lohr 2006). An issue to keep in mind is that since outsourcing seems to be very cost-effective for big business, it is likely to expand steadily, taking increasingly more American middle-class jobs.

While outsourcing is a common practice, a less prominent trend involving domestic positions entails importing individuals from other countries as hi-tech workers. The H-1B visa program offers three-year visas with one renewal to skilled foreigners who obtain positions with American firms. The program issues 195,000 visas a year, and the modal H-1B employee is a 28-year-old Indian computer programmer who earns about $45,000—much less than American counterparts but much more than he or she would receive at home (Hyde 2003, 125–26).

The modern American economy provides good opportunities for the selected foreign workers able to find jobs, but for many citizens the employment options have deteriorated. **Temporary (temp) work**, which involves jobs produced when a company contracts with an agency to supply it employees, has become prevalent. About 4 percent of the workforce, around 11.4 million individuals a year, work for temp staffing agencies, which receive a percentage of people's pay as long as they are employed at the firm that provides the job (Novak 2008). Companies find that temp work is a cheap way of hiring new employees—often less expensive than outsourcing. Furthermore some job holders respond positively to this arrangement, accepting lower wages and fewer benefits than the firm's regular staff because they recognize that they work for different companies than the full-time employees (Hyde 2003, 106).

Middle-class employees' reaction to temp work varies, depending on the job situation. One study involved permatemps who are long-term workers in a company called CompTech, a prominent manufacturer of computers and computer technology. Temps who were hired for 18 months and often rehired after a mandatory three-month layoff pursued a variety of tasks, including such complex activities as the calculation of schedules for filling orders, the assignment of team tasks, and meeting with vendors to review recurring product defects. Like many other companies, CompTemp hired temps because the money saved allowed its executives to provide its regular employees excellent training, benefits, and job security. Apparently temps at CompTech were comfortable with this arrangement. One told the researcher that it was reasonable for management to be more inclined to protect its regular employees from firing. He observed that "if it's inevitable you're going to have some pain—where do you have it?" Clearly, he concluded, the temp workers should be the ones to lose out (Smith 2001, 114–15). The vast majority of the temp-work employees had held a series of unstable jobs before coming to CompTech, and most said that in spite of receiving less money than the permanent staff and having little hope to advance, this was the best position they had ever had. For most of these permatemps, the overriding desire was that someday they would be able to obtain a permanent position at CompTech (Smith 2001, 107).

At FlexTech, another hi-tech firm, the administration also claimed that it used temp work in order to protect the permanent employees. In other respects, however, the two firms were very different. There was no 18-month hire, and jobs were unstable and badly paid. An underlying condition at FlexTech was that it worked strictly on contracts, with no company capacity to develop products. In addition, the firm used so-called "just in time" manufacturing, where inventories were small to save money, and any sudden surge in production led to rapid shutdown and no pay for temp workers. Still the permatemps at FlexTech generally liked their jobs, comparing them to grimmer work situations where employees had no possibility of bonuses or raises (Chun 2001).

Furthermore, while temp workers generally make less money than their permanent counterparts, those in middle-class positions which are highly skilled, require extensive training, and are highly valued can sometimes obtain better pay than the average for permanent workers in the field. For instance, registered nurses who are temps earn a typical wage that is $4.93 per hour higher than the national average for registered nurses, and computer programmers in temp positions exceed the national group by fully $7.85 an hour (Kilcoyne 2004).

Overall, however, the picture for temp workers is not promising. Investigative reporters Barbara Ehrenreich and Ta Mara Draut indicated that an increasing proportion of middle-class workers experience "'real' jobs giv[ing] way to benefit-free contract work. Far from being on an elite perch in the 'knowledge economy,' the middle class hovers just inches above the working poor" (Ehrenreich and Draut 2008). The upcoming discussion addresses the issue of middle-class job instability.

The Middle-Class Struggle with Reemployment

When middle-class workers lose their jobs, they tend to be rehired at least 60 percent of the time but often at a lower rate of payment (Hira and Hira 2005, 129–30). Table 6.3 provides data involving reemployment of several large middle-class job categories. Some professionalized jobs, in which outsourcing and importing foreign employees have become common practices, are especially unstable. Between 2000 and 2004, over 180,000 computer programmers lost their jobs, producing an unemployment rate of about 10 percent for this type of work (Hacker 2006, 77).

Often the dismissal is a shock. Jim Rude, a computer programmer, who was a few hours short of having a master's in computer science, was suddenly told that he and 325 other colleagues would be dismissed in two months. During this final time period, Rude and his fellow programmers had to train their replacements. Rude explained, "And we were told, 'If you don't train these people, you will be terminated on the spot and you won't get your severance package'" (Bartlett and Steele 1996, 28). When his job ended, Rude went unemployed for two months and then found a job at about half his previous salary.

At another company Myra Bronstein had to train a H-1B holder receiving one-sixteenth her salary. "I was staring hard at my shoes and trying not to cry," Bronstein explained. "It was hideously awkward. . . . It was very deflating and dehumanizing to train your replacement. . . . It was as if they handed us a shovel and said, 'Here dig your own grave'" (Hacker 2006, 77–78).

TABLE 6.3 Displaced Workers in Several Categories of Middle-Class Jobs and Their Employment Status

January	Number of workers displaced in thousands	Percent reemployed, 2008
Total jobs lost, January 2005 through December 2007[1]	3,641	67.1
Management, business, and financial operations occupations	605	64.2
Professional and related operations	542	73.5
Sales and related occupations	413	68.6

[1]These workers had three or more years on the job.

While the majority of middle-class workers find new jobs, the positions often pay less well than the previous ones.
Source: U.S. Bureau of Labor Statistics. 2008. Table 5. "Displaced Workers by Occupation of Lost Job and Employed Status in January 2008." http://www/bis.gov/news.release/disp.t05.htm.

For many people, especially if they are in their fifties or more, finding reemployment is a formidable proposition. To experience how difficult the middle-class job market was, Barbara Ehrenreich, who was in her fifties, spent seven months job searching, primarily for a sales job, and she wrote a book about her experiences. Ehrenreich hired a specialist to provide an image makeover, paid for assistance to refine and later upgrade her résumé, networked in four cities, and received exactly two offers for sales positions. They were not, however, in Ehrenreich's estimation real jobs, just paying commissions and offering no salary, benefits, or a workplace. Surely, Ehrenreich assumed, there were real jobs that provided salary and benefits along with commission, but the catch was that such an arrangement required the employer to risk an investment in the prospective employee (Ehrenreich 2005, 189).

During her investigation Ehrenreich found many people who went from solidly middle-class jobs to minimum-wage employment—a former broadcast journalist looking for an entry-level position at Best Buy, Circuit City, or Home Depot; a computer specialist working at moving furniture; a former teacher employed at a number of minimum-wage jobs such as sorting UPS mail and laying tile and hardwood floors. One former marketing executive, who had spent several years at menial jobs, explained that in her present position "I've done everything from scrub toilets to clean out apartments in this complex for eight dollars an hour." The physically demanding nature of the work made her more respectful of her largely Hispanic coworkers and caused her to lose 20 pounds (Ehrenreich 2006, 206).

Job loss has produced a heavy toll on many individuals. An examination of laid-off workers revealed that while aware of the sharply changing working conditions in the United States, many displaced middle-class workers have tended to see their dismissal in personal terms—that "it was somehow their fault or their particular bad luck" (Uchitelle 2006, 180). This point of view seems consistent with traditional American ideology emphasizing that individuals or families are on their own, responsible for their own fate, regardless of impinging structural conditions outside their control.

Besides developing diminished self-images, displaced workers often encounter negative response from former colleagues. Richard Sennett, who studied middle-class men who had lost corporate jobs, found that they had become strangely "invisible," barred from occupational networks to which they once had access. Sennett wrote, "The silence which surrounds their marginality marks America's greatest social taboo, failure, our unmentionable subject" (Sennett 2006, 102).

In spite of many individuals experiencing job loss, lowered income is generally not an obvious problem for middle-class families. In fact, for median-earning married couples, where both spouses are working, the combined income total was about $35,000 greater in 2007 (adjusted for inflation) than it was in 1970 (Warren 2007). So if income is not the basic problem, why are so many middle-class families in difficult economic circumstances? We consider.

THE MIDDLE CLASS'S SLIPPERY SLOPE FOR MAKING ENDS MEET

In recent years financial difficulties for middle-class families have increased. Between 2001 and 2004, the middle three quintiles (20 percent segments) of the population based on their amounts of wealth greatly increased their ratio of debt to income, producing a sharp gain of over 40 percent in just three years (Wolff 2007). In 2008 middle-income households had an average of $8,650 in credit-card debt (Mooney 2008, 155).

Many Americans are likely to think that people in debt are heavy, irresponsible buyers of exorbitant, unnecessary items. Two myth-laden topics are apparent, involving who goes into debt and what items produce people's financial crisis.

On the first issue, one might begin by wondering what quality makes women most likely to file for bankruptcy. It is not being young with an addictive use of credit cards or being old with declining savings and failing bodies. Curiously it is having a child. In fact, middle-class couples with children are more than twice as likely to file for bankruptcy than their childless counterparts, and divorced women raising a child are more than three times as likely to go bankrupt than childless women (Warren and Tyagi 2003, 6). Couples or individuals with children have expenditures that make them particularly vulnerable to debt, and, in addition, mothers find their work schedules and thus their incomes adversely affected in various ways.

On the second issue, an examination of what are widely believed sources of middle-class debt suggests extensive misinformation on the topic. Consider clothes, which advertisers display in catalogues, on TV, and in magazines, often presenting a range of elegant, expensive choices—shoes, coats, jackets, suits, blouses, sweaters, and more. However, in the opening years of the twenty-first century, middle-class families have spent an impressive 32 percent less on clothes than their counterparts 30 years earlier.

Food is another notable consumer issue. While it is well known that middle-income families eat out much more than in the past, they spend about 18 percent less on food than 30 years earlier, largely because people shop more at large, heavily discounting super-centers and, at least until recent years, agribusiness's efficient food production has helped keep food costs fairly low.

The cost of buying appliances has also changed over time. Retail prices have decreased 52 percent from the early 1970s. Modern appliances are better made, last longer, and cost less than they did in the past. In addition, automobiles might appear to be more costly, especially because of a widely perceived preference for luxury models, but their prices declined 24 percent over 30 years.

So if these widely believed sources of middle-class debt have made limited contributions to it, what costs are largely responsible for it? There are several, including housing, health insurance, childcare, college, and taxes. Modern middle-income families own slightly larger houses than their early 1970s counterparts. However, the expense is much greater, with a mortgage that cost 76 percent more in 2007 than 30 years earlier and a monthly payment in inflation-adjusted dollars that went from $485 to $854. Middle-class parents often find that a key issue in buying a house is the school district in which it is located—a concern which can motivate them to buy houses that are larger and more expensive than they otherwise would purchase.

Compared to their 1970s counterparts, middle-income families in 2007 spent 74 percent more on healthcare, 52 percent more on transportation costs, and about $1,048 more a month on childcare (often not an expense in the 1970s with the wife frequently staying home). In addition, by 2007 the cost of college had doubled in 20 years, and taxes were 25 percent higher in 2004 for a two-income family than for a one-income family in 1972 (Warren 2007; Warren and Tyagi 2003, 8). Table 6.4 provides a summary of middle-class consumers' changing costs over time, singling out the major factors contributing to debt and bankruptcy.

Besides these high, fixed expenses, modern middle-class families face vulnerabilities that were less pronounced in the past. In the 1970s, for example, if a husband became ill or was killed, it was likely that the wife could enter the workforce, and while the income she earned might be less, it could probably maintain the family. Nowadays with both spouses usually working full-time to meet relentlessly rising expenses, no such safety net exists. If a spouse loses his or her job or gets a devastating illness, or the couple decides to divorce, the economic impact on the family is going to be substantial (Warren and Tyagi 2003, 87).

Another vulnerability involves healthcare, which middle-class workers have found increasingly costly over time. Political scientist Jacob Hacker pointed out that some corporate employers perversely argue that the losing this insurance is a positive outcome—that

TABLE 6.4 Noncontributors and Contributors to Middle-Income Families Debt

2007 costs for consumer items compared to the early 1970s

Clothes	32 percent less
Food	18 percent less
Appliances	52 percent less
Cars	24 percent less

2007 fixed expenses compared to the early 1970s

Home mortgage	76 percent greater
Health insurance	74 percent greater
Transportation	52 percent greater
Childcare	About $13,000 a year compared to negligible cost in the early 1970s when middle-class mothers typically cared for their young children
College	Doubled in cost in two decades
Taxes	25 percent higher for a two-income family in 2004 than a one-income family in 1972

Source: Elizabeth Warren. 2007. "The New Economics of the Middle Class: Why Making Ends Meet Has Gotten Harder." Testimony before Senate Finance Committee, May 10, 2007. http://www.finance.senate.gov/hearings/testimony/2007test/051007testew.pdf.

"[f]reed from the shackles of old-style risk protection, we can . . . [decide] how much risk to bear in the market, and enjoy the financial rewards of our newfound freedom" (Hacker 2006, 58). This is a version of the traditional American ideology emphasizing the primacy of individual achievement. The harsh reality involving healthcare is that left on their own, many middle-class people can afford only very limited or no healthcare.

Then they face a serious economic challenge if catastrophic illness or injury occurs. Hacker described the case of a university professor who spoke about costs after a lengthy, expensive hospitalization. The man explained, "If you're negotiating a car, you can always say, 'I'll walk off the lot.' If your one-year-old kid has an IV in his arm, you don't have the same situation" (Hacker 2006, 59).

The broad facts about healthcare coverage hardly seem liberating for most middle-class people:

- Healthcare premiums have been steadily rising in cost, increasing three times as rapidly as income between 2000 and 2008 and consuming an expanding portion of family income. A middle-class family earning $50,000 a year spends about 7 percent of its pre-tax income on healthcare insurance.
- Nearly three quarters of middle-class families receive healthcare coverage through employers, and therefore the growing unemployment rate, which rose from 4.9 percent in December 2007 to 9.1 percent in August 2011, could increasingly eliminate that support.
- Each year 15 million middle-class families experience a significant healthcare expense, which drains over 10 percent of the family income.
- About 30 percent of Americans with above-median income, that is about 14 million individuals, have no health insurance. Their hiring is taking place in an era where many of them do temp work for employers who subsidize neither healthcare expenses nor retirement costs (Bureau of Labor Statistics 2011; Rowland, Hoffman, and Mcginn-Shapiro 2009; Swartz 2006, 15–18).

Another growing vulnerability for middle-class workers involves retirement. Many employers no longer provide the pensions that were common in the past. Nowadays the most common retirement plan features 401(k)s, where workers invest in stock-market funds, deciding on their own whether and how much to contribute. Generally employers' contribution has declined, averaging 1.5 percent of employees' payroll in the late 1980s compared to a much more robust 3.5 percent a decade earlier. In spite of a stock-market boom in the 1990s, the average investment among 401(k) account holders was about $13,000 in 2005. With the rapid replacement of traditional pension plans with 401(k)s, Jacob Hacker observed that "the nation has engaged in a vast experiment to see how Americans fare in a world in which retirement planning is an individual responsibility and in which families bear resulting risks on their own" (Hacker 2006, 125).

In fact, Hacker indicated that the middle class has experienced "the great risk shift," where previous stability in jobs, healthcare coverage, and retirement programs has ceased, disrupting "the fragile balance sheets of American families" (Hacker 2006, 6).

To Elizabeth Warren and Amelia Warren Tyagi, the modern middle-class two-income American family "is walking on a high wire without a net; they pray there won't be any wind. . . . But if anything—anything at all—goes wrong, then today's two-income family is in big, big trouble" (Warren and Tyagi 2003, 54).

Diana, aged 36, was a licensed psychologist, with a PhD in clinical psychology. She and her husband, a technical writer for a patent attorney, had two children, with a third on the way. She was worried about how they would be able to afford this third child, who was unplanned. Between them Diana and her husband made $75,000 as contract workers, paid on a per-client or per-project basis. They had $17,000 in credit-card debt and had cashed in Diana's 401(k) to pay for her maternity leave.

When interviewed, Diana admitted that she and her husband were doing less well than her working-class parents, who owned a garage and raised five children, living simply but never feeling deprived. Diana's voice broke as she confessed to the fear of being unable to meet the combined expense of retirement, healthcare, and college payments. She added, "We've never had much, but before I always felt like . . . [w]e were working our way toward a more comfortable future. That doesn't seem true anymore" (Mooney 2008, 5). If one recalls Chapter 4's quotation from a Ronald Reagan speech, it is clear that Diana's statement did not represent his sense of the land of opportunity always seeking to provide a better life for its people.

However, Diana's perspective appears to be somewhat atypical for well-educated people. An ABC News Poll conducted in 2010 found that among citizens considering themselves middle class with a college degree, only 25 percent considered themselves struggling. In contrast, for respondents who placed themselves in the middle class and lacked a college degree the number of individuals who felt they were fighting to hold on was nearly double—49 percent (ABC World News Poll 2010).

Conclusion

An historical overview of the middle class opens the chapter. The preindustrial middle class contained farmers and small businessmen, who usually had modest success along with a distinctly independent life. Industry brought a massive economic expansion and for middle-class men a changed lifestyle, emphasizing a commitment to hard work, self-improvement, and a sharply reduced family involvement. Independence waned, with middle-class workers joining companies and seeking to climb the company ladder. During industrialization the family changed, and the mother assumed the responsibility for preparing children to enter the new, fast-changing world. The twentieth century was generally a prosperous time for the middle class. Starting in the 1930s, the government introduced various supportive social programs. In addition, a number of middle-class occupations expanded sharply during the century.

The two middle classes differ in their income and jobs, education, and the impact of the ecology of class. The chapter also examines the development of middle-class people generally, analyzing childhood, schooling, and networking. Historically Americans born into the middle class have been the beneficiaries of social reproduction, and Table 6.5 summarizes middle-class resources as capital types—issues examined throughout the chapter.

A major topic in this chapter involves the middle-class work setting, including an assessment of the qualities necessary to be successful in American business. Times, however, have been changing, and such work-related realities as downsizing, outsourcing, the increasing number of companies hiring temp workers as opposed to permanent workers, and the challenge of seeking reemployment have produced persistent struggle.

TABLE 6.5 A Summary of Modern Middle-Class Resources

1. Financial capital: Salaries of about $150,000 per year for upper-middle-class employees and about $70,000 for middle-class workers. Growing threats to financial stability include job uncertainty, rising fixed costs, and employers' declining contribution to healthcare and retirement funds

2. Human capital: Parents' frequent emphasis on residing within a high-quality school district, often necessitating the purchase of an expensive home with a substantial mortgage; college expenses doubling between 1987 and 2007

3. Social capital: Widespread recognition that joining groups can help accomplish goals; recent social-networking sites helping to build online communities of people sharing interests and activities; middle-class parents' development of social capital to promote children's effective school performance

4. Cultural capital: Considerable variation in the cultural capital middle-class parents provide their children, ranging from conscientious development of children's ability to express themselves well and make sensible decisions to a "sink-or-swim" approach, leaving children largely on their own to figure out how the social world functions

---

The final topic involves the growing economic problems many middle-class individuals and families face.

How will these disruptive economic conditions and the accompanying stress affect middle-class families' childrearing patterns? In the modern middle-class setting, recent research has suggested that families have provided their children various types of quality capital. In contrast, Elliott Currie's chilling research about middle-class children with substance-abuse problems presents a different, more ominous picture of highly detached, punitive socialization. Hopefully the increased stresses of modern middle-class life do not accelerate such destructive parenting.

Speaking of future trends, what about job prospects? Completing college early in the twenty-first century, graduates find more positions in some areas than others. For instance, federal-government employees are aging, opening up employment for young people. A problem is that many feel that government work is both insignificant and uninteresting. The challenge is for various federal agencies to come up with strategies highlighting the appeal their jobs offer prospective workers (Barr 2007).

The aerospace industry confronted a similar situation, with workers aging and replacements being needed. Other industries facing work shortages can save money by outsourcing overseas, but with defense contracts, which are a substantial part of its business, aerospace companies cannot pursue that option because of restrictions involving national-security clearance.

A major challenge this industry faces is to find effective ways to contact well qualified recruits. While aerospace personnel used to believe that face-to-face meetings at luncheons or job fairs was the best approach, the sense has been growing that virtual connections might be more effective. Lockheed Martin Corporation, one of the industry's leaders, set up a chat room on its website, hosting daily one-on-one instant-messaging exchanges with job seekers. At Boeing, recruiters invited interns to join a Facebook group started by a company staff member (Chang 2007).

This is not an era that inspires optimism about middle-class job prospects. Which occupations seem likely to do particularly well? On a much larger scale, can one visualize a global scenario that would include an economically revitalized American middle class?

Key Terms in the Glossary

Blue-collar (job holders) *153*
Downsizing *169*
Ecology of class *158*
Functional literacy *157*

Intersectionality *156*
Outsourcing *170*
Redlining *151*
Social-networking site *167*

Temporary (temp) work
171
White-collar (job holders)
153

Discussion Topics

1. Examine the economic and noneconomic changes that middle-class people experienced with the arrival of the industrial era.
2. Analyze the differences between the two middle classes on the following dimensions—income and jobs, families and education, and the ecology of class.
3. Is it true that Annette Lareau's research on children in three classes found remarkably few differences in the parents' childrearing approaches? In responding to the question, refer to different types of capital.
4. What educational advantages do middle-class children experience?

5. How does the Internet promote middle-class networking?
6. What are three important qualities that successful corporate managers need to possess?
7. Analyze the impact of downsizing, outsourcing, and temp work on the modern middle-class workforce.
8. What are common outcomes for middle-class individuals seeking reemployment?
9. Is it clear that most indebted Americans are irresponsible, uncontrolled consumers? Discuss, supplying relevant data.

Research Papers

1. Focus on middle-class education, starting with sources in this chapter and obtaining others that also illustrate how the four different types of capital can contribute to effective schooling.
2. Reread the brief discussion of the ecology of class. Think of another topic where this concept applies and write a short analysis of it.
3. Gather information and data about the functions that online communities can provide individuals and groups. Is there a downside? In assessing both the positives and negatives, it might be useful to specify the conditions under

which online communities make positive contributions.
4. Indicate how middle-class work has changed over time by investigating employees' experiences. Include the concepts downsizing, outsourcing, temp work, and any others that might prove useful.
5. In the twenty-first century, how does social reproduction impact the middle class? Address this question, using the chapter's section "The Middle Class's Slippery Slope for Making Ends Meet" as a starting point. Bring in different types of capital when useful.

Informative Websites

The American Medical Association (http://www .ama-assn.org/) represents about 135,000 physicians who belong to an upper-middle-class occupation. The American Nurses Association (http://www.nursingworld.org/)

serves a less affluent professional group, which possesses about 180,000 members.
SchoolMatters (http://www.schoolmatters.com/ schools.aspx/q/page=sp/sid=99695) provides current or prospective parents some

useful information about schools their children attend or might attend.

Linkedin (http://press.linkedin.com/about) is a social-networking site whose spokespeople claim that 75 million professionals use it to exchange job-related information.

If corporate executives access Outsource2india's website (http://www.outsource2india.com/ why_india/article_index.asp), they find a list of reasons to outsource hi-tech jobs to that country.

Individuals facing bankruptcy and seeking an attorney can find many websites. The following site (http://www.bankruptcylawyer connecticut.com/) offers legal assistance to people in my locale.

Bibliography

ABC World News Poll. 2010. "Within the Middle Class, Four in 10 Are Struggling." http://abcnews.go.com/images/PollingUnit/1106a1middleClass.pdf.

Achinstein, Betty, Rodney T. Ogawa, and Anna Speiglman. 2004. "Are We Creating Separate and Unequal Tracks of Teachers? The Effects of State Policy, Local Conditions, and Teacher Characteristics on New Teacher Socialization." *American Educational Research Journal* 41 (Autumn): 557–603.

Allen, Tammy D., Mark L. Poteet, and Joyce E.A. Russell. 2000. "Protégé Selection by Mentors: What Makes the Difference?" *Journal of Organization Behavior* 21 (May): 271–82.

Aoki, Naomi. 2001. "Women Helping Women on Rise; Female Pioneers Serve as Mentors to the Next Generation." *Boston Globe* (May 9): F1.

Appleby, Joyce. 2001. "The Social Consequences of American Revolutionary Ideals in the Early Republic," pp. 31–49 in Burton J. Bledstein and Robert D. Johnston, *The Middling Sorts: Explorations in the History of the American Middle Class*. New York: Routledge.

Applegate, Debby. 2001. "Henry Ward Beecher and the 'Great Middle Class': Mass-Marketed Intimacy and Middle-Class Identity," pp. 107–34 in Burton J. Bledstein and Robert D. Johnston (eds.), *The Middling Sorts: Explorations in the History of the American Middle Class*. New York: Routledge.

Barr, Stephen. 2007. "Bringing Generation Y into the Fold." *Washington Post* (September 24): D1.

Bartlett, Donald L., and James B. Steele. 1996. *America: Who Stole the Dream?* Kansas City, MO: Andrews and McMeel.

Barvosa, Edwina. 2008. *Wealth of Selves: Multiple Identities, Mestiza Consciousness, and the Subject of Politics*. College Station: Texas A & M University Press.

Bashaw, David J., and John S. Heywood. 2001. "The Gender Earnings Gap for U.S. Physicians: Has Equality Been Achieved?" *Review of Labor Economics & Industrial Revolution* 15 (September): 371–91.

Beckery, Sven. 2001. "Properties of a Different Kind: Bourgeoisie and Lower-Middle Class in the Nineteenth-Century United States," pp. 288–95 in Burton J. Bledstein and Robert D. Johnston (eds.), *The Middling Sorts: Explorations in the History of the American Middle Class*. New York: Routledge.

Bernhardt, Annette, Martina Morris, Mark S. Handcock, and Marc Scott. 2000. "Trends in Job Instability and Wages for Young Men," pp. 111–41 in David Newmark (ed.), *On the Job: Is Long-Term Employment a Thing of the Past?* New York: Russell Sage Foundation.

Birkbeck, Morris. 1818. *Notes on a Journey in America, from the Coast of Virginia to the Territory of Illinois*. London: Severn & Company.

Bishop, Libby, and David I. Levine. 1999. "Computer-Mediated Communication and Employee Voice: A Case Study." *Industrial and Labor Relations Review* 52: 213–33.

Blumin, Stuart M. 1989. *The Emergence of the Middle Class: Social Experience in the American City, 1760–1900*. Cambridge, England: Cambridge University Press.

Bower, Bruce. 2002. "Night Patrol for Tired Cops." *Science News* 161 (April 6): 212.

Brady, Marilyn Dell. 1991. "The New Model Middle-Class Family [1915–1930]," pp. 83–115 in Joseph M. Hawes and Elizabeth I. Nybakken (eds.), *American Families: A Research Guide and Historical Handbook*. New York: Greenwood Press.

Brown, Clair, John Haltiwanger, and Julia Lane. 2006. *Economic Turbulence: Is a Volatile*

Economy Good for America? Chicago: University of Chicago Press.

Bureau of Labor Statistics. 2008a. "Occupational Employment and Wages News Release." (May 9). http://www.bls.gov/news.release/ocwage.htm.

Bureau of Labor Statistics. 2008b. "Displaced Workers by Occupation of Lost Job and Employment Status in January 2008." (August 26). http://www.bls.gov/news.release/disp.t05.htm.

Bureau of Labor Statistics. 2011. "Labor Force Statistics from the Current Population Survey." http://www.bls.gov/cps/.

Carlan, Philip E. 2007. "The Search for Job Satisfaction: A Survey of Alabama Policing." *American Journal of Criminal Justice* 32 (September): 74–86.

Chang, Alicia. 2007. "Aerospace Industry Pushes Recruiting into Cyberspace." *Los Angeles Times* (May 21): C3.

Chun, Jennifer Ji Hye. 2001. "Flexible Despotisms: The Intensification of Insecurity and Uncertainty in the Lives of Silicon Valley's High-Tech Assembly Workers," pp. 127–54 in Rick Baldoz, Charles Koeber, and Philip Kraft (eds.), *The Critical Study of Work: Labor, Technology, and Global Production*. Philadelphia: Temple University Press.

Cohen, Andrew Wender. 2001. "Obstacles to History? Modernization and the Lower Middle Class in Chicago, 1900–1940," pp. 189–200 in Burton J. Bledstein and Robert D. Johnston (eds.), *The Middling Sorts: Explorations in the History of the American Middle Class*. New York: Routledge.

Cohen, Stephen S., and Gary Fields. 2000. "Social Capital and Capital Gains: An Examination of Social Capital in Silicon Valley," pp. 190–217 in Martin Kenney (ed.), *Understanding Silicon Valley: The Anatomy of an Entrepreneurial Region*. Stanford: Stanford University Press.

Conant, James Bryant. 1967. *The Comprehensive High School: A Second Report to Interested Citizens*. New York: McGraw-Hill.

Conrad, Peter. 1988. "Learning to Doctor: Reflections on Recent Accounts of the Medical School Years." *Journal of Health and Social Behavior* 29 (December): 323–32.

Coombs, Robert Holman. 1998. *Surviving Medical School*. Thousand Oaks, CA: Sage.

Currie, Elliott. 2004. *The Road to Whatever: Middle-Class Culture and the Crisis of Adolescence*. New York: Metropolitan Books.

Damast, Alison. 2008. "MBA Applications Surge Again." *Business Week* (August 27). http://www.businessweek.com/bschools/content/aug2008/bs20080826_158181.htm.

Darbyshire, Philip, and Suzanne Gordon. 2005. "Exploring Popular Images and Representations of Nurses and Nursing," pp. 69–92 in John Daly, Sandra Speedy, Debra Jackson, Vickie A. Lambert, and Clinton E. Lambert (eds.), *Professional Nursing: Concepts, Issues, and Challenges*. New York: Springer Publishing Company.

Davis, Clark. 2001. "The Corporate Reconstruction of Middle-Class Manhood," pp. 201–16 in Burton J. Bledstein and Robert D. Johnston (eds.), *The Middling Sorts: Explorations in the History of the American Middle Class*. New York: Routledge.

Dellarocas, Chrysanthos. 2003. "The Digitization of Word of Mouth: Promise and Challenges of Online Feedback Mechanisms." *Management Science* 49 (October):1407–24.

Demo, David H., and Martha J. Cox. 2000. "Families with Young Children: A Review of Research in the 1990s." *Journal of Marriage and the Family* 62 (November): 876–95.

Dill, Bonnie Thornton, Amy E. McLaughlin, and Angel Davis Nieves. 2007. "Future Directions of Feminist Research: Intersectionality," pp. 629–37 in Sharlene Nagy Hesse-Biber (ed.), *Handbook of Feminist Research: Theory and Praxis*. Thousand Oaks, CA: Sage.

DiMaggio, Paul, Eszter Hargittai, W. Russell Neuman, and John P. Robinson. 2001. "Social Implications of the Internet." *Annual Review of Sociology* 27: 307–36.

Doob, Christopher Bates. 2005. *Race, Ethnicity, and the American Urban Mainstream*. Boston: Pearson Allyn & Bacon.

Doster, Adam. 2006. "White-Collar Workers Unite." *In These Times*. (December 14). http://www.inthesetimes.com/article/2938/white_collars_workers_unite/.

Dye, Thomas R. 2002. *Who's Running America? The Bush Restoration*, 7th ed. Upper Saddle River, NJ: Prentice-Hall.

Ehrenreich, Barbara. 2005. *Bait and Switch: The (Futile) Pursuit of the American Dream*. New York: Metropolitan Books.

Ehrenreich, Barbara, and Ta Mara Draut. 2006. "Downsized but Not Out." *Nation* (October 19). http://www.thenation.com/doc/20061106/ehrenreich.

Facebook. 2008. "About Facebook." http://www.facebook.com/about.php.

Fields-Smith, Cheryl. 2007. "Social Class and African-American Parental Involvement," pp. 167–202 in Jane A. Van Galen and George W. Noblit (eds.), *Late to Class: Social Class and Schooling in the New Economy*. Albany: State University of New York Press.

Finney, Karen. 2009. "Physicians' Job Satisfaction Varies by Specialty." University of California: UC Newsroom. http://www.universityofcalifornia.edu/news/article/22241.

Forrester Research. 2008. "Research Focus." http://www.forrester.com/rb/analyst/john_mccarthy.

Frank, Robert H. 2007. *Falling Back: How Rising Inequality Harms the Middle Class*. Berkeley: University of California Press.

Gilbert, Dennis. 2011. *The American Class Structure in an Age of Growing Inequality*, 8th ed. Los Angeles: Pine Forge Press.

Gordon, Larry, and Victoria Kim. 2008. "Hovering Parents No Big Deal for Freshmen." *Los Angeles Times* (January 24): B1.

Gorman, Thomas J. 2000. "Reconsidering Worlds of Pain: Life in the Working Class(es)." *Sociological Forum* 15: 693–717.

Group, Thetis M., and Jean I. Roberts. 2001. *Nursing, Physician Control, and the Medical Monopoly*. Bloomington, IN: Indiana University Press.

Gulwadi, Gowri Betrabet. 2006. "Seeking Restorative Experiences: Elementary School Teachers' Choices for Places That Enable Coping with Stress." *Environment and Behavior* 38 (July): 503–20.

Hacker, Jacob S. 2006. *The Assault on American Jobs, Families, Health Care and Retirement and How You Can Fight Back*. New York: Oxford University Press.

Haveman, Robert, and Timothy Smeeding. 2006. "The Role of Higher Education in Social Mobility." *The Future of Children* 16 (Autumn): 125–50.

Heckscher, Charles. 1995. *White-Collar Blues: Management Loyalties in an Age of Corporate Restructuring*. New York: Basic Books.

Hira, Ron, and Anil Hira. 2005. *Outsourcing America: What's Behind Our National Crisis and How Can We Reclaim American Jobs*. New York: Amacom.

Hoogstra, Lisa. 2005. "The Design of the 500 Family Study," pp. 18–38 in Barbara Schneider and Linda J. Waite (eds.), *Being Together, Working Apart: Dual-Career Families and the Work-Life Balance*. New York: Cambridge University Press.

Horvat, Erin McNamara, Elliot B. Weininger, and Annette Lareau. 2003. "From Social Ties to Social Capital: Class Differences in the Relations between Schools and Parent Networks." *American Educational Research Journal* 40 (Summer): 319–51.

Huston, Carol J. 2006. *Professional Issues in Nursing: Challenges & Opportunities*. Philadelphia: Lippincott, Williams & Williams.

Hyde, Alan. 2003. *Working in Silicon Valley: Economic and Legal Analysis of a High-Velocity Labor Market*. Armonk, NY: M.E. Sharpe.

Illick, Joseph E. 2002. *American Childhoods*. Philadelphia: University of Pennsylvania Press.

Ip, Greg. 2008. "The Declining Value of Your College Degree." *Wall Street Journal* (July 17): D1.

Jackall, Robert. 2010. *Moral Mazes: The World of Corporate Managers*, 2nd ed. New York: Oxford University Press.

Johnson, Susan Moore, and Sarah E. Birkeland. 2003. "Pursuing a 'Sense of Success': New Teachers Explain Their Career Decisions." *American Educational Research Journal* 40 (Fall): 518–617.

Kane, Sally. 2008. "Legal Career Satisfaction." *About.com*. (February 10). http://legalcareers.about.com/b/2008/02/10/legal-career-satisfaction.htm.

Karabel, Jerome. 2005. *The Chosen: The Hidden History of Admission and Exclusion at Harvard, Yale, and Princeton*. Boston: Houghton Mifflin Company.

Kehrer, Barbara H. 1976. "Factors Affecting the Incomes of Men and Women Physicians: An Exploratory Analysis." *Journal of Human Relations* 11 (Autumn): 526–45.

Kilcoyne, Patrick. 2004. "Occupations in the Temporary Help Services Industry." Bureau of Labor Statistics. http://www.bls.gov/oes/2004/may/temp.pdf.

Kozol, Jonathan. 1991. *Savage Inequalities: Children in America's Schools*. New York: Crown Publishers.

Kraut, Robert E., M. Patterson, V. Lundmark, Sara Kiesler, T. Mukophadhyay, and W. Scherlis. 1998. "Internet Paradox: A Social Technology That Reduces Social Involvement and Psychological Well-Being?" *American Psychologist* 53: 1017–31.

Landon, Bruce E. 2004. "Career Satisfaction among Physicians." *JAMA* 291 (February 4). http://jama.ama=assn.org/cgi/content/full/291/5/634.

Lareau, Annette. 2002. "Invisible Inequality: Social Class and Childrearing in Black Families and White Families." *American Sociological Review* 67 (October): 747–76.

Lareau, Annette. 2003. *Unequal Childhoods: Class, Race, and Family Life*. Berkeley, CA: University of California Press.

Lareau, Annette. 2007. "Unequal Childhoods: Class, Race, and Family Life," pp. 537–48 in David B. Grusky and Szonja Szelényi (eds.), *The Inequality Reader: Contemporary and Foundational Readings in Race, Class, and Gender*. Boulder: Westview Press.

Leigh, Paul, Daniel J. Tancredi, and Richard L. Kravitz. 2009. "Physician Career Satisfaction with Specialties." *BMC Health Services Research* 9. http://www.biomedcentral.com/1472-6963/9/166.

Lengermann, Patricia Madoo, and Gillian Niebrugge. 2008. "Modern Feminist Theory," pp. 319–71 in George Ritzer, *Modern Sociological Theory*, 7th ed. New York: McGraw-Hill.

Leonhardt, David. 2005. "The College Dropout Boom." *New York Times* (May 24): A1+.

Lin, Nan. 2000. "Inequality in Social Capital." *Contemporary Sociology* 29 (November): 785–95.

Lohr, Steve. 2006. "Study Plays Down Export of Computer Jobs." *New York Times* (February 23). http://www.cs.rice.edu/-vardi/jmtf06.html.

Maag, Christopher. 2008. "A Neighborhood Is Reborn After a Killing on Prince Avenue." *New York Times* (September 27): A18.

Maier, Kimberly S. 2005. "Transmitting Educational Values: Parent Occupation and Adolescent Development," pp. 396–418 in Barbara Schneider and Linda J. Waite (eds.), *Being Together, Working Apart: Dual-Career Families and the Work-Life Balance*. New York: Cambridge University Press.

Marchena, Elaine. 2005. "Adolescents' Assessments of Parental Role Management in Dual-Earner Families, pp. 333–60 in Barbara Schneider and Linda J. Waite (eds.), *Being Together, Working Apart: Dual-Career Families and the Work-Life Balance*. New York: Cambridge University Press.

Massey, Douglas S., and Nancy A. Denton. 1993. *American Apartheid: Segregation and the Making of the Underclass*. Cambridge, MA: Harvard University Press.

Mayclim, Troy. 2009. "Job Satisfaction Climbs during Downturn." *Execunet.com,* (July 7).

Mendenhall, Ruby, Ariel Kalil, Laurel J. Spindel, and Cassandra M.D. Hart. 2008. "Job Loss at Mid-Life: Managers and Executives Face the 'New Risk Economy.'" *Social Forces* 87 (September): 185–209.

Miller, Larry, and Michael Braswell. 2002. *Human Relations and Police Work*, 5th ed. Long Grove, IL: Waveland Press.

Mills, C. Wright. 1956. *White Collar*. New York: Oxford University Press.

Mooney, Nan. 2008. *(Not) Keeping Up with Our Parents*. Boston: Beacon Press.

Moskowitz, Marina. 2001. "Public Exposure: Middle-Class Material Culture at the Turn of the Twentieth Century," pp. 170–84 in Burton J. Bledstein and Robert D. Johnston (eds.), *The Middling Sorts: Explorations in the History of the American Middle Class*. New York: Routledge.

Mullings, Leith, and Amy J. Schulz. 2006. "Intersectionality and Health: An Introduction," pp. 3–17 in Amy J. Schulz and Leith Mullings (eds.), *Gender, Race, Class & Health*. San Francisco: Jossey-Bass.

Newmark, David, David Polsky, and Daniel Hansen. 2000. "Has Job Stability Declined Yet? New Evidence for the 1990s," pp. 70–110 in David Newmark (ed.), *On the Job: Is Long-Term Employment a Thing of the Past?* New York: Russell Sage Foundation.

Nie, Norman, and Lutz Erbring. 2000. "Internet and Society: A Preliminary Report." Stanford Institute for the Quantitative Study of Society: Stanford University. (http://www.stanford.edu/group/siqss/Press_Release/Preliminary_Report-4-21.pdf)

Novak, Candice. 2008. "What's Good and Bad About Temp Work." *US News and World Report* (August 9). http://www.usnews.com/articles/business/careers/2008/07/15/whats-…

Nursing. 2005. "What Nurses Do and Don't Like." 35 (June): 33.

Oliver, Melvin L., and Thomas M. Shapiro. 2006. "Black Wealth/White Wealth: A New Perspective on Racial Inequality," pp. 258–65 in Melvin M. Oliver and Thomas M. Shapiro, *Contemporary and Foundational Readings in Race, Class, and Gender.* New York: Routledge.

Ornstein, Allan. 2007. *Class Counts: Education, Inequality, and the Sinking Middle Class.* Lanham, MD: Rowman & Littlefield.

Pattillo, Mary E. 1998. "Sweet Mothers and Gangbangers: Managing Crime in a Black Middle-Class Neighborhood." *Social Forces* 76 (March): 747–74.

Perrucci, Robert, and Earl Wysong. 2008. *The New Class Society: Goodbye American Dream?*, 3rd ed. Lanham, MD: Rowman & Littlefield.

Proweller, Amira. 1998. *Constructing Female Identities: Meaning Making in an Upper Middle Class Youth Culture.* Albany: State University of New York Press.

Pryor, Frederic L., and David Schaffer. 1997. "Wages and the University Educated: A Paradox Resolved." *Monthly Labor Review* (July). http://www.bls.gov/opub/mlr/1997/07/art1full.pdf.

Ray, Dana. 1995. "Confront Call Reluctance." *Personal Selling Power* (September): 46–51.

RN. 2005. "Job Satisfaction at Issue in ANA Survey." 68 (June): 18.

Robinson, Simon, Ross Dixon, Christopher Preece, and Kristen Moodley. 2007. *Engineering, Business and Professional Ethics.* Amsterdam: Elsevier.

Rodgers, Bruce A. 2006. *Psychological Aspects of Police Work: An Officer's Guide to Street Psychology.* Springfield, IL: Charles C. Thomas.

Rodgers, Daniel T. 1978. *The Work Ethic in Industrial America, 1850–1920.* Chicago: University of Chicago Press.

Rotundo, E. Anthony. 1983. "Body and Soul: Changing Ideals of American Middle-Class Manhood, 1770–1920." *Journal of Social History* 16 (Summer): 23–38.

Rowland, Diana, Catherine Hoffman, and Molly McGinn-Shapiro. 2009. "Focus on Health Reform: Health Care and the Middle Class: More Costs and Less Coverage." *The Henry Kaiser Family Foundation.* http://www.kff.0rg/healthreform/759/.cfm.

Sandefur, Rebecca L. 2001. "Work and Honor in the Law: Prestige and the Division of Lawyers' Labor." *American Sociological Review* 66 (June): 382–403.

Sasser, Alicia C. 2005. "Gender Differences in Physician Pay: Tradeoffs between Career and Family." *Journal of Human Resources* 40 (Spring): 477–504.

Scott, Janny. 2005. "Life at the Top Isn't Just Better, It's Longer." *New York Times* (May 16): A1+.

Sennett, Richard. 2006. *The Culture of the New Capitalism.* New Haven: Yale University Press.

Sheshabalaya, Ashutosh. 2005. *Elephant: The Growing Clash with India over White-Collar Jobs and the Meaning for Americans and the World.* Monroe, ME: Common Courage Press.

Slavin, Robert E. 1994. "After the Victory: Making Funding Equity Make a Difference." *Theory into Practice 33 (Spring):* 98–103.

Slavin, Robert E. 1999. "How Can Funding Equity Ensure Enhanced Achievement?" *Journal of Education Finances* 24: 519–28.

Smith, Vicki. 2001. *Crossing the Great Divide: Worker Risk and Opportunity in the New Economy.* Ithaca, NY: ILR Press.

Stewart, Mary W. 2005. "The Social Context of Professional Nursing," pp. 111–27 in Kathleen Masters (ed.), *Role Development in Professional Nursing Practice.* Sudbury, MA: Jones and Bartlett.

Swartz, Katherine. 2006. *Reinsuring Health: Why More Middle-Class People Are Uninsured and What Governments Can Do.* New York: Russell Sage Foundation.

Tribble, Sarah Jane. 2008. "The Social Network as a Career Safety Net." *New York Times* (August 14): C6.

Uchitelle, Louis. 2006. *The Disposable American: Layoffs and Their Consequences.* New York: Alfred A. Knopf.

U.S. Census Bureau. 2007a. Table P-45. "Occupation of Longest Job—Full-Time, Year-Round Workers (Both Sexes Combined) by Median and Mean Earnings: 1982 to 2001." *Historical Incomes Tables—People.* http://www.census.gov/hhes/www/income/histinc/p45.html.

U.S. Census Bureau. 2007b. Table P-45A. "Occupation of Longest Job—Full-Time, Year-Round Workers (Both Sexes Combined) by Median and Mean Earnings: 2002 to 2007." *Historical Incomes Tables—People.* http://www.census.gov/hhes/www/income/histinc/p45A.html.

U.S. Department of Commerce. 2010. "Middle Class in America." http://commerce.gov/s/groups/public@doc/@os/@opa/documentss/content/prod01.

Vallas, Steven P. 1987. "White-Collar Proletarians? The Structure of Clerical Work and Levels of Class Consciousness." *Sociological Quarterly* 28 (Winter): 523–40.

Valleta, Robert G. 2000. "Declining Job Security," pp. 227–56 in David Newmark (ed.), *On the Job: Is Long-Term Employment a Thing of the Past?* New York: Russell Sage Foundation.

Ward, Stephanie Francis. 2007. "Pulse of the Legal Profession." *ABA Journal.* http://www.abajournal.com/magazine/article/pulse_of_the_legal_profession.

Warren, Elizabeth. 2007. "The New Economics of the Middle Class: Why Making Ends Meet Has Gotten Harder." Testimony before Senate Finance Committee, May 10, 2007. http://finance.senate.gov/hearings/testimony/2007test/051007testew.pdf.

Warren, Elizabeth, and Amelia Warren Tyagi. 2003. *The Two-Income Trap: Why Middle-Class Mothers and Fathers Are Going Broke.* New York: Basic Books.

Weir, Margaret. 2002. "The American Middle Class and the Politics of Education," pp. 178–203 in Oliver Zunz, Leonard Schoppa, and Nobuhiro Hiwatari (eds.), *Social Contracts under Stress: The Middle Classes of America, Europe, and Japan at the Turn of the Century.* New York: Russell Sage Foundation.

Wellman, Barry. 2001. "Computer Networks as Social Networks." *Science* 293 (September 14): 2031–34.

Wentzel, Kathryn. 2002. "Are Effective Teachers like Good Parents? Teaching Styles and Student Adjustment in Early Adolescence." *Child Development* 73 (January–February): 287–301.

Westphal, James D., and Ithal Stern. 2006. "The Other Pathway to the Boardroom: Interpersonal Influence Behavior as a Substitute for Elite Credentials and Majority Status in Obtaining Board Appointments." *Administrative Science Quarterly* 51 (June): 169–204.

Whyte, William H., Jr. 1956. *The Organization Men.* Garden City, NY: Doubleday Anchor Books.

Wills, John. 2000. "Provincial Lives: Middle-Class Experience in the Antebellum Middle West." *Economic History Review* 53 (August): 599–600.

Wolff, Edward N. 2007. "Recent Trends in Household Wealth in the United States: Rising Debt and the Middle-Class Squeeze." *Working Paper No. 589,* http://www.levyinstitute.org/pubs/wp_589.pdf.

Wyatt, Ian D., and Daniel E. Hecker. 2006. "Occupational Changes during the 20th Century." *Monthly Labor Review* (March), pp. 35–57. http://www.bls.gov/opub/mlr/2006/03/art-3full.pdf.

Xiao, Hong. 2000. "Class, Gender, and Parental Values in the 1990s." *Gender & Society* 14 (December): 785–803.

CHAPTER 7

Working Class: Estranged from Entitlement

When she entered a prominent university, Julie Ann, whose background was working-class, explained that she "never shared the sense of entitlement felt by many of my peers." Julie Ann felt insecure, always expecting "to be 'discovered' . . . I still remember how lucky I was to be 'allowed' to attend a university" (Cannon 2006, 101). Alfred Lubrano, a well-known writer, expressed a similar insecurity, indicating that in college he had suffered "imposter syndrome" and that even when receiving good grades, it did not seem his As were equal to middle-class students' (Lubrano 2004, 89–90).

Working-class people's location in the class-stratification system has often been precarious: generally employed, yes, but often not economically comfortable. And because of restricted financial, cultural, human, and social capital, working-class people frequently do not feel prepared to move into the middle-class world.

From the country's early years, working-class individuals and families found life difficult and demanding.

WORKING-CLASS HISTORY

In a newly settled, undeveloped land, common laborers did just that—labored for most of their waking hours. Accounts of seventeenth-century English workers in the middle colonies described men in sweat-soaked, woolen clothes, trapped in areas made torturous by fierce heat, humidity, mosquitoes, poisonous snakes, and blistered hands produced by wielding axes and hoes throughout the day. With nightfall the exhausted workers usually experienced little relief, finding themselves forced to grind corn into corn bread or hominy (Jones 1999, 22–23).

One prominent category of labor was indentured servants. In the seventeenth-century settlements in Virginia and Maryland, 75 to 85 percent of the 130,000 settlers were indentured servants. Three fourths were single men between the ages of 15 and 24. In exchange for four to seven years of servitude, they obtained their freedom, payment of the passage from Europe, a fresh set of clothes, a few tools, and 50 acres of land. This was a great opportunity for these impoverished individuals—possibly their only chance to acquire such a large plot of land. Working conditions, however, were very oppressive: Indentured servants faced masters who forced them to labor long and hard and readily imposed harsh punishments for any infractions. The result was that nearly two thirds died before their terms expired (Levine, Brier, Brundage, Countryman, Fennell, and Rediker 1989, 50–52).

Indentured servants as well as other categories of colonial manual workers were expected to labor "the whole day"—six days a week, from dawn to dusk in winter, and from 10 to 12 hours in summer. However, work itself was much more irregular, with farm labor taking much more time in the summer than winter and colonial shops and businesses often setting uneven work hours (Rodgers 1978, 18).

In the seventeenth and eighteenth centuries, a worker's legal status—indentured servant, convict laborer (deported from England), or family member—was more important than the specific kind of work in shaping his or her life. While daily existence might be physically demanding and unrewarding for family members, they were less exploited and better treated than indentured servants and convicts, who ran away in droves, producing a steady stream of announcements about their escapes in colonial newspapers operating in towns and cities along the Atlantic coast (Jones 1999, 39).

For workers family life was difficult, barely maintained above subsistence level. While Benjamin Franklin and other leaders lauded the newly formed nation as the land of opportunity, such employees as laborers, seamen, artisans, shoemakers, and tailors tended to remain propertyless, with stagnant incomes and no occupational mobility. Workers could seldom afford to own their homes, and they faced an economy where costs for such basic items as heating fuel and clothing were high and often increasing (Illick 2002, 76–77).

By the mid-nineteenth century, working-class members were diversified occupationally, serving as unskilled laborers, artisans, outworkers, and factory workers:

Unskilled laborers: During the 1800s massive expansion and building occurred, and while much of the work was unskilled, it required considerable physical strength and endurance to dig the canals, lay the track, build the roads, and carry out the myriad other tasks that various machines performed in the twentieth century. Between 1820 and 1860, the real wages of unskilled day laborers rose about 12 percent per decade, but for a pair of reasons the standard of living did not improve dramatically. First, competition, particularly from newly arrived immigrants desperate for any jobs, helped hold wages down. Second, jobs seldom lasted more than several weeks, sometimes only a day or two. Unskilled laborers generally ended up working no more than 200 days a year, leaving their families in difficult economic circumstances. Other family members contributed, with wives sometimes taking in boarders or doing outwork, where they made various saleable products at home. Children worked in factories, or, in the case of girls became live-in domestics. Sometimes minorities were hired. In the early 1860s, a burning question was whether seemingly puny Chinese men would be strong enough to build the transcontinental railroad. Charles Crocker, a contractor for the Central Pacific Railroad, decided to give them a trial. Although scornfully called "Crocker's pets," they proved to be excellent workers in treacherous, physically demanding conditions. Once the Chinese presence was accepted, they provided four out of every five new laborers on the transcontinental railroad.

Artisans: In the late eighteenth century, these craftsmen worked in small teams, with a master at the head. They served as tailors, shoemakers, barrelmakers, tanners, blacksmiths, printers, glassmakers, cabinetmakers, and in many other trades, often making a good living. Early in the nineteenth century, however, preindustrial employers took advantage of expanding markets and began dividing the expensive skilled operations into simpler tasks, and many artisans either had to accept lower pay or lose their jobs to women, children, or recent immigrants eager to do the work (Doob 1999, 61; Levine, Brier, Brundage, Countryman, Fennell, and Rediker 1989, 240–246). In the mid-nineteenth century, skilled artisans in such occupations as shoemaking or glassmaking found their crafts disappearing, replaced by various factory jobs in which workers performed specific tasks and produced the respective items more quickly and cheaply (Rodgers 1978, 22–23).

Outworkers: From the 1820s onward, outworkers, who labored in their homes, made products for low wages and minimal overhead costs. The workers were sometimes women who were the wives and daughters of poor laborers and were unwilling or unable to leave their homes. However, the majority of outworkers were female household heads, who were either abandoned by their husbands or widowed. For outworkers technological advances did not necessarily improve their lives. In 1846 the invention of the sewing machine, for example, did reduce the labor required to make garments, but the chief beneficiaries were employers, who dropped the piece rates so low that women had to work 15 to 18 hours on the new machines to earn as much as they had previously.

Factory workers: The first American factory was in Pawtucket, Rhode Island, where in 1790 Samuel Slater, an English immigrant, mechanized the spinning of cotton. By the middle 1830s, factories in southern New England were common—difficult places to work with low pay, long hours, and unhealthy, physically dangerous conditions. In this era increasing competition from new firms brought down prices, encouraging the bosses to speed up production and to lower the payment for each piece completed (LeBlanc 1999, 29–30; Levine, Brier, Brundage, Countryman, Fennell, and Rediker 1989, 249–54). The early factory system effectively represented Karl Marx's claim that capitalists engage in ever-expanding exploitation of their workers.

While employers exploited their workers, they also had trouble disciplining them. The most irregular production came from casually supervised outworkers alone in their own homes. However, even in the fairly controlled New England textile factories, managers were hard pressed to keep machines running on hot summer days. In 1878 one textile manager observed, "Our mill operatives are much like other people, and take their frequent holidays for pleasure and visiting" (Rodgers 1978, 162). In addition, a certain segment of workers frequently changed jobs, especially in prosperous times. The limited research on the topic suggested no clear motive for most departures: only that the workers involved felt dissatisfied and restless in a certain job but that its replacement was likely to be no more satisfying (Rodgers 1978, 164–65).

Working-class members toiled but generally remained poor or close to it. Between 1870 and 1890, 40 percent of industrial workers fell below the poverty line of $500 a year, and another 45 percent were barely above that level. The top 15 percent were craftsmen, usually Protestant and native born, who might earn three times as much as other working-class members. Furthermore craftsmen were fairly autonomous, often informally establishing "stints" (output quotas) and using their superior knowledge of the production process to defeat employers' efforts to wring more work from them.

All members of nineteenth-century working-class families worked hard. Many children had jobs in factories and in other settings, and among immigrant families, which were usually desperately poor, wives would frequently seek employment.

Second-generation families tried to keep the wife out of the workforce to do the formidable, full-time job of homemaking. Even in cities it often included raising their own vegetables, poultry, and livestock; making meals, with few or no prepared foods, not even bread; hauling water for cooking, cleaning, and laundering from outside the home; and tending and cleaning wood and coal stoves, which took hours of toil and produced an outpouring of soot making housework even more arduous (Coontz 1999, 99–102; Montgomery 1979, 12).

All in all, nineteenth-century working-class life was difficult. Low pay and poor working conditions encouraged high turnover, with annual rates often attaining 100 to 250 percent of the original labor force. To stabilize his workforce, Henry Ford in 1914 initiated his famous five-dollar-a-day minimum wage (Montgomery 1979, 41; Raff and Summers 1987).

In the opening two decades of the twentieth century, employers in different industries increasingly planned both the production of materials and workers' role in the productive operations. Ford's unprecedented wage, for instance, was a carefully calculated tactic that permitted bosses to demand whatever tempo of work they desired (Montgomery 1979, 101–02). Employers were exerting increasing control. It is hardly surprising that in some factories labor unions sought to improve factory workers' lives.

The Union Response

Historically many Americans have considered labor unions troublesome or insignificant. Several decades ago a successful young entrepreneur who owned a small, growing manufacturing business told me that he informed his workers that if they wanted to unionize it was fine with him, but they would find that his pay scale was better. But was that the only issue to consider? What about unions' struggles for benefits, improved working conditions, or possible protections against layoffs? The business owner did not necessarily consider such possible contributions, but unions do.

A **labor union** is an organization that legally represents the interests of a set of job holders in respect to wages, benefits, and working conditions. One of the earliest efforts to organize a union involved female factory workers in the Lowell (Massachusetts) textile mills, who issued the following statement: "As our fathers resisted unto blood the lordly avarice of the British ministry, so we, their daughters, never will wear the yoke that has been prepared for us" (LeBlanc 1999, 32).

In 1877, in response to years of 12-to-14-hour days and steady wage cuts, trainmen at the Baltimore and Ohio Railroad went on strike, and other railroads around the country took up the cause. In Pittsburgh federal troops brought in to break up the strike fired into the crowd and killed about 20 people, including three children. In the wake of this uprising, labor leaders formed the Knights of Labor, which took the unusually progressive positions of accepting all races and women as members and advocating equal pay for equal work, the female vote, and reduced working hours. This early union did obtain 700,000 members, but a coalition of big-business interests including newspapers destroyed it (LeBlanc 1999, 45–46).

Throughout the second half of the nineteenth century, one of the Knights' central issues—the length of the work day—became a popular rallying point. In the words of labor leader Samuel Gompers, the shorter workday was "the question of questions," the only one which "reaches the very root of society," addressing the intense desire of workers to obtain daily relief from lengthy toil (Rodgers 1978, 156). It was an issue that unified large numbers of working people, and it inspired two crusades—one in the middle 1860s and the other 20 years later. In spite of many strikes and increased union membership, especially in the Knights of Labor, the crusades did little to reduce workers' hours.

In fact, by the late nineteenth and early twentieth centuries, most workers who walked off their jobs struck over wage-related issues (Rodgers 1978, 156–58). At this time wages were slowly rising, but most working-class individuals could not support families on just their earnings. Wives took in laundry, looked after boarders, and made clothes to sell. Even though school attendance was rising, many children went to work at 12 or 13. As late as the middle 1920s, over half of working-class homes lacked indoor plumbing. Many of these families lived in rundown rural or urban areas.

Besides low income, working-class job holders often faced dangerous conditions. Factory employees sometimes encountered destructive chemical exposure, often unaware of the dangers they faced. Inhaling toxic dust killed miners and textile workers, and individuals exposed to petrochemicals could suffer lead poisoning, shaking violently and hallucinating. The most dangerous working-class jobs, however, involved mining and railroads. Between 1870 and 1920, cave-ins, fires, and explosions killed 75,000 miners, and from 1890 to 1920, accidents led to the death of 86,000 railroad workers (Ziegler and Gall 2002, 9–12).

Job conditions produced intense dissatisfaction, promoting widespread strikes. Between 1914 and 1920, an average of over 3,000 strikes a year occurred. The outstanding year was 1919 when 4 million individuals, 21 percent of the labor force, went on strike. In 1919 and 1920, 400,000 steel workers walked off the job (LeBlanc 1999, 70; Ziegler and Gall 2002, 37).

The arrival of the Great Depression brought hard times for many people and also for unions, whose membership, never more than 10 percent of the workforce, fell to 7 percent in 1930. Five years later, however, the passage of the National Labor Relations Act created a framework supporting workers' rights to organize into unions, to engage in collective bargaining with management, and to strike against their employers. Supported by this legislation and the Roosevelt administration, unions began organizing among such groups as auto and steel workers, commercial cannery and laundry employees, sharecroppers, and tenant farmers. By 1941 about a third of the labor force was unionized. In the South, however, owners and management used intimidation and violence to subdue the union efforts. Racism was a frequent theme, with steel employers stating that unions' intention of bringing blacks and whites together was inherently destructive to the "Southern way of life" (Jones 1999, 191; LeBlanc 1999, 89–91).

Since winning World War II was their mutual priority, unions and management cooperated with each other between 1941 and 1945. After the war, however, organized labor was stronger than ever before, comprising 14.5 million members and 35 percent of the civilian labor force (Ziegler and Gall 2002, 144). Union strength encouraged militancy, with 3.5 million members striking in 1945 and 4.6 million walking off the job the following year. Such actions brought increased pay for union members in the striking industries. Indeed, for the next 30 years, industrial unions provided workers rising buying power and an improved living standard. Average wages adjusted for inflation rose 250 percent. Meanwhile Walter Reuther, the president of the United Auto Workers, sought to ensure that consumers were not burdened by the expense of workers' raises (LeBlanc 1999, 96–98). During that era, however, unions were starting to face fierce political opposition. In 1947 an anti-labor Congress passed the Taft Hartley Act, which eliminated such powerful organizing tools as the closed shop requiring all workers at a place of employment to be union members and also the sympathy strike permitting individuals in one industry to stop work in support of those in another (Sweet and Meiksins 2008, 33).

Inevitably American unions always lacked the substantial support their counterparts in many European countries received. In western Europe, for example, working-class parties have bolstered the labor movement, obtaining a variety of benefits for both union members and the overall working-class citizenry—national healthcare, decent low-income housing, unemployment insurance, and universal high-quality education (LeBlanc 1999, 110). Furthermore in western Europe, Australia, New Zealand, and Canada, labor leaders have often been directly involved in political parties' policy decisions. For instance, in Great Britain, the Trades Union Congress, which is the umbrella organization for British labor unions, participates in Labour Party discussions and policy-making decisions (Ziegler and Gall 2002, 231). Because foreign labor unions tend to be more integrated into their nations' political structure than they are in the United States, they often are more powerful and influential than their American counterparts. It is hardly surprising to see Table 7.1's information showing that the United States has had consistently lower labor-union membership than most other developed countries. In recent decades American unions' membership has steadily declined.

TABLE 7.1 Union Membership as Percentage of the Workforce in 14 Technologically Advanced Nations

	1970	1980	1990	2000	2003
Australia	50.2%	49.5%	40.5%	24.7%	22.9%
Austria	62.8	56.7	46.9	36.5	35.4
Belgium	42.1	54.1	53.9	55.6	55.4
Canada	31.6	34.7	32.9	28.1	28.4
Denmark	60.3	78.6	75.3	73.5	70.4
Finland	51.3	69.4	72.5	75	74.1
France	21.7	18.3	10.1	8.2	8.3
Germany	32	34.9	31.2	25	22.6
Italy	37	49.6	38.8	34.9	33.7
Japan	35.1	31.3	25.4	21.5	19.7
Norway	56.8	58.3	58.5	53.7	53.3
Sweden	67.7	78	80.8	79.1	78
United Kingdom	44.8	50.7	39.3	29.7	29.3
United States	23.5	19.5	15.5	12.8	12.4

Over a 33-year period, the majority of the countries represented here, except for the Scandinavian nations and Belgium, have shown a decline in union membership. A prominent factor contributing to that decline has been the steady loss of manufacturing plants, sites where historically unionization has been prominent. Over time the United States has displayed a lower percentage of union membership than every nation in this table with the exception of France.

Source: Jelle Visser. 2006. "Union Membership Statistics in 24 Countries. *Monthly Labor Review.* V. 129 (January), pp. 38–49.

With the expanding global economy of the 1970s, working-class prosperity began to wane. At that point the Business Roundtable and other corporation-sponsored organizations launched a campaign mobilizing politicians' and media support for the idea that inflation and other economic problems resulted from workers' dangerously high wages.

Then in 1981 when a large strike of air traffic controllers occurred, President Reagan, who had jurisdiction over these federal employees, jailed the leaders of the Professional Air Traffic Controllers Organization and after giving the striking controllers two days to return to work, Reagan surprised the public and shocked the controllers by firing over 11,500 of them. The strike and the rapid firing were highly publicized. A more obscure but significant fact is that in the following years, the president appointed individuals to the National Labor Relations Board who were hostile to unions, generally siding with management's illegal efforts either to prevent union organizing or to break up unions (LeBlanc 1999, 122; Ziegler and Gall 2002, 256). Both of these actions signaled a powerful federal mobilization against labor unions. As a pair of labor experts asserted, "High wages and secure employment, the touchstone of the . . . [Roosevelt administration's] system of labor relations, suddenly came to seem counterproductive, divisive, and vaguely unpatriotic" (Boris and Lichtenstein 2003, 474).

In recent decades the commercial media, notably TV, have projected an indifferent or hostile image of labor unions, portraying their leaders as greedy, overpaid, and sometimes corrupted by connections to organized crime. In the popular series *The Sopranos*, some story lines touched on the connection between labor and organized crime, displaying a distinctly negative sense. For instance, one program showed the "business arrangement" between mobster Tony Soprano and the head of an African American jointfitters union (Kendall 2005, 152).

Labor unions have suffered. Not only have many of them lost membership, but they have become less militant, in large part because both government and management have become more punitive toward protests. As Figure 7.1 indicates, the number of work stoppages have steadily decreased over time. In 1960 there were 222, with the number peaking at 381 in 1970 and then steadily declining to 15 in 2008 (U.S. Census Bureau 2010, Table 647).

Furthermore since the 1990s, employers have used the fragile employment scene to discourage workers from starting unions. For instance, from 1993 to 1995, 50 percent of all firms and 65 percent of manufacturing companies that were targets for union organizing campaigns threatened to shut down their businesses and relocate if the workers decided to organize. Usually the threat worked, convincing employees not to organize (Pollin 2005, 55).

In spite of unions' problems in recent decades, they continue to provide their members better wages than their nonunion counterparts receive. In March 2001 Bureau of Labor Statistics data indicated that wages and salaries for private-sector union workers averaged $18.36 an hour compared with $14.81 for nonunion workers (Foster 2003). A more recent study using Current Population Survey data found a smaller but still substantial difference, concluding that unionized workers earned 9 percent more than their nonunion counterparts (Eren 2009).

While such disadvantaged groups as women and minorities readily appreciate the benefits of union membership, many unions have a history of excluding them. In modern times women's union membership has sharply increased, but they have distinctly

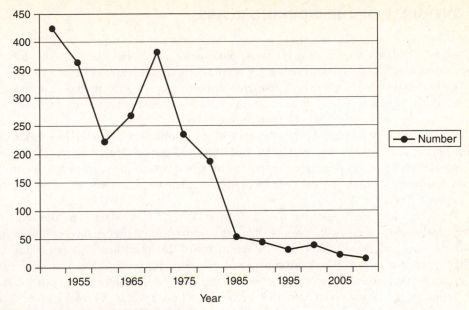

FIGURE 7.1   Work Stoppages over 58 Years

These data suggest that over time work stoppages, which involve at least 1,000 workers and last more than a day, have persistently decreased. A sharp decline started in the 1970s and persisted in the 1980s when the Reagan administration fiercely opposed unions. The number of stoppages shrunk from 381 in 1970 to 15 in 2008—less than one twenty-fifth the earlier figure.

Source: U.S. Census Bureau. 2010. Table 647. "Work Stoppages." *Statistical Abstract of the United States: 2010.* http://www.census.gov/compendia/statab/cats/labor_force_emp.

fewer opportunities than men to obtain union offices, especially the more elevated ones (Lepadatu and Thompson 2005).

Unions, however, possess a well-positioned opportunity to promote racial and/ or gender equality. In 1937 Myles Horton worked for the Textile Workers Organizing Committee. He was white, some of the workers were black, and in this sharply segregated world where unions had always excluded blacks, a white organizer was highly suspicious. While white workers readily approached Horton to sign up for the union, black workers walked away when he spoke to them. What was he going to do? Horton asked around, locating a black man considered a leader among the African American workers. They met; the man was noncommittal. Horton indicated that it was understandable how the man felt but that presently the blacks had no protection on the job. He added, "But, what you've got to think about is that maybe they'll be treated like anybody else, and protected if they join the union, and I'm telling you the truth. One way you've got a gambler's chance of protection, the other way you've got nothing" (Horton 1998, 90). The next day the man signed up, and a day later all the blacks joined him. Realistic prospects of raised salary and other benefits accompanying union membership overcame their reluctance. Horton always promoted racial equality, in part by helping disadvantaged people appreciate how union membership would enhance their lives.

Whether unionized or not, working-class individuals and families, like the members of all classes, have distinctive qualities.

AN OVERVIEW OF THE WORKING CLASS

Occupationally working-class members, who represent about 30 percent of the population, include craftsmen such as carpenters, plumbers, and electricians, unskilled factory and construction workers, and retail sales workers. Income averages about $40,000 per year (Gilbert 2011, 244, 249–48). Craftsmen—skilled workers—are included in this class because both American tradition and experts have considered the nature of their work, which is manual, distinctly blue-collar (working-class).

Racial differences have been apparent in working-class membership. Data comparing blacks and whites between 1850 and 1990 indicate a steady increase in blacks' working-class proportion over time, with African Americans at the turn of the twenty-first century showing a higher percentage in that class than whites (Horton, Allen, Herring, and Thomas 2000).

Working-class members are the core members of Karl Marx's **proletariat**, the workers, who do not own the means of production and are the victims of the capitalist order (Marx and Engels 1959, 4). The members of this class are also associated with another Marxist concept. **Work alienation** is an outcome job holders face when they lose control over either the work process, the product of their labor, or both (Shepard 1970; Sulek 2010). Marx concluded that in an era where machinery and a complicated division of labor had developed, work had lost "all individual character" and "all charm." The workman "becomes an appendage of the machine, and it is only the simplest, most monotonous, and most easily acquired knack that is required of him" (Marx and Engels 1959, 14).

Economist Michael Zweig, indicated that working-class jobs, while quite diverse, share certain distinct negative traits—the employees have little control over the pace and content of their work; and they seldom are anybody's boss. Since the early 1980s, the various global forces described in earlier chapters have produced lower real income, longer hours at work, and fewer protections by union or governmental regulation (Zweig 2000, 4–5). The most enduring element of work alienation seems to be the "simplest, most monotonous" quality of many working-class jobs. Factory jobs seem the epitome of work alienation. One individual indicated that he was employed at a margarine factory, picking up thousands of tubs of margarine each day and putting them in boxes. On the Internet he asked, "Has anyone ever been through this? How do you cope? Please give me an awesome answer so I can commit to working there" (Reddit 2010). Like this comment, the various employees' statements in this article are all attuned to Marx's observation about the worker as an appendage of the machine.

For his account about growing up in the working class, writer Alfred Lubrano conducted over 100 interviews with individuals born into that class. From these respondents along with a variety of other sources, Lubrano described the following traits of blue-collar life. They include:

- A well-developed work ethic, staying locked into a task until the job is finished.
- A great respect for parents, usually obeying them unquestioningly.
- Close relationships with extended family members, who often possess the right to exercise extensive authority over youthful relatives.
- An open honest manner without any hidden intentions and goals.
- An appreciation of what it takes to achieve goals in circumstances lacking the extensive resources that middle-class children often possess (Lubrano 2004, 17–19).

While the American working class appears to have distinct qualities, its members, who are part of "a profoundly individualistic social order," have generally not thought of themselves as belonging to a class (Ziegler and Gall 2002, 49). Material in Chapter 4 about both class and ideology suggests that such a response is typically American.

Research evidence indicates that some more prosperous working-class members might have a split perspective, considering themselves working-class on the job and middle-class in their consumption and living arrangements (Blumin 1989, 296).

Sociologist Diana Kendall suggested that the mass media have supported various stereotypes about the working class, including the following two:

- Working-class members as "white trash": On the long-time popular TV program *Roseanne*, the show featured a working-class family, which often described itself as "trashy." At one point Roseanne compared her family to old furniture, saying, "We're white trash and we'll stay white trash until they haul us out to the curb" (Kendall 2005, 157). In the news media, the term can be used to promote a negative outlook toward an individual. When Paula Jones alleged that then Governor Bill Clinton had propositioned her, James Carville, one of Clinton's advisors, accused Jones of being "trailer park trash." In short, Carville implied, her working-class origin discredited her testimony. Carville's reference to trailer park trash sparked extensive media coverage, both on TV and in newspapers. Journalists commenting on the Paula Jones situation indicated that because of her class background, she was treated differently from middle-class women.

- Blue-collar workers, particularly men, as various forms of lowlife: Starting with *The Life of Riley* in 1949, many TV actors portrayed the blue-collar lead characters as inept bunglers devoid of intelligence and ambition. The best-known illustrations have included bus driver Ralph Kramden in *The Honeymooners*, dockworker Archie Bunker in *All in the Family,* quarry crane operator Fred Flintstone in *The Flintstones*, and low-level nuclear-power technician Homer Simpson in *The Simpsons*. These half-hour comedies revolved around a humorous but problematic predicament, which was usually the central male character's creation. Invariably he needed help to solve a problem, and frequently assistance came from his wife, who tended to be more intelligent, mature, and socially skilled than her husband. One implicit but clearly conveyed message such programs project is the idea that working-class men are sufficiently incompetent that they require steady supervision both on the job and at home. Beyond their ineptitude most of the lead working-class male characters appeared to be buffoons, namely ridiculous or bumbling people. Homer Simpson has been a leading case in point. Besides creating a lengthy list of problems he has been unable to solve, Simpson has been a consistently negative role model for his children—staying glued to the TV, gorging on junk food, swilling beer, and spending much of his free time at Moe's bar (Kendall 2005, 158–65).

This Homer Simpson doll represents Simpson in a typical pose, eating doughnuts and drinking beer.

One might argue that all of these programs are comedies—that the characterizations should not be taken too seriously. While perhaps this is a point to consider, the stereotypes these shows display are likely to be influential in a society providing little information about the working class.

In contrast to the media, sociologists and other social scientists have recognized that growing up in the American working class is a unique experience shared by nearly a third of the citizenry and worthy of thorough study.

WORKING-CLASS DEVELOPMENT

As it does in all classes, social reproduction prevails in the working class. Its members often have fewer valued resources, both financial and nonfinancial, than their middle-class counterparts. As a result they tend to be less successful, at least by middle-class standards, in such important activities as communicating with their children or relating to their teachers. We examine childrearing, schooling, and community ties.

Childrearing

Various studies on working-class upbringing have indicated that blue-collar parents emphasize the importance of following rules and respecting parents, other relatives, and elders generally. For working-class parents, priorities have often been to maintain control and to receive respect. As part of childrearing, mothers and fathers belonging to this class have often resorted to physical punishment (Barbour and Barbour 2001, 65); Sailor 2004, 19; Shostak 1969, 136–37). Sociologist Melvin L. Kohn indicated that whereas middle-class parents emphasize self-direction, their working-class counterparts value conformity. Kohn explained, "The essential difference between the terms, as we use them, is that self-direction focuses on *internal* standards for behavior; conformity focuses on *externally* imposed rules" (Kohn 1969, 35). In other words Kohn suggested that working-class children's socialization downplayed autonomy, with parents imposing rules on their children instead of emphasizing their development into independent beings.

In her study of 88 children, Annette Lareau had a working-class segment with the following distinct childrearing-related traits:

> **The organization of daily life:** Often the children simply "hung out," particularly with relatives. In contrast to their middle-class peers, who tended to have planned activities, these children occupied themselves watching TV, entertaining themselves with video games, and playing outside. The class differences are significant and also understandable. Compared to their middle-class counterparts, working-class parents tended to place less emphasis on the importance of planned activities and, perhaps more significant, were less likely to have the money to pay for them.

> **Language use:** Parents provided directives, often as terse commands of no more than a few words. Children were told to do certain things—shower or take out the garbage—and not to do others—curse or talk back. Working-class childrearing is like the military, Alfred Lubrano suggested, with the parents barking orders. Children were seldom encouraged to express themselves (Hart and Risley 1995; Lareau 2007, 338–344; Lubrano 2004, 56, 93). Working-class and middle-class parents developed in distinctly different settings, and working-class mothers and fathers tended to reproduce as childrearers the kinds of relationships they experienced in their families, schools, and jobs.

Parents' relationships with institutions: Compared to their middle-class counterparts, working-class mothers and fathers were less likely to become involved in monitoring their children's institutional experiences. In Lareau's study it was clear that Wendy Driver's working-class mother (mentioned in Chapter 1) cared about her daughter and wanted to help her overcome her serious learning disabilities. Wendy's teachers described her mother as "very loving" and "supportive," but they wished she would take a more active, interventionist role. Ms. Driver was always willing to do what the teachers suggested and was confident in their judgment, not seeing any need nor, in fact, knowing how to take initiative to help her daughter. Unlike many middle-class parents, she did not ask a lot of questions about her child's school performance; nor did she seek an assessment from outside the school. In fact, she did not appear to fully grasp her daughter's problems, speaking vaguely about them and seeming not to understand the educators' terminology that specified just what the disabilities entailed. To Ms. Driver's way of thinking, her inability to understand Wendy's learning disability was not a problem. Lareau concluded that what Ms. Driver failed to appreciate was that the teachers wanted her to engage in a "pattern of 'concerted cultivation' where she actively [monitored] and . . . [intervened] in her child's schooling. The teachers asked for a complicated mixture of deference and engagement from parents" (Lareau 2007, 547). It appears that Ms. Driver's working-class experience affected this situation in two ways. First, unlike her middle-class counterparts, she had learned to consider teachers as experts who should be left to do educating without parents' involvement. Second, the teachers probably did not recognize that the "complicated mixture of deference and engagement" they sought from parents was probably more familiar and easier for middle-class parents to provide than it was for individuals like Ms. Driver.

Consequences for working-class children: Compared to their middle-class counterparts, they matured in a social setting that was narrower, provided fewer supportive resources, and instilled less sense of entitlement (Lareau 2007, 538).

While traditional child-rearing approaches continue, changes in outlook and behavior have been occurring. In her study of 162 working-class families in cities around the country, sociologist Lillian Rubin concluded that some working-class parents have become more flexible on traditionally controversial issues. For example, many of Rubin's female respondents indicated that mothers belong at home bringing up their children and should only have a job out of necessity, but then later in the interview they were likely to indicate many things they enjoyed about work. Parents who had previously condemned homosexuality often took another look when their own child came out of the closet. At first mothers and fathers might chastise God or blame themselves, but following such displays they usually supported their child. Rubin found a similar process unfolded when daughters planned to obtain an abortion: The parents tended to agonize, to vacillate on what to do, and then eventually to go along with an abortion. Finally these working-class women were critical of feminism, saying that its proponents are too pushy, loud, and hard, but many acknowledged the outcomes of feminist efforts, which include equity on the job, effective measures against sexual harassment, and the push against the glass ceiling (Rubin 1994, 63–72).

The college experience often created situations challenging working-class students' upbringing. For instance, one of the frequent tenets of the academic world has been that there exists more than one way to evaluate an issue—an idea that clashes with the blue-collar outlook, "where the rules are pretty much cast in concrete, and the primary colors are black and white" (Lubrano 2004, 59).

Just as working-class children's socialization can leave them feeling unentitled, their educational experience can produce a similar result.

Schooling

In the late nineteenth century, conflict sometimes occurred between working-class parents and their children's teachers. In particular, teachers and other education officials were becoming increasingly adverse to the use of physical punishment, which working-class fathers and mothers still used widely. In addition, some ethnic groups, perhaps most notably Italians, opposed compulsory education, feeling that no more than a basic literacy was necessary for children who would enter the work world at an early age and start contributing to the family income (Lassonde 2005, 54–56).

Working-class Italian parents considered schooling "economically disastrous" for girls, who were supposed to focus on getting married and producing a family and in their estimation needing only the most rudimentary education (Covello 1967, 292). As a result of this parental hostility, Italian immigrants' children tended to leave school at an early age and often developed an antagonistic relationship with the educational experience, displaying frequent truancy and for the boys high juvenile-delinquency rates (Lassonde 2005, 57–59). The opposition to schooling took its toll, with Italians experiencing less upward mobility in the first third of the twentieth century than any other white group (Perlmann 1988, 119–21).

For working-class families who accepted public education for their children, other issues arose. Many of the students found themselves in vocational education, also known as career-technical education, where they received preparation for jobs in manual activities. In the United States, a sharp distinction commonly exists between individuals who do skilled blue-collar work and those involved in white-collar activity. Researcher Mike Rose indicated that Americans' choice of words is quite explicit, making "substantial distinctions between work of body and brain, of white collar and blue—these days expressed as the new knowledge work versus old-style industry and service. Neck up and neck down" (Rose 2004, 148–49).

The widespread perception is that vocational education is for students preparing to work in "neck down" capacities. About 16 percent of high-school courses are in the career-technical area, preparing students for blue-collar jobs (Bishop and Mane 2005, 329). A study following eighth graders from 1988 intermittently to 2000 found that students who completed training for specific vocational jobs spent a higher portion of time employed, found better jobs, and earned more money than those seeking similar positions but not completing that training (Bishop and Mane 2005, 349–50).

While career-technical education has helped prepare large numbers of individuals effectively for the workplace, criticisms are widespread. Educators have pointed out that because of the "neck up and neck down" distinction the establishment of career-technical programs means two categories of citizens—one receiving vocational job training and the other benefiting from a more flexible, more promising general education (Goodlad 1984; Grubb and Lazerson 2004, 131; Wilms 1988, 90). In high school Mike Rose completed a vocational program and indicated that it represented one side of an existing dichotomy within the high-school curriculum, where the instruction received, one's fellow students, and one's sense of his/her status in public settings were distinctly negative realities (Rose 2004, 166). Economist Michael Yates emphasized that placement in either the vocational or academic portion of a high-school program has been largely based on one's ability in intelligence tests that are widely believed to be significantly flawed and that tend to reward affluent, white children, who have had the cultural and human capital that often more effectively prepare them for the tests. In school, however, Yates concluded, administrators and teachers usually overlook such opportunity differences, considering test scores strictly a matter of individual achievement. Yates himself was a case in point. He observed, "I would go to college because I deserved it, and you would go to the factory for the same reason" (Yates 2007, 158).

Working-class students' chances to attend college are fairly limited. Even if they feel mobilized to go, they are likely to find the quest difficult to achieve. A study of a working-class community concluded that 40 percent of high-school seniors indicated that they wanted to go to college. However, only 27 percent took the SATs, and among that group the average scores were not good enough for them to enter the state university. These students only qualified for the local community college, whose graduates tended to end up with lower-paying white-collar jobs (Weis 1990, 27).

In dealing with the education system, working-class students are likely to find themselves facing a troubling perception. A **sense of entitlement** is the conviction that one deserves to receive some valued opportunity or reward. In affluent high schools or colleges, working-class students sometimes feel that they are unentitled, do not belong—for example, Lubrano's imposter syndrome mentioned earlier. Sociologist Allison Hurst's study of 21 working-class students suggested various factors that could preclude a sense of entitlement, including middle-class peers who conveyed the conviction that working-class individuals neither belonged in college-preparatory courses nor college; parents who knew nothing about applying to college and lacked money to help pay for it; and counselors and teachers who apparently felt working-class students were not college material (Hurst 2009).

Some working-class students receive more support. A pair of academic writers indicated that they were able to teach history and English at the college level because as working-class college students themselves they were fortunate enough to have found passionately involved, caring mentors. Historian Richard Greenwald indicated that "the faculty in the history department at Queens College recognized me as a human being and engaged my mind in ways that were unknown to me" (Greenwald and Grant 1999, 34–35). Clearly these mentors nurtured the students' sense of entitlement. It would be interesting to know whether this experience is common—that working-class individuals who have succeeded in upper-middle-class occupations have had mentors playing a prominent role. Certainly working-class people use social capital.

Community Ties

In the late 1960s, many blue-collar workers were living and working in social networks involving personal affiliations with neighbors, kin, and sometimes fellow workers. The primary settings nurturing these contacts were taverns for men and coffee klatsches (where people gathered for coffee and conversation) and church services for women. The focus was the enjoyment of social relationships (Shostak 1969, 106).

Sociologist E.E. LeMasters's study of about 50 men and women who met regularly at a tavern found that the vibrant peer life contributed to the job satisfaction of these skilled workers. Shared activities included car pooling, working together in small crews, eating lunch as a group, and drinking beer at the end of the day. There was rich, often intense interaction—lots of practical jokes and horseplay (LeMasters 1975, 21).

Communities promoting such working-class solidarity, though less common, still exist. Laurence Harbor is a settlement with a small-town atmosphere in Middlesex County, New Jersey. While middle-class individuals and families have been buying up some of its winterized bungalows built in the first third of the twentieth century, others are sold to relatives or friends before realtors are contacted, helping to retain Laurence Harbor's working-class character. The mayor, a life-long resident of the town, explained that "Laurence Harbor is a state of mind. It's always been a closely knit, God-fearing, working-class community of affordable houses . . . where people know their neighbors and the streets are filled with children" (Cheslow 2004, 11).

For many working-class families, however, the kind of close-knit communities that Laurence Harbor and its predecessors have represented started fading from reality in the 1950s and 1960s. In 1950 economist Michael Yates moved with his family from a blue-collar town to a suburb, where they were to achieve the much-advertised "good life" of owning their own home. In the suburbs life was different—more isolated. Yates indicated that his parents' "lives devolved away from work and class solidarity toward a more limited and insular family life" (Yates 2007, 157). The old network of kin, neighbors, and friends had become much more distant.

Whether living in suburban or urban areas, working-class families are likely to view social networking quite differently from their middle-class counterparts—as a dirty word involving situations where opportunistic individuals make contacts simply to serve self-centered ends. It is often seen as taking advantage of others. However, upwardly mobile working-class young people learn to overcome this antipathy and take advantage of available opportunities (Lubrano 2004, 144–47).

These opportunities are likely to be better for some individuals within the working class than for others. As far as the potential for social capital is concerned, race can be a significant divider. A study of 25 black and 25 white males who graduated from a vocational high school in Baltimore indicated that while the white teachers helped members of both racial groups, they offered more active assistance to the white students, providing them more job-vacancy information, referrals, job-recruitment contacts, formal and informal training, and leniency in supervision (Royster 2003, 181). In addition, the whites were more likely to locate good jobs because of contacts their family members, neighbors, and friends provided while blacks had a much less well developed network of family and friends, supplying few if any leads for the kinds of jobs for which they had been trained. As a result of their deficient social capital, the young blacks were seldom able to remain in the trades they had studied, often ending up in the service sector, employed either in retail sales or food production (Royster 2003, 182–83).

Darren's case illustrates how teachers would help working-class white students establish themselves in the job world. Mr. Wooten, one of Darren's teachers his sophomore year, encouraged him to apply for a machinist's job, passing on the strategic information that this company had an effective in-house apprentice program. In addition, Mr. Wooten bent the rules, realizing that this program was a very good fit for Darren and so releasing him for work study even though that privilege was supposed to be reserved for juniors or seniors. At the time of the interview, Darren had been employed five years and had advanced from minor duties on the shop floor to machinist/journeyman. As previously noted, black students had no comparable success stories featuring teachers' useful aid (Royster 2003, 137–38).

Other factors affect the potency of working-class social networks. A study in a small town found that people's secure economic positions were often the foundation for building effective social capital. For instance, individuals with tools, skills, and money were likely to use these resources to help others in the community, thereby building a social network. Individuals without these resources were unable to produce such a support system. An illustration involved Eric Donohue, who had a good-paying working-class job in the municipal water system. Donohue's wages helped finance a small garage where he repaired cars. In exchanging information about car repairs with friends and acquaintances, Donohue developed a social network of individuals possessing a variety of desirable attributes, including skills, knowledge, and physical strength. Then when he and his wife decided to build their own home, they contacted network members. Donohue explained, "We needed sheetwork moved one day. It was a four-man job. We would just call people and they would come" (Nelson and Smith 1999, 174). The people working with the Donohues, in turn, learned a lot about home construction that some of them were able to use in building their own houses.

It has been apparent that working-class individuals and families have different types of capital—social (networks), human (schooling), and cultural (family) that provide some benefits though often not the kind that either produces a sense of comfort and entitlement or helps them obtain security in the labor force. The focus shifts to the work setting.

WORKING-CLASS EMPLOYMENT: CAN THE DREAM SURVIVE?

We consider the general nature of blue-collar work over time and then examine the current employment picture.

To begin, a broad appraisal of working-class jobs indicates that the majority have three negative associations: using limited skills, requiring minimal personal judgment, and providing almost no autonomy (Rubin 1976, 158).

Historically a segment of the working class has performed skilled labor. A **skilled-labor job** is a working-class position using a detailed body of knowledge and sometimes requiring specialized training or schooling. Individuals in such crafts as carpentry, electronics, welding, plumbing, bricklaying, roofing, and sheet-metal work have often received good pay and benefits and, thanks to frequent union membership, consistent job security. In many instances the work is interesting, involving a wide range of tasks, and the job site is largely unsupervised, with employees often passing the entire day without seeing their foremen. These individuals are likely to evaluate their working circumstances as considerably superior to those their peers in factories experience. Work alienation is minimal. A carpenter explained, "I see the auto workers in Detroit want early retirement. I don't blame the poor bastards. I would want to retire at thirty-five if I had to stand in one place and put left fenders on all day" (LeMasters 1975, 22).

Many people recognize that carpenters, electricians, plumbers, and welders, for instance, are extensively trained, highly competent job holders, who possess the skills to perform their respective tasks well. On the other hand, various blue-collar jobs like

Like other skilled blue-collar employees, carpenters tend to have jobs that provide good pay and positive working conditions.

waiting tables are underrated, requiring a distinct set of abilities that are learned on the job and go widely unappreciated. One requirement is physical adeptness—the capacity, for instance, to stack and carry a large number of plates and glasses in dangerously busy areas. A second necessity is an excellent memory—not only recalling who gets what dish(es) but other requests not recorded. Finally the individual needs interpersonal skills, dealing with and seeking to satisfy customers, cooks, and management in what are often tense, rushed circumstances (Rose 2004, 2–3).

Many observers of blue- and white-collar jobs emphasize the brain/hand distinction between white- and blue-collar activities, with the quality of cerebral action in the first invariably considered far superior to that in the second. Yet the reality is that many working-class jobs have a distinctly understated cerebral component. Just as a surgeon feels beneath the body's surface for a tumor or a blood vessel and, sight unseen, makes a diagnosis, a plumber reaches behind a wall to examine and diagnose the condition of a valve. To decide the most effective action to take, the two job holders draw on their respective storehouses of knowledge about the feel of things (Rose 2004, 151).

Admittedly many blue-collar job holders such as factory workers have boring, repetitive tasks, but so do some professionals. Several years ago in my course on social inequality, I had an auditor who had been a podiatrist. During a class in which we had been discussing the repetitive quality of many working-class jobs, he explained that the main reason he retired early was that he belonged to a practice in which his colleagues strongly encouraged him to make his primary function performing a fairly routine operation over and over again. "It might have surprised people to know this," the podiatrist explained, "but I began to feel as if I was working on an assembly line." Is this man unusual? It is entirely possible that a distinct number of middle-class, even professional workers suffer work alienation normally linked to working-class jobs.

Using some of the points raised in this section, one can see that not only do working-class jobs differ, but as Table 7.2 indicates, they roughly break down into two categories.

Regardless of the quality of working-class jobs, nowadays the people who fill them face stiff challenges.

Working-Class Jobs Today

Since the 1970s many of the better paying, more unionized blue-collar positions have been lost. Between 1979 and 2001, over 3.3 million manufacturing jobs disappeared (Perrucci and Wysong 2008, 64). Then from 2003 through 2007, an additional 1.9 million factory workers lost their positions (U.S. Bureau of Labor Statistics 2006; U.S. Bureau of Labor Statistics 2008).

In the twenty-first century, reemployment rates for working-class individuals have averaged about 65 percent—specifically, 65 percent in construction and 64 percent in manufacturing (U.S. Bureau of Labor Statistics 2008).

Did these reemployed blue-collar workers achieve their previous income level? The overall answer is negative. For instance, in the middle 1980s, employees displaced from the auto, steel, and meatpacking industries lost about 44 percent in income compared to their previous earnings in the two years following their layoffs. Then during the period from 1999 to 2000, two million workers lost factory jobs they had held for three or more years. By 2002 only 62 percent were reemployed in full-time wage jobs. So it seems safe to assume that those 38 percent representing nearly two fifths of the total were in a

TABLE 7.2 A Hypothetical Dichotomy of Blue-Collar Jobs

Examples	"Bad" positions	"Good" positions
	Assembly line, custodial, or equipment cleaning jobs	Carpentry, electrical work, plumbing, long-shoring
Characteristics		
1. Skill level	Unskilled	Highly skilled
2. Pay and benefits	Modest or low, few if any benefits	Good, with health insurance and a pension
3. Unionized	Seldom	Often
4. Job security	Little or none	Substantial, often backed by strong union advocacy
5. Peer support on the job	Limited	Extensive

While working-class jobs do not divide neatly between bad and good, this scheme loosely outlines the broad traits associated with such a hypothetical breakdown.

greatly diminished economic situation. Among the reemployed, 50 percent earned less than previously, and half of that half, namely 25 percent of the total, received at least 20 percent less than their income on the lost job. Older employees, those 45 to 64, experienced the most income decline in their new positions (Perrucci and Wysong 2008, 64–65). In 2007 a loss of over a quarter-million factory jobs signaled the sharpest decline in manufacturing since 2003 (Richards 2008, 20).

Over more than a 30-year period, real income for those in the working class has declined—for male high-school graduates from an entry-level payment of $13.39 in 1973 (in 2005 dollars) to $10.93 in 2005 and for female high-school graduates $9.81 in 1973 to $9.08 in 2005. For individuals without a college degree, finding "a good job" is increasingly problematic. Only half of young workers aged 18 to 34 without a college degree hold a full-time, permanent job (Perrucci and Wysong 2008, 66). Table 7.3 indicates that for over a 30-year span, American workers' hourly wages have declined compared to their counterparts in various technologically advanced nations. Table 7.4 points out that in the twenty-first century many working-class jobs have lost income, but others, the more highly skilled ones, have gained slightly (U.S. Census Bureau 2009).

While working-class jobs vary in income and other attributes, temp work often ranks quite low for reasons that become clear.

TABLE 7.3 Factory Workers' Hourly Pay over Time in US Dollars for the United States and 12 Other Nations

	1975	1980	1985	1990	1995	2000	2005
Australia	$4.87	$7.31	$6.98	$11.09	$12.75	$11.68	$19.85
Austria	3.53	6.79	5.59	13.20	18.26	13.87	21.44
Belgium	4.44	9.20	6.24	12.91	18.02	13.78	21.56
Canada	5.56	7.93	9.81	14.07	13.67	13.90	19.21
Denmark	6.01	10.30	7.65	17.88	23.85	20.14	31.82
France	3.34	6.47	5.30	10.75	13.33	10.71	16.93
Italy	3.12	5.72	5.33	11.74	10.73	9.50	14.54
Japan	2.67	4.84	5.49	10.89	20.02	18.28	18.06
Mexico	1.33	1.99	1.42	1.40	1.50	1.83	2.35
Norway	5.68	9.49	8.44	17.55	20.64	19.03	31.30
Sweden	5.54	9.04	6.75	14.57	15.37	14.51	20.66
United Kingdom	2.97	6.17	5.29	10.71	11.83	13.81	20.91
United States	5.16	7.84	10.24	11.80	13.56	15.69	18.32

Over 30 years the hourly wage for factory workers in a given country has maintained a fairly consistent rank order compared to other nations listed here. However, the US wage, which was fifth in 1975, slipped to ninth in 2005. Nonetheless, at that time the American wage was nearly eight times higher than its Mexican counterpart, encouraging some corporations to relocate plants there.

Source: U.S. Bureau of Labor Statistics. November 2006. Table 7. "Hourly Direct Pay in U.S. Dollars for Production Workers in Manufacturing, 33 Countries or Areas and Selected Economic Groups, 1975–2005." ftp://ftp.bls.gov/pub/special.requests/ForeignLabor/ichccsuppt07.txt.

TABLE 7.4 Full-Time Employees' Yearly Income[1] in Various Working-Class Occupations

	Healthcare support[2]	Food preparation and serving[3]	Maintenance[4]
2002	$29,497	$28,391	$29,497
2004	30,155	22,242	27,090
2006	27,949	25,534	29,895
2008	28,466	25,167	27,639
	Construction and extraction[5]	Production[6]	Transportation and material moving[7]
2002	$44,250	$39,066	$42,393
2004	43,279	40,088	42,474
2006	42,344	39,912	40,823
2008	44,848	40,005	40,719

[1]An occupational group's mean income in 2008 dollars
[2]Such as home health aids, nursing aids, orderlies, and attendants
[3]Such as chefs, waiters and waitresses, and fast-food employees
[4]Such as custodians, landscapers, housekeepers, and ground-maintenance workers
[5]Such as electricians, painters, roofers, miners, carpenters, and plumbers
[6]Such as tool and die makers, bakers, butchers, and printing, sewing, and textile-cutting machine operators
[7]Such as bus drivers, taxi drivers, deckhands, and train conductors

These data indicate that in the opening years of the twenty-first century, income in less skilled working-class job categories has tended to decline, but it has slightly increased in skilled areas involving construction and extraction, and production.

Source: U.S. Census Bureau. 2009. Table P–45A. "Occupation of Longest Job—Full-Time, Year-Round Workers (Both Sexes Combined) by Median and Mean Earnings: 2002 to 2008." *Historical Income Tables—People.* http://www.census.gov/hhes/www/income/histinc/incpertoc.html.

BLUE-COLLAR TEMP WORK: AN EXPANDING REALITY Russell Kelly, the founder of Kelly Services, developed the term "temp work." In the 1940s Kelly found it difficult to convey a sense of temp work to company executives, who failed to grasp his meaning when he indicated that the workers were his own employees. As a result Kelly had to laboriously keep explaining the difference between an employment agency, which for a fee locates individuals who become workers at a company, and a temp agency, which sends its own employees to a company to complete short-term jobs.

Once grasping the concept, however, American executives have increasingly invested in temp work. In the 1960s and 1970s, the number of temp workers steadily grew, but when companies started cutting back expenses by downsizing workers, the growth in temp work accelerated—from about 735,000 workers in 1985, to about a million in the middle 1990s, two million by 2000, and about 5 million by 2008. In the 1990s the American Staffing Association reported a $46.4 billion growth in revenues from temp work. Between 1998 and 2008, temporary employment increased more than ten times faster than regular employment. A substantial number of American businesses now include temp work. In November 2010, for example, 80 percent of the 50,000 private-sector hirings involved temp employees. These workers tend to be both younger and less educated than the general workforce, and temp agencies are most likely to be located in less affluent areas, where they can readily recruit low-income individuals (Novak 2008; Rich 2010, A1; U.S. Bureau of Labor Statistics 2005; Van Arsdale 2008, 77–81).

Both the organizations that provide temp workers and those that hire them gain from the arrangement. Such agencies as Kelly Services, Manpower, and Labor Ready usually receive half or more of the income from their employees' services. At the same time, the companies hiring the temp workers benefit because they generally avoid paying the healthcare premiums and pension payments full-time job holders often receive (Van Arsdale 2008, 93).

Using temp workers is likely to be a significant factor in a company's commitment to its regular work staff. A case in point would be the so-called "transplants"—Japanese auto firms like Honda, Nissan, and Toyota—which have built assembly plants in several midwestern and southern states. At these plants, which employ between two and three thousand individuals, the companies have made firm no-layoff commitments in exchange for high production to perhaps 60 percent of the workforce. The others, temp workers, are vulnerable to layoff when changing economic conditions encourage the company to cut back production (Perrucci and Wysong 2008, 121). Temp workers, in short, are a useful means of helping protect a company financially.

While temp agencies and companies benefit economically from temp work, the workers themselves face bleak prospects. In his participant-observation study of industrial temporary workers in Syracuse, New York, sociologist David Van Arsdale indicated that his respondents often referred to "a revolving door," a three-step process of waiting at a temp agency for a job, getting a job, and then returning to the agency and waiting for another job (Van Arsdale 2008, 82). These three steps follow:

Waiting for work: Van Arsdale's study focused on two temp agencies, and he spent many hours in their waiting rooms, both seeking jobs himself and informally interviewing the men waiting for such temp work as recycling waste, assembly-line duty, landscaping, roofing, and general labor at construction sites. Waiting, which could go on for hours, was very taxing. One day Van Arsdale and Slim had been at one of the agencies for two hours, and from a roomful of men only three had obtained jobs. Slim noted that as time passed and nothing happened, the men became increasingly edgy (Van Arsdale 2008, 88).

On a ticket: The men at the job had no real job security. The closest resemblance to a shred of security was a return ticket, which was a form extending the job to the following week day. So jobs changed frequently. One respondent indicated that in recent months he had been employed in a host of capacities—that it almost seemed an easier proposition to ask what jobs he had not had (Van Arsdale 2008, 89–90). Even when they were working steadily, the men suffered economically. They received barely enough wages to pay for food and lodging, and since wages were never more than a daily allotment, they could not afford to pay more than a weekly rent and buy more than a day's worth of groceries. This financial plight took a toll. Dee explained that such a deprived lifestyle eliminated marriage, a home, and other elements of an ordinary existence (Van Arsdale 2008, 90).

The revolving door: For many of these men, the experience of temp work was very stressful. Ricky indicated that many times he had hoped to get a permanent position, and each time it failed to happen he felt completely defeated (Van Arsdale 2008, 82). And so back he went, usually the next day, to the waiting room to get another job. Van Arsdale asked Slim, his most helpful respondent, why he did not seek a full-time job. Slim said that a major reason was that it seemed unlikely that companies would pay for his full-time services when they could hook up with temp agencies to get him and his colleagues cheap. In addition, Slim said that he had become dependent on the day-to-day situation. While Slim would have liked a full-time job, he had neither a phone nor a permanent address. No prospective employer would be able to contact him. His most effective way to obtain a job was to show up each morning at the temp agency (Van Arsdale 2008, 93). Van Arsdale learned that many other respondents shared Slim's views.

While temp agencies and companies profit nicely from temp work, the workers themselves suffer economically and psychologically. The fact that the number of temp workers is likely to grow in the years ahead indicates that this phenomenon is one of many outgrowths of the modern economy where selected working-class individuals are suffering a diminished quality of life. In a survey by the Pew Research Center, 62 percent of self-described working-class people indicated that they were falling behind the cost of living (Pew Research Center for the People & the Press 2008).

One of the assets of effective job training is that it might help individuals avoid such a predicament.

Blue-Collar Workers' Challenges

Locating competent, affordable job training and childcare are critical services that working-class employees can find difficult to obtain.

THE PURSUIT OF JOB TRAINING   The U.S. Bureau of Labor Statistics has indicated that a number of skilled blue-collar workers such as plumbers, structural iron and steel workers, electricians, elevator installers, commercial and industrial equipment electrical repairers, and aircraft mechanics often receive lengthy trainings or apprenticeships that can last up to three or four years and lead to yearly income that are generally over the annual U.S. median of $43,000 (Lorenz 2008).

However, training for many jobs, including apprenticeships for the skilled trades just cited, can be problematic. An **apprentice** is an individual who agrees to work for low wages for a specified length of time, learning from his or her employer the range of skills required in that trade (Bilginsoy 2003, 55). A study of apprenticeship programs in the construction industry involving carpenters, electricians, pipefitters, plumbers, and sheetmetal workers disclosed that 47 percent of the 12,715 apprentices had left the program, 39 percent had completed it, and the remaining 14 percent were still in it (Bilginsoy 2003, 58).

In American business, apprenticeship programs have played a much smaller role in training skilled workers than in many European countries. Germany has about 350 kinds of apprenticeships, involving bakers, hairstylists, bank clerks, video editors, and even such university-trained individuals as biotech or aerospace specialists. These programs appear to be a major reason why Germany's youth unemployment rate is less than half what it is in 10 other European Union nations. Austria, Denmark, and Switzerland also have well developed apprenticeship programs and youth unemployment below the European average (Elbaum 1989; Ewing 2009).

In top American business circles, leaders recognize that the limited development of training programs has become a serious problem. The Business Roundtable has called for the expansion of apprentice programs in the various construction trades as a means for relieving a chronic shortage of skilled workers (Bilginsoy 2003, 56).

The previously cited study of apprenticeship programs in the construction industry found that people in those programs where there was union-management collaboration were more likely to complete training and receive job classification than individuals enrolled in employer-only programs. One reason for this higher completion rate appeared to be that workers in the joint program faced a union requirement to finish the program while workers in the employer-only arrangement had no such requirement. In addition, white and male apprentices were more likely to complete apprentice programs, perhaps benefiting from the fact that they could more readily network with the primarily white males who were supervising their work (Bilginsoy 2003, 64–66).

One specific disadvantage that women and minorities sometimes face in seeking to enter training for skilled trades is that they are less likely to score high on qualifying tests, primarily because they are less inclined to have taken courses in such areas as mechanical reasoning and spatial relations, which provide information that often helps boost scores on those tests (Castellano 1997, 206–07).

Working-class women have encountered other difficulties in training programs. A study of 100 randomly chosen women who obtained training following the closing of the Tennessee textile plant where they had worked indicated that the short, usually six-month training they received did not prepare them for better-paying jobs with benefits. An advisory committee of these respondents said that training would prove helpful if:

- It prepared individuals for specific jobs in the immediate area.
- It had a longer duration and a more detailed process, allowing workers to master the skills associated with the new jobs.
- The 26 weeks of unemployment pay was extended. Six months of support was clearly insufficient to subsidize effective retraining for radically different work (Merrifield 1997, 289–90).

Research indicates that working-class women continue to experience more limited job-training opportunities than men. Over time these differences are likely to diminish but to persist, both because women are sometimes treated as second-class citizens and because their responsibilities for their children can restrict job training and advancement (Escriche 2007; Smith, Flynn, and Isler 2006).

Like job training, childcare is an important issue affecting people's work lives.

EMPLOYED WORKING-CLASS WOMEN'S PROCUREMENT OF CHILDCARE   It seems useful to set the context for this issue. In her study of working-class families, sociologist Lillian Rubin found that many parents were ambivalent about women working. Men tended to both appreciate the money and to discover that their wives developed greater understanding of what they faced on the job. However, some expressed a sense of personal failure in their wives' working. Doug Wright, a white, 30-year-old forklift operator, spoke for many when he said, "I know she doesn't mind working, but it shouldn't have to be that way" (Rubin 1995, 78). Working-class women also expressed ambivalence about seeking employment. "I like to work; it makes me feel good about myself," said Julia

Rumsford, a black, 28-year-old mother of two. "But I have to admit I never feel like a full mom, and that bothers me a lot" (Rubin 1995, 79).

For most working-class women, however, the need for income outweighs any qualms about working, and they seek childcare, sometimes encountering problems. One issue involves the challenge of coordinating the arrangement made with their work schedule. The vast majority of daycare operations function during regular working hours. Working-class employees, however, often have irregular schedules, serving on night shifts or suddenly receiving notice that they must work overtime. Such irregular job scheduling can make it difficult to locate childcare arrangements (Cherlin 2004). This situation involves **intersectionality**—the recognition that a woman's oppressions, limitations, and opportunities result from the combined impact of two or more influential statuses. In this instance the necessity for working-class women to make certain that their children obtain care can adversely affect their potential as workers.

Traditionally working-class families have faced a disadvantaged situation for childcare compared to the middle class, whose members are usually better equipped to pay for such services, and the poor, who can often receive subsidized care (Perry-Jenkins 2005, 465). With welfare reform, however, poor families have steadily lost some of that subsidized childcare, and as Table 7.5 indicates, working-class families have recently had a higher percentage of children in organized programs than poor families. These programs represent a distinct challenge. To begin, they are costly. An added problem is that corporate employers are likely to give their female blue-collar employees less flexibility in their working hours than they provide their white-collar counterparts (Haley, Perry-Jenkins, and Armenia 2001). Furthermore working-class parents sometimes feel awkward or out-of-place in the middle-class childcare world, ill-equipped to negotiate with caretakers about their children's particular sensitivities or needs (Cherlin 2004).

Reviewing the development of the American working class, we see that existence for its members has always been challenging and often alienating.

TABLE 7.5 Childcare Arrangement for Preschoolers under Five Years Old Living with Their Mothers[1]

Yearly income	Parents	Other relations	Various organized programs[2]
Under $18,000	17%	32.7%	31.7%[3]
$18,000–$35,999	19.8	28.1	35.6
$36,000–$53,999	22.7	33.9	40.1
$54,000+	20.9	30.8	53.2

[1]The mothers' marital status varies.
[2]The various programs include daycare centers, preschool nurseries, and Head Start.
[3]For the three lower income groups, some information is absent, producing a total under 100 percent. For the $54,000 and up category, a number of parents specified two choices, producing a total over 100 percent.

The roughly working-class group ($36,000–$53,999) is more likely to obtain organized childcare programs than the two least affluent categories but is distinctly less inclined to use those facilities than the largely middle-class set of parents in the upper bracket represented here ($54,000 and up).

Source: U.S. Census Bureau. 2005. Table 1A. "Child Care Arrangements of Preschoolers under 5 Years Old Living with Mother, by Employment Status of Mother and Selected Characteristics." *Who's Minding the Kids? Child Care Arrangements: Spring 2005.* http://www.census.gov/population/www.socdemo/child/pp1-2005.html-13k.

Conclusion

Historically many working-class individuals and families have had an unrewarding employment experience—jobs requiring long hours, considerable physical labor, little or no stability, limited appeal, and low pay. As recently as the late nineteenth century, the majority of working-class job holders were poor, with about 15 percent distinctly more prosperous, earning perhaps three times the average blue-collar wage. Prosperous times for the working class developed during the 30 years after World War II. Later the global economy brought downsizing and outsourcing of various industries, distinctly weakening labor unions, which the Reagan administration fiercely attacked and further undermined. The once vibrant labor movement has become a mere shadow of its former self. Modern working-class employees generally face declining real wages, the prospect of expanding temp work, challenges obtaining and completing training for skilled blue-collar jobs, and difficulties finding effective, inexpensive childcare.

As far as capital resources are concerned, working-class individuals tend to have the following prospects:

Financial capital: Money is likely to be scarce, making it difficult to pay for anything beyond basic necessities. Whereas middle-class families might be able to afford to move to more expensive housing to enroll their children in a high-quality school, their working-class counterparts are much less likely to be able to afford a housing upgrade. Data in this chapter indicate that modern working-class Americans' income is decreasing over time, and that factory workers' earnings are progressively falling farther behind their counterparts in most other affluent nations. Skilled-labor jobs, however, offer better pay and more interesting work than other blue-collar positions.

Human capital: Unlike middle-class families, where extensive spending occurs on schooling, lessons, books, computer products, and other education-related experiences and items, blue-collar parents lack the funds for such expenditures. Blue-collar education can be debilitating, and students who have completed vocational schooling sometimes reported it produced a negative self-image. Training programs for skilled jobs vary, with those sponsored solely by employers maintaining a lower completion rate than the programs supported by both employers and unions.

Cultural capital: Because of their isolation from middle-class schooling and jobs, working-class parents often lack the language abilities, values, and outlooks that could help prepare their children to succeed in the mainstream world. Lillian Rubin, however, indicated that when dealing with their children, some of her blue-collar respondents showed greater flexibility on such issues as abortion or homosexuality than they had in the past.

Social capital: A study reported in this chapter indicated that sometimes working-class parents lacked the experience to work with teachers on behalf of their children. However, other research demonstrated that some blue-collar people use social capital well, involving themselves extensively in their communities and sharing information and resources with their peers. The Royster research emphasized an important but troubling reality: that sometimes job-locating networks are racially biased.

A final commentary: Certain blue-collar work will continue indefinitely. Reg Theriault, a longshoreman turned writer, indicated that a case in point involves new houses, which cannot have their wiring, roofing, and plumbing outsourced. Theriault concluded, "This, in addition to their skills, is one of the major reasons the organized building trades workers have stayed healthy and continue to make decent wages" (Theriault 2003, 190). While in recent years the housing market has faltered, the construction of buildings, whether they are houses, retail stores, other businesses, or public structures, will always require a steady supply of workers to complete the necessary tasks.

Although skilled blue-collar workers can have good prospects, other working-class job holders face a less optimistic future. Interviewing 18 auto workers, Louis Uchitelle found that they all indicated that working conditions, which had been improving as recently as the 1990s, were distinctly in decline in 2007, and as a result many were planning to leave, accepting buyouts or retirement.

Kenneth Doolittle, once a supervisor for a team of assembly-line workers at General Motors, had loved his job. Then his plant was closed, and he was offered a position back on the assembly line, a demotion Doolittle considered humiliating. He decided to retire, gaining a pension that gave him about 60 percent of his old pay. To make up some of the difference, he started doing maintenance work for Sears at $10 an hour.

The new job did not engage Doolittle. He missed the old work, the income, and the camaraderie at the auto plant. "My children and my grandchildren will never have an opportunity to work at GM," Doolittle said. "My dad made a good living there. So did my brother and my brothers-in-law. That is all over now" (Uchitelle 2007, 3.1). In recent decades blue-collar workers in many others businesses could offer similar testimonies about the unhappy end of a family's long, successful relationship with a prominent American business.

Key Terms in the Glossary

Apprentice *207*

Intersectionality *209*

Labor union *189*

Proletariat *194*

Sense of entitlement *199*

Skilled-labor job *201*

Work alienation *194*

Discussion Topics

1. List and describe the conditions affecting working-class life in early industrial times.
2. How has TV programming generally represented the American working class?
3. Discuss working-class networking.
4. Evaluate this statement: Working-class jobs are usually boring and repetitive, lacking any cerebral component.
5. Examine income from working-class jobs over time, including the impact of reemployment.
6. Assess in detail the effect of temp work on the corporations receiving the workers' services, those businesses' full-time employees, and the temp job holders themselves.
7. What are qualities that make working-class job-training programs successful? Discuss.

Research Papers

1. Starting with material in this chapter, write about the activities of labor unions over time, evaluating their level of success. It might be helpful to follow a particular union, tracing its ups and downs through the years.
2. Are modern working-class Americans' lives consistent with the Marxist theory? Obviously the response is neither yes or no. Raise several, carefully documented points, providing both support for the theory and criticism of it.
3. Analyze the differences in working-class and middle-class experience in one of the following areas: family life; schooling; or work. Document the conclusions thoroughly, using references in Chapter 6 and this chapter as foundational sources.
4. Write about the challenges of doing blue-collar temp work or working-class job training. While material in the chapter can provide some sources, it will be helpful to obtain additional information.

Informative Websites

Visit the Web site of the Change to Win Federation (http://www.changetowin.org/aboutus.html) to learn about the efforts of five unions to revitalize the declining American labor movement.

This site (http://news.minnesota.publicradio.org/features/200) contains a detailed interview with Alfred Lubrano, who elaborates on the text's discussion about experiencing the transition from a working-class to a middle-class world.

The Vocational Information Center (http://www.khake.com/page23.html) provides extensive data about many types of blue-collar jobs.

The websites for Kelly Services (http://www.kellyservices.com/web/global/services/en/pages/index.htm) and Manpower Inc. (http://www.manpower.com/) describe the economic services that these two venerable, global temp agencies provide their corporate customers.

JobTrain (http://www.jobtrainworks.org/) offers hundreds of young people aged 14 to 21 training in seven vocational work spheres.

Bibliography

Barbour, Chandler, and Nita H. Barbour. 2001. *Families, Schools, and Communities: Building Partnerships for Educating Children*, 2nd ed. Upper Saddle River, NJ: Prentice-Hall.

Bilginsoy, Cihan. 2003. "The Hazards of Training: Attrition and Retention in Construction Industry Apprenticeship Programs." *Industrial and Labor Relations Review* 57 (October): 54–67.

Bishop, John H., and Ferran Mane. 2005. "Economic Returns to Vocational Courses in U.S. High Schools," pp. 329–62 in Jon Lauglo and Rupert Maclean (eds.), *Vocationalisation of Secondary Education Revisited*. Dordrecht, the Netherlands: Springer.

Blumin, Stuart M. 1989. *The Emergence of the Middle Class: Social Experience in the American City, 1760–1900*. Cambridge, England: Cambridge University Press.

Boris, Eileen, and Nelson, Lichtenstein. 2003. "Mobile Capital, Migratory Workers," pp. 473–75 in Eileen Boris and Nelson Lichtenstein (eds.), *Major Problems in the History of American Workers: Documents and Essays*, 2nd ed. Boston: Hougton Mifflin.

Cannon, Julie Ann Harms. 2006. "White, Working Class, and Feminist: Working within the Master's House and Finding Home Again," pp. 101–16 in Stephen Muzzatti and C. Vincent Samarco (eds.), *Reflections from the Wrong Side of the Tracks: Class, Identity, and the Working Class Experience in Academe*. Lanham, MD: Rowman & Littlefield.

Castellano, Marisa. 1997. "'It's Not Your Skills, It's the Tests': Gatekeepers for Women in the Skilled Trades," pp. 189–213 in Glynda Hull (ed.), *Changing Work, Changing Workers: Critical Perspectives on Language, Literacy, and Skills*. Albany: State University of New York Press.

Cherlin, Andrew J. 2004. "The Child-Care Squeeze for Working-Class Families." http://www .popcenter.umd/events/nichd/papers/ cherlin.pdf.

Cheslow, Jerry. 2004. "An Old Haunt Re-emerges on Raritan Bay." *New York Times* (October 26): 11.7.

Coonz, Stephanie. 1999. "Working-Class Families, 1870–1890," pp. 94–127 in Stephanie Coonz, Maya Parson, and Gabrielle Raley (eds.), *American Families: A Multicultural Reader*. New York: Routledge.

Covello, Leonard. 1967. *Background of the Italo-American School Child: A Study of the Southern Italian Family Mores and Their Effect on the School Situation in Italy and America*. Leiden, Netherlands: E.J. Brill.

Doob, Christopher Bates. 1999. *Racism: An American Caldron*. Boston: Addison Wesley Longman.

Elbaum, Bernard. 1989. "Why Apprenticeship Persisted in Britain but Not in the United States. *Journal of Economic History* 69 (June): 337–49.

Eren, Ozkan. 2009. "Does Membership Pay Off for Covered Workers? A Distributional Analysis of the Free Rider Problem." *Industrial and Labor Relations Review* 62 (April): 367–80.

Escriche, Luisa. 2007. "Persistence of Occupational Segregation: The Role of the Intergenerational Transmission of Preferences." *Economic Journal* 117 (April): 837–57.

Foster, Ann C. 2003. "Differences in Union and Nonunion Earnings in Blue-Collar and Service Occupations." *U.S. Bureau of Labor Statistics*. (June 25). http://www.bls.gov/ opub/cwc/cm20030623ar01p1.htm.

Gilbert, Dennis. 2011. *The American Class Structure in an Age of Growing Inequality*, 8th ed. Los Angeles: Pine Forge Press.

Goodlad, John I. 1984. *A Place Called School*. New York: McGraw-Hill.

Greenwald, Richard A., and Elizabeth Grant. 1999. "Reversals of Fortune: Downward Mobility and the Writing of Nontraditional Students," pp. 30–44 in Sherry Lee Linkon (ed.), *Teaching Working Class*. Amherst: University of Massachusetts Press.

Grubb, W. Norton, and Marvin Lazerson. 2004. *The Education Gospel: The Economic Power of Schooling*. Cambridge, MA: Harvard University Press.

Haley, Heather-Lyn, Maureen Perry-Jenkins, and Amy Armenia. 2001. "Workplace Policies and the Psychological Well-Being of First-Time Parents: The Case of Working-Class Parents," pp. 227–50 in Rosanna Hertz and Nancy L. Marshall (eds.), *Working Families: The Transformation of the American Home*. Berkeley: University of California Press.

Hart, Betty, and Todd R. Risley. 1995. *Meaningful Differences in the Everyday Experiences of Young American Children*. Baltimore: P.H. Brookes.

Horton, Hayward Derrick, Beverly Lundy Allen, Cedric Herring, Melvin E. Thomas. 2000. "Lost in the Storm: The Sociology of the Black Working Class, 1850 to 1990." *American Sociological Review* 65 (February): 128–37.

Horton, Myles. 1998. *The Long Haul: An Autobiography*. New York: Teachers' College Press.

Hurst, Allison L. 2009. "The Path to College: Stories of Students from the Working Class." *Race. Gender & Class* 16: 257–81.

Illick, Joseph E. 2002. *American Childhoods*. Philadelphia: University of Pennsylvania Press.

Jones, Jacqueline. 1999. *A Social History of the Laboring Classes: From Colonial Times to the Present*. Oxford: Blackwell.

Kendall, Diana. 2005. *Framing Class: Media Representation of Wealth and Poverty in America*. Lanham, MD: Rowman & Littlefield.

Kohn, Melvin L. 1969. *Class and Conformity: A Study in Values*. Homewood, IL: Dorsey Press.

Lareau, Annette. 2007. "Unequal Childhoods: Class, Race, and Family Life," pp. 537–48 in David B. Grusky and Szonja Szelényi (eds.), *The Inequality Reader: Contemporary and Foundational Readings in Race, Class, and Gender*. Boulder: Westview Press.

Lassonde, Stephen. 2005. *Learning to Forget: Schooling and Family Life in New Haven's Working Class, 1870–1940*. New Haven: Yale University Press.

LeBlanc, Paul. 1999. *A Short History of the U.S. Working Class: From Colonial Times to the Twenty-First Century*. Amherst, NY: Humanity Books.

LeMasters, E.E. 1975. *Blue-Collar Aristocrats: Life-Styles at a Working-Class Tavern*. Madison: University of Wisconsin Press.

Lepadatu, Darina, and Timothy Thompson. 2005. "The US Labor Unions and Their (non) Response to Workplace Diversity." *American Sociological Association annual meeting*, pp. 1–20.

Levine, Bruce, Stephen Brier, David Brundage, Edward Countryman, Dorothy Fennell, and Marcus Rediker. 1989. *Working People and the Nation's Economy, Politics, Culture, and Society*. New York: Pantheon Books.

Lorenz, Mary. 2008. "Today's Top 10 Blue Collar Jobs." http://jobs.aol.com/article/_a/todays-top-10-blue-collar-jobs/200709…

Lubrano, Alfred. 2004. *Blue-Collar Roots, White-Collar Dreams*. Hoboken, NJ: John Wiley & Sons.

Marx, Karl, and Friedrich Engels. 1959. "The Manifesto of the Communist Party," pp. 1–41 in Lewis S. Feuer (ed.), *Basic Writing on Politics & Philosophy*. Garden City, NY: Anchor Books.

Merrifield, Juliet. 1997. "If Job Training Is the Answer, What Is the Question?," pp. 273–94 in Glynda Hull (ed.), *Changing Work, Changing Workers: Critical Perspectives on Language, Literacy, and Skills*. Albany: State University of New York Press.

Montgomery, David. 1979. *Workers' Control in America*. Cambridge: Cambridge University Press.

Nelson, Margaret K., and Joan Smith. 1999. *Working Hard and Making Do: Surviving in Small Town America*. Berkeley: University of California Press.

Novak, Candice. 2008. "Behind the Rise of Temp Work." *U.S. News and World Report*. (July 15). http://www.usnews.com/articles/business/careers/2008/07/15/behind-…

Perlmann, Joel. 1988. *Ethnic Differences: Social Structure among the Irish, Italians, Jews, and Blacks in an American City, 1880–1935*.

Cambridge, England: Cambridge University Press.

Perrucci, Robert, and Earl Wysong. 2008. *The New Class Society: Goodbye American Dream?*, 3rd ed. Lanham, MD: Rowman & Littlefield.

Perry-Jenkins, Maureen. 2005. "Work in the Working Class: Challenges Facing Workers and Their Families," pp. 453–72 in Suzanne M. Bianchi, Lynne M. Cooper, and Rosalind Berkowitz King (eds.), *Work, Family, Health and Well-Being*. Mahwah, NJ: Lawrence Erlbaum Associates.

Pew Center for the People & the Press. 2008. "Economic Discontent Deepens as Inflation Concerns Rise." http://pewresearch.org/pubs/734/economy.

Pollin, Robert. 2005. *Contours of Descent: U.S. Economic Fractures and the Landscape of Global Austerity*. London: Verso.

Raff, Daniel M.G., and Lawrence H. Summers. 1987. "Did Henry Ford Pay Efficiency Wages?" *Journal of Labor Economics* 5 (October): 557–86.

Reddit. 2010. "Have You Guys Worked Boring, Repetitive, Assembly Line Jobs?" http://www.redditgadgetguide.com/r/AskReddit/comments/amyi2/have_you_guys_worked_boring_repetitive_assembly/.

Richards, Robyn J. 2008. "Payroll Employment in 2007: Job Growth Slows." *Monthly Labor Review* 131 (March): 19–31.

Rodgers, Daniel T. 1978. *The Work Ethic in Industrial America, 1850–1920*. Chicago: University of Chicago Press.

Rose, Mike. 2004. *The Mind at Work: Valuing the Intelligence of the American Worker*. New York: Viking.

Royster, Deidre A. 2003. *Race and the Invisible Hand: How White Networks Exclude Black Men from Blue-Collar Jobs*. Berkeley: University of California Press.

Rubin, Lillian Breslow. 1976. *Worlds of Pain: Life in the Working-Class Family*. New York: Basic Books.

Rubin, Lillian Breslow. 1994. *Families on the Fault Line: America's Working Class Speaks about the Family, the Economy, Race, and Ethnicity*. New York: HarperCollins.

Sailor, Dorothy Holin. 2004. *Supporting Children in Their Home, School, and Community*. Boston: Allyn & Bacon.

Shepard, Jon M. 1970. "Functional Specialization, Alienation, and Job Satisfaction." *Industrial and Labor Relations* 23 (January): 207–19.

Shostak, Arthur B. 1969. *Blue-Collar Life*. New York: Random House.

Smith, Vicki, Heather Kohler Flynn, and Jonathan Isler. 2006. "Getting Jobs and Building Careers: Reproducing Inequality in State-Sponsored Job Search Organizations." *Research in the Sociology of Work* 16: 375–402.

Sulek, Antoni. 2010. "Teaching with Melvin Kohn." *Polish Sociological Review*: 261–64.

Sweet, Stephen, and Peter Meiksins. 2008. *Changing Contours of Work: Jobs and Opportunities in the New Economy*. Thousand Oaks, CA: Pine Forge Press.

Theriault, Reg. 2003. *The Unmaking of the American Working Class*. New York: New Press.

Uchitelle, Louis. 2007. "The End of the Line as They Knew It." *New York Times* (April 1): 3.1.

U.S. Bureau of Labor Statistics. 2005. "Contingent and Alternative Employment Arrangements, February 2005." (July 27). http://www.bls.gov/news.release/conemp.nr0.htm.

U.S Bureau of Labor Statistics. 2006. "Worker Displacement, 2003–2005." (September 15). http://bls.gov/news.release/disp.nr0.htm.

U.S. Bureau of Labor Statistics. 2008. "Displaced Workers Summary." (August 20). http://www.bls.gov/news.release/disp.nr0.htm.

U.S. Census Bureau. 2009. Table P–45A. "Occupation of Longest Job—Full-Time, Year-Round Workers (Both Sexes Combined) by Median and Mean Earnings: 2002 to 2008." *Historical Income Tables—People*. http://www.census.gov/hhes/www/income/histinc/incpertoc.html.

U.S. Census Bureau. 2010. Table 647. "Work Stoppages." *Statistical Abstract of the United States: 2010*. www.census.gov/compendia/statab/cats/labor_force_emp.

Van Arsdale, David. 2008. "The Recasualization of Blue-Collar Workers: Industrial Temporary Help Work's Impact on the Working Class." *Labor Studies in Working-Class History of the Americas* 5: 75–99.

Weis, Lois. 1990. *Working Class without Work: High School Students in a Deindustrializing Economy*. New York: Routledge.

Wilms, Wellford W. 1988. "Captured by the American Dream: Vocational Education in the United States," pp. 81–93 in Jon Lauglo and Kevin Lillis (eds.), *Vocationalizing Education: An International Perspective*. Oxford: Penguin Press.

Yates, Michael D. 2007. *More Unequal Aspects of Class in the United States*. New York: Monthly Review Press.

Ziegler, Robert, and Gilbert J. Gall. 2002. *American Workers, American Unions: The Twentieth Century*, 3rd ed. Baltimore: John Hopkins University Press.

Zweig, Michael. 2000. *The Working Class Majority: America's Best Kept Secret*. Ithaca: ILR Press.

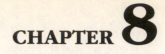

CHAPTER 8

American Poverty: The Dream Turned Nightmare

A 17-year-old college student from an impoverished neighborhood in Chicago estimated that about 40 percent of the people in his locale were alcoholics; many others were in the street just hanging out, experiencing an unplanned, purposeless life. He explained, "They live based on today. [They say,] 'Oh, we gonna get high today.' 'Oh, whoopee!' 'What you gonna do tomorrow?' 'I don't know, man. I know when it gets here.'" The man added that he understood such behavior—that being among confused, unmotivated people produced such an outcome (Wilson 1997, 8).

Is it personal failure or circumstances that contribute more substantially to people's poverty? Like this student sociologists favor the latter factor. This chapter examines the history of American poverty, the official definition of poverty, contemporary living for poor Americans, and the enactment of welfare reform. In the upcoming section, it becomes apparent that poverty has always been a reality in American society.

A basic concept throughout the chapter is the **cycle of poverty**, which is a circular process in which a set of interrelating large structures, primarily institutions, lock individuals and families into a low-income condition. The concept is provocative because it analyzes poverty as dynamic and interactive, and it also encourages speculations about attacking poverty—breaking the cycle. The reality that the concept describes focuses on several issues—in particular, schools, employment, and housing. In the American system of public education, poor people generally attend inferior schools where the level of learning is low and the dropout rate is high. As a result such individuals receive little effective preparation for employment, usually finding that only low-skill, low-paying jobs are available to them. If desperate for money, they sometimes turn to the informal sector for income, perhaps selling drugs or other illegal goods. These ventures further alienate them from the mainstream economy because such sources of income do not develop mainstream skills that can appear on a résumé. Low income forces people to start their own families in poor districts, where their children grow up, attend inferior schools, and repeat the cycle. Additional factors like racial discrimination, delinquent and criminal activity, and illegal drug use also promote repetition of the cycle of poverty (Marger 2010, 162–63; Rank and Hirschl 2001; Wilson 2009, 19–20). This concept addresses stark instances of social reproduction.

People engaged in "blaming the victim" maintain a sharply different outlook from those appreciating the cycle of poverty. **Blaming the victim** is a perspective that focuses on an individual's personal deficiencies, downplaying or ignoring such structural influences as the family's economic status or its access to quality education (Ryan 1976). In American history both of these points of view have been apparent.

THE AMERICAN POOR THROUGH THE CENTURIES

During the colonial era, male breadwinners were often killed or seriously injured in warfare, fires, epidemics, or work-related accidents, leaving their families instantly impoverished (Nash 2004, 9–12).

By the early nineteenth century, periodic depressions and increasing mechanization on farms put many farmers, unskilled laborers, and craftsmen out of work. These former holders of stable employment became a "floating proletariat," often traveling long distances to find jobs (Iceland 2006, 12; Katz 2003, 228; Trattner 1994, 22). Yet the myth prevailed that work was available for every able-bodied person. Some individuals attacked that belief. Referring to a group of 700 unemployed job seekers, Josiah Quincy, future president of Harvard University, told a roomful of scholars, "These men long for work; they anxiously beg for it; yet it is not to be found" (Katz 2003, 228).

In the middle nineteenth century, thousands of workers illustrated Quincy's conclusion, traveling hundreds of miles to dig canals for a dollar a day from which was deducted one-and-a-half to two dollars a week for room and board. They were working in marshy conditions which often made them sick. At the end of jobs, many returned to their families with little cash and their health ruined. However, other men were so desperate for money that they readily replaced those who departed (Katz 2003, 228).

Besides the toll taken on men, other family members also suffered. In the late eighteenth and early nineteenth centuries in Philadelphia, poor infants died in greater numbers from intestinal diseases and parasites caused by spoiled food, polluted water, and inadequate hygiene than more affluent youngsters. Poor children were also much more likely to be dropped, burned, or scalded than their wealthier counterparts. A significant contributor to these accidents was that members of poor families usually drafted all adults and older children into the workforce, leaving infants and toddlers either unattended or under young siblings' precarious supervision. Poor women were also disproportionately victimized. They were three times as likely as other women to die in childbirth. In such situations babies seldom survived (Klepp 2004, 72–73).

Religious and political leaders took few measures to help the poor, holding many of them responsible for their poverty. Once the Puritans accepted Newton's law of gravity, which denied God a role in that process, they concluded that the deity should not be held responsible for outcomes in the natural world. That outlook included the immediate society, where the Puritans asserted that individuals, not God, were responsible for results. In the case of poverty, people needed to be willing to work hard to escape its painful effects (Olivas 2004, 270–78).

Drawing inspiration from the Elizabethan Poor Law of 1601, colonial government officials distinguished between the "deserving poor" and the "undeserving poor."

- The **deserving poor** included the aged, infants, and people with serious illness or physical disability, who were incapable of work and thus qualified for charitable support and a sympathetic evaluation.

- The **undeserving poor** were individuals who simply avoided work out of apparent lethargy or because alcohol, drugs, or some other debilitating influence caused physical and/or mental decline. They were contemptible and needed to be coerced into the workforce (Iceland 2006, 12). With the undeserving poor, a blaming-the-victim outlook prevailed.

In 1834 the Reverend Charles Burroughs made a statement typical of contemporary leaders who distinguished between the deserving and undeserving poor. Burroughs declared that God's inscrutable wisdom caused individuals to be members of the deserving poor. "It is the result, not of our faults, but of our misfortunes . . . [The undeserving poor are] the consequence of willful error, of shameful indolence, of vicious habit" (Iceland 2006, 12).

Many nineteenth- and early twentieth-century leaders expressed deep concern and even fear of those they considered the undeserving poor. In 1854 Charles Loring Brace, the head of New York City's Children's Aid Society, declared that the country's greatest future danger was the persistence of "an ignorant, debased, and permanently poor class in the great cities." Brace warned that these people had the most contemptible passions and habits. He added, "They corrupt the lowest class of working-poor who are around them. The expenses of police, prisons, of charities and means of relief arise mainly from them" (Katz 1993, 9).

The distinction between the deserving and undeserving poor was a salient concern when officials began providing poor people assistance.

Governmental Efforts to Reduce Poverty

In colonial times the general outlook was that men were supposed to work and support themselves and their families. Single mothers, whether widowed, deserted, or never married, were usually not expected to provide for their children, and they became the earliest beneficiaries of arrangements where town officials found household heads willing to supply food and shelter in exchange for indentured servitude. This aid was usually for brief periods, supplied until the mother could find a more permanent source of income. Only white women received this aid. Town officials usually monitored free women of color but seldom sponsored their relief. Often they were expelled from the town, forced to fend for themselves and their children (Handler and Hasenfeld 2007, 151–52).

Starting in the 1830s state governments passed laws requiring counties to maintain "indoor relief"—poor farms or poorhouses which were sufficiently forbidding that they deterred all but the most desperate individuals and families from seeking help. Poorhouse occupants were generally designated "undeserving," expected to work long, hard hours as a combination of punishment, education, and reform. By the 1850s most poorhouses had become highly dysfunctional organizations. They tended to be badly built, poorly heated and ventilated, and crowded, with largely untrained, often incompetent directors and staff. Rowdiness, even chaos tended to prevail. Nonetheless until the early twentieth century, poorhouses remained prominent, only falling out of favor when public officials and poverty workers started realizing that these structures not only failed to reduce poverty but often destabilized already weakened families (Iceland 2006, 12; Katz 2003, 241).

In 1910 the first welfare program known as Aid to Dependent Children (ADC) started in Illinois, and by the end of the decade most states had similar initiatives. State statutes were usually broad enough to include all divorced, separated, or deserted mothers. However, ADC officials almost always restricted recipients to "deserving" mothers, who supplied a "suitable home," where the mother as homemaker provided a healthy setting for the moral, physical, and emotional development of her children. No explicit standards designated what constituted a suitable home, and as a result most local offices fell back on traditional assessments, usually excluding mothers with illegitimate children and families of color.

By the late 1950s and early 1960s, however, the ADC standards started to change. As African-American families moved from the South into northern cities, they often encountered unemployment and persistent poverty. At first ADC officials resisted the addition of large numbers of traditionally "undeserving" families to the rolls. However, civil-rights organizations, welfare-rights groups, and some Democratic politicians applied pressure on ADC leaders. The increase was significant. In 1960 there were 3.1 million ADC recipients. That total rose to 4.3 million in 1965, 6.1 million in 1969, and 10.8 million in 1974 (Handler and Hasenfeld 2007, 156–58).

In that era the federal government initiated a program to fight poverty and seek to curtail welfare. It was the so-called "War on Poverty," which President Lyndon Johnson proposed in recognition of President Kennedy's support for such an initiative. Considerable optimism greeted the program's development. Community organizer and writer Michael Harrington attended a party where many of the guests were prominent citizens in their communities. A well-known union official asserted that the upcoming moon mission made most earthly challenges seem quite modest. The prevailing feeling among those present was that if we could land on the moon, "why can't we put an end to the slums? [Everyone] . . . there, knew that our capacities were boundless, that we could deal with ghettos as well as outer space" (Harrington 1984, 2).

It turned out to be much simpler to land a man on the moon than to wage a successful war on poverty. Many problems arose. The program was controversial, with liberal and conservative politicians differing on how the money should be spent. Then after riots occurred in many cities, the officials running the program, fearing poor people's militancy, tried to cut back local residents' participation on agencies' boards of directors, further arousing activists. In addition, from the beginning the War on Poverty was seriously underfunded, making it impossible to provide its clients either jobs or income supports. Then as the Vietnam War escalated and became increasingly expensive, the modest support for that other war became more and more meager (Seccombe 2007, 35–36).

As welfare rolls grew through the 1960s and 1970s, many Americans reacted negatively, assuming that all or nearly all welfare families were headed by undeserving mothers. A blaming-the-victim perspective was in vogue. In the 1980s President Reagan coined the term "welfare queen," referring to African American unwed mothers who would allegedly have children to get on welfare and then would raise their children inadequately, leading to a repetition of the same process along with involvement in crime and drug abuse. The idea of the welfare queen is a combination of two negative perceptions—a contemporary image of the "undeserving poor" and a racist stereotype. Like President Reagan many critics of the welfare system tend to "race code" their analysis of it, tapping into Americans' tendency to perceive the program's deficiencies as produced by its black clientele (Gilens 1999; Williams 2000). Later in the chapter it becomes apparent that such negative generalizations about welfare recipients are gross distortions.

Besides Reagan many other political leaders became increasingly critical of the program, citing its rising cost. Some observers raised what struck them as a burning question: With a steadily expanding number of women entering the general workforce, why should welfare women be exempt? By 1996 about 14 million individuals, almost 5 million families, received what was now called Aid to Families with Dependent Children (AFDC).

Plans to change the welfare program were in the offing. In both 1967 and 1988, Congress passed legislation seeking to bring welfare mothers into the workforce. In both instances, however, financial allotments were modest, meaning the prospective job holders received little training or schooling, or childcare subsidy. Neither effort led to significant reduction of the welfare rolls (Handler and Hasenfeld 2007, 179–80). When Congress enacted welfare reform in 1996, the legislators might have assessed the reasons why the earlier programs failed. However, the politicians and their constituents appear to have had other priorities.

Bolstered by public support, conservative legislators fixated on the "welfare queen" issue. They were aware of the statistical pattern—for instance that in 1994, 79 percent of African American births were out-of-wedlock, and over half of those involved poor children, many of whom were on welfare. AFDC, the critics declared, was creating dependency and destroying families. Whether clients were black or white families, welfare had to cease. These female family heads needed to get jobs, thereby restoring morality and a work ethic. Public attention focused on this perception and ignored certain significant statistical trends—that African American women's number of children was declining and that the total count of out-of-wedlock births and the welfare rolls had begun to drop (Handler and Hasenfeld 2007, 182). In the middle 1990s, however, the only statistics regarding welfare that impacted the public were those backing a blaming-the-victim image and the urgent need to terminate AFDC. In 1996 Congress passed the Personal Responsibility Work and Opportunity Reconciliation Act, and President Clinton signed it into law. Temporary Assistance for Needy Families (TANF) replaced AFDC. Welfare reform, which we examine later in the chapter, had begun.

An analysis of this program makes it apparent that underlying realities affecting welfare recipients are often more complex than politicians and most other public players indicate. In fact, simply measuring poverty is complicated and controversial.

WHO IS POOR?

A necessary foundation for a discussion about poverty is a designation of what constitutes being poor. To begin, an **absolute threshold of poverty** is a cutoff point establishing the minimal level of income below which families are unable to purchase sufficient food, clothing, and shelter to maintain themselves in good health (Walker and Walker 1995, 655). The **official U.S. measure of poverty** is an absolute standard employing a two-step process—assessing the minimal cost for a nutritionally healthy diet and then tripling that figure to compute the threshold for a poverty income. It was Mollie Orshansky of the Social Security Administration who did the initial research on which the official U.S. measure of poverty is based. Orshansky used the "Economy Food Plan" from the U.S. Department of Agriculture to determine the expense of the lowest-cost nutritious if monotonous diet. Then from the 1955 Household Food Consumption Survey, she learned that families of three or more spent about one third of their after-tax income on food.

TABLE 8.1 Poverty Threshold for 2009 by Size of Family	
One person (under 65)	$11,161
Two people (under 65)	14,366
Three people[1]	16,781
Four people	22,128
Five people	26,686
Six people	30,693
Seven people	35,316
Eight people	39,498
Nine people or more	47,514

[1]No age limits are specified for three or more people.

Source: U.S. Census Bureau. 2010. "Poverty Thresholds 2009." http://www
.census.gov/hhes/www/poverty/threshld/thres09.html

Each year the poverty thresholds have been updated for inflation (Iceland 2006, 22). As Table 8.1 indicates, the 2009 thresholds ranged from $11,161 for one person to $47,514 for nine or more persons (U.S. Census Bureau 2010a).

This approach to measuring poverty has both strengths and weaknesses. A positive attribute is that it has achieved a consensus of what constitutes being poor. This situation has proved particularly useful for researchers who can generally feel confident that since the middle 1960s a consistent standard for establishing poverty thresholds has existed.

On the other hand, the official U.S. measure of poverty has received several severe criticisms. To begin, the measure focuses on food costs, which have dropped to about a sixth of the family budget. Meanwhile the U.S. measure ignores such critical, often rising expenses as transportation costs, childcare fees, healthcare expenditures, and rental payments. In addition, the current measure provides a single threshold for a given sized family, not acknowledging the significant variations in the cost of living around the country. Furthermore the mere existence of an official U.S. measure of poverty draws a sharp line between the poor and everyone else. Is that realistic? What about the family with an income that falls $1 or $50 above the official threshold? Are they safely removed from poverty status, or are they also significantly endangered? (Handler and Hasenfeld 2007, 6; Iceland 2006, 23–24; Seccombe 2000, 1096–97).

A study by researchers at the Economic Policy Institute addressed such concerns. It found that in hundreds of communities across the nation the cost of basic expenses, which included funds for housing, childcare, healthcare, food, transportation, and taxes, was about twice the poverty threshold for a four-member family (Books 2004, 22). It appears hard to dispute two conclusions—that the official measure is outmoded and that were Mollie Orshansky, who always based her computations on current sources, active today, she would call for a significant revision of the antiquated scheme.

In short, the official U.S. measure of poverty seems defective. In addition, it is apparent that the current approach understates the breadth and depth of poverty, perhaps lessening public concern about the issue and helping to tamp down welfare programs' expenditure.

A distinctly different approach for assessing the extent of poverty involves using an international perspective. At the turn of the twenty-first century, the US rate of poverty, which in this study involved family income that was less than half the national median income, was 17.8 percent—substantially higher than any of the other major developed nations in the study. Italy was a somewhat distant second at 13.9 percent, followed by the United Kingdom, Canada, and Spain (Smeeding, Rainwater, and Burtless 2001).

Among developed nations the United States is near the top in the size of its child-poverty segment. Using the aforementioned measure of poverty, one finds that the US has a higher percentage of children growing up poor—21.9 percent—than 24 of 25 other wealthy nations. Only Mexico, which has a per-capita income that is barely one fifth the American total, has a higher rate. The United States's peers in per-capita income trail distantly, with Italy and New Zealand next in line at 16.6 and 16.3 percent respectively (UNICEF Innocenti Research Centre 2005). Table 8.2 displays the percentages of child poverty for all 26 wealthy countries.

The statistics for the American poor are impressive, exceeding some developed nations' total populations. In 2008 13.2 percent of American inhabitants were officially poor, meaning 39.1 million people (U.S. Census Bureau 2009b). Table 8.3 focuses on

TABLE 8.2 Child Poverty in 26 Wealthy Nations[1]

Country	Percentage of child poverty	Country	Percentage of child poverty
Denmark	2.4	Greece	12.4
Finland	2.8	Poland	12.7
Norway	3.4	Spain	13.3
Sweden	4.2	Japan	14.3
Czech Republic	6.8	Australia	14.7
		Canada	14.9
Switzerland	6.8	United Kingdom	15.4
France	7.5		
Belgium	7.7	Portugal	15.6
Hungary	8.8	Ireland	15.7
Luxembourg	9.1	New Zealand	16.3
The Netherlands	9.8	Italy	16.6
Austria	10.2	United States	21.9
Germany	10.2	Mexico	27.7

[1]To qualify as poor, a child must live in a family with less than half the national median income.

Except for Mexico, which has a per-capita income that is scarcely one fifth the American figure, the United States leads these developed nations in its percentage of child poverty. In fact, the four Scandinavian countries all have less than one fifth the United States figure.

Source: UNICEF Innocenti Research Centre. 2005. Figure 1. "The Child Poverty League." *Child Poverty in Rich Countries 2005.* http://www.unicef-irc.org/publications/pdf/repcard6e.pdf

TABLE 8.3 Racial Characteristics of Families below the Poverty Line

	Number of families below the poverty levels (in thousands)	Percent of the group below the poverty level
Total	7,623	9.8%
Asian	261	7.9
Black	2,043	22.1
Hispanic	2,045	19.7
White	3,184	8.9

In 2007 white families represented nearly half of all officially poor families, but blacks and Hispanics had higher rates of family poverty.

Source: U.S. Census Bureau. 2010. Table 700. "Families below Poverty Level by Selected Characteristics: 2007." *Statistical Abstract of the United States: 2010.* http://www.census.gov/compendia/statab/cats/income_expenditures_poverty_wealth.html.

poor families' racial characteristics. Frequently sociologists have divided low-income Americans into two classes—the working poor and the underclass.

The working poor earn about $25,000 per year and are employed as service workers, childcare attendants, maids, custodians, and as employees in many other low-income, low-skill positions. While some members of the working poor complete high school, the prevailing reality is that schooling does little to provide them critical skills (Gilbert 2011, 244, 248; Shipler 2004, 239).

Their work is often physically demanding. Journalist Barbara Ehrenreich held three low-income jobs in order to experience working-poor people's lives. She wondered whether home owners were aware how physically taxing it was to clean people's houses, making them "motel-perfect." Her team of maids inhabited "a world of pain—managed by Excedrin and Advil, compensated for with cigarettes and, in one or two cases and then only on weekends, with booze" (Ehrenreich 2002, 89).

Can members of this class move a comfortable distance from poverty? One analysis suggested a "perfect lineup of favorable conditions" is necessary—job-related attributes such as a distinct set of work skills and a position that provides both a living wage and prospects of promotion; personal qualities like a focused sense of purpose, solid self-esteem, and freedom from illness, addiction, and debt; and finally, if necessary, assistance from family, friends, and government agencies. Any gap in this array of conditions means the people in question are unprotected and are likely to slip back into poverty (Shipler 2004, 4–5). Researcher David Shipler indicated that an impoverished, minimally educated individual facing the mainstream work world is like the prospect of "playing quarterback with no helmet, no padding, no training, and no experience, behind a line of hundred-pound weaklings . . . [A] poor man or woman gets sacked again and again" (Shipler 2004, 5).

National statistics indicated that in 2007 about 11 percent of poor people 16 and over worked full-time year-round, 25 percent worked but not both full-time or year-round, and 64 percent, nearly two thirds, did not work (U.S. Census Bureau 2010b).

The poor people who do not work generally fall into the underclass category. This poorest class contains a set of individuals and families that comprises about 12 percent of the population and have a yearly income of about $15,000 or lower. Few underclass members have completed high school, their job skills are limited, and many have physical and/or mental disabilities. Such qualities make it unlikely that they will have successful work histories (Gilbert 2011, 244, 248–49). While various critics have suggested that the term "underclass" is cold, impersonal, or even racist, targeting blacks and Hispanics, its use has remained prevalent, recognizing the harsh reality that confronts the poorest of the poor (Auletta 1999, 12; Gans 2010, 104).

Many underclass members believe that a steady job is essential and yet feel that their current circumstances make it impossible to obtain one. Some of these individuals, however, might be able to achieve that goal. For instance, a number of underclass high-school students might possess the potential to enter the job world but lack the information and guidance to make the move; high-school teachers and counselors can provide critical assistance here.

Eventually a certain segment of the underclass enters the informal sector, where, as Chapter 3 indicates, commercial activity is neither monitored nor taxed. Sociologist William Wilson suggested that the more marginal a neighborhood, the less restraint its members encounter to engaging in behavior that is illegal or widely considered inappropriate. Whether they are involved in street vending, unlicensed childcare, drug dealing, illegal gambling, or prostitution, participants in the informal sector become increasingly marginalized from the mainstream world, removed from its demands for tight scheduling and discipline and also its opportunities. (Wilson 1997, 69–75).

Both the underclass and the working poor are likely to experience a range of family problems.

The young man who is selling drugs functions within the informal sector.

THE PAIN OF FAMILY POVERTY

For poor Americans the struggle is unrelenting. In their study of working-poor families in five cities, social workers Roberta Iversen and Annie Armstrong commented on their respondents, declaring that "[i]n the richest large country in the world, they work full time year round, but they still do not earn enough to support their families" (Iversen and Armstrong 2006, 1).

Low-income individuals suffer **structural vulnerability**, meaning a distinct likelihood of encountering major difficulties or threats because of such deficient capital resources as money, education, or important information (Rank 2004a; Rank 2004b, 477–78). Certain difficulties are common in these families:

- Poor children are more likely than their affluent peers to encounter a lengthy list of health problems. These include mothers' inadequate prenatal care; low birth weight; high infant mortality; iron deficiency; a high risk of exposure to toxic lead; hunger and malnutrition; and elevated rates of heart disease, diabetes, hypertension, cancer, asthma, and dental problems (Handler and Hasenfeld 2007, 264–66; Iversen and Armstrong 2006, 62–63; Lichter and Crowley 2002; Rank 2004b, 478; Seccombe 2002; Seccombe 2007, 99). The health problems poor children face, however, go beyond a list of diseases and destructive conditions. Sue Books, an educator whose research focuses on poor children, declared, "Perhaps most devastating is the sometimes hidden but nevertheless debilitating anxiety created by living in crowded, run-down spaces with chronic shortages of money and fears of eviction, family dissolution, and random street violence" (Books 2004, 37–38).
- Another distinct vulnerability involves the quality of parental relations. As a result of the financial and psychological stresses associated with poverty, poor parents compared to their more affluent counterparts are inclined to be less nurturing and more controlling and to administer harsher physical discipline (Seccombe 2002, 387). In addition, low-income families provide less intellectual stimulation than more affluent families even when parents' education, ethnic and racial groups, and family structure are statistically controlled (McLoyd 1998).

   The volume of communication between adults and children varies markedly by class. A study of language use for children aged one to three found that parents in professional jobs used about 2,200 words per hour speaking to their children. Working-class mothers and fathers averaged about 1,300 words per hour. Finally welfare parents, the representatives of the poor in this research, used less than half the working-class figure—about 600 (Barr and Parrett 2007, 113). Besides speaking fewer words, poor parents are less likely to read with and teach their children than higher-status mothers and fathers (Handler and Hasenfeld 2007, 107). Poor children tend to arrive at school distinctly disadvantaged compared to age peers in other classes.
- In addition, a significant perception problem exists with poor single-parent families. Researchers, social workers, and government officials interacting with such units often fail to appreciate the contribution that extended-family networks make. An **extended-family network** is an interrelated kinship group which plays a role in members' care, particularly children's health and well-being. In poor African American and Latino single-parent families, aunts, uncles, cousins, and grandparents

often make significant contributions (Jones, Zalot, Foster, Sterrett, and Chester 2007; Sarkisian, Gerena, and Gerstel 2006). White middle-class outsiders tend to focus on the nuclear-family unit, not recognizing the important role that extended kin sometimes play. These relatives can be critically important to incorporate when social workers, healthcare personnel, and others are trying to help poor children with various issues.

In poor families parents and older siblings seldom serve as models for success. In sociologist Jay MacLeod's study of young men in a public-housing project, he learned that only two parents had graduated from high school and that those who found work could just obtain menial, unstable, low-paying jobs. Based on their own experience, the parents had distinctly modest aspirations for their children. MacLeod asked his respondents what kind of jobs mothers or fathers wanted them to do for a living, and they provided the following kinds of answers:

Boo-Boo: Anything . . . as long as I'm working.

Jinx: They don't talk about it. . . . Just as long as I'm not out of work. My mother hates when I'm unemployed.

(MacLeod 2009, 58)

While poor families are more exposed to various major problems than their more affluent counterparts, certain parental traits increase vulnerability. For instance, when low-income parents start their families in their teens or drop out of school, they are likely to have difficulties establishing themselves solidly in the job world. The economic impact is obvious—sustained, often extreme poverty. As a result children in these homes are likely to suffer very low birth weights, inadequate healthcare, and substandard schooling. In addition, they become almost certain victims of the cycle of poverty.

Another vulnerability involves single-parent families, whose poverty level is over three times as high as their dual-earner counterparts. One of Iversen and Armstrong's respondents expressed the enormity of being a poor single parent trying to improve life for her family. The woman explained, "I need to save money to move out [of dilapidated public housing]. I was trying to find an easier way but can't find no easier way out, it is just like me and the kids doing everything" (Iversen and Armstrong 2006, 70).

An additional difficulty for single-parent families is that the majority receive no child support. Reasons for this outcome include fathers' disappearance, their commitment to new partners and children, and their modest incomes failing to meet more than their own expenses (Iversen and Armstrong 2006, 70–71; Rainwater and Smeeding 2003).

Not only does poverty promote these families' vulnerabilities, it reduces the likelihood of marriage and the formation of an economically secure partnership (Rank 2004b, 479). Without steady work adults—men in particular—commit less strongly to their partners and children. William Wilson interviewed a researcher who had conducted interviews with inner-city fathers over three decades—from a prosperous era when factory jobs were plentiful in low-income areas to a time when unemployment had become widespread. The researcher stressed that at the later date family members were less likely to encourage fathers' relationships with their children. He explained that compared to the earlier era, "I found no instance, for example, of families urging their children to marry or even to live together" (Wilson 1997, 102).

While they face severe challenges, poor people have some compensations. In contrast to many middle-class mothers and fathers who find their relatives either too far away or too busy to help with children or some other issue, poor families display little physical mobility, meaning parents, siblings, and other relatives are likely to be living nearby and available when needed. In her study of about 600 welfare recipients, sociologist Karen Seccombe found that most of her respondents relied on local relatives for help—mothers, sisters, cousins, or adult daughters. Such extended-family networks can make a significant difference for single parents struggling with both time and money.

Kim, a 29-year-old African American woman, had three children and worked part-time and was looking for a full-time position after having completed a certificate program at a local community college. As Kim worked and searched for a job, her relatives played a crucial support role. She explained that "[b]etween my mom or sisters, someone is always there" (Seccombe 2007, 140). This quotation suggests a quality that successful poor families possess.

Resiliency refers to effective adjustment to adversity—the ability to survive when facing risks or to rebound following a crisis (Seccombe 2002, 388). Various studies concluded that certain poor parents' practices help create resilient families. These practices include frequent displays of warmth, affection, and emotional support; clear, reasonable expectations for children coupled with definite but not overly harsh discipline; the development of specific family routines and shared celebrations; and the maintenance of common values about money management and the use of leisure. In resilient poor families, other relatives step in to fill the parental role effectively if mothers and fathers are unavailable (Cauce, Stewart, Rodriguez, Cochran, and Ginzler 2003, 355; Owens and Shaw 2003, 273; Seccombe 2002, 388).

Poor children growing up in resilient families have received significant support for doing well as they enter the social world—starting in daycare programs and then in schooling.

POOR CHILDREN'S CHILDCARE AND SCHOOLING

Some critics assert that impoverished parents are often unconcerned about their children's education. However, Iversen and Armstrong's study of low-income families in five cities indicated that poor parents considered that schooling provided their children a major avenue for obtaining social mobility and avoiding the dire problems they themselves had endured. Elizabeth Seabrook, a respondent, who was struggling to move her children to better schools outside of her low-income district, declared, "Education is so important and I will tell that to my children until I can't breathe anymore" (Iversen and Armstrong 2006, 176). Both childcare and schooling often provide major challenges when families are poor.

Childcare in Poverty Areas

Because of cost or irregular working hours (evenings or weekends), poor parents are more likely than more affluent counterparts to use informal childcare—in particular, grandparents or siblings (Iversen and Armstrong 2006, 257–58). Many poor mothers and fathers are convinced that high-quality daycare provides a positive foundation for

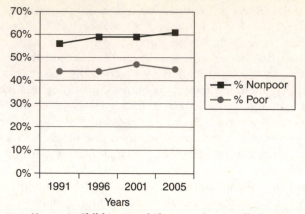

FIGURE 8.1   Poor[1] versus Nonpoor Children Aged Three to Five Enrolled in Center-Based Early Childhood Care, 1991–2005

[1]Children qualify as poor if family income is below the official poverty threshold.

Over a 14-year period, nonpoor families were distinctly more likely than poor families to enroll their three-to-five-year-old children in center-based early childhood care—an experience which research has shown provides cognitive advantages.

Source: National Center for Educational Statistics. 2007. Table 2-1. "Percentage of Preprimary Children Ages 3–5 Who Were Enrolled in Center-Based Early Childhood Care and Education Programs, by Child and Family Characteristics: Various Years, 1991–2005." http://nces.ed.gov/programs/coe/2007/section 1/table.asp?table ID=662.

effective school performance. However, those parents face a formidable barrier—the expense. A respondent in Iversen and Armstrong's study listed the deficiencies in her child's current program, but there was one asset—it was cheap. Unrealistic though it was financially, she longed to have a superior program where "someone will spend time with her, someone who will cultivate her mind. She understands nearly everything" (Iversen and Armstrong 2006, 65). Figure 8.1 demonstrates that over time, poor three- to five-year-olds have been consistently less often placed in organized childcare programs than their more affluent counterparts.

Research indicates the quality of care children receive affects their development. One revealing study assessed the impact of different programs on children whose single mothers had recently left welfare for work. Conducting this research over five years with 451 families in three cities, the investigators found that on various cognitive measures involving such issues as the children's ability to reason and to solve problems, those in center-based programs scored consistently higher than those in informal care (Handler and Hasenfeld 2007, 276). In short, compared to their affluent peers, poor children are less likely to attend center-based programs, and as Table 8.4 indicates, that result contributes to their entering school with less developed school-related skills.

Like the quality of childcare for low-income families, the effectiveness of schooling links to finances.

Poor Children's Education

Educator David Fulton indicated that the most important question to raise about American schooling is whether poor children have the same chance of obtaining a quality education

TABLE 8.4 A Comparison of Poor and Nonpoor Children's School Readiness Skills in 1993 and 2007[1]

	Recognizes all letters		Counts to 20 or more		Writes names		Reads or pretends to read storybooks[2]	
	1993	2007	1993	2007	1993	2007	1993	2007
Poor	12%	21%	41%	48%	41%	46%	64%	54%
Nonpoor	24	35	57	67	53	64	74	75

[1]The data describe children aged three to five not yet enrolled in kindergarten. They qualify as poor if family income is below the official poverty threshold.
[2]This issue uses 2005 as the more recent date.

In all categories displayed here, nonpoor children scored distinctly higher than poor children. Over 14 years the gap between the two income categories increased, hardly suggesting optimistic prospects for poor students entering school.

Source: U.S. Census Bureau. 2010. Table 230. "Children's School Readiness Skills: 1993 and 2007." *Statistical Abstract of the United States: 2010.* http://www.census.gov/compendia/statab/cats/education/elementary_and_secondary_education_special_topics.htm.

as their more affluent counterparts. Fulton responded, "For most industrialized countries, the answer is yes. For us, it's an embarrassing no" (Fulton 2000). At the core of the embarrassment lies the American system of public-school funding, where a substantial amount of a school district's financing comes from that specific locale. The result is often big disparities in districts' school funding, which do not occur in other westernized nations where the federal government distributes funds equitably. The US system has powerful negative impacts.

FUNDING INEQUITIES   Conducting a large study involving 47 states, the Education Trust found that in 30 of them school districts with high-poverty rates had significantly less state and local funding than districts with a low-poverty proportion. In the early 2000s, New York led the nation with a disparity of over $2,100 per student between the school districts with the 25 percent lowest poverty rate and those with the 25 percent highest measure of poverty. Illinois's gap was only slightly less—$2,060 (Books 2004, 64).

Because of their funding disadvantage, poorer school districts lose out in several ways. First, they cannot afford to compete for highly educated, more experienced teachers, who are usually the best prepared instructors to encourage a vibrant, achievement-oriented classroom (Lankford, Loeb, and Wyckoff 2002; Prince 2002; Rouse and Barrow 2006, 111). Across the nation almost one third of students in high-poverty middle schools take a course with a teacher who neither majored nor minored in the subject. Quality math teachers are particularly scarce. While about 27 percent of math teachers in affluent districts lack a math background, the level of unprepared instructors in poverty locales is 43 percent (Books 2004, 106). In fact, some poor districts have an even greater predicament. The math supervisor for New Haven's middle and high schools told me that each year one of her most difficult tasks was to locate math teachers for poorly funded schools. Sometimes she could not find instructors to fill certain positions, and the courses limped along with a succession of minimally qualified substitute teachers (Doob 2005, 200).

Another trait of poor schools that disadvantages them is class size. Wealthier districts are able to afford smaller classes, which appear to promote better learning, especially in early grades and for poor and minority students (Biddle and Berliner 2002; Darling-Hammond and Post 2000). A large experimental study involving 11,600 students randomly placed them in three groups—small classes of 13 to 17 students per teacher, large classes of 22 to 25 members, and large classes with a teacher aide. A pair of school finance experts concluded, "The data have been analyzed by a variety of researchers, with a remarkably consistent finding: smaller classes result in higher achievement" (Rouse and Barrow 2006, 113).

Poverty hurts schools in other ways. Because of economic limitations and discrimination, low-income families tend to concentrate in selected areas that are already poor and dilapidated. Within the nation's 60 largest urban school systems, more than three quarters of the student body is composed of people of color, and practically two thirds are poor, qualifying for a federally funded lunch. Inundated by students who are not well prepared for formal learning, schools in these districts often barely function (Books 2004, 103–4). The president of the Los Angeles teachers' union charged, "We have kids without teachers, teachers without classrooms, and a district without a clue. The system is broken. Students and teachers are a forgotten priority in the poor city schools" (White 1999, 3). Furthermore within these low-income districts, school buildings tend to be old and large, often causing their occupants to feel isolated and alienated.

A set of researchers developed a concept to characterize such areas. An **urban war zone** is a poor, crime-laden district in which deteriorated, violent, even war-like conditions and underfunded, largely ineffective schools promote inferior academic performance, including irregular attendance and disruptive or noncompliant classroom behavior (Espinosa and Laffey 2003; Garbarino, Dubrow, Kostelney, and Pardo 1992). Yet even in such difficult settings, students can be stimulated in the classroom. In a study of one low-income elementary school, the researchers found that children, who were often sullen and noncompliant when required to sit quietly in large groups and not move about, became engaged and attentive when involved in computer sessions where the tasks were highly individualized and adjusted to match students' interests and ability levels (Espinosa and Laffey 2003, 151).

A number of studies have demonstrated that children living in poverty districts also do better academically when both their school buildings and districts are smaller (Howley and Bickel 2002; Howley and Howley 2004).

Certain deficiencies of less well-funded schools are sufficiently impactful to deserve special attention here. Parents' responses and reform measures are also worth examining.

TRACKING IN POVERTY DISTRICTS   **Tracking** is a process where educators evaluate students and then place them in programs with a curriculum that supposedly is appropriate for their abilities (LeTendre, Hofer, and Shimizu 2003, 43–44). Criticism of tracking has been widespread, leading to such reforms as permitting low-tracked students more course options. Nonetheless students continue to be classified into tracks according to their short-term performance, and courses continue to be labeled, designating students' eligibility to enter them. In fact, many schools systems use math performance as a basis for allocating students' placement in other courses. While no research findings support this approach, it is likely, given low-income schools' frequent scarcity of effective math teachers, to prove particularly disadvantageous to poor students (Grusky 2001, 575; Moore 2001, 539).

Overall whether they are by themselves in a large urban schools or in a multi-class curriculum, poor students plagued by educational disadvantage dating back to infancy are likely to end up in general-education courses with watered-down offerings like "opportunity math" (designed for students who cannot learn algebra) or vocational preparation. As a rule the slow-learning tracks receive the most inexperienced teachers, who are likely to use the most mundane, unchallenging instructional techniques such as worksheets and drills (Barr and Parrett 2007, 144).

At the lower end of the academic curriculum, many poor students fail to master basic skills and are forced either to repeat the grade or are tracked into a lower level. Caught in a debilitating educational cycle, these students almost never catch up with their age peers and often do not advance from the slow-learning track. In many states under-achieving students, who are disproportionately poor, male, and minority-group members, have been removed from regular facilities and placed in alternative low-performing schools where the goal is behavior modification, not educational achievement. A Texas research program involving over 100,000 K–12 students found that these low-achieving research subjects often received only two hours of instruction a day, obtained no evaluation for reading levels, and were placed in a multi-grade classroom (Barr and Parrett 2007, 28).

Tracking is a particularly harsh representation of social reproduction. Educators Robert Barr and William Parrett summarized its impact, indicating that because of their educational disadvantage, poor students have been much more likely than more affluent peers to obtain low test scores, readily leading to their being labeled "dumb." With such a label, they have often been tracked into "a less challenging curriculum where they had almost no opportunity to succeed academically. The result has been a vicious cycle of low expectations, which results in underachievement" (Barr and Parrett 2007, 144).

It is common for the victims of such systems to feel responsible for their mediocre performances, promoting social reproduction. In *Ain't No Makin' It: Aspirations & Attainment in a Low-Income Neighborhood*, sociologist Jay MacLeod found that his black respondents felt they had been either lazy, stupid, or undisciplined. Mike, a respondent, explained, "I used to do good. I got all A's in grammar school. Now I'm doing shitty. I guess I started out smart and got stupider" (MacLeod 2009, 102). Like a sociologist Mike visualized his educational experience as a process involving a set of steps. The stark difference, however, was that he considered his lack of success strictly a personal responsibility, largely overlooking structural vulnerabilities he and other poor students collectively suffered.

Testing has also victimized low-income children.

HIGH-STAKES TESTING   In the 1940s Henry Chauncey, the founder of the Educational Testing Service, suggested that multiple-choice variations on intelligence tests could be used to sort individuals into categories based on their abilities. Chauncey had so much faith in these tests that he believed that the results should determine both the schooling and the jobs individuals in different categories ought to receive. Chauncey even felt that the existing elite should be replaced, with those at the top of the economic and political structures being the individuals who scored the highest in his tests (Afflerbach 2002, 349–350). It is doubtful that members of the power elite ever endorsed such a plan. In educational circles, however, Chauncey was influential.

It appears that Chauncey was the first advocate of **high-stakes testing**, a situation in which the outcome of a standardized test becomes the sole basis for determining students' educational progression. Over half (26) of the states rely heavily on test scores for determining students' promotion and graduation (Dworkin 2005, 170).

Many teachers are ambivalent about standardized testing and high-stakes testing in particular. They want their students to do well, recognizing that good scores are important for success in school. However, studies have shown that teachers feel the emphasis on testing hurts student performance in the classroom. They are bothered about the time that standardized test preparation takes from their own curriculum. For many teachers a strong suspicion exists that preparation for the standardized tests and the tests themselves provide students few learning benefits. In poor areas where test scores have generally been low, school officials often have an additional concern, worrying that low scores could lead to the state taking over their schools (Barone 2006, 154–55; Calkins, Montgomery, Santman, and Falk 1998; Hoffman, Assaf, and Paris 2001).

As the last point suggests, high-stakes testing is particularly problematic for poor schools. Critics have emphasized that:

- Students should not be held to the mainstream test standards when they attend schools that are grossly underfunded and possess many uncertified teachers, large classes, outdated texts, and limited access to computers and other modern technology.
- In particular, poor schools are less likely to afford the actual books, supplies, and practice exams that expressly prepare students for standardized tests.
- An implication of the previous two points is that because of the especially disadvantaged conditions they suffer, poor students over time will steadily lose ground in testing to their more affluent peers. When students of varied backgrounds and resources receive the same test, the general pattern is that the affluent will be the winners and the poor the losers (Afflerbach 2002, 356; Barone 2006, xv–xvii; Dworkin 2005, 172).

In the first quarter of the twentieth century, several prominent psychologists administered early versions of intelligence tests in English to various European groups, interpreting lower scores for Italians, Jews, or Poles as indications of biological inferiority. The fact that many members of these groups knew little or no English was simply ignored (Kamin 1974, 15–19). In a similar way, many advocates of high-stakes testing downplay or overlook poor children's various disadvantages.

Besides such questionable practices as high-stakes testing and tracking, poor children's everyday routine is also nonproductive.

THE PEDAGOGY OF POVERTY   Educator Martin Haberman concluded that in the academically undernourished context of poor schools a **pedagogy of poverty** prevails—a set of ineffective, even destructive teaching practices often imposed on poor children. These practices include:

A passive, teacher-centered classroom setting: Studies have demonstrated that among young children an effective learning process requires frequent hands-on assignments. Such practices compel students to be actively involved. In contrast, a distinctly passive learning experience dominates if the teacher directs all or most of the coursework, telling a largely noninteractive group what to do.

Low-quality schooling coupled with low expectations: Teachers in poor districts, many of whom are new and inexperienced, often do not think their students can perform at a high level. In many primary schools, children spend a significant amount of time making collages and posters and coloring pictures as intended demonstrations of "hands-on learning." Meanwhile basic reading and math skills receive scant attention. Within a few years, many of those students end up tracked into general-education courses and away from the more advanced academic offerings (Barr 2007, 30–31).

The concept pedagogy of poverty is useful because it encourages an observer to look beyond the blaming-the-victim perspective and to appreciate the specific conditions prevailing in most poor classrooms.

Haberman contended that this concept is not a formal methodology that educators have developed and studied, producing a body of theories. Rather it is a set of practices which are destructive for students but have proved useful for many teachers and administrators—those who have low expectations for poor and minority children and who possess a narrow vision emphasizing that at-risk children are best served by a directed, controlled system. Eventually most of the students accept the pedagogy of poverty, complying quickly to teachers whose assignments involve taking out their dictionaries and copying down all words beginning with "h" and also responding apathetically or angrily to reform-minded instructors (Haberman 1991).

School officials' low expectations appear to be a fundamental prerequisite for the pedagogy of poverty. While new teachers might not share this outlook, their colleagues' positions on the issue and students' performances are likely to bring the recent arrivals' expectations into line. In the course of his research on poor young men, Jay MacLeod interviewed Bruce Davis, a young, enthusiastic guidance counselor in the Occupational Education Program. Davis predicted that like their relatives the students in this program were headed for unskilled work. He said, "They're generally from homes where people are laborers. . . . [K]ids who go to college are from homes where parents went to college. That's how it works, it seems to me" (MacLeod 2009, 116). Davis's expectation for his students was low—that they would be models of social reproduction, assuming the same occupational positions their parents have held. Teachers like Davis are not likely to feel motivated to challenge the pedagogy of poverty.

In poor schools, however, parents' intervention can oppose that process.

POOR PARENTS' PARTICIPATION IN SCHOOLING   A study of 88 third- and fourth-grade children and their parents from the middle, working, and poor classes found that almost all the middle-class, less than half the working-class, and only a third of the poor parents reported that they knew a teacher (Horvat, Weininger, and Lareau 2003, 33). In such a context, if poor children need teachers' assistance, their parents are often not well positioned to initiate it.

Because teachers are often out of touch with their poor students' parents, they tend to be unaware of the long work hours and inflexible schedules many of them face, simply concluding that the parents, even when problems occur in school, are uninvolved with and unconcerned about their children's education (Iversen and Armstrong 2006, 197). The reality is more complicated. Data drawn from the National Longitudinal Survey of Youth involving 1,878 families found that when comparing children at risk for low scores in reading or math or for behavioral problems, low-income mothers were less likely than their more affluent counterparts to have flexible schedules or paid leave (Heymann and Earle 2000). Thus the poor mothers had less chance to meet with teachers or take other steps to help their children.

Because of their demanding work lives and limited relations with teachers, many poor parents feel isolated from their children's school. In Iversen and Armstrong's study of low-income families in five cities, Aida, whose eight-year-old son Juan had both behavioral and academic problems, complained that the teacher provided little information about his performance. After a long, exhausting work day, she tried to tutor Juan. Aida explained that "when I pick him up and bring him [home], he would sit there and look somewhere else. I am like 'I am telling you to read this word'" (Iversen and Armstrong 2006, 180).

The Iversen and Armstrong study also described a low-income family in which a child named Shalon, a first grader, had read over 300 books and performed at least one grade level and perhaps two above her present grade—a significant achievement in one of Philadelphia's so-called "failing" schools. When asked why she had not had Shalon tested for the gifted program, the teacher said it was because the student might barely qualify for that program. At that point one of the researchers asked if anything would be lost if Shalon took the test and failed. Nothing would be lost, the teacher admitted, but she simply had not felt Shalon should take the test. Frustrated by the teacher's inaction, Shalon's mother searched hard to find a stimulating program for her daughter, eventually enrolling her for a year in a school that was supposed to be somewhat more academically challenging than the previous one. However, even though Shalon's performance continued to be good, the teachers in the new school made no effort to have her tested for a gifted program (Iversen and Armstrong 2006, 181). Shalon's case suggests that even when poor students become academic stars, the pedagogy of poverty is likely to persist and hold them back.

As Table 8.5 indicates, it is hardly surprising to learn that poor parents have somewhat fewer positive impressions of their children's schools than either those who are near poor or nonpoor. It is also not surprising to learn that the educational outcomes for poor children are less satisfactory than they are for more affluent students. A half-dozen studies conducted during the 1990s found that poor children received lower grades, obtained lower scores on standardized tests, were less likely to finish high school, and less often attended or graduated from college than nonpoor youth (Seccombe 2000, 1104). Examining college students' socioeconomic backgrounds, economist Robert Haveman and political scientist Timothy Smeeding indicated that poor children enter the "college education game" later and with fewer resources than their more affluent peers. Poor students, they noted, are often "less well prepared academically; ill prepared to select colleges, apply for admission, and secure acceptance; and poorly informed about the cost of attending college and the availability of needs-based financial aid" (Haveman and Smeeding 2006, 125).

TABLE 8.5 Percentage of Parents with Differing Income Levels Who Are Very Satisfied with Their Children's School[1]

	Child's school			Child's teachers		
	1993	1999	2003	1993	1999	2003
Poverty status[2]						
Poor	51.9%	53.8%	54%	58.3%	60.5%	56.5%
Near poor	54.1	49.4	55.1	57.3	55.3	61
Nonpoor	58.7	54	59.5	58.8	56	59

	School's academic standards		
	1993	1999	2003
Poverty status			
Poor	53.3%	58.8%	54.4%
Near poor	56	53.7	56.5
Nonpoor	61.1	57.4	60.4

[1]The data display the percentage of parents very satisfied with the topic in question. These respondents had children in grades three through twelve and attended both public and private schools.

[2]"Poor" involves those families below the poverty threshold; "near poor" specifies families with income that is 100 to 199 percent of the poverty threshold; "nonpoor" refers to families whose income is at least 200 percent of the poverty threshold.

Over a decade poor parents were somewhat less likely than their near poor and nonpoor counterparts to be very satisfied with key elements of their children's schooling. However, the differences among the three categories were not very great. Considering the extensive criticism of schools in low-income districts, the extent of poor parents' satisfaction expressed in this table is surprising. Perhaps one contributing factor might be that low-income parents have more modest expectations.

Source: National Center for Education Statistics. 2006. Table 38–1. "Percentage of Children in Grades 3–12 with Parents Who Were Very Satisfied with Aspects of the School Their Child Attends, by Selected Characteristics: 1993, 1999, and 2003." http://nces.ed.gov/programs/coe/2006/section4/table.asp?tableID=507.

The conclusion seems clear: that schooling for poor children has been relatively unsuccessful. The potentially good news is that using the information they have gathered in recent decades, researchers and educators know what steps could improve schooling in poverty districts.

MEASURES TO IMPROVE POOR CHILDREN'S EDUCATION   This process should begin at the preschool level, thereby providing children with a firm foundation for their primary education. Research done by the Brookings Institution and Princeton University concluded that high-quality, center-based early childhood education is the most productive programmatic approach for low-income three- and four-year-olds. The criteria for a high-quality center include a high teacher-pupil ratio, instructors who are college graduates with training in early childhood education, and a well-planned, cognitively stimulating curriculum.

In poor areas effective education at all levels features teachers who can work well with children possessing mild to serious health or behavioral problems (Rouse, Brooks-Gunn, and McLanahan 2005, 12–13). To provide such teaching for all poor schools, of course, would be expensive.

While the amount of funding affects school quality, other factors can also influence it:

- ***The active participation of parents and community organizations with schools in poor districts.*** Substantial evidence indicates that sometimes low-income parents have not only become involved with their children's learning but with the schools themselves (Barr 2004, 81). In fact, the evidence of 30 years of research is compelling, demonstrating that when schools in poverty areas achieve academic success, productive partnerships with families and community organizations have been established (Chadwick 2004, 14).
- ***Movement toward alignment.*** This point extends the previous one, emphasizing that in poor areas school officials often find it fruitful to take concrete steps to promote parental involvement. Teachers and administrators sometimes fail to appreciate that rigid work schedules make it impossible for many low-income parents to be involved in school trips or programs or even to pick up their children's report card at school. The city of Seattle formed an Office of Community Learning, and one of its functions involved the engagement of students' families (Iversen and Armstrong 2006, 195–97). This unit was able to find ways to alleviate low-income parents' difficult, often alienated relations with their children's schools. For instance, its Family Partnerships Project helped parents learn to conduct productive conversations with their children about the curriculum and encouraged them to develop connections with other parents at the school (Seattle Public Schools 2009).
- ***Good teaching as a critical component.*** As I have noted, all too often poor districts receive young, inexperienced teachers with few tactics to combat the pedagogy of poverty. Over time, however, some instructors in poor classrooms develop the requisite qualities to excel. Martin Haberman, who spent decades observing successful classrooms in poor schools, indicated that effective teachers in those settings recognize that their students often face a number of debilitating conditions, including inadequate healthcare and nutrition and various forms of abusive treatment, and that a significant part of the teacher's job must be engaging their students in spite of these hindrances. If the students disengage, these effective teachers persist, seeking new ways of involving them and never forgetting that an important task for all participants in education is to learn about themselves and the world. (Books 2004, 8–9; Haberman 1995, 3–21).

In the fifth grade at Howard, a high-poverty elementary school, Mr. Bussoni was a highly successful teacher. He usually placed his students at tables, working with small groups or individuals instead of teaching from the front of the room. Often he sat beside a student, discussing at length what he or she was reading or writing. Others respected these private times and did not break in but waited for their special time with the teacher. Mr. Bussoni constantly encouraged and complimented his students and always expected and demanded quality work. When children were asked about reading and writing in elementary school, many singled out Mr. Bussoni, stressing that he encouraged them to read and helped them to improve their writing (Barone 2006, 175).

Chapter 11 provides further evidence involving successful schools in poor districts. Like schools other organizations and groups in poverty areas are often ineffective.

LOW-INCOME COMMUNITIES AND THEIR SOCIAL CAPITAL

It is apparent that two types of social capital exist in communities—the local organizations providing financial, medical, and other types of basic assistance; and family, neighborhood, and other nearby networks supplying information and support. A half-dozen studies conducted in the 1990s indicated that over time poor children and their families have become more physically isolated from the nonpoor in their neighborhoods and communities (Seccombe 2000, 1106). For poor blacks this pattern has been particularly virulent, with low-income African American families, powerless to do anything about it, often funneled into highly segregated areas, causing those areas to become steadily poorer and more segregated (Massey and Denton 1993, 118–25).

Such areas are likely to have lost their historic sources of income and social capital—factories, banks, large grocery stores, and a host of small businesses that link people both to the labor market and to what were once vibrant local communities. In the Woodlawn neighborhood located on the South Side of Chicago, there were over 800 commercial and industrial establishments in 1950. Forty-five years later only about 100 small businesses survived. Sociologist William Wilson explained that what had once been a vibrant neighborhood, which was crowded at rush hour, was now deserted, "an empty, bombed-out war zone," with broken glass and garbage scattered around the vacated, boarded-up buildings. The few active businesses were "liquor stores and currency exchanges, these 'banks of the poor,' where one can cash checks, pay bills and buy money orders" (Wilson 1997, 5).

The residents of the Woodlawn neighborhood are among the large numbers of Americans deprived of effective healthcare. A study of low-income families in three cities found that because of declining earnings after the recession of 2003, they had to rotate paying the bills, with rent the top priority. Almost none of these families had employer-sponsored health insurance, and even those who did had trouble keeping up with the premiums. Many of the respondents had substantial medical bills produced either by one-time problems like an accident, a major operation, or a chronic condition such as heart disease or cancer. The study concluded that for most of these research subjects the opportunity to obtain healthcare coverage to protect themselves from such debt was simply out-of-reach (Handler and Hasenfeld 2007, 118–19).

Between 2000 and 2004, the number of uninsured Americans increased by six million, primarily because of cutbacks in employer-sponsored health insurance. The poor and near poor were the most frequent victims, with two thirds of those losing their coverage having incomes below 200 percent of the poverty threshold (Holahan and Cook 2005, 1). Table 8.6 displays the relationship between household income and healthcare coverage.

Multiple millions of Americans unable to afford health insurance often turn to the organizations of last resort—the emergency rooms of the nation's 1,300 public hospitals. Since the middle 1970s, however, these facilities have been forced to serve increasing numbers of impoverished patients, and 300 of them have gone bankrupt. The chief of medicine at one of these public hospitals, Grady Memorial in Atlanta, called these bankruptcies "the canary in the coal mine" (Dewan and Sack 2008, A18).

TABLE 8.6 Healthcare Coverage for Different Income Groups

Household income	Percent of income category not covered by government or private health insurance
$75,000 or more	7.8%
$50,000–$74,999	14.5
$25,000–$49,999	21.1
Less than $25,000	24.5
Persons below poverty threshold	30.9

Not surprisingly the lower people's income, the more likely they are without healthcare coverage.

Source: U.S. Census Bureau. 2010. Table 149. "Health Insurance Coverage Status by Selected Characteristics." *Statistical Abstract of the United States: 2010.* http://www.census.gov/compendia/statab/cats/health_nutrition .html.

In 2008 Grady Memorial had lost money in 10 of the previous 11 years, with a deficit of $53 million projected for 2008. For the hospital's survival, deep cuts seemed necessary. In spite of these financial woes, the staff persevered, providing high-level medical care to a vast overload of individuals and families otherwise deprived of it.

Because of its limited funding, the hospital had to function with antiquated equipment, even in the emergency room. That unit lacked an X-ray machine, and so before operating on a man with a gunshot wound in the chest, a portable machine had to be obtained. As they waited, the man said to the doctor that he had been born in this hospital. "Don't let me go out in pain," he said. The doctor smiled slightly and declared, "Well, tonight, he's not going to die at this hospital" (Dewan and Sack 2008, A18). The X-rays were produced on films, not digitally, causing a 10-minute delay. Other equipment problems complicated the operation, and yet it was a success. Six days later the patient left in good condition.

The emergency room most graphically displayed the hospital's overload of patients, serving about 300 daily. One typical night the hallways "were chockablock with stretchers—one man, shackled to his gurney, writhing through an acid trip; a woman fighting seizures; asthma patients sucking down oxygen" (Dewan and Sack 2008, A18).

Another problematic trait about poor communities is their high rates of violent and property crime—as much as four times higher than national averages (Iversen and Armstrong 2006, 76; Seccombe 2000, 388). In Iversen and Armstrong's study of low-income parents and children, 39 of 66 children (59 percent) mentioned the violence they faced daily in their neighborhoods. Fearing the violence, parents like Aida Gomez restricted their children's activities, protecting them to be sure but also limiting their development of social capital.

Isolation, in fact, is another troubling issue, with poor people often unable to combat it effectively. In various rural communities, where families have often lived for generations, the mere mention of a last name can be sufficient to convey a sense of whether someone is a good or a bad person. The poor have "bad names"; they are "undeserving"—believed to be lazy or troublesome and as a result deprived of access to hospitals, jobs, and a variety of other necessities. One woman explained that in her town people were informed about each other's families. She added, "Now my family, they've been a bad family. There are places we can't even rent a house because of our last name. And that's just the way it is. You can't change it" (Duncan 2001, 67).

While poor people sometimes experience negative social capital, they can also encounter positive forms of it. In her study of over 600 female respondents either on welfare or moving off of it, Karen Seccombe found that most of the women had supportive networks: Family members were usually the preferred source for assistance, but some sought help from neighbors and friends either instead of or in addition to family members. Some respondents considered it important to avoid the family, fearing criticism for being on welfare.

Seccombe found that in public-housing projects inhabitants varied in the extent to which they developed social networks. Some opted not to seek local contacts, proudly emphasizing their independence and self-reliance; a number relied on a few, perhaps a pair of friends or neighbors; and others developed a wide circle of friends. During an hour-and-a-half interview with Janie, a 19-year-old mother of an infant daughter, four interruptions occurred—telephone calls or visits to borrow an item or to see if Janie needed anything from the grocery store. Referring to her network of friends, Janie indicated that she and her daughter were not alone. She concluded, "We have an extended family of sorts" (Seccombe 2007, 145).

In attempting to escape poverty, individuals and families can find that two sources of social capital prove helpful. There is emotional and financial support from their families—even when such assistance represents a sacrifice—and also various programs exposing them to experiences, information, and skills that have helped them advance educationally and occupationally (Duncan 2001, 79).

An experiment done in five US cities illustrated the impact of effective programs. Low-income families with children living in high-poverty, publicly financed housing were randomly assigned to one of three treatment groups—the experimental unit whose members relocated to private-market apartments in poor areas, receiving housing vouchers, help in locating their residences, and several other types of organizational assistance; the comparison segment that was provided vouchers but no other types of aid; and the control unit, which obtained no assistance. Between two and four years later, the study revealed that the experimental group achieved certain advancements over the other two categories of respondents, including better self-reports of parents' physical and mental health along with higher quality of parenting, and also children's superior results, particularly more reduction in antisocial behavior, better performances in reading, math, and standardized tests, greater declines in asthma attacks and injuries requiring medical treatment, fewer criminal victimizations, and lessened depression and anxiety (Ludwig 2003).

The previous experiment suggests that fairly modest inputs of organizational assistance to poor families can significantly affect outcomes. In the mid-1990s the Boston Housing Authority (BHA) obtained federal funding for Mission Main and Orchard Park, two large housing programs. On the face of it, the developments appeared to encounter a similar set of conditions—demolition of all or most units; replacement with low-density buildings; income-mixing of the new tenants; and efforts to integrate the new developments into the surrounding neighborhoods.

Offsetting these similarities, however, the two projects displayed distinctly different planning processes. At Orchard Park major conflicts were resolved along the way. A significant factor was the positive relationship between the tenants and the BHA team, especially its architect, who had worked well with the Orchard Park Tenants Association in an earlier rehabilitation. Furthermore the BHA and the Orchard Park tenants consistently sought to communicate their plans to the surrounding neighborhood in which residents were low-income like themselves and were pleased to learn that any vacant land would be returned to residential use. Some residents' fears of public housing were relieved by BHA staff, who explained that the new units would be carefully managed and that many if not most tenants would be employed, thus making it probable that they would be reliable neighbors.

In contrast, at Mission Main the BHA team and the architects did not develop a trustful relationship with tenants. Furthermore the two developers did not have effective relationships with each other or with the BHA. Initial differences and misunderstandings mushroomed to substantial distrust. In addition, many black residents often had a difficult time with their neighbors, resisting efforts to relate to this larger community, which was primarily middle-class and white.

All in all, differences between the two tenants groups and their relationships with both the BHA and the neighboring communities—the development of trust at Orchard Park and its absence at Mission Main—significantly impacted quality of life within the two public-housing projects. It appears that over time Orchard Park residents would be likely to have much more productive social-capital development with their neighbors and other outsiders than would their counterparts at Mission Main (Keyes 2001, 145–47).

In recent years Americans have increasingly recognized the importance of social capital. This section has demonstrated that social networks develop in a variety of contexts, including some helping to obtain jobs.

POOR PEOPLE'S WORK

Sociologist Jay MacLeod concluded that ours is a very unequal society [where] "[t]here are simply not enough good jobs to go around. For every boss there are many workers, and the gap in their pay is unparalleled among industrialized nations" (MacLeod 2009, 241).

Has the American economy been purposely structured for inequality? In particular, have business leaders committed themselves to developing a reserve army of labor (discussed in Chapter 2)? What analysts can readily substantiate is that the economy has been structured to produce increasing business profits and that this focus has often been detrimental for various income groups including the poor. Figure 8.2 shows that over time the top 5 and top 20 percent of the population have increased their portion of income while the bottom 20 percent has received a declining portion.

A number of factors have affected poor people's employment opportunities:

- *Deindustrialization and globalization.* Starting in the 1970s, manufacturing jobs have been disappearing. Previously individuals with limited education employed in that sector could make a decent living, supporting a family reasonably well. Nowadays it is often cheaper for companies to downsize and outsource.
- *Technological change.* The development of computers has eliminated the need for many typists, secretaries, clerks, and other types of limited-skill workers.
- *The decline of unions.* As Chapter 7 detailed, the number of unionized workers has decreased in recent decades. It is a well established fact that unionized employees obtain higher wages than their nonunionized counterparts.

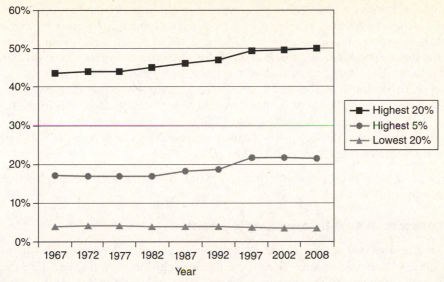

FIGURE 8.2   Share of the Total Income Received by the Lowest 20 Percent, the Highest 20 Percent, and the Top 5 Percent

These data reveal a distinct pattern of growing income inequality over 41 years. The lowest 20 percent representing the poor and near poor displays a percentage of the total income that between 1967 and 2008 dropped slightly from 4 to 3.4 percent while over the same time period the highest 20 percent obtained a robust increase in its portion, rising from 43.6 to 50 percent. The top 5 percent has also steadily increased its percentage over time.

Source: U.S. Census Bureau. 2010. Table H-1. "Income Limits for Each Fifth and Top 5 Percent." *Historical Income Tables.* http://www.census.gov/hhes/www/income/data/.

- *A domino effect.* In difficult economic times, middle-income individuals are likely to settle for jobs they would not ordinarily take, pushing the poor even lower or out of the labor market. In recent years college graduates have often found themselves seeking lower-paid openings in areas like retail sales that normally they would have ignored. Less educated job seekers have lost out, particularly young people, including black males in their late teens and early 20s without more than a high-school education.
- *The minimum wage.* Is the minimum wage, which rose to $7.25 an hour in 2009, a living wage? Many experts feel it is insufficient to lift families out of poverty. This is an important deficiency since about two thirds of minimum-wage earners are 20 years or older, and about 40 percent of them are the sole providers for their families (Bluestone and Harrison 2000, 190–97; Brady and Wallace, 2001; Iceland 2006, 77–78; Seccombe 2000, 1099–1100; Smith 2009; U.S. Bureau of Labor Statistics 2007). In *Nickle and Dimed: On (Not) Getting by in America*, Barbara Ehrenreich claimed that jobs for the working poor never proved to be economically viable. Furthermore living on minimum wage did not inspire revelations about ingenious means of saving money unknown to the middle class; economic worries were unrelenting. In her research Ehrenreich noted that housing "is the principal source of disruption in their lives, the first thing they fill you in on when they arrive for their

shifts" (Ehrenreich 2002, 25). This comment might bring to mind an earlier observation—that a significant oversight in the official U.S. measure of poverty involves its omission of several major expenses for poor people, including housing costs.

• ***Increase in part-time work and jobs without benefits.*** In 1988 part-time workers were about one quarter of the labor force, and by 2005 the proportion had become over a third—about 37 percent. Through the 1990s part-time employees and other members of the working poor experienced a steady decline in fringe benefits; by 2005 nearly a third of poor people (30.6 percent) had no health-insurance coverage. (Seccombe 2000, 1100; U.S. Census Bureau 2008, Table 146 ; U.S. Department of Labor Statistics 2007, Report 1001).

These influences on work are apparent when one examines the employment process poor people face.

The Prospects of Low-Income Employment

In Jay MacLeod's study of young men living in a public-housing project, he asked his respondents about their job plans. They were usually reluctant to reply, realizing that with their limited schooling their work potential was sharply limited. MacLeod found that no matter how hard he pressed Jinks, the young man "refused to articulate his aspirations: 'I think you're kiddin' yourself to have any. We're just gonna take whatever we can get.'" Jinks's assessment, MacLeod conceded, seemed accurate (MacLeod 2009, 63).

As MacLeod's respondents appreciated, the brutal fact is that poorly educated individuals have few good job prospects. A study using data from the National Current Population Survey found that only about a fifth of the positions held by people without at least some college credits involved filling such "starter" positions as bank tellers, roofers, or data entry keyers requiring little or no training and experience while leading to good-paying positions. For most poorly educated, low-income individuals, prospects for such climbs up the occupational ladder are remote.

In Iversen and Armstrong's study of low-income families in five cities, the parents' jobs usually displayed a number of undesirable traits: Wages were too low to maintain families with children; relations with supervisors or bosses featured ineffective communication or mistrust; employer-provided benefits were either unaffordable or nonexistent; workplace scheduling almost never displayed flexibility for accommodating such family needs as a child's illness or a doctor's appointment; no protection from economic downturn existed, with low-income workers the most vulnerable to layoffs and declining wages in subsequent jobs (Iversen and Armstrong 2006, 171). Even during the boom years of the late 1990s, nearly three in ten working-poor families with children under 12 had insufficient income to meet the calculated expense of what constituted a basic family budget (Appelbaum, Bernhardt, and Murnane 2003, 1).

Low-income workers faced with such an economic squeeze are likely to consider changing jobs, finding that training is often essential if they are going to advance. How much training do less educated job seekers need to propel themselves into an upwardly mobile path? Data from the National Adult Literacy Survey revealed that 200 hours of education or training—the equivalent of a full semester's course load—can produce $10,000 more annual income for individuals who have completed high school. On the other hand, high-school dropouts require more extensive training, up to several years, to advance themselves economically (Carnevale and Desrochers 1999).

The length of training these students receive is an important factor that will help determine if they are effectively prepared to do weatherization and other green jobs.

Many respondents in Iversen and Armstrong's study sought job training. Most of them appreciated the importance of both the "soft skills," which help develop manners, personal habits, communication abilities, and friendliness in order to relate to co-workers, bosses, and the public, and also the "hard skills," that involve specific teachable abilities associated with a particular job. Some informants felt that even a brief training, four weeks or even less, produced a combined sense of confidence and knowledge that transferred positively to the job site.

Nonetheless throughout their research, Iversen and Armstrong heard students, instructors, and employers express a common lament—that training programs less than a year long were ineffective. Wendy, for instance, was preparing to become a health-insurance representative. She claimed that the trainers did not provide enough specific information. While they expressed personal preferences about what job candidates should learn, "they are not educating you on what the . . . [workplace terminology is] going to be or what the health industry is all about. With a little more education it [would be] much better" (Iversen and Armstrong 2006, 105).

In transferring individuals from welfare to work, job-training agencies often supplied a case manager, whose duties involved an on-going assessment of the clients' success both in training and in the actual entrance into the job world. The case manager monitored participation in such activities as current drug-treatment programs, high-school completion (GED) study, and supportive counseling. Agencies supplying case managers varied on the issues they considered priorities. Staff members associated with social-service organizations tended to be adept at evaluating emotional and social issues and to possess limited knowledge about the labor market while their counterparts in workforce-development agencies displayed a reversed pattern (Iversen and Armstrong 2006, 108; Relave 2001).

As they move toward and then into the job world, often for the first time, welfare recipients can benefit from a case manager's workforce mentoring. For instance, Isabel, who had a new job, a new residence, and had just been reunited with one of her two children, also planned to go to school, attending a training program. She felt overwhelmed and turned to her case manager. Isabel said, "She was great, and she told me, 'God, you are nervous, but don't worry about it. School will still be there; you can do . . . [it] in June'" (Iversen and Armstrong 2006, 110). As a result of this important exchange, Isabel postponed training for several months, a decision that promoted success both in her relationship with her son and at work.

Once on the job, many low-income workers are strongly motivated to increase their income.

Battling on Up?

If low-income job holders seek to make more money, they usually require training. What such individuals generally discover is that (a) such programs are much more plentiful for the pre-employment than the post-employment phase and that (b) such assistance is much more likely to go to high-skilled, well educated workers than to low-skilled, less educated job holders (King 2004; O'Leary, Straits, and Wandner 2004).

While most poor workers face a training disadvantage, some do manage to advance themselves. Using national data from the Longitudinal Employer-Household Dynamics Program, a team of researchers learned that about 42 percent of low-wage workers who chose to change jobs and then stayed with their new employers escaped poverty completely. In sharp contrast, only 17 percent passed beyond the poverty threshold when staying with their original employer. The key factor in escaping poverty has been job holders' ability to locate higher-paid positions in such industries as construction, manufacturing, transportation/utilities, or wholesale trades (Andersson, Holzer, and Lane 2005, 78–90).

Although the successful move out of poverty has unquestionable benefits, many workers are unwilling to make the leap. Sometimes they feel secure in their present position and realize than in the new one they could fail, bringing economic devastation to the family. A case in point would be Maya Vanderhand from the Iversen and Armstrong study. She held an entry-level position at an insurance company where on-the-job training and advancement were available. However, Maya felt certain conditions made changing jobs too risky: Her husband was only intermittently employed, leaving Maya the primary breadwinner for a family of six; in addition, without a high-school diploma or GED, her educational credentials represented a weakness in a competitive job market. Maya explained, "I don't want to change departments any time; there is a lot going on. I have so much on my plate that I don't want to screw that up" (Iversen and Armstrong 2006, 147).

On the other hand, sometimes low-income workers remain in their jobs because they are generally pleased with their employment and expect their income to increase. In many of these positive instances, leaders within the firms in question are likely to view their job holders as partners whose needs and interests are integral to the overall success of the organization. One firm committed to a positive partnership with workers was the Financial Services Company (researchers' pseudonym), which besides the prospect of improving pay provided its workers the following supports:

- A volunteer mentoring program, which is uncommon in a highly competitive labor market, and offers a chance to help develop the job holder's career plans, including various skill upgrades
- A positive work setting for women and minorities, providing tangible benefits for children such as movie passes and "take your children to work" days
- An official flextime policy, which makes it much easier for employees to attend to their children's medical and school needs
- "Lunch and learn" meetings, introducing workers to the availability of company-financed training in computer skills and customer-service competencies (Iversen and Armstrong 2006, 172)

Table 8.7 indicates that at any given moment nearly two thirds of poor adults are not working (U.S. Census Bureau 2010b). The upcoming discussion of welfare reform examines the complex challenge of bringing former recipients into the workforce.

THE WELFARE REFORM ERA

Did welfare reform truly introduce an improved program, or did it continue the long-time war on the poor? As previously noted, the Personal Responsibility and Work Opportunity Reconciliation Act of 1996 became law, eliminating Aid to Families with Dependent Children and providing Temporary Assistance for Needy Families (TANF). As Figure 8.3 indicates, the passage of this act signaled a steady financial decline in welfare support involving schooling, job training, and other vital services that would have facilitated clients' successful movement into the long-term job world.

TABLE 8.7 Poor People's Work Experience in 2007[1]

	Worked full-time year-round	Worked but not both full-time and year-round	Did not work
Poor workers in millions	2.8	6.3	1.6
Percentages for poor workers	10.9%	25%	64%
Poor male workers in millions	1.5	2.6	5.9
Percentages for poor male workers	15.1%	26.2%	58.8%
Poor female workers in millions	1.2	3.7	10.2
Percentages for poor female workers	8.2%	24.7%	67.3%

[1]Individuals included here have an income below the poverty threshold and are 16 years old and over.

These startling statistics indicate that in 2007 nearly nine tenths of poor adults did not work full-time and year-round and that almost two thirds did not work at all.

Source: U.S. Census Bureau. 2010. Table 692. "Work Experience of People during Year by Selected Characteristics and Poverty Status of People 16 and Over: 2007." *Statistical Abstract of the United States: 2010.* http://www.census.gov/compendia/statab/cats/income_expenditures_poverty_wealth.html.

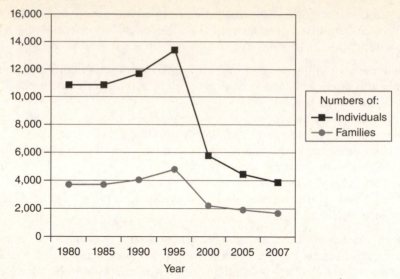

FIGURE 8.3   The Decline in Numbers of Public-Assistance Payments over Time[1]

[1]The numbers represent thousands of either families or recipients.

These data indicate that between 1980 and 1995 the number of public-assistance payments to poor families or individuals (called Aid to Families with Dependent Children) increased. Then in 1995, the year before passage of welfare-reform legislation, those payments began to decline, with between 1995 and 2007 a falloff of 65.1 percent in the number of families and a drop of 71 percent in the number of individuals. Supporters of the reform program have considered such numbers proof of its success. However, these numbers do not reveal the often destructive impact of welfare-to-work reform on both families and individuals.

Source: U.S. Census Bureau. 2012. Table 565. "Temporary Assistance for Needy Families (TANF)— Families and Recipients: 1980 to 2009." *U.S. Statistical Abstract: 2012.* www.census.gov/compendia/statab/2012/tables/12s0565.xls.

Analysis of welfare reform can be divided into two broad parts: reasons individuals seek welfare, including information about those returning to it after time in the job market; and evaluation of the welfare-reform system. The most prominent sources in this section are two studies of former welfare participants—sociologist Karen Seccombe's research on about 600 female welfare clients in Florida and Oregon and Steven G. Anderson, Anthony P. Halter, and Brian M. Gryzlak's social-work research involving 51 women in Chicago, most of whom had left welfare and returned to it. While negatives outweigh positives in the upcoming discussion, the welfare-reform program has produced some effective outcomes.

Running the TANF Gauntlet

Arguably the most pervasive motivator for remaining on welfare has been the absence of jobs that would elevate an individual's or family's economic condition. The majority of individuals coming off TANF have found that the kind of positions for which they qualify are often scarce and always low-paid. Unemployment rates have been particularly high among young African Americans and other minorities without a high-school degree. Many women on welfare often look hard for jobs but without success. Sarah, a 30-year-old divorced mother, had such accomplishments as a high-school certificate, current college attendance, and many years of work experience. She indicated that employers were picky or only hired individuals they knew or had been referred to them. As a result her job search was long and difficult. Sarah said, "I've applied for 20 to 100 a month. . . . It's not that I'm not qualified. I've had six years of management" (Seccombe 2007, 83–84).

Recent welfare recipients who find jobs sometimes discover that they are worse off employed than when receiving TANF support. One individual, who eventually returned to TANF, valued her job as a teacher's assistant and appreciated supporting herself. However, a comparison of the total income and benefits she received on welfare with her work earnings indicated that while "I was struggling on public aid, now I was working very hard every day, and I was getting $80 a month less by working" (Anderson, Halter, and Gryzlak 2004, 188).

Was such a case unusual? During the late 1990s, the advocates of welfare reform had touted the program as impressively successful. Indeed, between 1991 and 2000, income for poor mothers increased over 4 percent, with growth in earnings and the Earned Income Tax Credit, which has provided low-income families tax reductions and wage supplements, the major contributors. However, from 2000 to 2005, the income of poor families fell, with both dwindling earnings and the declining Earned Income Tax Credit contributing significantly (Bernstein 2007).

Some TANF recipients indicated that a major reason why women coming off of welfare can only find low-paying jobs is that the system gives them little chance to obtain schooling or training, simply rushing them into the first job available (Weaver, Risler, Nackerud, and Ellett 2007). Respondents appreciated the value of education. One woman stated, "It's easy to go out and get a $5 job, but you need your GED or high school diploma—some type of schooling to keep moving forward" (Anderson, Halter, and Gryzlak 2004, 188). The jobs, in short, paid too little, and the prospects they offered were too flimsy to make it economically feasible for many former TANF members to stay employed.

Another incentive to remain on TANF or return to it can be concern about Medicaid subsidy. In fact, family heads with serious medical problems or with children suffering them indicated that healthcare can be more important than TANF support. Kelly had Tourette's syndrome, Parkinson's disease, obsessive-compulsive disorder, and bipolarity while her son suffered from attention-deficit/hyperactivity disorder. Not surprisingly she worried, wondering about getting medication and whether she could survive without financial aid. She said, "It's really scary. For me, the only thing that I do worry about is . . . what's going to happen to me" (Seccombe 2007, 86–87).

Childcare is another factor making it difficult to move off welfare. Bureaucratic rules can be a complicating factor. While low-income families in Illinois are supposed to receive subsidy for this service, the regulations have been complicated, sometimes confusing recipients. One employed respondent applied for childcare support and was told she was making too much money. She explained, "So when I quit my job and went on {TANF] they paid for it." The interviewer asked whether TANF paid because she started going to school. "Exactly . . . [they didn't] want to do this when I'm trying to work, O.K., so I'll go to school" (Anderson, Halter, and Gryzlak 2004, 188).

Scheduling childcare is often a problem particularly for individuals moving into various types of service work. Such individuals often need to work nights and on weekends and can find it difficult or impossible to locate someone to provide childcare. Rhonda indicated that she could find a job. Her major challenge was finding someone to take care of her son at odd hours because "I ain't got nobody on weekends to watch him. . . . It's like they always want nights and weekends. . . It's hard" (Seccombe 2007, 88). While such difficulties exist, it is important to note that the welfare-reform initiative has provided significant childcare support. In 1997 the program supplied about $4 billion for childcare; the figure rose steadily, reaching $11.9 billion in 2004. This aid went primarily to poor working women, improving their chances of holding a job (Parrott and Sherman 2006, 9).

Child support is an additional issue that can affect women leaving the welfare system. In spite of the fact that most fathers have been identified, many avoid any regular contribution. When asked about receiving child support, a divorced African American mother of two indicated that the system appeared to let fathers keep their money while mothers and children remained impoverished. She declared, "I don't think the government should have to take care of a man's kids, especially if he can take care of his own kids. . . My kids deserve that money" (Seccombe 2007, 91).

Overall, however, the child-support program has improved over time. As part of reform, Congress reorganized the collection process. As a result between 1996 and 2004 the segment of families receiving child support rose from 20 to 51 percent, and the total amount collected increased from $12 to $22 billion (Parrott and Sherman 2006, 9).

Finally, in some cases a key factor in low-income women's ability to hold jobs is transportation. In a nation with limited effective mass transit, poor women entering the job market are likely to find that they face a long, sometimes complicated (requiring transfers), and expensive commute. A car would be helpful, but few women coming off welfare can afford a reliable model, ending up instead with one needing constant, often expensive repairs. One respondent indicated the negative role that transportation could play in transitioning from welfare. Not only was it costly, but "it was difficult because the shift that I was working was three to twelve—three in the afternoon to twelve at night" [and few buses ran late at night] (Seccombe 2007, 94). This respondent mentioned one of several disconnects with the transit system TANF recipients often experience. **Poor workers' temporal mismatch** refers to the fact that these individuals are on the job during evening and weekend shifts when local transportation is either less or not operative. In addition, **poor workers' spatial mismatch** is the reality that while these job seekers tend to live in urban districts, most economic expansion is in the suburbs (Amedee 2005).

In the course of their efforts to leave welfare, TANF recipients have ample opportunity to assess the welfare reform system.

Evaluation of Welfare Reform

When Karen Seccombe asked her respondents about the positive aspects of the welfare system, they would laugh then "grimace, shake their head in disbelief, stare back blankly, comment that they needed more time to think about an answer, or curtly retorted, 'There are none!'" (Seccombe 2007, 168).

Once past the initial jolt of surprise, some respondents mentioned a few positive attributes. First, a number of individuals conceded that the system, though meager in its allotments, did provide some financial support. Without it many poor families would be forced to live on the streets or in a homeless shelter. As one woman said, "It keeps me out of dumpsters." Second, as part of the welfare package, respondents belonged to various programs, which provided critical services these recipients could not have obtained elsewhere. Seccombe's informants most frequently mentioned Medicaid, which financed medical assistance to clients who otherwise could not have afforded it, and also food stamps. Many prized these two benefits more highly than the welfare check itself. Third, the women spoke favorably about several forms of financing that directly bolstered their job-seeking efforts, particularly childcare payments and transportation vouchers. Besides the money, these programs represented a morale boost for women making a strong effort to move off welfare. As one beneficiary said, "The system tries to help those who help themselves" (Seccombe 2007, 170).

While clients had selected positive observations about the TANF system, they had many criticisms of it. To begin, most emphasized that the financial value of the TANF package was low. One woman was angry that a wealthy country accepted such degraded living for poor children. She wondered how children who went to bed cold and hungry could perform effectively the next day in school. She asked, "How can anyone grow up normal, intelligent, and become a productive member of society living like that?" (Seccombe 2007, 71).

Another deficiency TANF recipients cited involved the delivery of services, with clients complaining that the system provided too little one-on-one help; was geared simply to lowering the number of clients through job placement, regardless of the job's quality; and was generally ineffective and impersonal. On the last point, respondents mentioned a number of particulars. Two factors contributing to the system's ineffectiveness were case workers' large client loads, meaning that a given welfare recipient received very limited attention, and rapid case-worker turnover, making it difficult or impossible to develop an effective relationship with a TANF representative over time. The women's most heated complaint about staff members focused on their tendency to look down on welfare recipients. One respondent explained, "To me their job is to downgrade us. They don't like us, they don't respect us as human beings, they feel that we are the ones that are in need . . . and that they can treat us like low people that are in poverty" (Anderson, Halter, and Gryzlak 2004, 190).

A third criticism of the TANF system has been the loss of all previous benefits—cash grants, food stamps, housing subsidies, and Medicaid—the moment a person received a job. Holding a low-paying position, the newly employed head of household often found herself worse off economically than when she was on welfare (Seccombe 2007, 173).

Besides their general evaluation of the TANF system, clients singled out certain questionable priorities welfare reform has featured. Time limits was one major issue, with opponents claiming that they are arbitrary and punitive, failing to address a variety of personal needs that could necessitate more than several years of TANF support. In most states the time limit is 60 months. One respondent conceded that she could understand that a strategy was necessary to get people off of welfare. However, she questioned this approach. "Oh, God, this is amusing. . . . . Setting an arbitrary time limit on a system that is so dysfunctional to begin with that, you know, it's amazing that anyone gets off it" (Seccombe 2007, 174).

Another related, often mentioned emphasis involved pushing clients into jobs, failing to assess their job prospects thoroughly. While the majority of respondents generally supported recipients' employment, they expressed distinct reservations about the sense of urgency—emphasizing that parents seeking jobs should have their children in school; that heads of household obtaining education should be allowed to finish their programs; that the job should pay above minimum wage in order to cover families' basic needs; that such critical benefits as food stamps and housing subsidies should be phased out, not abruptly eliminated (Seccombe 2007, 178); and finally that TANF clients obtaining positions in custodial work or sales that require a GED within a year or two of obtaining the job almost always need more time to prepare for the test (Cooney 2010).

In an examination of Mississippi's TANF system, a team of researchers concluded that "what now needs to be done is to shift the focus of welfare policies from caseload reduction to poverty, inequality, and social justice" (Parisi, Harris, Grice, Taquino, and Gill 2005). In short, there needs to be a thorough, dispassionate assessment of a family head's circumstances, not a blaming-the-victim display.

Besides using clients' comments as a basis for evaluation, analysts can judge the TANF program by examining relevant data. For instance, has welfare-reform altered the poverty rate? Official figures reveal some change over time. In 1959 20.8 percent of families fell below the poverty threshold. A decade later it had dropped by half—to 10.4 percent. When welfare reform legislation passed in 1996, the figure was 12.2 percent, declining to 9.6 percent in 2000 and then rising to 11.5 percent in 2008 (U.S. Bureau of the Census 2009a). From the late 1960s, the perceived percentage of poor families has been fairly constant. At the same time, it should be remembered that the measurements for determining poverty thresholds are distinctly suspect, undoubtedly underestimating the number of people who are poor.

Examination of clients who obtained jobs and those who did not can provide another evaluation of the TANF program:

- **_Entering the job world._** At any given moment, about three in five former TANF recipients are working. Typically wages are low, around $7 to $8 an hour, but former recipients with jobs generally have slightly higher income than when they received TANF support (Parrott and Sherman 2006, 10–11). However, a study conducted in Michigan found that when female household heads leaving welfare were compared to those who remained, they suffered a similar number of financial crises involving health insurance, rent and utilities, and food purchase (Danziger, Heflin, Corcoran, Oltmans, and Wang 2002). In fact, a study of low-income women in three cities concluded that unless other family members made substantial contributions, former TANF recipients' movement into employment had little or no long-term income impact (Moffitt and Winder 2004). A few welfare-to-work programs were unusually successful. A Portland (Oregon) program secured higher-paying jobs than recipients normally found. The program planners created an effective set of building blocks—a thorough identification of clients' career interests and job skills; provision of training opportunities for recipients to receive occupational certificates that increased the likelihood of obtaining well-paying jobs; and the referral of trained individuals to promising job locations (Parrott and Sherman 2006, 11).

- **_Not entering the employment market after exhausting TANF support._** At any moment about 1 million poor single mothers and about 2 million children are neither on TANF nor is the family head employed. Early in the twenty-first century, this segment of poor people increased. Between 2000 and 2004, the number of children living in families with cash income below one half the poverty threshold rose by nearly 800,000. TANF officials created various techniques to trim down the number of recipients—discouraging families from applying for assistance; immediately terminating support to clients for missing appointments or not completing paperwork; and eliminating TANF recipients for failing to meet work requirements even if they were temporarily or permanently unable to work (Parrott and Sherman 2006).

Scholars at the Brookings Institution developed a concept that characterized the victims of such treatment. A **floundering family** is a household in which the breadwinner(s) appear(s) to lack the ability to establish financial independence. The family heads thrown off the welfare rolls often have serious barriers to employment—major mental or physical impairments, the need to care for family members or friends with long-term health problems, low-level schooling often linked to limited cognitive functioning, substance abuse, and victimization by domestic violence. Sometimes the problems these heads of household experience are acute. One mother was so physically impaired that she could not lift a milk container off the table. Another was too depressed to maintain basic hygiene. Some family heads displayed cognitive functioning so low that they could not read simple words or numbers or tell time (Handler and Hasenfeld 2007, 343–44; Hill and Kauff 2002; Parrott and Sherman 2006, 12–13). How could anyone reasonable consider it possible for people with such problems to be competent job holders? In such cases two outcomes seem certain. Families without either TANF or job support suffer significantly, having trouble obtaining food and paying bills, including fees for medical emergencies. In addition, the family heads find themselves isolated from the various job-related resources that TANF provides (Parrott and Sherman 2006).

What policy should government programs follow? On the one hand, it is probably both practical and humane to take into account the bad news that research revealed—that at any moment about one million single mothers and two million children reside in families where the parents lack the physical and/or mental capacities to succeed in the job world (Parrott and Sherman 2006). On the other hand, the good news is that like the previously mentioned Oregon program, carefully planned training can be very effective with poor parents who are ready to enter the job world. A resounding case in point involves the state of New Jersey, which sponsored a year-long program administered through its One-Stop Career Centers to develop Internet technology skills for 128 women who were members of the working poor, with about three fifths having a high-school diploma or less and averaging $16,900 in income. While these women were not in the TANF program, where some members encounter major barriers to entering the workforce, they were only modestly equipped for success in the job world, and so their experiences seems suggestive for poor women generally.

In this setting each participant received a computer, printer, Internet access, and the availability of online courses. At the state's centers, a trainee obtained a coach who worked with the student to identify her current skills, the abilities required to move into a better-paying job, and also her progress to date. In addition, this program partnered with gender-equity researchers at the Rutgers University Center for Women and

TABLE 8.8 Poverty Rates[1] in 24 Developed Nations

Country	Poverty rate based on household income	Poverty reduction by income-transfer programs[2] and taxes	Net poverty rate
Denmark	24%	18%	5%[3]
Sweden	27	21	5
Czech Republic	28	22	6
Austria	23	16	7
Finland	18	10	7
France	31	24	7
Iceland	20	13	7
Norway	24	17	7
Luxembourg	29	21	8
The Netherlands	25	17	8
Slovakia	27	19	8
United Kingdom	26	18	8
Belgium	33	24	9
Germany	34	23	11
Italy	32	22	11
New Zealand	27	16	11
Australia	29	16	12
Canada	23	11	12
Portugal	29	16	13
Ireland	31	16	15
Japan	27	12	15
Korea	18	3	15
Poland	38	23	15
United States	26	9	17

[1]Based on less than half the median income and involving data from around the year 2005

[2]These programs involve such issues as health, family, old age, and disabilities. Some countries including the United States also have private programs, which can influence the poverty rate.

[3]In some countries, primarily ones belonging to the European Union, the impact of the social transfers exceeds the numbers listed for the programs. Thus in Denmark's case, the net poverty rate is lower than the numbers in the first two columns would suggest.

Compared to the other nations represented here, the United States has a below-average poverty rate based on household income. However, the net poverty rate is the highest because the country's poverty reduction by income transfers and taxes is the second lowest of the 24 countries in the list.

Source: Koen Caminada and Kees Goudswaard. 2009. "Social Expenditure and Poverty Reduction in the EU15 and other OECD Countries." SSRN: http://papers.ssrn.com/sol3/papers.efm?abstract_id=1553803.

Work, who evaluated ways to either alleviate or eliminate the kind of barriers to employment previously discussed—involving childcare, irregular work hours, and transportation. Furthermore the program offered regular meetings where trainees and instructors could address such issues as the sense of inadequacy many felt working with computers and the Internet and some individuals' reluctance to communicate with their peers and instructors about program issues. As interpersonal relations improved, many felt that a distinct sense of community was developing.

The results were impressive. Ninety-two percent of the participants completed the program—an exceptionally high number. All of the graduates obtained jobs and averaged a 14 percent increase in income. In addition, 15 percent of the participants sought further schooling at either a community college or a university (Appelbaum and Gatta 2006). Clearly the plan was to provide the participants a high-quality training experience that confronted the major barriers to successful employment—not to rush them out into the job world. With some adjustment this program's optimistic, highly practical insights would appear applicable to many TANF recipients.

A pair of long-time poverty analysts summarized how the TANF program could refocus its goals most effectively to assist largely single-mother families—"help adults get and keep jobs, and help them get the education and training they need to make full use of their talents and the childcare they need to be able to stay employed." Sometimes, however, jobs are not available, and so TANF should supply "a decent safety net for families who have no other source of income" (Edelman and Ehrenreich 2010). Unfortunately like earlier government programs, welfare reform has not effectively attacked the conditions that make people poor. In fact, Table 8.8 demonstrates that over time most other developed nations have been more successful at curtailing that cyclical process.

Conclusion

Since the late eighteenth century, American organizations and individuals have made some effort to alleviate poverty, often drawing a distinction between the "deserving" and the "undeserving" poor. Starting early in the twentieth century, the state of Illinois began providing welfare support to white, "deserving" mothers. From that time until the late 1960s, the program expanded, with opposition to it building from the 1970s into the 1990s and eventually leading to federal legislation initiating welfare reform.

In modern times there is an official definition of poverty, which has some assets but receives sharp criticisms from many experts on the subject. While the official definition appears to understate the number of poor, all experts seem to agree that individuals and families falling below the poverty threshold are indeed poor.

As far as resources are concerned, the poor are significantly challenged. They receive little financial capital, with the minimum wage insufficient to elevate families above the poverty level. Employers of the poor have increased the number of part-time and temporary jobs, which generally offer neither stability nor a reasonable opportunity to expand income over time.

Deprived of sufficient financial capital, poor families must live in areas offering substandard human capital—childcare and schools. Low-income families are unlikely to be able to afford quality childcare programs, putting their children at a cognitive disadvantage before starting formal education. Major drawbacks to poor schools include less effective teaching, large classes, and dysfunctional exposure to tracking and high-stakes testing.

Because of the various deprivations in their lives, poor parents provide their children less effective cultural capital than that their more affluent counterparts supply. In particular, poor parents talk less and are more controlling, curtailing the development of abilities useful for success in school.

Finally, whether it involves negotiations with school officials to obtain tutoring to improve reading skills or a business contact to secure a job, low-income individuals generally possess less effective social capital than their middle-class counterparts.

Research suggests that the welfare reform legislation, which was signed into law in 1996, did not take into account the various capital-related deficiencies poor heads of household possess. The proponents of this program, in short, appear to have subscribed to a blaming-the-victim approach. The outcome has been that the majority of TANF recipients have either ended up with low-level, low-paying jobs, have returned to welfare after brief employment, or lost TANF support after they exceeded the time limit. A significant segment of family heads with neither jobs nor welfare are individuals who face one or more severe barriers to entering the job world.

Once people are locked into the cycle of poverty, its impact on their lives is formidable. The black CEO of an inner-city wholesale firm described his sense of the effects. If there is "a bunch of poor people together . . . I don't give a damn whether they're white, green or grizzly . . . You're going to create crime and everything else that's under the sun." When asked, the business man conceded that he could understand some employers' reluctance to hire poor blacks (Wilson 1997, 130).

This quotation addresses the impact of the cycle of poverty, including an additional specific element in its perpetuation—prospective employers sometimes shying away from job applicants just because they live in certain low-income areas.

The cycle of poverty accelerates from the interaction of a set of factors. To break the cycle, outside intervention is necessary. Academic experts and program developers have focused on different entry points where intervention can be effective—notably children's healthcare, childcare, schooling, housing assistance, and job training and retraining (Cizon 1966; Fuller, Caspary, and Gauthier 2002; Grant 2006; Sen 1999). Illustrations in this chapter have suggested that well-organized, substantial intervention at any point increases poor people's chances of materially improving their lives. When provided critical supports, many, perhaps most poor heads of household try hard to function productively in the job world. The issue that the rest of the citizenry should assess is whether they consider it a worthwhile expenditure to subsidize effective means of breaking the cycle of poverty and bringing millions of poor families into the relative comfort of the economic mainstream.

Key Terms in the Glossary

Absolute threshold of poverty *220*
Blaming the victim *216*
Cycle of poverty *216*
Deserving poor *217*
Extended-family network *225*

Floundering family *251*
High-stakes testing *232*
Official U.S. measure of poverty *220*
Pedagogy of poverty *232*
Poor workers' spatial mismatch *248*

Poor workers' temporal mismatch *248*
Resiliency *227*
Structural vulnerability *225*
Tracking *230*
Undeserving poor *218*
Urban war zone *230*

Discussion Topics

1. Describe the distinction between the "deserving" and the "undeserving poor."
2. What are the primary strengths and weaknesses of the U.S. official measure of poverty?
3. What are three structural vulnerabilities poor families face? Discuss.
4. Summarize three important qualities a successful daycare program for poor children should possess.
5. Examine in detail the major factors undermining effective schooling in poor districts.
6. Can poor families possess potent sources of social capital? How can government programs help build social capital in poor communities?
7. What factors have contributed to poor people's declining work opportunities since the 1980s?
8. Discuss the primary contributions that a job-training program for poor people must provide to be successful.
9. As clients have left the TANF program, what challenges have they faced dealing with job searches?
10. According to welfare clients, what are two strengths and two weaknesses of welfare reform?
11. Why is the cycle of poverty an illustration of social reproduction?

Research Papers

1. Write a paper about the cycle of poverty, using various studies that reveal different phases of the process.
2. Analyze the relationship between an absolute threshold of poverty and the official U.S. measure of poverty, incorporating various sources to indicate how the U.S. measure could be most effectively revised to approach the absolute threshold.
3. Obtain information about the pedagogy of poverty, providing detail about its practices and case-study information about teachers who have defeated this common condition in their classrooms.
4. Examine studies to determine the accuracy of the following assertion: The TANF program, which has significantly cut the welfare rolls, has been an unqualified success.
5. Use current research to analyze why some families have been unable to enter or remain in the job world and the consequences for such families.

Informative Websites

The Wire is a six-year TV series—a tour de force set in the poor city of Baltimore, which uses beautifully written and directed scripts and a talented array of actors to illuminate such previously discussed issues as family conflicts, community relations, working-poor and underclass job struggles, and most notably the unfolding of the pedagogy of poverty in a poor urban school.

The site for the National Center for Children in Poverty (http://www.nccp.org/projects/) provides a wealth of information about poor American children, including state profiles, publications, and projects for fighting child poverty.

The site Access Quality Education: Inequality and Inadequacy in America's Schools (http://www.schoolfunding.info/issues/issues.php3) supplies detail about the public-school funding issue, notably funding differences within states and news about the steady flow of developing court cases to equalize public-school funding within individual states.

Teach for America (http://www.teachforamerica.org/) is an organization which provides young teachers who serve for two years in one of 39 poor urban or rural districts. Since its inception in 1990, over 20,000 teachers have participated in the program. The site provides basic information about Teach for America and encourages individuals to apply.

The Center for Women and Work at Rutgers University (http://www.cww.rutgers.edu/)

offers an informative site developed by the professional women who advised the successful job-training program in New Jersey discussed in the chapter. In particular, click "Working Families."

Bibliography

Afflerbach, Peter. 2002. "Essay Books Review: The Road to Folly and Redemption: Perspectives on the Legitimacy of High-Stakes Testing." *Reading Research Quarterly* 37 (July–August–September): 348–60.

Amedee, George. 2005. "Closing the Transportation Divide: Linking TANF and Transportation." *Race, Gender & Class* 12: 86–106.

Anderson, Steven G., Anthony P. Halter, and Brian M. Gryzlak. 2004. "Differences after Leaving TANF: Inner-City Women Talk about Reasons for Returning to Welfare." *Social Work* 49 (April): 185–94.

Andersson, Fredrik, Harry J. Holzer, and Julia I. Lane. 2005. *Moving Up or Moving On: Who Advances in the Low-Wage Labor Market*. New York: Russell Sage Foundation.

Appelbaum, Eileen, Annette Bernhardt, and Richard J. Murnane (eds.). 2003. *Low Wage America: How Employers Are Reshaping Opportunity in the Workplace*. New York: Russell Sage Foundation.

Applebaum, Eileen, and Mary Gatta. 2006. "Crossing Over: From Working Poverty to Self-Sufficiency via Job Training That Is Flexible in Time and Space." *American Sociological Association Annual Meeting,* pp. 1–39.

Auletta, Ken. 1999. *The Underclass*, rev. ed. Woodstock, NY: Overlook Press.

Barone, Diane M. 2006. *Narrowing the Literacy Gap: What Works in High-Poverty Schools*. New York: Guilford Press.

Barr, Robert D., and William H. Parrett. 2007. *The Kids Left Behind: Catching Up the Underachieving Children of Poverty*. Bloomington, IN: Solution Tree.

Bernstein, Jared. 2007. "A Tale of Two Time Periods for Low-Income Families." *Economic Policy Institute*. http://www.epi.org/content.cfm/webfeatures_snapshots_20070606.

Biddle, Bruce J., and David C. Berliner. 2002. "A Research Synthesis: Unequal School Funding in the United States." *Educational Leadership* 59 (March): 1–15.

Bluestone, Barry, and Bennett Harrison. 2000. *The Battle for Growth with Equity in the Twenty-First Century*. Boston: Houghton Mifflin.

Books, Sue. 2004. *Poverty and Schooling in the U.S.: Context and Consequences*. Mahwah, NJ: Lawrence Erlbaum Associates.

Brady, David, and Michael Wallace. 2001. "Deindustrialization and Poverty: Manufacturing Decline and AFDC: Recipiency in Lake County, Indiana 1964–93." *Sociological Forum* 16 (June): 321–58.

Calkins, Lucy, Kate Montgomery, Donna Santman, and Beverly Falk. 1998. *A Teacher's Guide to Standardized Reading Tests: Knowledge Is Power*. Portsmouth, NH: Heinemann.

Carnevale, Anthony P., and Donna M. Desrochers. 1999. *Getting Down to Business*. Princeton: Educational Testing Service.

Cauce, Ana Mari, Angela Stewart, Melanie Domenech Rodriguez, Bryan Cochran, and Joshua Ginzler. 2003. "Overcoming the Odds? Adolescent Development in the Context of Urban Poverty," pp. 343–91 in Suniya S. Luthar (ed.), *Resilience and Vulnerability: Adaptation in the Context of Childhood Adversities*. Cambridge: Cambridge University Press.

Cizon, Francis A. 1966. "Problems in Breaking the Poverty Cycle." *AgEcon Search*: 84–91. http://ageconsearch.umn.edu/bitstream/17533/1/ar660084.pdf.

Chadwick, Kathy Gordon. 2004. *Improving Schools through Community Engagement: A Practical Guide for Educators*. Thousand Oaks, CA: Corwin.

Cooney, Kate. 2010. "The Promise and Pitfalls of Employer-Linked Job Training for

Disadvantaged Workers." *Administration in Social Work* 34 (January): 27–48.

Danzinger, Sheldon, Colleen M. Heflin, Mary E. Corcoran, Elizabeth Oltmans, and Hui-Chen Wang. 2002. "Does It Pay to Move from Welfare to Work?" *Journal of Policy Analysis and Management* 21 (Autumn): 671–92.

Darling-Hammond, Linda, and Leslie Post. 2000. "Inequality in Teaching and Schooling: Supporting High-Quality Teaching and Leadership in Low-Income Schools," pp. 127–67 in Robert D. Kahlenberg (ed.), *A Nation at Risk: Preserving Public Education as an Engine for Social Mobility*. New York: Century Foundation Press.

Dewan, Shaila, and Kevin Sack. 2008. "A Safety-Net Hospital Falls into Financial Crisis." *New York Times* (January 9): A1+.

Doob, Christopher B. 2005. *Race, Ethnicity, and the American Urban Mainstream*. Boston: Pearson Allyn and Bacon.

Duncan, Cynthia. 2001. "Social Capital in America's Poor Rural Communities," pp. 60–86 in Susan Saegert, J. Phillip Thompson, and Mark R. Warren (eds.), *Social Capital and Poor Communities*. New York: Russell Sage Foundation.

Dworkin, A. Gary. 2005. "The No Child Left Behind Act: Accountability, High-Stakes Testing, and Roles for Sociologists." *Sociology of Education* 78 (April): 170–74.

Edelman, Peter, and Barbara Ehrenreich. 2010. "What Really Happened to Welfare." *Nation* 290 (April 12): 15+.

Ehrenreich, Barbara. 2002. *Nickel and Dimed: On (Not) Getting By in America*. New York: Owl Books.

Espinosa, Linda, and James M. Laffey. "Urban Primary Teacher Perceptions of Children with Challenging Behaviors." *Journal of Children & Poverty* 9 (Fall): 135–56.

Fuller, Bruce, Sharon L. Kagan, Gretchen L. Caspary, and Christiane A. Gauthier. 2002. "Welfare Reform and Child Care Options for Low-Income Families." *Future of Children* 12 (Winter–Spring): 97–119.

Fulton, David. 2000. "Teach the Children: Who Decides." *New York Times* (September 19): A19.

Gans, Herbert. 2010. "Deconstructing the Underclass," pp. 102–08 in Paula S. Rothenberg (ed.), *Race, Class and Gender in the United States*, 8th ed. New York: Worth.

Garbarino, James, Nancy Dubrow, Kathleen Kostelney, and Carol Pardo. 1992. *Children in Danger: Coping with the Consequences of Community Violence*. San Francisco: Jossey Bass.

Gilbert, Dennis. 2011. *The American Class Structure in an Age of Growing Inequality*, 8th ed. Thousand Oaks, CA: Pine Forge Press.

Gilens, Martin. 1999. *Why Americans Hate Welfare: Race, Media, and the Politics of Antipoverty Policy*. Chicago: University of Chicago Press.

Grant, Neva. 2006. "Helping Dropouts Break the Cycle of Poverty." *NPR*. (March 27). http://www.npr.org/templates/story/story.php?storyId=5300726.

Grusky, David B. 2001. "Review." *Contemporary Sociology* 30 (November): 574–76.

Haberman, Martin. 1991. "The Pedagogy of Poverty versus Good Teaching." *Phi Delta Kappan* 73 (December): 290–94.

Haberman, Martin. 1995. *Star Teachers of Children in Poverty*. Indianapolis: Kappa Delta Pi Publications.

Handler, Joel F., and Yeheskel Hasenfeld. 2007. *Blame Welfare, Ignore Poverty and Inequality*. New York: Cambridge University Press.

Harrington, Michael. 1984. *The New American Poverty*. New York: Holt, Rinehart and Winston.

Haveman, Robert, and Timothy Smeeding. 2006. "The Role of Higher Education in Social Mobility." *Future of Children* 16 (Fall): 125–50.

Heymann, S. Jody, and Alison Earle. 2000. "Low-Income Parents: How Do Working Conditions Affect Their Opportunity to Help School-Age Children at Risk?" *American Educational Research Journal* 37 (Winter): 833–48.

Hill, Heather, and Jacqueline Kauff. 2002. "Living on Little: The Stories of Families with Very Low Income and Lessons for TANF Reauthorization." *Policy & Practice* 60 (Spring): 14–18.

Hoffman, James, Lori Assaf, and Scott G. Paris. 2001. "High-Stakes Testing in Reading: Today in Texas, Tomorrow?" *Reading Teacher* 54 (February): 482–94.

Holahan, John, and Allison Cook. 2005. *Change in Economic Conditions and Health Insurance Coverage, 2000–2004*. Washington, DC: Urban Institute.

Horvat, Erin McNamara, Elliot B. Weininger, and Annette Lareau. 2003. "From Social Ties to Social Capital: Class Differences in the Relations between Schools and Parent Networks." *American Educational Research Journal* 40: 319–51.

Howley, Craig, and Robert Bickel. 2002. "The Small Schools Make a Difference for Children from Poor Families." *American School Board Journal* 189 (March): 28–30.

Howley, Craig B., and Aimee A. Howley. 2004. "School Size and the Influence of Socioeconomic Status on Student Achievement: Confronting the Threat of Size Bias in National Data Sets." *Education Policy Analysis Archives.* http://epaa.asu.edu/epaa/v12n52/.

Iceland, John. 2006. *Poverty in America: A Handbook.* Berkeley: University of California Press.

Iversen, Roberta Rehner, and Annie Laurie Armstrong. 2006. *Jobs Aren't Enough: Toward a New Economic Mobility for Low-Income Families.* Philadelphia: Temple University Press.

Jones, Deborah J., Alecia A. Zalot, Sarah E. Foster, Emma Sterrett, and Charlene Chester. 2007. "A Review of Childrearing in African American Single Mother Families: The Relevance of a Coparenting Framework." *Journal of Children and Family Studies* 16 (October): 671–83.

Kamin, Leon J. 1974. *The Science and Politics of IQ.* New York: Wiley.

Katz, Michael B. 1993. "The Urban 'Underclass' as a Metaphor of Social Transformation," pp. 3–23 in Michael B. Katz (ed.), *The "Underclass" Debate: Views from History.* Princeton: Princeton University Press.

Katz, Michael B. 2001. *The Price of Citizenship: Redefining America's Welfare State.* New York: Metropolitan Books.

Katz, Michael B. 2003. "In the Shades of the Poorhouse: A Social History of Welfare in America," pp. 225–53 in Dalton Conley (ed.), *Wealth and Poverty in America: A Reader.* Malden, MA: Blackwell.

Keyes, Langley C. 2001. "Housing, Social Capital, and Poor Communities," pp. 144–47 in Susan Saegert, J. Phillip Thompson, and Mark R. Warren (eds.), *Social Capital and Poor Communities.* New York: Russell Sage Foundation.

King, Christopher T. 2004. "The Effectiveness of Publicly Financed Training in the United States: Implications for WIA and Related Programs," pp. 57–99 in Christopher J. O'Leary, Robert A. Straits, and S.A. Wandner (eds.), *Job Training Policy in the United States.* Kalamazoo: W.E. Upjohn Institute for Employment Research.

Klepp, Susan E. 2004. "Malthusian Miseries and the Working Poor in Philadelphia, 1780–1830," pp. 63–92 in Billy G. Smith (ed.), *Down and Out in Early America.* University Park, PA: Pennsylvania State University Press.

Lankford, Hamilton, Susanna Loeb, and James Wyckoff. 2002. "Teacher Sorting and the Plight of Urban Schools: A Descriptive Analysis." *Educational Evaluation and Policy Analysis* 24 (Spring): 37–62.

LeTendre, Gerald K., Barbara K. Hofer, and Hidetada Shimizu. 2003. "What Is Tracking? Cultural Expectations in the United States, Germany, and Japan." *American Educational Research Journal* 40 (Spring): 43–89.

Lichter, Daniel T., and Martha L. Crowley. 2002. "Poverty in America: Beyond Welfare Reform." *Population Bulletin* 57 (June): 1–36.

Ludwig, Jens. 2003. "Improving Neighborhoods for Poor Children," pp. 136–55 in Isabel V. Sawhill (ed.), *One Percent for the Kids: New Policies, Brighter Futures for America's Children.* Washington, DC: Brookings Institution Press.

Marger, Martin N. 2010. *Social Inequality: Patterns and Processes*, 5th ed. New York: McGraw-Hill.

Massey, Douglas S., and Nancy A. Denton. 1993. *American Apartheid: Segregation and the Making of the Underclass.* Cambridge, MA: Harvard University Press.

MacLeod, Jay. 2009. *Ain't No Makin' It: Aspirations & Attainment in a Low-Income Neighborhood*, 3rd ed. Boulder: Westview Press.

Mayer, Susan E. 2001. "How Did the Increase in Economic Inequality between 1970 and 1990 Affect Children's Educational Attainment?" *American Journal of Sociology* 107 (July): 1–32.

McLoyd, Vonnie C. 1998. "Socioeconomic Disadvantage and Child Development." *American Psychologist* 53 (February): 185–204.

Moffitt, Robert, and Kate Winder. 2004. "Does It Pay to Move from Welfare to Work? A Comment on Danziger, Heflin, Corcoran, Oltmans, and Wang." http://www.jhu.edu/~welfare/moffitt_winder_v4c.pdf.

Moore, Mignon R. 2001. "Review." *American Journal of Sociology* 107 (September): 538–40.

Nash, Gary B. 2004. "Poverty and Politics in Early American History," pp. 1–39 in Billy G. Smith (ed.), *Down and Out in Early America*. University Park, PA: Pennsylvania State University Press.

O'Leary, Christopher J., Robert A. Straits, and S.A. Wandner (eds.). 2004. *Job Training Policy in the United States*. Kalamazoo: W.E. Upjohn Institute for Employment Research.

Olivas, J. Richard. 2004. "'God Helps Those Who Help Themselves': Religious Explanations of Poverty in Colonial Massachusetts," pp. 262–88 in Billy G. Smith (ed.), *Down and Out in Early America*. University Park, PA: Pennsylvania State University Press.

Organization for Economic Cooperation and Development. 2008. "Are We Growing Unequal? New Evidence on Changes in Poverty and Incomes over the Past 20 Years." http://www.oecd.org/dataoecd/48/56/41494435.pdf.

Owens, Elizabeth. B., and Daniel .S. Shaw. 2003. "Poverty and Early Childhood Adjustment," pp. 267–92 in Suniya S. Luthar (ed.), *Resilience and Vulnerability: Adaptation in the Context of Childhood Adversities*. Cambridge, UK: Cambridge University Press.

Parisi, Domenico, Deborah A. Harris, Steven Michael Grice, Michael Taquino, and Duane A. Gill. 2005. "Does the TANF Work-First Initiative Help Low-Income Families Make Successful Welfare-to-Work Transitions?" *Journal of Poverty* 9: 65–81.

Parrott, Sharon, and Arloc Sherman. 2006. "TANF at 10: Program Results Are More Mixed than Often Understood." *Center on Budget and Policy Priorities*. http://www.cbpp.org/8-17-06tanf.pdf.

Prince, Cynthia D. 2002. "Attracting Well-Qualified Teachers to Struggling Schools." *American Educator* (Winter): 16–21+.

Rainwater, Lee, and Timothy M. Smeeding. 2003. *Poor Kids in a Rich Country*. New York: Russell Sage Foundation.

Rank, Mark R. 2004a. *One Nation Underprivileged: Why American Poverty Affects Us All*. New York: Oxford University Press.

Rank, Mark R. 2004b. "The Disturbing Paradox of Poverty in American Families: What We Have Learned over the Past Four Decades," pp. 469–89 in Marilyn Coleman and Lawrence H. Ganong (eds.), *Handbook of Contemporary Families: Considering the Past, Contemplating the Future*. Thousand Oaks, CA: Sage.

Rank, Mark R., and Thomas A. Hirschl. 2001. "The Occurrence of Poverty across the Life Cycle: Evidence from the PSID." *Journal of Policy Analysis and Management* 20 (Autumn): 737–55.

Relave, Nanette. 2001. "Using Case Management to Change the Front Lines of Welfare Service Delivery." *Welfare Information Network*. http://www.financeproject.org/Publications/casemanagementissuenote.htm.

Rouse, Cecilia Elena, Joanne Brooks-Gunn, and Sara McLanahan. 2005. "Introducing the Issue. School Readiness: Closing Racial and Ethnic Gaps." *Future of Children* 15 (Spring): 5–14.

Rouse, Cecilia Elena, and Lisa Barrow. 2006. "U.S. Elementary and Secondary Schools: Equalizing Opportunity or Replicating the Status Quo?" *Future of Children* 16 (Autumn): 99–123.

Ryan, William. 1976. *Blaming the Victim*, rev. ed. New York: Vintage Books.

Sarkisian, Natalia, Mariana Gerena, and Naomi Gerstel. 2006. "Extended Family Ties among Mexicans, Puerto Ricans, and Whites: Superintegration or Disintegration?" *Family Relations* 55 (July): 331–44.

Seattle Public Schools. 2009. "Office for Community Learning." http://www.seatttleschools.org/area/ocl/index/xml.

Seccombe, Karen. 2000. "Families in Poverty in the 1990s: Trends, Causes, Consequences, and Lessons Learned." *Journal of Marriage and the Family* 62 (November): 1094–1113.

Seccombe, Karen. 2002. "'Beating the Odds' versus 'Changing the Odds': Poverty, Resilience, and Family Policy." *Journal of Marriage and the Family* 64 (May): 384–94.

Seccombe, Karen. 2007. *"So You Think I Drive a Cadillac?" Welfare Recipients' Perspective on the System and Its Reform*, 2nd ed. Boston: Pearson Allyn and Bacon.

Sen, Amartya K. 1999. "Investing in Early Childhood: Its Role in Development." *Inter-American Development Bank*. http://www.iadb.org/sds/SOC-114E.pdf.

Shipler, David K. 2004. *The Working Poor: Invisible in America*. New York: Alfred A. Knopf.

Smeeding, Timothy A., Lee Rainwater, and Gary Burtless. 2001. "U.S. Poverty in a Cross-National Context," pp. 162–89 in Sheldon H. Danziger and Robert Haveman (eds.), *Understanding Poverty*. Cambridge, MA: Harvard University Press.

Smith, Aaron. 2009. "Higher Minimum Wage Coming Soon." *CnnMoney.com* (July 7). http://money.cnn.com/2009/07/06/news/economy/minimum wage/index.htm.

Stricker, Frank. 2007. *Why America Lost the War on Poverty—and How to Win It*. Chapel Hill: University of North Carolina Press.

Trattner, Walter I. 1994. *From Poor Laws to Welfare State*. New York: Free Press.

UNICEF Innocenti Research Centre. 2005. Figure 1. "The Child Poverty League." *Child Poverty in Rich Countries 2005*. http://www.unicef-irc.org/publications/pdf/repcard6e.pdf

U.S. Bureau of Labor Statistics. 2007. "A Profile of the Working Poor, 2005." Report 1001. http://www.bls.gov/cps/cpswp2005.pdf.

U.S. Census Bureau. 2008a. Table 146. "Health Insurance Coverage Status by Selected Characteristics 2004 and 2005." *Statistical Abstract of the United States: 2008*. http://www.census.gov/compendia/statab/cats/health_nutrition.html.

U.S. Census Bureau. 2008b. Table 225. "Children's School Readiness Skills: 1993 and 2005." *Statistical Abstract of the United States: 2008*. http://www.census.gov/compendia/statab/cats/education.html-103k.

U.S. Census Bureau. 2009a. Table 2. "Poverty Status of People by Relationship, Race, and Hispanic Origin: 1959 to 2008." *Historical Poverty Tables—People*. http://www.census.gov/hhes/www/poverty/histpov/perindex.html.

U.S. Census Bureau. 2009b. "Poverty: 2007 and 2008 American Community Surveys." *American Community Survey Reports*. http://www.census.gov/prod/2009pubs/acsbr08-1.pdf.

U.S. Census Bureau. 2010a. "Poverty Thresholds 2009." http://www.census.gov/hhes/www/poverty/threshld/thres09.html

U.S. Census Bureau. 2010b. Table 692. "Work Experience of People during Year by Selected Characteristics and Poverty Status of People 16 and Over: 2007." *Statistical Abstract of the United States: 2010*. http://www.census.gov/compendia/statab/cats/income_expenditures_poverty_wealth.html.

Walker, Alan, and Carol Walker. 1995. "Poverty," pp. 655–57 in Adam Kuper and Jessica Kuper (eds.), *The Social Science Encyclopedia*, 2nd ed. London: Routledge.

Weaver, Robert D., Edwin A. Risler, Larry G. Nackerud, and Alberta Ellett. 2007. "After the Bubble Bursts: Welfare Reform in an Era of Economic Decline." *Journal of Policy Practice* 6: 63–81.

White, Kerry A. 1999. "L.A. Board Names CEO with Broad Powers." *Education Week* (October 20): 3.

Williams, Johnny E. 2000. "Race and Class: Why All the Confusion?", pp. 215–27 in Berel Lang (ed.), *Race and Racism in Theory and Practice*. Lanham, MD: Rowman & Littlefield.

Wilson, William Julius. 1997. *When Work Disappears: The World of the New Urban Poor*. New York: Vintage.

Wilson, William Julius. 2009. *More than Just Race: Being Black and Poor in the Inner City*. New York: W. W. Norton & Company.

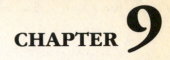
Racism: A Persistent American Presence

Is active, even violent hatred toward certain minority groups an outmoded trend that ceased about a century ago? While many Americans might think that is the case, hateful, sometimes violent racist incidents persist.

Mexican immigrants can find themselves in a very hostile world, where some native citizens subscribe to a centuries-old belief that they represent an alien culture and are stealing Americans' jobs. Between 2004 and 2007, the number of hate crimes against Latinos increased. In Auburn, Washington, a man was charged with violating the state's hate crime law when he pointed a gun at three Hispanic neighbors and threatened to shoot them. In his words they were "disrespecting him in his own country." What they had done was simply to ask him to lower the volume on his radio. In May 2010 Gary Thomas Kelley faced charges for killing John Varela. "Hurry up and go back to Mexico or you're gonna die," Kelley shouted before shooting Varela in the neck. The dead man was a third-generation American (Keller 2010). Throughout this chapter it is apparent current racist displays can be as ferocious and, as the last example suggests, as primitive as any in the past.

Racism is a belief that real or alleged traits of one race establish its superiority over another or others. A pure racist outlook refuses to assess impinging circumstances, concluding that it is solely racial traits that account for a racial group's limitations. In modern times racism is often quite subtle, toned down. Other concepts amplify its meaning.

A distinction exists between individual and institutional racism. **Individual racism** is a person's or group's action that produces racial abuse—for example, verbal or physical mistreatment. Frequently this type of racism is intentional, but it need not be. One might argue, for instance, that individual racism occurs when a white customer seeking information approaches a group of five employees and addresses the only white member, simply assuming that this individual is better informed and more authoritative than the others.

While individual racism probably occurs less often than in the past, the impact of particular incidents can be shocking. Consider the response to a questionnaire item in which a graduate student asked her respondents whether they had ever been the victims of racism. A 24-year-old black woman explained that she was going to cross the street "when about five white males ran the red light, drove as close to the curb as possible, and screamed in my face, 'Run the nigger over! I jumped back to avoid getting hit and looked in bewilderment, searching for this 'nigger.' That was my first racist experience . . . I became overwhelmed with hate, anger, and fear" (Doob 1999, 7).

Institutional racism, unlike individual racism, is not an immediate racist action but a collective reality. **Institutional racism** refers to the discriminatory racial practices built into organizations and groups within the political, economic, and educational systems. The idea of institutional racism is distinctly sociological, recognizing that social structures establish norms guiding people's behaviors. By accepting the norms maintained in their structures, individuals often perpetuate discriminatory conditions. Institutional racism can involve standards that are explicitly racist or simply ones that are not obviously discriminatory against minorities but prove consistently disadvantageous—a heavy weighting of SAT scores for college admittance, involving outcomes from tests that favor white, middle-class students' backgrounds. Institutional racism is common practice.

Minority-group members entering white-controlled organizations can find themselves exposed to institutional racism. Black journalist Nathan McCall, who had been imprisoned for armed robbery, never revealed the conviction during his job interview at the renowned *Atlanta Journal-Constitution*, fearing he would not be hired. After several years of productive work, McCall felt he had earned the right to expose the truth, and so he spoke to his celebrated, highly principled editor, who was white.

"There's something I need to talk with you about."

"O.K." He sat erect. "What is it?"

I got right to the point. "I have served time in prison."

"Oh? What for?" His tone and expression didn't change."

"Armed robbery." I waited for a visible reaction. There was none. Then he gave me a strange look, as if he were wondering why I had bothered wasting his time with such trivia. After a few minutes, he said, "Is that all?"

I thought, *Is that all? Is that all!* [his italics] It was enough to make some white folks run screaming from the room, with their arms flailing. I cleared my throat and answered, "Yes."

"Is anybody giving you shit about it?"

"No."

"If anybody gives you shit about it, let me know."

That was it. I sat there a minute, waiting to see if he had anything else to say. He said nothing. I looked into his eyes, and he looked into mine. Then I rose and walked out of his office, stunned, wondering if that scene had actually **occurred.**

(McCall 1994, 356)

McCall was startled to discover an important staff member who would summarily reject institutionally racist standards. As in this case, institutional racism can involve an organization's discriminatory rules about hiring black ex-convicts, or it can concern the varied access to valued resources that structures and organizations provide different racial groups—such as poorly funded schools or medical facilities disproportionately serving low-income blacks and Hispanics. Racism, this concept emphasizes, can reside in structures, not just in individuals.

Racism affects social stratification. A **majority group** is a category of people within a society who possess distinct physical or cultural characteristics and maintain superior power, wealth, and other valued resources. Whites, particularly whites of British and other northern European descent, have always been the majority group in American society. In contrast, a **minority group** is a category of people with recognizable racial or ethnic traits that place it in a position of restricted power and inferior status so that its members suffer limited opportunities and rewards. It is important to recognize that these two terms do not refer to size—that minority groups can be larger than majority groups or whatever—but involve access to valued resources.

Besides majority and minority groups, analysts sometimes use the terms "dominant group" and "subordinated group." Majority or minority status not only derives from racial membership but also from **ethnicity**—the classification of people into categories with distinct cultural or national traits.

In dealing with the members of either ethnic or racial groups, individuals experience **social distance**—people's willingness to engage in different degrees of closeness with members of various racial and ethnic groups. Sociologist Emory Bogardus developed a scale containing seven degrees of social distance, ranging from acceptance of the group in question as a close relative by marriage to the most extreme rejection—exclusion from one's country. Throughout its lengthy use in the United States, the Bogardus scale has revealed fairly consistent group rankings—at the top with the least social distance, white Americans and northern European ethnic groups; at the next level of social distance people of southern and eastern European ancestry; and finally various racial minorities. Recent exceptions have included rising scores for African and Italian Americans (Bogardus 1947; Martin, Pescosolido, Olafsdottir, and McLeod 2007; Wark and Galliher 2007).

Finally sociologists Howard Omi and Michael Winant (1994; 2009) developed several provocative concepts that can help interpret the major developments that occur in the course of racial events. To begin, a **racial formation** is the socio-historical process of creating and changing race-related structures and meanings. The concept addresses the interrelationship of major structures and racial conditions, with economic, political, judicial, educational, and other institutional factors affecting racial meanings and those meanings, in turn, impacting the prominent structures. The content of a racial formation depends on how its society is organized and ruled (Omi and Winant 1994, 55–61). A case in point might involve the Jim Crow South where from the Civil War until the 1950s black and white children had to attend segregated public schools. When the Supreme Court in the celebrated case of *Brown v. Board of Education of Topeka* declared segregation unconstitutional, the administrative machinery was set in motion to integrate public schools and significantly change the racial formation. While it was an arduous, sometimes even bloody process, it seems indisputable that this judicial decision led to increased interracial contacts and thus altered relations and outlooks between white and black children.

Within modern American society the racial formation undergoes a **trajectory**, a cyclical pattern of disruption and restoration, with racial projects a key component in this process. A **racial project** consists of an interpretation or explanation of racial events that promotes the mobilization of new organizations and groups along with altered everyday behavior. Racial formations provide the settings in which racial projects evolve (Omi and Winant 1994, 56–58). Racial projects, which can be large or small, are ideologically charged engines for change. For instance, one might consider what Omi and Winant referred to as "the great transformation," initiated by the 1950s civil-rights movement as a major racial project to alter perceptions and relations involving race, using a variety of organizations (Omi and Winant 1994, 95–97). Like any racial project, the great transformation concerned itself with both racial meaning and social structure and action. In the course of this chapter, there are several references to Omi and Winant's concepts.

As discussion progresses from the upcoming historical material to the contemporary topics of the family, peers, schools, and the work world, it is apparent that many Native Americans, African Americans, Hispanic Americans, and Asian Americans continue to experience minority status.

PASSAGE TO RACISM

Writing to the King and Queen of Spain about the Indians he encountered, Christopher Columbus was complimentary, indicating that they were peaceful and loving toward their neighbors and that "their discourse is ever sweet and gentle, and accompanied with a smile; and though it is true they are naked, yet their manners are decorous and praiseworthy" (Brown 1972, 1). To Columbus and the hoards that followed, these positive qualities were signs of weakness. The Indians were sweet, pliable, but definitely savage people, who, Columbus believed, should be "made to work, sow, and do all that is necessary and to *adopt our ways*" (Brown 1972, 2). The European authorities would provide religion and schooling but also would relentlessly appropriate land and impose an alien and alienating way of life—a highly controlled, exploitative racial formation.

The impact of the invaders was quickly felt. Their trade activities disrupted intertribal relations that had existed for centuries. More important they brought new diseases—smallpox, influenza, and measles—that would often sweep through a village, killing large numbers. The settlers' domestic animals were also destructive as cows and horses destroyed corn fields, and all grazing animals competed with deer and later bison for the limited supply of grass (Nichols 2003, 29–30).

Certainly the early English settlers did not perceive themselves as troublesome intruders. They were the descendants of a society whose members considered themselves at the center of the civilized world. Other nations with different cultural standards were summarily deemed inferior. Native Americans were considered both profoundly alien and exploitable (Wood 1997, 20–21).

As settlement moved westward, government officials signed treaties with the Indians, pledging time after time not to move beyond a certain boundary. For instance, in 1829 President Andrew Jackson decided the best solution was to move most Indians west of the Mississippi, where he promised them that whites will make "no claim to the land, and you can live upon it, you and all your children, so long as the grass grows or the water runs, in peace and plenty" (Bailyn, Davis, Donald, Thomas, Wiebe, and Wood 1977, 441).

Within a few years settlers were pouring across the Mississippi into the western lands, and by 1890 nearly all Indians had to leave the open range and were forced to settle on reservations. Once a tribal group ended up on a reservation, its lifestyle options sharply declined. At that point, regardless of tribal tradition, Native Americans had to engage in farming, often with poor soil, limited water, and great distances from possible markets (Nichols 2003, 146). Sometimes reservation-bound Indians were relocated to provide land for end-of-the-century whites moving into the locale (Nichols 2003, 148).

Indian leaders told government officials that placement on reservations would devastate their people. In 1867 during treaty negotiations, a Kiowa chief bluntly stated,

"I don't want to settle there. [W]hen we settle down we grow pale and die." Three years later the renowned Lakota Sioux warrior Red Cloud described his reservation as "nothing but an island. When we first had this land we were strong. Now we are melting like snow on the hillside" (Nichols 2003, 149).

Whether on or off reservations, Native Americans suffered significant losses over time. In 1500 the American Indian population was between two and 18 million, declining to only 250,000 in 1900 (Oswalt and Neely 1999, 7; Page 2003, 105). The numbers for land loss have been nearly as drastic. In 1887 American Indians, who once controlled the entire continent's land, possessed about 154 thousand acres, approximately the equivalent of the state of Texas. A half-century later the total was scarcely a third—about the acreage of Mississippi (Indian Land Tenure Foundation 2009; Page 2003, 330). Native Americans have also suffered physically. Compared to the overall population, modern American Indians are four times more likely to die of tuberculosis, six times more often succumb to alcoholism, and nearly twice as often die by homicide (Page 2003, 394).

While Native Americans were severely oppressed, they were seldom enslaved. One reason was that the use of captive workers normally took place in the Indians' own locale, and escape was fairly simple. In addition, the white inhabitants often wanted to engage in trade with indigenous people, and it hardly enhanced their commercial reputation to enslave some of their trading partners' tribal peers (Wood 1997, 75). Africans' enslavement was a distinctly different proposition.

For the first 40 years of British settlement, indentured servitude was more common than slavery. Eventually, however, several factors suggested that slavery was more efficient. First, since slaves were owned, they could be forced to accept whatever living and working conditions would be most advantageous to their owners. Indentured servants, in contrast, could become troublesome, sometimes even suing their masters for contract violations. Second, even though plantation owners could recruit a certain number of servants, there never were enough to work on the steadily growing number of tobacco, rice, indigo, and later cotton plantations. Third, and probably most significant, keeping slaves was distinctly cheaper than hiring indentured servants (Franklin and Moss 1988, 32). So what became known as "the peculiar institution," meaning an arrangement distinctive to the South, thrived in that region and represented the most repressive type of racial formation.

The proponents of slavery shared racist beliefs that rationalized the practice. Besides the overall sense of English cultural superiority already cited, images of Africans as inferior, potentially exploitable beings became prevalent over time. In the seventeenth and eighteenth centuries as English explorers entered Africa, they considered the inhabitants' blackness both fascinating and repellant. For the English, blackness had long epitomized sinfulness and evil, and so they readily attributed these traits to dark-skinned Africans. Furthermore these explorers found African cultural standards strange and alien—their allegedly superstitious, magical beliefs and practices along with a stubborn refusal to embrace Christianity; marriage and family arrangements that seemed savage and inferior to English practices; and inhabitants' brazen tendency to wear little clothing, particularly women's baring their breasts. While struck with what they considered Africans' uncivilized qualities, explorers also observed them doing agricultural work and concluded that most of them would make hard-working, capable field laborers (Camp 2006, 91; Wood 1997, 23–24). The English explorers were particularly impressed with African women's strength, concluding that they gave birth "without payne" and that these women were "of a cruder nature and stronger posture than the Females in our Lands in Europe" (Camp 2006, 91). Stereotypes about blacks were developing.

From early contacts with Africans, the English started creating stereotypes about Africans. A **stereotype** is a set of largely negative traits that prejudiced people apply to all members of the group against whom they are prejudiced. The concept involves images, images that can trigger such powerful emotions as fear, anger, resentment, or contempt toward a group or an individual and that are much more powerful and explosive than many holders of stereotypes appreciate. Several references to the impacts of stereotypes appear later in the chapter. Once slavery was underway, stereotypes about slaves abounded, claiming blacks were primitive, simpleminded, lazy, violent, and oversexed.

Slavery was always most widely practiced in the South, which, unlike the New England and Middle Atlantic states, had large plots of agricultural crops that could effectively use the primarily unskilled labor of a large slave population; by the early nineteenth century, the northern states had outlawed slavery. Until the end of the War of 1812, in fact, the growth of slavery was relatively slow, even in the South. Then, with the virtual elimination of war in the Western world, unlimited trade with Europe became possible, and soon a great demand for cotton developed. Massive cotton production depended on large numbers of unskilled laborers, and with the growing demand, slavery expanded. In 1790 there were fewer than 700,000 slaves; by 1830 the number had reached 2 million; at the last census before the Civil War, the slave population had nearly doubled to 3,953,760 (Franklin and Moss 2000, 139).

Southern whites often justified slavery by contending that blacks were inferior, representing an irreversible deterioration from the original white race. Whites being dominant and blacks being subservient, they argued, were inevitable outcomes of the alleged racial differences (Fredrickson 2002, 79–80). During this period of slavery, intellectuals argued that not only were blacks inferior, fated to be a subservient class, but that such an arrangement assured a productive, stable society. In his *Sociology for the South* (1854) and *Cannibals All!* (1857), social theorist George Fitzhugh asserted that the abolition of slavery would produce a chaotic society in which merciless employers would brutally exploit black workers. Slavery, Fitzhugh claimed, was a relatively benign system that protected blacks (Bailyn, Davis, Donald, Thomas, Wiebe, and Wood 1977, 581).

To regulate slavery, each state using the practice developed **slave codes**, a body of laws covering all major issues in slaves' lives. While the slaves codes differed from state to state, the dominant theme was that slaves were property, not people—that the laws were supposed to protect ownership of that property and to ensure that slaves remained in highly controlled conditions that would promote a maximum level of production (Franklin and Moss 2000, 140–41).

After the Civil War, most ex-slaves found little reason to celebrate their recent freedom. The war had devastated the land, with many blacks and even some whites suffering from disease and starvation. Whites in the ex-slave states, determined to retain as much power as possible over blacks, passed the infamous black codes, which locked African Americans into a racial formation that offered scarcely more rights and opportunities than slavery.

Then, for a moment, it appeared there would be a miraculous change. Historian Lerone Bennett, Jr., concluded, "Never before had the sun shone so bright" (Bennett 1982, 214). Congress passed the Reconstruction Act of 1867, requiring all southern states to convene racially mixed constitutional conventions, eliminating race as a criterion for determining a person's right to possess and inherit property and extending the vote to all black males. In the next few years, blacks were elected to a variety of high-level political positions and appointed to numerous other posts (Edwards 1996; Franklin and Moss 2000, 266–69).

But it was no more than a quick burst of sunshine. Faced with white southerners' continuous resistance, northern congressmen gradually withdrew from the difficult struggle for blacks' rights, and in 1877 federal troops meant to ensure the implementation of Reconstruction-era laws were removed from the South (Smith 1997). The message was clear: No lasting economic, political, or social reforms would take place—in particular, no guaranteed 40 acres of land (as one congressman had advocated) that would have provided black families a solid foundation on which to build their economic future. If southern blacks had received that land, it seems nearly certain that they and their descendants would have had chances to establish themselves securely in the nineteenth-century economy instead of suffering poverty, isolation, and physical threat. In fact, a study of 20 successful African Americans, including Oprah Winfrey and the former track star Jackie Joyner-Kersee, supported this conclusion, indicating that three quarters of these individuals descended from families that owned property by 1920—a date when scarcely one quarter of black families were property owners (Gates 2010, 329).

That was the heart of the **Jim Crow era**—a period of time ranging from Reconstruction to the 1960s during which laws and customs mandated a caste-like separation of blacks and whites, featuring blacks' subordination and oppression. The common rule was a **separate-but-equal standard**—a legal doctrine legitimating segregated services and facilities for blacks and whites. The separate-but-equal standard received a huge boost when in 1896 seven of the eight members of the Supreme Court in the famous *Plessy v. Ferguson* case ruled that the state of Louisiana had the right to designate separate railroad cars for blacks and to compel them to sit there. Three years later the doctrine was applied to public schools (Elliott 2006; Fireside 1997). Subsequently the doctrine was accurate in one regard: Separation of the races prevailed. Equality was another story. For instance, in 1929 southern school districts averaged over two-and-a-half times as much funding for white children as for their black age peers (Southern Education Foundation 2002).

During both slavery and its aftermath, stereotypes of blacks served the majority group, sometimes altering over time to correspond with whites' changing motivations. The "Sambo," an image which dominated during slavery, represented blacks as contented, even happy, thus justifying the system's persistence. In the course of slavery, however, a new stereotype of blacks developed—the "coon," who was not contented and was lazy, slow, and unreliable. "The coon was a Sambo gone bad" (Pilgrim 2000), sociologist David Pilgrim suggested. By 1900 white racists identified older, more docile blacks, who accepted the Jim Crow standards, as Sambos and younger, particularly urban blacks, who disrespected whites and needed to be controlled and disciplined, as coons (Bogle 2004; Pilgrim 2000).

Violence was common during the Jim Crow era, striking with full force at the turn of the century, primarily in the South. Two broad sentiments seemed to lie behind the beatings, shootings, and lynchings—the desire to drive blacks out of political activity initiated during Reconstruction and into terrorized submission; and an effort to alleviate a widespread sense of social crisis generated by economic depression, with blacks serving as scapegoats for frustrated, stereotype-prone whites. A study of lynchings occurring in Georgia between 1890 and 1900 found that counties demonstrating intense economic competition between blacks and whites had a greater number of lynchings than counties where that competition was less intense.

Between 1889 and 1899, lynching was most prevalent, with on average one victim murdered every other day. In the nearly 40-year span from 1889 to 1936, almost 4,000 black men, women, and children were lynched. Some were simply hung, but many were extensively tortured. While still alive, victims were sometimes roasted slowly over fires or had limbs or sexual organs amputated. Castration occurred in hundreds of lynchings, with the impulse to castrate black males popularized in literature and folklore. After death, pieces of the victim were routinely distributed to onlookers who wanted souvenirs of the grisly event. For many of the perpetrators, these killings were simultaneously an effort to intimidate and subdue blacks and a celebration of white supremacy (Aronson 2007, 168–69; Marable 1994, 71; Shapiro 1988, 30–31; Soule 1992).

Until World War I, most blacks lived in the South, but then several conditions encouraged them to join what became known as the Great Migration. Floods, the impact of the cotton-destroying boll weevil, and low cotton prices forced many southern planters to shift from growing cotton to producing food crops and livestock, which required fewer workers. So many blacks lost jobs or received sharp wage cuts. Simultaneously the outbreak of World War I both increased the need for more factory workers to produce war supplies in the North and largely cut off the flow of Europeans who had previously filled these positions. Finally "Northern fever" became prevalent, with gossip, letters, and articles in black newspapers spreading the word about better wages and working conditions in the industrial belt. By 1930 about 1.3 million African Americans born in the South had left that area, primarily moving to northeastern and midwestern cities (Franklin and Moss 1988, 251–52, 305–06; Reich 2007, 152; Massey and Denton 1993, 29; Tolnay and Beck 1992; Ziegler 2007, 71).

In the 1890s the typical African American resident of a northern city lived in an area that was 90 percent white. When large numbers of southern black workers started to arrive, whites' views toward African Americans quickly hardened. Between 1900 and 1920, local whites often ransacked or burned blacks' homes located outside recognized "black" neighborhoods, compelling them to move to areas designated for African Americans.

By the late 1920s, urban whites had replaced violence with a nonviolent, legal technique—the **racially restrictive covenant**, which was a contract among property owners prohibiting specified minorities from buying, leasing, or occupying property in their locale (Massey and Denton 1993, 29–31; Schaefer 1993, 196). For racist whites this novel racial project worked well. One enthusiastic judge, who was a member of the Chicago Real Estate Board, declared that these covenants were "like a marvelous delicately woven chain armor . . . [excluding] any members of a race not Caucasian" (Jones-Correa 2001, 559).

The outcome was **de facto segregation**, which is the separation of racial groups resulting from common practice and involving such issues as residential patterns or school enrollment. These two conditions are often related. The schools black children attend are usually based on their place of residence which can be impacted by racially restrictive covenants and other segregation strategies. In Chicago the percentage of children attending primarily (90 percent or more) black schools rose sharply from a modest 8 percent in 1915 to a formidable 84 percent in 1930 (Neckerman 2007, 84). By 1940 northeastern and midwestern cities had established segregated urban housing patterns that marked the perimeters of the modern black ghettoes (Massey and Denton 1993, 31).

Historically African Americans and Native Americans were the two most prominent victims of racism. European, Asian, and Hispanic immigrants, however, also suffered discriminatory treatment.

Who's White and Who's Not

The Naturalization Act of 1790 set the early racial tone for the nation, declaring that only the "free white person" could obtain the rights and privileges of US citizenship (Rees 2007, 56). There was, however, considerable ambiguity about who was white. Among early immigrants Germans were the principal group that could claim a broadly shared biological heritage with the British, allowing them to escape a racially inferior designation (Rees 2007, 47).

In the 1830s the alleged scientific study of race—the measurement of facial features and head size—received extensive attention in popular newspapers and magazines, suggesting a connection between a group's physical features and its mental and moral traits. Anglo Saxons, individuals of English and Scottish descent, were the decided winners of these supposedly objective evaluations, and all others were believed to be outside the inner circle of whiteness.

Yet as the case of the Irish demonstrates, racial placement could be highly unstable. In 1860 cutting-edge "scientific" assessments concluded that the Irish did not qualify as white, but several decades later the Democratic Party's need to enlist immigrant voters prompted its leaders to support Irish claims to whiteness. Furthermore by the 1870s about 60 percent of Irish job holders were making a steady income, establishing themselves as reputable working-class members and helping to bolster their claims of whiteness (Kenny 2000, 129; Rees 2007, 48–49). The Chinese were not so fortunate. To quell the violence against Chinese miners and other laborers and to protect whites' jobs, Congress passed the Chinese Exclusion Act of 1882, abruptly halting the influx of immigrant workers (Chin 2003; Gyory 1999).

Social Darwinism prevailed at this time. **Social Darwinism** was a doctrine emphasizing that the most inherently capable groups will rise to the top of economic, political, and social hierarchies, ensuring the most productive arrangement for the distribution of wealth and power for society at large (Bender 2008; Hofstadter 2006; Tontonoz 2008). In the 1880s immigrants from southern and eastern Europeans found themselves classified as "in-between" people—above Africans and Asians but below the resident "whites" (Rees 2007, 50). Educators, business people, and politicians from the established white groups organized to confront what they considered an invasion of alien people.

The mobilization featured the **eugenics movement**, which was an initiative founded by prominent intellectuals who claimed that scientists could lead an organized effort to ensure "the purification of the Anglo-Saxon race." Well-known physical and biological scientists, sociologists, and psychologists along with an array of wealthy and powerful economic and political leaders supported this influential racial project. Academic leaders made highly supportive statements. For instance, William Ripley, a Harvard economist, claimed that the new wave of immigrants was "a menace to our Anglo-Saxon civilization," with cities now reduced to reproducing "a swarthy and black-eyed primitive-type" population (Muller 1993, 39–40).

In his famous *The Passing of the Great Race* (1916), Madison Grant borrowed some of Ripley's allegedly scientific terminology to divide Europeans into three races, with the supposedly tall, blond Nordics representing "the great race" or "the master race," superior to the other two categories in their intelligence and contribution to civilization. Without prompt action, Grant warned the Anglo Saxon public, the inferior hoards would swamp the nation and quickly destroy its racial purity (Rees 2007, 53–54). Strong support existed for restrictive legislation.

Congress passed the National Origins Act of 1924, requiring that a quota based on national origin be established, and with minor variations that standard persisted until 1965. The so-called Johnson-Reed Act declared that the size of any nationality's annual quota of immigrants could be 2 percent of that group's American population based on 1890 census figures. Asians, described as "nonwhite" by the Naturalization Act of 1790, were simply barred admittance. The use of the 1890 population profile was the legislation's master stroke. At that date the flood of immigrants from southern and eastern Europe had barely started, and so with the passage of the 1924 law the number of potential new arrivals representing those nationalities shrunk drastically. For Italy and Russia together, average annual immigration for the first two decades of the twentieth century was 270,000, slipping to 6,000 with restrictive legislation. Greeks faced an even more drastic reduction, going from 17,000 annually in the century's opening two decades to a legislated quota of 100 (Muller 1993, 43–47). Congressional members felt that they had saved the country from invading hoards of racially inferior people. Senator David Reed, who composed the law, declared, "The American people want us to discriminate" (Aronson 2007, 200).

The impact of this racial project reverberated throughout society. In F. Scott Fitzgerald's *This Side of Paradise* (originally published in 1920), Amory Blaine, the upper-class hero, was taking a train from Washington to Princeton, New Jersey. World War I had broken out, and the soldiers in the sleeping berths across from Blaine "were . . . stinking aliens—Greeks, he guessed, or Russians." Life was simpler and more pleasant, he thought, when soldiers in earlier wars shared a common background. That night he stayed awake "listen[ing] to the aliens guffaw and snore as they filled the car with the latest scent of America" (Fitzgerald 2000, 132). Clearly Blaine would have been an ardent supporter of restrictive legislation.

While the Johnson-Reed Act drew distinctions among European immigrants, it did acknowledge that all of them were white and that it was at least possible for them to become citizens. For 40 years the so-called "nonwhite" groups had few such privileges (Rees 2007, 56–57).

The Immigration Act of 1965 discarded the 1890 census standard for determining a country's yearly quota and replaced it with an annual maximum of 20,000 immigrants per country. Preferential applications came from family members, professionals, and skilled workers. Within a few years, most congressional members were surprised, even shocked to discover that the priority given to family members greatly expanded Asian immigration to about 2.7 million a year in the 1980s. Currently after priority for family members and preferred occupations, immigrants enter on a first-come, first-serve basis, with the annual maximum per country now raised to about 28,000 individuals (Fernandez 2000, 18–21).

Has racism in the US also altered over time?

Modern Racial Isolation and Oppression

Open, defiant racism is less common today, and yet many modern policies incorporate racist oppression, with urban-renewal projects in numerous cities serving as cases in point. During the 1950s and 1960s, various large businesses as well as universities, hospitals, libraries, and foundations lobbied the federal government to help clean up their cities by reorganizing the poor, rundown areas in which large numbers of minorities, primarily blacks, resided. Relief came with two housing acts that provided local political leaders funds to purchase slum properties, clear "blighted" areas of residents and buildings, and then "redevelop" districts for business, high-priced apartments, hospital extensions, university buildings, and other facilities that the urban elite valued. Psychologist William Ryan commented on the program's intent, suggesting without using the terminology that each initiative featured a relentless racial project, which had nothing to do with politicians' public claims about providing the poor quality housing. Instead the aim was simply "to get rid of a slum neighborhood (and the 'undesirables' who lived there) to make room for 'higher uses'" (Ryan 1976, 185).

The individuals choosing the location for public housing have picked low-value pockets of land located next to or within recognized ghettoes. Because of budgetary restrictions, the amount of housing built has never been enough to make up for what has been torn down, and residents normally find themselves living in areas that are as rundown and dangerous as those in which they previously resided. In addition, local political leaders usually authorize drab, poorly constructed, multi-unit, often high-rise projects, where most tenants feel little if any pride in their apartments and the surroundings and limited incentive to maintain them in good condition (Essoka 2010; Ryan 1976, 182–88).

In both cities and suburbs, racially segregated housing persists. Data using the index of dissimilarity make this clear. The **index of dissimilarity** indicates the percentage of a particular racial group that would need to change residential location in order to achieve racial evenness—to disperse its membership throughout the city so that census tracts average that group's percentage of inhabitants in the city (Massey and Denton 1993, 20). Consider, for instance, a city where a certain group is 20 percent of the overall population, but that group represents 60 percent of the population in the census tracts where its members are living. In this case the group has an index of dissimilarity of 40, meaning that 40 percent of its members would need to move into other census tracts to establish racial evenness throughout the city. High indices of dissimilarity illustrate high levels of housing segregation.

Census data comparing 1990 to 2000 dissimilarity indices for the three largest minority groups living in American cities and suburbs provide the following figures:

- Asian/Pacific Islanders: 41.2 percent to 41.4 percent
- Hispanics: 49.7 percent to 51 percent
- African Americans: 67.8 percent to 64.3 percent
  (Center for Regional Policy Studies 2001)

For Asian/Pacific Islanders and Hispanics, the indices have risen slightly while for African Americans, whose index has always been higher, a small decline has occurred.

Sociologists Douglas Massey and Nancy Denton noted that compared to Asian and Hispanic Americans, African Americans' indices of dissimilarity do not reduce significantly as their income rises. They wrote, "The residential segregation of African Americans cannot be attributed in any meaningful way to the socioeconomic disadvantages they experience, however serious those may be" (Massey and Denton 1993, 88).

Overall, however, some improvements are occurring. Local fair-housing organizations have conducted so-called "tester" studies, where 4,600 "tests" in 20 major cities matched realtors' reactions to white couples and similarly credentialed black or Hispanic couples working for the research team. Compared to a decade earlier, the surveys completed in 2000 indicated that for black renters and homebuyers and for Hispanic homebuyers discriminatory treatment declined. For Hispanic renters, however, information about the availability of housing remained a serious problem, with testers less likely to hear about advertised units or to be allowed to inspect them than their Hispanic counterparts a decade earlier. While African Americans generally encountered more receptive realtors, they also experienced a sharp increase in **steering**, a realtor's effort to dissuade minority clients from seeing residences in all-white or largely all-white areas, instead seeking to interest them in homes in what are wholly or primarily minority areas (Ross and Turner 2005).

People's residential location affects their health, safety, access to social capital, and the quality of their schools. As we have noted in previous chapters, wealthier districts generally have higher-quality schooling and a high proportion of white students. Average white children often live in fairly affluent districts and attend well-funded, educationally effective schools where about 80 percent of the students are white, and most of the remaining are either Asian or Hispanic. In contrast, blacks and Hispanics often reside in less affluent districts and attend lower-quality schools where the minority population is high (Aronson 2007, 258–59).

Schooling illustrates a widespread trend in modern America—that chances for valuable resources are **racialized**—meaning that people's racial classification significantly affects their access to valued economic, political, and social resources. Because of the American system of educational funding discussed in Chapter 8, poor children, a disproportionate number of whom are black and Hispanic, receive less effective, racialized schooling, and that disadvantage handicaps them significantly in the job world. A study of jobless men within 331 American metropolitan areas revealed another destructive racialized effect—that unemployed black men, many of whom lived in highly segregated poor districts, were considerably more isolated from employed men than jobless men in the other three major racial groups. As a result these unemployed black men had much less chance to build social capital that might lead to jobs than their counterparts in other racial group, and, in addition, they were more exposed to the persistently negative effects of joblessness (Wagmiller 2005).

In modern life racism can appear in its individual form, but as the situation involving poor blacks' inferior schooling indicates, minorities' racialized life chances are more likely to unfold in an institutionally racist setting.

THE VARIED IMPACT OF RACE ON FAMILIES

Whites often find themselves living quite isolated from minorities. In a study of 200 families from Boston, St. Louis, and Los Angeles with diverse class and racial backgrounds and at least one school-aged child, many of the white respondents indicated that they chose their residential location carefully. Laurie, a parent, indicated that she and her husband bought a house in an area where the schools were good and the problems of the inner city were far away. Laurie explained that if the family of her husband's black colleague who shared a similar background and aspirations moved next door, she would be comfortable having her children spend time with them. However, Laurie was frightened of inner-city families with "parents who are on crack and who don't care about [their children] and don't feed them and have drugs and guns lying around . . . to bring to school." She admitted to being "a racist deep down inside" (Johnson and Shapiro 2003, 175).

The researchers concluded that Laurie's race-related preferences for housing location and schooling are typical for middle-class whites (Johnson and Shapiro 2003, 175). If Laurie was unusual, it was in the way she spoke candidly about her perceptions. The nature of white privilege is that the majority of white people are able to live out their daily routine without addressing the impact of race, without assessing the advantages their majority status bestows upon them. An operative concept is **color-blind racism**— whites' assertion that they are living in a world where racial privilege no longer exists, but their behavior supports racialized structures and practices. The color-blind racist endorses what is often a widely shared racial project, contending that ours is an open society, which offers opportunity and success to all groups, and that more than a cursory concern with race-related issues and, in particular, with limitations or restrictions particular groups face is neither necessary nor appropriate. Two studies on color-blind racism indicated that nearly 90 percent of respondents resided in neighborhoods with few black or minority residents. Residential segregation, in short, appears to promote this outlook (Bonilla-Silva 2001, 140–41; Bonilla-Silva 2010, 105–15, 211; Bonilla-Silva, Goar, and Embrick 2006, 37).

Whites seldom discuss racial issues in depth with their children, and yet using cues that are "indirect, unintentional, and invisible" (Rockquemore and Laszloffy 2005, 61), these parents convey to their offspring how to perceive the racialized world and how to treat the members of other racial groups. While such parents would make the same choices for the same reasons that Laurie did, they would probably be less forthcoming, asserting that race had nothing to do with their decision.

In contrast to whites, minority parents are often convinced they have no option but to engage in racial socialization. They recognize that it can be a daunting task for minority-group individuals to develop and maintain a healthy identity in American society (Constantine and Blackmon 2002; Miller and McIntosh 1999; Stevenson, Reed, Bodison, and Bishop 1997). Therefore minority parents are likely to conclude that the cultural capital they provide their children on this topic is critical. A study of 141 black college students indicated that those respondents who grew up receiving racial socialization messages about pride in their African heritage and about the harsh realities of racism tended to be better adjusted academically, showing more satisfaction with their courses and a clearer sense of purpose in college (Anglin and Wade 2007).

An investigation involving 247 black college freshmen also addressed the issue of racial pride, finding that parents' communications about this issue were more effective in reducing race-related stress than familial messages emphasizing the importance of such race-related resources as extended kin or religious/spiritual support (Bynum, Burton, and Best 2007).

Additional research involving 20 successful black college students and their parents found that racial socialization played a significant part in mapping out the road to effective adjustment in school, with parents' contribution in the forefront of this racial project supporting young African Americans' development. One student observed, "My parents taught me to know that, because I was black and female, I would face obstacles but could still excel academically" (Herndon and Hirt 2004, 501).

Parents' impact on their children's outlook on race often appears to be more important than other factors. Research involving college-aged Chinese Americans and Filipino Americans suggested that discussions with parents influenced their children's perception of racism more than such factors as the number of ethnic-study courses or the racial composition of one's closest peers (Alvarez, Juang, and Liang 2006).

Sometimes parents' influence regarding racial issues is significant even though the amount of time spent together is modest. In an autobiographical account, Willi Coleman explained how her very busy mother provided quality time imparting a black woman's perspective on survival in a racist setting. While she spent her work days cleaning white women's homes, she reserved Saturday evenings for doing her girls' hair and sharing candid accounts of experiences that would have embarrassed her to discuss at other times—about "how she had triumphed over 'folks that were lower than dirt' and 'no-good snakes in the grass.' She combed, patted, twisted and talked" (Collins 1999, 210).

Two of the previous sources involve socialization that considers the impact of both race and gender. Unquestionably intersectionality, which involves the combined impact of at least two minority statuses, is relevant to the discussion of racism, but the many topics that need to be covered in this chapter make it preferable to postpone its lengthy discussion until Chapter 10. Interracial families also must deal with combined impact—in this instance of two or more races.

Parents of children with mixed racial heritage tend to have options in shaping their children's racial identity. For instance, in black/white interracial families, children might identify as black, white, biracial, or belonging to no specific race. This situation requires parents to be aligned with each other, making certain that they send children consistent messages about their racial membership.

Using several sources of information involving national data, researchers revealed the following trends about parents' impact on their interracial children's racial identification in black-white marriages:

- That the racial breakdown of the residential community parents chose impacted on their children's sense of identity. If blacks lived close by, it communicated the idea that they were valued and should serve as a source of identification while their absence conveyed an opposing message.
- That since 2000 when the census provided the option of "interracial" as an individual's racial classification, the majority of married black-white parents chose that option for their children.
- That the greater spouses' level of education in black-white marriages, the higher the probability that they picked the "interracial" identity for their children. It appeared that the more educated parents were willing to look beyond the traditionally restrictive categories of "white" and "black" and to embrace a more complex, less definite classification (Rockquemore, Laszloffy, and Noveske 2006, 212; Roth 2005).

Some black-white parents who are highly sensitive to the racist nature of modern society are likely to impress their children with the prospect that most people will simply see them as black. Singer Lenny Kravitz said that many interracial children he met growing up wanted to be white—that it is too hard to be black. Kravitz explained that he never had such a wish—that his mother taught him that "if you're mixed, accept the advantage of two cultures, but understand you are black . . . [I]f you have a spot of black, you are black. So get over it" (Rockquemore, Laszloffy, and Noveske 2006, 214).

Do self-identified interracial adolescents display different patterns from their monoracial age peers? A representative sample of American students in grades seven through twelve indicated that the interracial respondents were more likely to be depressed, to feel alienated in school and to skip classes, and to use tobacco or alcohol but that they were also more inclined to be socially active, discussing problems with friends, getting along with peers, and belonging to various in-school organizations and teams. The researchers speculated that compared to their monoracial peers the interracial individuals grew up in a very different social world, experiencing multiple self-images that produced stress but also supplied diverse perspectives for developing social interactions and skills (Cheng and Lively 2009).

Race also produces a significant impact on the following activites.

THE INFLUENCE OF RACE ON PEER AND FRIENDSHIP PATTERNS

In modern American society, where color-blind racism is prominent, whites often make inflated claims of friendships with blacks in order to demonstrate that they are free of racism. For instance, in a study of college students, close to 50 percent claimed to have good or even best friends who were black, but scrutiny of the claims revealed that no more than 3 percent actually had black friends (Bonilla-Silva, Goar, and Embrick 2006).

Research on middle-class blacks growing up in predominantly white areas indicates that color-blind racism has an impact. Janice, who had only two other African Americans in her school, indicated that she experienced social isolation, making some friends at school but finding it impossible to extend the relationships outside of it. In adolescence Janice's white girl friends never introduced her to their brothers or male friends, and nobody ever asked her out. Janice commented on the high-school scene where race was not discussed and color-blind racism prevailed. She said, "I didn't really see my blackness in high school at all. I mean I was aware of how I was treated differently . . . [but I would say] 'we don't see color here. Everyone is friends and they treat me the same'" (Tatum 2004, 122).

Although Karen had more white friends than Janice, she always felt somewhat set apart by them. She was offended when these friends declared in a seemingly complimentary manner that she was "not really black." Karen observed, "Obviously they think that everyone who's black is either carrying a gun or talking in some sort of slang" (Tatum 2004, 123). Other stances her friends took also seemed bothersome. Karen explained that her white friends told her that since colleges prized minorities, she would easily gain acceptance. Karen retorted that just like them she has been "going to school. . . , [not] sitting in my room everyday going 'Oh, when it's time to apply to college, it's not going to matter anyway.' . . . I was very pissed off" (Tatum 2004, 123–24).

A variety of early studies involving elementary-school students demonstrated that majority-group children displayed an in-group bias, preferring friends from their own group. In contrast, minority groups often had no distinct preference or preferred peers from the majority group (Robinson 1998, 79).

Later research, however, found that racial distributions within schools seemed to affect peer groups' racial memberships. When African American and Hispanic American students found themselves in racially diversified school settings where their respective racial groups were quite large, they were as inclined as whites to concentrate on same-race peers. Their peer choices only became more racially inclusive in school settings where their own racial groups were small (Neal 2008).

National survey data involving Asian American and Hispanic American adolescents found that such ethnic groups as Chinese Americans, Vietnamese Americans, Puerto Ricans, and Mexican Americans preferred peers from their own groups. In line with the pattern previously cited, the willingness to engage in interracial and interethnic peer relations increased in settings featuring few members of their own group (Kao and Joyner 2006).

Are there any other conditions influencing the race factor in children's friendships? Research using the National Longitudinal Study of Adolescent Health provided some clues. First, it appeared that residential segregation—the "bus stop effect" of frequent friendships with children generally living within a couple of hundred yards— explained about a third of racially segregated peer relations in school. Second, the key to an expansion in interracial friendships was the setting where students made contact. The racial diversity of the student body was less important than the presence of select circumstances encouraging interracial friendships—classroom and out-of-class settings promoting participants' equality and interdependent action (Moody 2001; Mouw and Entwisle 2006).

High-achieving students frequently illustrate the second situation. They can find themselves in schools where many or most of their racial peers are minimally motivated academically, and so they seek like-minded associates from other racial groups.

Under certain conditions adolescents of various racial groups can relate well, benefiting all participants.

A Mexican student in a study on three racial groups said that his friends were "mostly Asian students, because they are more [his] type . . . unlike . . . the guys that hang out by the gym . . . never go to class, have low grades and tend to be different." An Advanced Placement student, who had recently immigrated from Peru, said, "I don't associate with those other Latinos because . . . they belong to this gang or that gang and they don't even go to class. I mean, they bring their mess to our school, they bring their mess to our learning environment" (Conchas 2006, 67).

Besides academic performance social activities or skills can affect peer-group membership, sometimes encouraging cross-race affiliations. A study of 260 elementary-school students suggested that individuals belonging to the numerical majority, whether black or white, who possessed a friend belonging to the numerical minority, whether black or white, were (according to classmates' evaluations) better adjusted socially, were more popular, and had more positive behavioral characteristics than their counterparts who lacked a cross-racial friendship (Lease and Blake 2005). This finding is consistent with earlier research suggesting that majority-race individuals with minority-race friends are respected and well adjusted socially (Granovetter 1983). Possible reasons for this outcome include the likelihood that the superior assets the children with cross-race friendships possess are the precise qualities that make it possible for those children to develop these relationships. For instance, this category of students is likely to have well developed listening skills that might prove necessary for allowing them to move beyond stereotypes and to understand and appreciate racial groups' differences in outlook and behavior. In addition, sometimes cross-race friends might be a valuable commodity, allowing majority-race children to "buy" popularity that derives from association with individuals who have valued abilities or characteristics such as athletic or artistic skills (Lease and Blake 2005, 36).

In many instances, however, peers share a common racial heritage.

Minorities' Frequent Preference for Racially Homogenous Peers

In high school and college, serious students often associate with same-race peers who can help them in significant, concrete ways. In a small study of African American men at six universities, the researcher found that black peers engaged in racial projects, providing new students considerable help in adjusting to the university and reducing any sense of isolation. Arnold, a senior at Indiana University, described his participation in the Pharaoh's Club, a support group for African American males, especially first-year students with whom he shared classes and other experiences. He said, "I felt really connected to the guys in that group, so I really connected with the university from the start. Since then, I was like, 'Okay, this was a good experience'" (Harper 2006, 348).

Respondents in this investigation also indicated that their peers in primarily African American organizations helped them develop leadership skills. Paul, a student at Illinois University, indicated that fellow members in his group "motivated me with their world and their affirmations of the things I was doing . . . , and they thought more positively of me than I was thinking of myself" (Harper 2006, 349).

High-achieving students can also be engaged in providing mutual assistance for same-race peers. In the previously cited study of Mexican American, African American, and Vietnamese American high-school students, the researcher found that the Vietnamese group was the most committed to supporting its members' academic success. One Vietnamese student said, "[Vietnamese] believe in all this brotherhood thing where if one [Vietnamese] needs help . . . the whole group of [Vietnamese] comes out to help" (Conchas 2006, 107–08). While the Vietnamese American students often preferred to associate and work with members of their own group, the atmosphere could become competitive and tense.

Another factor can encourage racial-group members to be racially exclusive in their choice of peers. In *Why Are All the Black Kids Sitting Together in the Cafeteria?*, psychologist Beverly Tatum (2003) indicated that when minority children enter adolescence, new identity issues arise, with racial topics often in the forefront. The cute seven-year-old black child finds that at 15 nobody considers him cute—that sometimes white people cross the street to avoid him and that at the mall security guards often follow him. It is not just shared negative experiences that prompt racial minorities to hang out with same-sex peers. Whether the context is a cafeteria, a classroom, or out-of-school setting, activities often seem most comfortably shared with their own group's members. Even minorities who have previously lived in integrated settings often favor this adjustment.

Clearly race relations are a complicated entity, with interracial relations sometimes proving an asset and sometimes not. A study of nine, nonsexual relationships involving black and white women concluded that:

- These friendships invariably involved strains and tensions resulting from different backgrounds and the persistent impact of racism. Over time the friends were often tolerant but also vulnerable to outbursts of racially associated anger (McCullough 1998, 189). The majority of the respondents asserted that women belonging to the two races have had different life experiences producing contrasting, potentially incompatible styles—that black women are "assertive, confrontive, direct, honest, caring, quick tempered, blunt, open, impulsive, and loud" while white women are "reserved, shy, indirect, nit-picky, polite, always wanting reasons for things, and quiet" (McCullough 1998, 177). Some of these distinctions might derive from class backgrounds or represent oversimplifications, but most of the research subjects agreed about these race-related sets of traits.
- Women's cross-racial connections make them activists in examining and challenging traditional racist oppression. When asked why her relationship with Ruby was unique, Eartha said, "I think it makes me feel I am living out what I believe, that actions speak louder than words, that if I am really believing in equality, I had better prove it" (McCullough 1998, 188).

Peers are one of several factors influencing different racial groups' educational achievement.

RACE, SCHOOLING, AND ACADEMIC SUCCESS

In a study of a multiracial high school in northern California, Rocio, a Salvadoran student, concluded that each of the four major racial groups has a widely shared image that includes a perception of members' typical academic performance. He noted that "society says that [you] are Latino and lazy, that you are Asian, you are smart, if you are white, Oh God, the best, and if you are black, you are bad, horrific" (Conchas 2006, 64). It is a stark summary, representing many people's highly stereotyped views.

As Table 9.1 indicates, race plays an important role in influencing students' educational opportunities. Consider, for instance, the issue of tracking. While racial stereotyping

TABLE 9.1	Amount of Schooling Obtained by the Employed Members of the Four Major Racial Groups[1]			
	Asians	**Blacks**	**Hispanics**	**Whites**
No high-school diploma	999 (11%)	3,761 (17.1%)	9,643 (38.9%)	21,102 (13.2%)
High-school graduation	1,858 (20.3%)	7,884 (35.9%)	7,191 (29%)	50,340 (31.6%)
Some college, no degree	893 (9.8%)	4,160 (18.9%)	3,176 (12.8%)	26,927 (16.9%)
Associate's degree	609 (6.7%)	1,881 (8.6%)	1,489 (6%)	14,080 (8.8%)
Bachelor's degree and more	4,750 (52.1%)	4,268 (19.4%)	3,292 (13.3%)	46,815 (29.4%)

[1]All numbers represent thousands.

Source: Bureau of Labor Statistics. 2008. Table 3. "Employment Status of Persons 25 and Over by Educational Attainment, Sex, Race, and Hispanic or Latino Ethnicity, 2007 Annual Averages." *Labor Force Characteristics by Race and Ethnicity, 2007.* http://www.blsgov/cps/cpsrace2007.pdf.

appears to influence racial minorities' disproportionate appearance in low tracks, weak educational backgrounds also contribute. Once located in lower-level classrooms, children's learning opportunities are diminished (Burris and Welner 2007, 211). Across classes and racial groups, certain factors—what psychologists Clark McKown and Michael J. Strambler designated "direct effects"—strongly influence children's educational success, with race threading through the different issues.

Direct Effects

These factors concern families and quality of schooling.

THE FAMILIES   To begin, studies have found that income and income-linked resources such as tutoring services accounted for a substantial amount of racial groups' differences in standardized test scores (Hedges and Nowell 1999; Magnuson and Duncan 2006). Yearly income totals reveal that Asians and whites are much better positioned economically to support their children's schooling than Hispanics and blacks. The respective family median incomes figures are Asian American $77,133; white $64,427; Hispanic American $40,566; and black $40,143 (U.S. Census Bureau 2010).

Among minorities three aspects of parental behavior affect academic achievement (McKown and Strambler 2008, 372–76). First, the features of family relationships impact on children's educational advancement. For instance, research on African American children has revealed that in low-income neighborhoods more demanding, restrictive maternal childrearing appears to produce better schooling results while in more affluent settings, a more relaxed, lenient maternal style seems to promote academic success (Baldwin and Cole 1990; Gonzales, Cauce, and Mason 1996).

Second, racial socialization can be an important parental element. Investigation of African American children and college students has suggested that proactive parental socialization that both prepares children for the possibility of obstacles to their educational and occupational advancement and teaches them racial pride strongly associates with academic success (Mandara 2006; McKown and Strambler 2008, 374–75).

Third, there is parents' engagement with teachers and administrators, an issue discussed at length in all of the class chapters. As we have seen, more affluent, better educated parents have the knowledge and sense of entitlement (cultural capital) and the friends and acquaintances (social capital) to intervene more effectively on behalf of their children's schooling interests than their lower-status counterparts. While all four major racial groups are diversified in income and education, the general pattern is that Asian Americans and whites, who tend to be more affluent, are more effectively prepared for this engagement than Hispanic Americans and blacks.

Parents best equipped to champion their children's rights are more likely to be their active advocates while others tend to be less visible. Maria Teresa Palmer, an educational researcher, attended a high-school orientation for rising ninth graders, where an administrator told the students and parents that if a problem developed, they needed to seek help. Palmer wrote, "The parents in attendance were upper-middle class and established members of the community. No Latino families, no public housing parents, no Spanish translation." Furthermore unlike their less affluent counterparts, the parents at the orientation were hard-nosed, relentless promoters of their children's interests (Palmer 2007, 143–44).

Another factor influencing students' performance is the educational setting.

QUALITY OF SCHOOLING   Race links to school quality. Data from the National Center for Education Statistics indicated that in 2005 black and Hispanic students were more likely to attend high-poverty schools than Asians and whites. In addition, the majority of black and Hispanic children found themselves in classes where 75 percent or more of their fellow students were minority members (National Center for Education Statistics 2007a). Such oppressive, overburdened schools provide students few productive chances to meet peers, teachers, or administrators who can help promote their educational success.

Because of either the schools they attend or tracking within schools, Hispanic and African American students are more likely than their Asian American or white counterparts to have less experienced teachers, larger classes, less parental outreach, greater conflict with teachers, especially when they do not belong to students' racial group, and placement in lower-track classrooms (Entwisle, Alexander, and Olson 1997; Lee and Burkam 2002; Lucas and Berends 2002; Oakes 2005; Saft and Pianta 2001). The realities of tracking are devastating. A pair of educational researchers observed, "Whatever the reason for placing students of color in lower-tracked classes, the result is that these children are offered diminished learning opportunities" (Burris and Welner 2007, 211).

Low-tracked students are prominent candidates for school suspension. Throughout the country, especially in large urban districts, zero-tolerance practices provide immediate, often harsh punishments for violating certain rules in school; common practice involves suspensions for a variety of offenses ranging from violent behavior and truancy to dress-code violations. While no evidence indicates the use of zero tolerance has either increased school safety or improved overall student behavior, its practice has accelerated since the early 1990s. African Americans are much more likely to be suspended than whites. A study of over 9,000 middle schools indicated that black males (28 percent) were almost three times as frequently suspended at least once than their white counterparts (10 percent), and for girls the black percentage (18 percent) was more than four times the white figure (4 percent). In poor urban districts, the black suspension rates are often considerably higher. The report of these findings did not attempt to assess the extent to which racist treatment came into play in reaching the decision to suspend. Regardless of that determination, the racialized trend is troubling. Students missing school are distinctly disadvantaged. In addition, research has indicated that once in middle school the children most at risk for later incarceration were readily identifiable, having struggled consistently in school (Losen and Skiba 2010). African Americans, in short, can suffer a serious disadvantage which extends from childhood into their adult years.

Besides the direct effects linking race and schooling, minority students can encounter another negative influence of race that unfolds in school.

Impact of Stereotype Threat

A concept that addresses the potential influence of racism in schools is **stereotype threat**, which is the distinct risk that the members of a group widely believed to possess inferior abilities will fall victim to that diminished expectation (McKown and Strambler 2008, 381–82; Zirkel 2005, 110–11).

Studies demonstrate the impact of this process. When African Americans recorded their racial membership before taking a difficult test, they performed less well than when they were not asked to provide the racial information. It appears that the act of designating their race unleashed a stereotype threat. (Steele and Aronson 1995). In addition, a set of studies found that stereotype threat weakened performance when members of a group faced a test where teachers referred directly to tasks in which the group in question has been stereotyped as deficient—African Americans on intellectual issues, girls or women on mathematical ability, and white males considered inferior to Asian American boys or men on math skills. On the other hand, when teachers avoided references to groups' stereotypes, the scores rose significantly (Steele 1997; Zirkel 2002).

While stereotype threat is powerful, little children do not detect stereotypes and thus are largely immune. Research has shown that between six and ten, African American and Hispanic American children became aware of racial stereotypes about ability, and as a result their scores on tests presented to them as diagnosing certain stereotype-related skills tended to decline from the group averages while their test results not characterized beforehand as assessing stereotype-linked abilities generally remained stable. As they grew up, Asian Americans and whites gradually recognized the existence of these stereotypes, but they were usually not victims of stereotype threat and thus suffered no impact on their test scores (McKown and Weinstein 2003).

Teachers have a chance to either perpetuate or combat stereotype threat. Researcher Christine E. Sleeter suggested that to be successful new teachers from white, middle-class backgrounds need to be disposed to treat children of diverse backgrounds equitably. In many cases they write off blacks and Latinos, believing they are already too far behind, too disinterested, or too deficient in home support. The issue, Sleeter declared, was not job competence "but rather . . . one of understanding students through a cultural deficiency worldview that results in low expectations and teaching geared accordingly." Individuals with such an outlook, Sleeter asserted, should not be allowed to teach (Sleeter 2007, 176).

An effective antidote for stereotype threat involves relationships in which students of color and teachers are able to develop effective working ties, collectively envisioning positive educational or occupational opportunities in the future (Zirkel 2002).

Because of various disadvantages, racial minorities' academic performances tend to be less effective than whites'. As Figure 9.1 indicates, National Assessment of Educational Progress standardized tests in reading and math administered to large representative samples of both fourth and eighth graders revealed that on a 500-point scale blacks,

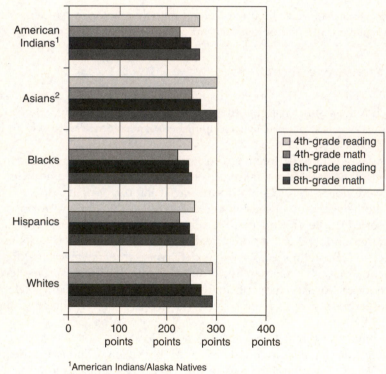

¹American Indians/Alaska Natives
²Asian/Pacific Islanders

FIGURE 9.1   Racial Groups' Results on National Assessment of Educational Progress Test

The data reveal a distinct pattern—that in all four national tests reported here Asian/Pacific islanders and whites scored higher than the other three groups. This result is sobering if not surprising, suggesting as information throughout the text supports that the two highest-scoring groups, which overall are more affluent, possess distinct advantages in financial, cultural, and human capital when it comes to taking standardized tests.

Sources: National Center for Education Statistics. 2007. Table 7. "Percentage of Fourth-Grade Public School Students and Average Scores in NAEP Reading, by Selected Student Groups and State: 2007." *The Nation's Reading Card: Reading 2007.* http://nces.ed.gov/nationsreportcard/pdf/main2007496.pdf; National Center for Education Statistics. 2009. Table A-12. "Average Scores and Achievement-Level Results in NAEP Mathematics for Fourth-Grade Public School Students, by Race/Ethnicity and State/Jurisdiction: 2009." *The Nation's Report Card: Mathematics 2009.* http://nces.ed.gov/nationsreportcard/pdf/main2009/2010451.pdf.

Hispanics, and Native Americans tended to score lower than Asian/Pacific islanders and whites (National Center for Education Statistics 2007b; National Center for Education Statistics 2009).

In addition, black and Hispanic students tend to score lower on SATs and other standardized tests that college officials often weigh heavily when evaluating candidates for admittance. Ardent proponents of testing claim that it is a serious error to admit students with low SAT scores. Yet some research suggests otherwise. In 1989 28 elite colleges and universities accepted a diverse student group in which minorities averaged between 100 and 300 points lower than whites. Yet after six years the graduation rates were fairly similar—namely, whites 86, Hispanics, 81, and blacks 75 percent. In contrast, six years after matriculation at 300 large, somewhat less prominent colleges and universities, the graduation rates were distinctly lower—59 percent for whites and 40 percent for blacks. The key difference in the two settings seems to have been the support and counseling the elite schools often provided (Brown, Carnoy, Currie, Duster, Oppenheimer, Shultz, and Wellman 2003, 115–16). High college graduation rates are very significant, meaning more students have earned a critical credential for success in the middle-class job world.

Just as stereotypes play a significant role in the education process, they are a prominent influence in the upcoming context.

COLLISION OF MASS MEDIA AND RACE

On the evening news when the 1960s inner-city riots were at their height, I saw a reporter standing in the middle of an Iowa corn field a hundred miles from the nearest city. "It's curious," he explained, "that out here where black people are almost nonexistent local residents who watch the nightly news are much more fearful of riots and rioters than city dwellers." More than four decades later, stereotypes remain powerful and pervasive, influencing individuals' self-images as well as their opportunities in such key domains as schooling and employment. This section examines the racist images and stereotypes media can project and also their destructive impact on people of color, especially children. The focus primarily involves television.

Racial Minorities' Participation

Analysis emphasizes two themes that are common within various mass-media forms, particularly TV and films: first, that some racial groups are significantly underrepresented or are represented negatively; and second, that TV programming or other media sources often highlight racial stereotypes (Deo, Lee, Chin, Milman, and Yuen 2008, 149).

On the first point, the media tend to underplay minorities in heroic or admirable roles, more readily representing them as victims or failures. During the media coverage of Hurricane Katrina and its aftermath, most reporting focused on white rescuers and black victims. The reality, however, was much less clear-cut, with a substantial number of black rescuers and white victims (Deo, Lee, Chin, Milman, and Yuen 2008, 149). The major racial groups vary considerably in their appearances on TV. Asian Americans, who represent about 5 percent of the population, are nearly invisible, comprising about 1.3 percent of the lead roles in film and TV. In prime-time TV, they provide about 2 percent of the characters (Deo, Lee, Chin, Milman, and Yuen 2008, 151). An analysis of 63 prime-time programs with 748 speaking characters found that 74 percent were white, 3 percent Hispanic, 18 percent African American, and the remaining 5 percent, including Asian

Americans, unspecified (Conners 2004, 209). In summary, whites and blacks are slightly overrepresented compared to their proportions of the population, and Hispanic and Asian Americans significantly underrepresented.

Sometimes minorities are overrepresented but portrayed unfavorably. A study of the introductory economics texts with pictures of poor people revealed that African Americans were overrepresented—serving as over 60 percent of the subjects while at that time blacks were only about 23 percent of the poor (Clawson 2002, 355).

On the second issue, mass media nurture popular stereotypes. Children of all races describe white characters on TV as affluent, well-educated, and competent in leadership. In contrast, those same groups identify television minority characters as lazy, goofy, law-breaking, and poor (Levin and Carlsson-Paige 2003, 430).

Media stereotypes vary for different racial groups. Asian American men in prime-time drama series often appear as sexually undesirable, nerdy, passive, unaggressive, and overachieving (Deo, Lee, Chin, Milman, and Yuen 2008, 154–55). In both prime-time TV and film, Asian American women tend to be presented as exotic and sexualized—either as deferential, giggling sex machines considered "China dolls" or "lotus blossoms," or manipulative, untrustworthy, and back-stabbing "dragons ladies" such as the character Ling Woo, a lawyer turned judge, who used sexual intrigue to manipulate men in the long-running TV series *Ally McBeal* (Fung 1994; Kang 2002, 77; Larson 2006, 70–71).

Stereotypes of Native Americans in film and TV represent either "good" or "bad" Indians. Those in the first category are powerless, cooperative, often spiritually pure individuals, who willingly, even happily adopt a subservient role. For instance, in the 1969 film *Tell Them Willi Boy Is Here*, a "good" Indian tried to teach whites the meaning of love. In contrast, "bad" Indians are either sadistic or degraded. In countless western films and TV programs, Indian men appeared as war-crazed, bloodthirsty, cruel warriors, who enjoyed torture and mutilation. A different stereotype of Indian men in films and TV presents them as unsuccessful, weak, unmotivated, and often chemically dependent (Bird 1999; Churchill 1998; Larson 2006, 47–50).

Like other racial minorities, Hispanics have been stereotyped in TV and film. A dominant image has pictured emotional, dishonest, treacherous, violent killers—"el bandido," a representation dating back to silent films. Such 1990s movies as *Carlito's Way*, *Mi Vida Loca*, and *The Mambo Kings* have presented consistently degraded characters. Another prominent stereotype involving Latinos is the "greaser" image, a term derived from the use of nineteenth-century Mexicans to grease wagon wheels and representing Hispanic individuals as lazy, immoral, untrustworthy, dirty, and stupid. A popular female image involves hot-tempered, aggressive, highly sexed sirens enslaved by their own passions (Doob 1999, 217; Larson 2006, 59–60)—creatures "who fume and fornicate without substance, and without much intelligence" (Rodriguez 1997, 181). In both old and recent films, these female characters have been punished for their sexual indiscretions, particularly if they violate segregation standards by liaisons with white men. Then they suffer, either dying themselves or forced to watch a lover's death (Larson 2006, 61).

Historically blacks have also had highly stereotyped images in the mass media. Since *Birth of a Nation* (1915), movies have presented a steady supply of oversexed, frenzied, violent black male characters. That film, which was the most celebrated, largest grossing of its era, featured a scene where a white woman fled a black man's advances. At the time

James Weldon Johnson, a black writer and activist, suggested that the startling stereotype the film unleashed would have a momentous effect. He wrote, "A big, degraded looking Negro . . . chas[es] a little golden-haired white girl for the purpose of outraging her; she, to escape him, goes to her death by hurling herself off a cliff." Johnson speculated that the impact of this scene was especially powerful among less informed whites who were avid moviegoers but never read books or attended plays (Johnson 2004, 613).

In both TV shows and films, black women are often represented as Jezebels—wicked, oversexed women, appearing frequently as prostitutes, tempters of men, or sexual victims (Larson 2006, 29–30).

Stereotyped images of African Americans have also flourished in some specific segments of the media such as sports coverage. For instance, a study of Division 1A football and basketball telecasts found that black players tended to be described as high-quality physical specimens with God-given athletic ability while whites were portrayed as hardworking, intellectually endowed competitors—in short, a racially stereotyped division endowing the body to blacks and the mind to whites (Rada and Wulfemeyer 2005)—a distinction where authority and control clearly lies with the more cerebral group to the detriment of the other.

A key element in blacks' media-enhanced stereotype is violence.

SPECTER OF BLACK VIOLENCE   When the first major urban riot of the 1960s occurred in Watts, the leading newspapers blamed African American rioters, describing them as "irrational, hysterical, and insane." The black press, however, focused elsewhere, pinning responsibility on "white indifference, police brutality, and racism" (Jacobs 2000, 80). In mainstream TV some version of the first position has often prevailed.

Many whites fear blacks, visualizing themselves as prospective victims. One way that the media contribute is by producing an exaggerated sense of African Americans' numbers. A study conducted when blacks were 12 percent of the population found that white subjects' average estimate was over two-and-a-half times greater—32 percent. When asked why she thought that the nation was 55 percent black and 45 percent white, Kelly explained, "It just seems . . . if I'm watching the news and there are crimes committed, [t]hey are usually by blacks and Hispanics" (Gallagher 2003, 385). Most likely the programming that contributed to Kelly's inflated sense of blacks' numbers was local news.

The majority of TV news viewers watch the local variety (Gilliam and Iyengar 2000, 560; Schaffner and Gadson 2004, 607), and that programming generally contains a predictable script: that crime is violent and the perpetrators are "nonwhites," namely blacks and Hispanics (Gilliam and Iyengar 2000).

Does local programming affect whites' perceptions? Experiments conducted with 390 whites in the greater Los Angeles area assigned their subjects to different groups. All the participants saw a 12-minute news clip about local crime, but these clips varied in whether or not they included a five-second black person's or white person's mug shot or the absence of a mug shot. The respondents exposed to a photo of a black suspect demonstrated two distinct outlooks. The subjects living in all-white or nearly all-white areas expressed more stereotypic evaluations of African Americans, more hostility toward them, and greater support for punitive policies toward them than other respondents. When whites living in more racially diversified areas were exposed to the photo of the black suspect, their responses were less stereotyped, hostile, and punitive (Gilliam, Valentine, and Beckman 2002). When interviewed about race, people like the respondents living in largely white areas are likely to express colorblind racism, but this study suggested that behind probable denials of racist feelings and perceptions, stereotyped, punitive outlooks lurk.

Besides thrusting racial stereotypes on the public, the mass media, particularly TV, have another destructive impact.

THE MEDIA INGREDIENTS IN A LETHAL COCKTAIL   The principal ingredients are residential location and TV exposure. About 80 percent of black children live in areas that are poor and vulnerable to local violence (Jipguep and Sanders-Phillips 2003, 380). They are also extensively exposed to TV violence, watching, according to one study, nearly twice as much television as white children (Ward 2004, 285).

Exposure to both community violence and media violence appear to reinforce certain distinct results—high levels of aggression, anxiety, alcohol use, and other destructive and self-destructive reactions (Kuther and Wallace 2003; Villani 2001). One team of researchers indicated that TV images of violence and risk-taking provide what some viewers are likely to consider a tantalizing prospect. It is "a world in which unhealthy behavior such as physical aggression, unprotected sex, and smoking and drinking are glamorous and risk free" (Jipguep and Sanders-Phillips 2003, 385).

While TV can be a potent negative force for minority children, positive exceptions exist. A study involving black high-school students demonstrated that when they identified with such reputable, successful characters as Darrell on *The Hughleys*, they had higher self-esteem than if they identified with a white individual such as Chandler on *Friends*. These students indicated that Darrell's positive role model represented a welcomed exception to the frequent stereotyped portrayal of their racial group (Ward 2004, 281).

All in all, media and race maintain an important but elusive relationship. In particular, stereotypes are like a virus that penetrates the media and seeps steadily into people's minds, creating self-doubting stereotype threat and a variety of other negative effects. Stereotypes also have a powerful impact in the job world.

WORK AND RACIAL INEQUALITY: CONTRIBUTING FACTORS

The upcoming subject examines two job-related issues—the distinctly disadvantaged conditions affecting certain racial minorities, particularly blacks and Hispanics; and analysis about the impact of discrimination and stereotyping in the work setting. Data from Figure 9.2 and Tables 9.2 and 9.3 are frequently relevant. While job discrimination persists, Table 9.2 indicates that in general racial minorities' income prospects have modestly improved over time. For many families, however, poverty remains a persistent reality.

Disadvantaged Context: Minority-Group Members' Unrelenting Battle against Poverty

In *Open Wounds: The Long View of Race in America*, historian William Evans indicated that "the imprint of slavery on the nation is still visible" (Evans 2009, 1). In other words social reproduction still unfolds along racial lines. The influence of race, Evans suggested,

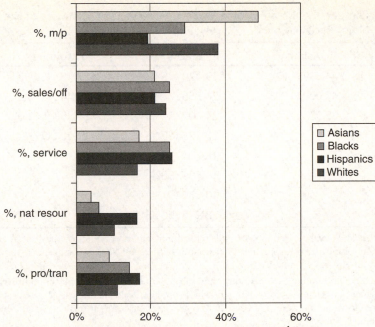

FIGURE 9.2   Percentages Employed in Major Occupational Categories[1] by Race

[1]Reading top to bottom, the employment categories are management, professional and related occupations; sales and office occupations; service occupations; natural resources, construction, and maintenance occupations; and production, transportation, and moving occupations. Individuals aged 16 or older are included in these statistics.

These data indicate that occupational distributions vary significantly for different racial groups. With more effective human and financial capital, Asians and whites have better opportunities than blacks and Hispanics to move into the higher paying, more prestigious white-collar positions represented by the top two job categories, especially the first.

Source: Bureau of Labor Statistics. 2010. Table 10. "Employed Persons by Occupation, Race, Hispanic or Latino Ethnicity, and Sex." *Labor Force Characteristics by Race and Ethnicity, 2007.* http://www.bls.gov/cps/tables.htm.

can be obscured, with public figures often applauding the majority group's achievements and paying scant attention to their advantages and minorities' persistent disadvantages (Evans 2009, 237). Such commenters assert that individuals succeed in the work world strictly because of effort, intelligence, initiative, and other personal traits consistent with the American ideology. Such an outlook overlooks Evans's "long view"—that historical circumstances have often encouraged social reproduction, including minority groups' disproportionately low-level employment.

The various racial minorities face different challenges on the job. Compared to whites and Asian Americans, Latinos and blacks tend to grow up in families disadvantaged in all four types of capital.

Figure 9.2 indicates that black and Hispanic American workers represent a lower percentage in the management/professional category and a greater percentage in services and production, transportation, and moving operations than either Asian Americans or whites (Bureau of Labor Statistics 2008). To a significant extent, different racial groups

TABLE 9.2 Comparative Mean Income Figures over Time for Members of the Four Major Racial Groups[1]

Years	Asians	Blacks	Hispanics	Whites
2007	$44,359 (113%)	$29,429 (75%)	$27,755 (54%)	$39,321
2000	42,009 (109%)	28,355 (73%)	26,466 (51%)	38,686
1995	35,307 (104%)	24,002 (71%)	22,254 (66%)	33,838
1985		20,223 (69%)	21,208 (72%)	29,158
1975		18,704 (67%)		27,959
1965		14,799 (58%)		25,528
1955		10,556 (51%)		20,892
1948		8,917 (50%)		17,781

[1]The figures list mean annual income in 2007 dollars for the members of the four largest racial groups. The minimum age for inclusion was 14 until 1980 when it became 15. No data are available for Asians before 1995 and for Hispanics before 1985.

Each group's income tends to increase over time, and through the years Asians', blacks', and Hispanics' respective percentages of whites' income has generally risen. For blacks the increase is sharpest, rising 25 percent compared to whites between 1948 and 2007. Since 1995 Asian Americans have been the racial group possessing the highest income.

Source: U.S. Bureau of the Census. 2010. Table P-4. "Race and Hispanic Origin of People (Both Sexes Combined) by Median and Mean Income: 1947 to 2009." *Historical Income Tables—People.* http://www.censusbureau.biz/hhes/income/histinc/p04.html.

do different work. Table 9.3 reveals the dollar value of schooling, showing, for instance, that for employed blacks and whites finishing high school meant about $10,000 more income a year than for members of their groups not completing high school. For Asian and Hispanic Americans, the advantage is also substantial (U.S. Bureau of the Census 2008a).

Since the 1970s many blacks living in urban areas have experienced a deteriorating work environment. Factories, which had provided good, steady wages to modestly educated workers, began leaving northern and midwestern cities. A resident of one of the poorest, largely black neighborhoods on the South Side of Chicago explained, "You could walk out the house and get a job. Maybe not what you want but you could get a job. Now, you can't find anything" (Wilson 1997, 36).

Studying 26 young black men living in poor areas in Detroit, sociologist Alfred Young, Jr., found that the decline in auto making and other manufacturing has meant that his respondents could not find blue-collar jobs. While over two thirds had graduated from high school, they tended to have abbreviated work histories, primarily in the fast-food industry. Often their tenure was brief, with respondents reporting that because of abundant surplus workers, bosses were unwilling to invest time and energy resolving problems or conflicts. Brian's demotion was typical. He was an assistant manager at McDonald's, one of only three black people, and some cash disappeared. Brian noted that because he handled money, "I'm the first person they looked at—when it turned out that one of . . . [them], uh, the actual manager was stealing money—and I got bumped back out to a crew member." Disillusioned, Brian left the job in about eight months (Young 2006, 152).

TABLE 9.3 Mean Yearly Earnings for Workers in the Four Major Racial Groups Divided by Educational Attainment

	All workers	Asians	Blacks	Hispanics	Whites
Overall mean	$42,064	$49,517[1]	$33,333	$29,910	$45,542
Not finished high school	$21,484 (9.6%)[2]	$21,305 (14.2%)	$17,439 (10.6%)	$21,303 (32%)	$23,015 (5.5%)
High school graduate	$31,286 (29.1%)	$28,773 (17.8%)	$27,179 (34.4%)	$27,604 (31%)	$33,094 (28.7%)
Some college/ associate's degree	$35,138 (29.9%)	$34,423 (23.3%)	$32,787 (33.3%)	$31,040 (23.2%)	$36,290 (31.1%)
Bachelor's degree	$57,181 (20%)	$54,451 (22.7%)	$46,502 (15.4%)	$44,696 (9.8%)	$59,727 (22.7%)
Advanced degree	$80,977 (10.7%)	$81,943 (22%)	$64,247 (6.3%)	$73,111 (4.1%)	$82,900 (12%)

[1]Income figures for racial groups are higher in this table than in the previous one because only workers 18 and older are included.

[2]Percentage represented in the schooling category in question.

Clearly education pays off. These data suggest that the greater amount of schooling the members of a racial group obtain, the higher their yearly income. However, the amount of schooling is not the sole determinant of income. For instance, data in this table indicate that Asians have more schooling than whites, but in the top two levels of educational attainment their income is slightly lower.

Source: U.S. Census Bureau. 2008. Table A-3. "Mean Earnings of Workers 18 and Over, by Educational Attainment, Race, Hispanic Origin, and Sex: 1975 to 2007." *Current Population Survey. Historic Tables.* http://www.census.gov/population/socdemo/education/cps2008/tabA-3.csv.

Recognizing that the road to better employment involves improved work skills, many of these young men sought job training. Like Darryl some were pleased to have mastered skills that were previously unknown to them. Darryl listed what he had learned in his training—how to write a résumé, to do an effective job interview, to resolve feuds, and to relate effectively with coworkers and supervisors (Young 2006, 174).

Research involving training programs for noncollege low-income young people suggests that young black men like the respondents in the previous study often have nearly as much schooling as their white peers. As a result they are likely to have a skill foundation that can benefit considerably from on-the-job training. Focused human capital can make trainees much more effective workers (Nightingale and Sorensen 2006, 206).

Not all job training, however, provides practical benefits. Henry, a respondent in the Young investigation, pointed out that job training would only be effective if it were geared closely to the individual's eventual work tasks. He explained that at A-Plus Certification the training program involved assembling a single type of computer. He added, "Why not have you build . . . multiple computers, break it down and do it again so you're going to have experience and you actually know exactly what you [need to] know" (Young 2006, 177).

Like blacks, Hispanic Americans are often disadvantaged occupationally and economically. Figure 9.2 indicates that of the four major racial groups Hispanics have the distinctly smallest segment of workers in the management/professional category—less than a fifth of their total (Bureau of Labor Statistics 2008). Table 9.2 points out that since 1995 Hispanic Americans have had the lowest mean income of the four major racial groups.

It is notable that in 1985 mean Hispanic income was higher than African Americans' (U.S. Census Bureau 2008b). A major factor in reversing that trend has been the steady flow of Latino immigrants from Mexico, Central America, and elsewhere. They have tended to be young, limited in schooling and in English proficiency, undocumented in immigrant status, and employed in low-wage jobs (Valenzuela 2006, 144). A significant determinant of whether or not Hispanic immigrants advance occupationally is the combination of language ability and schooling, with foreign-born individuals at a distinct disadvantage in both areas. In 1999 native-born Hispanic men earned 31 percent less and foreign-born Hispanic men 59 percent less than white males (Tiendra and Mitchell 2006, 90).

While normally one distinguishes between first-generation and second-generation members' extent of achievement in these areas a further refinement proves useful. The **1.5 generation** refers to immigrants who reach the new host country before the age of 13 and thus have the chance to achieve mastery of its language and also to obtain extensive American schooling. Because of these opportunities, the 1.5 generation of Latinos arriving in the United States has obtained occupational levels that equal those of second-generation members and are considerably better than those achieved by first-generation workers (Shin and Alba 2006).

In contrast, Latino workers who are young, limited in schooling and English proficiency, and undocumented almost invariably end up in low-paying, strenuous, and unstable employment. In Los Angeles, where undocumented, largely Hispanic immigrants contribute significantly to the local informal sector, they work in factories, mills, restaurants, warehouses, nursing homes, office buildings, and private houses (Vogel 2007, 61).

Many Latinas work as housekeepers or nannies, finding if disagreements with employers arise that their undocumented status precludes any assistance from authorities. Speaking of her former bosses, one ex-nanny explained, "They treated me poorly. They were asking me to do more and more" (Creary 2007, A24).

Hispanic men have also been extensively exploited. In carwashes, which are prevalent in Los Angeles, bosses often claim to pay minimum wage or more, but many just allow their employees tips. "It's bad," explained a Mexican worker, his eyes nervously shifting toward his manager's office. "Other carwashes are the same, no?" Pedro Guzman, an undocumented immigrant from Honduras, said his boss insured a furious pace by regularly posing a two-word ungrammatical question in Spanish: "Quiere casa?" ("Want to go home?") (Nazario and Smith 2008, A1).

Nearly half of American Indians reside on reservations, where low academic achievement and high unemployment along with an array of social problems often plague people's existence. Overall Native American income is well below average, and their poverty rate is the highest of any racial group. Since the middle 1980s, however, some job-creating growth opportunities have occurred, notably tribal enterprises in casinos, hotels, and restaurants, and also the extension of tribal governments into social-service sectors which the federal government formerly maintained (Gitter and Reagan 2002; Kamper 2006; Massey 2004; Rombough and Kelthly 2005).

If this Latina nanny is an undocumented immigrant as many are, then her life is seldom as enjoyable as the photo suggests.

Compared to American Indians, Latinos, and blacks, Asian Americans are very well off occupationally and economically. Their 48 percent in the management/professional category (Bureau of Labor Statistics 2008) and $49,517 mean annual income for workers 18 and over (U.S. Census Bureau, 2008b) are the highest figures for the major racial groups.

Some members of the category, however, are more advantaged than others. Education plays an important role. Research reveals that controlling for the amount of schooling the different categories receive, US-born whites, US-born Asians, and all US-educated Asians average similar incomes, but foreign-educated Asians earn 16 percent less (Zeng and Xie 2004). In addition, for Asian Americans a pattern develops that is similar to that cited in the earlier study showing that Hispanics' 1.5 generation equals the second generation and exceeds the first generation in earnings (Shin and Alba 2006).

Figure 9.3's findings indicate that blacks and Hispanic Americans have higher percentages of their members below the official poverty threshold than either whites or Asian Americans.

While such human-capital factors as language ability, schooling, and job training affect minority groups' employment success, another is also influential—discrimination.

Stereotype Fallout and the Employment Process

Stereotype fallout refers to the significant penalty minority-group members can suffer when influential, sometimes powerful individuals embrace an established stereotype of

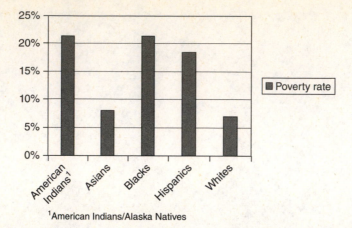

¹American Indians/Alaska Natives

FIGURE 9.3   Racial Groups' Rates of Family Poverty

Whites and Asian Americans have distinctly lower family poverty rates than the other three racial groups.

Source: U.S. Census Bureau. 2010. Table 36. "Selected Characteristics of Racial Groups and Hispanic Population: 2007. *Statistical Abstract of the United States: 2010.* http://www.census.gov/compendia/statab/cats/population.html.

that minority group, promoting its toxic impact on their life chances. Both stereotype threat and stereotype fallout concern outcomes, but stereotype threat focuses on victims' perceptions affecting behavior while stereotype fallout involves actions against minorities such as exclusion from such critical opportunities as schooling and jobs. For instance, data from the California Workforce Survey indicated that when Latino men and women had limited schooling and low-level fluency in English, they became objects of negative perceptions, receiving low wages. In contrast, Asian American employees with similar educational and language skills obtained better pay (Yang 2005). It appears that in such situations many Hispanic Americans but not Asian Americans experience stereotype fallout. When they possess limited schooling and ability in English, Latinos are likely to trigger the kind of stereotype described in the media section—the "greaser" image as lazy, immoral, and stupid—and thus to racist employers seemingly fit for only the most menial, low paying jobs.

Because they are not hampered with this potent stereotype, Asians with limited schooling and ability in English escape an income-related penalty. In another context, however, Asian Americans are vulnerable to stereotype fallout. A review of research on Asian Americans in management and professional positions suggested that in spite of their unquestioned educational and occupational achievements, they obtained limited promotions, finding themselves "significantly underrepresented in positions of authority, leadership, and decision-making in the private sector, government agencies, and institutions of higher learning" (Varma 2004, 297). It is likely that the stereotype of Asian American men described in the section on mass media—that they are nerdy, passive, and unaggressive—generally supports this discrimination. A trainer working for a network of Asian American executives at IBM suggested that, in fact, Asian Americans have been socialized not to question authority and to be quiet in meetings, providing bosses the sense that they lack the aggressiveness and dynamism executives must possess (Wong 2006). In the federal workforce, where Asian American employees are distinctly underrepresented in the higher pay grades, barely a tenth of the Asian American respondents who indicated in a Gallup poll that they had experienced discriminatory or unfair treatment filed a complaint (Rosenberg 2009).

African Americans can be victims of stereotype fallout, with a study of 150 white male respondents ranging in age from 18 to 73 serving to illustrate the process. These men examined résumés that varied in applicants' amount of schooling and the quality of their work history. A racially stereotypical name—such as Lee Chang, Jamal Jenkins, José Gonzales, or James Sullivan—identified the applicant's race. Regardless of the quality of their résumés, the black applicants were often viewed negatively, assessed as unqualified for all but low-status jobs (King, Madera, Hebl, Knight, and Mendoza 2006).

As the media discussion indicates, black men have often been stereotyped as violent and frenzied, and an experimental study demonstrated how such perceptions have influenced prospective white employers. Sociologist Devah Pager (2007; Pager and Quilliam 2005) conducted a tester study of 350 job audits, using male college students from Milwaukee and providing 150 audits by a white pair of students and 200 by a black pair, whose basic characteristics such as age and amount of schooling were matched. Each member of a racial duo received a random assignment to apply for one of 15 entry-level positions; additionally one member of each pair represented himself as an ex-offender who had served 18 months for a drug conviction.

After the interview 34 percent of the white audits without a criminal record received a callback compared to just half that figure—17 percent—among those with a criminal record (Pager 2007, 67–68).

A positive interview for a white ex-offender developed in this manner.

> Bill, one of the white testers, applied in person at a furniture sales company. The owner of the company was on site to look over Bill's completed application. The owner read through the application, looked Bill up and down, then looked back at the application. "So it says here you were at the Winnebago Correctional Facility," he stated matter-of-factly, but clearly looking for an explanation. "Yes, served time for a drug conviction. I made a big mistake in my life and I'm looking to move on. " Bill gave the scripted response. The owner looked at him for a moment, seemed satisfied, and went on to ask Bill some questions about his work experience and interests. "Well, you seem okay to me," the owner concluded. Bill seemed to have made a positive impression despite the awkward beginning.

(PAGER 2007, 102)

The black testers tended to receive a more negative response. Even though their credentials matched their white counterparts, only 14 percent of the blacks without a criminal record received a callback, a smaller percentage than that for whites who had supposedly served prison time, and among the convicted barely a third that modest number—5 percent—obtained a callback. The following audit described the typical experience for black ex-offenders.

> Jerome arrived at a branch of a national restaurant chain in a suburb twenty miles from Milwaukee. He immediately sensed that he was the only black person in the place. An employee hurried over to him, "Can I help you with something?' "I'm here about the job you advertised," he replied. The employee nodded reluctantly and went off to produce an application form. Jerome filled out the form, including information about his fictitious criminal record. He was given a math test and a personality test. He was then instructed to wait for the manager to speak with him. The manager came out about ten minutes later, looked over Jerome's application, and frowned when he noticed the criminal history information. Without asking any questions about the context of the conviction, the manager started to lecture: "You can't be screwing up like this at your age. A kid like you can ruin his whole life like this." Jerome began to explain that he had made a mistake and had learned his lesson, but the manager cut him off. "I'll look over your application and call if we have a position for you."
>
> (PAGER 2007, 100)

The vignettes suggested that the interviews the two sets of testers received provided distinct hints about the chances for a callback.

Several months after the audits were completed, Pager conducted a survey of the employers previously tapped in the tester phase, providing them a vignette of one job candidate who was represented half the time as black and half as white and who had served 12 months for a drug offense. In spite of the sharp preference previously shown for white testers, these interviewees reversed themselves, indicating that they were about equally inclined to hire both the black and white applicants (Pager and Quilliam 2005, 363–64). Color-blind racism seems to have been operative. It is apparent that the tester research was more effective than interviews at revealing those employers' different perceptions of black and white applicants, particularly their inclination to mobilize stereotype fallout against black applicants.

Such findings make it hardly seem surprising that the intergenerational mobility in income for whites is higher than for blacks. Drawing from data in the Panel Study of Income Dynamics discussed in Chapter 4, researchers compared economic mobility of black and white families. The most prominent finding was that at each of the five income levels represented in the research, blacks were less likely than whites to have higher income than their parents (adjusted for inflation). The disparity was greatest in the middle quintile, where the comparative figures for children's higher income were 68 percent for whites and 31 percent for blacks and the second highest quintile displaying 67 and 49 percent, respectively (Isaacs 2007).

When the three largest racial minorities were surveyed about job prospects, some opinion differences emerged. Three quarters of Latinos and two thirds of Asians indicated that they would progress if they worked hard, but less than half of blacks—44 percent— shared that conclusion. Furthermore about two thirds of African Americans indicated that all individuals do not have the same chance to succeed (Preston 2007). Loosely speaking, these perceptions seem in line with the information in this chapter. A review of the chapter's content follows, often emphasizing the close association between racism and poverty.

Conclusion

In starting to examine this topic, individuals not only need to recognize the meaning of racism but also the distinction between individual and institutional racism. The United States has a lengthy racist tradition, developing racial projects that have targeted not only American Indians and blacks but various European, Asian, and Hispanic groups. Urban-renewal programs and real-estate activities are prominent areas where minorities still encounter racist treatment.

Unlike white parents, who tend to conclude that racial issues have been solved, minority parents often decide that they must carefully prepare their children for a racism-ridden world. In interracial families mothers and fathers must select a racial group for their children.

In children's peer groups, race can have an impact, with conditions sometimes encouraging and sometimes discouraging interracial membership.

The members of the four major racial groups have different educational opportunities, with family traits and the quality of schooling contributing to success. In addition, black and Hispanic children are more vulnerable to the destructive impact of the zero-tolerance policy and stereotype threat. As a result of the educational disadvantages they face, blacks and Hispanics tend to score lower on standardized tests than Asians and whites.

Evidence indicates that racism is widespread in the news media. On TV racial minorities are often both underrepresented in speaking roles and are stereotyped in distinct ways involving both their racial group and sex. In addition, blacks' portrayal on local news contributes to the nurturing of stereotypes, especially for whites living isolated from blacks.

Since the 1970s poor blacks have found it increasingly difficult to locate employment.

Job training can be helpful, particularly if it provides the specific knowledge one needs at work. Hispanic Americans have also been disadvantaged educationally and occupationally, particularly the flow of young immigrants. Overall American Indians have below-average income and the highest poverty rate of all major racial groups. In many occasions racial minorities are vulnerable to stereotype fallout, with Devah Pager's research displaying its destructive impact for black men.

Charles Dickens's famous juxtaposition—that it is the best of times; it is the worst of times—applies very well to the current American racial picture. Barack Obama's election to the presidency has inspired a sense of racial renewal not only in this country but also internationally. Shortly after the election, Helen Grant, who grew up in public housing and eventually became a successful lawyer, decided to run for the British Parliament as the Conservative Party's first black female candidate. She observed that Obama has been "an inspiration to a whole generation. He's caught the imagination of millions of people, who will say, 'Maybe I'll try it myself'" (Sullivan 2008, A17).

In contrast, many more millions—poor African Americans, Latinos, Asian Americans, and American Indians in the United States along with minorities in other countries—find themselves trapped in the cycle of poverty discussed in Chapter 8. At each stage of the cycle, there might be an asterisk, signaling the exacerbating impact of racism—the disproportionate chance of living in a poor area and ending up in low-quality schooling; the heightened danger of experiencing stereotype threat affecting performance in school and at work; or the widespread exposure to stereotype fallout on the job.

In this chapter we have seen that individuals who have very limited quantities and qualities of valuable capital are particularly vulnerable to the damages racism produces. I have sought to provide detail, introducing concepts like stereotype threat and stereotype fallout to display how these damaging processes unfold.

Key Terms In The Glossary

1.5 generation *290*
Color-blind racism *273*
De facto segregation *268*
Ethnicity *263*
Eugenics movement *269*
Index of dissimilarity *271*
Individual racism *261*
Institutional racism *262*
Jim Crow era *267*
Majority group *262*

Minority group *263*
Racial formation *263*
Racial project *263*
Racialized *272*
Racially restrictive
    covenant *268*
Racism *261*
Separate-but-equal standard
    267
Slave codes *266*

Social Darwinism *269*
Social distance *263*
Steering *272*
Stereotype *266*
Stereotype fallout *291*
Stereotype threat *281*
Trajectory *263*

Discussion Topics

1. Define institutional racism. Illustrate it by discussing a hypothetical or an actual organization's discriminatory practices.
2. While the early treatment of Native Americans and blacks differed in specific regards, certain general racist patterns victimized both groups. List and discuss three major ways government and citizen groups oppressed both Indians and blacks.
3. Has the perception of being white changed in the past century? Discuss.
4. Does the idea of color-blind racism make sense? What illustrations of it come to mind?
5. Consider how minority families can mobilize to help their children deal with racism.

6. Does your experience suggest that race affects peer-group membership among students? Comment on both high-school and college settings.
7. Examine two important issues about school that minority parents are likely to discuss with their children.
8. What are several memorable racial stereotypes you have seen in films or TV? Did those stereotypes influence your perception of the groups in question?
9. Discuss in detail two important disadvantages racial minorities are likely to face in seeking employment.

Research Papers

1. Examine the development and meaning of the separate-but-equal standard and assess whether or not it continues to exist in modern times.
2. Starting with the text's discussion of the different factors influencing the racial composition of young people's peer groups, gather additional information. Indicate why one or two factor(s) is (are) more influential than others.

3. Discuss the occurrence of racial stereotypes in modern mass media, focusing on either TV, the Internet, films, or books and magazines.
4. Develop a paper about racism in the job world, bringing in the following concepts—individual racism, institutional racism, stereotype, stereotype fallout, and, if possible, color-blind racism.

Informative Websites

The Southern Poverty Law Center's Hatewatch (http://www.splcenter.org/blog/) provides up-to-date information about hate crimes, hate groups, and analysis of various means to combat such extreme racism.

The Website for Institutional Racism in America (http://academic.udayton.edu/race/2008electionandracism/raceandracism/RaceandRacism.htm) supplies extensive data about current political, economic, and mass-media topics addressing both institutional and individual racism.

The National Coalition on Sports in the Media (http://www.aimovement.org/ncrsm/) formed in 1991 to battle major media's involvement in perpetuating oppressive representations of American Indians, particularly racist mascots, and the organization continues to focus on that issue.

The following sites supply abundant information about the outlooks and activities for long-established advocacy organizations representing major racial groups: (African Americans) The National Association for the Advancement of Colored People (NAACP) (http://www.naacp.org/programs/). (American Indians) The American Indian Movement (http://www.aimovement.org/). (Asian Americans) Asian American Legal Defense and Education Fund (http://www.aaldef.org/) (Hispanic Americans) National Council of La Raza (http://www.nclr.org/).

Bibliography

Alvarez, Alvin N., Linda Juang, and Christopher T. H. Liang. 2006. "Asian Americans and Racism: When Bad things Happen to 'Model Minorities.'" *Cultural Diversity and Ethnic Minority Psychology* 12 (June): 477–92.

Anglin, Deidre M., and Jay C. Wade. 2007. "Racial Socialization, Racial Identity, and Black Students' Adjustment to College." *Cultural Diversity and Ethnic Minority Psychology* 13 (July): 207–15.

Aronson, Marc. 2007. *Race: A History beyond Black and White.* New York: Ginee Seo Books.

Bailyn, Bernard, David Brion Davis, David Herbert Donald, John L. Thomas, Robert H. Wiebe, and Gordon S. Wood. 1977. *The Great Republic.* Lexington, MA: D.C. Heath.

Bender, Daniel E. 2008. "Perils of Degeneration: Reform, the Savage Immigrant, and the Survival of the Unfit." *Journal of Social History* 42 (Fall): 5–29.

Bennett, Lerone. 1982. *Before the Mayflower: A History of Black America,* 5th ed. Chicago: Johnson Publishing Company.

Berthrong, Donald J. 1986. "Legacies of the Dawes Act: Bureaucrats and Land Thieves at the Cheyenne–Arapaho Agencies of Oklahoma, pp. 204–17 in Roger L. Nichols (ed.), *The American Indian: Past and Present,* 3rd ed. New York: Alfred A. Knopf.

Bird, S. Elizabeth. 1999. "Gendered Construction of the American Indian in Popular Media." *Journal of Communications* 49 (Summer): 61–83.

Bogardus, Emory S. 1947. "Measurement of Personal-Group Relations." *Sociometry* 10 (November): 306–11.

Bogle, Donald. 2004. *Toms, Coons, Mulattoes, Mammies, and Bucks,* 4th ed. New York: Continuum.

Bonilla-Silva, Eduardo. 2001. *White Supremacy & Racism in the Post-Civil Rights Era.* Boulder: Lynne Rienner.

Bonilla-Silva, Eduardo. 2006. "Black, Honorary White, White: The Future of Race in the United States?," pp. 33–48 in David L. Brunsma (ed.), *Mixed Messages: Multiracial Identities in the "Color-Blind" Era.* Boulder: Lynne Rienner.

Bonilla-Silva, Eduardo. 2010. *Racism without Racists: Color-Blind Racism & Racial Inequality in Contemporary America,* 3rd ed. Lanham, MD: Rowman & Littlefield.

Bonilla-Silva, Eduardo, Carla Goar, and David G. Embrick. 2006. "When Whites Flock Together: White Habitus and the Social Psychology of

Whites' Social and Residential Segregation from Blacks." *Critical Sociology* 32: 229–55.

Brown, Dee. 1972. *Bury My Heart at Wounded Knee*. New York: Bantam Books.

Brown, Michael K., Martin Carnoy, Elliott Currie, Troy Duster, David B. Oppenheimer, Marjorie M. Shultz, and David Wellman. 2003. *Whitewashing Race: The Myth of a Color-Blind Society*. Berkeley: University of California Press.

Bureau of Labor Statistics. 2008. Table 4. "Employed Persons by Occupation, Sex, Race, and Hispanic or Latino Ethnicity, 2007 Averages." *Labor Force Characteristics by Race and Ethnicity, 2007*. http://www.bls .gov/cpsrace2007.pdf.

Burris, Carol Corbett, and Kevin G. Welner. 2007. "Classroom Integration and Accelerated Learning through Detracking," pp. 207–27 in Erica Frankenberg and Gary Orfield (eds.), *Lessons in Integration: Realizing the Promise of Racial Diversity in American Schools*. Charlottesville: University of Virginia Press.

Bynum, Mia Smith, Thomaseo Burton, and Candace Best. 2007. "Racism Experiences and Psychological Functioning in African American College Freshmen: Is Racial Socialization a Buffer?" *Cultural Diversity and Ethnic Minority Psychology* 13 (January): 64–71.

Camp, Stephanie M. H. 2006. "The Pleasures of Resistance: Enslaved Women and Body Politics in the Plantation South, 1830–1861," pp. 87–124 in Edward E. Baptist and Stephanie M. H. Camp (eds.), *New Studies in the History of American Slavery*. Athens, GA: University of Georgia Press.

Center for Regional Policy Studies. 2001. "Census 2000 Fact Sheet: Residential Segregation in United States Metropolitan Areas." http:// www.sppsr.ucla.edu/lewis.

Chang, Iris. 2003. *The Chinese in America: A Narrative History*. New York: Viking.

Chen, Chuansheng, and Harold W. Stevenson. 1995. "Motivation and Mathematics Achievement: A Comparative Study of Asian-American, Caucasian-American, and East Asian High School Students." *Child Development* 66 (August): 1215–34.

Cheng, Simon, and Kathryn J. Lively. 2009. "Multiracial Self-Identification and Adolescent Outcomes: A Social Psychological Approach to the Marginal Man Theory." *Social Forces* 88 (September): 61–98.

Churchill, Ward. 1998. *Fantasies of the Master Race: Literature, Cinema and the Colonization of American Indians*. San Francisco: City Lights Books.

Clawson, Rosalie A. 2002. "Poor People, Black Faces: The Portrayal of Poverty in Economics Textbooks." *Journal of Black Studies* 32 (January): 352–61.

Collins, Patricia Hill. 1999. "Shifting the Center: Race, Class, and Feminist Theorizing about Motherhood," pp. 197–217 in Stephanie Coontz, Maya Parson, and Gabrielle Raley (eds.), *American Families: A Multicultural Reader*. New York: Routledge.

Conchas, Gilberto Q. *The Color of Success: Race and High-Achieving Youth*. New York: Teachers College Press.

Conners, Joan L. 2004. "Color TV? Diversity in Prime-time TV," pp. 206–12 in Rebecca Ann Lind (ed.), *Race/Gender/Media: Considering Diversity across Audiences, Content, and Producers*. Boston: Pearson Allyn & Bacon.

Constantine, Madonna G., and Sha'Kema M. Blackmon. 2002. "Black Adolescents' Racial Socialization Experiences: Their Relation to Home, School, and Peer Self-Esteem." *Journal of Black Studies* 32 (January): 322–35.

Creary, David. 2007. "Domestic Workers Labor in the Shadows: Female Immigrants, Many Undocumented, Get Little or No Pay for Torturous Jobs." *Los Angeles Times* (November 4): A24.

Deo, Meera E., Jenny J. Lee, Christina B. Chin, Noriko Milman, and Nancy Wang Yuen. 2008. "Missing in Action: 'Framing Race on Prime-Time Television." *Social Justice* 35: 145–62.

Doob, Christopher Bates. 1999. *Racism: An American Cauldron*, 3rd ed. Reading, MA: Longman.

Edwards, Laura F. 1996. "The Disappearance of Susan Daniel and Henderson Cooper: Gender and Narratives of Political Conflict in the Reconstruction-Era South." *Feminist Studies* 22 (Summer): 363–86.

Elliott, Mark Emory. 2006. *Color-Blind Justice: Albion Tourgée and the Guest for Racial Equality from the Civil War to PI*. Oxford: Oxford University Press.

Entwisle, Doris R., Karl Len Alexander, and Linda Steffel Olson. 1997. *Children, Schools, and Inequality*. Boulder: Westview Press.

Essoka, Jonathan D. 2010. "The Gentrifying Effects of Brownfields Redevelopment." *Western Journal of Black Studies* (Fall): 299–315.

Evans, William McKee. 2009. *Open Wound: The Long View of Race in America*. Urbana: University of Illinois Press.

Feagin, Joe R. 1991. "The Continuing Significance of Race: Antiblack Discrimination in Public Places." *American Sociological Review* 56 (February): 101–16.

Fernandez, Ronald. 2000. *America's Banquet of Cultures: Harnessing Ethnicity, Race, and Immigration in the 21st Century*. Westport, CT: Praeger.

Fireside, Harvey. 1997. Plessy v. Ferguson: *Separate but Equal?* Springfield, NJ: Enslow Publishers.

Fitzgerald, F. Scott. 2000. *F. Scott Fitzgerald: Novels and Stories 1920–1922*. New York: Library of America. Originally published in 1920.

Fletcher, Anne C., Alethea Rollins, and Pamela Nickerson. 2004. "The Extension of School-Based Inter- and Intraracial Children's Friendships: Influences on Psychosocial Well-Being." *American Journal of Orthopsychiatry* 74 (July): 272–85.

Franklin, John Hope, and Alfred A. Moss, Jr. 1988. *From Slavery to Freedom: A History of Negro Americans*, 6th ed. New York: Alfred A. Knopf.

Franklin, John Hope, and Alfred A. Moss, Jr. 2000. *From Slavery to Freedom: A History of African Americans*, 8th ed. Boston: McGraw-Hill.

Fredrickson, George M. 2002. *Racism: A Short History*. Princeton: Princeton University Press.

Fung, Richard. 1994. "Seeing Yellow: Asian Identities in Film and Video," pp. 161–71 in Karin Anguilar-San Juan (ed.), *The State of Asian America: Activism and Resistance in the 1990s*. Boston: South End Press.

Gallagher, Charles A. 2003. "Miscounting Race: Explaining Whites' Misperceptions of Racial Group Size." *Sociological Perspective* 46 (Fall): 381–96.

Gates, Henry Louis, Jr. 2010. "Forty Acres and a Gap in Wealth," pp. 328–30 in Paula S. Rothenberg (ed.), *Race, Class, and Gender in the United States*, 8th ed. New York: Worth Publishers.

Gilliam, Franklin D., Jr., and Shanto Iyengar. 2000. "Prime Suspects: The Influence of Local Television News on the Viewing Public." *American Journal of Political Science* 44 (July): 560–73.

Gilliam, Franklin D., Jr., Nicholas A. Valentine, and Matthew A. Beckmann. 2002. "Where You Live and What You Watch: The Impact of Racial Proximity and Local Television News on Attitudes about Race and Crime." *Political Research Quarterly* 55 (December): 755–80.

Gitter, Robert J., and Patricia B. Reagan. 2002. "Reservation Wages: An Analysis of the Effects of Reservations on Employment of American Indian Men." *American Economic Review* 92 (September): 1160–68.

Gonzales, Nancy A., Ana Marie Cauce, and Craig A. Mason. 1996. "Interobserver Agreement in the Assessment of Parental Behavior and Parent-Adolescent Conflict: African American Mothers, Daughters, and Independent Observers." *Child Development* 67 (August): 1483-98.

Goyette, Kimberly A., and Xie Yu. 1999. "Educational Expectations of Asian American Youths: Determinants and Ethnic Differences." *Sociology of Education* 72 (January): 22–36.

Granovetter, Mark. 1983. "The Strength of Weak Times: A Network Theory Revisited," pp. 201–33 in Robert Collins (ed.), *Friendships and Social Relations in Children*. New York: Wiley.

Grant, Madison. 1916. *The Passing of the Great Race*. New York: Charles Scribner's Sons.

Gyory, Andrew. 1998. *Closing the Gate: Race, Politics, and the Chinese Exclusion Act*. Chapel Hill: University of North Carolina Press.

Harper, Shaun R. 2006. "Peer Support for African American Male College Achievement: Beyond Internalized Racism and the Burden of 'Acting White.'" *Journal of Men's Studies* 14 (Fall): 337–58.

Hedges, Larry, and Amy Nowell. 1999. "Changes in the Black-White Gap in Achievement Test Scores." *Sociology of Education* 72 (April): 111–35.

Herndon, Michael K., and Joan B. Hirt. 2004. "Black Students and Their Families: What Leads to

Success in College." *Journal of Black Studies* 34 (March): 489–513.

Hofstadter, Richard. 2006. *Social Darwinism in American Thought*. Boston: Beacon Press. Originally published in 1944.

Indian Land Tenure Foundation. 2009. "Indian Land Foundation—FAQs." http://www.indianlandtenure.org/faqs/faqs.html.

Isaacs, Julia B. 2007. "Economic Mobility of Black and White Families." *Pew Charitable Trusts: Economic Mobility Project*. http://www.economicmobility.org/assets/pdfs/EMP_BlackandWhite_ChapterVI.pdf.

Jacobs, Ronald N. 2000. *Race, Media and the Crisis of Civil Society: From Watts to Rodney King*. Cambridge: Cambridge University Press.

Jipguep, Marie-Claude, and Kathy Sanders-Phillips. 2003. "The Context of Violence for Children of Color: Violence in the Community and in the Media." *Journal of Negro Education* 72 (Fall): 379–95.

Johnson, Heather Beth, and Thomas M. Shapiro. 2003. "Good Neighborhoods, Good Schools: 'Good Choices' of White Families," pp. 173–87 in Ashley W. Doane and Eduardo Bonilla-Silva (eds.), *White Out: The Continuing Significance of Race*. New York: Routledge.

Johnson, James Weldon. 2004. *Writings*. New York: The Library of America.

Jones-Correa, Michael. 2001. "The Origins and Diffusion of Racial Restrictive Covenants." *Political Science Quarterly* 115 (Winter): 541–68.

Kamper, David. 2006. "Organizing in the Context of Tribal Sovereignty: The Navaho Area Indian Health Service Campaign for Union Recognition." *Labor Studies Journal* 30: 17–39.

Kang, Laura Hyun-Yi. 2002. "The Desiring of Asian Female Bodies: Interracial Romance and Cinematic Subjection," pp. 71–100 in Peter X. Feng (ed.), *Screening Asian Americans*. New Brunswick, NJ: Rutgers University Press.

Kao, Grace, and Kara Joyner. 2006. "Do Hispanic and Asian Adolescents Practice Panethnicity in Friendship Choices?" *Social Science Quarterly* 87 (December): 972–92.

Katz, Michael B., and Mark J. Stern. 2006. *One Nation Divisible: What America Was and What It Is Becoming*. New York: Russell Sage Foundation.

Keller, Larry. 2010. "Anti-Latino Hate Crimes Seen from Baltimore to Arizona." *Southern Poverty Law Center*. http://www.splcenter.org/blog/2010/08/23/anti-latino-hate-crimes-seen-from-baltimore-to-arizona/.

Kenny, Kevin. 2000. *The American Irish: A History*. New York: Longman.

King, Eden B., Juan M. Madera, Mikki R. Hebl, Jennifer L. Knight, and Saad A. Mendoza. 2006. "What's in a Name? A Multiracial Investigation of the Role of Occupational Stereotypes in Selective Decisions." *Journal of Applied Social Psychology* 36 (May): 1145–59.

Kuther, Tara L., and Scyatta A. Wallace. 2003. "Community Violence and Sociomoral Development: An African American Cultural Perspective." *American Journal of Orthopsychiatry* 73 (April): 177–89.

Larson, Stephanie Greco. 2006. *Media & Minorities: The Politics of Race in News and Entertainment*. Lanham, MD: Rowman & Littlefield.

Leaper, Campbell, and Carly Kay Friedman. 2007. "The Socialization of Gender," pp. 561–87 in Joan E. Grusec and Paul D. Hastings (eds.), *Handbook of Socialization: Theory and Research*. New York: Guilford Press.

Lease, A. Michele, and Jamilia J. Blake. 2005. "A Comparison of Majority-Race Children with and without a Minority-Race Friend." *Social Development* 14 (February): 20–41.

Lee, Valerie E., and David T. Burkam. 2002. *Inequality at the Starting Gate: Social Background Differences in Achievement as Children Begin School*. Washington, DC: Economic Policy Institute.

Levin, Diane E., and Nancy Carlsson-Paige. 2003. "Marketing Violence: The Special Toll on Young Children of Color." *Journal of Negro Education* 72 (Autumn): 427–37.

Losen, Daniel J., and Russell Skiba. 2010. "Suspended Education: Urban Middle Schools in Crisis." Southern Poverty Law Center. http://www.splcenter.org/get-informed/publications/suspended-education.

Lucas, Samuel R., and Mark Berends. 2002. Sociodemographic Diversity, Correlated Achievement, and De Facto Tracking." *Sociology of Education* 75 (October): 328–48.

Magnuson, Katherine A., and Greg J. Duncan. 2006. The Role of Family Socioeconomic

Resources in the Black-White Test Score Gap among Young Children." *Developmental Review* 26 (December): 365–99.

Mandura, Jelan. 2006. "The Impact of Family Functioning on African American Males' Academic Achievement: A Review and Clarification of the Empirical Literature." *Teachers College Record* 108 (February): 318–37.

Marable, Manning. 1994. "The Black Male: Searching Beyond Stereotypes," pp. 69–77 in Richard G. Majors and Jacob D. Gordon (eds.), *The American Black Male: His Present Status and His Future*. Chicago: Nelson-Hall.

Martin, Jack K., Bernice A. Pescosolido, Sigrun Olafsdottir, and Jane D. McLeod. 2007. "The Construction of Fear: Americans' Preferences for Social Distance from Children and Adolescents with Mental Health Problems." *Journal of Health and Social Behavior* 48 (March): 50–67.

Massey, Douglas S., and Nancy A. Denton. 1993. *American Apartheid: Segregation and the Making of the Underclass*. Cambridge: Harvard University Press

Massey, Garth M. 2004. "Making Sense of Work on the Wind River Indian Reservation." *American Indian Quarterly* 28 (Summer/Fall): 786–816.

McCall, Nathan. 1994. *Makes Me Wanna Holler: A Young Black Man in America*. New York: Random House.

McCullough, Mary W. 1998. *Black & White Women as Friends: Building Cross-Race Friendships*. Cresskill, NJ: Hampton Press.

McKown, Clark, and Michael J. Strambler. 2008. "Social Influences on the Ethnic Achievement Gap," pp. 366–96 in Stephen M. Quintana and Clark McKown (eds.), *Handbook of Race, Racism, and the Developing Child*. Hoboken, NJ: John Wiley & Sons.

McKown, Clark, and Rhona S. Weinstein. 2003. "The Development and Consequences of Stereotype Consciousness in Middle Childhood." *Child Development* 74 (March/April): 498–515.

Miller, David E., and Randall McIntosh. 1999. "Promoting Resilience in Urban African American Adolescents: Racial Socialization and Identity as Protective Factors." *Social Work Research* 23 (September): 159–70.

Moody, James. 2001. "Race, School Integration, and Friendship Segregation in America." *American Journal of Sociology* 107 (November): 679–717.

Mouw, Ted, and Barbara Entwisle. 2006. "Racial Segregation and Interracial Friendship in Schools." *American Journal of Sociology* 112 (September): 394–441.

Muller, Thomas. 1993. *Immigrants and the American City*. New York: New York University Press.

National Center for Education Statistics. 2007a. "Status and Trends in the Education of Racial and Ethnic Minorities." http://nces.ed.gov/pubs2007/minoritytrends/.

National Center for Education Statistics. 2007b. Table 7. "Percentage of Fourth-Grade Public School Students and Average Scores in NAEP Reading, by Selected Student Groups and State: 2007." *The Nation's Report Card: Reading 2007*. http://nces.ed.gov/nationsreportcard/pdf/main2007496.pdf.

National Center for Education Statistics. 2009. Table A-12. "Average Scores and Achievement-Level Results in NAEP Mathematics for Fourth-Grade Public School Students, by Race/Ethnicity and State/Jurisdiction: 2009." *The Nation's Report Card: Mathematics 2009*. http://nces.ed.gov/nationsreportcard/pdf/main2009/2010451.pdf.

Nazario, Sonja, and Doug Smith. 2008. "A Times Investigation: Workers Getting Soaked at Southland Carwashes." *Los Angeles Times* (March 23): A1.

Neal, Jennifer Watling. 2008. "Hanging Out: Features of Elementary Students' Classroom Social Networks." *American Sociological Association annual meetings,* pp. 1–19.

Neckerman, Kathryn M. 2007. *Schools Betrayed: Roots of Failure in Inner-City Education*. Chicago: University of Chicago Press.

Nichols, Roger L. 2003. *American Indians in U.S. History*. Norman: University of Oklahoma Press.

Nightingale, Demetra Smith, and Elaine Sorensen. 2006. "The Availability and Use of Workforce Development Programs among Less-Educated Youth," pp. 185–210 in Ronald B. Mincy (ed.), *Black Males Left Behind*. Washington, DC: Urban Institute Press.

Oakes, Jeannie. 2005. *Keeping Track: How Schools Structure Inequality*, 2nd ed. New Haven: Yale University Press.

Omi, Michael, and Howard Winant. 1994. *Racial Formation in the United States: From the 1960s to the 1990s*, 2nd ed. New York: Routledge.

Omi, Michael, and Howard Winant. 2009. "Thinking through Race and Racism." *Contemporary Sociology* 38 (March): 121–25.

Oswalt, Wendell H., and Sharlotte Neely. 1999. *This Land Was Theirs: A Study of Native Americans*, 6th ed. Mountain View, CA: Mayfield.

Page, Jake. 2003. *In the Hands of the Great Spirit: The 20,000 Year History of American Indians*. New York: Free Press.

Pager, Devah. 2007. *Marked: Race, Crime, and Finding Work in an Era of Mass Incarceration*. Chicago: University of Chicago Press.

Pager, Devah, and Lincoln Quillian. 2005. "Walking the Talk? What Employers Say versus What They Do." *American Sociological Review* 70 (June): 355–80.

Palmer, Maria Teresa Unger. 2007. "'Desperate to Learn:' The Schooling Experience of Latinas in North Carolina," pp. 120–44 in Erica Frankenberg and Gary Orfield (eds.), *Lessons in Integration: Realizing the Promise of Racial Diversity in American Schools*. Charlottesville: University of Virginia Press.

Pilgrim, David. 2000. "The Coon Caricature." http://www.ferris.edu/jimcrow/coon/.

Planty, Michael, William Hussar, Thomas Snyder, Stephen Provasnik, Grace Kena, Angelina KewalRamani, and Jane Kemp. 2008. "The Condition of Education 2008." National Center for Education Statistics. http://nces.ed.gov/pubs2008/2008031.pdf.

Preston, Julia. 2007. "Survey Points to Tensions among Chief Minorities." *New York Times* (December 13): A33.

Prokos, Anastasia, and Irene Padavic. 2005. "An Examination of Competing Explanations for the Pay Gap among Scientists and Engineers." *Gender & Society* 19 (August): 523–43.

Rada, James A., and K. Tim Wulfemeyer. 2005. "Color Coded: Racial Descriptors in Television of Intercollegiate Sports." *Journal of Broadcasting & Electronic Media* 49 (March): 65–85.

Rawick, George P. (ed.). 1972. *The American Slave: A Composite Autobiography: Unwritten History of Slavery*. Vol. 18. Westport, CT: Greenwood.

Rees, Richard W. 2007. *Shades of Difference: A History of Ethnicity in America*. Lanham, MD: Rowman & Littlefield.

Reich, Steven A. 2007. "The Great War, Black Workers, and the Rise and Fall of the NAACP in the South," pp. 147–77 in Eric Arnesen (ed.), *The Black Worker: Race, Labor, and Civil Rights since Emancipation*. Urbana, IL: University of Illinois Press.

Robinson, Julia Ann. 1998. "The Impact of Race and Ethnicity on Children's Peer Relations," pp. 76–88 in Phillip T. Slee and Ken Rigby (eds.), *Children's Peer Relations*. New York: Routledge.

Rockquemore, Kerry Ann, and Tracey Laszloffy. 2005. *Raising Biracial Children*. Lanham, MD: Rowman & Littlefield.

Rockquemore, Kerry Ann, Tracey Laszloffy, and Julia Noveske. 2006. "It All Starts at Home: Racial Socialization in Multiracial Families," pp. 203–16 in David L. Brunsma (ed.), *Mixed Messages: Multiracial Identities in the "Color-Blind" Era*. Boulder: Lynne Rienner.

Rodriguez, Clara E. 1997. "Keeping It Reel? Films of the 1980s and 1990s," pp. 180–84 in Clara E. Rodriguez (ed.), *Latin Looks: Images of Latinas and Latinos in the U.S. Media*. Boulder: Westview Press.

Rombough, Shirley, and Diane C. Kelthly. 2010. "Native Americans, the Feudal System, and the Protestant Work Ethic: A Unique View of the Reservation." *Race, Gender & Class* 12: 104–20.

Rosenberg, Alyssa. 2009. "Asian-American Employees Underreport Discrimination, Report Finds." *Government Executive.com*. http://www.govexec.com/dailyfed/0109/012009ar1.htm.

Ross, Stephen L., and Margery Austin Turner. 2005. "Housing Discrimination in Metropolitan America: Explaining Changes between 1989 and 2000." *Social Problems* 52 (May): 152–80.

Roth, Wendy D. 2005. "The End of the One–Drop Rule? Labeling of Multiracial Children in Black Intermarriages." *Sociological Forum* 20 (March): 35–67.

Ryan, William. 1976. *Blaming the Victim*, rev. ed. New York: Vintage Books.

Saft, Elizabeth W., and Robert C. Pianta. 2001. "Teachers' Perceptions of Their Relationships with Students: Effects of Child Age, Gender, and Ethnicity of Teachers and Children." *School Psychology Quarterly* 16 (June): 125–41.

Schaefer, Richard T. 1993. *Racial & Ethnic Groups*, 5th ed. New York: HarperCollins.

Schaffner, Brian F., and Mark Gadson. 2004. "Reinforcing Stereotypes? Race and Local Television Coverage of Congress." *Social Science Quarterly* 85 (September): 604–23.

Shapiro, Herbert. 1988. *White Violence and Black Response: From Reconstruction to Montgomery*. Amherst, MA: University of Massachusetts Press.

Shin, Hyoung-jin, and Richard Alba. 2006. "The Economic Value of Bilingualism for the 1.5 and the 2nd Generation Hispanic and Asian Workers." *American Sociological Association annual meetings*, pp. 1–18.

Sleeter, Christine E. 2007. "Preparing Teachers for Multiracial and Historically Underserved Schools," pp. 171–89 in Erica Frankenberg and Gary Orfield (eds.), *Lessons in Integration: Realizing the Promise of Racial Diversity in American Schools*. Charlottesville: University of Virginia Press.

Smith, Dinitia. 1997. "Reconstruction's Deep Imprint." *New York Times* (June 18): C13.

Soule, Sarah A. 1992. "Populism and Lynching in Georgia, 1890–1900." *Social Forces* 71 (December): 431–49.

Southern Education Foundation. 2002. "1916–1931: Jim Crow Segregation." http://www.sefatl.org/1916.asp.

Steele, Claudia M. 1997. "A Threat in the Air: How Stereotypes Shape Intellectual Identity and Performance." *American Psychologist* 52 (June): 613–29.

Steele, Claudia M., and Joshua Aronson. 1995. "Stereotype Threat and the Intellectual Test Performance of African Americans." *Journal of Personality and Social Psychology* 69 (November): 797–811.

Stevenson, Howard C., Jocelyn Reed, Preston Bodison, and Angela Bishop. 1997. "Racism Stress Management: Racial Socialization Beliefs and the Experience of Depression and Anger in American Youth." *Youth and Society* 29 (December): 197–222.

Sullivan, Kevin. 2008. "Europeans Foresee Their Own Obama Emerging One Day." *Washington Post* (November 13): A17.

Tatum, Beverly Daniel. 2003. *Why Are All the Black Kids Sitting Together in the Cafeteria?: A Psychologist Explains the Development of Racial Identity*, rev. ed. New York: Basic Books.

Tatum, Beverly Daniel. 2004. "Family Life and School Experience: Factors in the Racial Identity Development of Black Youth in White Communities." *Journal of Social Issues* 60 (March): 117–35.

Tienda, Marta, and Faith Mitchell (eds.). 2006. *Multiple Origins, Uncertain Destinies: Hispanics and the American Future*. Washington, DC: National Academies Press.

Tolnay, Stewart E., and E. M. Beck. 1992. "Racial Violence and Black Migration in the South, 1910 to 1930." *American Sociological Review* 57 (February): 103–16.

Tontonoz, Matthew J. 2008. "The Scopes Trial Revisited: Social Darwinism versus Social Gospel." *Science as Culture* 17 (June): 121–43.

Troutman, Phillip. 2006. "Correspondences in Black and White: Sentiment and the Slave Market Revolution," pp. 211–42 in Edward E. Baptist and Stephanie M. H. Camp (eds.), *New Studies in the History of American Slavery*. Athens, GA: University of Georgia Press.

U.S. Census Bureau. 2008a. Table A–3. "Mean Earnings of Workers 18 and Over, by Educational Attainment, Race, Hispanic Origin, and Sex: 1975 to 2007." *Historical Tables*. http://www.census.gov/population/socdemo/education/cps2008/tabA-3.csv.

U.S. Census Bureau. 2008b. Table P-4. "Race and Hispanic Origin of People (Both Sexes Combined) by Median and Mean Income: 1947 to 2007." *Historical Income Tables—People*. http://www.censusbureau.biz/hhes/income/histinc/p04.html.

U.S. Census Bureau. 2009. Table 577. "Marital Status of Women in the Civilian Labor Force: 1970 to 2007." *Statistical Abstract of the United States: 2009*. http://www.census.gov/compendia/statab/tables/09s0577.pdf.

U.S. Census Bureau. 2010. Table 680. "Money Income of Families—Percent Distribution by Income Level in Constant (2007) Dollars: 1980 to 2007." *Statistical Abstract of the United States: 2010*. http://www.census.gov/

compendia/statab/cats/income_expenditures-poverty-wealth/family_income.html.

Valenzuela, Abel, Jr. 2006. "Economic Development in Latino Communities: Incorporating Marginal and Immigrant Workers," pp. 141–58 in Paul Ong and Anastasia Loukaitou-Sideris (eds.), *Jobs and Economic Development in Minority Communities*. Philadelphia: Temple University Press.

Varma, Roli. 2004. "Asian Americans: Achievements Mask Challenges." *Asian Journal of Social Science* 32: 290–307.

Villani, Susan. 2001. "Impact of Media on Children and Adolescents: A 10-Year Review of the Research." *Journal of the American Academy of Child and Adolescent Psychiatry* 40 (April): 392–401.

Vogel, Michael D. 2007. "Harder Times: Undocumented Workers and the U.S. Informal Economy," pp. 57–66 in Michael D. Yates (ed.), *More Unequal: Aspects of Class in the United States*. New York: Monthly Review Press.

Wagmiller, Robert. 2005. "Race, Residential Segregation, Suburbanization, and the Spatial Segregation of Jobless Men." *American Sociological Association annual meeting*, pp. 1–26.

Ward, L. Monique. 2004. "Wading through the Stereotypes: Positive and Negative Associations between Media Use and Black Adolescents' Conception of Self." *Developmental Psychology* 40 (March): 284–94.

Wark, Colin, and John F. Galliher. 2007. "Emory Bogardus and the Origins of the Social Distance Scale." *American Sociologist* 38 (December): 383–95.

Wilson, Leslie Owen. 2005. "Wilson Curriculum Pages." http://www.uwsp.edu/Education/wilson/curric/curtyp.htm.

Wilson, William Julius. 1997. *When Work Disappears: The World of the New Urban Poor*. New York: Vintage Books.

Wood, Betty. 1997. *The Origins of American Slavery: Freedom and Bondage in the English Colonies*. New York: Hill and Wang.

Wong, Dan. 2006. "Why Are Asian American Executives Scarce?" *Multicultural Advantage*. http://www.multiculturaladvantage.com/leader/workplace-leadership/Why-Are-Asian-American-Executives-Scarce.asp.

Yang, Song. 2005. "English Non-fluency and Income Penalty for Hispanic Workers." *American Sociological Association annual meeting*, pp. 1–26.

Young, Alfred A., Jr. 2006. "Low-Income Black Men on Work Opportunity, Work Resources, and Job Training Programs," pp. 147–84 in Ronald B. Mincy (ed.), *Black Males Left Behind*. Washington, DC: Urban Institute Press.

Zeng, Zhen, and Yu Xie. 2004. "Asian Americans' Earnings Reexamined: The Role of Education." *American Journal of Sociology* 109: 1075-1108.

Ziegler, Robert H. 2007. *For Jobs and Freedom: Race and Labor in America since 1865*. Lexington, KY: University Press of Kentucky.

Zirkel, Sabrina. 2002. "Is There a Place for Me? Role Models and Academic Identity among White Students and Students of Color." *Teachers College Record* 104 (March): 357–76.

Zirkel, Sabrina. 2005. "Ongoing Issues of Racial and Ethnic Stigma in Education 50 Years after *Brown v. Brown*." *Urban Review* 37 (June): 107–26.

CHAPTER 10

Women's Oppression: Sexism and Intersectionality

In the late nineteenth century, Charlotte Gilman wrote *Women and Economics: A Study of the Economic Relations between Men and Women as a Factor in Social Evolution*. While the majority of her feminist contemporaries were focused on enfranchising women, Gilman's concerns about inequality ran broader and deeper. Gilman recognized that people's position in a social-stratification system depended on their location in the division of labor. For the majority of women, who were housewives, Gilman declared, "[W]ork is not such as to affect her economic status." The quantity and quality of a woman's household labors did nothing to determine her material benefits. "These things bear relation only to the man she marries, the man she depends on—to how much he has and how much he is willing to give her" (Gilman 1898, 21). In Gilman's thinking the housewife had no personal location in the division of labor. She was an appendage.

Furthermore Gilman emphasized the critical impact of socialization. She stated, "From the time our children are born, we use every means known to accentuate sex-distinction in both boy and girl" (Gilman 1898, 51). As a child grows older, "every step of the human creature is marked 'male' or 'female'—surely, this is enough to show our [overemphasis on gender]" (Gilman 1898, 52–53).

In spite of this relentless child-rearing, some changes began to appear. Gilman noted that "[l]ittle by little, very slowly, and with unjust and cruel opposition, . . . it is being established by many martyrdoms that human work is woman's as well as man's" (Gilman 1898, 53).

While the following concept did not exist in Gilman's era, she dedicated her life to destroying the reality it described. **Sexism** is a set of beliefs claiming that real or alleged differences between women and men establish the superiority of men. Real differences would involve physical traits such as the existence of distinctive sexual organs while alleged differences would include undocumented claims that men are more intelligent, more capable of leadership, and emotionally more stable. Through American history sexism has been a ferocious, common presence.

Sexism like racism is divided into two types. **Individual sexism** is a person's or group's action that produces abuse against girls or women. It can be verbal, psychological, or physical. **Institutional sexism** involves the discriminatory practices built into organizations and groups within the political, economic, and educational systems. Like its racial counterpart, institutional sexism has been a common, widely accepted practice—for instance, in a variety of organizational settings "business as usual" means women face repeated discriminations when engaging in schooling and work.

This chapter's opening section examines the sexist conditions that have prevailed through the American centuries. Then the focus shifts to the present, describing major sources of sexism. The final subject is intersectionality, revealing the impact on women of two or more influential statuses.

A HISTORY OF SECOND-CLASS CITIZENRY

In the preindustrial life of early America, work was usually home-centered, with family members dependent on each other for basic sustenance. While fathers and sons were farmers, shopkeepers, laborers, and other job holders, wives and daughters cooked, cleaned, engaged in childcare, spun and wove, and made clothes, candles, soap, and shoes.

Women, however, were not restricted to household tasks. Some, primarily widows of business men, took their husbands' place, serving as innkeepers, merchants, printers, craft workers, physicians, tavern owners, and shopkeepers (Hesse-Biber and Carter 2005, 21–22; Padavic and Reskin 2002, 60). In his autobiography Benjamin Franklin described a printer's widow who took over her husband's business, proving more successful than he had been. One reason for her success was that in her native Holland a woman's standard education included bookkeeping. Ever the practical man, Franklin noted that if widowed, women would find this training "of more use to them and their children . . . than either music or dancing, . . . enabling them to continue, perhaps, a profitable mercantile house" (Franklin 1962, 95). Franklin's recommendation received scant attention, and so such women were more the exception than the rule. In most families a sharply gendered division of labor prevailed.

In the nineteenth century, industrial growth started to provide new jobs for both men and women. Men dominated most occupations, including some like clerical work, which eventually became women's domain. Most women employed outside the home labored 12 hours a day for low wages in factories, mills, sweatshops, or as servants (Padavic and Reskin 2002, 61).

More affluent women, however, tended to have a better arrangement. A few worked as teachers or nurses. Many nineteenth-century, middle-class Americans considered teaching a special calling for women, because, as the well-known educator Catherine E. Beecher declared, a "[w]oman's great mission is to train immature, weak, and ignorant creatures, to obey the laws of God; the physical, the intellectual, the social, and the moral—first in the family, then in the school" (Beecher 2006, 294). Writing in 1872, Beecher indicated that in the family and in the school a woman is a "complete autocrat" with "supreme control" over the development of children's intellect and habits. She also controlled "a husband, whose character, comfort, peace, and prosperity are all in her power" (Beecher 2006, 296). Woman, Beecher contended, has a moral power that is "more controlling and abiding than the inferior, physical power conferred on man" (Beecher 2006, 297).

Historically other categories of traditional women were sometimes able to exert considerable power. Among many American Indian tribes, the standard practice was that men hunted and fished while women farmed. The more prominent part agricultural work played within an Indian society, the greater women's power. In Native American farming communities, women often controlled tools, land, and surplus food, sometimes enabling them to exert formidable political clout. For instance, if Iroquois women opposed a particular raid, they might forestall the violence by refusing to turn over cornmeal needed to sustain the attack force (Hesse-Biber and Carter 2005, 28–29).

Clearly the conception of womanhood has varied across time and space. A sharp contrast existed in the pre-Civil War South, where white women living on plantations were coddled, idealized, and protected while black women had to labor long hours and face the ever-present prospect of cruel punishment. Pregnancy offered no escape. A common method for whipping pregnant slaves was to force them "to lie face down in a specially dug depression in the ground, a practice that provided simultaneously for the protection of the fetus and the abuse of the mother" (Hesse-Biber and Carter 2005, 25).

While hardly as oppressive as slavery, middle-class women's subjugated condition at the dawn of the twentieth century nurtured many discontents. By 1900 divorce was rising, women's militant organizations were mushrooming, pressure for equal voting rights was increasing, and press coverage of "the woman question" was ever expanding. The organized women's movement seized on suffrage as the central issue, but Charlotte Gilman and some of the era's most articulate and sophisticated feminists took a broader view, emphasizing a major economic reality—that women were largely excluded from employment. Historian Daniel Rodgers put it simply: What women "needed above all else was to go to work" (Rodgers 1978, 184).

In the intervening century, large numbers of women have moved into the job world. Figure 10.1 indicates that the proportion of working women in different marital statuses has increased steadily through the twentieth century and into the twenty-first century. Perhaps most notably the percentage of married women in the workforce expanded from 5.6 percent in 1900 to 61.4 percent in 2008—more than a tenfold increase (U.S. Bureau of the Census 2003; U.S. Bureau of the Census 2010).

In spite of such increases in employment, women are still more likely than men to find themselves in low-wage, dead-end jobs, often segregated from the male-dominated, prestigious, high-paying positions (Katz and Stern 2006, 76–77).

A relevant concept is the **index of occupational segregation**, which represents the proportion of females (or males) who would need to change to jobs where their sex is underrepresented, thereby producing a sexually integrated occupational structure. Most occupations fall far short of a complete integration. Women tend to be heavily represented in a few job areas—especially in secretarial work, retail sales, school teaching, nursing, and cashiering and bookkeeping. At the turn of the twenty-first century, the index of occupational segregation was 31, meaning that nearly a third of employed American woman would have needed to shift to predominantly male jobs to produce full occupational integration (Padavic and Reskin 2002, 65–67). Table 10.1 lists women's and men's percentages in five broad occupational categories.

In any segregated situation, the less elevated group is likely to be significantly disadvantaged—a topic discussed at length in the section on work later in the chapter. Figure 10.2 illustrates that while over time women's income has grown closer to men's, the significantly segregated work world still displays a gender gap in earnings. In fact, a survey of 22 developed nations indicated that men's full-time earnings averaged 17.6 percent higher than women's; in the United States, the gap is slightly above average—19 percent (Organization for Economic Cooperation and Development 2010; Rampell 2010). Besides economic discrimination sexism produces other negative experiences for women.

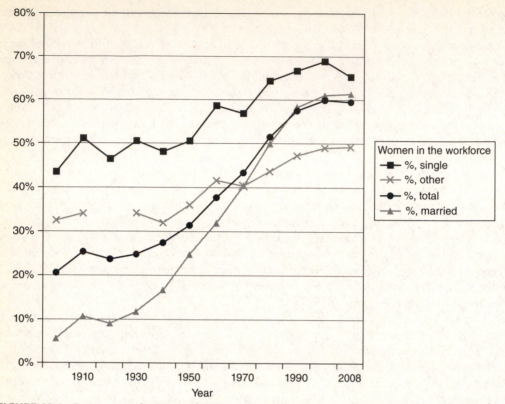

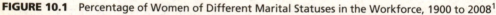

FIGURE 10.1 Percentage of Women of Different Marital Statuses in the Workforce, 1900 to 2008[1]

[1]Comments on the categories: Since 1955 "married" refers to husbands living in the household, and "other" means widowed, divorced, or separated. In 1920 "other," then meaning widowed or divorced, was included with single, and thus as the figure indicates, no data for "other" were available at that time. The data represent women 16 and older.

Over more than a century, women of all major marital statuses have increased their workforce participation. The greatest growth has involved married women.

Sources: U.S. Census Bureau. No. HS-30. "Marital Status of Women in the Civilian Labor Force: 1900 to 2002." *Statistical Abstract of the United States: 2003*. http://www.census.gov/statab/hist/HS-30.pdf; U.S. Census Bureau. Table 584. "Marital Status of Women in the Civilian Labor Force: 1947 to 2008." *Statistical Abstract of the United States: 2010*. http://www.census.gov/compendia/statab/cats/labor_force_employment_earnings.html.

THE PERSISTENCE OF SEXISM

In the well-known article "Doing Gender," Candace West and Don Zimmerman (1987) indicated that at birth a standard sequence of events occurs. Basing their judgment on an examination of newborn infants' genitalia or occasionally their chromosomal typing, adults attending at births assign children to a sex category. From that moment everyone, eventually including the children themselves, start **doing gender**, acting in ways considered appropriate toward members of the designated sex category. Throughout the life span, doing gender has a persistent impact on everyone involved.

TABLE 10.1 Percentage of Women and Men in Broad Occupational Categories

	Total	Management, professional, and related positions	Service jobs	Sales and office	Natural resources, construction, and maintenance positions	Production, transportation, and material moving jobs
Women	46.7%	50.8%	57.2%	63.2%	4.2%	22.4%
Men	53.3	49.2	42.8	36.8	95.8	77.6

These statistics suggest that men and women often have different kinds of jobs. In 2008 women's proportion of sales and office positions and service jobs was much higher than men. In contrast, women's percentage in natural resources etc. and production etc., was much lower than men's.

Source: U.S. Bureau of the Census. 2010. Table 603. "Employed Civilians by Occupation, Sex, Race, and Hispanic Origin: 2008." *Statistical Abstract of the United States: 2010.* http://proximityone.com/statab/guide/index .htm?laborforce_employment.htm

According to writer R.W. Connell, modern societies practice **hegemonic masculinity**—an established gender hierarchy in which masculine qualities, opportunities, and privileges receive greater recognition than feminine ones (Connell 1995, 35–37). This trend is apparent in the upcoming discussions of families, peers, the mass media, and work.

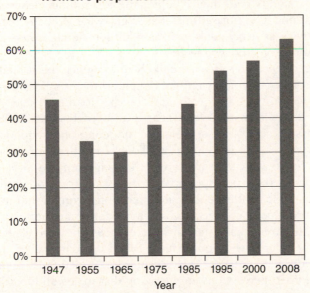

Women's proportion of men's median income

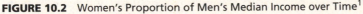

FIGURE 10.2 Women's Proportion of Men's Median Income over Time[1]

[1]In 2008 dollars

Since the middle 1960s, women's proportion of men's median income has risen steady, going from 30 percent in 1965 to more than double that figure—63 percent in 2008.

Source: U.S. Census Bureau. 2010. Table P-2. "Race and Hispanic Origin of People by Median Income and Sex." *Historical Income Tables—People.* http://www.census.gov/hhes/www/income/data/historical/ people/index.html.

The Family Impact

Since the 1970s hundreds of studies have indicated that before the age of five, children have developed both gender identity and gender stereotypes. By age three most are aware of being male or female, and by five "girls prefer dolls, doll accessories, soft toys, drawing, painting, cutting, and pasting while boys prefer blocks, small vehicles, tools, and rough-house play" (Hesse-Biber and Carter 2005, 115). When they saw pictures of unknown children in their age group, four- to ten-year-olds predicted girls would like "feminine" toys and boys "masculine" ones (Hesse-Biber and Carter 2005, 115).

Parents often support traditional gender-related identities and stereotypes. As a rule they interact more with infants of their own sex. For instance, fathers more frequently visit their newborn sons in the hospital, play more with them, and display more physical affection toward them. On the other hand, mothers tend to imitate, talk to, and play with their infant daughters more than with their sons.

Mothers and fathers often characterize their newborn children in broadly different ways—boys as "big, active, and alert . . . and girls as small, soft, fine-featured and inattentive" (Marmion and Lundberg-Love 2004, 2). In fact, the data indicate that the two sexes are similar in size, weight, and physical activity. Frequently parents often decorate their infant children's bedrooms in stereotyped ways, with a survey of bedrooms for 120 boys and girls under two revealing girls' rooms often displaying the color pink and containing dolls, doll houses, and children's furniture and boys' rooms featuring the colors blue and white along with sports equipment, tools, and vehicles (Marmion and Lundberg-Love 2004, 2). In addition, if parents read their children the top-selling picture books, they are exposing them to distinctly sex-biased material, with twice as many male title characters and also almost twice as many adult male as adult female characters in the stories (Hamilton, Broaddus, Anderson, and Young 2006).

Furthermore, the chores parents assign are likely to influence their children's gender perceptions and choices. Parents typically require daughters to do childcare and cleaning, initiating their intimacy with those traditionally female tasks at an early age; sons, in contrast, are more likely to do maintenance work (Leaper and Friedman 2007, 580).

Besides parents' assignment of tasks, their role modeling often supports their children's gender-role stereotypes. For instance, regardless of mothers' employment status, most women do more housework than men, and their children are aware of the discrepancy, which influences their perception of both sexes' appropriate domestic responsibility. On another topic, evidence indicates that both women and men consider that the subjects men introduce in conversation are more important and more worthy of discussion. Once again, if parents have standard preferences, they are likely to promote children's conventional gender-role outlook (Hesse-Biber and Carter 2005, 115–16).

All in all, the development of gender-role socialization is a cumulative process often promoting highly stereotyped perceptions emphasizing that males and females "differ in the levels of independence, aggression, activity, strength, fearlessness, dominance, obedience, expressiveness, concern with physical appearance, nurturance, intellectual ability, and mechanical competence" (Hesse-Biber and Carter 2005, 117).

In some instances, however, mothers' work experiences can promote their opposition to traditional gender roles. One study indicated that adolescents with employed mothers were more likely to express egalitarian gender-role views than homemakers' children (Gardner and LaBrecque 1986). Furthermore other research concluded that married women were more likely to be involved in egalitarian role sharing if their mothers had jobs during their childhood (Cunningham 2001).

Overall, however, most children grow up valuing gender distinctions. Parents and other adults reinforce such a reality, providing different clothes, toys, norms, and media images for the sexes. As children grow up in this controlled context, they develop a greater sense of **gender constancy**—the recognition that being female or male is a permanent part of one's identity, serving as the foundation for adult gender roles. Somewhere between the ages of five and seven, children achieve gender constancy, and it motivates them to identify more strongly with their own sex (Glick and Hilt 2000, 254; Miller, Trautner, and Ruble 2006, 298–99).

While the social environment promotes gender constancy, biological factors can have an impact, sometimes surprising parents. Having raised a daughter in a weapons-free environment, Holly Lutz looked forward to a similar result when she gave her son Carver a Barbie doll and a truck. She explained, "The little boy examined both and then proceeded to run Barbie over repeatedly with the truck. By 2, he was bending his sister's Barbies into L-shapes and using them as guns" (Turley 2007, B1).

Most of the time gender constancy is an important reality underlying children's relations with each other.

The Influence of Peers

From the age of two or three, children prefer to play with same-sex others, and that tendency increases until they are about 11. It seems apparent that peers are the strongest influence on gender-typed play. Children use same-sex peers as models for developing rules about gender. Both girls and boys are more likely to experiment with a gender-neutral or cross-gender toy if a same-sex peer does it first. However, most of the time same-sex peers disapprove of mixed-sex activities, and children usually internalize these conventional standards. Not surprisingly research has indicated that the longer children play with same-sex peers, the more conventionally gendered their behavior (Glick and Hilt 2000, 253; Leaper and Friedman 2007, 569).

Among young children same-sex peers have several ways of ensuring a traditional outlook on gender roles:

- Peers often display bias, convinced that members of their own sex are preferable. This same-sex support appears stronger for girls than for boys, with research in elementary school showing that girls like girls more than boys like boys. Possible reasons for this outcome are that girls dislike boys' tendency to dominate mixed-sex conversations and also resent their practices of barking orders and using physical intimidation, and so they respond by elevating their evaluation of their own sex (Marmion and Lundberg-Love 2004, 11–12). A study in which 8- to 10-year-olds designated personality traits as either feminine or masculine confirmed the existence of extensive sex-linked bias. Both boys and girls assigned more positive traits to their own sex and negative qualities to the other one. Notably the assignment of traits the children made bore little resemblance to whether they were considered traditionally feminine or masculine in adults' estimation. For instance, adults are likely to consider "strong" a positive quality associated with males and "gentle" a positive trait linked to females. However, in the research both girls and boys considered each of these characteristics positively related to their own sex (Powlishta 1995).

- Peers can act as gatekeepers, with boys and girls usually supporting tradition- alism and punishing deviations with critical remarks, attempting to change the deviant behavior, or even abandoning the troublesome individual. Many boys prefer same-sex peers who avoid talk about anxieties, fear, and other emotion- ally sensitive issues and act in physically aggressive, competitive, and emotionally detached ways (Marmion and Lundberg-Love 2004, 10–11; Spade and Valentine 2004, 174).

- Same-sex peers encourage segregation, with even children who are less strongly gender-typed still more likely to prefer same-sex playmates because they gener- ally share similar interests and interaction styles. In addition, spending time with same-sex companions supports children's powerful impulse to develop their gender identity. The resulting separation handicaps children's development of skills for relating to members of the other sex (Marmion and Lundberg-Love 2004, 111–12).

As sexual attraction develops in adolescence, the antagonistic competition abates. Vaguely grasping the situation, children contrive ways to defuse this new, confusing state of affairs. Frequently girls and boys tease each other about sexual attraction, sometimes turning the situation into a competition where the opposite-sex opponent is chased and if captured is "punished" with a kiss. This approach transforms a confusing, sexually tinged encounter into a familiar, hostile competition.

Eventually, however, sexual attraction becomes undeniable. Modern adolescents remain fairly traditional in their dating standards, with males often controlling such benevolently sexist patterns as opening doors and acting as the planners of dates and initiators of sexual activity. In adolescence, as in childhood, gender-role distinctions remain pronounced, but the chief difference is that teenage boys positively evaluate such traditional feminine traits as warmth and interpersonal skills (Glick and Hilt 2000, 258–60).

Females, however, pay a price. Studies have shown that in dating situations they still feel pressure to present themselves as less powerful and more vulnerable than males. To be successful in heterosexual situations, they learn to defer to males' choice of con- versation topics and to accept their interruptions. Their body language is supposed to be modest and reserved, meaning they can neither slouch nor sit with their legs spread apart but must look attentive, smile often, and frequently nod their heads (Hesse-Biber and Carter 2005, 122).

Most recent research suggests that the youthful dating world is one in which males confidently set the rules, control the action, and remain emotionally detached in the pur- suit of sexual conquest. While informative, this body of studies is limited, generally focus- ing on girls. An investigation drawn from a sample of 957 adolescents who had started dating included boys and found that many of them were neither confident nor emotion- ally aloof. Michael (aged 17) explained that relating to girls was terrifying.

"I was always nervous at asking them out, but that one experience where I crashed and burned that just killed my confidence completely" (Giordano, Manning, and Longmore 2006, 275). Furthermore contrary to prevailing beliefs, male respondents often indicated they were emotionally involved with their girlfriends. When asked how important his relationship was, Will (aged 17) replied that he would willingly give up his life for her—that "I wouldn't want to live without Jenny" (Giordano, Manning, and Longmore 2006, 277).

It appears that this student, seemingly eager to comment in class, is not intimidated by the hidden curriculum.

In schools, dating and other peer-related activities help shape children's educational experience.

Schools and the Gendered Hidden Curriculum

Traditionally the United States has emphasized that schools are settings where all children, no matter how modest their background, have a good opportunity to be successful. Such an outlook ignores the frequent existence of a **hidden curriculum**—the messages about values, beliefs, and behavior that teachers and administrators can unofficially communicate to students (Wilson 2005). Most of the time school officials, parents, and children pay little attention to the hidden curriculum because it is just that—hidden. However, in recent decades some educators have recognized that various vulnerable groups—children who are poor, belong to racial minorities, or are female—often fall victim to it. Focusing on the gender issue internationally, three educators contended that further evaluation is necessary to determine "whether education institutions allow girls effective participation, and whether the existing situations of girls and women are enhanced or diminished by the schooling they receive" (Aikman, Unterhalter, and Challender 2005, 45).

Research suggests that a gendered hidden curriculum is alive and well and operating in certain ways:

The academic program. A 1989 study of 62 children's picture books indicated that while the ratio of female to male human characters was about equal, male animal characters outnumbered their female counterparts three to one, and about two thirds of story illustrations featured males. Furthermore the stories described females as less adventurous, more vulnerable, and narrower occupationally (Purcell and Stewart 1990). Gender stereotyping also remained prevalent in more recent books (Gooden and Gooden 2001; Taylor 2003).

Beyond elementary school, history books still concentrate on men's domination in all important public activities, with no more than an occasional passing reference to such renowned women as Elizabeth I or Marie Curie.

Females are also underrepresented in certain academic areas. Teachers, administrators, and parents often consider math, science, and computers more appropriate interests for males, and so it is hardly surprising that women's choices of professions reflect this emphasis. Females are overrepresented in the humanities, social sciences, and biology while males dominate the physical and computer sciences, engineering, and mathematics (Basow 2004, 119). In 2005 this issue received widespread attention when Harvard president Laurence Summers publicly speculated that women might have less innate ability than men in science and math. The furor that arose forced Summers to resign the presidency shortly afterward (Bombardieri 2005).

In particular, many educators have believed that women have less math ability. To be successful, those interested in pursuing math must confront and defeat the widespread gender stereotypes about male superiority in math, dealing with the often low expectations many teachers and family members maintain (Meraz 2008, 102).

Gender roles in the classroom. Evidence suggests that many teachers pay more attention to boys in the classroom, calling on them more often and encouraging them to make lengthier statements. In addition, because of stereotyped notions about girls' abilities, particularly that they are less capable in mathematics, the sciences, and computer studies (Leaper and Friedman 2007, 578), some teachers take them less seriously as students than they do boys. In selected college classrooms, women are likely to receive less encouragement from teachers. These classes tend to be large, feature traditionally masculine topics such as math or physical sciences, and are male dominated numerically (Basow 2004, 123).

What happens, one may wonder, when a new program increasing girls' opportunities enters the traditionally gendered public-school system? A case in point involves the 1972 enactment of Title IX, the new national standard requiring federally funded educational programs to provide funds equally to both sexes. As a result girls' and women's athletic programs increased substantially, offering valuable experience and knowledge. Team sports develop such important skills as learning to contribute to group cohesiveness, discussing how to make one's own positive contribution to the team's activities, figuring out how to achieve both collective and personal goals, and learning how to function with impersonal, often troublesome rules (Hesse-Biber and Carter 2005, 119; Shakib and Dunbar 2002, 353).

In spite of female teams' increased opportunities to participate, however, they continue to be less favored than boys' teams. An illustration involves a study of 44 high-school basketball players, 25 females and 19 males coming from three public high schools and belonging to six teams (Shakib and Dunbar 2002, 357). Both the male and female respondents felt that the girls' teams, even the very good ones, were inferior to the boys' teams. Nicole, the top player on a very good team, conceded that while her team was league champion and the boys' team finished well down the ranks, "I think [if we played them], they would still beat us . . . 'Cause they are just a higher level," (Shakib and Dunbar 2002, 360).

For both sexes the consensus seemed to be that the girls' game is not as fast, physical, or entertaining and lacks the most spectacular element—the dunk.

Many of the male players contended that the apparent superiority of their game is simply an indicator of a greater truth—that males are better. Robert, who longed to become a professional ball player, explained how basketball served to demonstrate male domination. He said, "[Boys] are stronger than girls, faster than girls, tougher than girls, jump higher than girls. And guys were put on this planet just to beat them" (Shakib and Dunbar 2002, 365).

While the respondents' two-tiered perception of the basketball teams prevailed, existing programs did provide girls the sports-related experiences mentioned earlier. In addition, some girls obtained a potentially valuable piece of cultural capital—the opportunity to acquire certain practical "masculine" behaviors. Tiffany stated her view on this issue, indicating that without basketball she would not be "aggressive or tough. Being physically aggressive has helped me in balancing out so I won't be just completely girlie or completely tomboyish" (Shakib and Dunbar 2002, 370).

With sexism widely entrenched in schools, among peers, and in families, it is hardly surprising that it thrives in the media.

The Representation of Females in the Mass Media

Sexism in the media is apparent in two ways—in traditionally stereotyped representations and in male/female differences in participation. These two discriminations undermine both women's images and their opportunities in such key domains as schooling and employment.

STEREOTYPES AS A PERSISTENT PRESENCE While an emphasis on traditional gender roles and stereotyped representations of women in the media has continued over time, some changes have occurred. For two decades following World War II, most situation comedies featured men as workers and problem solvers and women in support roles as housewives.

By the 1970s as more women entered the working world, there developed a number of long-running shows featuring women on the job—*The Mary Tyler Moore Show*, *Rhoda*, and *Charlie's Angels*. Nonetheless more men's than women's parts were on display in evening TV, and the male roles were more diverse, with the majority of women being homemakers.

Between 1982 and 1988, *Cagney and Lacey* was a TV series which received high ratings while opposing entrenched gender stereotypes. Unlike any program before it,

Cagney and Lacey centered on a relationship involving two women—police officers who solved their own cases without men's help and off the job lived distinctly different, empowered lives. One was a single woman with an active dating and sex life, and the other was her family's chief breadwinner, who was sometimes shown initiating sex with her husband. The high ratings kept the program going, but from the beginning executives felt the women were too tough and aggressive—"too women's lib." In fact, after the pilot was aired, the bosses tried to alleviate this concern by replacing one of the two lead women with a seemingly more moderate, mainstream actress (Holtzman 2000, 77–79).

The following two decades provided some diverse female characters, but less traditional representations have been more the exception than the rule. Contemporary programming has demonstrated, however, that a skillfully written and performed series can raise searching questions about gender issues while presenting female characters in a variety of roles, especially traditional ones. A notable case in point has been the cable series *Mad Men*, which examines work and life for the employees of a prominent 1960s Madison Avenue advertising agency. While the central characters are "mad men," who go about their daily lives often making sexist wisecracks and a variety of underhanded moves, including cheating on their wives and seducing their female employees, three women are also featured. They are a secretary whose developing skills allowed her to become an account executive, the wife of the leading male character, and a secretary. Through the episodes they struggle with men, work, and above all their sense of self. As one analyst noted, "They are complicated, glamorous, ambitious, and stifled in a way that women in the 1960s television never were" (Smith 2008, E1). In short, *Mad Men* looks beyond the façade of conventional behavior, revealing the women beneath the gender stereotypes as well as the episodes of hegemonic masculinity unfolding in their lives.

Even more than regular TV programming, commercials have projected narrow, stereotyped gender images, with two prominent patterns. First, commercials display men in control and women in passive situations. One distinct indicator of this trend is that while overwhelmingly women demonstrate products, the unseen powers describing them—the voice-overs—are about 96 percent men (Cortese 2008, 58; Hesse-Biber and Carter 2005, 125).

Second, in commercials women appear in a narrow range of roles. According to sociologist Anthony Cortese, they are depicted as "sex objects or mindless domestics pathologically obsessed with cleanliness" (Cortese 2008, 58). Producers of commercials, particularly beauty products ads, have a huge stake in projecting a very specific ideal of femininity. As Cortese noted, "The exemplary female prototype in advertising, regardless of product or service, displays youth (no lines or wrinkles), good looks, sexual seductiveness, . . . and perfection (no scars, blemishes, or even pores)" (Cortese 2008, 59). Thinness is also a common requirement. Weight-loss programs are often the central topic in advertisements about health clubs, exercise equipment, diet drinks, and various food products. One analyst suggested that "[t]he obsession with thinness is about cutting girls and women down to size" [italics removed] (Kilbourne 2004, 105). Whether or not that is accurate, these ads accelerate profits. Media support for the thinness obsession seems problematic in a nation where one third of 12- to 13-year-old girls are actively trying to lose weight by dieting, vomiting, and/or taking pills (Kilbourne 2004, 104).

Besides how women are represented in the media, an important issue involves the extent to which they participate.

FREQUENCY OF WOMEN'S PARTICIPATION IN THE MASS MEDIA In newspapers and news magazines, men continue to dominate numerically in several ways. Male authors write two thirds of front-page articles and three quarters of opinion pieces, and about 85 percent of front-page stories focus on men. Furthermore when women appear in "hard" news stories, aspects of their lives that are usually downplayed or disregarded for men—their physical appearance or family information—tend to receive ample coverage (Hesse-Biber and Carter 2005, 124). As a result the emergent image for women is likely to be less focused, perhaps implying they are less worthy than their male counterparts.

Television also underrepresents women. A study of prime-time TV shows produced by the four leading networks involved 1,269 characters, with males having nearly twice (1.7 to 1) as much speaking time as females (Glascock 2001). These results were consistent with a long-term pattern stretching from the early 1950s to the early 2000s: that on television women play little more than one in every three roles (Hesse-Biber and Carter 2005, 124).

The prime-time TV study displays an even greater disparity in creative personnel behind the scenes; male producers, directors, writers, and creators outnumber their female counterparts 3.6 to 1 (Glascock 2001). A reality of television production appears to contribute to this trend. The primarily male owners and producers of TV programming make a lucrative living with skits and commercials that generally represent women in conventional, stereotyped ways, promoting the purchase of beauty and household products. These corporate officials are sensitive to the fact that female creative personnel, most decidedly those with feminist leanings, are likely to oppose or resist sexist representations (Holtzman 2000, 80–81).

On the other hand, when a TV series systematically analyzes issues involving gender roles, its staff is likely to reflect that pattern. Why? First, the actual willingness to support an examination of gender subjects means that the program's executives are more likely than most of their peers to commit to gender equal opportunity. In addition, they are likely to appreciate that a mixed-sex staff will be better equipped to produce their gender-sensitive programming than an all-male or largely male group. *Mad Men*, which was previously discussed, had an unusual number of women among its creative personnel, including a staff writer, a consulting producer, and two supervising producers (Smith 2008).

When children are the target audience, conventional gender roles and gendered stereotypes are also likely to be emphasized. In cartoons male characters are greatly overrepresented, and the members of both sexes are portrayed in highly stereotyped ways. In TV commercials for children's products, the target audiences are usually divided, with boys selling to boys and girls to girls. Furthermore boys are normally portrayed as more knowledgeable, active, aggressive, and goal-oriented. With both cartoons and commercials, the gender-biased quality has an impact. The more cartoons children watch, the more likely they express gender stereotypes. In addition, an experiment indicated that the more television advertising children saw, the greater the effect it had in determining their requests for gender-specific toys (Browne 1998; Leaper and Friedman 2007, 566–68).

Alleged experts on parenting are another mass-media source influencing individuals' perception of gender roles. Social worker Karin Martin examined 34 books and

42 articles on 15 websites providing advice to parents. She found that these sources described gender development as socially constructed and emphasized that parents' gender-related treatment of their children was varied and produced different outcomes. Most of the advisors approved of preschool boys playing with dolls, girls and boys playing together, and girls playing sports—all practices that were nearly taboo a half-century earlier. However, the experts did draw a line: They did not accept the idea of girls and boys growing up to think of themselves as similar. For instance, it is inappropriate, these child-rearing specialists agreed, for 10 or 12 year-old boys to play with dolls. Such behavior suggests what many considered the specter of homosexuality—an unacceptable outcome in most people's eyes. Homosexuality remains stigmatized and distinctly absent from the mainstream sources on parental advice (Martin 2005).

Martin used the phrase "a stalled revolution" to summarize the current state of affairs involving media sources on childcare advice. Could the phrase apply to women's situation on the job?

Women in the Modern Work World

A question: Does the work world significantly resemble young children's peer relations? The fact of the matter is that both tend to be quite segregated. In other words men and women often do different work. The U.S. Census Bureau distinguishes over 500 occupations, and every 10 years it determines what percentage of both sexes occupy each occupation. At the turn of the twenty-first century, 30 percent of women worked in just 10 of the 503 occupations. In order of frequency, those categories are:

> Cashiers
> Secretaries
> Salaried managers and administrators
> Salaried sales supervisors and proprietors
> Registered nurses
> Elementary-school teachers
> Nursing aids, orderlies, and attendants
> Bookkeeping, accounting, and auditing clerks
> Waitresses
> Receptionists

Men too tend to cluster occupationally, but their top 10 positions share only two categories with women—salaried managers and administrators, and salaried sales supervisors and proprietors. In most jobs men outnumber women, in some cases overwhelmingly so. For instance, there are 128 times more male car mechanics, 62 times more male carpenters, and nearly eight times more male motor vehicle and boat sales people (Padavic and Reskin 2002, 65–66). As previously noted, the index of occupational segregation is 31 (Gabriel and Schmitz 2007). Table 10.2 demonstrates that managerial and professional occupations display considerable gender segregation, with women numerically dominant in certain positions and significantly underrepresented in others.

The impressive numbers in the table, however, fail to tell the full story of gendered job segregation. Within some occupations in which women and men appear to be doing the same work, investigation reveals that this is not the case and that

TABLE 10.2	Employed Women in Selected Occupations in Management and the Professions	
	Number of women employed (in thousands)	**Percent women**
Total, 16 years and over	67,884	46.7%
Management occupations	5,929	37.4
Professional and related occupations	17,408	56.7
Selected occupations starting with the highest female frequency		
Preschool and kindergarten teachers	669	97.6%
Librarians	164	83.5
Elementary and middle-school teachers	2,402	81.2
Accountants and auditors	1,077	61.1
Veterinarians	32	56.7
Secondary-school teachers	678	56
Financial managers	640	54.8
Biological scientists	53	52.9
Pharmacists	126	51.8
Lawyers	349	34.4
Physicians and surgeons	267	30.5
Computer scientists and systems analysts	230	27.5
Dentists	41	27.2
Architects, except naval	58	24.8
Chief executives	387	23.4
Civil engineers	36	10.4
Aerospace engineers	14	10.3
Construction managers	102	8.2
Mechanical engineers	21	6.7
Engineering managers	7	6.3

The percentage of women in these different managerial and professional occupations showed great variation. Female participation ranged from nearly complete numerical domination of preschool and kindergarten teaching to a very limited presence in several types of engineering and construction management.

Source: Bureau of Labor Statistics. 2010. Table 11. "Employed Persons by Detailed Occupation and Sex, 2008 Annual Averages." *Women in the Labor Force: A Databook (2009 ed.).* http://www.bls.gov/cps/wlftable11.htm.

women perform less prestigious, often lower-paying tasks. For instance, at Deloitte & Touche, one of the world's largest professional-services firm, female accountants focus on clients in the healthcare and retail areas and rarely work on challenging, career-building assignments involving mergers and acquisitions, normally considered male reserves. Among writers there is a fairly even split between the sexes but not in the celebrated film industry where there are twice as many male screen writers (Padavic and Reskin 2002, 67).

Another largely hidden disadvantage women can face involves their limited advancement within management and the professions. Income figures support this conclusion. In management and professional specialties, women's earnings are about 71 percent of men's—actually falling 2.7 percent between 1996 and 2001 (Hesse-Biber and Carter 2005, 203).

The glass ceiling is one of the factors affecting women's earnings. A number of studies found that women and minorities often face a **glass ceiling**, where they encounter various distinct but often unseen barriers, including discrimination, in seeking to move into high-level positions (Cotter, Hermsen, Ovadia, and Vanneman 2001; Hesse-Biber and Carter 2005, 205–08; Neumann 2006; Prokos and Padavic 2005; Rosser 2004).

A federal government study of women in management in ten industries addressed the concept of glass ceiling, concluding that between 1995 and 2000 women fell farther behind their male counterparts in both pay and job mobility. The research found that female managers' salaries decreased in relation to men's in seven of the ten industries which employed three quarters of female managers. Often women were steered into jobs that were less critical to a company's operation—dead-end positions offering no upward mobility. Discrimination, however, was not the only factor producing the glass ceiling. This study revealed that while about 60 percent of male managers in these industries had children in their home, only about 40 percent of women working full or part time maintained such an arrangement. Childcare responsibilities appeared to be a major factor holding women back from breaking through the glass ceiling (Dingell and Maloney 2002).

A study using data from the National Panel Study of Income Dynamics concluded that both black and white women faced a glass ceiling, with high-earning women experiencing a growing income gap with their male counterparts in the later portion of their career—not something that lower-earning women encountered (Cotter, Hermsen, Ovadia, and Vanneman 2001, 671).

One factor relating to the gender gap in income is the complex issue of **pay equity**—the contention that women and men should receive similar compensation not only for equal work but also for work of equal value. In modern times two conclusions about pay equity seem important—first, the reality that in a variety of job areas when such important factors as credentials, work tasks, and opportunity structures are controlled, men's income is higher (Dinovitzer, Reichman, and Sterling 2009; Morgan 2008); and second, the recognition that "work of equal value" is hardly a widely recognized standard. A case in point would involve state jobs in Minnesota, for which investigators developed pay ratings based on scorings for schooling, training, complexity of customer relationship, and job responsibility. The assessment system rated nurses and vocational education teachers the same; however, the nurses, who were primarily women, received $1,732 a month while the vocational education teachers, who were mainly men, averaged $2,260 a month (Andre and Velasquez 2010).

The latter example addressed the issue of **comparable worth**—the conclusion that the definitive means of promoting pay equity is to base pay scales on a combined assessment of the worker's qualifications and the job's basic traits, considering irrelevant whether or not the position is traditionally associated with a particular sex. Advocates of comparable worth fear that its obvious absence in most work settings might produce growing female resentment, poorer job performance, and tensions between the sexes (Andre and Velasquez 2010). While this concern could remain a reality, comparable-worth standards are not going to be easy to establish. For instance, three job-evaluation firms rated 27 jobs in an actual company on the basis of comparable worth. The result was very different ratings, with the firms disagreeing markedly on the job trait or traits that should be most salient (Arnault, Gordon, Joines, and Phillips 2001). While comparable worth might be difficult to attain, its achievement would be very significant for women economically. The typical woman worker would receive about $5,710 (in 2008 dollars), and American women in the workforce would obtain an additional $319 billion (Institute for Women Policy Research 2008).

Besides economic issues women can face other difficult conditions on the job.

A PAIR OF CHALLENGES EMPLOYED WOMEN CAN ENCOUNTER   The positions in question involve two very different occupational situations women can experience—working with men in blue-collar jobs and facing childcare pressures that can force one's retirement. Sociologist Jeanie Greene interviewed 17 female blue-collar workers and aptly named her book *Blue-Collar Women at Work with Men: Negotiating the Hostile Environment*. The respondents were involved in trucking, construction, loading ships, manufacturing, policing, security, carpentry, printing, commercial painting, and various other jobs.

The research subjects reported that certain men, not only fathers but also brothers and sons, contributed to their atypical interests in these blue-collar positions. Sally, who drove tractor-trailers, indicated that since childhood she had always helped her father, and he had taught her many things, including car repairs. He told her, "'And you're gonna know, if something breaks on a car, how to fix it.' I guess he kind of brought me up . . . like . . . [his] right-hand man" (Greene 2006, 43).

While these women enthusiastically sought blue-collar jobs, they tended to have less effective social capital than men—family members, friends, or others in the locale who helped them find jobs or recommended them for positions. As a result their means of locating jobs was distinctly nontraditional, often involving considerable personal initiative. Gretchen, for instance, visited a national park with her family, and she was fascinated by it. She returned several times on her own—young, with long blond dreadlocks, and, most of all, inquisitive. Gretchen asked a lot of questions, and eventually one of the rangers, who happened to be the park historian, began paying attention to her. She asked many questions about the work. "And finally after seeing me a bunch of times, he said, 'You keep coming back here. You should get a job here.' And I said, 'You can do that?' So he said, 'Oh, yeah, you can do visitors' service or maintenance'" (Greene 2006, 58).

Once on the job, these female blue-collar workers often faced significant challenges. Many of them encountered new, sometimes formidable demands, notably physical challenges they never previously faced. While the challenges in themselves were significant, the tasks in question had to be performed in a way that was acceptable to their male peers. Chris commented on police training, which was always strenuous, putting her at distinct advantage to her male peers, who were more accustomed to such activities. She said, "I really had to prove myself and work twice as hard to be half as good, because of being female, because I didn't know what I was doing" (Greene 2006, 75).

For all the respondents in this study, the jobs were difficult and demanding. However, the quality of supervision could determine whether the work was tolerable or intolerable. Beth, who did electrical contracting, had a supervisor who applauded women's job performances and recruited her into the meter-repair-and-assembly shop, encouraging her to study the subjects to qualify for the position. The supervisor stated, "'Women are my best workers.' . . . And that was the way he let us know we were welcome there." Beth suggested that such a supportive outlook can eventually permeate an entire organization (Greene 2006, 118–19).

In contrast, difficult supervisors readily made a hard job intolerable, sometimes forcing women to leave their positions. The punitive supervisors were often more vigilant overseeing women's than men's work, particularly on the topic of sick and injury time—a sensitive subject because it relates to stereotypes of women being weak or lazy. Sonja indicated that two days after she was hurt in a fall her supervisor called to ask when she would return to work. She indicated that in several days she would have tests, and then she would let him know. The supervisor, in turn, declared that her work was not getting done at home. Sonja replied, "I fell. I hurt myself. I did not do it on purpose . . . , and if you're taking this personally, maybe you should talk to somebody because this isn't personal. This is a business" (Greene 2006, 119).

Like supervisors female workers' male peers responded in varied ways. On some jobs verbal harassment was common, letting women know they were unwelcome. The results could be painful and degrading, wearing them down over time. Verbal harassment included insulting sexual comments, mocking requests for dates, harsh

Sexual harassment is one of the difficult issues on the job that women are more likely to face than men.

invitations to have sex, or remarks about an individual's breasts or other body parts. These barrages often persisted, no matter how many times the women asked their coworkers to stop (Greene 2006, 149).

Hostility against female workers appeared in other ways. On the job women were often ignored, not given help when they needed it or not given credit for work they had done. When Claire and her male partner returned to the office after a day's painting, he bragged about his accomplishment, and his coworkers reacted positively, simply assuming that as a man he had done most of the work. "They'd say 'Oh, great job, Ed. . . . you really earned us the money today.' And I had a cut in the whole thing, and . . . he got credit for it" (Greene 2006, 153).

On the other hand, some male coworkers were supportive, even very supportive. They might tell sexual jokes around the women but not jokes meant to embarrass or degrade females. On occasion they might hug a female coworker but only in a fatherly or brotherly way. These friendly male coworkers supported their female colleagues when they had personal issues or problems on the job. Sonja described a male coworker's empathy for her struggles with the supervisor. Hugging her, he would say, "'I wish I could just beat . . . that guy [to a pulp]. Because I'm really sick of seeing this kind of thing happen.' He said, 'But its not you. . . .' I said, 'thanks a lot'" (Greene 2006, 155).

A very different set of working women also found their jobs posing significant challenges. A study focused on 43 women who had held professional or managerial jobs but left them to care for their children. Invariably the decision to leave work was a highly conflicted one, predicated on a number of factors. Statistics indicated that the respondents in the research fitted into a broader pattern: that professional women are about three times as likely as their male counterparts to be out of the labor force (Stone and Lovejoy 2004, 63).

The informants explained that the decision to leave their jobs was a complicated one. Nearly 90 percent expressed a moderate to high degree of ambivalence about giving up their positions—an often protracted struggle between a sense of their investment in and commitment to their careers versus an intense pressure to stay home. For months Claire Lott, a public utilities manager, struggled with her decision. She said, "Ironically, that Sunday, after I made the decision, the sermon at church was 'Loss of Identity because of Loss of Job or Spouse.' That kind of clicked with me" (Stone and Lovejoy 2004, 66).

One factor that influenced these women's decision was the perceived importance of having a full-time parent in the home. Vita Cornwall, who left her job after the birth of her first child, explained that she wanted her children exposed to cultural capital they would not receive if she were working. She said, "The reason [I quit] is I want them to, for better or worse, interpret my values, our moral system, speak in our cadence, with our grammatical errors or proper speech." Only then, Cornwall felt, would they develop as their children (Stone and Lovejoy 2004, 67).

Sometimes workplace inflexibility became a significant impediment to holding a job. Meg Romano, who had worked full- or part-time with the same firm for 15 years, took a leave of absence to attend to her child's medical problems. Then she planned to resume work. A part-time position opened up, and looking forward to returning to work, she made the childcare arrangements. At the last minute, however, "the big boss" refused to support the rehiring (Stone and Lovejoy 2004, 68)

Workplace inflexibility is most apparent in high-growth industries. Lynn Hamilton, an MD who was medical director of a start-up company, recalled the steady barrage of faxes requiring instant action and the grueling travel schedule she had faced. She observed "I think the punch line is, there's a reason why people that tend to be funded by venture capitalists are twenty and live on Doritos in their basement." When someone was twice that age with a family, such a lifestyle became virtually impossible (Stone and Lovejoy 2004, 71).

About a quarter of the respondents indicated that at their child's birth, an intense feeling of attachment and bonding developed. Women who felt this response and returned to work were often anguished—torn between career and child. Regina Donofrio, a senior publicist for a large media corporation, felt she was trapped in a nightmare. "When I was at work, I should have been at home. When I was at home, I felt guilty, [leaving the job] early to see the baby, and I had maybe left some things undone" (Stone and Lovejoy 2004, 73).

One more factor contributing to these women's departure from their jobs concerned their husbands, who like their wives often had positions requiring long hours and extensive travel. The research subjects seldom mentioned husbands' domestic contributions, making it apparent that they were unable or unwilling to provide much childcare assistance (Stone and Lovejoy 2004, 75).

On the job, in school, and elsewhere, a variety of women's traits impact their activities and outcomes.

SEXISM AND INTERSECTIONALITY: PROSPECTS FOR A DOUBLE NEGATIVE

Intersectionality is the recognition that a woman's oppressions, limitations, and opportunities result from the combined impact of two or more influential statuses—in particular, her gender, race, class, age, and sexual preference (Barvosa 2008, 76–77; Dill, McLaughlin, and Nieves 2007, 629; Lengermann and Niebrugge 2008, 353; Mullings and Schulz 2006, 4–5; Shields 2008; Strolovitch 2007, 6–7).

Power is a key component in the intersectional process. Sociologist Patricia Hill Collins (1990, 225–27) referred to "the matrix of domination," which involves the most powerful players in the class/gender/race complex, particularly the higher classes of white males, who exert oppressive control over less privileged groups.

Experts on intersectionality point out that when traditional analyses focus on a single factor—say gender or race—the tendency has been to dichotomize the factor into a privileged category and a degraded one—man versus woman, white person versus black person. Instead the intersectional strategy involves an appreciation of a broad social context, where investigation involves a thorough, dispassionate evaluation of the key statuses impacting women's lives as well as some assessment of how those factors interact with each other. That interaction, which one might describe as "status interlock," is often more discernable to the women experiencing intersectionality than to outside observers.

The intersectional approach can prove useful in analyzing important political or economic topics. Title VII of the Civil Rights Act of 1964 is supposed to eliminate all employment discrimination, but black women with job-related grievances have been strongly encouraged to choose to focus on either race or sex. The discriminatory reality they often face, however, is not one or the other but an intersectional combination—the impact of being black women (Collins 1990, 224–25). Most Americans, however, fail to appreciate such realities. Addressing minority women, questioners often assume that the impact of either gender or race dominates. Ancella Livers, a journalist and management specialist, explained that "the experiences of women of color belie these assumptions. They are 'both/and' not 'either/or'" (Livers 2006, 205).

As a case in point, sociologist Lynn Weber observed that intersectional analysis can provide detailed insights about the different dimensions of poor black women's lives. It can examine such basic realities as their educational attainment and yearly income and micro-level information about their everyday existence, where "we can learn how they live with financial constraints, how they feed their families, how they deal with the stresses they face, how they manage work and family life" (Weber 2004, 129).

In examining people's everyday lives, the intersectional approach highlights the significance of **standpoint**—a particular group's outlook on the workings of social relations and society (Harding 2007, 62–63; Lengermann and Niebrugge 2008, 355). The intersectional approach analyzes subjugated female groups' standpoints, which arise from their common experience. Collins noted that as African American women interact, "a collective, focused group consciousness becomes possible" (Collins 1990, 26).

Often the members of an oppressed group are aware of the intersectional nature of their standpoint. Respondents in a study of black female firefighters consistently asserted that the impact of gender and race intertwine in producing a discrimination-laden job setting. One subject concluded, "It is double-edged: being black and being female" (Yoder and Aniakudo 1996, 255).

Kimberle Crenshaw, who developed the concept of intersectionality, would endorse the above point, also emphasizing the impact of class. She indicated that poor women of color, who are burdened by a formidable set of conditions associated with their class, gender, and race, face greater disadvantage than privileged women in receiving help for personal crises. For instance, while information about rape-crises services readily reaches affluent women, poor women of color are likely to live in more marginalized areas where they will not learn about such services unless their locales are targeted. Furthermore once case workers encounter this set of victims, they find that unlike situations involving privileged women, the aftermath of rape can be a less pressing issue than such looming crises as impending eviction or the absence of money for food. Rape-crisis counselors, whose work is supposed to provide information and referrals about rape, are usually ill-equipped to deal with such persistent problems (Crenshaw 1997, 95–101).

In the upcoming illustrations of intersectionality, it is apparent that mainstream structures often deal ineffectively and harshly with various disadvantaged groups. We consider black and Hispanic women, lesbians, immigrant women, and learning-disabled students.

Intersectionality: Black and Hispanic Women

On the job black women have faced discrimination in hiring and in promotion and have been more vulnerable than other female workers to layoffs and firings (Branch 2007; England 1992; Ortiz 2008; Reid 2002). However, as the twentieth century ended, analysts expected that because of declining discrimination and growing employment opportunities the gap in income between black and white women would decline. They were wrong. That racial divide grew from 8 percent in 1980 to more than double that figure—17 percent—in 2002. The principal contributing factors hindering black women seem to have been less access to human capital—in particular, a fairly low rate of college graduation necessary for most better paying jobs along with limited completion of training and certification programs—and also greater vulnerability than whites to labor-market declines featuring the decreasing availability of clerical and manufacturing jobs and, in turn, the growing necessity to take low-paying service positions (Dozier 2006).

In seeking employment poor African American women face a host of challenges, including childcare responsibilities, deficient schooling, and limited job skills (Crenshaw 1997, 95–96). With such disadvantages how do they find jobs? Some poor black women possess a productive source of social capital—a network of family and friends. In a study of 169 randomly sampled low-income African American women in Chicago and Baltimore, 43 percent of the 108 employed respondents found their jobs through such social connections. One woman explained that the "best thing to do is to keep in touch with family members or friends." She indicated how the process worked: "You just generally have conversations. Different jobs come up and people talk about the things that they are doing. And before you know it, they are helping you find out about what it is that you really want to do" (Turney 2005, 10).

However, poor black women's social networks are not always helpful for finding work. A study of 105 low-income Africans Americans, most of whom (84 percent) had a high-school diploma or GED and half of whom were employed, indicated that they generally felt distrust (81 percent) about jobseekers in their social networks, fearing that the individuals lacked the motivation to follow through and get hired, were likely to be irresponsible on the job, or were going to prove too needy at work (Smith 2006).

In seeking to enter the job world, poor African American women face an additional barrier—domestic violence. A study of 776 poor black and Hispanic women indicated that current partner abuse significantly increased the likelihood that a woman was unemployed and on welfare. Sometimes abuse victims received visible injuries that made it embarrassing to appear in public; in addition, some abusive individuals stalked their partners at work or made harassing phone calls to the job site (Nam and Tolman 2002).

While middle-class black women often have well-paid, prestigious jobs, they can be disadvantaged compared to their white counterparts. For instance, black female lawyers are more likely to work in fairly low-paying public-sector jobs. A study of black female lawyers indicated that its respondents had often attended black or largely black law schools where they were less likely than students in more expensive programs, whether black or white, to receive mentoring about the kind of extracurricular activities in which they should engage to promote their careers; that job recruiters in the private sector often weighed such credentials more heavily with minority than majority candidates; and that African American women attending black law schools faced the additional drawback that their schools' officials generally lacked effective social capital to help them obtain positions with private firms (Higginbotham 2009, 44–45).

Entering management, African American women often find themselves isolated, with few colleagues who are black and even fewer who are black women. Seldom do they find individuals who could serve as mentors, assisting their career development (Crawford and Smith 2005). A frequent suggestion is to build social networks composed of majority-group members, particularly white males. These individuals, however, are likely to resist such efforts, preferring close affiliation with people like themselves. Black female managers often find themselves the victims of stereotypes challenging their competence for the job; they are likely to learn that their white bosses and peers are reluctant to accept them as authority figures while white women with equal credentials usually advance more quickly (Combs 2003; Giscombe and Mattis 2002, 104–05).

Participants in a focus group composed of mid-level African American female managers indicated that they worked in a setting offering little support—that "whereas white men and women do not have to go through proving themselves, for they ride on their past performance . . . African American women have to be validated over and over again" (Giscombe and Mattis 2002, 113).

In a small study of black female professionals, all of whom had at least a college degree, the women expressed various complaints, perceiving themselves as more exploited than their male counterparts—more often required to perform menial, distasteful tasks. For instance, one subject indicated that her colleagues chose her to tell a black client that he needed to eliminate his excessive body odor. Why, the woman asked angrily, did these people think this unpleasant assignment would be any easier for her than for them?

Some female respondents in this study also considered themselves branded with the Jezebel stereotype described in the mass-media discussion in Chapter 9. Georgia, a respondent, said that she received a phone call from a fellow worker who indicated that her husband reacted strongly to what he considered her provocative outfit. Georgia said, "First, this is a man who wears white socks all the time. Second, I don't want to know that her husband is checking me out in my suit." Georgia also wondered why this woman who had always been distant was suddenly confiding in her (Wingfield 2007, 204).

African American middle-class women working in a largely white world can encounter another oppressive reality—an abiding sense of inadequacy. Reasons for such a reaction include the awareness that many whites share stereotypes that represent them as inferior beings and also an uneasiness that being black is a major reason why they obtained their positions. Jan Carter-Black, who was a college professor in a social work department, indicated that being alone with such stressful concerns produced "moments when I am plagued with self-doubt and insecurity" (Carter-Black 2008, 119).

Is there a productive action black women can take to confront such isolation and stress on the job? A study of black female college administrators found that these women had very few peers in either the faculty or administration sharing both their sex and race. When such individuals existed, however, they often proved useful as mentors or guides, either helping to build a positive self-image on the job or providing critical information and social capital. One respondent's interest in social networking was specific, focused on locating black women who could help her understand the local political workings. She added, "I have spent more time trying to leverage the system, trying to get to know people as opposed to having a formal mentor or mentoring relationship" (Crawford and Smith 2005, 63).

Whether or not they have racial peers, most black and Hispanic women find themselves with white bosses, who sometimes discriminate against them. A large study of white and minority respondents in Atlanta, Boston, and Los Angeles found that compared to white men, black women and Latinas required more time at a job to receive a promotion (Smith 2005).

Hispanic women realize limited schooling can be a major impediment to job advancement, and so they emphasize the importance of education. Research on 20 undocumented Mexican women in South Carolina indicated that busy as their lives were with work and family responsibilities, most of them participated in adult-education programs focusing on such topics as English as a second language (ESL), basic literacy, computer processing, and a general equivalency diploma (GED). Lily, a respondent, indicated that "education is the key to the future. And I want to set a good example for my children" (Campbell 2008, 237–38). Table 10.3 summarizes school-completion rates for women in the four major racial groups over time, demonstrating the racialized disadvantage that Hispanic and black women have compared to their Asian and white counterparts.

For Latinas the task of learning English in school can be an elusive prospect. A study of immigrant Hispanic women in a high-school ESL (English as a second language) program indicated that many of the respondents faced family pressures to engage in childcare, housework, and other domestic tasks and to deemphasize their education. Once in school students and teachers often conveyed the idea that Latinas would only remain in school until they were married. Pilar explained. "Yes, we are seen as strange. [Even] people of our own race pretend to be Americanized. This is very grave. Here, the Americans look at us as though we travel on burros" (Williams, Alvarez, and Andrade Hauck 2002, 573).

Latina students said that for them to be mainstreamed, they had to speak English well. However, the instruction they received was inadequate, featuring 20 words a week that were matched with definitions and then laboriously repeated. With such inadequate instruction, the students showed little improvement in English and as a result remained isolated in their ESL classes (Williams, Alvarez, and Andrade Hauck 2002, 573–76). Unable to learn English well, they had very limited job prospects.

These Latinas lacked any effective social networks to convey complaints about their education. In contrast, a study of three middle schools in a major southwestern city indicated that each school had a community room, which was a safe, pleasant unrestricted space where students could enjoy the company of women whose children attended the school. There were refreshments, even a few meals, and the children could speak openly, sometimes complaining about teachers. Keenly aware that the students were often denied a quality education, the women sought to empower them. If necessary, one of the adults would contact a teacher. Cecilia, an eighth grader, spoke enthusiastically, indicating that the parent volunteers acted like helpful friends. "If we tell them that someone is bothering us, then they will go and look for that person and find out what's going on before it becomes a big problem" (López and Lechuga 2006, 19).

Like the children just described, professional Latinas often value social capital from their racial group. A study of 103 Hispanic women with jobs in business, academia, government, and politics indicated that nearly all of the respondents would have liked a mentor and would have preferred that person to be Hispanic. Reasons for that choice included Latinas' continuing commitment to their traditional culture, the difficulties and suspicions they encountered dealing with whites, and the recognition that often an Hispanic mentor would have experienced similar challenges and struggles (González-Figueroa and Young 2005, 220).

Undoubtedly many of these professional Latinas would applaud the Association for Latinas in Business (the ALB) located in Orange County, California. Interviews with 80 members revealed that the organizational founders helped develop social capital by promoting ties among successful Latinas and also emphasizing such critical skills as displaying a firm handshake, maintaining eye contact in conversation, remembering names, returning phone calls, and even learning to play golf because so much business

TABLE 10.3 School Completion Percentages for Women from the Four Major Racial Groups over Time

Women's completion percentages for four years of high school or more

Year	Total population (Both sexes)	All women	Asians	Blacks	Hispanics	Whites
2009	86.7%[1]	87.1%	86.6%	84.1%	63.3%	91.9%
2000	84.1	84	NA[2]	78.3	57.5	88.4
1995	81.7	81.6	NA	74.1	53.8	85.8
1990	77.6	77.5	NA	66.5	51.3	79[3]
1985	73.9	73.5	NA	60.8	47.4	75.1
1980	68.6	68.1	NA	51.3	44.1	70.1
1975	62.5	62.1	NA	43.3	36.7	64.1
1970	55.2	55.4	NA	34.8	NA	57.6

[1]The population comprises individuals who are 25 years and older.

[2]Not available

[3]For 1990 and earlier, data reported here are for "whites" and not the currently used "non-Hispanic whites."

Women's completion percentages for four years of college

Year	Total population (Both sexes)	All women	Asians	Blacks	Hispanics	Whites
2009	29.5%	29.1%	52.3%	20.6%	14%	31.9%
2000	25.6	23.6	NA	16.7	10.7	25.5
1995	23	20.2	NA	12.9	8.4	22.1
1990	21.3	18.4	NA	10.8	8.7	19[3]
1985	19.4	16	NA	11	7.3	16.3
1980	17	13.6	NA	8.1	6.2	14
1975	13.9	13.6	NA	6.2	4.6	11
1970	11	8.2	NA	4.4	NA	8.6

Perhaps the most obvious conclusion is that over time women in all four racial groups have significantly increased their amounts of schooling. For black and Hispanic women, however, the growth has been particularly impressive, with black women's percentage of high-school graduates expanding nearly two-and-a-half times between 1970 and 2009 and Hispanic women's proportion fairly close to doubling between 1975 and 2009. The increases for college graduation are even more impressive—a nearly fivefold percentage rise for black women and a threefold growth for Hispanic women over the time spans previously cited. Finally it is important to note that through the 29-year time span, black and Hispanic school-completion rates in both categories have remained significantly lower than the Asian and white totals.

Sources: U.S. Census Bureau. 2008. Table A-2. "Percent of People 25 and Over Who Have Completed High School or College, by Race, Hispanic Origin and Sex: Selected Years 1940 to 2008." *Current Population Survey*. http://www.census.gov/population/socdemo/education/cps2008/tabA-2.csv; U.S. Census Bureau. 2009. Table 1. "Educational Attainment of the Population 18 Years and Over, by Age, Sex, Race, and Hispanic Origin: 2009." *Current Population Survey*. http://www.census.gov/population/www/socdemo/education/cps2009.html.

is conducted in the course of a match. Individuals who developed these skills, ALB leaders emphasized, were likely to escape "the immigrant shadow" that plagues Latinas. A founding board member explained that they engaged in an unrelenting battle against stereotypes, displaying how well educated they are and "prov[ing] to everyone that we are here not because we are lazy and that we just want to speak Spanish and take over the country" (Vallejo 2007. 21). Because of their success, it is likely that income for the ALB is well above average for their racial group. Figure 10.3 provides income figures for women in the four major racial groups over time, offering evidence that the combined impact of race and gender affects black and Hispanic women adversely.

Like Latinas and black women, lesbians face distinct intersectional conditions.

Intersectionality: Lesbians' Challenge for Equality

A team of researchers on intersectionality indicated that lesbians are a group that has been "largely neglected and ignored," with "undiscovered points of intersection reveal[ing] the complexity of their lived experience" (Dill, McLaughlin, and Nieves 2007, 631). This discussion considers issues that address some of that complexity.

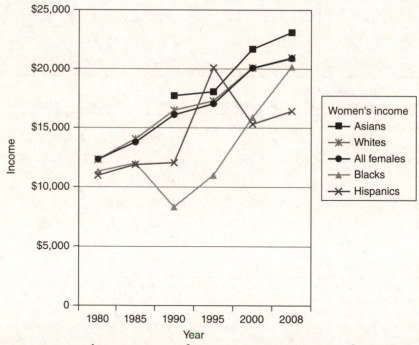

FIGURE 10.3 Median Income[1] Levels for Women[2] in the Four Major Racial Groups[3] over Time

[1]In 2008 dollars
[2]Aged 15 and over
[3]Data for Asian Americans only available from 1990

Asian and white women have consistently obtained higher income than their black and Hispanic counterparts. Over time all four female groups have distinctly increased their income.

Source: U.S. Bureau of the Census. 2010. Table P-2. "Race and Hispanic Origin of People by Median Income and Sex: 1947 to 2008." *Historical Income Tables—People.*

At the macro level, efforts to pass federal legislation prohibiting job discrimination against homosexuals started with a House bill on employment discrimination in 1975. In 2007 a version of that bill passed the House but failed to reach a vote in the Senate. Had the bill passed the Senate, the president was prepared to veto it, declaring it would be too burdensome on businesses and would produce too much litigation. A *New York Times* editorial asserted that such reasons "echo the ones given by opponents of every previous civil rights bill to pass Congress in the past 50 years or so" (*New York Times* 2007, A26).

Without such legislation the majority of states deny lesbians and gays a level playing field at work. Exceptions exist. Twenty states have passed antidiscrimination statutes regarding gender preference, meaning it is illegal for lesbians and gays to face bias in hiring, promotion, and firing. In addition, at least 350 big businesses have provisions extending such benefits as health insurance and retirement packages to lesbian and gay partners (*New York Times* 2007, A26; Van Wormer, Wells, and Boes 2000, 94).

Like others impacted by two or more intersecting statuses, lesbians sometimes describe the compounding effects. For instance, at Bienestar, a large Latino/Latina health organization which provides HIV/AIDS services for lesbians and gays, lesbian Latinas indicated that if interested in this line of work, they had few alternatives to this particular organization—that in white-run gay and lesbian groups they were outsiders because of race; that in straight Latino groups their sexual preference marginalized them; and in gay Latino structures they were unwelcome because of their sex.

Tina, a Latina staff member, summarized this apparent exclusion, indicating that "[y]ou're a woman, . . . [and as a result] you're not in a position of power. Apart from that, you're a lesbian. And the last part is you're a Latina. So you're triple-f---ed" (Ward 2004, 92). Tina emphasized that in this instance status interlock produced a negative outcome for lesbian job seekers.

Lesbians' work histories tend to be fairly different from straight women's. Traditionally they have been more inclined to seek employment because of being more independent than some heterosexual women and because of the recognition that once out of the closet their families might cut them out of their lives (Friend 1991; Jones and Nystrom 2002; Kimmel 1995). Two respondents in a study of lesbians who were 55 and older commented about their job histories. The first suggested that like her many lesbians, realizing they must be self-supporting, seek a profession's high income. The second individual, along with others, followed a varied career path. This woman explained, "I worked for Boeing. I worked for the shipyards, drove a school bus. I owned a tavern, ran an auto parts store for my parents." At most of the jobs, including at Boeing, she had the advantage over most of her female peers of receiving wages similar to men's (Jones and Nystrom 2002, 66).

Many lesbians pursue nontraditional jobs, often running a variety of small businesses that tend to provide less income than more conventional jobs in the private and public sectors. Another economic disadvantage some lesbians face is that they can find themselves excluded from partners' health-insurance and retirement programs, which are available to straight employees' spouses (Richard and Brown 2006).

While lesbians' type of employment and their limited access to benefits appear to disadvantage them, two studies suggest that their income equals or exceeds heterosexual women's earnings. National surveys with small samples of lesbians conducted over seven years indicated that lesbians earned at least 20 percent more than straight women.

A larger investigation in California found that the two categories of women obtained about the same income. In the latter study, lesbians, who at the time could not marry, were matched against straight women who were unmarried, and the comparison showed that lesbians were more educated (Black, Makar, Sanders, and Taylor 2003; Carpenter 2005). Since lesbians were more educated but had earnings about the same as straight women, it was possible that they were victims of discrimination.

Certainly lesbians fear that their sexual preference can hurt them economically. A physician had a thriving practice with "somewhat homophobic [patients] and had it been known, I would have lost a lot of money . . . So I just stayed in the closet in order to make a living" (Jones and Nystrom 2002, 65). Another respondent was also in a job where she had to hide her sexual preference, "I was in a youth organization, and that means being fired if you were found out. So for years I kept trying to find men that I could fall in love with" (Jones and Nystrom 2002, 65).

The academic world has often been more receptive to lesbians and gays than most other work settings. Barbara Gerber, a psychologist and counselor at the State University of New York at Oswego, indicated that she has never been treated badly. Gays and lesbians had always welcomed her. "Today 'straight' folks are sometimes surprised but often quite accepting—which I attribute as much to their good sense as to . . . acceptance and respect I have earned . . . on campus" (Gerber 1997, 71).

Dawn Bennett-Alexander, a law professor, also had a positive experience as a lesbian in an academic setting. She explained, "Being black and female, and thus understanding the importance of participating in the struggle for civil rights for race and gender, made me also understand the importance of doing so for gays and lesbians." She added that being black, female, and a lesbian who publishes in the areas of race, gender, and sexual preference "in a largely white, traditionally male, conservative academic setting gives me the chance to use my professional research as an opportunity to also provide food for thought for the academic community that benefits me personally" (Bennett-Alexander 1997, 22). This person, in short, found that intersectional analysis provided a provocative perspective on the setting in which she was located.

While many intersectional topics examine two statuses, the upcoming analysis focuses on three.

Intersectionality: Poor Immigrant Women

Sociologists Denise Segura and Patricia Zavella indicated that "[w]hen women become the center of the analysis, questions change and previously held assumptions become subjects of inquiry" (Segura and Zavella 2007, 19). In this instance the inquiry focuses on the subjects' three intersectional qualities—their poverty, immigrant status, and gender roles:

- As poor people they have limited resources—little money, low-quality education, restricted access to healthcare, ineffective social capital, and more.
- As immigrants these women sometimes face the disadvantages of arriving in the United States with little or no knowledge of English and/or the workings of various important institutional structures. In addition, prospective employers sometimes perceive them as undesirable or inferior aliens, significantly affecting job prospects. Furthermore if their immigrant status is undocumented, they can not obtain a legal job and are always vulnerable to deportation.

- As women these individuals often face highly traditional role expectations in their native cultures, including in their families, and in the United States sometimes less job opportunity and lower wages than men. Furthermore poor female immigrants are likely to find themselves severely overloaded, both running the household and maintaining an outside, often full-time job.

International studies of immigrant women have paid considerable attention to the impact of migration on women's relationship with family members. In particular, researchers have considered whether women's entrance into the labor force has increased their authority within the family and encouraged men to assume more responsibility for housework and childcare (Boyd 2003). Table 10.4 provides some key facts about immigrant women.

Investigations suggest that immigrant women often face highly traditional family expectations. In south Florida young female Cuban immigrants complained to researchers that their fathers and grandfathers were strict, seeking to control their choice of clothes, relations with boys and men, job options, and residential locations (Cooper, Linstroth, and Chaitin 2009). Sometimes parental expectations can be confusing and contradictory. Among the Hmong people, who are refugees from southeast Asia, some

---

TABLE 10.4 A Statistical Portrait of Immigrant Women

- 18.9 million immigrant women comprising 12 percent of all US women
- Total foreign-born population evenly split between women and men but proportions varying sharply among the countries of origin
- In 2008, 27 percent of foreign-born women from Mexico, 5 percent from the Philippines, 4 percent from India, 4 percent China, and 3 percent Vietnam
- 4.1 million immigrant women currently unauthorized
- About 52 percent of foreign-born women reporting their spoken English is not very good
- Sixty-eight percent of immigrant women possessing a high-school degree or more education; twenty-seven percent recipients of a bachelor's degree or more schooling
- Comparable figures for native-born women: 89 and 29 percent respectively
- Foreign-born full-time year-round workers earning 14 percent less than native-born counterparts
- Median income of family households with immigrant women the primary breadwinners (with no husband present) tallying 4 percent less than the median income of households headed by foreign-born men and 35 percent less than those with native-born men the primary breadwinners
- The nearly nine million immigrant female workers including 33 percent involved in service work (e.g., food preparation and health-care support), 22 percent in professional and related positions (e.g., teachers, school administrators, and healthcare practitioners), 12 percent in office and administrative support (e.g., clerks and secretaries), 11 percent in management, business, and financial occupations (e.g., retail-store managers or accountants), and 10 percent in sales and related occupations (real-estate broker or insurance agent). About 12 percent of the total did not have their jobs classified.

Source: Jeanne Batalova. 2008. "Immigrant Women." *Migration Information Source.* http://www .Migrationinformation.org/Usfocus/display.cfm?ID=763.

teenage daughters indicated that parents both expected them to do well in school and also to marry young and produce many children (Lie, Yang, Rai, and Vang 2004, 134).

Like parents, immigrant husbands can also be controlling. For instance, research indicated that first-generation Korean American men often insisted on a traditional order where women were responsible for the lion's share of household tasks, regardless of whether or not they had jobs (Sohng and Song 2004, 89). A study of low-income Latin American families indicated that some husbands kept their wives severely isolated. For instance, Yolanda, a 28-year-old Puerto Rican with five children, endured a marriage in which her husband was so determined to prevent her from making friends in the neighborhood that he screened her phone calls and followed her to see where she was going. To alleviate her sense of isolation and depression, Yolanda frequently called her sister in Puerto Rico. She explained, "She's the only one I always talk to. I tell her everything. I call her and I pay . . . whatever the cost is. That is my therapy exactly" (laughed) (Dominguez and Lubitow 2008, 424).

While fathers, husbands, and other relatives sometimes seek to control poor immigrant women, those women have one arena of persistent influence—the family, which in most cultures has traditionally been their domain. Thus it is hardly surprising that once established in the United States, these new arrivals often take a prominent role in developing their communities. Soon after settling in southern Illinois, Hispanic women began exploring local facilities—schools, daycare programs, church groups, and stores—and mobilizing their social networks to patronize those that seemed promising (Del Castillo 2007, 98–99).

Besides their domestic and community obligations, many poor immigrant women must find work. Often they are disadvantaged compared to men. First, they are sometimes less well equipped to enter the workforce. Coming from traditional societies where the dominant standard is that women focus on domestic roles, they are likely to reach the United States less educated and less experienced on the job than men. For instance, research among south Asian immigrants indicated that a substantial number of women were less well educated and less likely to be fluent in English than men (Ross-Sheriff and Husain 2007, 169). Furthermore when seeking jobs, female immigrants have the disadvantage of social networks primarily involving relatives while men's tend to contain co-workers. In part because of inferior social capital, immigrant women often have more localized, less well-paying jobs than men (Greenwell, Valdez, and DeVanzo 1997; Marsiglia and Menjivar 2004).

Nonetheless in spite of their employment disadvantages, poor immigrant women produce earnings that are a substantial contribution for their families. For instance, a study of Mexican women who came from a community where few jobs for people of limited schooling paid even half the minimum wage revealed that in Atlanta they could often obtain positions that paid slightly above the minimum wage, making it possible to support their families fairly well (Hirsch 2007, 450–51).

Sometimes immigrant women have the added value of being able to obtain jobs in locations where men's positions are scarce or nonexistent. In the Los Angeles area, the unending demand for nanny-housekeepers can alter families' migratory strategies. Emelia, who left her five children in Guatemala nine years earlier, explained that traditionally women had let husbands lead the way. She added, "But now since the man cannot find work here so easily, the woman comes first. Recently women have been coming and the man staying" (Hondagneu-Sotelo and Avila 2007, 399).

Immigrant women, however, have differing feelings about coming to the United States to work. In-depth interviews with Mexican women revealed that some felt that motherhood and employment were basically incompatible but that they had no option except to work, at least part-time. Angela, a full-time seamstress, was in tears when she told the interviewer about her childcare arrangement. Since her son was six, she had left him with a babysitter, who was unreliable. Angela explained that when she picked him up, her son "always had on dirty diapers and was starving . . . But there wasn't any other recourse. . . . I would just clean him and feed him when I got home" (Segura 2007, 378). In contrast, other Mexican immigrants felt quite comfortable having their children in daycare while they worked. One woman explained that her employment made it possible for her children to have a better life and that besides staying at home all day would be a stifling experience. She added, "And that way I wouldn't have the same desire to play with my daughters. But now, with the time we have together, we do things that we want to, like run in the park, because there's so little time" (Segura 2007, 380).

A painful child-related decision many mothers face is the one to migrate to the United States and leave their children at home. In this situation both central American and Mexican women stated a preference for grandmothers as the primary caregivers. As Velia, who did housecleaning, indicated, "If my children were with the woman next door [who babysits], I'd worry if they were eating well, or about men [coming to harass the girls]. Having them with my mother allows me to work in peace" (Hondagneu-Sotelo and Avila 2007, 401). However, when mothers who left young children return to the homeland, they are likely to find that their daughters and sons no longer relate to them as parents (Zuniga 2004, 186).

While intersectionality focuses on women, the central idea of the concept, namely the combined impact of two or more statuses on the people in question, can apply in such gender nonspecific contexts as the following one.

Intersectionality: Black Students in Special-Education Programs

African Americans are disproportionately represented in various special-education programs. As Table 10.5 indicates, data from the National Center for Education Statistics indicated that of the four largest racial groups, blacks had the highest rate of specific learning disability (National Center for Education Statistics 2007). Information provided by three national surveys involving 981 school districts pointed out that in over 90 percent of those districts black students' participation in programs for the Educable Mentally Handicapped (EMH) was overrepresented. EMH students supposedly display significantly below-average intelligence while those with a learning disability (LD) achieve below-normal academic success. Although a conceptual distinction exists between the two classifications, the basis for particular students' placement in one category or the other is often haphazard. Both sets of students are prime candidates for special-education designation (Harry and Klingner 2006, 124–25). In the 981 school districts with EMH programs, the proportion of black representation was nearly double the white percentage (Eitle 2002, 588).

One might assume that clear, nationally researched criteria exist for designating children learning-disabled and placing them in special-education programs. However,

TABLE 10.5 Number and Percentage of Children[1] of Different Races with Major Learning Disabilities[2]

	Total	American Indians/ Alaska natives	Asian/ Pacific Islanders	Blacks
Specific learning disability	2,789,875 (4.2%)[3]	48,645 (7.5%)	46,603 (1.7%)	561,623 (5.7%)
Language impairment	1,137,692 (1.7%)	14,487 (2.3%)	33,593 (1.2%)	180,761 (1.8%)
Summation of the two disabilities	3,927,587 (5.9%)	63,492 (9.8%)	80,196 (2.9%)	742,384 (7.5%)
	Hispanics	**Whites**		
Specific learning disability	550,723 (4.7%)	1,582,301 (3.9%)		
Language impairment	183,350 (1.6%)	725,141 (1.8%)		
Summation of the two disabilities	734,073 (6.3%)	2,307,442 (5.7%)		

[1]Aged 6 to 21 years

[2]In 2004

[3]Percentage of all students in the specified category

Compared to the other three major racial groups, blacks display a higher rate of learning disability (5.7%) and also a higher rate for the summation of learning disability and language impairment (7.5%). Only American Indians/Alaska Natives have greater proportions in these categories. In line with research cited in this chapter, one might speculate about the numbers, considering the distinct possibility that the comparatively high percentage of black children designated learning disabled partially results from discriminatory placement.

Source: National Center for Education Statistics. 2007. *Status and Trends in the Education of Racial and Ethnic Minorities.* Table 8.1b. "Number and Percentage of Children Ages 3 to 8 and 6 to 21 Served under the Individuals with Disabilities Education Act (IDEA), by Race/Ethnicity and Type of Disability: 2004." http://nces.ed.gov/pubs2007/minoritytrends/tables/table_8_1b.asp?referrer=report.

no such criteria exist. In fact, the large study that encompassed 981 school districts suggested that a couple of factors unrelated to the children themselves appeared to affect black students' placement in such programs. The factors are:

- That where the proportion of black and Hispanic students was high, then their representation in special-education programs was fairly low. In such districts whites had often abandoned the public schools and perhaps the area, and therefore because of their substantial presence African Americans possessed the power to oppose educating large numbers of their children outside of the curricular mainstream.
- That placement of students in special-education programs was greater if the district was under court order to desegregate, encouraging officials in white-controlled schools to use special education as a means of keeping blacks out of mainstream classes without explicitly segregating them. On the other hand, if a district was not pressured to integrate or if its various racial groups were residentially isolated, then whites' pressures to segregate black and Hispanic children would be minimal, and their placement in special-education programs would be fairly restricted (Eitle 2002).

Since blacks are designated for special education more often than whites, they are obviously less likely to be placed in the more flexible setting of general-education programs (Hehir, Figueroa, Gamm, Katzman, Gruner, Karger, and Hernandez 2005, 71), where they can downplay or even avoid a sense of being different and inferior. As information about cultural and social capital indicated in earlier chapters, middle-class parents compared to less affluent counterparts are likely to have both the experience and sense of entitlement facilitating intervention with teachers and administrators on behalf of their children. In this instance it is probable that the fact that white parents frequently possess higher class positions is a significant factor contributing to their children's greater likelihood of being mainstreamed and black children being placed in special education.

Thus when learning-disabled students are white, they are often mainstreamed, obtaining extra support services within the context of the general-education curriculum. These students, whose abilities range widely, often graduate with a conventional diploma and sometimes receive postsecondary education. In contrast, the majority of African Americans labeled learning-disabled, also widely varying in ability, are in programs where they spend 60 percent or more of their day in segregated special-education placements and 40 percent or less in general-education programs. Their teachers are frequently unlicensed or provisionally certified, and if they make it to graduation they are likely to receive a certificate of attendance/completion and not a high-school diploma (Blanchett 2008, xiii; Chamberlain 2005; LeRoy and Kulik 2003). In both instances the students have the same label—learning-disabled—but their schooling experiences are drastically different. These contrasting experiences promote opposing self-images. The middle-class students are likely to have a fairly positive self-image, but among poor and working-class blacks that is unlikely (Connor 2008, 15–16).

Often students try to hide the fact that they are in special education. From the moment educator David Connor started studying low-income black and Latino LD students, he discovered that many used various tactics to prevent general-education peers observing them in the classroom—choosing seats that made it difficult for passersby to see them; arriving late and leaving early to avoid discovery; or not telling friends about their LD status and sometimes being crushed when discovered and subsequently avoided (Connor 2008, 12).

Connor observed that in over 20 years of working with LD students, "what has always haunted me has been students' incomprehension of the label LD, particularly in relation to themselves." Their experience indicated that the term had not been useful to them, failing to offer insights into their own specific difficulties. Generally being LD is a taboo subject. When pressed in class to explain how they felt about the LD label, students expressed confusion, anger, sadness, and discomfort. It was "one of the few taboo subjects, a shameful secret momentarily allowed out into the open. Even to acknowledge it [is] an emotionally difficult task" (Connor 2008, 14). The label, in short, was a potent source of stereotype fallout.

Low-income black learning-disabled students are prime candidates for social reproduction. Michael was a poor black adolescent who lived in a public-housing project where children attended underfunded schools that generally did not prepare them well for either higher education or good-paying jobs. On top of this already difficult situation, Michael and many other students faced the added disadvantage of being LD, further restricting their educational and occupational advancement.

Yet in spite of being in a special-education program, Michael had worked hard and been fairly successful, eventually graduating from high school. Being designated LD bothered Michael. It was a label "[t]hat's basically saying you're not good at any subject." Michael indicated that for students' sake it is much more reassuring if teachers are specific, indicating that they are good at some subjects and not others. Then the students are likely to be motivated to work hard at all of them. On the other hand, individuals labeled learning-disabled are discouraged and inclined to give up in school. According to Michael, they are likely to tell themselves, "I'm special ed. I'm slow in all these classes. I don't need to do none of the work" (Connor 2008, 139).

Precious, another student, suspected that she was in special education because of a hearing impairment and because the impact of her mother's drug involvement led to her being classified LD. When child-welfare authorities found out about her mother's addiction, they put Precious in foster care, "and since I was away from my mother, I stopped talking. I stopped talking for a whole year. They thought I couldn't talk, so that's how I wound up being in special ed" (Connor 2008, 190). Precious considered that conversationally she was as intelligent as general-education students, but because special-education programs were less challenging, she had learned much less in school.

As high school progressed, Precious became discouraged, feeling her LD program did not provide the help and support she needed. She dropped out of school and worked in fast-food restaurants, where Precious suspected that many of her co-workers were special-education students. She said, "I never asked them you know—are they? It's that I felt more comfortable, and that I could talk to them" (Connor 2008, 193).

United by common experience, students in special education are likely to feel relaxed with each other. At the same time, they are likely to feel trapped—that their educational and occupational options are marginal and their future bleak.

As this discussion on gender-related issues draws to a close, we consider the principal topics covered in this chapter and then look toward the future.

Conclusion

Most preindustrial wives found themselves in full-time domestic roles. With industrial development some women labored long days in factories while more affluent females workers became teachers or nurses. Since 1900 an increasing percentage of women have moved into the job world. However, the index of occupational segregation indicates that women's present occupational dispersion is far removed from a complete occupational integration.

Sexism persists, with the family, peers, schools and the hidden curriculum, and the mass media all exerting influence. On the job women continue to face various disadvantages. Two studies—one involving female blue-collar workers in traditionally male positions and the other professionals and managers who had left their jobs to care for their children—detail some of the stressful problems the job world largely reserves for women.

The last major section examines intersectionality. After an overview of the topic, the focus shifts to four intersectional categories—black and Hispanic women, lesbians, poor immigrant women, and black students in special-education programs.

At this point I return to an issue raised earlier in the chapter. In 1981 Betty Friedan, who wrote *The Feminine Mystique*, which is widely considered a major contributor to the development of the modern feminist movement, produced another book—*The Second Stage*. While much less well known, its concern with the prospects for women who have been the beneficiaries of the struggles for equal rights resonates decades later. Friedan indicated that many of the seemingly fortunate women she interviewed expressed doubt, confusion, even bewilderment about the future. To illustrate their situation, Friedan cited several cases of successful young professional women immersed in important, demanding jobs. One concerned a surgeon with a staggering schedule who wondered whether it would be possible to have an intimate relationship and, even more problematically, a family (Friedan 1981, 16).

A study drawing from the Survey of the Practice Patterns of Young Physicians provides relevant information. The data indicated that a gap in work earnings and income has been increasing between female physicians with children and childless woman doctors and that a small but growing percentage of young physician mothers—between 5 and 7 percent among those aged 30 to 40—dropped out at least temporarily from the labor force (Boulis 2004).

Is it reasonable to conclude that the feminist movement has made women's lives miserable? That possibility suddenly received extensive public attention in 2009 when a study containing data from the General Social Survey claimed that women had become unhappier over time. Shortly afterward, however, a more dispassionate appraisal of the data indicated that between the 1970s and the 2000s very slight changes in women's happiness levels had occurred and that in the 2000s over 80 percent of both sexes claimed to be very or fairly happy (Pollitt; Stevenson and Wolfers 2009). In short, it appears that women's unhappiness has not changed appreciably over time. It seems likely, however, that through the decades their challenges have altered.

When married women and men who are employed full time and have children under 18 living at home are compared for the daily hours spent on household tasks and childcare, the women devote about 1.16 hours more per day to those duties. Fully employed women average nearly an hour less time on the job, suggesting that the time gap signals women's greater vulnerability both to lower pay and less likelihood of promotion. Then, as previously noted, there are the substantial number of married women who feel compelled to cut back to part-time employment or to leave the workforce (Bureau of Labor Statistics 2008).

Women make the basic decisions about their work lives. However, governments can be a significant influence. While the United States spends less than 0.1 percent of its gross domestic product on childcare, Denmark, Sweden, the United Kingdom, Norway, and Japan designate at least 0.3 percent of their gdp for that subsidy. Such countries as Austria, the Czech Republic, Finland, and Hungary provide up to three years of paid leave for mothers. In contrast, the United States supplies no paid maternal leave and only 12 unpaid weeks of job release (*Economist 2009;* Organization for Economic Co-operation and Development 2008). It appears that American mothers in the workforce receive substantially less government support than their counterparts in many other countries.

Key Terms in the Glossary

Comparable worth *320*
Doing gender *308*
Gender constancy *311*
Glass ceiling *320*
Hegemonic masculinity *309*

Hidden curriculum *313*
Index of occupational
  segregation *307*
Individual sexism *305*
Institutional sexism *305*

Intersectionality *324*
Pay equity *320*
Sexism *305*
Standpoint *325*

Discussion Topics

1. Consider how Charlotte Gilman's outlook on women's second-class citizenry differed from most early feminists' views.
2. Evaluate Catherine Beecher's contention about women's moral power over their families.
3. Examine the process of "doing gender," describing a hypothetical situation.
4. Explain your philosophy of gender-role socialization by addressing the following three issues comparing expectations for girls and boys: responsibility for household chores; opportunities in school; and occupational goals. Be frank and thorough.
5. Drawing on your own and others' experiences, comment on the complicated, confusing adolescent world of gender relations.
6. Is the gendered hidden curriculum alive and well? Discuss.
7. Pick a prominent mass-media form—TV programming, commercials, film, children's books, or whatever—and describe two scenes portraying both a traditional and a modern perspective on gender roles.
8. Analyze the modern job world, focusing on the concepts institutional sexism and hegemonic masculinity.
9. If you could make one gender-associated change in the structures or relations of the work world, what would it be? Explain.
10. Provide an illustration of intersectionality, explaining how the statuses in question affect a person's or group's life chances.
11. What impact does class have in affecting black women's and Latinas' lives? Explain.
12. Discuss lesbians' discrimination on the job. Cite illustrations.
13. Describe poor immigrant women's three intersectional statuses, offering concrete examples of each of them.
14. Do black LD students receive an effective education? Use material from the chapter and other information available to you. What steps could improve the programs in question?

Research Papers

1. Write about "doing gender" using studies that focus on some specific age in girls' development.
2. Make a well-documented response to this statement: In the twenty-first century, girls and women have the same educational opportunities as boys and men.
3. What is modern women's greatest challenge in the job world? Provide information to back up your conclusion.
4. Drawing heavily from source material, produce a report about the female members of a major racial group (perhaps considering American Indians) and discuss the different intersectional elements, specifying respective significances wherever possible.
5. What strikes you as the most interesting or compelling variety of intersectionality? Gather data and produce a paper about it.

Informative Websites

Both *Gilmore Girls* and *Sex in the City* were long-running, successful TV series. Their principal characters, however, displayed very different relations with men. In *Gilmore Girls* relations with men were important but hardly the dominant reality in their lives. In contrast, in *Sex and the City*, the central characters were emotionally dependent on men, focused on establishing long-term relationships with them.

The website for the National Organization for Women (NOW) (http://www.now.org/) is a good place to start to learn about a host of past and present feminist activities. At this site one finds out about this distinguished organization, which was founded in 1966 at the beginning of the modern women's movement.

The Institute for Women's Policy Research (http://www.iwpr.org/index.cfm) is a research organization, which conducts studies, disseminates its findings, and promotes public discussion and policy changes to strengthen women's and families' rights, particularly for those who are poor.

Feministing (http://feministing.com/) provides an Internet presence for young feminists, giving them a chance to discuss important issues affecting their present and future lives.

The National Gay and Lesbian Task Force (http://www.thetaskforce.org/) has focused on the grassroots power of lesbian, gay, bisexual, and transgender groups.

Bibliography

Aikman, Sheila, Elaine Unterhalter, and Chloe Challender. 2005. "The Education MDGs: Achieving Gender Equality through Curriculum and Pedagogy Change." *Gender and Development* 13 (March): 44–55.

Andre, Claire, and Manuel Velasquez. 2010. "Comparable Worth." *The Markkula Center for Applied Ethics*. http://www.scu.edu/ethics/publications/iie/v3n2/comparable.html.

Arnault, Jane E., Louis Gordon, Douglas H. Joines, and G. Michael Phillips. 2001. "An Experimental Study of Job Evaluation and Comparable Worth." *Industrial and Labor Relations Review 54 (July):* 806–15.

Baldwin, Alfred L., Clara Baldwin, and Robert E. Cole. 1990. "Stress-Resistant Families and Stress-Resistant Children," pp. 257–80 in Jon E. Rolf, Norman Garmezy, and Ann S. Masten (eds.), *Risk and Protective Factors in the Development of Psychopathology*. New York: Cambridge University Press.

Barvosa, Edwina. 2008. *Wealth of Selves: Multiple Identities, Mestiza Consciousness, and the Subject of Politics*. College Station: Texas A & M University Press.

Basow, Susan. 2004. "The Hidden Curriculum: Gender in the Classroom," pp. 117–31 in Michael A. Paludi (ed.), *Praeger Guide to the Psychology of Gender*. Westport, CT: Praeger.

Beecher, Catherine E. 2006. "Women's Profession as Mother and Educator," pp. 293–301 in S. T. Joshi (ed.), *A Documentary History of Prejudice against Women: In Her Place*. Amherst, NY: Prometheus Books. Originally published in 1872.

Bennett-Alexander, Dawn D. 1997. "Reflections on Being an Out Black Lesbian on a Southern Campus, pp. 15–22 in Beth Mintz and Esther Rothblum (eds.), *Lesbians in Academia: Degrees of Freedom*. New York: Routledge.

Black, Dan A., Hoda R. Makar, Seth G. Sanders, and Lowell J. Taylor. 2003. "The Earnings Effects of Sexual Orientation." *Industrial and Labor Relations Review* 56 (April): 449–69.

Blanchett, Wanda J. 2008. "Educational Inequities: The Intersection of Disability, Race, and Social Class," pp. xi–xvii in David J. Connor (ed.), *Urban Narratives: Portraits in Progress: Life at the Intersections of Learning Disability, Race, & Social Class*. New York: Peter Lang.

Bombardieri, Marcella. 2005. "Summers' Remarks on Women Draw Fire." *Boston Globe* (January 17).

Boulis, Ann. 2004. "The Evolution of Gender and Motherhood in Contemporary Medicine." *Annals of the American Academy of Political and Social Science* 596 (November): 172–206.

Boyd, Monica. 2003. "Women and Migration: Incorporating Gender into International Migration Theory." *Migration Information Source*. http://www.migrationinformation.org/feature/display.cfm?ID=106.

Branch, Enobong Hannah. 2007. "The Creation of Restricted Opportunity Due to the Intersection of Race & Sex: Black Women in the Bottom Class." *Race, Gender, & Class* 14: 247–64.

Browne, Beverly A. 1998. "Gender Stereotypes in Advertising on Children's Television in the 1990s: A Cross-National Analysis." *Journal of Advertising* 27 (Spring): 83–96.

Bureau of Labor Statistics. 2008. "Married People's Use of Time, 2003–2006." http://www.bls.gov/tus/.

Campbell, Wendy Sellers. 2008. "Lessons in Resilience: Undocumented Mexican Women in South Carolina." *Affilia: Journal of Women & Social Work* 23 (Fall): 231–41.

Carpenter, Christopher S. 2005. "Self-Reported Sexual Orientation and Earnings: Evidence from California." *Industrial and Labor Relations Review* 58 (January): 258–73.

Carter-Black, Jan. 2008. "A Black Woman's Journey into a Predominantly White Academic World." *Journal of Women and Social Work* 23 (May): 112–22.

Collins, Patricia Hill. 1990. *Black Feminist Thought: Knowledge, Consciousness, and Empowerment*. Boston: Unwin Hyman.

Combs, Gwendolyn. 2003. "The Duality of Race and Gender for Managerial African American Women: Implications of Informal Social Networks on Career Advancement." *University of Nebraska*. http://digitalcommons.unl.edu/managementfacpub/31.

Connell, R. W. 1995. *Masculinities*. Berkeley: University of California Press.

Connor, David J. 2006. "Michael's Story: 'I Get into So Much Trouble Just by Walking': Narrative Knowledge and Life at the Intersections of Learning Disability, Race, and Class." *Equity & Excellence in Education* 39 (May): 154–65.

Connor, David J. 2008. *Urban Narratives: Portraits in Progress: Life at the Intersections of Learning Disability, Race, & Social Class*. New York: Peter Lang.

Cooper, Robin, John P. Linstroth, and Julia Chaitin. 2009. "Negotiating the Transnationality of Social Control: Stories of Immigrant Women in South Florida." *Forum: Qualitative Social Research* 10 (September): 1–23.

Cortese, Anthony J. 2008. *Provocateur: Images of Women and Minorities in Advertising*, 3rd ed. Lanham, MD: Rowman & Littlefield.

Cotter, David A., Joan M. Hermsen, Seth Ovadia, and Reeve Vanneman. 2001. "The Glass Ceiling Effect." *Social Forces* 80 (December): 655–82.

Crawford, Kijana, and Danielle Smith. 2005. "THE WE AND THE US: Mentoring African American Women." *Journal of Black Studies* 36 (September): 52–67.

Crenshaw, Kimberle. 1997. "Mapping the Margins: Intersectionality, Identity Politics, and Violence against Women of Color," pp. 91–149 in Karen J. Maxchke (ed.), *The Legal Response to Violence Against Women*. New York: Garland Publishing.

Cunningham, Mick. 2001. "Parental Influence on the Gendered Division of Housework." *American Sociological Review* 66 (April): 184–203.

DeAnda, Roberto M. 2005. "Employment Hardship among Mexican-Origin Women." *Hispanic Journal of Behavioral Sciences* 27 (February): 43–59.

Del Castillo, Adelaida R. 2007. "Illegal Status and Social Citizenship: Thoughts on Mexican Immigrants in a Postnational World," pp. 92–105 in Denise A. Segura and Patricia Zavella (eds.), *Women and Migration in the U.S.-Mexico Borderlands*. Durham: Duke University Press.

Dill, Bonnie Thornton, Amy E. McLaughlin, and Angel Davis Nieves. 2007. "Future Directions of Feminist Research: Intersectionality," pp. 629–37 in Sharlene Nagy Hesse-Biber (ed.), *Handbook of Feminist Research: Theory and Praxis*. Thousand Oaks, CA: Sage.

Dingell, John D., and Carolyn Maloney. 2002. "A New Look through the Glass Ceiling: Where Are the Women?" *General Accounting Office*. http://www.equality2020.org/glass.pdf.

Dinovitzer, Ronit, Nancy Reichman, and Joyce Sterling. 2009. "The Differential Valuation of Women's Work: A New Look at the Gender Gap in Lawyers' Income." *Social Forces* 88 (December): 819–64.

Dominguez, Silvia, and Amy Lubitow. 2008. "Transnational Ties, Poverty, and Identity: Latin American Immigrant Women in Public Housing." *Family Relations* 57 (October): 419–30.

Dozier, Raine. 2006. "Accumulating Disadvantage: The Growth of the Black-White Wage Gap among Women." *American Sociological Association annual meeting*, pp. 1–21.

Economist. 2009. "Women in the Workforce: Female Power." (December 30). http://www.economist.com/displaystory.cfm?story_id=15174418.

Eitle, Tamela McNulty. 2002. "SPECIAL EDUCATION OR RACIAL SEGEGATION: Understanding

Variation in the Representation of Black Students in Educable Mentally Handicapped Programs." *Sociological Quarterly* 43 (Autumn): 575–605.

England, Paula. 1992. *Comparable Worth: Theories and Evidence.* Hawthorne, NY: Aldine de Gruyter.

England, Paula, Carmen Garcia Beaulieu, and Mary Ross. 2004. "Women's Employment among Whites, Blacks, and Three Groups of Latinas. Do More Privileged Women Have Higher Employment?" *Gender & Society* 18 (August): 494–509.

Flores, Glenda. 2008. "The Paradox of Race in the Workplace: Latina Teachers Navigating Racial/Ethnic Tensions and Opportunities on the Job." *American Sociological Association annual meeting,* pp. 1–37.

Franklin, Benjamin. 1962. *The Autobiography of Benjamin Franklin.* New York: Collier Books. Originally published in 1791.

Friedan, Betty. 1981. *The Second Stage.* New York: Summit Books.

Friend, Richard A. 1991. "Older Lesbian and Gay People: A Theory of Successful Aging." *Journal of Homosexuality* 20: 99–118.

Gabriel, Paul E., and Susanne Schmitz. 2007. "Gender Differences in Occupational Distributions among Workers." *Monthly Labor Review* 130 (June): 1–6.

Gardner, Kaye E., and Suzanne V. LaBrecque. 1986. "Effects of Maternal Employment on Sex Role Orientation of Adolescents." *Adolescence* 21: 875–85.

Gerber, Barbara W. 1997. "Becoming a Lesbian in Academia," pp. 69–73 in Beth Mintz and Esther Rothblum (eds.), *Lesbians in Academia: Degrees of Freedom.* New York: Routledge.

Gilman, Charlotte Perkins. 1898. *Women and Economics: A Study of the Economic Relations Between Men and Women as a Factor in Social Evolution.* Boston: Small, Maynard & Company.

Giordano, Peggy C., Wendy D. Manning, and Monica A. Longmore. 2006. "Gender and the Meaning of Adolescent Romantic Relationships: A Focus on Boys." *American Sociological Review* 71 (April): 260–87.

Giscombe, Katherine, and Mary C. Mattis. 2002. "Leveling the Playing Field for Women of Color in Corporate Management: Is the Business Case Enough?" *Journal of Business Ethics* 37 (April): 103–19.

Glascock, Jack. 2001. "Gender Roles on Prime-time Network Television: Demographics and Behaviors." *Journal of Broadcasting & Electronic Media* (Fall). http://www.entrepreneur.com/tradejournals/article/81767329_2.

Glick, Peter, and Lori Hilt. 2000. "Combative Children to Ambivalent Adults: The Development of Gender Prejudice," pp. 243–72 in Thomas Eckes and Hanns M. Trautner (eds.), *The Developmental Social Psychology of Gender.* Mahwah, NJ: Lawrence Erlbaum Associates.

Gonzáles-Figueroa, Evelyn, and Angela M. Young. 2005. "Ethnic Identity and Mentoring among Latinas in Professional Roles." *Cultural Diversity & Ethnic Minority Psychology* 11(August): 213–26.

Gooden, Angela M., and Mark A. Gooden. 2001. "Gender Representation in Notable Children's Picture Books: 1995–1999." *Sex Roles* 45 (July): 89–101.

Granovetter, Mark. 1983. "The Strength of Weak Times: A Network Theory Revisited," pp. 201–33 in Robert Collins (ed.), *Friendships and Social Relations in Children.* New York: Wiley.

Greene, Jeanie Ahearn. 2006. *Blue-Collar Women at Work with Men: Negotiating the Hostile Environment.* Westport, CT: Praeger.

Greenwell, Lisa, R. Burciaga Valdez, and Julie DaVanzo. 1997. "Social Ties, Wages, and Gender in a Study of Salvadoran and Filipino Immigrants in Los Angeles." *Social Science Quarterly* 78 (June): 559–77.

Hamilton, Mykol C., Michele Broaddus, David Anderson, and Kate Young. 2006. "Gender Stereotyping and Under-representation of Female Characters in 200 Popular Children's Picture Books: A Twenty-first Century Update." *Sex Roles* 55 (December): 757–65.

Harding, Sandra. 2007. "Feminist Standpoints," pp. 45–69 in Sharlene Nagy Hesse-Biber (ed.), *Handbook of Feminist Research: Theory and Praxis.* Thousand Oaks, CA: Sage.

Harry, Beth, and Janette Klingner. 2006. *Why Are So Many Minority Students in Special Education?: Understanding Race and Disability in Schools.* New York: Teachers College Press.

Hehir, Thomas, Richard Figueroa, Sue Gamm, Lauren I. Katzman, Allison Gruner, Joanne Karger, and Jaime Hernandez. 2005. *Comprehension Management Review and Evaluation of Special Education Submitted to the New York Department of Education.* New York City Department of Education. pp. 1–116. http://schools.nyc.gov/NR/donlyres/8843599E-FOAE-92D3968D9/0/FinalHehirReport092005.pdf.

Hesse-Biber, Sharlene, and Gregg Lee Carter. 2005. *Working Women in America: Split Dreams.* New York: Oxford University Press.

Higginbotham, Elizabeth. 2009. "Entering a Profession: Race, Gender, and Class in the Work Lives of Black Women Attorneys," pp. 22–49 in Bonnie Thornton Dill and Ruth Enid Zambrana (eds.). *Emerging Intersections of Race, Class, and Gender in Theory, Policy, and Practice.* New Brunswick: Rutgers University Press.

Hirsch, Jennifer S. 2007. "'En el norte la mujer manda:' Gender, Generation, and Geography in a Mexican Transnational Community," pp. 438–55 in Denise A. Segura and Patricia Zavella (eds.), *Women and Migration in the U.S.-Mexico Borderlands.* Durham: Duke University Press.

Holtzman, Linda. 2000. *Media Messages: What Film, Television, and Popular Music Teach Us about Race, Class, Gender and Sexual Orientation.* Armon, NY: M.E. Sharpe.

Hondagneu-Sotelo, Pierrette, and Ernestine Avila. 2007. "'I'm Here, but I'm There': The Meanings of Latina Transnational Motherhood," pp. 388–412 in Denise A. Segura and Patricia Zavella (eds.), *Women and Migration in the U.S.-Mexico Borderlands.* Durham: Duke University Press.

Institute for Women's Policy Research. 2008. "Improving Pay Equity Would Mean Great Gains for Women." http://www.iwpr.org/pdf/payequityrelease.pdf.

Jones, Teresa C., and Nancy M. Nystrom. 2002. "Looking Back . . . Looking Forward: Addressing the Lives of Lesbians 55 and Older." *Journal of Women and Aging* 14: 59–76.

Katz, Michael B., and Mark J. Stern. 2006. *One Nation Divisible: What America Was and What It Is Becoming.* New York: Russell Sage Foundation.

Kilbourne, Jean. 2004. "'The More You Subtract, the More You Add:' Cutting Girls Down to Size in Advertising," pp. 103–17 in Rebeccca Ann Lind (ed.), *Race/Gender/Media: Considering Diversity across Audiences, Content, and Producers.* Boston: Pearson.

Kimmel, Douglas C. 1995. "Lesbians and Gay Men Also Grow Old," pp. 289–303 in Lynne A. Bond, Stephen J. Cutler, and Armin A. Grams (eds.), *Promoting Successful and Productive Aging.* Thousand Oaks, CA: Sage.

Leaper, Campbell, and Carly Kay Friedman. 2007. "The Socialization of Gender," pp. 561–87 in Joan E. Grusec and Paul D. Hastings (eds.), *Handbook of Socialization: Theory and Research.* New York: Guilford Press.

Lengermann, Patricia Madoo, and Gillian Niebrugge. 2008. "Modern Feminist Theory," pp. 319–71 in George Ritzer, *Modern Sociological Theory,* 7th ed. New York: McGraw-Hill.

LeRoy, Barbara, and B. Kulik. 2003. "'Who's There?' Students in Inclusive Education Settings." *TASH Connections* 29: 26–28.

Lie, Gwat-Yong, Pahoua Yang, Kalyani Rai, and Pa Y. Vang. 2004. "Hmong Children and Families," pp. 122–45 in Rowena Fong (ed.), *Culturally Competent Practice with Immigrant and Refugee Children and Families.* New York: The Guilford Press.

Livers, Ancella. 2006. "Black Women in Management," pp. 205–21 in Margaret Foren Karsten (ed.), *Gender, Race, and Ethnicity in the Workplace: Issues and Challenges for Today's Organizations.* Vol. 1, *Management, Gender, and Ethnicity in the United States.* Westport, CT: Praeger.

López, Nancy, and Charlene E. Lechuga. 2006. "They Are like a Friend: Other Mothers Creating Empowering School-Based Community Livingrooms in Latino/a Middle Schools." *American Sociological Association Annual Meeting,* pp. 1–23.

Marmion, Shelly, and Paula Lundberg-Love. 2004. "Learning Masculinity and Femininity: Gender Socialization from Parents and Peers across the Life Span," pp. 1–26 in Michele A. Paludi (ed.), *Praeger Guide to the Psychology of Gender.* Westport, CT: Praeger.

Marsiglia, Flavio Francisco, and Cecilia Menjivar. 2004. "Nicaraguan and Salvadoran Children and Families," pp. 253–73 in Rowena Fong (ed.), *Culturally Competent Practice with Immigrant and Refugee Children and Families*. New York: The Guilford Press.

Martin, Karin A. 2005. "WILLIAM WANTS A DOLL. CAN HE HAVE ONE? Feminists, Child Care Advisors, and Gender-Neutral Child Rearing." *Gender & Society* 19 (August): 456–79.

Meraz, Sharon. 2008. "Women and Technology: How Socialization Created a Gender Gap," pp. 99–117 in Paula Poindexter, Sharon Meraz, and Amy Schmitz Weiss (eds.), *Women, Men, and News: Divided and Disconnected in the News Media Landscape*. New York: Routledge.

Miller, Cindy Faith, Hanns Martin Trautner, and Diane N. Ruble. 2006. "The Role of Gender Stereotypes in Children's Preferences and Behavior," pp. 293–323 in Lawrence Balter and Catherine S. Tamis-LeMonda (eds.), *Child Psychology: A Handbook of Contemporary Issues*, 2nd ed. New York: Psychology Press.

Morgan, Laurie A. 2008. "Major Matters: A Comparison of the Within-Major Gender Pay Gap across College Majors for Early-Career Graduates." *Industrial Relations* 47 (October): 625–50.

Mullings, Leith, and Amy J. Schulz. 2006. "Intersectionality and Health: An Introduction," pp. 3–17 in Amy J. Schulz and Leith Mullings (eds.), *Gender, Race, Class & Health*. San Francisco: Jossey-Bass.

National Center for Education Statistics. 2007. Table 8.1b. "Number and Percentages of Children Ages 3 to 5 and 6 to 21 Served under the Individuals with Disabilities Education Act (IDEA) by Race/ethnicity and Type of Disability: 2004." *Status and Trends in the Education of Racial and Ethnic Minorities*. http://nces.ed.gov/pubs2007/minoritytrends/tables/table_8_1b.asp?referrer=report.

Nam, Yunju, and Richard Tolman. 2002. "Partner Abuse and Welfare Receipt among African American and Latina Women Living in a Low-income Neighborhood." *Social Work Research* 26 (December): 241–51.

Neumann, Anna. 2006. "Review." *Contemporary Sociology* 35: 143–44.

Nichols, Roger L. 2003. *American Indians in U.S. History*. Norman: University of Oklahoma Press.

New York Times. 2007. "An Overdue Step for Equal Justice." (November 9): A26.

Organization for Economic Cooperation and Development. 2008. PF10: "Public Spending on Childcare and Early Education." http://www.oecd.org/dataoecd/45/27/37864.391.pdf.

Organization for Economic Cooperation and Development. 2010. "Women Still Earn Less than Men." *OECD: Factblog*. https://community.oecd.org/. . ./03/. . ,/women-still-earn-less-than-men.

Ortiz, Susan. 2008. "Still First-Fired?: An In-Depth Look at the Discrimination Experienced by African-American Women at Work." *American Sociological Association annual meeting*, pp. 1–26.

Padavic, Irene, and Barbara Reskin. 2002. *Women and Men at Work*, 2nd ed. Thousand Oaks, CA: Pine Forge Press.

Pollitt, Katha. 2009. "Are You Happy?" *Nation* (September 30). http://live.thenation.com/doc/20091019/pollitt.

Powlishta, Kimberly K. 1995. "Gender Bias in Children's Perceptions of Personality Traits." *Sex Roles* 32 (January): 17–28.

Prokos, Anastasia, and Irene Padavic. 2005. "An Examination of Competing Explanations for the Pay Gap among Scientists and Engineers." *Gender & Society* 19 (August): 523–43.

Purcell, Piper, and Lara Stewart. 1990. "Dick and Jane in 1989." *Sex Roles* 22 (February): 177–85.

Rampell, Catherine. 2010. "The Gender Wage Gap. Around the World." *New York Times* (March 9).

Reid, Lori L. 2002. "Occupational Segregation, Human Capital, and Motherhood: Black Women's Higher Exit Rates from Full-Time Employment." *Gender & Society* 16: 729–47.

Richard, Colleen. Anne, and Alison Hamilton Brown. 2006. "Configurations of Informal Support among Older Lesbians." *Journal of Women & Aging* 18: 49-65.

Rodgers, Daniel T. 1978. *The Work Ethic in Industrial America 1850–1920*. Chicago: University of Chicago Press.

Rosser, Sue V. 2004. *The Science Glass Ceiling: Academic Women Scientists and the Struggle to Succeed*. New York: Routledge.

Ross-Sheriff, Fariyal, and Altaf Husain. 2004. "South Asian Muslim Children and Families," pp. 163–82 in Rowena Fong (ed.), *Culturally Competent Practice with Immigrant and Refugee Children and Families*. New York: The Guilford Press.

Segura, Denise A. 2007. "Working at Motherhood: Chicana and Mexicana Immigrant Mothers and Employment," pp. 368–87 in Denise A. Segura and Patricia Zavella (eds.), *Women and Migration in the U.S.-Mexico Borderlands*. Durham: Duke University Press.

Segura, Denise A., and Patricia Zavella. 2007. "Introduction," pp. 1–32 in Denise A. Segura and Patricia Zavella (eds.), *Women and Migration in the U.S.-Mexico Borderlands*. Durham: Duke University Press.

Shakib, Sohaila, and Michele D. Dunbar. 2002. "The Social Construction of Female and Male High School Basketball Participation: Reproducing the Gender Order through a Two-Tiered Sporting Institution." *Sociological Perspectives* 45 (Winter): 353–78.

Shields, Stephanie A. 2008. "Gender: An Intersectionality Perspective." *Sex Roles* 59 (September): 301–11.

Smith, Lynn. 2008. "'Mad Men,' Strong Women. The Ladies of the AMC Series Might Seem to Conform to 1960s Gender Stereotypes. But the Show Invites Viewers to Look Deeper." *Los Angeles Times* (July 20): E1.

Smith, Sandra Susan. 2006. "A Question of Access or Mobilization?: Understanding Inefficacious Job Referral Networks among the Black Poor." *American Sociological Association annual meeting*, pp. 1–46.

Smith, Ryan A. 2005. "Do the Determinants of Promotion Differ for White Men Versus Women and Minorities?: An Exploration of Intersectionalism through Sponsored and Contest Mobility Processes." *American Behavioral Scientist* 48 (May): 1157–81.

Spade, Joan Z., and Catherine G. Valentine. 2004. *The Kaleidoscope of Gender: Prisms, Patterns, and Possibilities*. Belmont, CA: Wadsworth.

Stevenson, Betsey, and Justin Wolfers. 2009. "The Paradox of Declining Happiness." *General Social Survey*. http://www.norc.org/GSS+Website/Publications/Basic+Search/.

Stone, Pamela, and Meg Lovejoy. 2004. "Fast-Track Women and the 'Choice' to Stay Home." *Annals of the Academy of Political and Social Science* 596 (November): 62–83.

Strolovitch, Dara Z. 2007. *Affirmative Advocacy: Race, Class, and Gender in Interest Group Politics*. Chicago: University of Chicago Press.

Taylor, Frank. 2003. "Content Analysis and Gender Stereotypes in Children's Books." *Teaching Sociology* 31 (July): 300–11.

Turley, Jonathan. 2007. "My Boys Like Shootouts. What's Wrong with That?" *Washington Post* (February 25): B01.

Turney, Kristin. 2005. "Search Mismatch: An Exploratory Analysis of Job Search Strategies among Low-Income Black Women." *American Sociological Association annual meeting*, pp. 1–21.

U.S. Census Bureau. 2003. No. HS-30. "Marital Status of Women in the Civilian Labor Force: 1900 to 2002." *Statistical Abstract of the United States: 2003*. http://www.census.gov/statab/hist/HS-30.pdf.

U.S. Census Bureau. 2010. Table 584. "Marital Status of Women in the Civilian Labor Force." *Statistical Abstract of the United States: 2010*. http://www.census.gov/compendia/statab/cats/labor_force_employment_earnings.html.

Vallejo, Jody Agius. 2007. "Entering the Mainstream Economy: How Latina Professionals Combat Gender and Immigrant Stereotypes." *American Sociological Association annual meeting*, pp. 1–34.

Van Wormer, Katherine, Joel Wells, and Mary Boes. 2000. *Social Work with Lesbians, Gays, and Bisexuals: A Strengths Perspective*. Boston: Allyn and Bacon.

Varma, Roli. 2004. "Asian Americans: Achievements Mask Challenges." *Asian Journal of Social Science* 32: 290–307.

Ward, Jane. 2004. "Not All Differences Are Created Equal: Multiple Jeopardy in a Gendered Organization." *Gender & Society* 18 (February): 82–102.

Weber, Lynn. 2004. "A Conceptual Framework for Understanding Race, Class, Gender, and Sexuality," pp. 121–39 in Sharlene Nagy Hesse-Biber and Michelle L. Yaiser (eds.), *Feminist Perspectives on Social Research*. New York: Oxford University Press.

West, Candace, and Don Zimmerman. "Doing Gender." *Gender & Society* 2 (June): 121–51.

Williams, L. Susan, Sandra D. Alvarez, and Kevin S. Andrade Hauck. 2002. "My Name Is Not Maria: Young Latinas Seeking Home in the Heartland." *Social Problems* 49 (November): 563–84.

Wilson, Leslie Owen. 2005. "Wilson Curriculum Pages." http://www.uwsp.edu/Education/wilson/curric/curtyp.htm.

Wingfield, Adia Harvey. 2007. "The Modern Mammy and the Angry Black Man: African American Professionals' Experience with Gendered Racism in the Workplace." *Race, Gender, & Class* 14: 196–212.

Yoder, Janice D., and Patricia Aniakudo. 1996. "When Pranks Become Harassment: The Case of African American Women Firefighters." *Sex Roles* 35 (September): 253–70.

Zuniga, Maria. 2004. "Latino Children and Families," pp. 183–201 in Rowena Fong (ed.), *Culturally Competent Practice with Immigrant and Refugee Children and Families*. New York: The Guilford Press.

CHAPTER 11

Astride with the Best and the Wisest

Several days after Senator Edward M. Kennedy learned that he had a malignant brain tumor, he sought the advice of over a dozen national experts. Some flew to Boston, and others participated by telephone after receiving pertinent test results and medical records. For Kennedy this procedure was all too familiar. He had followed the same strategy when two of his children were diagnosed with cancer—a son with bone cancer who had part of a leg amputated and received an experimental form of chemotherapy; and a daughter with lung cancer which was successfully removed even though some specialists deemed it inoperable (Altman 2008).

In all three instances, Kennedy had both the wisdom and the resources to obtain highly privileged medical advice. Whether it is medical information or some other valued commodity, Kennedy's experiences bring to mind philosopher John Dewey's statement about leveling the playing field in public education. Dewey declared, "What the best and wisest parent wants for his child, that must be what the community wants for all its children" (Biddle and Berliner 2002, 11).

The implicit goal, in short, is to eliminate or at least curtail inequalities, with quality schooling providing all Americans a chance to establish themselves effectively in the occupational world. A number of innovators have not only shared Dewey's vision but attempted to implement it. The next section discusses such efforts.

CONTEMPLATING STRATEGIES FOR CHANGE

Before discussing means for alleviating social inequality, it seems useful to review central conditions relating to social stratification and social inequality, starting with several broad, persistent conditions describing wealthy, powerful groups' potent impact:

- Multinationals have had a pivotal role in the global economy, investing heavily in developing nations and profiting from their cheap labor and resources; since the middle 1980s, American corporations' investment abroad has increased more than thirteenfold.
- Superclass interests are strongly represented in the federal public-policy areas of taxation, budgeting, and business regulation.
- A few giant corporations control large segments of the mass media.
- Rich individuals and groups exert disproportionate political influence through lobbying and campaign giving.

Prevailing American views support social reproduction, including the tendency to downplay class issues and to promote an ideology that emphasizes individual achievement, the importance of hard work, equality of opportunity, and the preeminence of liberal capitalism.

A brief review of the major stratified groups featured in the different chapters demonstrates that while social reproduction prevails, some inequalities have been alleviated. An examination of the four types of capital structures this analysis:

Financial capital. The biggest winners are the upper class (the top 1 percent), whose share of net worth over time has remained a fairly stable third of the nation's total, and between 1983 and 2007 the wealthiest 1 percent's net worth was generally 100 times greater than the lower 40 percent's net worth while the upper class's share of income steadily increased. In the opening decade of the twenty-first century, tax policies benefited this affluent segment. Upper-middle-class earners (in the 2 to 10 percent bracket) have slightly increased their portion of the income total over time while the entire middle-class segment (2 to 25 percent bracket) has received a mildly declining share. Working-class employment reveals a split, with skilled job holders gaining slightly in income over time and unskilled individuals declining. In recent decades the poor have experienced an income loss; the least affluent 20 percent of the population composed of the poor and near poor obtained 4 percent of income in 1967 and slightly less—3.4 percent—in 2008. It is hardly an optimistic situation. Both the curtailment of public-assistance funding and analysts' and clients' commentary suggest that job preparation and training in the TANF program has generally not been effective. Over time Asians', blacks', and Hispanics' income has steadily risen compared to whites'. Many members of racial minorities, however, are vulnerable economically, experiencing higher poverty rates than most majority-group families. The same two conclusions apply to women. Their proportion of men's median income more than doubled between 1965 and 2008. On the other hand, some intersectional groups such as poor minority women, poor female immigrants, and lesbians can encounter disadvantages and discriminations in the workforce. All in all, American income inequality is pronounced, with greater disparities between the wealthy and poor than residents in other developed nations.

Cultural capital. Upper-class parents emphasize the importance of childrearing, and mothers often play a major role. Some wealthy children attend prestigious preschools. Many modern middle-class parents spend significant time with their children, helping them learn to express themselves effectively. In contrast, working-class mothers and fathers are more inclined simply to provide directives, less likely to consider conversation with children as a learning opportunity. Poor parents tend not to converse extensively with their children. Because of the financial and psychological stress of poverty, they tend to be less nurturing than their more affluent counterparts. Within racial groups an important issue involving cultural capital is the child's socialization to race-related issues—for instance, the encouragement of racial pride or, for interracial individuals, the development of a distinctive racial identity. Most parents "do gender," with traditional experiences and outlooks often shaping their relations with their children.

Social capital. The upper class possesses a rarefied version, well situated to use its connections obtained in their own extended families, prep schools and colleges, social clubs, and boardrooms to obtain valuable information and cement a wide range of outcomes. Middle-class individuals are also adept with social capital, using it at their children's schools and in other contexts, including social-networking sites. Once widespread, tightly knit working-class communities are less common now. However, some still exist, with networking opportunities remaining in play. Poor people can have productive social capital, drawing on extended family members for various types of assistance. However, for various reasons they often lack either access to networked personnel or the experience to use such contacts effectively. Such resources can prove very helpful. Research revealed that when poor families were provided social capital that assisted in locating residences, various long-term benefits resulted. Sometimes same-race peers can supply effective networking, promoting leadership skills, mutual assistance, or a shared sense of identity. American girls often find that the social capital they obtain in their peer contacts supports traditional gender-role outlooks and behavior. Intersectional groups encounter different experiences with this resource, sometimes finding as in the case of the Association for Latinas in Business that an organization offers invaluable job-related information and contacts.

Human capital. The upper class has the wealth and contacts that give them optimal access to the most prominent, prestigious education, ranging from preschool through graduate school. The contacts made are invaluable, particularly in well-known boarding schools and universities. Middle-class parents are concerned about the quality of their children's education, sometimes jeopardizing family finances by purchasing a house they cannot afford in order to gain access to a high-quality school district. Individuals with greater functional literacy are more likely to obtain jobs for which a college degree is the standard. Unlike other postindustrial nations, the United States obtains a substantial amount of public-school funding from local property tax. As a result some working-class and most poor families receive less effective schooling—less experienced and capable teachers, large classrooms, inadequate buildings and classroom materials, and among the poor a prevailing pedagogy of poverty. Historically blacks and Hispanics have been disproportionately exposed to poverty, and as a result they are particularly likely to find themselves in schools providing inferior learning, and blacks have been particularly vulnerable to the effects of tracking, suspension, and special-education placement. In the classroom girls have sometimes suffered sexist treatment, victimized by the hidden curriculum and by the widespread belief that they lack the ability to perform well in such fields as mathematics, the sciences, and computer studies. Data in the text suggest that education pays—that overall the more schooling individuals obtain, the higher their income.

This final assessment of the four types of capital does not suggest that any of the US social-stratification systems are undergoing major change. Perhaps with a persistently unpromising job market, some individuals will slip out of the upper-middle class or even the middle class into less affluent categories. Data from the last couple of decades suggests few prospects for widespread upper mobility. Table 11.1 compares the United States and other developed nations on social-inequality issues.

TABLE 11.1 The Lands of Opportunity: A Comparison between the United States and Other Developed Nations

Key resource distributions affecting social inequality

- The US has huge corporate wealth (notably in 2010 two of the top three and 19 of the top 50 multinationals in revenues were American), giving US corporate leaders considerably more wealth than their foreign counterparts to establish and influence the international and national policy-making processes. (Chapter 3)

- American expenditure on campaign spending is massive, with candidates not restricted in the amounts they can receive, and the Supreme Court lifting limitations on corporate contributions; in contrast, European countries operate with relatively stringent ceilings on how much money candidates can obtain. (Chapter 4)

- The US is one of few postindustrial nations not using a proportional-representation system, which means political activity is dominated by two large, wealthy parties, strongly discouraging smaller, less affluent parties' participation. (Chapter 4)

- The US is the only developed nation to rely heavily on local financial sources for public-school funding; in contrast, other developed nations tend to equalize monetary support among districts, sometimes allotting more funding to those which are disadvantaged. (Chapter 6)

- American union membership was lower than in 13 of 14 developed nations between 1970 and 2003. (Chapter 7)

Major differences on important social-inequality dimensions

- Of 24 developed nations, the US had the greatest disparity of income between the richest 10 percent and poorest 10 percent. (Chapter 1)

- American parents' income was more highly associated with children's income than it was in nine of eleven other developed nations. (Chapter 4)

- American parents' income was more closely linked to scores on an international science test than in almost all of 29 other countries. (Chapter 4)

- American factory workers' wages were fifth of 12 developed nations in 1975, slipping to ninth of 12 in 2005. (Chapter 7)

- The US possessed the highest net poverty rate among 24 developed countries. (Chapter 8)

- The US child poverty percentage was higher than in 24 of 25 wealthy nations. (Chapter 8)

- All of these statistical patterns support the conclusion that compared to other developed nations, the United States is most distinctly the land of social reproduction and most decidedly not the land of opportunity.

The United States is a society in which only the affluent, particularly the rich, have steadily improved their economic situation. Addressing the topic of income and wealth distribution, sociologist Dalton Conley raised a provocative question: Should individuals concerned about social inequality focus their energy on publicizing rich people's disproportionate assets or address subjects like globalization, immigration, and changeover to a postindustrial/information society that often extend beyond the power elite's control? Conley's choice is to downplay the upper class's disproportionate wealth and focus on issues that will improve opportunities for those suffering from inequalities, particularly lower-income groups (Conley 2009).

While applauding the development of effective programs to address major inequalities, I would suggest that it is also productive to examine and analyze rich people's wealth and power. Such information helps us to begin to learn how our society functions, and in these chapters we have seen evidence that the upper class, notably the power elite, plays a major role. In particular, detailed information exists about how past and current public policies involving budgeting, taxation, and regulation have contributed to private fortunes and deprived the nation of what are widely considered legitimate sources of revenue. With sufficient popular support, changes in these policies can occur.

One revealing topic is the recent history of rich people's taxation. From the 1930s through the 1970s, progressive taxation prevailed, with wealthy families paying a substantial share of citizens' total. During the 1930s affluent individuals paid as much as 94 percent of their income in taxes, and between 1939 and 1945 federal tax revenues escalated from $1 billion in 1939 to over $18 billion dollars in 1945. In spite of that expenditure, rich people did not go bankrupt nor did they lose the incentive to work. During the Reagan years, progressive taxation began to erode, and deterioration continued through the George W. Bush presidency. In 2007 the richest 1 percent of the citizenry paid just 34 percent of taxes, a sharp falloff from 1980 when they were responsible for 60 percent. The government collected almost 21 percent of the gross domestic product in taxes in 2000, but because of the tax cuts, four years later the figure had dropped to 16 percent (Mooney 2008, 206–07).

Economist Robert Frank proposed a means of addressing this decline in tax revenues—a progressive consumption tax. This arrangement would involve families reporting what they have earned and what they have saved. The difference would indicate the economic value of their consumption, and that sum would be taxed. This innovation, which would encourage people to save, is progressive because more affluent citizens, most notably the rich, would consume more and thus would need to pay more taxes (Frank 2007, 105, 120).

It seems useful to analyze the prevailing inequities in public policy, considering such progressive proposals as Frank's taxation scheme. At the same time, Conley had a worthy point—to consider how effective programming can curtail social inequalities.

CRITICAL ARENAS

Various factors contribute to conditions of social inequality, but as we have seen throughout the text, none affects it more than education and work. Public programs in these two areas can help people immeasurably, significantly improving their life chances.

The Schooling Revolution

In recent years innovative educators have founded and run successful public schools in low-income areas where scholastic achievement has been well below average. In *Sweating the Small Stuff: Inner-City Schools and the New Paternalism*, researcher David Whitman wrote about six secondary schools that have been able to remove students from an inner-city educational setting and elevate their scholastic performance so that they function competently in the educational mainstream. Whitman found that these six schools shared certain traits:

- High quality prevailed in the classroom, particularly dedicated teachers, a rigorous curriculum attuned to state standards, an extended school day and year, and small classes.
- The principals were unorthodox, minimally interested in relations with either central office personnel or teachers' unions, but stayed focused on overcoming students' achievement gap. These maverick principals roamed the halls, sat in on classes, and knew all students by name.
- The schools featured the so-called new paternalism, which involves a meticulous supervision of students' behavior along with punishment for misdeeds and rewards for good character and achievement (Shaughnessy 2008; Whitman 2008).

Many of the most successful educational revitalizations in poor areas, including some of the schools Whitman examined, occur within **charter schools**, which are publicly funded schools run by outside organizations, usually nonprofits, beyond the jurisdiction of local school boards (Tough 2008, 7). While charter schools tend to provide a fine, rigorous education to their students, they usually only help a small number of more promising children.

What Geoffrey Canada, the founder and president of Harlem Children's Zone, planned to do was to deny this exclusivity, making all the primarily black children in the Zone's 68-square block area eligible for a quality education. Canada explained, "The fact is . . . we're in the saving-kid business. That's not what schools traditionally do, but that's what we do" (Tough 2008, 170).

Charter schools often have innovative programs such as this hands-on robotics class at the Detroit Community School.

It has been a massive campaign. In one statement Canada summarized the benefits his students received. He said, "They get adults who love them and are prepared to do anything. And I mean I'm prepared to do anything to keep those kids on the right track" (Harvard Graduate School of Education 2009).

To address its diverse tasks, the Harlem Children's Zone maintains 1,200 employees and a $75-million annual operating budget. It provides a full-service community organization. The centerpiece is Promise Academy, which contains two charter schools—one at the primary and the other at the middle-school level—and associated preschool and afterschool programs. In addition, the Zone offers prekindergarten instruction, parental education, and such family services as foster-care prevention, tax preparation, and disease immunization (Bracey 2009; Harvard Graduate School of Education 2009; Tough 2008, 210–11).

Applicants to Promise Academy participate in a lottery. In 2004, the first year, 100 students joined the kindergarten and 100 the sixth grade. The plan has been that each year that procedure continues until all grades are filled, with 1,300 students extending from kindergarten through the twelfth grade. All charter schools must use lotteries, and in New York City any students in the city's five boroughs are eligible. Canada, however, has been expressly interested in students from central Harlem, especially low performers—the very individuals whose parents are unlikely to take the initiative to send them to a different school than the one to which they are assigned. So in the weeks leading up to the first lottery, Canada sent outreach workers to students' homes, encouraging them to sign up for the lottery (Tough 2008, 8–9).

Starting a new school in a poor district is a formidable task, but on top of that, recruiting the most unpromising students might seem both futile and masochistic. In fact, the first testing results were discouraging. Canada and other administrators had assumed that on standardized tests in math and English many of their students would be a year or perhaps two behind the national average. The scores were much lower. About two thirds of the incoming sixth graders were at least two years behind the national average in math, and nearly three fifths were three or more years behind in verbal ability (Tough 2008, 133).

Five years later Promise Academy had standardized test results showing that the typical eighth graders were higher than the national averages in both math and verbal ability (Brooks 2009; Dobbie and Fryer 2009). How did the school accomplish that transformation?

To begin, Canada's method for education has been eclectic, combining both liberal and conservative elements. He and his colleagues have embraced the liberal position that poor, minority students should receive a high-quality education. However, his approach to achieving that goal has been conservative, following a business model emphasizing that both school officials and students need to engage in a relentless pursuit of achievement. In teacher-student relations Promise Academy has firmly endorsed a version of the new paternalism.

At times Canada has worried that administrators and teachers have not been sufficiently committed to the required approach. At a board meeting in the Academy's second year, the principal of the primary school casually indicated that a number of students had already missed at least 20 days of school. Two wealthy board members who had invested heavily in the school were furious. Why, these men roared, were they spending so much money—so that the kids could stay home and watch TV? (Tough 2008, 135).

Student absenteeism was something Canada found intolerable, interfering with his goal-focused approach. He wanted his administrators to engage in disciplined planning: "start from the result you want to achieve, however improbable, and then work backward, figuring out every single thing you have to do in order to get there" (Tough 2008, 137).

Canada's administrative plan has been critical, but a practical element—funding—has also contributed to Promise Academy's success. While school officials engaged in fundraising, wealthy donors have played an important role. The foremost figure has been Stanley Druckenmiller, a billionaire hedge-fund manager, who has been chairman of the Harlem Children's Zone's board of directors since 1998, and the Academy's largest contributor (Tough 2008, 9–10). Druckenmiller and other wealthy businessmen's financial support have made it possible for Promise Academy and its associated programs to provide first-rate services, but the money has arrived with a firm expectation—that in short order the students' test performances would significantly improve.

The early results were not promising. In the Academy's second year, 40 percent of the sixth grade and 34 percent of the seventh grade were at or above grade level in math while verbal ability scores were much lower—25 percent and 24 percent respectively at or above grade level. The results made Geoffrey Canada feel physically ill (Tough 2008 172–73).

Drastic action was necessary. Canada fired the middle-school principal, who had always had mixed feelings about Promise Academy's unrelenting emphasis on standardized-test results. Glen Pinder, the new principal, was tougher and more exacting, challenging parents to become more involved in their children's schooling and emphasizing the importance of discipline. At the beginning of the third school year, Pinder singled out 29 "bad apples," who had persistent disciplinary problems the previous year and informed them that this was their last chance—either they cleaned up their act or they were out. It was an effective approach, and in the upcoming weeks 28 of 29 former troublemakers had made at least some effort to conform more closely with school rules.

Discipline, however, was not going to be the central means for raising test scores. Thanks to Stanley Druckenmiller's financial support, the afterschool program had been building, with 40 new part-time reading and math specialists hired for the second year. Canada appointed Kate Shoemaker as the new director for the academic afterschool program, where she had to manage 40 tutors and 200 students from 4:00 to 7:00 P.M. every week day and from 9:00 A.M. to 1 P.M. on Saturdays (Tough 2008, 183–85).

The tutors and the students worked long and hard. However, it was more than simply a question of putting in time. Many of these children faced difficult emotional and psychological issues—depression, anger-management struggles, or severely deficient parental relations. Sometimes in the course of this afterschool work, the students told the tutors about their pain. While Sophie Ricard was tutoring a child about test-taking strategy, he abruptly stopped working, saying that nobody cared about his performance, including he himself. Ricard disagreed, claiming that she cared.

[T]ears sprang to the boy's eyes and . . . [ran] down his face. "Why do you care?" he asked.

"Because this is your future, and I care very deeply about you."

(TOUGH 2008, 186)

It turned out that what made the difference for many students was a personal connection—something that was hard to measure but was critical both for their sense of well-being and their effective performance.

Indeed, the students' performance became effective, with sharp improvements over several years. An average student entered Promise Academy in the sixth grade, scoring in the 39th percentile in math among New York City students; by the eighth grade that average student had risen to the 74th percentile. For verbal ability the typical student also improved between the sixth and eighth grades—from the 39th to 53rd percentiles (Brooks 2009; Dobbie and Fryer 2009).

Catherine Bracy, the administrative director for the interdisciplinary Berkman Center at Harvard, concluded that Geoffrey Canada and his associates "had achieved the holy grail as far as education policy wonks are concerned—he's figured out a way to bring inner-city kids up to the same standard as their middle-class counterparts WITHOUT removing those kids from the inner city" (Bracy 2009). Roland Fryer, an economist who investigated the test results, declared that the Promise Academy scores were "the equivalent of curing cancer for these kids. It's amazing" (Brooks 2009, A31).

To produce an educational equivalent of a cure for cancer, Canada and his associates have had access to various forms of capital. Besides the subsidy they receive as a publicly financed school, their financial capital includes the support that Stanley Druckenmiller and other wealthy sponsors provide. Overall the funding for the Harlem Children's Zone of $75 million a year has made it possible to pay for a wide range of productive programming. In inner-city schools children often lack effective social capital putting them in touch with those who would help them resolve academic and psychological difficulties. Unlike most schools in poor areas, Promise Academy has meticulously provided such resources—in particular, competent tutors and counselors. Finally school officials have also supplied cultural capital, with cultural enrichment classes and emotional support from teachers and administrators.

Overall the Academy's potent package of capital resources has produced high-quality education—a pair of charter schools that abolished the pedagogy of poverty and produced an astounding success. Promise Academy and some other charter schools illustrate the educational attainments that effective organization, resources, and commitment can produce. Are there similar accomplishments in the jobs area?

The Revitalization of the Economy

Historian Tony Judt declared that because of the complexity of economic policy, "[w]e have been advised that these are matters for experts" (Judt 2010, 160). Judt concluded, however, that such restraint is unnecessary. Bolstered by informed sources, a nonexpert can make productive commentary about the impact ideas and initiatives can have on the economy. For instance, the goal of full employment at decent wages is a clear, simple conception (Pollin 2005, 177), and historical precedent for it exists.

In the wake of the Great Depression, the (Franklin) Roosevelt administration initiated the Works Progress Administration (WPA), a massive jobs program, which addressed the twin objectives of giving work to people in need of employment and supplying useful public improvements or services. Between 1935 and 1943, the program provided nearly eight million jobs and built roads, bridges, parks, schools, and hospitals (40,000 new and 85,000 refurbished buildings) and also offered numerous courses, childcare, job training, and a host of artistic and educational productions (Gabriel 2008, 39; Leighninger

1996, 227; Mooney 2007, 198–99; Potter and Goetzmann 1960, 52). Does the WPA offer valuable lessons for a current jobs program? .

A labor historian acknowledged that far-ranging government-sponsored initiatives and programs might seem like "pie in the sky but it is more practical than urging more tax cuts and nastier welfare policies, neither of which cure poverty or the jobs crisis" (Stricker 2007, 235). Broad measures that would be helpful for a fairly wide range of American citizens include:

Government initiatives that would target benefits for the less affluent half of the population. It would be a productive economic advancement if politicians and the Federal Reserve Board, which exercises control over such financial issues as interest rates and product prices, took actions that favored the general citizenry's needs over wealthy citizenry's preferences. For instance, in the early 1970s oil prices rose sharply, affecting the cost of most good and services and creating inflation and devaluation of currency. Inflation is a destructive development for all but the affluent few who obtain accelerated dividends from products' rising prices. Thus in such instances the vast majority of citizens would benefit from a price freeze, preventing the onset of inflation. However, politicians and the federal reserve board are unlikely to take such a decisive step unless large numbers of Americans, particularly empowered, knowledgeable middle-class citizens, apply extensive pressure (Mooney 2008, 198; Stricker 2007, 235).

Creation of good jobs. The WPA created jobs for millions of destitute Americans. While Great Depression unemployment rates no longer occur, modern government statistics, which only reveal about half the unemployed, set the rate at 9 percent of the workforce in 2011. How might the federal government proceed with this issue?

A distinctly promising option would be a push toward full employment, a goal that presidential administrations in both the 1930s and the 1960s envisioned. A current means of financing such a venture would be the diversion of substantial spending from costly military and fossil-fuel energy sectors that produce limited employment to intensive job development in such areas as healthcare, education, public infrastructure, and a clean-energy economy. These new jobs would be positions that cannot be outsourced. Such a drive toward full employment would curtail poverty and promote robust consumer activity, increasing business opportunities for both small and large firms (Bureau of Labor Statistics 2011; Gabriel 2008, 39; Pollin 2005; Pollin 2009; Stricker 2007, 235–36; Stricker 2008).

Economist Robert Pollin suggested that good jobs do not just happen—that legislation and union activity have made them possible, promoting good wage benefits, and working conditions. He illustrated by referring to employment at Walmart. "Historically it's a lousy job while working in a steel mill is a good job because steel mills were organized, and that took a long time." The key, Pollin claimed, is to follow the earlier factory model, developing legislation that encourages effective labor unions at Walmart and other such businesses, and those unions will relentlessly push for good-paying, decent jobs (Films for the Humanities and Sciences 2004).

Sustained support for workers' rising wages. In July 2009 Congress mandated an increase in the minimum wage, which rose to $7.25 an hour. At that minimum rate, a full-time worker would earn $15,080 a year, but at the nationwide work-week average of 33 hours, individuals would obtain just $12,441 a year. The government sets the poverty standard at $10,830 for one person or $22,050 for a family of four. Thus full-time employees with jobs paying a minimum wage are going to find themselves close to or below the poverty level. Matt Goldberg, a staff attorney at the Legal Aid Society-Employment Law Center, an organization that advocates for low-wage workers, concluded, "A minimum wage job might technically keep you above the poverty line. But the practical reality is that anyone trying to survive on minimum wage is in real, real dire straights" (Smith 2009). A substantial increase in the minimum wage, perhaps to $15 an hour, would not only raise workers' standard of living but also would force employers to consider them more valuable, making it more likely that they would invest in training, and that action, in turn, would increase employers' commitment and inhibit the likelihood of layoffs (Uchitelle 2006, 211).

Unions can significantly support workers' wages and jobs. Chapter 7 indicated that American union strength has declined in recent years but that in many other countries they continue to be strong. During the 1930s when the New Deal government programs were hiring unemployed individuals, they cooperated initially with unions, signing up workers at the "prevailing wage," which means a region's going rate for unionized jobs. Later when the WPA formed, federal officials tried to cut back wages, initiating much lower "sustainable wages" that were scarcely above poverty level, prompting the Workers Alliance of America, the union of unemployed workers, to picket at job sites and WPA offices throughout the 1930s. Eventually the turmoil and adverse publicity prompted the WPA director to raise payments to the prevailing wage (Gabriel 2008, 41).

Unions and many other activist organizations have provided growing support for a **living wage**, which is an hourly rate of pay that would ensure meeting a family's basic material needs without reliance on public assistance. Living-wage coverage needs adjustment to the area-specific costs of raising a family. Over 120 local governments around the country have passed living-wage ordinances and about as many are discussing and debating whether they should seek such a law. Living-wage standards are considerably higher than minimum-wage figures. For instance, while in 2011 the minimum wage in San Francisco, Chicago, and Boston was $8.00 an hour, the living wage, which adjusts for the number of family members, was much higher for families of two adults and two children—$32.70, $27.04, and $31.85 an hour respectively. Typically living-wage standards only apply to jobs in local government and businesses with which the city has dealings. It seems obvious that living-wage initiatives can transform families' lives; however, they are expensive, and corporations tend to resist them. It seems likely that given the widespread interest in the living-wage issue, discussion and action involving it will continue and that many more cities will pass living-wage ordinances (Living Wage Calculator 2011; Los Angeles Living Wage Study 2005; Universal Living Wage Campaign 2009).

Engagement in responsible restructuring. What measures can help protect workers when downsizing occurs? Instead of companies engaging in mass layoffs, 17 states encourage large employers to initiate work sharing, where reduced hours disperse throughout a workforce. For instance, if management needs to cut 20 percent of its total employee hours, it could either lay off 20 percent of its employees or use a work-sharing program to cut the entire full-time workforce's hours 20 percent. Many of those workers would receive about half of their lost pay through the program's jobless benefits. Generally the work-sharing system has

In recent years residents of hundreds of US cities have mobilized to demand a living wage.

been popular. Employers appreciate it because they can reduce payroll and retain experienced workers and do not need to recruit, hire, and train workers when the economy picks up. Employees like it because it improves the chances of avoiding layoff stresses and major income loss. Pam Thayer, the human-resources leader at the New Buffalo Shirt Factory in Clarence, NY, said that her workers realized that if their hours were cut back to four days a week for several months "they know they'll get that one day of unemployment, so they don't have to go out and look for another job, worried that, 'I don't have a steady income'" (Pugh 2009).

Work sharing is a productive action that can save people's jobs. However, it does not resolve a disturbing reality of modern American society—that both the public and the two major political parties have allowed businesses complete control over layoffs even though both victims and observers appreciate how economically and emotionally destructive their occurrence is (Uchitelle 2006, 205).

In contrast, other nations have provided some provocative approaches to responsible restructuring. Instead of the common American practice of announcing last-minute job dismissals, France and Germany require companies to show government labor inspectors that they have developed a reasonably satisfactory outcome for each downsized employee—for instance, offering a voluntary separation package or convincing suppliers or other businesses to hire former workers temporarily or permanently (Starcher 2009a). In addition, both Japanese and European companies have found that in the long run it is more profitable to engage in "lean management" with an emphasis on productivity improvements and the elimination of waste than to dismiss large numbers of employees (Starcher 2009b).

Perhaps most significantly a number of European countries have developed such innovative policies as co-determination and supervisory boards. Co-determination permits workers to elect some members of companies' supervisory boards, which oversee the managers handling of day-to-day operations. In Germany, the world's second largest exporter, fully half of the supervisory boards for the largest corporations are worker-elected while in Sweden the figure is one third. Evidence indicates that instead of promoting tension or cumbersome decision making, this new policy has increased cooperation between workers and management. A survey of Swedish businesses indicated that two thirds of executives interviewed felt that co-determination is "very" or "rather" positive. One can only imagine that if workers at Walmart could elect a third to half of a supervisory board, the change in treatment of employees would be significant (Hill 2010).

The focus in efforts to reform work and schools has been on large-scale projects led by established professionals and sometimes subsidized by significant private funding. Does that mean that efforts to overcome social inequality exclude less prominent, less affluent groups and individuals, including students? We consider.

Another Way

This discussion involves a central concept. A **social-change organization** is a nonprofit agency, which seeks to alter conditions in an effort to increase marginalized groups' and communities' power and income (Chetkovich and Kunreuther 2006, 14).

Investigators Carol Chetkovich and Frances Kunreuther studied 15 social-change organizations, interviewing their staff members in depth and discovering varying approaches to social change work. In all instances respondents maintained a significant level of engagement. Sometimes individual transformation played an important role, and in organizing groups there could be a linkage between individual transformation and collective action. College students in selected courses can have similar experiences. The following three points amplify these ideas:

Participants' active engagement. As an employee in an agency concerned with its neighborhood growth and development said, "[W]e think the leverage point in social change . . . is the ability for people who live here, versus institutions and organizations, to make change" (Chetkovich and Kunreuther 2006, 15). Such efforts, respondents indicated, can be difficult and demanding. At Respect, a low-income women's collective, the members addressed poor families' needs. At times, Linda Jefferson admitted, staff members' own poverty made the tasks arduous. She added, "And then you meet the next person. . . . And the next thing you know . . . you're giving them energy and they're giving you energy. And you begin to see that, yes, we can do this" (Chetkovich and Kunreuther 2006, 16).

Students too can become engaged in such settings. In a family-science course requiring community service, students' sense of engagement sometimes grew out of witnessing people's pain and deprivation. One student said that in the past she "was happy not knowing what was going on" but after the fieldwork she felt "it is my responsibility to help those in need." She would continue to work in various programs to help poor people and planned to lobby politicians to mobilize against poverty. She added, "Sometimes people need our help. They may not know how to get politically involved and with my education, I can teach them how" (Stanberry and Blackwell 2001, 77).

Individual transformation. Individuals coming into social-change organizations often do not appreciate their potential to improve systems and alleviate social inequality. To engage in such practices, they must alter their outlooks and approaches. Henry Mathis, a project director at an organization which helped low-income families become home owners, indicated that his staff told clients that their efforts did not involve "hand holding" but instead focused on "giv[ing] you the tools to deal . . . with the government agencies, . . . [going] to the department of finance and disput[ing] a tax bill" (Chetkovich and Kunreuther 2006, 18).

Maureen Lynch, an administrator at an agency helping homeless and other poor families move out of poverty, indicated that one of their basic functions was to help their clients "realize that they are a victim of the system. Lots of times they come in thinking they are the cause. . . . So [we're] helping them recognize that [larger system] and . . . become advocates for social change" (Chetkovich and Kunreuther 2006, 19).

In such settings students too can experience an expanding sense of self. At a college which required all freshmen to perform at least 50 hours of community service as part of a two-hour required course, students often found the fieldwork memorable. Nicholas Borgia concluded that it was "a transformational experience," providing "a front row seat to observe and question issues related to humanity and injustices in my small universe." These issues had been raised in class, but now they "were taken out of the academic environment and brought center stage" (Anker, Hillery, Thomas, and Gonzalez 2003, 54).

Individual transformation leading to collective action. Pete Veratek, the director of an agency that educated and mobilized local residents to demand various improvements in their community, applauded the program participants' ability to compel many substantial physical improvements in the neighborhood. He said their clients "just go, organize, prepare, research, act, and get it done. Large numbers of people, not just three leaders or ten pastors or—hundreds of people, thousands of people." Success, Veratek contended, drove these individuals toward more ambitious goals (Chetkovich and Kunreuther 2006, 24).

In a course on American society with a service-learning component, students and local residents worked together in small groups to evaluate photos the inhabitants had taken to reveal their community's strengths and weaknesses. As the residents and students interacted, initial shyness dissipated, replaced by an upbeat outlook emphasizing the community's potential. A student explained that after the meeting everyone was energized, wanting to keep discussing the photos. He added, "I got the feeling that everyone felt like something was actually being done, not just blowing smoke. I think that that in itself was very empowering" (Lewis 2004, 102).

Social-change organizations are diverse, addressing a wide range of economic issues and committed to varied strategies. Staff members within these organizations concern themselves with many economic activities, including food production, home building and rehabilitation, healthcare, manufacturing, and transportation. Decision makers involved with social-change organizations need to develop careful strategies, for instance, deliberating on how militant to be to present their causes in messages to the media or whether to encourage workers to initiate a strike or another form of protest. In addition, personnel in these organizations must decide when and how to affiliate with other grassroots groups, potentially forming coalitions that can broaden their appeal and impact (Grassroots Economic Organizing 2010).

We have discussed efforts to alleviate social inequality. If programs like the ones cited in this chapter are truly going to attack social inequality, what general traits do they require?

Conclusion

Once in the midst of a local activist group's planning session I attended, a member declared, "If we really want to take on the power elite, then we need to be as organized and committed as they are." What might represent useful, practical guidelines for individuals committed to reducing social inequality?

Effective leadership spearheading a powerful, promising, and concrete vision for program development. The principals at the six charter schools David Whitman described focused on overcoming students' achievement gap, mobilizing programs that featured dedicated teachers, a rigorous curriculum, and close working relations with students. In the 1930s Franklin Roosevelt and his associates initiated the WPA, providing an unprecedented 8 million government jobs to unemployed workers during the nation's worst economic depression.

Defensible if controversial goals. At Promise Academy Geoffrey Canada and the other administrators made standardized test scores a priority. Many educators would criticize this approach,

saying that such an emphasis makes students good test takers but does not effectively expose them to the creative thinking and skill development that are at the core of a good education. The rejoinder is that good test scores represent the only means of legitimating the school's success with the educational bureaucracy and their wealthy supporters. Furthermore Canada and his associates could also point out that they have emphasized cultural enrichment and high-quality teaching, which have provided students experiences and information that extend well beyond test-taking skills. In a different vein, the living-wage movement has been controversial. It is costly, requiring employers to pay people a substantial increase above minimum wage. However, what drives it is a powerful moral certainty about committed workers receiving enough money to raise their families decently.

Necessity of being cost-effective. While barely mentioned until now, this factor is important to sustain a strong program in a world where the bottom line is usually salient. Consider, for instance, a pair of successful initiatives with very young poor children. In the early 1970s, the Abecedarian Project, a publicly funded, highly intensive early-childhood program containing 111 poor children, extended from infancy until kindergarten entry and provided full-day, year-round, center-based care. The focus involved developmental skills in cognition and language. The results indicated that compared to nongraduates, the graduates of the project scored substantially higher in reading and math and were much more likely to have attended a four-year college and to have a skilled job. Furthermore a cost-benefit analysis indicated that for every taxpayers' dollar invested, the Abecedarian Project saved $2.50 because of graduates' higher incomes as well as less need for costly intervention by the criminal-justice system and remedial-education services (UNC: FPG Snapshot 2007).

A much larger program containing 1,539 low-income children born in Chicago in 1980 divided the research subjects into program participants who attended one of the Title I Chicago-Parent Centers involving either preschool or extended intervention for children four to six and a control group. The program graduates not only had better grades and higher school-completion rates but also much lower involvement with remedial-education services and juvenile delinquency. The cost-benefit analysis concluded that the preschool project provided $7.14 return for each public dollar invested, and the extended-intervention project returned $6.11 per tax dollar (Reynolds, Temple, Robertson, and Mann 2002).

Grassroots efforts incorporating marginalized people and students.
As earlier discussion suggests, this is a significant issue that establishes whether a given program is simply imposed on an apathetic community or whether members of that community have a chance to become empowered and transformed, assuming ownership in a process where they can both understand and implement inequality-reducing conditions.

Is it possible to mobilize an effective campaign against social inequality? As recently as the opening years of the twenty-first century, not even the most optimistic opponents of social inequality would have expected the passage of the first piece of major legislation in 45 years, in this instance involving healthcare, to include less affluent citizens as major beneficiaries. That was the case, however, when the president signed the Patient Protection and Affordable Care Act into law (Leonhardt 2010).

It was a highly publicized moment in which major political and economic groups participated. But are these the only significant players in such struggles? What is the potential impact of grassroots forces attacking various sources of social inequality? Such efforts receive little media attention and thus remain unknown or obscure to much of the public, and yet especially with the emergence of the Internet, current evidence indicates that a growing mobilization might develop in the decades ahead, potentially rewriting the fine print of social inequality throughout our society.

Key Terms in the Glossary

Charter school *353*   Living wage *358*   Social-change organization *360*

Discussion Topics

1. Evaluate the Geoffrey Canada's educational experiment, indicating both its strengths and weaknesses. Is this a model that is likely to be used widely and effectively with poor children?
2. Describe in detail the three most important factors to take into account in setting up a federal jobs-development initiative.

3. If you were committed to reducing social inequality, what issue would be your focus? Would it be productive to work with a grassroots organization? Explain.

Research Papers

1. Gather information about the Paradise Academy, comparing its effectiveness to other successful charter schools.
2. Drawing on sources in the chapter but expanding them, discuss and evaluate the federal government's record at and potential for both creating jobs and improving workers' economic welfare.

3. Write a paper that examines and assesses grassroots organizations' capacity to reduce social inequality. Cite the activities of specific social-change organizations.

Informative Websites

The site for the Harlem Children's Zone Project (http://www.hcz.org/) supplies updated information about the project, its programs, and its results.

The Living Wage Calculator (http://www.livingwage.geog.psu.edu/) is a remarkable source of information, providing living, poverty, and minimum wages for counties, cities, and towns within each state and also detailing expenses that produce the living-wage estimates.

Grassroots Economic Organizing (http://www.geonewsletter.org/) produces a newsletter authored by educators, researchers, and activists promoting a society that emphasizes democratic participation, citizens' ownership of sources of production, social and economic justice, and environmental health.

Bibliography

Altman, Lawrence K. 2008. "The Story Behind Kennedy's Surgery." *New York Times* (July 29): F1.

Anker, Laura, Barbara Hillery, Tonya Thomas, and Julia Gonzalez. 2003. "Civic Engagement and Inter-cultural Understanding: Course-embedded Community Field Work for First Year College Students." *International Journal of Diversity in Organizations, Communities and Nations* 8 (Winter): 49 –58.

Biddle, Bruce J., and David C. Berliner. 2002. "A Research Synthesis: Unequal School Funding in the United States." *Educational Leadership* 59 (March): 1–15.

Bracy, Catherine. 2009. "Just Finished Reading Whatever It Takes by Paul Tough." *Braceland* (May 4). http://blogs.law.harvard.edu/cbracy/2009/05/04/just-finished-reading-whatever-it-takes-by-paul-tough/.

Brooks, David. 2009. "The Harlem Miracle." *New York Times* (May 7): A31.

Bureau of Labor Statistics. 2011. "Labor Force Statistics from the Current Population Survey." http://www.bls.gov/cps/.

Chetkovich, Carol, and Frances Kunreuther. 2006. *From the Ground Up: Grassroots Organizations Making Social Change*. Ithaca: ILR Press.

Conley, Dalton. 2009. "Who Cares about the Excesses of the Rich? It's the Fate of the Poor That Matters." *American Prospect* (December 15). http://www.prospect .org/cs/articles?article=don't_blame_the_ billionaires.

Dobbie, Will, and Roland G. Fryer, Jr. 2009. "Are High-Quality Schools Enough to Close the Achievement Gap? Evidence from a Bold Social Experiment in Harlem." pp. 1–52. http://www.economics.harvard.edu/faculty/ fryer/files/HCZ_Nov_2010.pdf.

Films for the Humanities and Sciences. 2004. "A Question of Fairness."

Frank, Robert H. 2007. *Falling Behind: How Rising Inequality Harms the Middle Class*. Berkeley: University of California Press.

Gabriel, Jeanette. 2008. "A Twenty-First Century WPA: Labor Policies for a Federal Government Jobs Program." *Social Policy* 38 (Spring): 38–43.

Grassroots Economic Organizing. 2010. "News from the Frontlines of Economic Solidarity and Grassroots Globalization from Below: Themes and Topics." http://www.geonewsletter.org/ node/21.

Harvard Graduate School of Education. 2009. "Making a Difference: Geoffrey Canada and the Harlem Children's Zone." http:// www.gse.harvard.edu/impact/stories/alums_ students/hdp/canada.php.

Hill, Steven. 2010. "Europe's Answer to Wall Street." *Nation* 290 (May 10): 23–24+.

Judt, Tony. 2010. *Ill Fares the Land*. New York: Penguin Press.

Leighninger, Robert D., Jr. 1996. "Cultural Infrastructure: The Legacy of New Deal Public Space." *Journal of Architectural Education* 49 (May): 226–36.

Leonhardt, David. 2010. "In the Process, Pushing Back at Inequality." *New York Times* (March 24): A1+.

Lewis, Tammy L. 2004. "Service Learning for Social Change? Lessons from a Liberal Arts College." *Teaching Sociology* 32 (January): 94 –108.

Living Wage Calculator. 2011. "Introduction to the Living Wage Calculator." http://www .livingwage.geog.psu.edu/places/0607567000.

Los Angeles Living Wage Study. 2005. "Examining the Evidence: The Impact of the Los Angeles Living Wage Ordinance on Workers and Businesses." http://www.livingwage.geog .psu.edu/.

Mooney, Nan. 2007. *(Not) Keeping Up with Our Parents*. Boston: Beacon Press.

Pollin, Robert. 2005. *Contours of Descent: U.S. Economic Fractures and the Landscape of Global Austerity*. London: Verso.

Pollin, Robert. 2009. "Robert Pollin on Full Employment." *Tikkun Magazine* (January).

Potter, David M., and William Goetzmann. 1960. *The New Deal and Employment*. New York: Henry Holt and Company.

Pugh, Tony. 2009. "Obama Urged to Turn Successful State Job Program National." *McClatchy Newspapers*. (November 11). http://www.mcclatchydc.com/economy/ story/78720.html.

Reynolds, Arthur J., Judy A. Temple, Dylan L. Robertson, and Emily A. Mann. 2002. "Age 21 Cost-Benefit Analysis of the Title I Chicago Child-Parent Centers." *Educational Evaluation and Policy Analysis* 24 (Winter): 267–303.

Shaughnessy, Michael F. 2008. "An Interview with David Whitman: On Sweating the Small Stuff." *EducationNews.org*. http://www .ednews.org/articles/an-interview-with-david-whitman-on-sweating-the-small-stuff.

Smith, Aaron. 2009. "Higher Minimum Wage Coming Soon." *CNNMoney.com* (July 7). http://money.cnn.com/2009/07/06/news/ economy/minimum_wage/index.htm.

Stanberry, Anne M., and Ann P. Blackwell. 2001. "Marshalling Students to Action: The Community, Education and Policy Partnership." *Journal of Teaching in Marriage and Family* 1: 68–82.

Starcher, George. 2009a. "Best Downsizing Practices." *EBBF*. http://ebbf.org/blog/?p=474.

Starcher, George. 2009b. "Responsible Downsizing." *EBBF*. http://ebbf.org/blog/?p=464.

Stricker, Frank. 2007. *Why America Lost the War on Poverty—and How to Win It*. Chapel Hill: University of North Carolina Press.

Stricker, Frank. 2008. "Help Wanted: Too Many Workers, Not Enough Jobs." *National Jobs for All Coalition*. http://www.njfac.org/ stricker.htm.

Tough, Paul. 2008. *Whatever It Takes: Geoffrey Canada's Quest to Change Harlem and America.* Boston: Houghton Mifflin Company.

Uchitelle, Louis. 2006. *The Disposable American: Layoffs and Their Consequence.* New York: Alfred A. Knopf.

UNC: FPG Child Development Institute. 2007. "Poverty and Early Child Intervention." http://www.fpg.unc.edu/~snapshots/snap42.pdf.

Universal Living Wage Campaign. 2009. "Welcome to the Universal Living Wage Campaign." http://www.universallivingwage.org/.

Whitman, David. 2008. *Sweating the Small Stuff: Inner-City Schools and the New Paternalism.* Dayton, OH: Thomas B. Fordham Foundation.

PHOTO CREDITS

GLOSSARY

1.5 generation immigrants who reach the new host country before the age of 13 and thus have the chance to achieve mastery of its language and to obtain extensive American schooling

Absolute threshold of poverty a cutoff point establishing the minimal level of income below which families are unable to purchase sufficient food, clothing, and shelter to maintain themselves in good health

Apprentice an individual who agrees to work for low wages for a specified length of time, learning from his or her employer the range of skills required in that trade

Authority power derived from a person's location within an organization or structure

Blaming the victim a perspective that focuses on an individual's personal deficiencies, downplaying or ignoring such structural influences as the family's economic status or its access to quality education

Blue-collar (job holders) individuals who have obtained a high-school diploma or less schooling and do manual work, normally receiving an hourly wage

Bourgeoisie the class with ownership of the various means of production

Bureaucratic system of authority a structure that systematically administers the tasks controlling an organization's operation

Capital resources that people possess or acquire, finding them valuable in various settings

Capitalism a system in which economic production features private ownership in pursuit of profit

Charismatic system of authority a system at the core of which is an individual who pursues a mission driven by a powerful sense of divine purpose and draws followers who are committed to that mission

Charter school a publicly funded school run by outside organizations, usually nonprofits, beyond the jurisdiction of local school boards

Class a large category of similarly ranked people located in a hierarchy and distinguished from other categories in the hierarchy by such traits as occupation, education, income, and wealth

Color-blind racism whites' assertion that they are living in a world where racial privilege no longer exists, but their behavior supports racialized structures and practices

Comparable worth the conclusion that the definitive means of promoting pay equity is to base pay scales on a combined assessment of the worker's qualifications and the job's basic traits, considering irrelevant whether or not the position is traditionally associated with a particular sex

Conflict theory a perspective contending that the struggle for wealth, power, and prestige in society should be the central concern of sociology

Conspicuous consumption lavish expenditure on high-priced goods and services in order to flaunt one's wealth

Core nation a country which possesses a successful industrial history, exerts both political and economic influence in the world system, and enjoys a high standard of living

Corporate community a number of large businesses and banks which form a network for such mutual benefits as sharing information and developing economic and political policies

Cultural capital broadly shared outlooks, knowledge, skills, and behavior passed from one generation to the next

Cycle of poverty a circular process in which a set of interrelating large structures, primarily institutions lock individuals and families into a low-income condition

Deck stacking the process of loading most of the positions in the media companies—the editors, managers, and reporters—with unshakably loyal personnel

De facto segregation the separation of racial groups resulting from common practice and involving such issues as residential patterns or school enrollment

Deserving poor such people as the aged, infants, and individuals with serious illness or physical disability, who were incapable of work and thus qualified for charitable support and a sympathetic evaluation

Doing gender acting in ways considered appropriate toward members of the designated sex

Downsizing the deliberate reduction of permanent employees in an effort to provide an organization more efficient operation and/or cut costs

Ecology of class the largely unrecognized or acknowledged impact that residential or occupational location has on quality of life

Equality of opportunity a situation where people possess broadly similar chances for success in business, politics, and other prized endeavors

Ethnicity the classification of people into categories with distinct cultural or national traits

Eugenics movement an initiative founded by prominent intellectuals who claimed that scientists could lead an organized effort to ensure "the purification of the Anglo-Saxon race"

Extended family network an interrelated kinship group which plays a role in members' care, particularly children's health and well-being

False consciousness the proletariat's inability to perceive that the established economic and political forces inevitably maintain their domination and exploitation

Family office an organization formed when family members pool some of their resources and hire experts to evaluate investments, charitable activities, and perhaps even political donations

Financial capital monetary items such as wages and salaries or purchasable items such as computers or books that can contribute directly or indirectly to obtaining various valued resources representing other types of capital

Floundering family a household in which the breadwinner(s) appear(s) to lack the ability to establish financial independence

Foundation a tax-free organization, which spends money on research, education, the arts, and many other endeavors

Functional literacy the capacity to use basic skills in reading, math, and the interpretation of documents in work situations

Gender constancy the recognition that being female or male is a permanent part of one's identity, serving as the foundation for adult gender roles

Gini index a measurement of a nation's statistical distribution of income or wealth inequality

Glass ceiling distinct but often unseen barriers including discrimination women face in seeking to move into high-level positions

Globalization the increasing integration of nations in an age featuring highly reduced costs for communication and transportation along with the lowering of such "artificial barriers" as treaties or tariffs restricting the movement of goods, services, financial capital, and technology across borders

Habitas the set of attitudes, behavior, and experiences maintained by the people sharing a distinct social world

Hegemonic despotism a condition where modern firms can control operations by threatening workers with downsizing or even plant closure

Hegemonic masculinity an established gender hierarchy in which masculine qualities, opportunities, and privileges receive greater recognition than feminine ones

Hegemony a situation in which one nation has sufficient power and influence to impose its rules and goals globally in the economic, political, military, diplomatic, and even cultural realms

Hidden curriculum the messages about values, beliefs, and behavior that teachers and administrators can unofficially communicate to students

High-stakes testing a situation in which the outcome of a standardized test becomes the sole basis for determining students' educational progression

Human capital the attainment of skills, knowledge, and expertise people acquire to be successful in various valued ways

Hypergamy the ability to transcend normal rules and restrictions

Ideology the complex of values and beliefs that support a society's social-stratification systems and their distribution of wealth, income, and power

Income individuals' earnings obtained through wages, salaries, business profits, stock dividends, rents, and other means

Index of dissimilarity the percentage of a particular racial group that would need to change residential location in order to achieve racial evenness—to disperse its membership throughout the city so that census tracts average that group's percentage of inhabitants in the city

Index of occupational segregation the proportion of females (or males) who would need to change to jobs where their sex is underrepresented, thereby producing a sexually integrated occupational structure

Individual racism a person's or group's action that produces racial abuse—for example, verbal or physical mistreatment

Individual sexism a person's or group's action that produces abuse against girls or women

Informal sector jobs and businesses that government neither monitors nor taxes

Institutional racism the discriminatory racial practices built into organizations and groups within the political, economic, and educational systems

Institutional sexism the discriminatory practices against women built into organizations and groups within the political, economic, and educational systems

Intergenerational mobility a measure of social mobility comparing a child's and a parent's class location

Interlocking directorate a formal connection between two major corporations which develops when an officer from one company serves on the board of directors of another

Intersectionality the recognition that a woman's oppressions, limitations, and opportunities result from the combined impact of two or more influential statuses—in particular, her gender, race, class, age and sexual preference

Jim Crow era a period of time ranging from Reconstruction to the 1960s during which laws and customs mandated a castelike separation of blacks and whites, featuring blacks' subordination and oppression

Labor union an organization that legally represents the interests of a set of job holders in respect to wages, benefits, and working conditions

Legitimation individuals' willing acceptance of the dominant ideology and institutions and the social inequalities they promote

Liberal capitalism a combination of a democratic political system and a capitalist economy, supporting free trade and unrestricted economic competition

Lifestyle a particular set of behavioral patterns involving social relations, childrearing practices, language usage, and other activities deriving from members' consumption patterns

Living wage an hourly rate of pay that would ensure meeting a family's basic material needs without reliance on public assistance

Lobbying the process by which individuals or groups attempt to influence government officials to support legislation or policies sought by their clients, who can be corporations, professional and trade associations, or consumer and environmental groups

Lumpenproletariat the portion of the working class comprised of society's dregs—swindlers, brothel-keepers, beggars, and such—who are disengaged from the revolutionary struggle

Majority group a category of people within a society who possess distinct physical or cultural characteristics and maintain superior power, wealth, and other valued resources

Means of production the factories, farms, and businesses, where goods and services are developed and dispersed

Media framing the process of packaging information and entertainment in order to produce a distinct impact on an audience

Minority group a category of people with recognizable racial or ethnic traits that place it in a position of restricted power and inferior status so that its members suffer limited opportunities and rewards

Mode of production a society's organized system for developing goods and services such as feudalism, capitalism, or socialism

Modern world system a capitalist global economy which contains multiple states and a single dominant international division of labor

Multinational a large corporation which both produces and sells goods or services in various countries

Official U.S. measure of poverty an absolute standard employing a two-step process—assessing the minimal cost for a nutritionally healthy diet and then tripling that figure to compute the threshold for a poverty income

Outsourcing companies' subcontracting of services to other companies instead of continuing to provide those services themselves

PAC or **political action committee** a private fundraising group often affiliated with a corporation, labor union, or citizen group, permitting participants an additional $5,000 contribution on top of their individual giving

Pay equity the contention that women and men should receive similar compensation not only for equal work but for work of equal value

Pedagogy of poverty a set of ineffective, even destructive teaching practices often imposed on poor children

Peripheral nation a member of the poorest, least powerful, and least industrially developed set of countries

Petite bourgeoisie a small-business class, whose members never accumulate enough profit to expand their holdings and to challenge the bourgeoisie's economic supremacy

Pluralism a theory concluding that a dispersion of authority and control exists within government

Poor workers' spatial mismatch the reality that while these job seekers tend to live in urban districts, most economic expansion is in the suburbs

Poor workers' temporal mismatch the fact that these individuals are on the job during evening and weekend shifts when local transportation is either less or not operative

Power elite a number of high-status people, particularly in prominent corporate and political positions, who largely control the process of determining a society's major economic and political policies

Proletariat the workers, who do not own the means of production

Proportional representation an electoral formula attempting to match the national or regional votes a party receives with its legislative seats

Racial formation the socio-historical process of creating and changing race-related structures and meanings

Racialized meaning that people's racial classification significantly affects their access to valued economic, political, and social resources

Racially restrictive covenant a contract among property owners prohibiting specified minorities from buying, leasing, or occupying property in their locale

Racial project an interpretation or explanation of racial events that promotes the mobilization of new organizations and groups along with altered everyday behavior

Racism a belief that real or alleged traits of one race establish its superiority over another or others

Redlining the discriminatory practice of refusing to provide mortgage loans or property insurance or only providing them at accelerated rates for reasons not clearly associated with any conventional assessment of risk

Regulatory agency an independent governmental investigatory commission established by Congress to develop standards for some specific commercial activity and then to enforce those standards

Reserve army of labor the bourgeoisie's purposeful maintenance of a distinct level of unemployment as a bargaining chip for keeping wages low

Resiliency effective adjustment to adversity, namely the ability to survive when facing risks or to rebound following a crisis

Selective reporting a biased coverage of news issues that promotes corporate interests and downplays, denigrates, or ignores issues and groups challenging these interests

Semiperipheral nation an independent state which has achieved a moderate level of industrialization and development

Sense of entitlement the conviction that one deserves to receive some valued opportunity or reward

Separate-but-equal standard a legal doctrine legitimating segregated services and facilities for blacks and whites

Sexism a set of beliefs claiming that real or alleged differences between women and men establish the superiority of men

Skilled-labor job a working-class position involving specific knowledge or ability and sometimes requiring specialized training or schooling

Slave codes a body of laws covering all major issues in slaves' lives

Social capital those individuals, networks, groups, and organizations that can assist participants in pursuing valued objectives

Social-change organization a nonprofit agency which seeks to alter conditions in an effort to increase marginalized groups' and communities' power and income

Social Darwinism a doctrine emphasizing that the most inherently capable groups will rise to the top of economic, political, and social hierarchies, ensuring the most productive arrangement for the distribution of wealth and power for society at large

Social distance people's willingness to engage in different degrees of closeness with members of various racial and ethnic groups

Social inequality a situation in which individuals, families, or members of larger structures like neighborhoods or cities vary in access to such valued resources as wealth, income, education, healthcare, and jobs

Social mobility the movement of an individual or group up or down in a social hierarchy such as a class system

Social-networking sites Internet organizations that are seeking to build online communities of people sharing interests and activitie

Socialism an economic system in which the proletariat controls the means of production and the distribution of profits

Social reproduction analysis of the structures and activities that transmit social inequality from one generation to the next

Social stratification a deeply embedded hierarchy providing different groups varied rewards, resources, and privileges and establishing social relationships that both determine and legitimate those outcomes

Sociological theory a combination of observations and insights providing a systematic explanation of social life

Spin control various media practices meant to mobilize an audience's support for a corporate or superclass outlook

Squatters individuals or families who settle on land that does not belong to them

Standpoint a particular group's outlook on the workings of social relations and society

Steering a realtor's effort to dissuade minority clients from seeing residences in all-white or largely all-white areas, instead seeking to interest them in homes in what are wholly or primarily minority areas

Stereotype a set of largely negative traits that prejudiced people apply to all members of the group against whom they are prejudiced

Stereotype fallout the significant penalty minority-group members can suffer when influential, often powerful individuals embrace an established stereotype of that minority group, promoting its toxic impact on their life chances

Stereotype threat the distinct risk that the members of a group widely believed to possess inferior abilities will fall victim to that diminished expectation

Structural-functional theory a perspective suggesting that groups in interaction tend to adjust to one another in a fairly stable, conflict-free way

Structural mobility a type of social mobility where either technological or institutional change creates an increase or decrease in jobs within a certain class

Structural vulnerability a distinct likelihood of encountering major difficulties or threats because of such deficient capital resources as money, education, or important information

Substructure the material conditions of production such as gathering and hunting, agriculture, or industrial development

Superstructure the noneconomic parts or institutions of society—for instance, the political system, medicine and healthcare, the family, or education

Surplus value the difference between a product's economic worth and the worker's payment

Temporary (temp) work jobs produced when a company contracts with an agency to supply it employees

Think tank an organization that does the most systematic research and analysis in the policy-formation process

Tracking a process where educators evaluate students and then place them in programs with a curriculum that supposedly is appropriate for their abilities

Traditional system of authority a system which is usually patriarchal, with the dominant individual, whether a husband, father, master, chieftain, lord, or king, maintaining legitimacy based on established belief

Trajectory a cyclical pattern of disruption and restoration, with racial projects a key component in this process

Undeserving poor individuals who simply avoided work out of apparent lethargy or because alcohol, drugs, or some other debilitating influence caused physical and/or mental decline

Urban war zone a poor, crime-laden district in which deteriorated, violent, even war-like conditions and underfunded, largely ineffective schools promote inferior academic performance, including irregular attendance and disruptive or noncompliant classroom behavior

Wealth people's economic assets—their cars, homes, stocks, bonds, and real estate, which can be converted into cash

White-collar (job holders) individuals who are well educated or fairly well educated and perform nonmanual tasks in offices

Work alienation an outcome job holders face when they lose control over either the work process, the product of their labor, or both

Work ethic the conviction that unrelenting commitment to one's job is necessary both for occupational success and for building character

INDEX

Concepts that are boldfaced are defined in the book, often on the first page listed in the index and also in the end-of-text glossary.

1.5 generation, 386

A

Abecedarian Project, 363
abortion, 197
absolute threshold of poverty, 220
Achinstein, Betty, 164
A. C. Nielsen Company, 103
admission offices (universities), 133, 134
advice books for parents, 317–18
aerospace industry, 178
Afflerbach, Peter, 232
African Americans, 12, 132, 200–01, 237, 265–69,
    271–72, 273–74, 275–76, 277, 278, 279–81,
    282, 283, 284–85, 286, 287, 288–89, 294, 295,
    325–28, 349, 350
  income and jobs, 287–94
  mass media, 284–86
  poverty, 292
  parents, 273–74
  schooling, 273–74, 279–82, 289
  special education, 335–38
agriculture, 51, 57, 64, 148, 149
Ahrens, Frank, 40
Aid to Dependent Children, 218–19
Aid to Families with Dependent Children, 220
Aikman, Sheila, 313
Alba, Richard, 290, 291
Alderson, Arthur S., 59, 63
Aldrich, Nelson W., Jr., 130, 132
Alesina, Alberto, 86
Alexander, Herbert E., 98
Alexander, Karl Len, 280
Alger, Horatio, Jr., 1, 17, 82, 83, 90, 124
Allard, Kenneth, 105
Allen, Beverly Lundy, 194
Allen, Michael Patrick, 131, 135, 137
Allen, Tammy P., 168
Ally McBeal, 284
Alterman, Eric, 91
Altman, Lawrence K., 348
Alvarez, Alvin N., 274
Alvarez, Louis, 80
Alvarez, Sandra D., 328
Amedee, George, 248

American business, 4–7
American Enterprise Institute, 92, 94, 95, 141
American ideology, 82–86, 176, 287
American Indians
    See Native Americans
American Medical Association, 24–25
Amnesty International, 104
Anderson, Charles H., 30
Anderson, David, 30
Anderson, Jenny, 121
Anderson, Kim, 86
Anderson, Martin, 95
Anderson, Steven G., 244, 246, 247, 249
Andre, Claire, 320, 321
angioplasty, 159–60
Anglin, Deidre M., 273
Aniakudo, Patricia, 325
Anker, Laura, 361
Appelbaum, Eileen, 242, 253
Appleby, Joyce, 148
Applegate, Debby, 150
Apple's iPhone, 63
apprentices, 207–08
Argentina, 49
Armenia, Amy, 209
Armstrong, Annie Laurie, 87, 225–28, 234, 236, 238,
    242–45
Arnault, E. Jane, 321
Aron-Dine, Aviva, 107
Aronson, Joshua, 270
Aronson, Marc, 268, 272
artisans, 187–88
Asian Americans, 270, 271, 277, 280–84, 287, 291,
    292–93, 294, 295, 349
  income, 288
  jobs, 287, 289
  mass media, 283–84
  poverty, 292
  schooling, 279, 282, 289
Asian American women, 334
Assaf, Lori, 232
Association for Latinas in Business, 328–29, 350
Astor, John Jacob, 123, 125
Atlas, John, 111
Auletta, Ken, 224

Australia, 7, 49
authoritative parenting, 160, 181
authority, 33
authority
   systems, 33–35
auto industry, 51, 54–55
Avila, Ernestine, 334, 335

B
Bagdikian, Ben H., 100
Bailyn, Bernard, 264, 266
Baltimore and Ohio Railroad strike, 189
Baltzell, E. Digby, 133, 135, 136
Bank of the United States, 123
bankruptcy, 174
banks
   and the global economy, 4, 52
Barbour, Chandler, 196
Barbour, Nita H., 196
Barboza, David, 63
Bario, D., 57
Barone, Diane M., 232, 236
Barr, Robert D., 225, 231, 233, 236
Barr, Stephen, 178
Barrow, Lisa, 229, 230
Barstow, David, 105
Bartlett, Donald L., 172
Barvosa, Edwina, 156, 324
Bashaw, David J., 156
basketball, 315
Basow, Susan, 314
Beaulieu, Carmen Garcia, 325
Becht, Marco, 138
Beck, E.M., 268
Beckery, Sven, 150
Bednarzik, Robert, 89
Beebe, Lucius, 122
Beecher, Catherine E., 306
Beeghley, Leonard, 2
Beim, David, 133
Bellah, Robert N., 82
Beltran, Pedro, 129–30
Bender, Daniel E., 269
Bennett, Lerone, 267
Bennett-Alexander, Dawn D., 332
Bensman, David, 65
Berberoglu, Berch, 30, 56
Berends, Mark S., 280
Berenson, Alex, 113
Berkshire Hathaway, 137
Berliner, David C., 230, 348
Berndt, Christian, 64

Bernhardt, Annette, 242
Bernstein, Basil, 10
Bernstein, Jared, 247
Berruecos, Luis, 63
Bessemer process, 53
Best, Candace, 273
Bethleham Steel, 125
Bickel, Robert, 230
Biddle, Bruce J., 230, 348
Bilginsoy, Cihan, 207, 208
biomedical research, 126
Bird, S. Elizabeth, 284
Birkbeck, Morris, 148
Birkeland, Sarah E., 155, 156
Birth of a Nation, 284–85
Bishop, Angela, 273
Bishop, John H., 198
Bishop, Libby, 166
Biskupic, Joan, 57
Black, Dan A., 332
Blackmon, Sha'kema M., 273
blacks
   see African Americans
Blackwell, Ann P., 361
black women, 325–28
Blake, Jamilia J., 277
blaming the victim, 216, 218, 220, 233, 250, 254
Blanchett, Wanda J., 337
Blau, Peter M., 88
Blevins, Andy, 158
blue-collar job holders, 3, 153, 169, 202–09, 288, 321–23
Bluestone, Barry, 241
Blumin, Stuart M., 151, 195
Bodison, Preston, 273
Boeing, 126
Boes, Mary, 331
Bogardus, Emory S., 263
Bogle, Donald, 267
Bohemian Club, 41, 136–37
Bombardieri, Marcella, 314
Bonilla-Silva, Eduardo, 273, 275
Books, Sue, 221, 225, 229, 230, 236
Borgia, Nicholas, 361
Boris, Eileen, 192
Bosh, Chris, 83
Boston Housing Authority, 239–40
Boswell, Terry, 54, 57
Bourdieu, Pierre, 11, 12
bourgeoisie, 27–30, 32, 44, 60
Bowles, Samuel, 11, 87

BP, 51
Boulis, Ann, 339
Boyd, Monica, 333
Brace, Charles Loring, 218
Bracy, Catherine, 356
Bradbury, Katherine, 89
Bradshaw, York W., 49, 50, 58
Bradvik, 132
Brady, David, 241
Brady, Marilyn Dell, 149–151, 160
Branch, Enobong Hannah, 325
Braswell, Michael, 155
Brazil, 49, 60, 68–69
Brecher, Jeremy, 3
Bretton Woods conference, 4, 54
Brewer, Benjamin D., 53
Brier, Stephen, 186, 188
Broaddus, Michele, 310
Brookings Institution, 92, 141, 235
Brooks, Arthur C., 129
Brooks, David, 12, 356
Brooks-Gunn, Joanne, 235
Brown, Alison Hamilton, 331
Brown, Clair, 109
Brown, Dee, 264
Brown, Michael K., 283
Brown, Paul B., 10
Brown University, 134
Brown v. Board of Education of Topeka, 263
Browne, Beverly A., 317
Brundage, David, 186
Bryant, Kobe, 83
budgeting, 107–08
Buffett, Warren, 121, 137
Bunker, Stephen G., 53
bureaucratic system of authority, 33
Burkham, David T., 280
Burris, Carol Corbett, 279, 288
Burris, Val, 99, 129, 140
Burroughs, Charles, 218
Burtless, Gary, 222
Burton, Thomasco, 273
Bush, George H.W., 97, 136
Bush, George W., 77, 98, 103, 107, 108, 110, 136, 170
Bush (George W.) administration, 104–05, 352
Business Roundtable, 41, 93, 140, 141–42, 170, 192, 208
Byrd, Larry, 83

C

Cagney and Lacey, 315–16
Calkins, Lucy, 232

Calvinists, 84
campaign spending, 98–100, 121, 138, 351
Campbell, Wendy Sellers, 328
Canada, 108
Canada, Geoffrey, 353–56, 362
capital, 12, 48, 137
capitalism, 26, 29–33, 36, 59, 84, 85, 140, 188
capitalist class, 56, 121–44
    See also upper class
Carlan, Philip E., 155
Carlsson-Paige, Nancy, 284
(The) Carlyle Group, 97
Carnegie, Andrew, 124, 125, 138, 139, 141
Carnegie Endowment for International Peace, 141
Carnevale, Anthony P., 242
Carnoy, Martin, 283
Carpenter, Christopher S., 332
Carter, Gregg Lee, 306, 310, 312, 314, 316, 317, 320
Carter, Robert, 122
Carter-Black, Jan, 327
cartoons, 317
Carville, James, 195
carwashes, 290
Casals, Pablo, 129
Caspary, Gretchen L., 254
Castellani, John J., 93
Castellano, Marisa, 208
Cauce, Ann Mari, 227, 279
Centano, Miguel Angel, 59, 60, 63
CEOs, 6–7, 56, 106, 139, 168
Chadwick, Kathy Gordon, 236
Chaitin, Julia, 333
Challender, Chloe, 313
Chang, Alicia, 178
Chang, Iris, 275
charismatic system of authority, 34
charter schools, 353–56, 362
Chase-Dunn, Christopher, 49, 53, 54
Chauncey, Henry, 231–32
Chen, Chuansheng, 273
Cheng, Simon, 275
Cherlin, Andrew J., 209
Cheslow, Jerry, 200
Chester, Charlene, 226
Chetkovich, Carol, 360, 361
Chicago Real Estate Board, 268
childcare, 129, 175, 176, 209, 227–28, 247–48, 253, 320, 323–24, 339
children's books, 310, 314
child poverty, 222, 225–26, 227–37
child support, 226, 248

Chin, Christina B., 283, 284
China, 23, 29, 33, 60, 62–63, 65, 72
Chinese Americans, 269, 274
Chinese Communist Party, 60
Chinese Exclusion Act of 1882, 269
Chirot, Daniel, 50, 53–55, 57
Christie, Lee, 92
Chun, Jennifer Ji Hyde, 172
Churchill, Ward. 284
Ciccantell, Paul S., 53
Citizens United v. Federal Election Commission of 2010, 100
civil-rights movement, 263
class, 2, 12, 14–17, 25, 30–32, 35–37, 41, 44, 48, 56–57, 71, 78–82
  Marxist system, 27–28, 32, 37
  Weber's system, 31–34, 37
  Wright's system, 35–37
Class Action Fairness Act of 2005, 97–98
class-based lobbying, 97–98
Clawson, Rosalie A., 284
Clement, Wallace, 56
Clinton, Hillary, 91
Clinton, William, 54, 59, 77, 103, 195, 220
Cochran, Bryan, 227
Cockburn, Alexander, 137
Coddington, Ron, 99
co-determination, 360
Cohen, Andrew Wender, 150
Cohen, Stephen S., 166
Coleman, James, 12, 13
Coleman, Willi, 274
college, 157, 164, 175, 178, 197–98, 199, 234, 325–26, 350
Collins, Chuck, 77
Collins, Jane L., 66
Collins, Patricia Hill, 274, 324
color-blind racism, 273, 275, 286, 294
Columbia, 134
Columbus, Christopher, 264
Combs, Gwendolyn, 327
Commager, Henry Steele, 86
commercials, 316, 317
Committee for Economic Development, 39, 41, 93, 141, 142
communities, 165–67, 199–201, 237–40
company ladder, 150, 177
comparable worth, 320–21
computer specialists, 64, 72, 151, 172, 173
Conant, James Bryant, 159
Conchas, Gilberto Q., 277, 278
conflict theory, 23, 25, 26, 34

Conley, Dalton, 351
Connell, R. W., 309
Connelly, Marjorie, 82, 88
Conners, Joan L., 284
Connor, David J., 337
Conrad, Peter, 154
conspicuous consumption, 32–33, 125, 128
Constantine, Madonna G., 273
consumer costs, 174–76
Cook, Allison, 237
Coombs, Robert Holman, 153
Cooney, Kate, 250
"coons," 267
Coontz, Stephanie, 189
Cooper, Robin, 333
Corak, Miles, 90
Corcoran, Mary E., 250
core nations, 48, 49–50, 55–58, 63, 71
Cornwall, Vita, 323
corporate communities, 99, 114, 123–24
corporate leadership, 137–40
Cortese, Anthony J., 316
Costello, Tim, 3
Cotter, David A., 320
Council on Foreign Relations, 39, 93, 141, 142
Countryman, Edward, 186, 188
Coutsoukis, Platon E.,
Covello, Leonard, 198
Cox, Gena, 43
Cox, Martha J., 156, 160
Crawford, Kijana, 326
Creary, David, 290
Crenshaw, Kimberle, 325, 326
Crocker, Charles, 187
"Crocker's pets," 187
Crowley, Martha L., 225
Cuba, 29
Cuban Americans, 333
cultural capital, 13–16, 27, 40, 114, 129, 130–32, 138, 142, 157, 161, 178, 199, 210, 225, 254, 273, 280, 282, 315, 323, 337, 349, 356
Cunningham, Mick, 311
Curie, Marie, 314
Currie, Elliott, 84, 162, 178, 283
cycle of poverty, 216, 226, 254, 295
Czech Republic, 7

D

Dahl, Robert A., 38
Dalzell, Robert F., Jr., 124
Damast, Alison, 167
Dannon, 64, 72

Danzinger, Sheldon, 250
Darling-Hammond, Linda, 230
DaVanzo, Julie, 334
Davies, James, 49
Davis, Bruce, 233
Davis, Clark, 149, 150
Davis, David Brion, 264, 266
Davis, Kingsley, 24–25
Davis-Moore theory of social stratification, 24–25, 44
DeBarros, Anthony, 99
debt, 174–75
deck stacking, 103
de facto segregation, 268–69
DeFoe, Daniel, 52
deindustrialization, 240
de Kam, Flip, 107
de la Rocha, Mercedes González, 68
Del Castillo, Adelaida R., 334
Della Fave, L. Richard, 2, 86
Dellarocas, Chrysanthos, 166
Deloitte & Touche, 319–20
Delong, J. Bradford, 138
Demo, David H., 156, 160
Denton, Nancy A., 151, 237, 268, 269, 271–72
Deo, Meera E., 283
Depository Institutions Deregulatory and Monetary Control Act of 1980, 112
deregulation, 8, 112
Deripasta, Oleg V., 60
Desai, Sonalde, 60, 64
deserving poor, 217–19, 253
Desrochers, Donna M., 242
Deutsch, Claudia H., 93
Dewan, Shaila, 237, 238
Dewey, John, 348
Diamond, John B., 12
Dickens, Charles, 149, 295
digital spectrum, 101
Dill, Bonnie Thorton, 156, 324, 330
DiMaggio, Paul, 166
Dingell, John D., 320
Dinovitzer, Ronit, 320
d'Iribarne, Philippe, 64
D'Mello, Bernard, 65
Dobbie, Will, 356
doctrine of predestination, 84
doing gender, 308–09, 349
    basketball, 315
    family impact, 10–11
    jobs, 318–24, 349
    mass media, 315–18
    peer influence, 311–12

Domeritz, Janet, 100
domestic violence, 326
Domhoff, G. William, 39–41, 42, 43, 44, 91, 92, 93, 94, 98, 102, 124, 131, 132, 135, 136, 137, 140, 141, 142
Domhoff's power-elite theory, 39–41, 42, 43, 44, 140
Dominquez, Silvia, 334
Donald, David Herbert, 264, 266
Donohue, Eric, 201
Doob, Christopher B., 151, 188, 229, 251, 284
Doolittle, Kenneth, 211
Doster, Adam, 169
downsizing, 4, 154, 169–70, 358, 359–60
Dozier, Raine, 326
Draut, Ta Mara, 172
Dreier, Peter, 111
Drew, Christopher, 110
Druckenmiller, Stanley, 355
Dubrow, Nancy, 230
Duke, 134
Dunbar, Michele D., 314–15
Duncan, Cynthia, 239
Duncan, Otis Dudley, 88
DuPont Company, 125
Durbin, Richard, 98
Duster, Troy, 283
Dutch industries, 51–52
Dworkin, A. Gary, 232
Dye, Thomas R., 4, 39, 41, 42–43, 44, 78, 79, 91, 92, 93, 94, 96, 101, 103, 106, 107, 128, 129, 139, 140, 142, 154, 157
Dye's theory of the institutional elite, 42–43

E

Earned Income Tax Credit, 247
"eating clubs," 134–35, 138
Eckert, Craig, 94, 95, 142
ecology of class, 82, 158–60
Economic Growth and Tax Relief Reconciliation Act of 2001, 107
Economic Recovery Tax Act of 1981, 94
Edelman, Peter, 253
Educable Mentally Handicapped (EMH)
Education
    See schooling
Edwards, Laura F., 267
Ehrenreich, Barbara, 172, 173, 223, 241–42, 253
Einhorn, David, 112
Eisenhower, Dwight D., 54
Eitle, Tamela McNulty, 335, 336
Eitzen, D. Stanley, 6
Elbaum, Bernard, 207

electronic sweatshop, 8
Elizabethan Poor Law of 1601, 217
Elizabeth I, 314
Ellett, Alberta, 247
Elliott, Justin, 110
Ellison, Larry, 129
Embrick, David G., 273, 275
Engels, Friedrich, 26, 27, 29, 194
England, Paula, 325
English as a second language (ESL), 328
Entwisle, Barbara, 276
Entwisle, Doris R., 280
Environmental Protection Agency (EPA), 110
equality of opportunity, 85, 159
Erbring, Lutz, 166
Eren, Ozkan, 192
Esbenshade, Jill, 66
Escribe, Luisa, 208
Espinosa, Linda, 230
Essential Action, 103–04
Essoka, Jonathan D., 271
Etebari, Mehrun, 28
ethnicity, 42, 263, 276
eugenics movement, 269–70
Evans, William McKee, 286–87
Exploding ARM, 11–12
extended-family networks, 225–27
Exxon Mobil, 51

F

Fabrikant, Geraldine, 127, 128
Facebook, 167
factory workers, 56, 62–64, 67, 72, 188–190, 194, 201, 203, 204, 210, 240, 288, 351
Falk, Beverly, 232
false consciousness, 27, 30, 82, 104, 107
families, 129–31, 137, 149, 159–62, 196–98, 225–27, 272–75, 279–80
family offices, 137
Featherman, David L., 88
Federal Communication Commission (FCC), 109–10
Federal Election Commission (FEC), 98
federal lobbying, 96–97
Federal Reserve Board, 357
feeder factories, 51, 58, 62–65, 66
feminism, 197
Fennell, Dorothy, 186, 188
Fernandez, Ronald, 270
Feuer, Lewis S., 28
Field, Erica, 71
Fields, Gary, 166

Fields-Smith, Cheryl, 163
Figueroa, Richard, 337
Filipino Americans 274
finance industry, 113
financial capital, 13–16, 33, 40, 51, 52, 57, 60, 70–72, 113–14, 122, 129, 138, 142, 144, 165, 166, 178, 210, 253, 282, 287, 349, 356
Finland, 7
Finney, Karen, 154
Fisher, Daniel, 57
Fitzgerald, F. Scott, 270
Fitzhugh, George, 266
527s, 99
floundering families, 251
Flynn, Heather Kohler, 208
Food and Drug Administration (FDA), 110
Ford, Henry, 35, 125, 138, 189
Form, William H., 82
Foster, Sarah A., 226
foundations, 33, 42, 43, 91–92, 95, 138, 140, 141
401(k)s, 176
France, 25, 54, 85, 359
Francis, David R., 112, 142
Frank, Barney, 54, 112
Frank, Robert, 137
Frank, Robert H., 14, 163, 352
Franklin, Benjamin, 187, 306
Franklin, John Hope, 265, 266, 267, 268
Fredrickson, George M., 266
Freeman, John, 97
free world trade, 51, 53, 54, 58
Friedan, Betty, 338–39
Friedman, Carly Kay, 310, 311, 314
Friend, Richard A., 331
Fryer, Roland G., Jr., 356
Fuller, Bruce, 254
Fullerton, Andrew S., 6
Fulton, David, 228–29
functional literacy, 157–58, 350
Fung, Richard, 284
Furstenberg, Frank F., Jr., 13

G

Gabriel, Jeanette, 350, 357, 358
Gabriel, Paul E., 318
Gadson, Mark, 285
Gagné, Patricia, 27
Gail, Gilbert J., 190, 191, 192, 195
Gallagher, Charles A., 285
Galliher, John F., 263
Gamm, Sue, 337
Gans, Herbert, 224

Garbarino, James, 230
Gardner, Kaye E., 310
Garson, Barbara, 8
Gasol, Pau, 83
Gasper, Phil, 29
Gates, Bill, 40
Gates, Henry Louis, Jr., 267
Gates, Melinda, 40
Gatta, Mary, 253
Gauthier, Christiane A., 254
gender, 56, 156, 305–38
gender constancy, 311
General Motors, 114, 125, 211
Gerber, Barbara W., 332
Gerena, Mariana, 226
Germany, 31, 53, 54, 85, 207, 359, 360
Gerstel, Naomi, 226
Gerth, Hans, 31
GI Bill, 151
Giddens, Anthony, 30
Giesecke, Johannes, 56
Gilbert, Dennis, 14, 79, 81, 85, 88, 122, 153, 155,
    158, 194, 223, 224
Gilded Age, 125, 128, 140
Gilens, Martin, 219
Gilfoyle, Timothy J., 124
Gill, Duane A., 250
Gilliam, Franklin D., Jr., 285
Gilman, Charlotte Perkins, 305, 307
Gini index, 7, 77
Gintis, Herbert, 11, 87
Ginzler, Joshua, 227
Giordano, Peggy C., 312
Girard, Stephen, 123
Giroux, Henry A., 11
Giscombe, Katherine, 327
Gitter, Robert J., 290
giving/getting compact, 9
Glaeser, Edward, 86
Glascock, Jack, 317
glass ceiling, 320
Glick, Peter, 311
globalization, 3–10, 17, 39, 48–73, 88,
    125–27, 240
Goar, Carla, 273, 275
Goetzmann, William, 357
Goldberg, Matt, 358
Golden, Daniel, 134
Gompers, Samuel, 189
Gonzales, Nancy A., 279
Gonzalez, Julia, 361

González-Figueroa, Evelyn, 328
Gooden, Angela M., 314
Gooden, Mark A., 314
Goodlad, John I., 198
Goodman, Peter S., 4
Gordon, Alberta, 165
Gordon, Larry, 161
Gordon, Lovis, 321
Gorman, Thomas J., 14–15, 156, 162
Gould, Jay, 124
government, 49, 59, 64, 86, 96–99, 105–112
Grady Memorial (Atlanta), 237–38
Graham, Donald, 40
Granovetter, Mark, 277
Grant, Elizabeth, 199
Grant, Helen, 295
Grant, Madison, 270
Grant, Neva, 254
Great Britain, 48, 51–53, 55, 71
Great Migration, 268
Greece, 270
Greenberg, David, 77, 81
Greene, Jeanie Ahern, 321, 322, 323
Greenwald, Richard A., 199
Greenwell, Lisa, 334
Grice, Steven Michael, 250
Grodsky, Eric, 11
Group, Thetis M., 155
Groveland, 165
Grubb, W. Norton, 198
Grumman Aerospace, 126
Grund, Francis, 149
Grunner, Allison, 337
Grusky, David B., 231
Gryzlak, Brian M., 246, 247, 249
Guantanamo Bay detention center, 104–05
Gulf oil spill, 110
Gulwadi, Gowri Betrabet, 155
Guzman, Pedro, 290
Gyory, Andrew, 269

H
Haberman, Martin, 233, 236
habitas, 11, 15
Hacker, Jacob S., 10, 169, 172, 176
Haley, Heather-Lyn, 209
Hallett, Tim, 12
Halter, Anthony P. 246, 247, 249
Haltiwanger, John, 109
Hamilton, Mykol C., 310
Handcock, Mark S., 169

Handler, Joel F., 218–221, 225, 228, 237, 251
Hansen, David, 169
Han Young welding factory, 68
Happy Days, 23
Harding, Sandra, 325
"hard" money, 98–99
hard work, 84–85, 87, 149, 167–68
Hargittai, Eszter, 166
haringbuis, 51
Harlem Children's Zone, 354–56
Harper, Shaun R., 277
Harrington, Michael, 29, 30, 219
Harris, Deborah A., 250
Harrison, Bennett, 241
Harry, Beth, 335
Hart, Betty, 196
Hart, Cassandra M.D., 170
Harvard, 132–34, 165
Hasenfeld, Yeheskel, 218–221, 225, 228, 237, 251
Hashimoto, Kenji, 56
Hauck, Kevin S. Andrade, 328
Hauser, Robert M., 88
Haveman, Robert, 16, 157, 234
Head, Simon, 9
Head Start, 108
Heady, Christopher, 107
healthcare costs, 175–76, 237–38, 247
heart attacks, 159–60
Hebl, Mikki R., 293
Hecker, Daniel E., 151
Heckscher, Charles, 154, 169
hedge funds, 121
Hedges, Larry, 279
Heflin, Colleen M., 250
hegemonic despotism, 62
hegemonic masculinity, 309, 316
hegemony, 48, 53–55, 71
Hehir, Thomas, 337
Heintz, James, 66
"helicopter parents," 160–61
Henwood, Doug, 128
Heritage Foundation, 92
Herman, Edward S., 139
Hermsen, Joan M., 320
Hernandez, Jaime, 337
Hernandez, Raymond, 121
Herndon, Michael K., 274
Herring, Cedric, 194
Hertz, Tom, 88
Hesse-Biber, Sharlene, 306, 310, 312, 314, 316, 317
Hetherington, Marc J., 108

Heywood, John S., 156
hidden curriculum, 213, 350
  gendered, 314
Higginbotham, Elizabeth, 326
high-level management, 154
high-stakes testing, 231–32
Hill, Heather, 251
Hill, Steven, 360
Hillery, Barbara, 361
Hilt, Lori, 311
Hira, Anil, 5, 170, 172
Hira, Ronil, 5, 170–72
Hirsch, Jennifer S., 334
Hirschi, Thomas A., 216
Hirt, Joan B., 274
Hispanic Americans, 261, 271, 272, 275–76, 279, 280–82, 287, 289–90, 292, 294, 295, 327–30, 349, 350
  income, 288
  jobs, 287, 289
  mass media, 284
  parents, 280
  peers, 277
  schooling, 279, 280, 282, 289
Hispanic American women, 327–30
Hmong, 333–34
Hochshild, Jennifer I., 82
Hofer, Barbara K., 230
Hoff, Derek, 7
Hoffman, Catherine, 176
Hoffman, James, 232
Hoffman, Kelly, 59, 60, 63
Hofstadter, Richard, 269
Holahan, John, 237
holding companies, 137
Holland, 48, 51–55, 58, 71, 163, 306
Holtzman, Linda, 316
Holzer, Harry J., 244
Home Owners Loan Corporation, 151
homosexuality, 197
Honda, 206
Hondagneu-Sotelo, Pierrette, 334, 335
H-1B visa program, 171
Hong Kong, 49
Hoover Institution, 95
Horace Mann School, 134
Horton, Hayward Derrick, 194
Horton, Myles, 193
Horvat, Erin McNamara, 157, 163, 233
housing, 241–42
Howard, Adam, 121, 132

Howley, Aimee A., 230
Howley, Craig, 230
Hu, Winnie, 135
Huber, Joan, 82
Hughes, Mary Elizabeth, 13
human capital, 12, 14–16, 40, 57, 71, 72, 114, 134,
    138, 157, 161, 178, 199, 210, 253, 282, 287, 289,
    291, 325, 350
Hun Young Company, 68
Hurricane Katrina, 283
Hurst, Allison L., 199
Husain, Altaf, 334
Hyde, Alan, 166, 171
hypergamy, 143

I

Ibarra, Marilyn, 5
Iceland, John, 217, 218, 221, 241
ideology, 2, 17, 27, 28, 30, 51, 53–54, 82–86, 113,
    128, 132, 287, 349
Ignatius, David, 121
Illick, Joseph E., 149–151, 187
Immigrant women, 332–35
Immigration Act of 1965, 271
income, 6–8, 25, 31, 33, 49, 50, 90, 131, 137, 241,
    309, 330, 349, 351
  and schooling, 158, 164–65
  middle class, 157–58, 174–77
  poor, 220–23
  upper class, 131
  working class, 204–05
indentured servants, 186–87, 218, 265
index of dissimilarity, 271
index of occupational segregation, 307, 318,
    338
India, 33, 60, 64–65, 72, 170–71
Indian land, 265
individual achievement, 2, 83–84, 87, 143, 176
individual racism, 261, 295
individual sexism, 305
Industrial Age, 149–51
Industrial growth, 52–53
inflation, 357
informal sector, 57, 70, 216, 224, 290
informal social control, 165
institutional racism, 262, 272, 295
institutional sexism, 305
insurance industry, 113
intelligence tests, 232
intergenerational mobility, 87, 88, 294
interlocking directorates, 40, 42, 43, 44, 91, 99,
    101, 114, 123, 141, 142, 168

International Monetary Fund (IMF), 54, 60
Internet, 166–67
interracial families, 274–75, 295, 349
intersectionality, 156, 209, 274, 324–38, 350
Interstate Commerce Commission (ICC), 108
invisible empire, 91–105
Ip, Greg, 167
Iraq War, 94, 126
Irish Americans, 269
Irish "potato famine," 57
Iriquois, 306–07
Isaacs, Julia B., 90, 294
Ishida, Hiroshi, 56
Ishmail, Mohd Nazari, 58
Isler, Jonathan, 208
Italy, 85, 222, 270
Iversen, Roberta Rehner, 87, 225, 226, 227, 228,
    234, 236, 238, 242, 243, 244, 245
Iyengar, Shanto, 285

J

Jackall, Robert, 139, 167, 168
Jackson, Andrew, 264
Jackson, James K., 5
Jacobs, Ronald N., 285
Jahr, Nicholas, 111, 112
James, LeBron, 83
Japan, 3, 7, 24, 33, 38, 49, 54
Jefferson, Linda, 360
Jefferson, Thomas, 86, 148
Jelin, Elizabeth, 68
Jenkins, J. Craig, 94, 95, 142
Jewish Americans, 133
Jim Crow era, 263, 267
Jipguep, Marie-Claude, 288
jobs, 6, 8–10, 27–28, 31, 35–37, 84–85, 87–89,
    137–40, 152–56, 201–09, 241–45, 286–94, 307,
    318–24, 349, 356–60
  men, 309
  women, 307–09
  See also class and racial categories
Jobs and Tax Relief and Reconciliation Act of 2003,
    107
job training, 207–08, 210, 242–44, 247, 251, 253,
    289, 295
Johnson, Earvin, Jr. (Magic), 83
Johnson, Heather Beth, 273
Johnson, James Wheldon, 285
Johnson, Lyndon Baines, 219
Johnson, Susan Moore, 155, 156
Joines, Douglas H., 321
Jones, Deborah j., 226

Jones, Jacqueline, 186, 187, 190
Jones, Paula, 195
Jones, Teresa C., 331, 332
Jones-Correa, Michael, 268
Jordan, Michael, 83
Josephson, Matthew, 124
Joyner, Kara, 276
Joyner-Kersee, Jackie, 267
Juang, Linda, 274
Judt, Tony, 7–8, 356

K

Kagan, Sharon L., 254
Kalil, Ariel, 170
Kamin, Leon J., 232
Kamper, David, 290
Kane, Sally, 154
Kang, Laura Hyun-Yi, 284
Kao, Grace, 13, 276
Kaplinsky, Raphael, 53, 54, 58, 62
Karabol, Jerome, 133, 164, 165
Karger, Joanne, 337
Karle, Wolfgang, 56
Katz, Jane, 89
Katz, Michael B., 217, 218, 307
Katzman, Lauren I., 337
Kauff, Jacqueline, 251
Kawano, Yukio, 53
Kay, David, 106
Keefe, Bob, 104, 108
Keefe, William J., 108
Kehrer, Barbara H., 156
Keister, Lisa A., 128, 134
Kelley, Gary Thomas, 261
Kelly, Russell, 205
Kelly Services, 205
Kelthly, Diane C., 290
Kendall, Diana, 80, 104, 125, 129, 131, 192, 195
Kennedy, Edward M., 348
Kennedy, John F., 34, 219
Kennedy, Paul, 52
Kennedy, Robert F., 34
Kentor, Jeffrey, 54, 57
Kenya, 69–71
Kenyan Homeless People's Federation, 71
Kerbo, Harold, 57, 58
Keyes, Langley C., 240
Keynes, John Mayard, 54
Khan, Mafruza, 101, 102, 109
Kiberia (Kenya), 69–71, 72
Kiesler, Sara, 166
Kilbourne, Jean, 316

Kilcoyne, Patrick, 172
Kim, Victoria, 161
Kimmel, Douglas C., 331
Kinealy, Christine, 57
King, Christopher T., 244
King, Eden B., 293
King, Martin Luther, Jr., 34
Kingston, Paul W., 12
Kinzie, Susan, 11
Kioko, Winnie, 70
Kison, Victoria, 161
Klepp, Susan E., 217
Klinger, Janette, 335
Knickerbocker (club), 136
Knight, Graham, 66–68
Knight, Jennifer L., 293
Knights of Labor, 189–90
Kohn, Melvin L., 196
Kolker, Andrew, 80
Koncz, Jennifer, 5
König, Wolfgang, 56
Kostelney, Kathleen, 230
Kovner, Bruce, 94
Kozol, Jonathan, 163
Kramer, Andrew E., 60
Kraut, Robert E., 166
Kravitz, Lenny, 274–75
Kravitz, Richard L., 154
Kroll, Luisa, 81
Krugman Paul, 7, 140
Kukdong plant, 66–68
Kulik, B., 337
Kunreuther, Frances, 360, 361
Kusserow, Adrie S., 11
Kuther, Tara L., 286
Kuttner, Robert, 108

L

Labaton, Stephen, 121
labor unions, 4, 62–68, 72, 79, 80, 94, 104,
    189–193, 210, 240, 351, 357, 358
LaBrecque, Susanne V., 310
Ladd, Everett Carll, 82, 85
Laffey, James M., 230
Lamont, Michelle, 12
Landon, Bruce, 154
Lane, Julia I., 169, 244
Lankford, Hamilton, 229
Lapham, Lewis H., 133
Lareau, Annette, 12, 14, 15, 157, 161, 163, 196,
    197, 233
Larson, Stephanie Greco, 284, 285

Lassonde, Stephen, 198
Laszloffy, Tracey, 273, 275
Latin America, 60, 63–64, 72
Latinos
   See Hispanic Americans
Laurence Harbor, 200
lawyers, 154, 326
Lazerson, Martin, 198
Leaper, Campbell, 310, 311, 314
Learning Disabled (LD), 335, 337–38
Lease, A. Michele, 277
LeBlanc, Paul, 189, 190, 192
Lechuga, Charlene E., 328
Lee, Cheal-Sung, 59, 63
Lee, Jenny J., 283, 284
Lee, Valerie E., 280
legitimation, 82
Leigh, Paul, 154
Leighninger, Robert D., Jr., 350
Lekachman, Robert, 5
LeMasters, E. E., 200, 201
Lengermann, Patricia Madoo, 156, 324, 325
Leonhardt, David, 127, 158, 363
Lepadatu, Darina, 193
Lerner, Max, 33
LeRoy, Barbara, 337
lesbians, 330–32
Leser, Eric, 97
LeTendre, Gerald K., 230
Levine, Bettijane, 106
Levine, Bruce, 186
Levine, David I., 166
Levine, Diane E., 284
Levine, Jason K., 100
Lewis, Charles, 97
Lewis, Daniel, 166
Lewis, Ethan, 84, 143
Lewis, Michael, 112
Lewis, Tammy L., 361
Liang, Christopher T. H., 274
liberal capitalism, 85–86
Lichtenstein, Nelson, 192
Lichter, Daniel T., 225
Lie, Gwat-Young, 334
lifestyle, 81
Lin, Nan, 13
Lincoln, Abraham, 83, 148
Linkedin, 167
Links (club), 41, 136
Linstroth, J. P., 333
Liptak, Adam, 100

Lively, Kathryn J., 275
Livers, Ancella, 325
living wage, 65, 94, 241, 358, 359, 362
"loans for shares," 59
lobbying, 94–98, 113, 121, 138, 142, 144, 348
local news, 285–86
Lochbaum, David, 110
Lockheed Corporation, 178
Loeb, Susanna, 229
Lohr, Steve, 93, 171
Longmore, Monica A., 312
López, Nancy, 328
Lorenz, Mary, 207
Lorien, Jasny, 140
Losen, Daniel J., 281
Lott, Claire, 323
Louisiana Purchase, 148
Lovejoy, Meg, 323, 324
lower-middle class, 56, 57
Lubitow, Amy, 334
Lubrano, Alfred, 186, 194, 196, 198
Lucas, Samuel R., 280
Ludden, David, 3
Ludwig, Jens, 239
lumpenproletariat, 28
Lundberg-Love, Paula, 310–12
Lundmark, V., 166
Lüttinger, Paul, 56
Lutz, Erbring, 184
lynchings, 268

M

Maag, Christopher, 166
MacLeod, Jay, 10, 11, 16, 226, 231, 233, 240, 242
Madera, Juan M., 293
Mad Men, 316, 317
Magao, Cathryn, 13
Mahan, Alfred Thayer, 53–54
Maier, Kimberly S., 162
majority group, 262, 275
Makar, Hoda R., 332
Malaysia, 49
Malcolm X, 34
Maloney, Carolyn, 320
management, 137–40, 154–55, 157, 167–69, 319, 323, 324, 326–27
Mandura, Jelan, 280
Mane, Ferran, 198
Mann, Emily A., 363
Manning, Wendy D., 312
Mantsios, Gregory, 80

Marable, Manning, 268
Marger, Martin, 79, 82, 216
Marmion, Shelly, 310–12
Marshall Plan, 3, 53
Marsiglia, Flavio Francisco, 334
Martin, Frederich Townsend, 124
Martin, Jack K., 263
Martin, Karin A., 318
Martin, William G., 53
Marxist theory, 23, 25–30, 32, 35–38, 44, 60
    capitalist class system, 27–28, 30
    revolution and its aftermath, 28–32
    strengths, 29–30
    weaknesses, 29
Marx, Karl, 17, 25–31, 35, 37, 44, 82, 104, 188, 194
Mason, Craig A., 279
Massey, Douglas S., 268, 269, 271–72
Massey, Garth M., 290
mass media, 29, 42, 79, 80, 100–05, 195–96,
    283–86, 315–18
    See also Press
mass-media conglomerates, 101–02
math teachers, 229
Mattis, Mary C., 327
Mayclim, Troy, 154
Mazur, Jay, 65
McCain, John, 103
McCall, Nathan, 262
McCarthy, John C., 170
McChesney, Robert W., 101, 109, 110, 127
McCullough, Mary W., 278
McDonnell Douglas, 126
McGauchery, Deanna, 27
McGinn-Shapiro, Molly, 176
McIntosh, Randall, 273
McKown, Clark, 279–281
McLanahan, Sara, 236
McLaughlin, Amy E., 156, 324, 330
McLeod, Jane D., 263
McLoyd, Vonnie C., 225
means of production, 27, 28, 34, 35, 37, 44
media framing, 80
Media Matters for America, 103
Medicaid, 247, 249
medical doctors, 24–25, 153–54, 156, 157,
    332, 339
Medicare, 108
Meier, Kenneth J., 109
Meiksins, Peter, 191
Mellon, Andrew, 138
Mendenhall, Ruby, 170

Mendoza, Saad A., 293
Menjivar, Cecilia, 334
mentors, 326–28
Meraz, Sharon, 314
Merrill Lynch, 137
Merryfield, Juliet, 208
merry-go-round, 70
Merton, Robert K., 33, 83
Messere, Ken, 107
Mexican Americans, 68, 261
Mexican American women, 334–35
Mexican Businessmen's Association, 68
Mexico, 49, 53, 59, 60, 62, 63–64, 66–68, 222
middle class, 2, 11, 12, 14–16, 29, 37, 41, 56, 79,
    148–77, 307, 337, 349, 350
    childrearing, 150–51, 160–62
    income, 152, 153
    jobs, 152–56, 167–74, 178
    reemployment, 172–74
    schooling, 14–16, 17, 156–58, 162–65, 167, 337
middle class (or lower-middle class), 155–56, 177
Miele, Jean, 159–60
military, 49, 51, 53–54, 126, 144
Miller, Cindy Faith, 311
Miller, David E., 273
Miller, Larry, 155
Miller, Matthew, 77, 81
Miller, William, 124
Mills, C. Wright, 31, 38–39, 43, 148, 149
Mills's power-elite theory, 38–39, 43
Millward, Bob, 29
Milman, Noriko, 283, 284
Minerals Management Service, 110
minimum wage, 357–58
mining, 190
minorities
    See racial minorities
minority group, 263, 275
Mishel, Lawrence, 6
Mission Main (Boston), 239, 240
Mitchell, Faith, 290
mode of production, 25–26, 29, 30, 32
modern world systems, 48–72
Moffitt, Robert, 250
Montgomery, David, 189
Montgomery, Kate, 232
Moody, James, 276
Moody's, 112
Mooney, Nan, 148, 151, 155, 174, 352, 357
moon landing, 219
Moore, Wilbert E., 24–25

Morgan, J. P., 124, 138
Morgan, Laurie A., 320
Morgans, Howard, 139–40
Morris, Martina, 169
Morse, Robert, 123
Moscowitz, Marina, 149
Moss, Alfred A., Jr., 265, 266, 267, 268
Moss, David A., 8
Mouw, Ted, 276
Moyers, Bill, 101
Mukophadhyay, T., 166
Muller, Thomas, 270
Müller, Walter, 56
Mullings, Leith, 156, 324
multinationals, 3–5, 10, 49, 51, 54, 55, 56, 57–58, 59, 64, 66, 71–72, 126, 127, 348, 351
Muravchik, Joshua, 29
Murnane, Richard J., 242
Murray, Nina Chandler, 128
MySpace, 167

N

Nackerud, Larry G., 247
Nam, Yunju, 326
nannies, 290, 291
Nash, Gary B., 217
National Labor Relations Act of 1935, 190
National Labor Relations Board, 192
National Origins Act of 1924, 270
Native Americans, 56, 264–65, 282, 284, 287, 290, 295, 306–07
   mass media, 284
   schooling, 282
Naturalization Act of 1790, 269
Nazario, Sonja, 290
Ndunge, Sabina, 70
Neal, Jennifer Watling, 276
Neckerman, Kathryn M., 269
Neely, Sharlotte, 265
Nelson, Margaret K., 201
Neoconservative movement, 93–95, 141, 142
Netherlands
   See Holland
net worth, 130
Neuman, W. Russell, 166
Neumann, Anna, 320
Neuwirth, Robert, 68–71
New Engand,
   early industrial development, 52
Newmark, David, 169
new rich, 128–29, 134
Newton's law of gravity, 217

New Zealand, 49, 222
Nichols, Roger L., 264, 265
Nie, Norman, 166
Niebrugge, Gillian, 156, 324, 325
Nielson, François, 59, 63
Nieves, Angel Davis, 156, 324, 330
Nightingale, Demetra Smith, 289
Nike, 66–67
Nissan, 206
Nixon, Richard, 136
Norris, Floyd, 93
Novak, Candice, 171, 206
Novak, Kristen, 99
Noveske, Julia, 274, 275
Nowell, Amy, 279
Nuclear Regulatory Commission (NRC), 110
nurses, 155, 172
Nystrom, Nancy M., 331, 332

O

Oakes, Jeannie, 280
Obama, Barack, 91, 100, 295
Obera, Michael, 69–70, 71
O'Brien, Patricia, 168
Office of Community Learning (Seattle), 236
official U.S. measure of poverty, 220–21, 242, 253
Ogawa, Rodney T., 164
Olafsdottir, Sigrun, 263
old rich, 127–28, 129, 130, 134
O'Leary, Chistopher J., 244
Olivar, J. Richard, 217
Oliver, Melvin L., 151
Ollman, Bertell, 30
Olson, Linda Steffel, 280
Oltmans, Elizabeth, 250
Omi, Michael, 263
1.5 generation, 290, 291
One-Stop Career Center (New Jersey), 251
Oppel, Richard A., Jr., 110
Oppenheimer, David B., 283
Orchard Park (Boston), 239–40
Ormrod, David, 52
Ornstein, Allan, 164
Orshansky, Mollie, 220, 221
Ortiz, Susan, 325
Ostrander, Susan A., 129, 133
Oswalt, Wendell H., 265
outsourcing, 4, 64, 170–71, 357
outworkers, 188
Ovadia, Seth, 320
Overton, Spencer, 100
Owens, Elizabeth B., 227

P

PACs, 99–100
Padavic, Irene, 306, 307, 318, 320
Page, Jake, 265
Pager, Devah, 293–95
Palmer, Maria Teresa Unger, 280
Palpacuer, Florence, 58
Panoptimex (factory), 66
Pardo, Carol, 230
Paris, Scott G., 232
Parisi, Domenico, 250
Parrett, William H., 225, 231
Parrott, Sharon, 248, 250, 251
Parsons, Talcott, 23, 24
Patient Protection and Affordable Care Act of
    2010, 363
patrons, 168
Patterson, M., 166
Pattillo, Mary E., 165
Paul, Ron, 54
pay equity, 320
pedagogy of power, 232–33, 236, 350, 356
peripheral nations, 48, 49–50, 54, 57
Perlman, Janice, 68
Perlman, Joel, 198
Perrucci, Robert, 3–5, 36–37, 88, 91, 96, 97, 102–04,
    108, 134, 141, 153, 157, 169, 203–06
Perry-Jenkins, Maureen, 78, 209
Personal Responsibility and Work Opportunity Act
    of 1996, 220, 245
Pescosolido, Bernice A., 263
Pessen, Edward, 124
petite bourgeoisie, 28, 29
Petras, James, 60, 65
Phillips, G. Michael, 321
Phillips, Kevin, 123, 125, 127
Philipse, Frederick, 122
Phillips Exeter, 132, 133
physicians
    See medical doctors
Pieterse, Jan Nederveen, 49
Pietrangelo, Anthony R., 110
Piggott, Rhyne, 99
Pilgrim, David, 267
Pinder, Glen, 355
Planta, Robert C., 280
Plessy v. Ferguson, 267
pluralism, 38, 39, 44
police officers, 155
policy-making organizations, 39, 41–43, 92–93,
    95, 140
political parties, 86, 98–100, 103–04, 108

Pollin, Robert, 192, 356, 357
Pollitt, Katha, 339
Polsky, David, 169
poor, 49, 56, 57, 108, 216–54, 292, 349, 350, 351
    childcare, 227–28, 247–48, 253
    designation, 220–23
    families, 225–27
    healthcare, 237, 238, 247
    housing, 216
    income, 223, 224, 241
    jobs, 216, 217, 228, 240–45, 249, 250, 251, 253
    racial composition, 223
    schooling, 216, 228–37, 247, 254
poorhouses, 218
poor workers' spatial mismatch, 248
poor workers' temporal mismatch, 248
Porcellian, 134
Portes, Alejandro, 13
Portland (Oregon) job-training program,
    250, 251
Post, Leslie, 230
Potter, David M., 357
poverty
    See poor
Powell, Arthur G., 134
power, 25, 29, 38, 44
power elite, 17, 23, 38–44, 91–105, 140–42, 144,
    170, 231–32, 351–52, 362
power-elite theories, 17, 23, 38–43, 44
Powlishta, Kimberly K., 311
Prabhakar, A. C., 49
Prante, Gerald, 6
press
    hype about news, 103
    opinion-shaping strategy, 103–05
    power, 100–05
Preston, Julia, 294
Prince, Charles O., III, 4
Prince, Cynthia, 229
Prince Heights, 165–66
Princeton, 132, 133, 135, 165, 235
privateering, 123
Professional Air Traffic Controllers
    Organization, 192
professions, 153–54, 319, 323, 324
progressive income tax, 107
Prokos, Anastasia, 320
proletariat, 27–30, 32, 194
Promise Academy, 354–56, 362
proportional representation, 86, 98, 351
Protect Mark L., 168
Proweller, Amira, 163

Pryor, Frederic L., 158
psychological empowerment, 143
public assistance, 44, 109, 218–20, 245–51, 253, 349
public housing, 239–40
public policy, 77, 105–13, 140, 141, 348, 352
public-school funding, 14, 159, 162–63, 229–30, 272, 350, 351
Puette, William J., 104
Pugh, Tony, 359
Pun, Ngai, 62, 65
Purcell, Piper, 314
Puritans, 84
Pusey, Nate, 130
Putin, Vladimir, 60
Putnam, Robert D., 13

Q

Quilliam, Lincoln, 293, 294
Quincy, Josiah, 217

R

racial formations, 263–66
racialized, 272, 281
racially restrictive convenants, 268
racial minorities
    families, 272–75, 279–80
    jobs, 286–94
    learning disabilities, 336
    mass media, 283–86
    peers and friendship patterns, 275–78
    poverty, 292
    schooling, 278–83
racial pride, 273–74, 349
racial projects, 263–64, 269–271, 273, 277, 295
racism, 68–69, 200–01, 261–96
Rada, James A., 285
Radhakrishnan, Smitha, 64
Raff, Daniel, M. G., 189
Rai, Kalyani, 334
railroads, 149, 187, 190
Rainwater, Lee, 222, 226
Rampell, Catherine, 90, 307
Rank, Mark R., 216, 225, 226
rape-crisis services, 325
Reagan, Patricia B., 290
Reagan, Ronald, 82, 93, 108, 177, 192, 219, 220, 352
real-estate industry, 113, 272
Reconstruction, 267, 268
Red Cloud, 265

Reddit, 194
Rediker, Marcus, 186, 188
redlining, 151
Reebok, 64–65
Reed, Bruce, 86
Reed, David, 270
Reed, Jocelyn, 273
reemployment, 172–74
Rees, Richard W., 269
regulatory agencies, 108–13
Reich, Steven A., 268
Reichman, Nancy, 320
Reid, Lori I., 325
Relave, Nanette, 244
reserve army of labor, 29, 240
resiliency, 227
Reskin, Barbara, 306, 307, 318
retirement, 176
Reuther, Walter, 190
Reynolds, Arthur J., 363
Ricard, Sophie, 355
Richard, Colleen Anne, 331
Richards, Robyn J., 204
Ripley, William, 270–71
Risler, Edwin A., 247
Risley, Todd R., 196
Ritzer, George, 78
Rivoli, Pietra, 66
"Robber barons," 124, 128
Roberts, Bryan R., 68
Roberts, Jean I., 155
Robertson, Dylan L., 363
Robertson, Susan L., 13
Robinson, John P., 166
Robinson, Julia Ann, 275
Robinson, Michael, 103
Robinson, William I., 54
Rockefeller, David, 4, 124, 129–30
Rockefeller Family and Associates, 137
Rockefeller, John D., 35, 124, 125, 136, 138–39
Rockefeller, John D., Jr., 136
Rockefeller, John D., III, 136
Rockwell International, 99
Rocquemore, Kerry Ann, 273, 274, 275
Rodgers, Bruce A., 155
Rodgers, Daniel t., 84, 149, 187, 188, 190, 307
Rodriguez, Clara E., 284
Rodriguez, Melanie Domenech, 227
Roig, Carlos, 99
Roman, Joseph, 66
Romano, Meg, 323

Rombaugh, Shirley, 290
Roosevelt, Eleanor, 134–35
Roosevelt (Franklin) administration, 356
Roosevelt, Franklin D., 134–35, 190, 362
Roosevelt, Theodore, Jr., 130
Roosevelt, Theodore, Sr., 130
Rose, Mike, 198, 199, 202
Roseanne, 195
Rosen, Michael, 27
Rosenberg, Alyssa, 293
Ross, Mary, 325
Rosser, Sue V., 320
Ross-Sheriff, Fariyal, 334
Roth, Wendy D., 274
Rothgeb, John M., Jr., 65
Rothkopf, David, 39, 141
Rotundo, E. Anthony, 149
Rouse, Cecilia Elena, 229, 230, 235
Rouse, Lori, 101
Rowland, Diana, 176
Royal Dutch Shell, 51
Royster, Deidre A., 201, 210
Rubin, Irene S., 107
Rubin, Lillian Breslow, 197, 201, 208, 209
Ruble, Diane N., 311
Rude, Jim, 172
Ruder, David, 113
Rumsfeld, Donald, 105
Rumsford, Julia, 208–09
Russell, Joyce E. A., 168
Russia, 29, 54, 59–60, 72, 270
Rutgers University Center for Women and Work, 251–52, 253
Ryan, William, 217, 271
Rytina, Steven, 87

S

Sacerdote, Bruce, 86
Sack, Kevin, 237, 238
Safa, Helen, 68
Saft, Elizabeth W., 280
Sailor, Dorothy Holin, 196
Salem (Massachusetts), 123
Salzinger, Leslie, 66
"Sambos," 267
Samuelson, Robert J., 79
Sandefur, Rebecca L., 154
Sanders, Seth G., 332
Sanders-Phillips, Kathy, 286
Sandstrom, Susanna, 49
Santman, Donna, 232

Sarkisian, Natalia, 226
Sasser, Alicia C., 156
Satterthwaite, David, 71
"savage inequalities," 163
Schaefer, Richard T., 268
Schaffer, David, 158
Schaffner, Brian F., 285
Scherlis, W., 166
Schervish, Paul G., 84, 143
Schmitz, Suzanne, 318
schooling, 14–16, 59, 85, 131–35, 163–65, 198–99, 216, 228–37, 247, 254, 278–83, 313–15, 328, 334, 335–38, 350, 352–56
    and jobs, 85, 87, 94, 167, 201, 228–36, 242, 272, 283
Schorr, Daniel, 141
Schuler, Doug, 58
Schultz, Amy J., 156, 324
Schumer, Charles. 121
Schwartz, Nelson D., 93
Scott, Janny, 160
Scott, Marc, 169
Seabrook, Elizabeth, 227
Seattle
    Office of Community Learning, 236
Seccombe, Karen, 219, 221, 225, 227, 234, 237, 239, 241, 242, 246, 247, 248, 249, 250
Segura, Denise A., 332, 335
selective reporting, 104
semiperipheral nations, 48, 49–50, 54, 57, 60, 62–65
Sen, Amartya K., 254
Sennett, Richard, 4, 10, 13, 173–74
sense of entitlement, 161, 186, 199, 337
separate-bit-equal standard, 267
sexism, 56, 66, 68–69, 305–38
sexual harassment, 322–23
sewing machines, 188
Shah, Anup. 54
Shakib, Sohaila, 314–15
Shapiro, Herbert, 268
Shapiro, Thomas M., 151, 273
Sharkey, Joe, 143
Shaughnessy, Michael F., 353
Shaw, Daniel S., 227
Shepard, Joe M., 194
Sherman, Arloc, 248, 251
Sheshabalaya, Ashutosh, 170, 171
Shields, Stephanie A., 324
Shimizu, Hidetada, 230
Shin, Hyoung-jin, 290, 291

shipbuilding, 51–52
Shipler, David K., 223
Shoemaker, Kate, 355
Shorrocks, Anthony, 49
Shostak, Arthur B., 196, 199
Shultz, Marjorie M., 283
Sicakyuz, Achrene, 56
Siegel, Paul, 126
Simpson, Homer, 195
Singapore, 49
Singer, Peter, 25
single-parent families, 225–27
SITEMEX (union), 67–68
Skiba, Russell, 281
skilled-labor jobs, 201, 210
Skrzyeki, Cynthia, 110
Skull and Bones, 134, 135
Slater, Samuel, 188
slave codes, 266
slavery, 50, 265–66, 286, 307
Slavin, Robert E., 14, 162–63
Sleeter, Christine E., 281–82
small-business owners, 150
Smeeding, Timothy A., 16, 108, 157, 222,
    226, 234
Smith, Aaron, 241, 358
Smith, Brendan, 2
Smith, Danielle, 326
Smith, Dinitia, 267
Smith, Doug, 290
Smith, Joan, 201
Smith, Lynn, 316, 326
Smith, Ryan A., 327
Smith, Sandra Susan, 326
Smith, Vicki, 171, 172, 208
So, Alvin Y., 60
social capital, 12, 15, 16, 40, 41, 60, 67, 70, 72, 97,
    114, 122, 131, 133, 134, 138, 141–44, 157, 161,
    163, 165–67, 178, 199–201, 210, 237–40, 272,
    280, 321, 326–28, 332, 337, 350, 356
social-change organizations, 360–62
social clubs, 12, 38, 41, 42–44, 122, 135–37, 138,
    141, 142
social Darwinism, 269
social distance, 263
social inequality, 2, 6–8, 12–14, 16, 348–52, 363
socialism, 25, 28–30, 59
social mobility, 79, 87–90, 148, 227
    myths, 87
social networking, 165–67, 326, 328–29
social-networking sites, 166–67, 350
Social Register, 41, 127–28

social reproduction, 1, 10–12, 14, 16, 17, 25, 40,
    44, 57, 71, 72, 90, 113, 122, 124, 129, 130, 148,
    177, 196, 216, 231, 233, 286, 337, 349, 351
    and schooling, 14–16, 159
social security, 151
social stratification, 2
    theories, 23–44
sociological theories, 24
"soft" money, 98–99
Soltow, Lee, 123
Soprano, Tony, 192
Sorensen, Elaine, 289
Soule, Sarah A., 268
South Korea, 49
Soviet Union, 23
Spade, Joan Z., 312
Spain, 52, 54
spatial empowerment, 143
special education, 335–38
Speiglman, Anna, 164
Spillane, James P., 12
spin control, 104–05, 107
Spindel, Laurel J., 170
squatter communities, 68–71
squatters, 68
Stanberry, Anne M., 361
Standard & Poor's, 112
Standardized Aptitude Tests (SATs), 164–65, 199
standardized tests, 231–32, 279, 282–83, 295, 354–56,
    362
standpoint, 325
Starcher, George, 360
steel mills, 357
Steele, Claudia M., 281
Steele, James B., 172
steering, 272
Steinreich, Dale, 25
stereotype fallout, 291–96, 337
stereotypes, 266, 267, 278–79, 283–86, 292, 295,
    310, 314, 317, 322, 326–27, 330
stereotype threat, 281–83, 286, 292, 295, 296
Sterling, Joyce, 320
Stern, Ithal, 168
Stern, Mark J., 307
Sterrett, Emma, 226
Stevenson, Betsey, 339
Stevenson, Harold W., 273
Stewart, Angela, 227
Stewart, Lara, 314
Stiglitz, Joseph E., 2, 54
Stone, Pamela, 323, 324
Story, Louise, 8, 121

Straits, Robert A., 244
Strambler, Michael J., 279–281
Stricker, Frank, 357
strikes, 67–68, 190
Strolovitch, Dara Z., 324
structural-functional theory, 23–25, 44
structural mobility, 87–89
structural vulnerability, 225, 231
"subprime mortgage," 110–11
substructure, 26, 30
Sulek, Antoni, 194
Sullivan, Kevin, 295
Summers, Lawrence H., 189, 314
superclass, 91–105, 113–14, 127–44, 348
    See also upper class
superstructure, 26–27, 30, 32
supervisory boards, 360
surplus value, 27
Svendsen, Gert Tiggaard, 12
Svendsen, Gunnar, 12
Swartz, Katherine, 176
sweatshops, 62, 65–68, 72
Sweden, 360
Sweet, Stephen, 191

T

Tabb, William K., 144
Taft Hartley Act of 1947, 190–91
Tancredi, Daniel J., 154
Taquiro, Michael, 250
tariffs, 4, 53, 58, 59
Tatum, Beverly Daniel, 275, 278
taxation, 106–07, 352
tax beaks, 121, 126, 352
tax reform, 144, 352
Tax Reform Act of 1986, 95
Taylor, Frank, 314, 332
teachers, 132, 155–56, 163–64, 199, 200–01, 216,
    232–33, 234, 236, 281–82, 306
technology, 59, 240
Telecommunications Act of 1996, 101, 109, 127
Temple, Judy A., 363
temporal empowerment, 143
Temporary Assistance for Needy Families (TANF),
    108, 220, 245, 246–51, 253, 254, 349
temporary (temp) work, 171–72, 177, 205–07
tent cities, 111
Terkel, Studs, 85
tester studies, 272, 293–94
textile factories, 51, 188, 189
Textile Workers Organizing Committee, 193
Thayer, Pam, 359

Theodos, Brett, 89
Theriault, Reg, 88, 211
The Simpsons, 195
think tanks, 42, 43, 91–92, 95, 133, 138,
    140, 141
Thomas, John L., 264, 266
Thomas, Melvin E., 194
Thomas, Tonya, 361
Thompson, Gabriel, 94
Thompson, Timothy, 193
Thorton, Bridget, 101
Tiendra, Marta, 290
Title 1 Chicago Parent Centers, 363
Title VII of the Civil Right Act of 1954, 324–25
Title IX of 1972, 314
Tolman, Richard, 226
Tolnay, Stewart A., 268
Tontonoz, Matthew J., 269
Tough, Paul, 353–55
Toyota, 206
tracking, 230–31, 279, 280–81
Trades Union Congress (Great Britain), 191
traditional system of authority, 33–34
trajectory (racial), 263
transportation, 248
Trattner, Walter I., 217
Trautner, Hanna Martin, 311
Tribble, Sarah Jane, 167
"trickle-down" economics, 27
Trumbull, Mark, 114
trust, 10
Tucker, Robert C., 25
Tumin, Melvin, 24–25
Turley, Jonathan, 311
Turney, Kristin, 326
Tyagi, Amelia Warren, 174, 175

U

Uchitelle, Louis, 173, 211, 358, 359
underclass, 70, 79, 223–24, 238
undeserving poor, 218, 219, 253
unemployment insurance, 151
Union of Concerned Scientists, 110
unions
    See labor unions
United Auto Workers, 114
United Food and Commercial Workers, 104
United Provinces
    See Holland
universities, 38, 42, 92, 95, 133–34, 138, 141
unskilled laborers, 187
Unterhalter, Elaine, 313

upper class, 38–43, 56, 57, 63, 78, 90, 122, 127–44, 349, 350, 352
  corporate leadership, 137–42
  families, 129–31
  jobs, 122–24, 137–40
  power elite and, 38–43, 140–42
  schooling, 131–35
  social clubs, 135–37
  wealth and income, 78, 122, 137
upper-middle class, 56, 57, 78–80, 153–55, 156, 177, 349
urban renewal, 271
urban war zone, 230
Useem, Michael, 40–42, 140, 141

V

Valdez, R. Burciaga, 334
Valentine, Catherine G., 312
Valenzuela, Abel, Jr., 290
Vallejo, Jody Agius, 330
Vallely, Paul E., 105
Valleta, Robert G., 169
Van Arsdale, David, 206–07
Vanderbilt, Cornelius, 123
Van der Galien, Michael, 127
Vanderhand, Maya, 244
Vang, Pa Y., 334
Vanneman, Reeve, 320
Van Wormser, Katherine, 331
Varma, Roli, 292
Vaznis, James, 133
Veblen, Thorstein, 32, 125
Velasquez, Manuel, 320, 321
Veratek, Pete, 361
Vietnamese Americans, 277–78
Vietnam War, 23, 219
Villani, Susan, 286
Viser, Matt, 134
vocational education, 198–99, 210
Vogel, Michael D., 290

W

Wacquant, Loic J. D., 11
Wade, Dwayne, 83
Wade, Jay C., 273
Wagmiller, Robert, 272
Walford, Geoffrey, 11
Walker, Alan, 220
Walker, Carol, 220
Wallace, Michael, 6, 241
Wallace, Scyatta A., 286
Wallerstein, Immanuel, 48, 49, 51–55

Walmart, 9, 51, 56–58, 62, 63, 357, 360
Walters, Britt, 101
Wandner, S. A., 244
Wang, Hong-zen, 66
Wang, Hui-Chen, 250
Ward, Jane, 331
Ward, L. Monique, 286
Ward, Peter M., 68
Ward, Stephanie Francis, 154
Wark, Colin, 263
War on Poverty, 219
Warren, Elizabeth, 14, 148, 163, 174, 175
wealth, 25, 31, 33, 44, 80, 122, 137, 144
"wealthfare," 126–27
Weaver, Robert D., 247
Weber, Lynn, 325
Weber, Max, 17, 29, 30, 31–35, 37, 44, 81, 84, 128
Weber's theory of class, status, and party, 31–35, 37, 44
Wecter, Dixon, 125
Weidenberg, Murray, 95
Weininger, Elliot B., 12, 157, 163, 233
Weinstein, Rhona S., 281
Weintraub, Ellen L., 100
Weir, Margaret, 157
Weis, Lois, 199
Weiss, Philip, 94
welfare
  See public assistance
"welfare queens," 219, 220
welfare reform, 245–53
  evaluation, 248–51, 253
Wellman, Barry, 166
Wellman, David, 283
Wells, Donald, 66, 67, 68
Wells, Joel, 331
Welner, Kevin G., 279, 280
Wentzel, Katherine, 164
West, Candace, 308
Westphal, James D., 139, 168
Weyerhaeuser family, 130–31
White, Kerry A., 230
White, Theodore, 100
white-collar job holders, 3, 153, 169, 202–03
whites, 272–73, 275, 279–284, 286, 287, 290, 294, 336, 349
  income, 288, 289
  jobs, 287
  parents, 272–73
  peer and friendship relations, 275, 277
  poverty, 292
  schooling, 279, 282, 289

Whitman, Christine Todd, 110
Whitman, David, 352–53, 362
Whyte, William H., Jr., 150
Wiebe, Robert H., 264, 266
Williams, Johnny E., 219
Williams, L. Susan, 328
Williams, Robin, Jr., 82, 85, 86
Wills, John, 151
Wilms, Welford W., 198
Wilson, Charles Henry, 52
Wilson, Will, 160
Wilson, William Julius, 216, 224, 226–27, 237, 254, 288
Winant, Howard, 263
Winder, Kate, 250
Winfrey, Oprah, 267
Wingfield, Adia Harvey, 327
Wolfers, Justin, 339
Wolff, Edward N., 49, 81, 174
Wolff, Tobias, 133
women, 305–38
    families, 149, 150–51
    income, 309, 349
    jobs, 318–24, 325–35
    management and professions, 319
    math and science, 314
    schooling, 313–15, 329
women's liberation movement, 23
Wong, Dan, 293
Wood, Betty, 264, 265
Wood, Gordon S., 264, 266
Woodlawn neighborhood (Chicago), 237
work
    See jobs
work alienation, 194, 201, 203
Workers Alliance of America, 358
work ethic, 2, 84, 148, 167, 220
working class, 2, 10–12, 14–16, 30, 56, 57, 65, 79, 156, 187–209, 349, 350
    childcare, 208–09
    childrearing, 196–97
    families, 188–89, 196–97
    jobs, 79, 201–09, 321–23
    media representation, 195
    schooling, 14–17, 198–99
    traits, 194
working conditions, 62, 63, 65, 186, 190
working poor, 61, 79, 223, 225, 241–42
"working rich," 153
working women, 66, 162, 174, 175, 189, 197, 208

work sharing, 358–59
Works Progress Administration (WPA), 356–58, 362
work stoppages, 193
World Bank (WB), 54, 60
world systems, 48–55
World Trade Organization (WTO), 53, 54, 65
Wright, Doug, 208
Wright, Erik Olin, 17, 28, 29, 35–36, 37, 44
Wright, Melissa W., 66
Wright's perspective on class, 35–36, 37, 44
Wulfenmeyer, K. Tim, 285
Wyatt, Ian D., 151
Wyckoff, James, 229
Wysong, Earl, 3, 4, 5, 36–37, 88, 91, 92, 96, 97, 99, 102–04, 108, 134, 141, 153, 157, 169, 203, 204, 206

X

Xiao, Hong, 162
Xie, Yu, 291

Y

Yale, 132, 133, 165
Yang, Pahoua, 334
Yang, Song, 292
Yankelovich, Daniel, 10
Yates, Michael D., 199
Yeskel, Felicia, 77
Yoder, Janice D., 325
Young, Alfred A., Jr., 12, 288, 289
Young, Angela M., 328
Young, Kate, 310
Yu, Xiaomin, 62, 65
Yuen, Nancy Wang, 283, 284

Z

Zajac, Edward J., 139
Zalot, Alecia A., 226
Zavella, Patricia, 332
Zeng, Zhen, 291
Zepezauer, Mark, 106, 126
zero-tolerance practices, 280–81, 295
Ziegler, Robert, 190, 191, 192, 195
Ziegler, Robert H., 268
Zimmerman, Don, 308
Zinn, Maxine Baca, 6
Zirkel, Sabrina, 281, 282
Zuniga, Maria, 335
Zweig, Michael, 79, 194